Literature of the Romantic Period

Literature of the Romantic Period

A Bibliographical Guide

Edited by
Michael O'Neill

CLARENDON PRESS · OXFORD
1998

Oxford University Press, Great Clarendon Street, Oxford OX2 6DP

Oxford New York

Athens Auckland Bangkok Bogota Bombay Buenos Aires
Calcutta Cape Town Dar es Salaam Delhi Florence Hong Kong
Istanbul Karachi Kuala Lumpur Madras Madrid Melbourne
Mexico City Nairobi Paris Singapore Taipei Tokyo Toronto Warsaw

and associated companies in
Berlin Ibadan

Oxford is a trade mark of Oxford University Press

Published in the United States by
Oxford University Press Inc., New York

A catalogue record for this book is available from the British Library

Library of Congress Cataloging in Publication Data
Literature of the romantic period : a bibliographical guide / edited
    by Michael O'Neill.
        Includes bibliographical references (p.) and index.
        1. English literature—19th century—History and criticism—
    Bibliography.   2. English literature—18th century—History and
    criticism—Bibliography.   3. Romanticism—Great Britain—
    Bibliography.   I. O'Neill, Michael, 1953–   .
    Z2013.L58 1998 [PR457] 016.8209'007–dc21   97–33299

ISBN 0–19–871120–4
ISBN 0–19–871121–2 (pbk.)

Typeset by Graphicraft Typesetters Ltd., Hong Kong
Printed in Great Britain
on acid-free paper by
Biddles Ltd.,
Guildford & Kings Lynn

Preface

THE present volume seeks to give readers a critical guide to the best and the typical in scholarship and criticism devoted to literature of the Romantic period (a period defined as running roughly from 1785 to 1830). Contributors have been asked to keep an undergraduate audience in mind, though the volume is also intended to be of use to postgraduates, lecturers, Romantic specialists, and interested general readers. There are individual chapters on Blake, Wordsworth, Coleridge, Byron, Shelley, Keats, Clare, Scott, Mary Shelley, Peacock, and Austen. The justification for this is twofold: it is helpful for the reader who has as a priority bibliographical information about individual authors of the period, and it is a form of organization suggested by much of the book's subject matter (that is, much criticism concentrates on individual authors). To take account of the abundance of fine and often overlooked writing in the period, there are a number of chapters concerned with more than a single author. Many challenges to the idea that Romantic literature consists, essentially, of the writings of six great male poets have been mounted over the last two decades. These challenges explain, in part, the present volume's existence, and they are taken on board by the contributors.

The volume provides extensive and up-to-date treatment of work on widely studied Romantic writers; considerable discussion of work on less well-known figures in whom there has been an explosion of interest in recent years; informed judgements about the current state of editions (especially important at a time when many canonical and non-canonical Romantic writers are being re-edited or newly edited); and chapters dealing with work on fiction and prose, reflecting the changing emphases of much contemporary criticism of Romantic literature. Throughout, contributors have been encouraged to be evaluative and to concentrate on work which they regard as valuable. Each chapter concludes with a 'References' section that lists works mentioned in the chapter (and, on occasion, works not mentioned in the chapter). It is my hope and belief that, through the explorations of individual contributors and the interactions between their perspectives, the volume will help to clarify and advance the current debate about the nature of 'Romanticism' and 'the Romantic period'.

M.O'N.

Acknowledgements

I SHOULD like to thank Andrew Lockett at OUP for suggesting to me that I might edit the present volume and Jason Freeman who has seen it through the press. Jackie Pritchard copy-edited the typescript with exemplary meticulousness and attention to detail and Jane Horton compiled the index. I am grateful to all the contributors for their patience, good humour, hard work, and prompt responses to editorial letters and e-mail messages. To Michael Rossington, who coped expertly with a late request that he include Burns in his important chapter, I owe a particular debt. My colleagues at Durham, Pamela Clemit, Fiona Robertson, and J. R. Watson, made searching and helpful comments on my own chapter. The anonymous readers for the Press have been constructive in their criticisms. Stanley Wells's *Shakespeare: A Bibliographical Guide: New Edition* (Oxford, 1990) has provided the volume with an inspiring and adaptable model.

M.O'N.

Contents

CONTENTS

1. *General Studies of the Romantic Period*

MICHAEL O'NEILL

In recent years Romantic studies, always abundant, have multiplied at a head-spinning rate. In this chapter I make no attempt at inclusiveness; even representativeness is a chimerical ambition. Instead, I draw highly selective attention to general studies of Romanticism and the Romantic period which may be regarded as significant, or particularly helpful for students, or both. For the most part, I concentrate on work from 1970 to the present, discussing studies of poetry, and studies of poetry and fiction, before studies of fiction.

Overlap with later chapters has been kept to a minimum, though it is unavoidable in some cases: many books of a general kind contain discussions of individual authors, while many books focusing on specific authors contain innovative general discussions. Because 'Romantic Gothic' and 'Fiction of the Romantic Period (Godwin, Wollstonecraft, Bage, Edgeworth, Burney, Inchbald, Hays, and Others)'—and the questions raised by such titles—are the subjects of chapters by Peter Garside and Susan Matthews, respectively, my treatment of these topics is brief. Again, since Robert Morrison has written a chapter on 'Essayists of the Romantic Period' and John Whale a chapter on 'Political Prose' of the period, the reader is referred to those chapters for books containing relevant general discussions. Michael Rossington's and Jennifer Breen's chapters make it unnecessary for me to talk in much specific detail about issues to do with the Romantic poetic canon or the impact of feminism on our reading of Romantic poetry, though both topics are mentioned in ensuing pages.

'The Romantic period' or 'Romanticism': the choice of terms may indicate a critic's allegiances in the debate about the Romantic which has rekindled over the last decade or so. As Jerome J. McGann remarks, 'the romantic period and its correspondent breeze, the romantic movement, are not the same thing' (McGann 1993). 'Romanticism', like 'the romantic movement', is a term that can speak of the desire to identify certain essential constituents in a body of work which, so far as British Romanticism is concerned, has traditionally been identified with the poetry of six male poets, Blake, Wordsworth, Coleridge, Byron, Shelley, and Keats. 'The Romantic period' refers to a historical period,

roughly 1785–1830 (though these dates are themselves the subject of controversy), during which different kinds of work were written, many of which
might not be regarded as 'Romantic' as that vexed term was defined by René
Wellek ('imagination for the view of poetry, nature for the view of the world,
and symbol and myth for poetic style'). Seeking to gift Romanticism with an
essence, Wellek's description contests Arthur O. Lovejoy's emphasis on the
need 'to use the word "Romanticism" in the plural'. Much current work on
'the Romantic period' is on Lovejoy's side in its opposition to the notion that
'Romantic' is most appropriately applied to the work of the 'big Six'; forgotten or marginalized figures have rarely had it so good. Yet 'Romanticism' is a
category that refuses to go away, if only because so much has been invested
in the attempt to describe it. To write about, or, indeed, to organize a bibliography around, 'the Romantic period' is necessarily to enter into debate about
the nature of 'Romanticism'.

ANTHOLOGIES, BIBLIOGRAPHIES, TEXTUAL STUDIES

Anthologies are a catwalk for critical fashions to display themselves, and a
number, each reflecting a different conception of the period, can be recommended. They include *Romantic Poetry and Prose*, edited by Bloom and Trilling,
a monument to 'High (or Yale) Romanticism' in its selections and commentary; McGann's 1993 anthology which contains poetry by many different
authors and is organized chronologically by the year of publication (contro-
versially excluding poems unpublished in the period); Jennifer Breen's widely
available selection of women Romantic poets (see also Ashfield's larger edition); and Duncan Wu's *Romanticism* which offers newly edited texts of a wide
range of writings, mainly poems. McGann's and Wu's anthologies, in particular, show how richly textual scholarship serves a fuller understanding of the
period. The series of facsimile reprints of works from the period published by
Woodstock Books with introductions by Jonathan Wordsworth (gathered
together in *Ancestral Voices* and *Visionary Gleam*) are invaluable; readers unable
to get to a research library can now read Wordsworth's *The Excursion* in a
facsimile of the 1814 edition that Byron, Shelley, and Keats read. Jeffrey Cox's
anthology of Gothic drama is helpful for the specialist.

Useful selections of Romantic critical prose are edited by David Bromwich
and Peter J. Kitson. Kitson's volume contains, among other things, the 1800
preface to *Lyrical Ballads* as well as selections from *A Defence of Poetry*, *The
Statesman's Manual*, *Biographia Literaria*, *The Spirit of the Age*, and Scott's 'Life
of Horace Walpole'. John Spencer Hill has edited a convenient if now rather
dated Casebook volume on *The Romantic Imagination*. In Jonathan Bate's selec-

tion of writings by the Romantics on Shakespeare, Coleridge and Hazlitt are well represented, but there are also sizeable extracts from A. W. Schlegel and Hegel. Reviews of the major poets are best sampled in Donald Reiman's nine-volume *The Romantics Reviewed*, or, if something less bulky is desired, in Theodore Redpath's selection. Reviewing practice in the period is studied by John O. Hayden.

Bibliographies and regular critical round-ups include the MLA's critically incisive *English Romantic Poets* (the fourth edition of which appeared in 1985); volume iv (1800–1900) of the *Cambridge Bibliography of English Literature* (3rd edn.); the annual listings in the *Keats–Shelley Journal*; the annual review article in *Studies in English Literature*; the autumn reviews issue of *The Wordsworth Circle*; the annual evaluative chapters in *The Year's Work in English Studies* and *The Romantic Movement* (edited by David Erdman); and J. R. de Jackson's exhaustive listing of *Romantic Poetry by Women*. The new database *Annotated Bibliography for English Studies* (ABES) will include regularly updated and evaluative entries on criticism dealing with the period. Among the proliferation of relevant web-sites (and offering a gateway to them) is *Romantic Circles*, edited by Steven E. Jones and others; the resources of *Romantic Circles* include hypertext editions and lists of recent publications in the field of Romantic studies. Bibliographical guides to English poetry and the English novel (both edited by A. E. Dyson) are still worth consulting for their concise chapters on authors in the period.

Increasingly central to thinking about the Romantic period are some difficult editorial considerations. What, for instance, *is* Wordsworth's *The Prelude*? Jonathan Wordsworth, the poet's most influential editor, surveys the various forms taken by the poem as a result of Wordsworth's revisions and concludes: 'As far as I can see, we can read whatever text we please—as long as we don't think it's the right one. There could be no such thing.' Brinkley's and Hanley's *Romantic Revisions*, in which Jonathan Wordsworth's essay appears, adopts what Walter Pater calls a 'relative spirit' towards the editorial problems thrown up by the attempt to arrive at texts for poets such as Wordsworth and Coleridge who revised their work intensively. The volume's introduction and seventeen essays ground theoretical issues—is there (for instance) such a thing as a determinate text?—in discussions of particular works. Stephen Gill describes how recent preferences for early texts of Wordsworth have transformed study of the poet; J. C. C. Mays (editor of the forthcoming edition of Coleridge's poems for the Bollingen *Collected Works*) suggests that much-revised poems have a multiple identity as 'versions'; Donald Reiman reminds us that Shelley's manuscripts reveal a decidedly effectual process of creative shaping; Timothy Webb explores the smoothing-out of tensions evident in Leigh Hunt's revisions for his *Autobiography*; and Jack Stillinger wonders whether it is appropriate to see Keats as an 'intentional' poet.

MICHAEL O'NEILL

Reiman's *Romantic Texts and Contexts* and *The Study of Modern Manuscripts* offer ponderable reflections on the theory and practice of editing Romantic texts, including in the latter volume a useful distinction between private, public, and confidential manuscripts. Zachary Leader explores the compositional and revising practices of the Romantics in a study that questions a number of received wisdoms, including the notion that Clare is best served by editors who use the poet's unaltered manuscripts as copy text and the view that Shelley's involvement in the writing of *Frankenstein* was regrettable (Leader sees Percy Shelley as collaborating with Mary Shelley). Most work to date, as suggested, has concentrated on the editing of poetry, but there is likely to be a growth in work on the critical implications of the editing of Romantic prose, given the number of big prose editions recently published and in the pipeline.

CRITICAL STUDIES

An idiosyncratic but brilliant work, guaranteed to provoke thought about Romanticism (in which category *Moby-Dick*, French Symbolist poetry, and Kierkegaard are rounded up), is W. H. Auden's *The Enchafèd Flood*. Deftly illustrated aphorisms blaze throughout: 'To the romantic . . . childhood is over, its island is astern, and there is no other.' Equally clear and worthwhile is Northrop Frye's study of English Romanticism in terms of its 'informing structures' or 'myths'; chief among Romanticism's concerns, for Frye, in a typically suggestive formulation, 'is a romance with the poet for hero'. The book contains a valuable exposition of *Prometheus Unbound* as a 'comedy' with Shakespearian parallels. Mario Praz's *The Romantic Agony*, first published in 1933, studies Romantic literature with special emphasis on its dark side and its 'erotic sensibility'. Praz takes in European as well as British authors, and interprets Romanticism to include 'Decadent' authors such as Baudelaire and Poe in an elegant, erudite typology of various forms of Romantic morbidity. Frank Kermode's *Romantic Image* also sees connections between Romantic poetry and later work. Especially in Yeats Kermode traces an ultimately Romantic obsession with the image and the isolation of the artist, the 'symbol-making power' intermittently redeeming the poet from what Yeats calls 'dissipation and despair'. A major (and readable) philosophical work on 'the making of the modern identity' which has much to say about the Romantic period is supplied by Charles Taylor. The surveys by Renwick and (especially) Jack are still worth consulting; Fiona Robertson has been commissioned to write the relevant volume in the *New Oxford English Literary History*. M. H. Abrams's collection of essays, *English Romantic Poets*, contains many famous pieces, including Lovejoy's 'On the Discrimination of Romanticisms' and W. K. Wimsatt's subtle study of 'The Structure of Romantic Nature Imagery'.

Frances Ferguson contributes to Greenblatt and Gunn a difficult, clever chapter on what has been going on in 'Romantic Studies'. She is good at getting back to 'the arguments that underlie the disputes', pointing out, for example, that 'The question of periodization . . . becomes a critical version of the question of unity so prominent and so vexed in Romantic aesthetic theory'. Paul Fry writes with originality about recent developments in Romantic criticism and about Romantic poetry (especially in his chapters on Wordsworth, Byron, and Keats) in his attempt to produce *A Defense of Poetry*, a defence based on the notion that literature puts us in touch with the 'preconceptual'. J. R. de J. Jackson's *Poetry of the Romantic Period* gives a crisply unpretentious 'history of poems rather than of poets', setting well-known poems cheek by jowl with work by 'the illustrious obscure'. A well-written account of the poetry of the 'big Six' that stresses the affinities rather than differences between the poets is *English Romanticism: The Grounds of Belief* by John Clubbe and Ernest J. Lovell, Jr. Kelvin Everest supplies an informative introduction to the poetry of the period and its contexts, sharpened throughout by awareness of 'The problem of how to integrate literary and historical judgement'.

Everest's volume should be read alongside Marilyn Gaull's impressive study. Gaull does much more than sketch in 'The Human Context' (her subject in the first part): she supplies well-organized essays on the many facets of Romanticism, including incisive accounts of 'Bards and Minstrelsy' (running from Percy's *Reliques* to Carlyle's fictionalizing of history) and 'Science', with which, as Gaull shows, Romantic poetry had a close if difficult relationship, now embracing it as offering a common understanding of creativity and life, now condemning it as reductive and opposed to the imagination. H. W. Piper studies ' "Romantic Pantheism" and its part in the development of the Romantic theory of the Imagination'. His book is of value for its account of Joseph Priestley's and Erasmus Darwin's belief in 'the active force of matter', its readings of Wordsworth's and Coleridge's early poetry, and its description of the influence of *The Excursion* on Shelley and Keats. Desmond King-Hele traces instructively 'the effect of [Erasmus] Darwin's ideas, images and words on the poets of the next two generations'.

Carl Woodring's *Politics in English Romantic Poetry* expounds the political dimension of Romantic poetry with clarity and wit. So Woodring describes Blake's experience of 'the difficulty of dealing imaginatively with current politics without the disjunction of wrath and pity', Wordsworth's 'democratic individualism' in *Lyrical Ballads*, and the mixture in Shelley's *Peter Bell the Third* of 'Fun and sadness . . . with satire'. More detailed historical accounts of the period include Linda Colley's study of 'the evolution of Britishness' from 1707 to 1837, from, that is, the Act of Union to Queen Victoria's accession to the throne. Colley does not discuss literature of the Romantic period, but her emphasis on the importance of Protestantism for the invention of British identity helps to contextualize the discoveries of poetic vocation in *The Prelude* and *Jerusalem*. Colley is also critical of the notion that it was 'only through oppositional activity that men and women outside the governing élite advanced their claims'. Here she modifies the trenchant position articulated by E. P. Thompson in his study of the making of the working class, a book still of unrivalled importance for understanding social forces at work in the period. Standard and still valuable histories are provided by Elie Halévy and R. J. White. Ian R. Christie, concentrating on the period from 1760 to 1815, 'tells the story of a nation's survival at peace with itself in an age of wars and revolution'. In a thoughtful study John W. Derry defends the record of the much-maligned Pitt and Liverpool administrations. More specifically, Robert Walmsley reappraises an event of immense symbolic importance: the Peterloo Massacre of August 1819. E. J. Hobsbawm supplies 'interpretation' rather than 'detailed narrative' as he traces the changes brought about by the French and Industrial Revolutions between 1789 and 1848.

There are many works on the French Revolution: two of the liveliest are Carlyle's famous attempt to see with 'the eye of History' and Simon Schama's richly humane if arguably counter-revolutionary narrative. George Lefebvre's two-volume work is still a standard account; so, too, is William Doyle's readable book. Marilyn Butler (1984) has edited a source-book of prose writings by Burke, Paine, Godwin, and others that respond polemically to the French Revolution, while H. T. Dickinson's *Britain and the French Revolution* includes pieces by Marianne Elliott on 'Ireland and the French Revolution', John Stevenson on 'Popular Radicalism and Popular Protest', and Iain Robertson Scott on 'the Literary Response'; Robertson Scott points out 'that those authors who embraced conservative ideas after 1803 did not merely accept the state of things as they are', an important insight if Wordsworth, Coleridge, and Southey are to receive their due. Political caricature—a flourishing genre in the period—can be studied in M. Dorothy George's two-volume work, while the *Radical Underworld* is explored by Iain McCalman. Raymond Williams's famous study lays the ground for much subsequent reflection on the inter-relations between literature and culture; he sees both professional self-interest and humane value in writers' emphases 'on the special nature of art-activity as a means to "imaginative truth" ' and 'on the artist as a special kind of person'. Seamus Deane analyses the 'reception of the French Enlightenment and Revolution' in England. Particularly illuminating are his readings of James Mackintosh (in *Vindiciae Gallicae* and other works) and Shelley (responding to La Mettrie's attack on 'remorse' and Cabanis's positing of 'a physiological basis for an altruistic morality').

J. R. Watson gives a vivid overview of the poetry of the period in his volume in Longman's Literature in English series. To accessible readings of texts and contexts, the second edition adds a judicious assessment of current debates about the nature of the Romantic. Watson has also co-edited with Jean Raimond *A Handbook to English Romanticism* (containing alphabetically ordered entries that range from the Abolition of the Slave Trade to Edward Young). He has edited, too, *An Infinite Complexity* (see especially the essays by David Fuller on Blake and David Constantine on Clare) and a collection of historically informed essays on 'The French Revolution in English Literature and Art' (including essays by Vincent Newey on Keats (collected in Newey 1995), Nicholas Roe on Wordsworth and Milton, Richard Gravil on *The Prelude*, and Tom Furniss on Burke and Paine and their 'contending economic and linguistic models'). Geoff Ward's volume on the period is not dissimilar in conception to Raimond's and Watson's *Handbook*; again, there are alphabetically arranged entries. Ward also includes lively essays on 'Romantic Poetry and Literary Theory' (Philip Shaw), 'Women, Romanticism, and the Gothic' (Alison Milbank), and 'Theatre and European Romanticism' (Edward Burns). His own essay on 'The Persistence of Romanticism' is a sharply written piece on Romanticism's pursuit of empathy and attendant self-questioning.

David Pirie has edited an excellent volume for *The Penguin History of Literature* on *The Romantic Period*. Paul Hamilton's outstanding account of Coleridge, Kelvin Everest's equable and elegant chapter on Shelley, and Pirie's detailed politicizing of Keats are the highlights of a volume which, among other things, has a chapter on Jane Austen (Margaret Kirkham) and a fine discussion of politics and the novel (Peter Garside), as well as wide-ranging, innovative studies of two subjects on which much has been written recently: reader relations (Kathryn Sutherland) and Orientalism (Marilyn Butler). Drawing on the work of critics such as Jon Klancher for whom reading in the period 'became the scene of a cultural struggle demanding a new mental map of the complex public and its textual desires', Sutherland paints a fascinating picture of publishing and reading practices in the period: a period in which the great periodicals (like the *Edinburgh Review* and its Tory rival, the *Quarterly Review*) staged many of its central intellectual contests (such as the value of Wordsworth's poetry, denigrated by Francis Jeffrey in the *Edinburgh Review*). Sutherland is interesting on poetry's decline in status after the 1820s, a decline that she relates to 'advancements in technology' and 'the consequent diversification and cheapening of print for a growing reading public'. Butler's discussion of Romantic Orientalism, that is, the way that poets of the period represented the East, is tied to a larger argument that 'Romantic world-making had real-life, complex applications'. She discerns in Southey's *The Curse of Kehama* both an illiberal ambition to traduce Hinduism in the interests of evangelizing Christianity and the first stirrings of the theme of 'Empire as a Western sickness' explored by Conrad's *Heart of Darkness*.

Current accounts of Romanticism are often in adversarial dialogue with the work of M. H. Abrams. Much debated and attacked in recent years, its scope, lucidity, and humaneness still make it indispensable. *The Mirror and the Lamp* is a 'history of aesthetic theory' that describes the aesthetic attitudes and ideas of major Romantic poets. Abrams depicts a shift from an eighteenth-century emphasis on the mind as a 'reflector of the external world' to the new, Romantic version of the mind as a lamp creatively illuminating external reality. The influential account of 'Coleridge and the Aesthetics of Organism' describes how in Coleridgian thought 'belief in the complete autonomy and the unique originality of the individual work went hand in hand with a confidence in universal principles of value'. This describes a belief and a confidence that have been largely set aside in recent criticism of the Romantic period.

The later study, *Natural Supernaturalism*, is Abrams's outstanding contribution to Romantic studies. A formidable work that sees Wordsworth as the master-poet of his age and controversially omits Byron because of his 'satirical perspective on the vatic stance of his Romantic contemporaries', the book's central concern is 'with the secularization of inherited theological ideas and ways of thinking' in England and Germany, 'two great Protestant nations with a history of theological and political radicalism'. Romanticism's 'high argument', on Abrams's reading, is succinctly set out in Wordsworth's prospectus to *The Recluse* which asserts the superiority of the poet's 'vision . . . of the awesome depths and height of the human mind' over 'Milton's Christian story'. Romantic poetry is viewed by Abrams as offering a secular, humanist version of the Christian story of the fall of mankind and subsequent redemption. This version adapts ideas of apocalypse and places its trust less in 'political revolution' than in 'the powers inherent in human consciousness', powers shown, as Wallace Stevens's lines have it, 'in the act of finding | What will suffice'. (There is an excellent section of a chapter on the 'post-Romantic' that looks at authors such as Baudelaire, Rimbaud, Hopkins, Plath, and Ginsberg.) Abrams, however, makes clear the importance of the French Revolution for the structures of feeling found in literature of the period: hope and despondency nearly always, for Abrams, represent an internalizing of political response.

Natural Supernaturalism is almost too fine and compendious a book for its own good. It is troubling to see how often its nuances and subtleties are misrepresented and simplified. If its larger affirmations about Romanticism have been influential, it is also the case that few studies give so powerful or so moving a sense of the various spiritual struggles and crises endured by Romantic writers and inspiring their quest for a lost 'home'. Abrams's collection of essays, *The Correspondent Breeze*, is also essential reading; it includes his 'English Romanticism: The Spirit of the Age' (first published in 1963), in which he argues for the importance of the 'epic events of their revolutionary era' for an understanding of the Romantics (especially for the poets who reached maturity in the 1790s) and asserts that 'It is by a peculiar injustice that Romanticism is often described as a mode of escapism'. At the same time he points out that the great Romantic poems were written 'in the later mood' of 'disillusionment or despair'. Abrams's essay in the same volume on 'Structure and Style in the Greater Romantic Lyric' (first published in 1965) explores the 'repeated out-in-out process'—'out' being the movement from mind to natural landscape—in Romantic lyrics, a process inaugurated, for Abrams, by Coleridge.

Before his defence of 'The Western Canon', Harold Bloom was best known for his theory of the anxiety of influence, which in an exuberant mingling of Freud and the cabbala saw post-Enlightenment poets as engaged in imaginative struggle with their predecessors. He is, in essence and at his best, a responsive and rhetorically skilful reader of Romantic and post-Romantic poetry. *The Visionary Company* contains condensed yet accessible reports on the major (and some of the minor) Romantic poets; it is composed in a style that, in its unmelodramatic urgency and swiftness of transition, is answerable to the poetry it discusses. So Bloom writes that 'The ruin and desolation that shadow the heart's affections in *Prometheus* haunt all of [Shelley's] later poetry', and that in *Dejection: An Ode* 'the voice is turned against itself with an intensity that only the greatest poets have been able to bring over into language'. Bloom lays emphasis on 'The Internalization of Quest Romance' (to quote the title of an essay gathered in *The Ringers in the Tower*), writing that 'The high cost of Romantic internalization, that is, of finding paradises within a renovated man, tends to manifest itself in the arena of self-consciousness.' He is preoccupied by the tragic power of the Romantic concern with 'inwardness', and he sees the modernist enterprise associated with T. S. Eliot as a flawed (and largely unconscious) effort to evade this concern. In fact, Bloom's work frequently proposes exciting continuities (masking and masked by agonistic struggle) between the Romantics and later poets such as Tennyson, Yeats, Stevens, and Hart Crane. Always he is alert to the 'cost' exacted by quest, and the resulting tendency of the Romantic poets to write 'crisis poems': Wordsworth's 'Ode: Intimations of Immortality' and Shelley's 'Ode to the West Wind' are examples. *A Map of Misreading* and *Poetry and Repression* are difficult, sometimes maddening, but often enthralling attempts to flesh out the view proposed by *The Anxiety of Influence* that poems come into being through 'misreadings'—prompted by the desire for individuality—of precursor poems. What is most valuable in Bloom's work is a troubled refusal to let go of the imaginative and aesthetic worth of poetry, a refusal evident in the coda of his book on Wallace Stevens.

Bloom's reputation was at its height in the mid-1970s, as can be seen by the respectful references to his work in Thomas Weiskel's profound grappling with *The Romantic Sublime*. Weiskel sees the 'sublime' as involving a desire for transcendence; employing Kantian and Freudian ideas in an unreductive way, he investigates the rhetoric, structure, and psychology of the Romantics' sublime moments. The backlash against the stress laid by Bloom and others on 'consciousness' and 'inwardness' is apparent in Marilyn Butler's wittily iconoclastic, socially directed study of 1981. Sceptical of the notion that Romanticism is 'a single if complex theoretical movement', Butler relishes the variety of movements and styles between 1760 and 1830. One reason for placing her opening date as early as 1760 is to suggest provocative continuities between Enlightenment rationalism and the Wordsworth of the preface to the *Lyrical Ballads* or the Blake of the *Songs*. Coleridge's great poetry of the late 1790s is seen, by contrast, as part of a counter-revolutionary reaction, pushing to 'an expressive extreme art's retreat from ideas'. Putting the Romantics into contexts allows Butler to question the assumptions of Abrams, Bloom, and others; her book tilts against Romantic self-aggrandizing, especially when, in her view, that self-aggrandizing is duplicated in the work of its (male) critics. Butler's book is a fund of brilliant hints and suggestions: she sketches the ideological struggles at work in the period, in, say, the second generation's turning away from German models to Mediterranean precursors as it reacts against supposed Coleridgean mystification; and she gives equal weight to the importance and achievement of prose writers of the period, offering as the two major writers of the period (partly because they possessed complex historical imaginations) Shelley and Scott.

Butler's influential book relies on width of reading and knowledge and on uncommon common sense. A more theorized interrogation of Romanticism was provided two years later by Jerome J. McGann in *The Romantic Ideology*. McGann finds fault with commentators on Romanticism (including his earlier self) for their 'uncritical absorption in Romanticism's own self-representations'. The 'Ideology' of the title is constructed both by poets of the period who practise 'displacement' (that is, they resituate 'in a variety of idealized localities' what McGann calls 'actual human issues') and by critics complicit in these acts of displacement. It would appear that McGann's real target is the latter rather than the former group, but he is hard to pin down here; if he seems to praise poets of the Romantic period for enacting 'the emotional experience of contradiction' in their work, in the same breath he says that they do so 'in the form of Romantic ideology'. In *The Beauty of Inflections* McGann practises a 'historical criticism' that, by virtue of its historical awareness, 'systematically opposes its own reification': the results include the crucial attempt to bring 'Historical Method' to bear on Keats's work, the questioning of periodization in an essay on Crabbe, and inquiries into the meaning of the meanings attributed to *The Ancient Mariner* and 'the social and historical ground' of Byron's work. The centrality of Byron to McGann's reading of the Romantic period makes a pointed contrast with Abrams's marginalization of the poet.

Yet McGann is himself implicated in the ideology he deplores, according to Clifford Siskin, whose book is engaged in an austere search for 'a kind of knowledge that historicizes its own disciplinary procedures within an analysis of the literary institution's production of value'. Whether Siskin is right to say censoriously that McGann 'reproduces a particular form of the human' by insisting on the 'historical uniqueness of subject and object' will depend, finally, on one's values and assumptions. It may be that Siskin alerts one to the fact that—like many Romantic poems—McGann's 1983 book is fascinatingly, even creatively, riven by conflicting impulses. Siskin's book analyses the implications of the fact that 'almost all our literary histories of the late eighteenth and early nineteenth centuries are themselves Romantic'. 'Literature' itself and 'the deep self' are, for Siskin, ideological constructions determined by changing social relations; for him, it is the critic's duty to historicize such constructions.

Siskin contrasts McGann's procedures with those of critics such as L. J. Swingle who 'have sought a stylistic or rhetorical theory of the workings of Romantic poems'. Swingle himself is concerned with the various exploratory and questioning modes by which Romantic poets and novelists resist 'dogmatic assertion' in favour of 'inquiry'; he seeks to approach these issues historically and provides an elegant account of many Romantic works, including a good chapter on the Romantic novel that contains a deft discussion of the way Scott's endings 'unsettle our complacency'. Certainly, the turn to the historical in the 1980s was at once a reaction against and a sometimes less than amicable ally of the deconstructive or rhetorical reading of Romantic literature associated, above all, with the work of Paul de Man. De Man's 'The Rhetoric of Temporality' and *The Rhetoric of Romanticism* are classic deconstructions of what might be termed Coleridgian Romanticism. Whereas Coleridge values symbol, de Man argues in 'The Rhetoric of Temporality' that early Romantic literature (especially that by Rousseau and Wordsworth) 'finds its true voice' when it forsakes 'symbol' for 'allegory', the latter word meaning for de Man a mode of writing that concedes the gap between 'image' and 'substance' and 'prevents the self from an illusory identification with the non-self'. Whereas Coleridge finds in the artwork a system of harmonized coherences, de Man discovers in Romantic literature attempts to evade or confront the 'conflict between a conception of the self seen in its authentically temporal predicament and a defensive strategy that tries to hide from this negative self-knowledge'. Rhetorical reading is particularly interested in investigating the linguistic symptoms of these defensive strategies. To 'allegory' de Man links 'irony' as central to the Romantics' 'Rhetoric of Temporality'; he writes on irony as 'unrelieved *vertige*' involving, for writers such as Friedrich Schlegel and Baudelaire, 'an endless process that leads to no synthesis'.

De Man's practice of rhetorical reading has been influential; the 'figures' of few Romantic poems have escaped being decomposed (to adapt the title of Cynthia Chase's study) and in works such as J. Hillis Miller's *The Linguistic Moment* the Romantic and post-Romantic tradition has been scrutinized with fascinated scepticism. Tilottama Rajan's *Dark Interpreter* also probes the self-divided dynamics of Romantic poems in the light of various Romantic and post-Romantic schemes of thought, such as Schiller's distinction between the naive and the sentimental and Nietzsche's dialogue in *The Birth of Tragedy* between the Apollonian and the Dionysian. Rajan has more interest than de Man in the imaginative benefits of self-division. While her book would be impossible without de Man's exposure of Romanticism as a rhetoric, her readings trace inner conflicts in a spirit that is far from demystifying. David Simpson (1979) has stressed how, in its linguistic workings as in its philosophical underpinnings (there are helpful pages on Kant and Hegel), 'Romanticism . . . conceived and exploited and perhaps suffered the radical instability of the "self" '; through close attention to a number of poems and passages he argues that 'Romantic poetry is organised to make us confront the question of authority'.

Susan Wolfson's *The Questioning Presence* is indebted to but not overpowered by deconstruction as it investigates the status and process of questioning in Romantic poetry, with particular regard to Wordsworth and Keats. Wolfson writes with a vigilant sensitivity that mirrors her view that 'questioning does not just subvert meanings and closure; it also tests the possibility of new meanings and projects'. Her book teems with suggestive insights such as the remark that there is in Keats a 'tension of poetic voice against authorial design'. Arden Reed's edited collection, *Romanticism and Language*, contains important essays that do not necessarily sign up to deconstruction but do 'find the dissonances and differences of Romantic literature to be irresolvable'. A valuable reading of 'Language as Living Form' in poets including Wordsworth, Shelley, and Byron is provided by Isobel Armstrong who takes her cue from Hegel's notion (as articulated by Armstrong) that 'Being . . . is the continual and reciprocal construction and deconstruction of self and other'. Marjorie Levinson raises vital issues in her attempt to answer the question 'Why *Romantic* fragment poems?'; she reads the Romantic fragment poem as engaged in complex ways with a dormant or explicit aesthetic of incompletion.

Much recent criticism has stressed the links between English and Continental, especially German, Romanticism; German Romanticism, in its analogies with and possible influence on British Romanticism, raises large questions about the relationship (or discontinuity) between literature and philosophy. A good starting point is the lucid chapter on 'German Ideas' in Wimsatt's and Brooks's study whose synthesizing ambitions do not preclude some sharply individual points, as when they remark of Kant's aesthetic theory that 'here was a system which conceived Homer and Shakespeare as less aesthetically pure than wallpaper'. Some sense of the ferment of ideas in 'German Aesthetic and Literary Criticism from Lessing to Hegel', as the book's subtitle has it, can be gained by reading in David Simpson's *The Origins of Modern Critical Thought*.

Lilian R. Furst's slim anthology also gives access to 'European Romanticism', while her *Romanticism in Perspective* is full of interest as it compares and contrasts writers from different cultures, juxtaposing, for example, Lamartine's 'Au rossignol' and Keats's 'Ode to a Nightingale'. A major idea from German Romanticism to affect study of English authors is 'Romantic Irony', the ability of a writer and text simultaneously to hold an idea or attitude and undercut it in the name of creative freedom. Anne K. Mellor's *English Romantic Irony* is helpful on the topic, seeing it as a more positive force than some other commentators do. The essay by John Francis Feltzer in Hoffmeister's collection of essays is also of use. Mark Kipperman considers the implications for Romantic poetry of Kantian idealism, insisting as it did 'that the world, even in its most fundamental properties of space and time, answers our questions with our own voice'. Particularly useful are sophisticated readings of Shelley and Byron that discover in 'romantic quest' 'a mobility greater than enchantment or disillusionment'. Kathleen Wheeler has written acutely on the links between Shelley, Hegel, and Nietzsche on the one hand and Derrida on the other; her expositions of Shelley and Hegel and her critique of new historicism are especially thought-provoking.

Though not concerned primarily with Romantic philosophy, Michael Cooke in *Acts of Inclusion* considers the difference between the mode of argument in Romantic poetry and analytical thought. Cooke is good on the way that 'The romantic mind sets itself in opposition to mere opposition.' The collection edited by Porter and Teich contains essays that explore how diverse Romanticisms took place in different countries and how 'these different national Romanticisms coexisted in symbiotic relations to each other'. The editors argue that 'The Romantics liked to forge solacing ideologies for the developing bourgeois societies they so profoundly despised.' Equally contentious is David Simpson (1993), who seeks to link British reactions to the French Revolution with a current 'antitheoretical bandwagon' he finds alarming.

A robust questioning of Romanticism has been carried out by critics interested in issues of gender. Barbara Schapiro mixes gender issues with psychoanalytical insights in her description of Shelley, Keats, Coleridge, and Wordsworth as ambivalently and narcissistically fixated, to varying degrees, on the 'mother imago'. The danger of 'reductionism' of which the author is aware is not wholly avoided. But there is much of interest in the book, as when Schapiro sees Moneta's face (in *The Fall of Hyperion*) as symbolizing 'a vision of a whole reality that includes both love and loss'. Anne Mellor's *Romanticism and Gender* (following on from her important edited collection *Romanticism and Feminism*) argues that accounts of Romanticism—whether humanist, deconstructive, or historicist—have been 'unwittingly gender-biased'. Her answer is to set up, yet also suggest the theoretical limitations of, a 'polarity' between 'masculine' and 'feminine' Romanticisms. The book is, arguably, valuable less for its struggles to define what is 'masculine' and 'feminine' than for its readings of works by women writers of the period in relation to its supposedly dominant values and ideologies, sketched with great if at times arguable clarity by Mellor. So a chapter looks at the way that a central Romantic notion—the sublime ('associated', for Mellor, 'with an experience of masculine empowerment')—is domesticated by Ann Radcliffe, Lady Morgan, and Susan Ferrier. Felicia Hemans and Letitia Landon are explored through a perceptive discussion of their acceptance of 'the hegemonic construction of the ideal woman'.

Meena Alexander examines the different meanings of 'freedom' for male and female authors in Romantic writing, studying how in the work of Mary Wollstonecraft, Dorothy Wordsworth, and Mary Shelley 'The claims of Romantic subjectivity are questioned, undermined and finally refashioned.' Marlon Ross writes powerfully about the implications of gender in Romantic poetry by men and women. Taking his cue from a later essay by McGann (1992), Philip Cox argues, refreshingly, that 'Romantic texts frequently challenge what has been reductively thought of as their singular "ideology"'; his reading of the way genre and gender interact is alert to complexity, finding in, say, *Tintern Abbey*'s 'masculine accommodation of the feminine' scope for a positive account of the poem. Finally, Jerome McGann's most recent book (1996) explores the poetry of 'sensibility' and 'sentiment' chiefly by women writers such as Ann Yearsley, Mary Robinson, Hemans, and Landon. In an apparent reversal of his position in *The Romantic Ideology*, McGann urges respect for 'the aesthetic character and value' of poetry; he is concerned by 'the tendency to approach all art . . . in rational—in theoretical and philosophical—terms'. If the implicit reprimand is hard to accept from an author so committed in his 1983 book to a decidedly 'theoretical' project, the resulting readings are still in thrall to dominant conceptual categories. That said, McGann's readings are exciting, affecting, and inward, especially when dealing with the link between the imaginative and the socio-economic in the work of Hemans and Landon.

Two fine books on Romantic poetry's reworking of traditional genres have been written by Brian Wilkie and Stuart Curran. Wilkie attends to poems 'in which the epic intention is central'; his study includes a serviceable chapter on Southey and Landor as well as chapters on Wordsworth, Shelley, Keats, and Byron. It disputes the idea that Romantic poets rebelled 'against the literary forms consecrated by the past', and it discusses, for example, the 'epic pattern' of *The Prelude* in relation to Homer's flashback technique in *The Odyssey*. There are also astute chapters on *The Revolt of Islam*, *Hyperion*, and *Don Juan*. Stuart Curran's satisfyingly distilled and wide-ranging volume explores how 'major forms of earlier poetry are resuscitated and transformed in the Romanticism of Great Britain'. The genres discussed exclude satire, but embrace the sonnet, the hymn and ode, the pastoral, the romance, the epic, and what Curran calls 'composite orders', a category including *Prometheus Unbound* (a 'lyrical drama') and *Don Juan*, 'a tour de force of generic capaciousness'.

Lucy Newlyn's *'Paradise Lost' and the Romantic Reader* is also concerned with Romantic reworkings of past literature, specifically Milton's great epic. Organized round themes ('Allusion', 'Politics', 'Religion', 'Sex', 'Subjectivity', 'Imagination') and finishing with a reading of Blake's *Milton*, this thoughtful book proposes a Milton who was himself far more indeterminate than is often allowed and whose influence on the Romantics was liberating rather than constraining. In a complex but rewarding study E. Douka Kabitoglou detects affinities between Platonic dialectic and Romantic poetry. Kabitoglou views Plato as a thinker who delights in the interplay of contraries. Jonathan Bate (1986; corr. 1989) has produced a clear and sensitive book on 'Shakespeare's influence on the minds and works of the major English Romantic poets', while Ralph Pite valuably explores Dante's impact on Romantic writing.

Aidan Day's volume helpfully charts 'Constructions of the Term "Romantic" ', in the words of one chapter title. He points out that 'Romantic' was not a term much used by the Romantics themselves, Byron being typically ironic in a letter to Goethe about the possibility of there being in England 'a great struggle about what they call *"Classical"* and *"Romantic"* '. Yet writers of the time were aware of what Shelley in *A Defence of Poetry* called 'the electric life which burns within [the] words' of Romantic works. Day is good on twentieth-century political constructions of Romanticism: condemned by Irving Babbitt for laying 'the ground for the horrors of revolutionary collectivism', yet seen by Albert Guerard (in 1942) as having dark affinities with a proto-Fascist cult of irrationality. Complementing Day's volume and more ambitious in scope are the essays in Curran's *The Cambridge Companion to British Romanticism*: the best pieces, such as 'Romanticism and Language' by William Keach and 'Romantic Hellenism' by Timothy Webb, are original (rather than merely synthesizing), while Marshall Brown writes thought-provokingly on Romanticism's complex relations with the Enlightenment (the topic of a full-length study by him). Brown argues that 'The new [Romanticism] turns against the old [the Enlightenment], but it does so from a historical logic already inscribed in the old, and still preserved in the new.'

A convenient way of sampling some of the most challenging recent accounts of Romanticism is provided by two collections: Cynthia Chase's volume in the Longman Critical Readers series (1993) and Duncan Wu's *Romanticism: A Critical Reader*. Possibly because of commercial pressures, both collections, for all their alertness to new critical approaches, focus on a small group of authors traditionally thought to be 'Romantic'. Chase's introduction analyses the strategies employed by new historicism and deconstruction (or 'rhetorical reading'). She points out that political readings of Romantic poetry such as Marjorie

Levinson's critique of *Tintern Abbey* (a poem faulted by Levinson for not say-ing anything about the plight of vagrants camped in the Abbey's grounds) ignore the fact that 'literary language means in another way, and that engage-ment with historical and political realities does not necessarily take the form of literal statements about empirical facts'. And she notes that 'rhetorical read-ing' runs the risk 'of claiming that a text *can* control and know its own struc-tures'. Chase writes especially well about Paul de Man, one of whose essays is included in the volume. The volume also features examples of feminist or gender-based criticism by Margaret Homans on *Frankenstein* as 'about the death and obviation of the mother and about the son's quest for a substitute object of desire'; and by Karen Swann who discusses *Christabel*'s cunning invest-ment in and critique of the 'cultural fantasy' that dramatizes the opposition between ' "manly" speech and "feminine bodies" ', in Swann's words from a companion article. Duncan Wu's collection contains that companion article by Swann, as well as Homans's piece on *Frankenstein*. It also includes Nelson Hilton's 'Blakean Zen', in which a tricksy poststructuralism catches up with and, in places, overtakes Blake; Alan Liu's historicized reading of Wordsworth (emphasizing that the poet recognized that 'history was there before, and will be there after, the agony of consciousness'); Peter Manning's brilliant account of Byron's creative entanglement in the webs of a language that inevitably precedes and defines him; Leon Waldoff on the way Keats's odes attempt 'to restore a lost inner world'; Tom Paulin's impassioned and beautifully written advocacy of Clare's poetry as 'a form of Nation Language beating its head against the walls of urbane, polished Official Standard'; and Edward Said's provocative reading of *Mansfield Park* as a novel that 'connects the actualities of British power overseas to the domestic imbroglio within the Bertram estate'.

There has been a good deal of work on the relations between art (and the theory of art) and literature. J. R. Watson (1970) examines the influence upon the major Romantic poets 'of current habits of viewing landscape, chiefly those associated with the cult of the picturesque'; his book can be recommended for its lucid readings of many central poems in the period. Hugh Honour's volumes on neoclassicism and Romanticism in the visual arts are clearly written and well illustrated; John Buxton's civilized *The Grecian Taste* links literature written between 1740 and 1820 to 'The Greek Revival' celebrated by Winckelmann. One reason why painting rather than music is often related to literature of the period is that there are major British Romantic artists who compel comparison with Romantic writers. The connection between Word-sworth and Constable is treated by Karl Kroeber (1975), who has also edited with William Walling a collection of essays that explore the interrelations between literature and art: Carl Woodring discusses 'What Coleridge Thought of Pictures'; Jean H. Hagstrum shows that Blake was related to the contem-porary art scene through 'a network of complex and elusive ties'; and James

A. W. Heffernan looks at colour in the work of the English Romantics, explor-ing, for instance, how 'Like Turner's *Slavers* . . . the seascape of [*The Ancient Mariner*] is dominated by the color of fire and blood' (on the fascinating topic of 'colour' part I of Richard Cronin's study is illuminating).

The relevant volume (edited by Michael Booth and others) of *The Revels History of Drama* offers helpful information about theatrical practices during the period. More critically penetrating on the subject of Romantic drama are the essays in Richard Allen Cave's edited collection, especially Timothy Webb's outstanding piece, 'The Romantic Poet and the Stage: A Short, Sad, History'. Joseph W. Donohue, Jr., has written a useful book on *Dramatic Character in the English Romantic Age*. Jonathan Bate (1989) is both influenced by and resistant to new historicism in his 'account of how Shakespeare was constituted in England in the eighteenth and early nineteenth centuries, and how cultural life during that period was by constitution Shakespearean'. He endorses Frank Kermode's view that 'the books we call classics possess intrinsic qualities that endure', yet he is alive to the way 'appropriation may slide into misappropri-ation'. John Kerrigan's wide-ranging *Revenge Tragedy* includes a scintillating chapter on 'Revolution, Revenge, and Romantic Tragedy'. Among other things, the chapter proposes a Nietzschean reading of Beatrice in *The Cenci* as bravely choosing 'the course which she must take'.

The best introductory survey of fiction in the period is Gary Kelly's Longman volume. Kelly stresses 'the social function of fiction', interpreting the genre's increasing 'literariness' as part and parcel of the process by which the 'gentrified professional classes' formed a sense of identity and legitimacy. Their great champion, according to Kelly, was Jane Austen, about whom Kelly writes well, shrewdly noting the meanings implicit in the novelist's formal devices and commenting on Austen's corrective response to 'the Romantic cul-ture of the self'. But Kelly's overall design is to lure us away from the notion of Jane Austen as the one great novelist of the period. He writes acutely, too, about the 'ideologically motivated' fusion of discourses in Scott's fiction (the motive being the wish to present the ' "modernization" of Scottish society' from a perspective attuned to 'social change' but sympathetic to 'comprom-ise'). Going far beyond fresh appraisals of these two famous novelists, Kelly's book includes an impressively contextualized account of the variety of fiction in the period: there is an especially lively account of Peacock as a novelist con-cerned with 'the limitations . . . of Romantic discourse'.

Kelly is also the author of a book on *The English Jacobin Novel 1780–1805*. This is a ground-breaking study that looks at novels by Robert Bage, Elizabeth Inchbald, Thomas Holcroft, and William Godwin, novelists said to share a 'philosophically motivated search for "unity of design" '. Kelly argues that the tumultuous events of the 1790s affected the novelists; he discovers in Godwin's *St Leon* (1799), for instance, 'a note of pessimism, even an elegiac note suggesting that the heroic age of public action was past'. Pamela Clemit's *The Godwinian Novel* lucidly studies Godwin's creation of a novel form able to serve as the vehicle for the imaginative pursuit of rational inquiry. This form is seen as being inherited and modified by Mary Shelley and Charles Brockden Brown, both of whom receive substantial treatment. A strength of the book is its recognition of the marshalling intelligence of the novelists with whom it deals: Godwin and Mary Shelley emerge as novelists in control of their readers —to whom, none the less, considerable responsibility is given through the use of multiple narrations and first-person narrators.

Yet psychoanalytical interest in the 'Romantic Unconscious' fruitfully persists in the work of many critics, notably David Punter, whose work on Romantic Gothic seeks to marry Freudian and Marxist approaches to texts. His chapters in *The Literature of Terror* on 'The Classic Gothic Novels' (principally those by Radcliffe and Lewis) and 'Gothic and Romanticism' (including Blake, Coleridge, Shelley, Byron, Keats, John Polidori, and Mary Shelley) are remarkably suggestive, especially about Gothic fiction and 'the development in sophistication' it displays. Romantic Gothic has, indeed, attracted much attention from critics often impelled by the desire to widen the canon and redefine Romanticism. Fred Botting gives a succinct reprise of current developments: Gothic 'signifies a writing of excess'; it is haunted by uncertainties about rational and political structures (including assumptions about gender— hence the emergence of interest in so-called 'female Gothic'); linked to 'fears of social disintegration', it is ambivalently transgressive. In a book that is out of step with much recent work on Gothic fiction, Elizabeth Napier seeks to analyse ways in which Gothic fails: chiefly, on her reading of *The Castle of Otranto*, *The Mysteries of Udolpho*, *The Monk*, and *The Italian*, through its inability to offer its reader 'the complex response of ambivalence that the form ideally demands'. This is a provocative and stimulating work. E. J. Clery's well-researched volume in the formidably historicist Cambridge Studies in Romanticism series suggests a 'gendered differentiation of Gothic modes': female authors such as Radcliffe (under cultural pressure to be didactic) explain the supernatural; male authors allow themselves the non-didactic *frisson* associated with sublime indeterminacies.

George Levine seeks to 'take the word *realism* and the idea of representation seriously'. Defining realism as 'an attempt to use language to get beyond language', but never minimizing the difficulty and elusiveness of the concept or the sophistication of his chosen writers, he links early nineteenth-century fiction to Victorian works and includes chapters on Austen and Scott. In an informed, alert study, Ian Duncan seeks to rehabilitate the genre of 'romance', a vehicle, in the case of Radcliffe's fiction, for making history 'visible' if 'alien' and, in the case of Scott's novels, for 'the representation of a public, national life'. The impact of eighteenth-century notions of sensibility and sentimentalism on Romanticism is a recurrent topic in recent work. In a lively book Nicola J. Watson looks at the 'fate of the letter within the novel as a pointer to the changing concerns of literary-political discourse over the period': on her argument, conservative authors such as Austen suppress the epistolary form in favour of third-person narration that is more suited to 'the disciplining of individual desire by social consensus'; other writers, such as Maturin, Hazlitt, and Hogg, push 'sentimental paradigms to their furthest extreme'.

Feminist treatment of fiction during the period is wide-ranging. An influential text is Gilbert's and Gubar's *The Madwoman in the Attic*. Gilbert and Gubar trace a tradition of female writing that centres on the fact that 'the artists . . . studied were literally and figuratively confined'. They discern in writings of the nineteenth century 'a common, female impulse to struggle free from social and literary confinement through strategic redefinitions of self, art, and society'. Jane Austen emerges as self-divided, fascinated by the imagination yet anxious that it is 'unfeminine'; Mary Shelley confronts 'Milton's bogey' (Virginia Woolf's phrase) by writing a novel, *Frankenstein*, that is full of shape-changing and duplication that hide and reveal the feminist truth that 'for Mary Shelley the part of Eve *is* all the parts'. Mary Poovey's *The Proper Lady* has also been influential in its discernment of tension between social role and imaginative ambition in women writers of the period.

Nancy Armstrong thinks that Gilbert and Gubar 'virtually ignore the historical conditions that women have confronted as writers'. Her book attempts to put 'domestic fiction' within the context of its 'historical conditions'; she discusses *Emma* as 'striving to empower a new class of people' ('polite country gentlefolk') and has comments on the political implications of the figure of 'the monstrous woman' that emerges fully blown in Victorian fiction. Helen Small writes about the treatment of female insanity in fiction from 1800 to 1865. The dates of her study, running from the 'decline of sentimentalism' to 'the emergence of sensation fiction', unsettle traditional groupings to good effect. Her discussion includes an analysis of *Sense and Sensibility* as an attempt to 'express the demands of feeling' without having recourse to sentimentalism, as well as stimulating accounts of *The Bride of Lammermoor*, *Jane Eyre*, *Great Expectations*, and *The Woman in White*. Not the least of its virtues is its awareness of links between the 'Romantic' and the 'Victorian'.

A level-headed history of women's writing in the period (concentrating on the three writers mentioned below) is provided by Gary Kelly (1993). For Kelly writing by women participates in a 'cultural revolution' that pivots on 'the relationship of class and gender'; women writers of the period seek 'to reshape civil society' in ways that are 'at times contradictory'. If in the 1790s Helen Maria Williams 'feminized' revolutionary culture and Mary Hays flirted with a 'Rousseauist sense of liberation', Elizabeth Hamilton took 'the "anti-Jacobin", counter-feminist line'; in the 'Revolutionary aftermath' Williams and Hays were forced to take up new modes of non-confrontational 'feminist critique' (Hays's biographies of women are an example), while Hamilton, on Kelly's reading, 'moved closer to Revolutionary feminism after 1800'.

What, then, does the future hold for Romantic criticism? A likely possibility, in the short term, is that Romanticism will be seen by many critics less as an identifiable literary essence than as a complex, fraught, and fascinating bundle of differing practices and achievements. A number of collections of essays that build on recent work reveal in their titles a wish to aspire beyond the restraining medium of the category of the Romantic. *Beyond Romanticism*, edited by Stephen Copley and John Whale, seeks to resist Romanticism's 'idealizing power'. The fact that it succeeds in doing so will not strike all readers as unequivocally desirable. Yet in its emphasis on materialist approaches, lucid critiques, and authors usually thought of as peripheral to Romanticism, it gives a very good sense of where a major line of British Romantic criticism had reached by the start of the 1990s. In *Re-visioning Romanticism* Carol Shiner Wilson and Joel Haefner bring together essays that 'suggest ways in which women's texts force us to rethink British Romanticism'. Katharine M. Rogers strikes a typical note in her essay on Charlotte Smith's fiction when she says of Smith—by no means to her disadvantage—that she 'could not make the enormous claims of men possessed by the Romantic imagination'. Especially good essays by Susan Wolfson and Jerome J. McGann that revalue the poetry of Felicia Hemans lend distinction to this attempt to rethink Romanticism. The editors side with Lovejoy against Wellek in believing that Romanticism is not a 'monolithic field of study'. They anticipate that future study will be preoccupied by the attempt to identify schools of Romanticism.

John Beer's edited collection argues in sophisticated detail and from a variety of critical positions that Romanticism should be regarded less as 'a defined entity' than as 'a site of questioning'. Mary A. Favret and Nicola J. Watson have edited a volume of essays that seek to situate themselves *At the Limits of Romanticism*. A sharp introduction surveys recent work to argue that 'Predicated on the history of readings and institutions that have preceded it, romanticism at the limits reflects upon that history in order to project its own'. That Romantic literature cannot be read on its own terms is a premiss of much recent work, work intelligently exercised by problems of historical distance. Still, for those such as the present writer (see O'Neill) who believe that the effort to imagine such a reading is not wholly worthless, Charles Altieri's attempt to discover a 'possible positive role for poetic eloquence' marks a high point in a fine collection of essays edited by Kenneth R. Johnston and others. (See also Thomas McFarland's *Romanticism and the Heritage of Rousseau* for an affecting attempt to 'hear once more the plangency of Romantic activity'.) In Johnston's volume both new historicists (James Chandler and Marilyn Butler) and those such as M. H. Abrams who believe that *Tintern Abbey* 'speaks to enduring constants amid the ever-changing conditions of what it means to be human' have their voice. My guess is that thinking about literature of the Romantic period will continue to provoke rewarding critical conflict and to show an increasingly pragmatic acceptance of different approaches.

REFERENCES

Abrams, M. H., *The Mirror and the Lamp: Romantic Theory and the Critical Tradition* (Oxford, 1953).

—— *Natural Supernaturalism: Tradition and Revolution in Romantic Literature* (New York, 1971).

—— (ed.), *English Romantic Poets: Modern Essays in Criticism* (2nd edn., London, 1975).

—— *The Correspondent Breeze: Essays on English Romanticism* (New York, 1984).

Alexander, Meena, *Women in Romanticism: Mary Wollstonecraft, Dorothy Wordsworth and Mary Shelley* (Basingstoke, 1989).

Annotated Bibliography for English Studies, ed. Robert Clark (Lisse, 1996).

Armstrong, Isobel, *Language as Living Form in Nineteenth-Century Poetry* (Brighton, 1982).

Armstrong, Nancy, *Desire and Domestic Fiction: A Political History of the Novel* (New York, 1987).

Ashfield, Andrew (ed.), *Romantic Women Poets, 1770–1838* (Manchester, 1995).

Auden, W. H., *The Enchafèd Flood: or, The Romantic Iconography of the Sea* (London, 1951).

Bate, Jonathan, *Shakespeare and the English Romantic Imagination* (1986; Oxford, 1989, with corr.)

—— *Shakespearean Constitutions: Politics, Theatre, Criticism 1730–1830* (Oxford, 1989).

—— (ed.), *The Romantics on Shakespeare* (Harmondsworth, 1992).

Beer, John (ed.), *Questioning Romanticism* (Baltimore, 1995).

Bloom, Harold, *The Visionary Company: A Reading of English Romantic Poetry* (1961; rev. and enlarged edn., Ithaca, NY, 1971).

—— (ed.), *Romanticism and Consciousness: Essays in Criticism* (New York, 1970).

—— *The Ringers in the Tower: Studies in Romantic Tradition* (Chicago, 1971).

—— *The Anxiety of Influence: A Theory of Poetry* (New York, 1973).

—— *A Map of Misreading* (New York, 1975).

—— *Poetry and Repression: Revisionism from Blake to Stevens* (New Haven, 1976).

—— *Wallace Stevens: The Poems of our Climate* (Ithaca, NY, 1977).

—— and Trilling, Lionel (eds.), *Romantic Poetry and Prose*, The Oxford Anthology of English Literature (New York, 1973).

Booth, Michael R., et al., *The Revels History of Drama in English, volume vi: 1750–1880* (London, 1975).

Botting, Fred, *Gothic*, The New Critical Idiom (London, 1996).

Breen, Jennifer (ed.), *Women Romantic Poets 1785–1832: An Anthology* (London, 1992).

Brinkley, Robert, and Hanley, Keith (eds.), *Romantic Revisions* (Cambridge, 1992).

Bromwich, David (ed.), *Romantic Critical Essays* (Cambridge, 1987).

Brown, Marshall, *Preromanticism* (Stanford, Calif., 1991).

Butler, Marilyn, *Romantics, Rebels and Reactionaries: English Literature and its Background 1760–1830* (Oxford, 1981).

—— (ed.), *Burke, Paine, Godwin, and the Revolution Controversy* (Cambridge, 1984).

Buxton, John, *The Grecian Taste: Literature in the Age of Neo-Classicism 1740–1820* (London, 1978).

Bygrave, Stephen (ed.), *Approaching Literature: Romantic Writings* (London, 1996).

Cambridge Bibliography of English Literature Third Edition, iv: *1800–1900*, ed. Joanne Shattock (Cambridge, 1998).

Carlyle, Thomas, *The French Revolution* (1837), ed. K. J. Fielding and David Sorensen (Oxford, 1989).

Cave, Richard Allen (ed.), *The Romantic Theatre: An International Symposium* (Gerrards Cross, 1986).

Chase, Cynthia, *Decomposing Figures: Rhetorical Readings in the Romantic Tradition* (Baltimore, 1986).

—— (ed. and introd.), *Romanticism*, Longman Critical Readers (London, 1993).

Christie, Ian R., *Wars and Revolutions: Britain, 1760–1815* (Cambridge, Mass., 1982).

Clemit, Pamela, *The Godwinian Novel: The Rational Fictions of Godwin, Brockden Brown, Mary Shelley* (Oxford, 1993).

Clery, E. J., *The Rise of Supernatural Fiction 1762–1800* (Cambridge, 1995).

Clubbe, John, and Lovell, Ernest J., Jr., *English Romanticism: The Grounds of Belief* (London, 1983).

Colley, Linda, *Britons: Forging the Nation 1707–1837* (London, 1992).

Cooke, Michael G., *Acts of Inclusion: Studies Bearing on an Elementary Theory of Romanticism* (New Haven, 1979).

Cooper, Andrew M., *Doubt and Identity in Romantic Poetry* (New Haven, 1988).

Copley, Stephen, and Whale, John (eds.), *Beyond Romanticism: New Approaches to Texts and Contexts 1780–1832* (London, 1992).

Cox, Jeffrey N. (ed.), *Seven Gothic Dramas 1789–1825* (Athens, Oh., 1992).

Cox, Philip, *Gender, Genre and the Romantic Poets: An Introduction* (Manchester, 1996).

Curran, Stuart, *Poetic Form and British Romanticism* (New York, 1986).

—— (ed.), *The Cambridge Companion to British Romanticism* (Cambridge, 1993).

Day, Aidan, *Romanticism*, The New Critical Idiom (London, 1996).

Deane, Seamus, *The French Revolution and Enlightenment in England 1789–1832* (Cambridge, Mass., 1988).

de Man, Paul, 'The Rhetoric of Temporality', in his *Blindness and Insight: Essays in the Rhetoric of Contemporary Criticism* (2nd edn., London, 1983), 187–228.

—— *The Rhetoric of Romanticism* (New York, 1984).

Derry, John W., *Politics in the Age of Fox, Pitt and Liverpool: Continuity and Transformation* (Basingstoke, 1990).

Dickinson, H. T. (ed.), *Britain and the French Revolution, 1789–1815* (Basingstoke, 1989).

Donohue, Joseph W., Jr., *Dramatic Character in the English Romantic Age* (Princeton, 1970).

Doyle, William, *The Oxford History of the French Revolution* (Oxford, 1989).

Duncan, Ian, *Modern Romance and Transformations of the Novel: The Gothic, Scott, Dickens* (Cambridge, 1992).

Dyson, A. E. (ed.), *English Poetry: Select Bibliographical Guides* (London, 1971).

—— (ed.), *The English Novel: Select Bibliographical Guides* (London, 1974).

Erdman, David V. (ed.), *The Romantic Movement: A Selective and Critical Bibliography* (New York and West Cornwall, Conn., 1980–).

Everest, Kelvin, *English Romantic Poetry: An Introduction to the Historical Context and the Literary Scene* (Milton Keynes, 1990).

Favret, Mary A., and Watson, Nicola J. (eds.), *At the Limits of Romanticism: Essays in Cultural, Feminist, and Materialist Criticism* (Bloomington, Ind., 1994).

Feldman, Paula R., and Kelley, Theresa M. (eds.), *Romantic Women Writers: Voices and Countervoices* (Hanover, NH, 1995).

Ferguson, Frances, 'Romantic Studies', in Stephen Greenblatt and Giles Gunn (eds.), *Redrawing the Boundaries: The Transformation of English and American Literary Studies* (New York, 1992), 100–29.

Fry, Paul H., *A Defense of Poetry: Reflections on the Occasion of Writing* (Stanford, Calif., 1995).

Frye, Northrop, *A Study of English Romanticism* (1968; Brighton, 1983).

Furst, Lilian R., *Romanticism in Perspective: A Comparative Study of Aspects of the Romantic Movements in England, France and Germany* (London, 1969).

—— (ed.), *European Romanticism: Self-Definition: An Anthology* (London, 1980).

Gaull, Marilyn, *English Romanticism: The Human Context* (New York, 1988).

George, M. Dorothy, *English Political Caricature: A Study of Opinion and Propaganda*, 2 vols. (Oxford, 1959).

Gilbert, Sandra M., and Gubar, Susan, *The Madwoman in the Attic: The Woman Writer and the Nineteenth-Century Literary Imagination* (New Haven, 1979).

Halévy, Elie, *The Liberal Awakening (1815–1830)*, trans. E. I. Watkin, vol. iii of *A History of the English People* (1926; London, 1987).

Hall, Jean, *A Mind that Feeds upon Infinity: The Deep Self in English Romantic Poetry* (London, 1991).

Hayden, John O., *The Romantic Reviewers 1802–1824* (Lincoln, Nebr., 1969).

Hill, John Spencer (ed.), *The Romantic Imagination: A Casebook*, Casebook Series (Basingstoke, 1977).

Hobsbawm, E. J., *The Age of Revolution: Europe 1789–1848* (1977; London, 1986).

Hoffmeister, Gerhart (ed.), *European Romanticism: Literary Cross-Currents, Modes, and Models* (Detroit, 1990).

Homans, Margaret, *Bearing the Word: Language and Female Experience in Nineteenth-Century Women's Writing* (Chicago, 1986).

Honour, Hugh, *Neo-classicism* (Harmondsworth, 1968).

—— *Romanticism* (London, 1979).

Jack, Ian, *English Literature 1815–1832*, vol. x of *The Oxford History of English Literature* (Oxford, 1963).

Jackson, J. R. de J., *Poetry of the Romantic Period*, vol. iv of *The Routledge History of English Poetry* (London, 1980).

—— (comp.), *Romantic Poetry by Women: A Bibliography, 1770–1835* (Oxford, 1993).

Johnston, Kenneth R., et al. (eds.), *Romantic Revolutions: Criticism and Theory* (Bloomington, Ind., 1990).

Jones, Steven E., et al. (eds.), *Romantic Circles* (http://www.inform.umd.edu: 8080/RC/rc.html).

Jordan, Frank (ed.), *The English Romantic Poets: A Review of Research and Criticism* (4th edn., New York, 1985).

Kabitoglou, E. Douka, *Plato and the English Romantics* (London, 1990).

Kelly, Gary, *The English Jacobin Novel 1780–1805* (Oxford, 1976).

—— *English Fiction of the Romantic Period 1789–1830*, Longman Literature in English Series (London, 1989).

—— *Women, Writing, and Revolution 1790–1827* (Oxford, 1993).

Kermode, Frank, *Romantic Image* (1957, 1961; London, 1971).

Kerrigan, John, *Revenge Tragedy: From Aeschylus to Armageddon* (Oxford, 1996).

King-Hele, Desmond, *Erasmus Darwin and the Romantic Poets* (Basingstoke, 1986).

Kipperman, Mark, *Beyond Enchantment: German Idealism and English Romantic Poetry* (Philadelphia, 1986).

Kitson, Peter J. (ed.), *Romantic Criticism 1800–1825* (London, 1989).

Kroeber, Karl, *Romantic Landscape Vision: Constable and Wordsworth* (Madison, 1975).

—— and Walling, William (eds.), *Images of Romanticism: Verbal and Visual Affinities* (New Haven, 1978).

Leader, Zachary, *Revision and Romantic Authorship* (Oxford, 1996).

Lefebvre, Georges, *The French Revolution*, i: *From its Origins to 1793*, trans. Elizabeth Moss Evanson (London, 1962); ii: *From 1793 to 1799*, trans. John Hall Stewart and James Friguglietti (London, 1964).

Levine, George, *The Realistic Imagination: English Fiction from Frankenstein to Lady Chatterley* (Chicago, 1981).

Levinson, Marjorie, *The Romantic Fragment Poem: A Critique of a Form* (Chapel Hill, NC, 1986).

Lovejoy, Arthur O., 'On the Discrimination of Romanticisms', *Publications of the Modern Language Association of America*, 39 (1924), 229–53.

McCalman, Iain, *Radical Underworld: Prophets, Revolutionaries and Pornographers in London, 1795–1840* (Cambridge, 1988).

McFarland, Thomas, *Romanticism and the Heritage of Rousseau* (Oxford, 1995).

McGann, Jerome J., *The Romantic Ideology: A Critical Investigation* (Chicago, 1983).

—— *The Beauty of Inflections: Literary Investigations in Historical Method and Theory* (1985; Oxford, 1988 with corr.).

—— 'Rethinking Romanticism', *English Literary History*, 59 (1992), 735–54.

—— (ed.), *The New Oxford Book of Romantic Period Verse* (Oxford, 1993).

—— *The Poetics of Sensibility: A Revolution in Literary Style* (Oxford, 1996).

Mellor, Anne K., *English Romantic Irony* (Cambridge, Mass., 1980).

—— (ed.), *Romanticism and Feminism* (Bloomington, Ind., 1988).

—— *Romanticism and Gender* (New York, 1993).

Miller, J. Hillis, *The Linguistic Moment: From Wordsworth to Stevens* (Princeton, 1985).

Napier, Elizabeth R., *The Failure of Gothic: Problems of Disjunction in an Eighteenth-Century Literary Form* (Oxford, 1987).

Newey, Vincent, *Centring the Self: Subjectivity, Society and Reading from Thomas Gray to Thomas Hardy* (Aldershot, 1995).

Newlyn, Lucy, 'Paradise Lost' and the Romantic Reader (Oxford, 1993).

O'Neill, Michael, Romanticism and the Self-Conscious Poem (Oxford, 1997).

Paulson, Ronald, Representations of Revolution (1789–1820) (New Haven, 1983).

Piper, H. W., The Active Universe: Pantheism and the Concept of Imagination in the English Romantic Poets (London, 1962).

Pirie, David B. (ed.), The Romantic Period, vol. v of The Penguin History of Literature (London, 1994).

Pite, Ralph, The Circle of our Vision: Dante's Presence in English Romantic Poetry (Oxford, 1994).

Poovey, Mary, The Proper Lady and the Woman Writer: Ideology as Style in the Works of Mary Wollstonecraft, Mary Shelley, and Jane Austen (Chicago, 1984).

Porter, Roy, and Teich, Mikuláš (eds.), Romanticism in National Context (Cambridge, 1988).

Praz, Mario, The Romantic Agony, trans. Angus Davidson, 2nd edn. with foreword by Frank Kermode (1st edn. 1933; Oxford, 1951).

Punter, David, The Literature of Terror: A History of Gothic Fictions from 1765 to the Present Day (1980; 2nd edn., London, 1996).

—— The Romantic Unconscious: A Study in Narcissism and Patriarchy (New York, 1989).

Raimond, Jean, and Watson, J. R. (eds.), A Handbook to English Romanticism (Basingstoke, 1992).

Rajan, Tilottama, Dark Interpreter: The Discourse of Romanticism (Ithaca, NY, 1980).

—— The Supplement of Reading: Figures of Understanding in Romantic Theory and Practice (Ithaca, NY, 1990).

Redpath, Theodore, The Younger Romantics and Critical Opinion 1807–1824: Poetry of Byron, Shelley, and Keats as Seen by their Contemporary Critics (London, 1973).

Reed, Arden (ed.), Romanticism and Language (London, 1984).

Reiman, Donald H. (ed.), The Romantics Reviewed, 9 vols. (New York, 1972).

—— Romantic Texts and Contexts (Columbia, Mo., 1987).

—— The Study of Modern Manuscripts: Public, Confidential, and Private (Baltimore, 1993).

Renwick, W. L., English Literature 1789–1815, vol. ix of The Oxford History of English Literature (Oxford, 1963).

Ross, Marlon B., The Contours of Masculine Desire: Romanticism and the Rise of Women's Poetry (New York, 1989).

Schama, Simon, Citizens: A Chronicle of the French Revolution (Harmondsworth, 1989).

Schapiro, Barbara A., The Romantic Mother: Narcissistic Patterns in Romantic Poetry (Baltimore, 1983).

Simpson, David, Irony and Authority in Romantic Poetry (London, 1979).

—— (ed.), The Origins of Modern Critical Thought: German Aesthetic and Literary Criticism from Lessing to Hegel (Cambridge, 1988).

—— Romanticism, Nationalism and the Revolt against Theory (Chicago, 1993).

Siskin, Clifford, The Historicity of Romantic Discourse (New York, 1988).

Small, Helen, Love's Madness: Medicine, the Novel, and Female Insanity, 1800–1865 (Oxford, 1996).

Swingle, L. J., The Obstinate Questionings of English Romanticism (Baton Rouge, La., 1987).

Taylor, Charles, *Sources of the Self: The Making of the Modern Identity* (Cambridge, 1989).

Thompson, E. P., *The Making of the English Working Class* (1963; rev. edn. 1968; Harmondsworth, 1982).

Walmsley, Robert, *Peterloo: The Case Reopened* (Manchester, 1969).

Ward, Geoff (ed.), *A Guide to Romantic Literature: 1780–1830*, Bloomsbury Guides to English Literature (1993; London, 1994).

Watson, J. R., *Picturesque Landscape and English Romantic Poetry* (London, 1970).

—— (ed.), *An Infinite Complexity: Essays in Romanticism* (Edinburgh, 1983).

—— *English Poetry of the Romantic Period 1789–1830* (London, 1985; 2nd edn., 1992).

—— (ed.), 'The French Revolution in English Literature and Art: Special Number', *Yearbook of English Studies*, 19 (London, 1989).

Watson, Nicola J., *Revolution and the Form of the British Novel, 1790–1825: Intercepted Letters, Interrupted Seductions* (Oxford, 1994).

Weiskel, Thomas, *The Romantic Sublime: Studies in the Structure and Psychology of Transcendence* (Baltimore, 1976).

Wellek, René, 'The Concept of Romanticism in Literary Scholarship' (1949), in *Concepts of Criticism* (New Haven, 1963).

Wheeler, Kathleen M., *Romanticism, Pragmatism and Deconstruction* (Oxford, 1993).

White, R. J., *Waterloo to Peterloo* (1957; London, 1963).

Wilkie, Brian, *Romantic Poets and Epic Tradition* (Madison, 1965).

Williams, Raymond, *Culture and Society 1780–1950* (Harmondsworth, 1963).

Wilson, Carol Shiner, and Haefner, Joel (eds.), *Re-visioning Romanticism: British Women Writers, 1776–1837* (Philadelphia, 1994).

Wimsatt, William K., Jr., and Brooks, Cleanth, *Romantic Criticism*, vol. iii of *Literary Criticism: A Short History* (1957; London, 1970).

Wolfson, Susan J., *The Questioning Presence: Wordsworth, Keats, and the Interrogative Mode in English Poetry* (Ithaca, NY, 1986).

Woodring, Carl, *Politics in English Romantic Poetry* (Cambridge, Mass., 1970).

Wordsworth, Jonathan, *Ancestral Voices: Fifty Books from the Romantic Period* (Oxford, 1991).

—— *Visionary Gleam: Forty Books from the Romantic Period* (London, 1993).

Wu, Duncan (ed.), *Romanticism: An Anthology* (Oxford, 1994).

—— (ed.), *Romanticism: A Critical Reader* (Oxford, 1995).

2. *William Blake*

DAVID FULLER

TEXTS AND FACSIMILES

There are three independent complete modern editions of Blake's writings, those of Keynes, Erdman, and Bentley. The Keynes text is chronological in arrangement, gives variant readings in the main text, is modernized in punctuation, and has only a limited textual apparatus. The Erdman *Concordance* is keyed to this edition. Erdman's text (which has become standard for scholarly use) separates the works in illuminated printing from letterpress and manuscript texts (and within this latter grouping also separates poetry and prose). With the poetry (both engraved and manuscript) in order to present an uncluttered reading text it gives variants in textual notes; revisions of prose, however, are retained in the text. The text is not modernized in punctuation or accidentals (which, since Blake's punctuation is idiosyncratic, can make for difficulties—though on some views these are essential to the sense-making experience). It has a brief but good critical commentary by Harold Bloom. Like Erdman, Bentley separates the illuminated books from the rest of Blake's writings. He gives the texts in a somewhat modernized punctuation, with a textual apparatus which signals his emendations, and he gives bibliographic information on each work. Among the many virtues of Bentley's edition the most important is that he also prints (in black and white) about three-quarters of the designs. Since Blake produced almost all his poetry in the form of illuminated books with text and designs engraved on copper, printed and usually hand-coloured, it is important wherever possible to read the poetry in its illuminated form. The text of Alicia Ostriker's edition is based on Erdman. It is unmodernized, but, while variants of the engraved poems are given in textual notes, revisions of poems which exist only in manuscript are given in the text. The annotation is brief but good. The best edition for student use (though of the poetry only) is that of W. H. Stevenson. This uses Erdman's text, which it modernizes, and has excellent annotation. No designs are reproduced, but the designs are described briefly in the notes. The Ellis/Yeats and Sloss/Wallis editions are both of historical interest, but neither is a good reading text. The best selection is that of Grant and Johnson: it is comprehensive, well annotated, and contains a selection of designs as well as critical essays. Michael Mason's selection is generous and well annotated, but his decision to print different aspects of individual long poems in different sections (*Milton* and *Jerusalem* have to be assembled from three different places) is unsatisfactory.

Beginning with *Jerusalem* (1951), coloured facsimiles of all Blake's works in illuminated printing (as well as his designs for the poems of Gray and for the Book of Job) have been produced by the Trianon Press for the Blake Trust, almost all under the editorship of Sir Geoffrey Keynes. These are hand-coloured facsimiles, made using stencils cut from originals. They reproduce well the texture of watercolours, though naturally the colour match is occasionally less exact than in photographic facsimiles. The Blake Trust has also produced a complete edition in six volumes of the illuminated books in photolithographic facsimile under the general editorship of David Bindman (1991–5). Each volume has a critical and scholarly commentary of high quality. No photographic method can reproduce the radiance of texture or the detail of watercolour, but the photolithographic process often matches the colours of the originals better than the Trianon Press method was able to do. These are, therefore, the best facsimiles now available, and the best form in which to read the canon of Blake's illuminated work, but other facsimiles are also listed in the bibliography because different copies of the illuminated books are often substantially different. All the illuminated books are reproduced in black and white by David Erdman (1975), with a plate-by-plate commentary.

Of the reproductions of individual works the most important are Erdman's edition of the Notebook and the Bentley and Erdman/Magno facsimiles of *The Four Zoas*. Blake composed many of the *Songs of Innocence and of Experience* and designs for the emblem series *The Gates of Paradise* in his Notebook, which is therefore revealing about his methods of composition. The Erdman/Moore facsimile used infra-red photography to show lines not now visible to the naked eye, and prints the written text in typographical imitation of Blake's vigorously haphazard use of the manuscript. Infra-red photography was also employed for the Erdman/Magno facsimile of *The Four Zoas*. Blake worked on this poem over perhaps ten years, adding to and correcting the text in many layers in a way that can only be fully reflected by a facsimile. Infra-red photography is here peculiarly important because it reveals sexually explicit designs, some of which have been partially erased (when or by whom is not known). A few designs are also reproduced with their colour washes. These improvements in technology apart, Bentley's earlier sumptuous reproduction gives a better sense of the manuscript. An ongoing supplement to these sources is *Blake: An Illustrated Quarterly*. *BIQ* publishes scholarly and critical work, and is particularly important for its detailed checklists of publications and information on art sales related to Blake and his circle.

permanent structure of ideas'. His book is beautifully written, full of creative thinking, and wide in scope because Frye believed he had discovered through his struggles with Blake a grammar of symbolism underlying all imaginative writing. But the book is difficult, remote from the problematic minutiae of Blake's texts, and imposes an unduly stable order on the structure of Blake's myth. Blake did indeed have a will towards system, but he also invented and discarded with prodigality the schemes which Frye's pattern-making rigidifies. Also, though Frye had not in 1947 formalized the anti-Leavisite purity of criticism-as-inductive-science elaborated in *Anatomy of Criticism* (1957), his account of Blake is in part based on a view of the nature of literature and the function of criticism which Blake did not share. In *Anatomy of Criticism* Frye treats metaphors and ideas as having the same status in a work: both are there to give an aesthetic experience. But for Blake ideological content is more important than Frye's principles allow. Poetry makes things happen, if not by affecting action directly, then certainly by changing consciousness—though with Blake it is also always important to remember that 'ideas cannot be given but in their minutely appropriate words' (*Notebook*, 62). Finally Frye fathered onto Blake the mythic pattern of the so-called 'Orc cycle', the pattern evident in so many revolutions by which rebellion, once successful, becomes a new tyranny. This is the pattern of the manuscript (though not the engraved) versions of the lyric 'The Grey Monk', but Blake's grand myths are more hopeful. Nevertheless, despite objections to its view of Blake, for the quality of its thought and of its writing *Fearful Symmetry* has a classic status in Blake criticism.

Frye's magisterial schematization of Blake has often been challenged, though some of the early challenges were either in part demonstrably wrong, or sketchy on Blake's later writings. E. D. Hirsch, for example, in an interesting mixture of truth and error, offers elaborated readings only of the *Songs*; and his argument that in later life Blake repudiated early works, including *The Marriage of Heaven and Hell*, is contradicted by the bibliographical evidence. Morton Paley (1970) is much more consistently good, but he sticks to the dual theme of his title, the shift of Blake's positive interests from liberation through release of energy (the myth of Orc) to regeneration through imaginative struggle (the myth of Los), and does not therefore expound a total view of Blake's development. He is helpful in reading individual works, though (quite properly) only in so far as they are concerned with his underlying subjects. My own book likewise challenges the Frye view, throughout tracing developments in Blake's ideas on politics, religion, and sexuality. It also gives critical accounts of each of Blake's works (concentrating on the long poems), and discusses some of the main issues of Blake criticism—the relation of poetry and design, the rhythmic structures of Blake's long-line verse, Blake's relations to his own time, and to various traditions of thought often adduced as influences. The final chapter is a polemic, arising out of the account of Blake, arguing for a more explicit articulation of the values in relation to which literary-critical interpretations are formulated.

At the opposite extreme from Frye, attending not to myth and archetype but to the history Frye deliberately excludes, is Erdman (1954/1977). The basis of Erdman's work is the wholly legitimate view that Blake is a socially conscious writer who needs to be understood partly in terms of his social context —as he already was in the accounts of Jacob Bronowski and Mark Schorer. Even in Blake's later work, where he concentrates more on the transforming powers of the imagination and less is expected from social change, the poet is haunted by the cry of the poor, or investigates the London slums with a view to finding out what has gone wrong and how to take action—though the actions adumbrated may be remote from those a politician would conceive. But with Erdman the recognition that Blake is always in some sense a political poet often means seeing Blake as writing covert political allegory. This particularly distorts his reading of *The Four Zoas* in which his historical identifications (Urizen and Ahania are Nelson and Lady Hamilton, and so forth) were based on the Sloss/Wallis text from which he derived too simple a view of the poem's processes of composition. Erdman gives a vivid sense of Blake's times, and of the immediate milieu in which Blake worked; and he is right about the broad directions of Blake's politics. But his insistence on detailed historical allegory inverts the proper method of Blake's poetry which is, as Blake puts it, 'to show the historical fact in its poetical vigour so as it always happens' (*A Descriptive Catalogue*, V). For Steven Vine, however, even Erdman is so dominated by Frye as to be ashamed he is not an idealist. Vine seeks a non-idealist focus by concentrating on Blake's myth of the Spectre, with all that figure suggests about relentless negation and the failure of poetic and prophetic vision.

Blake has often been presented, most famously by T. S. Eliot, as an eccentric solitary. He has also been seen within various religious, political, and intellectual traditions. E. P. Thompson, the great historian of working-class culture in the Romantic period, sets Blake (as A. L. Morton had done) in a tradition of religious and political antinomian dissent stemming from the Civil War, and sees him as in a dialogue of qualified sympathies with Enlightenment and Jacobin ideas—Painite radicalism, and deism. Thompson never falls into the common source-study error of limiting Blake to rehearsing the views of others. It is clear from Blake's annotations of intellectual friends and enemies that he was energized by opposition, and in Thompson's vivid and beautifully written account sources provide a vocabulary, a symbolic structure, an ideological stance, from which Blake explores, or with which he quarrels creatively. On similar political themes Jon Mee is less convincing. This is historical and political criticism investigating writings which it presents as outside the domain of standard literary history. Mee traces sources and analogues for Blake's style in the 1790s in popular traditions of millenarianism and antinomianism, literary primitivism, mythography, and scriptural criticism, and explicates the politics supposedly encoded in the style. But all that is valid in his readings could have been achieved without the historical paraphernalia. Behind Mee lies the critical practice of Jerome McGann, who produces another kind of political reading, underlying which is an attack on the whole Arnoldian idea of poetry derived from the Romantics themselves: poetry is no longer to be seen as the representation of the best that has been known and thought, or of a human power to transcend circumstance; beauty is no longer a fundamental category of the artistic. We must cast aside what McGann presents as the Kant/ Coleridge formalist tradition of thought about poetry as symbolic structure (for example, the Frye reading of Blake): poetry has a kind of truth which such readings cannot reveal. The excitements of the new mode of understanding begin (as usual with McGann) with bibliography—attention to a work's institutions of production and consumption. McGann comments well that with respect to truth experience always outruns conception. But what applies to the formulations of poetry seems not to apply to those of criticism. By virtue of mere historical belatedness the critic understands conceptually what the poet could not. In a sort of materialist-deconstructive reading material features of Blake's illuminated texts bear witness against his own conscious beliefs, especially Christianity and the transcendent imagination. Once again the Real Blake has a remarkable (coincidental) resemblance to his critic. Less partial than any of these writers is Michael Ferber (1985). Ferber's methodology is derived from the neo-Marxist Frankfurt School, the ideas of which he has thoroughly absorbed so that they constitute not just an applied theory but a genuine view of the world, though one held with the flexible intelligence which allows it to interact with, not dominate, the subject matter. As Ferber explains in a preface, his book began from his (thoroughly Blakian) experience as a draft refuser in America during the Vietnam War, and, though this experience does not reappear, it is everywhere evident in the book's sense that the issues are not (in the pejorative sense) 'academic' but can make a real difference to people's lives. Ferber combines in decently tentative ways the systemizing of Frye with the contextualizing of Erdman to show how Blake contested the dominant ideologies of his time, and that much in this contesting has lost none of its relevance. Unlike many writers whose primary reference is either idealist or materialist, Ferber recognizes that for Blake religion and politics are inextricably intertwined. The book assumes a good knowledge of Blake's texts. But it also explains itself to the patient reader, and moves supply between particular readings and its large issues of what Blake has to say about brotherhood, nature, liberty, labour, history and eternity, and universal redemption.

Blake's most prolific modern expositor, Kathleen Raine, takes a quite different view from Thompson and Mee of the traditions with which Blake is to be connected. Her *Blake and Tradition* (1968) continues a kind of commentary begun by Damon and Joseph Wicksteed, developed in different ways by Milton O. Percival and Ruthven Todd, and extended by George Mills Harper (Neoplatonism) and Désirée Hirst (Paracelsus, Boehme, William Law). She is concerned with learned traditions stemming predominantly from Plotinus and the Neoplatonists—though the net can be cast very wide (to include, for example, the *Bhagavadgita*, Zoroaster, the Hermetica, and the kabbala): the spiritual wisdom of diverse civilizations is seen as in fundamental agreement. The esoteric nature of some of the traditions of knowledge invoked means that Blake is partly seen as deliberately obscure: the aim is to put off readers who hope for improbably easy access to spiritual truth. This is a view of Blake that has been adopted by different perspectives: it can be too fruitful a supposition for the eager exegete. Given that there are few meanings that ingenuity cannot make some show of justifying, the difficulty is to find acceptable criteria by which obscured meanings discovered by spiritually informed contemplation can be distinguished from an interpreter's fancies. Raine is too serious a critic lightly to abuse the freedoms of her presuppositions, and much of the material she adduces is evidently resonant with Blakian analogies, but her opposition to positivist criteria about evidence can make her mode of argument seem, to anyone caught in the toils of such criteria, slippery. One thing that is certainly un-Blakian about Raine's view is her attitude to politics: it is a materialist delusion. Blake's work embodies an 'everlasting gospel', out of tune with the materialist presuppositions of his own age as with ours: mind, not matter, is the ground of being. Raine writes out of a long love and study of her subjects (both Blake and his supposed sources), and she has given deep and imaginative consideration to the issues. But she is opposed to some of Blake's views on politics, sexual relations, and religion, and her account bends Blake's views on these subjects towards her own. How to combine a right use of learning with a properly imaginative love and wonder is one of the great problems of Blake criticism. With Raine there is no lack of either love or learning. The filtering that her commitments necessitate is the price to be paid for the provocative engagement of her criticism.

Though few things were more important to him, Blake's Christianity perhaps admits of, and has certainly given rise to, more latitude of interpretation than anything else. Despite the admired antinomian Jesus of *The Marriage of Heaven and Hell*, Blake's repeated attacks on the Church, and his late portrayal of himself as a contrary reader of the Bible (reading black for the orthodox Christian's white), in the Anglican account of J. G. Davies, Blake is almost as orthodox as piety could wish. In the contrary account of Thomas Altizer (fresh from completing *The Gospel of Christian Atheism* (1966)) Blake's beliefs are similarly found to be much like the author's own. Even the more precise issue of whether or not the development of *The Four Zoas* shows that Blake experienced some kind of 'conversion' to Christianity in middle age is disputed between those who best understand the textual evidence (Bentley 1963, Erdman 1964). An intelligently suggestive (though brief and selective) account of Blake's Christianity is that of Kathleen Raine (1979). Morton Paley (1979) deals well with Blake's important but problematic relation to the Swedish Christian mystic and dissident Emanuel Swedenborg. That Blake saw the Bible as 'the great code of art' is the starting point of Leslie Tannenbaum's superbly well-informed study. Tannenbaum examines the interpretative traditions through which Blake's understanding of the Bible was mediated, and the ways in which he borrowed or deviated from those traditions in terms of prophetic form, figurative language, and understanding of typology to construct his own 'Bible of Hell' in the so-called Lambeth books.

If you cannot love the sounds and shapes made by the words in a poem you can scarcely start to love it as poetry at all. But in learning to hear the rhythms of Blake's long-line verse it is not helpful to think, as Alicia Ostriker does (1965), in terms of the usual scansion of English verse derived from classical metres. A more suggestive attempt is that of Morton Paley (1983). Paley uses Blake's own account of his style as variously 'terrific', 'mild and gentle', and 'prosaic', and, by examining the verbal changes in passages transferred from *The Four Zoas* to *Jerusalem* in these terms, and by looking at Blake's rhythms in relation to the Bible and other possible influences, aims to establish that Blake observes a linguistic decorum partly of his own devising and related to his own expressive needs.

Several critics have applied to Blake's style modern theories of textuality. Nelson Hilton (1984), using Derridian ideas about the instability of language, attempts to show that puns and other forms of verbal play are common in his poetry. (More in the same kind, and from a variety of voices, can be found in Hilton and Vogler; and (with feminist and Lacanian pieces) in Miller, Bracher, and Ault.) Blake saw these potentials of language, and turned them to account in some manuscript work. But in his poetry—except in naming some figures in his myth—his impulse is to resist this potential, not exploit it. It is in his fallen state that Los utters 'ambiguous words blasphemous': the inspired Los demands 'explicit words'. Where every word has unlimited potential no word has the single precise significance which allows error to be snared and truth to be told so as to be irresistibly understood. Language then becomes the Babel by which Nimrod maintains his archetypal tyranny. Robert Essick (1989) makes a more interesting and historically grounded use of poststructuralist linguistics. His basic subject is a battle between structuralist and phenomenological views of language; or (in Blake's terms) Locke, for whom the relation of sign to referent is arbitrary, versus Boehme and Swedenborg, who postulate a spiritually enlightened language-user able to perceive the motivated nature of the apparently conventional sign. Amongst Essick's well-informed delvings in eighteenth-century linguistics, particularly interesting are Wilhelm von Humboldt, for whom language is both potential prison house and liberating discoverer of the previously unknown, and Lessing, for whom poetic language, especially metaphor, is able to reduce the inevitable gap between sign and referent. The language of Blake's poetry is 'incarnational' because it calls into question the boundaries between the literal and the figurative: his language is not the Saussure/Derrida system of differences with no positive terms, but—largely because of the figurative possibilities of poetry—it is the Heideggerian system of transactions between consciousness, signs, and things. Essick establishes his subject by some fanciful readings of Blake pictures, and in his readings of Blake's poetry the linguistic theme becomes a Procrustean bed. But this is a shapely book with an interesting argument, engaged with current critical fashions without being enslaved to them.

Similarly well informed about contemporary theory, but never credulous of its clichés, is V. A. De Luca on Blake's language and eighteenth-century and modern theories of the sublime. He argues that though Blake ostensibly repudiated Burke's aesthetics because of the Lockian basis of his view of mind and because his notion of the sublime involved the indeterminate against Blake's ideals of determinacy and precision, nevertheless Blake was imaginatively drawn to Burke. But Blake typically replaced the obscurities of the Burkian natural sublime with the sublime of the obstacle-ridden text—that is, with the difficulties of reading an alluring and baffling combination of eloquent simplicity and tantalizing but obscure adumbrations of a positive gnosis which just escapes the reader's grasp. These notions of the sublime provide exemplary instances of some of the difficulties of reading which preoccupy contemporary criticism, just as their vocabulary of gaps, barriers, abysses, and labyrinths parallels its characteristic rhetoric. The relevant theories are brought to bear, but not in any mechanical way. De Luca is alert to the tone and movement of Blake's verse, shows a real and subtle sense of aesthetic effect, and moves from poetry to context to theory with clear fundamental directions of argument. The limitation of his view is that, despite a healthy scepticism about contemporary obsessions with language, and (as with Essick) a specifically anti-Derridian argument about textual plenitude, it is so determinedly linguistic. If a text is allowed to point to the world we are supposed in danger of oppressive programmes. But attention to Blake's subjects need not degenerate into treating poetry as propaganda. On the contrary, for Blake poetry and painting 'exist and exult in immortal thoughts', and criticism that shies away from Blake's direct engagement with religious, political, epistemological, and other issues risks degenerating into a narrow aestheticism.

Any historical criticism accepts that a writer must be read first in terms of his or her age. That Blake's later readers should conceive of emancipation in terms somewhat different from his own is inevitable: it is merely parochial to measure the past by the present on the assumption that our own ideological embeddedness is apparent to us and the present represents unalloyed progress, in whatever area. Nevertheless, from the perspective of feminist criticism it may appear that Blake is, in culpable ways, only dividedly liberationist. Clearly Blake was, at one level, concerned with issues of women's emancipation, in *Visions of the Daughters of Albion* and elsewhere; and his own positive values are often prominently conveyed through female personifications—Oothoon, Ololon, Jerusalem—just as his negatives are prominently conveyed by male figures—Urizen, Satan, the Spectre. But in certain of his metaphors and personifications Blake is held by some feminist critics to mistake the social (what might be transformed by the radical stances he elsewhere proposes) for the natural, the permanently human within any social structure or set of values. The obvious answers—that Blake's male and female personifications are not equivalent to actual men and women, and that all are aspects of a total psyche which in its ideal form Blake conceives as androgynous—lead only to further criticism of how that ideal itself is conceived. The main issues of the feminist critique are well canvassed by Anne Mellor (1982–3), and, in the context of Blake's overall view of sexuality, by Alicia Ostriker (in the same issue of *BIQ*; reprinted in Hilton 1986). Eugenie Freed offers some answers.

Much of the most ambitious criticism of Blake has focused on his non-lyric poetry. Hazard Adams attempts to apply the schemes of *Fearful Symmetry* to the lyrics. Adams presents Blake as in these poems too employing a traditional archetypal symbolism, which he explains (as he explains much else) with the aid of diagrams. All Blake's lyrics are referable to a total 'central form'; all his poems are variations on a single theme. These assumptions work best with the later lyrics. Anyone interested in the poems of the 'Pickering [Ballads] Manuscript' (especially 'The Mental Traveller') should try Adams. The problems of his method can be sampled in his account of 'The Tyger': its daunting (and false) implication is that unless you have read everything you cannot understand anything. Quite the opposite is Zachary Leader, Blakian in his insistence that scholarly learning (for example, about a supposed Blakian 'system') may be imaginative ignorance, and that true knowledge of poetry depends on imaginative receptivity and attention to verbal nuance. Leader examines the *Songs* as a carefully organized volume, at once both verbal and visual, and offers many good readings. But with *Songs of Experience* his fundamental solution for critical disagreements is to suppose that the Bard has interiorized the infections he beholds, and so a great deal that might be read straight has to be read ironically. In addition, while on principle not invoking later poetic compositions to interpret the *Songs*, Leader bases his interpretations on copy Z (c.1826), brushing aside the problem that its style of colouring and its ordering of the poems are quite different from those of any copy contemporary with the work's composition. One great difficulty of the *Songs* (particularly of *Songs of Innocence*)—a difficulty to which Leader presents one extreme solution—is to mark the limits of their irony. This often means deciding whether, and in what ways, the two collections comment on each other. Stanley Gardner argues that *Songs of Innocence* should not be read with *Songs of Experience* as a commentary because they were written by a hopeful Blake, persuaded by philanthropic activity in his neighbourhood that social evil might be overcome in an evolutionary way. Gardner's view is strengthened by research about life in Blake's immediate environment, but the character trusting to philanthropy that he imagines is difficult to fit into any probable sense of Blake's development. The engraving 'Albion Rose' (1780) shows Blake in as revolutionary a vein before *Innocence* as the Lambeth books show him after it; the tractates, engraved immediately before *Innocence*, show a similar continuity with the revolutionary *Marriage of Heaven and Hell*, engraved immediately after. The motto Blake considered for the songs ('The good are attracted by men's perceptions | And think not for themselves') shows him thinking of Innocence as naive just after he finished the collection. A more dialectical reading of the two collections is offered by Andrew Lincoln (Bindman 1991). Like many critics he insists—I think too much—on obliquity and irony: the speakers in *Songs of Experience* are always seen as victims of the limitations they attempt to repudiate; as in Zachary Leader's account, the prophetic bard—who according to Blake sees past, present, and future—is never, on this view, heard speaking unequivocally. But some of Lincoln's readings are exemplary, and show that, when not forced to compromise with theories that insist criticism be more flamboyant in its pretensions, historically based close reading with a proper reverence for art can still fulfil the genuine critical function of deepening understanding.

ART SCHOLARSHIP AND CRITICISM

Blake is one of very few creative artists to work with equal force in two media. During his lifetime, though he was hardly known as a poet he enjoyed some recognition within a small circle as a painter, particularly in his final years, and he earned his living as an engraver. He also produced important series of watercolour illustrations for the poetry of Young, Gray, Milton, and Dante, and over 150 illustrations of biblical scenes. (Reproductions of these are listed in the bibliography.) Since, in addition, almost all Blake's poetry is accompanied by designs, it is at least peculiarly difficult—arguably impossible—to understand him as a poet without some reference to his graphic work. Martin Butlin's catalogue raisonné of the paintings and drawings is one of the essential tools of Blake scholarship—a mine of information with largely good reproductions.

Robert Essick's meticulous catalogues of the so-called 'separate plates' (about fifty plates published as independent works) and the commercial book engravings are also standard. The major collections of Blake's work and catalogues of large exhibitions provide reproductions, scholarly information, and critical comment.

When Blake wrote about his own pictures he often did so turning image to idea: 'the strong man represents the human sublime; the beautiful man represents the human pathetic', and so forth. The interpreter's task is to discuss Blake's art in similar terms, remembering also his injunction to 'make a friend or companion of these images of wonder'. Interpretation has constantly to refer to analogous work in Blake's poetry, but not in a formulaic way which ignores Blake's particular articulations, either verbal or visual. The vices of criticism of Blake's visual art are, either to ignore his poetry, or (the reverse) not to trust to visual values but to look for a caption from Blake's writings which is then treated as a dogma. David Bindman (1977) is quite free of this. He offers a complete survey of Blake's work, from an art-historical viewpoint, but arguing for the unity of Blake's various activities. He complements his account of Blake's graphic work with the necessary understanding of the texts of the illuminated books, so that his interpretations draw, interchangeably but flexibly, on Blake's verbal and visual statements. Morris Eaves extrapolates from Blake's writings an expressive-organic-Romantic theory of art—of the artist, the work of art, and the audience—and sets this in the context of the discourses about literature and art of Blake's time. Blake's emphasis on line above colour is not, as for Bindman, evidence that at bottom he adhered to neoclassical principles, because Blake associates outline not with fidelity to natural forms but with strength and clarity of imagination.

Blake's designs in the illuminated books function in a variety of ways—as decoration, as straightforward illustration, as commentary on the verbal text, to highlight central characters or issues, or to introduce issues not present in the verbal text alone. The central possibilities are considered by Frye ('Poetry and Design' (1951; reprinted in Frye 1966)). Frye's approach is developed by Jean Hagstrum, who places Blake in a tradition of poetry and painting as 'sister arts' working in various kinds of integrated relationship. W. J. T. Mitchell sees this relationship in more various terms, of dialectical interplay, independence, even rivalry, and enforces his view by extended accounts of *Thel*, *Urizen*, and *Jerusalem*—works chosen to represent different periods, themes, and styles of 'composite art'. Mitchell's subtle but clearly written book is suggestive and open-ended. With very wide-ranging illustration Behrendt (1992) argues for a yet more open text view of how the reader's creativity is invoked to make sense of the peculiar enigmas of Blake's mixed-media texts. By contrast Erdman's plate-by-plate commentary on the illuminated books (1975) is at times unduly dogmatic or over-ingenious. Morton Paley (1983) comments well

that the designs are not puzzles but 'educts of the imagination'. The interpretations offered in his *Jerusalem* facsimile (Bindman 1991) are in keeping with
Blake's own stated aims of rousing the faculties to act. Paley describes alternative interpretations in terms of 'analogies': any one image may, for example,
properly suggest several related figures of Blake's myth; its significance lies not
in some particular identification but in the kinds of issues or characteristics it
embodies.

The techniques by which Blake produced the illuminated books have been
exhaustively studied by Robert Essick (1980), and more recently by Joseph
Viscomi, whose conclusions supersede previous discussions of Blake's print-
making processes. Both men stress the critical importance of the materiality
of Blake's work. Viscomi, a printmaker himself, has reconstructed every aspect
of Blake's technique. His main conclusion is that, at least before 1795 (by which
time, in terms of number of copies, Blake had produced 75 per cent of his
extant illuminated *œuvre*), Blake printed his books, not individually whenever
he had a buyer, but in small editions of perhaps ten copies in a printing ses-
sion. These were then coloured using a similar palette, style, and even placement of colours. It remains true, however, that the significance of Blake's
images changed for him as he reprinted them at different periods of his life,
change being pointed by an added inscription, or different styles of colouring,
the emphasizing or painting over of different details, or a different juxtaposi-
tion of the plates. Whenever Blake reprinted a work it changed and developed
as a later self saw in it new possibilities of emphasis, or even a radically different significance. Viscomi remarks (as others have done) one general change:
later copies are more elaborately coloured, showing a shift from emphasis on
the poetic text to a primarily visual artefact.

Blake's illustrations of other writers are a form of creative criticism central
to his *œuvre*. Their aim is to help us read the text which is Blake's subject
with more full engagement and appreciation by presenting an epitome of that
text in an alternative medium. Beginning from Albert Roe's account of the
Dante series, criticism of the illustrations has often seen them as embodying
continuous elaborate critiques of their subjects by reference to Blake's own
ideas and mythology. I criticize this approach in my own essay on the Dante
series as a kind of interpretative reading which has Blake trapped in solipsism,
seeing only himself, never the otherness of his subjects. This line of argument,
initiated by Bo Lindberg (1973), is extended by Christopher Heppner into
more general principles of interpretation with readings of the Colour Prints
of 1795, the Young illustrations, and certain of the paintings of biblical scenes.
In illustrating other poets or the Bible Blake may, as in his famous account of
Milton (as 'of the Devil's party without knowing it'), draw out 'against the
grain' or latent meanings. But he was not (as the Roe view implies) painting
for a coterie audience and using a private code to express highly idiosyncratic

personal views. Like the Renaissance painters he admired, Blake drew on his biblical and theological knowledge and his knowledge of iconographic convention. Reading the results requires an informed reader, but not the breaking of a code. Fundamentally the issue is inseparable from that of the kind of poet and artist one sees Blake as being. Criticism that draws Blake into an esoteric frame of reference and implies a reader whose access to the mysteries depends on arcane preparation is basically on a wrong track. Blake is certainly a difficult writer, and he expects the reader to know what every reader once did—the Bible and Milton. But the demands he places on the reader are not in terms of esoteric knowledge but of intensity of attention, openness to experience, and preparedness to take art utterly seriously in relation to that experience.

REFERENCES

TEXTS AND FACSIMILES

Collections

Bentley, G. E., Jr. (ed.), *William Blake's Writings*, 2 vols. (Oxford, 1978).

Bindman, David (gen. ed.), *The Illuminated Books of William Blake*, 6 vols. (London, 1991–5) (vol. i: *Jerusalem*, ed. Morton D. Paley, 1991; vol. ii: *Songs of Innocence and of Experience*, ed. Andrew Lincoln, 1991; vol. iii: *The Early Illuminated Books*, ed. Morris Eaves, Robert N. Essick, and J. Viscomi, 1993; vol. iv: *The Continental Prophecies*, ed. D. W. Dörrbecker, 1995; vol. v: *'Milton a Poem' and the Final Illuminated Works*, ed. Robert N. Essick and J. Viscomi, 1994; vol. vi: *The Urizen Books*, ed. David Worrall, 1995).

Ellis, E. J., and Yeats, W. B. (eds.), *The Works of William Blake: Poetic, Symbolic and Critical*, 3 vols. (London, 1893).

Erdman, David V. (ed.), *The Complete Poetry and Prose of William Blake*, with a commentary by Harold Bloom (New York, 1965; rev. edn., 1988).

—— (ed.), *The Illuminated Blake* (London, 1975).

Grant, John, and Johnson, Mary Lynn (eds.), *Blake's Poetry and Designs* (New York, 1979).

Keynes, Geoffrey (ed.), *The Complete Writings of William Blake* (London, 1957; rev. edn., 1966).

Mason, Michael (ed.), *William Blake* (Oxford, 1988).

Ostriker, Alicia, *William Blake: The Complete Poems* (Harmondsworth, 1977).

Sloss, D. J., and Wallis, J. P. R. (eds.), *The Prophetic Writings of William Blake*, 2 vols. (Oxford, 1926).

Stevenson, W. H. (ed.), *Blake: The Complete Poems*, text by D. V. Erdman (London, 1971; rev. edn., 1989).

Individual Works

Bentley, G. E., Jr. (ed.), *William Blake, 'Vala or The Four Zoas': A Facsimile of the Manuscript, a Transcript of the Poem, and a Study of its Growth and Significance* (Oxford, 1963).

—— (ed.), *'Tiriel': Facsimile and Transcript of the Manuscript, Reproduction of the Drawings, and a Commentary on the Poem* (Oxford, 1967).

Bogan, Nancy, *The Book of Thel: A Facsimile and a Critical Text* (Providence, RI, 1971).

Easson, K. P., and Easson, R. (eds.), *The Book of Urizen* (London, 1979).

—— —— (eds.), *Milton* (London, 1979).

Erdman, David (ed.), with the assistance of Donald K. Moore, *The Notebook of William Blake* (Oxford, 1973; rev. edn., 1977).

—— and Magno, Cettina Tramontano (eds.), *'The Four Zoas' by William Blake: A Photographic Facsimile of the Manuscript with Commentary on the Illuminations* (Lewisburg, Pa., 1987).

Keynes, Geoffrey (ed.), *The Letters of William Blake, with Related Documents* (London, 1956; 3rd edn., Oxford, 1980).

—— (ed.), *Songs of Innocence and of Experience* (London, 1967).

—— (ed.), *The Marriage of Heaven and Hell* (London, 1975).

Margoliouth, H. M. (ed.), *William Blake's 'Vala'* (Oxford, 1956).

Phillips, Michael (ed.), *An Island in the Moon* (Cambridge, 1987).

Graphic Works

Bindman, David, assisted by Deirdre Toomey, *The Complete Graphic Works of William Blake* (London, 1978).

—— with an essay by Bo Lindberg, *Colour Versions of William Blake's Book of Job Designs* (London, 1987).

Butlin, Martin, *The Paintings and Drawings of William Blake*, 2 vols. (New Haven, 1981).

Essick, Robert N., *The Separate Plates of William Blake: A Catalogue* (Princeton, 1983).

—— *William Blake's Commercial Book Illustrations* (Oxford, 1991).

—— and Paley, Morton D., *Robert Blair's 'The Grave' Illustrated by William Blake* (London, 1982).

Grant, John, Rose, E. J., and Tolley, Michael, co-ordinating editor David Erdman, *William Blake's Illustrations to Edward Young's 'Night Thoughts'*, 2 vols. (Oxford, 1980).

LITERARY SCHOLARSHIP AND CRITICISM

Biography and Bibliography

Ackroyd, Peter, *Blake* (London, 1995).

Bentley, G. E., Jr., *Blake Records* (Oxford, 1969).

—— *Blake Books* (Oxford, 1977).

—— *Blake Records Supplement* (Oxford, 1988).

—— *Blake Books Supplement* (Oxford, 1995).

Erdman, David, et al., *A Concordance to the Writings of William Blake*, 2 vols. (Ithaca, NY, 1967).

Gilchrist, Alexander, *Life of William Blake, 'Pictor Ignotus'*, 2 vols. (London, 1863; rev. edn., 1880).

Johnson, Mary Lynn, 'William Blake', in Frank Jordan (ed.), *The English Romantic Poets: A Review of Research and Criticism* (4th edn., New York, 1985), 113–253.

DAVID FULLER

Keynes, Geoffrey, and Wolf, Edwin, II, *William Blake's Illuminated Books: A Census* (London, 1953).

Natoli, Joseph, *Twentieth Century Blake Criticism: Northrop Frye to the Present* (New York, 1982).

Wilson, Mona, *The Life of William Blake* (London, 1927; rev. edn., ed. Geoffrey Keynes, Oxford, 1971).

Literary Criticism

Adams, Hazard, *William Blake: A Reading of the Shorter Poems* (Seattle, 1963).

Altizer, Thomas, *The New Apocalypse: The Radical Christian Vision of William Blake* (Ann Arbor, 1967).

Beer, John, *Blake's Humanism* (Manchester, 1968).

—— *Blake's Visionary Universe* (Manchester, 1969).

Behrendt, Stephen, *Reading William Blake* (Basingstoke, 1992).

Bentley, G. E., Jr. (ed.), *William Blake: The Critical Heritage* (London, 1975).

Blackstone, Bernard, *English Blake* (Cambridge, 1949).

Bloom, Harold, *Blake's Apocalypse: A Study in Poetic Argument* (London, 1963).

Bronowski, Jacob, *A Man without a Mask (William Blake: 1757–1827)* (London, 1944; rev. as *William Blake and the Age of Revolution*, New York, 1965).

Clark, Steve, and Worrall, David (eds.), *Historicizing Blake* (Basingstoke, 1994).

Curran, Stuart, and Wittreich, Joseph A., Jr. (eds.), *Blake's Sublime Allegory: Essays on 'The Four Zoas', 'Milton' and 'Jerusalem'* (Madison, 1973).

Damon, S. Foster, *William Blake: His Philosophy and Symbols* (London, 1924).

—— *A Blake Dictionary: The Ideas and Symbols of William Blake* (1965; rev. edn., ed. Morris Eaves, Providence, RI, 1988).

Damrosch, Leopold, Jr., *Symbol and Truth in Blake's Myth* (Princeton, 1980).

Davies, J. G., *The Theology of William Blake* (Oxford, 1948).

De Luca, Vincent Arthur, *Words of Eternity: Blake and the Poetics of the Sublime* (Princeton, 1991).

Eliot, T. S., 'William Blake' (1920), in *Selected Essays* (London, 1932; 3rd rev. edn., 1951), 317–22.

Erdman, David V., *Blake: Prophet against Empire* (Princeton, 1954; 3rd rev. edn., 1977).

—— 'The Binding (et cetera) of Vala', *Library*, 5th seri. 19 (1964), 112–29.

Essick, Robert N., *William Blake and the Language of Adam* (Oxford, 1989).

—— and Pearce, Donald, *Blake in his Time* (Bloomington, Ind., 1978).

Ferber, Michael, *The Social Vision of William Blake* (Princeton, 1985).

—— *The Poetry of William Blake* (Harmondsworth, 1991).

Freed, Eugenie R., *'A Portion of his Life': William Blake's Miltonic Vision of Women* (Lewisburg, Pa., 1994).

Frye, Northrop, *Fearful Symmetry: A Study of William Blake* (Princeton, 1947).

—— 'Notes for a Commentary on *Milton*', in Vivian de Sola Pinto (ed.), *The Divine Vision: Studies in the Poetry and Art of William Blake* (London, 1957), 97–137.

—— (ed.), *Blake: A Collection of Critical Essays* (Englewood Cliffs, NJ, 1966).

—— *The Stubborn Structure: Essays on Criticism and Society* (London, 1970).

42

Fuller, David, '*Milton* and the Development of Blake's Thought', in J. R. Watson (ed.), *An Infinite Complexity: Essays in Romanticism* (Edinburgh, 1983), 46–94.

—— *Blake's Heroic Argument* (London, 1988).

Gardner, Stanley, *Blake's Innocence and Experience Retraced* (London, 1986).

Gleckner, Robert F., *The Piper and the Bard: A Study of William Blake* (Detroit, 1959).

Glen, Heather, *Vision and Disenchantment: Blake's 'Songs' and Wordsworth's 'Lyrical Ballads'* (Cambridge, 1983).

Hagstrum, Jean H., *William Blake, Poet and Painter: An Introduction to the Illuminated Verse* (Chicago, 1964).

Harper, George Mills, *The Neoplatonism of William Blake* (Chapel Hill, NC, 1961).

Hilton, Nelson, *Literal Imagination: Blake's Vision of Words* (Berkeley, 1984).

—— (ed.), *Essential Articles for the Study of William Blake, 1970–84* (Hamden, Conn., 1986).

—— and Vogler, Thomas A. (eds.), *Unnam'd Forms: Blake and Textuality* (Berkeley, 1986).

Hirsch, E. D., *Innocence and Experience: An Introduction to Blake* (Chicago, 1964).

Hirst, Désirée, *Hidden Riches: Traditional Symbolism from the Renaissance to Blake* (London, 1964).

Holloway, John, *Blake: The Lyric Poetry* (London, 1968).

Keynes, Geoffrey, *Blake Studies* (London, 1949; 2nd rev. edn., Oxford, 1971).

Larrissy, Edward, *William Blake* (Oxford, 1985).

Leader, Zachary, *Reading Blake's 'Songs'* (London, 1981).

McGann, Jerome J., *Towards a Literature of Knowledge* (Oxford, 1989).

Mee, Jon, *Dangerous Enthusiasm: William Blake and the Culture of Radicalism in the 1790s* (Oxford, 1992).

Mellor, Anne K., *Blake's Human Form Divine* (Berkeley, 1974).

—— 'Blake's Portrayal of Women', *Blake: An Illustrated Quarterly*, 63 (1982–3), 148–55.

Miller, Dan, Bracher, Mark, and Ault, Donald (eds.), *Critical Paths: Blake and the Argument of Method* (Durham, NC, 1987).

Mitchell, W. J. T., *Blake's Composite Art: A Study of the Illuminated Poetry* (Princeton, 1978).

Morton, A. L., *The Everlasting Gospel* (London, 1958).

Nurmi, Martin K., *William Blake* (London, 1975).

Ostriker, Alicia, *Vision and Verse in William Blake* (Madison, 1965).

Paley, Morton D., *Energy and the Imagination: A Study of the Development of Blake's Thought* (Oxford, 1970).

—— '"A New Heaven is Begun": William Blake and Swedenborgianism', *Blake: An Illustrated Quarterly*, 50 (1979), 64–90.

—— *The Continuing City: William Blake's 'Jerusalem'* (Oxford, 1983).

—— and Eaves, Morris (eds.), *Blake: An Illustrated Quarterly* [formerly *Blake Newsletter*, 1967–77] (Rochester, NY).

—— and Phillips, Michael (eds.), *William Blake: Essays in Honour of Sir Geoffrey Keynes* (Oxford, 1973).

Percival, Milton O., *William Blake's Circle of Destiny* (New York, 1938).

Phillips, Michael (ed.), *Interpreting Blake* (Cambridge, 1978).

Raine, Kathleen, *Blake and Tradition*, 2 vols. (Princeton, 1968).

—— *Blake and the New Age* (London, 1979).

Rosenfeld, Alvin, (ed.), *William Blake: Essays for S. Foster Damon* (Providence, RI, 1969).

Schorer, Mark, *William Blake: The Politics of Vision* (New York, 1946).

Swinburne, A. C., *William Blake: A Critical Essay* (London, 1868).

Tannenbaum, Leslie, *Biblical Tradition in Blake's Early Prophecies: The Great Code of Art* (Princeton, 1982).

Thompson, E. P., *Witness against the Beast: William Blake and the Moral Law* (Cambridge, 1993).

Todd, Ruthven, *Tracks in the Snow* (London, 1946).

Vine, Steven, *Blake's Poetry: Spectral Visions* (Basingstoke, 1993).

Viscomi, Joseph, *Blake and the Idea of the Book* (Princeton, 1993).

Wicksteed, Joseph, *Blake's Innocence and Experience* (London, 1928).

Wittreich, Joseph Anthony, Jr., *Angel of Apocalypse: Blake's Idea of Milton* (Madison, 1975).

ART SCHOLARSHIP AND CRITICISM

Behrendt, Stephen, *The Moment of Explosion: Blake and the Illustration of Milton* (Lincoln, Nebr., 1983).

Bindman, David, *William Blake: An Illustrated Catalogue of Works in the Fitzwilliam Museum, Cambridge* (Cambridge, 1970).

—— *Blake as an Artist* (Oxford, 1977).

—— *William Blake: His Art and his Times* (London, 1982).

Blunt, Anthony, *The Art of William Blake* (London, 1959).

Butlin, Martin, *William Blake, 1757–1827*, Tate Gallery Collections 5 (London, 1990).

—— *William Blake* (Catalogue of the 1978 Tate Gallery exhibition; London, 1978).

—— and Gott, Ted, *William Blake in the National Gallery of Victoria* (Melbourne, 1989).

Eaves, Morris, *William Blake's Theory of Art* (Princeton, 1982).

Essick, Robert N., *William Blake: Printmaker* (Princeton, 1980).

—— *The Works of William Blake in the Huntington Collections* (San Marino, Calif., 1985).

Fuller, David, 'Blake and Dante', *Art History*, 11 (1988), 349–73.

Heppner, Christopher, *Reading Blake's Designs* (Cambridge, 1995).

Keynes, Geoffrey, *William Blake's Illustrations to the Bible* (Paris, 1957).

Lindberg, Bo, *William Blake's Illustrations to the Book of Job* (Abo, 1973).

Raine, Kathleen, *The Human Face of God: William Blake and the Book of Job* (London, 1982).

Roe, Albert S., *William Blake's Illustrations to 'The Divine Comedy'* (Princeton, 1953).

Tayler, Irene, *Blake's Illustrations to the Poems of Thomas Gray* (Princeton, 1971).

Wicksteed, Joseph, *Blake's Vision of the Book of Job* (London, 1910; 2nd edn., 1924).

3. *William Wordsworth*

NICHOLAS ROE

TEXTS

For many years the standard edition was de Selincourt's and Darbishire's *Poetical Works of William Wordsworth*, which followed the text of 1849–50, the last prepared with Wordsworth's supervision. Modern editorial work has sought to establish the earliest versions of the poems; see for example *The Ruined Cottage* and *The Pedlar* in J. Wordsworth (1969); Gill's 'Original *Salisbury Plain*'; and 'A Night-Piece' and 'The Discharged Soldier' in Darlington (1970). The Cornell Wordsworth Series (1975–   ) brings 'early Wordsworth into view' through editorial reconstruction and inclusive presentation of manuscript sources and printed texts. This ambitious series is an indispensable research resource, although it has provoked controversy on the grounds that it misrepresents Wordsworth's intentions for his work and obscures his later career.

De Selincourt's edition of *The Prelude* (1926) printed for the first time the poem completed in May 1805 alongside the poem published (after Wordsworth's death) in July 1850. The Norton *Prelude* (1979a) includes the 'Two-Part *Prelude*' of 1798–9 with the 1805 and 1850, plus manuscript drafts and critical responses: a useful volume, readily available. J. Wordsworth's *The Prelude: The Four Texts* (1995) adds an earlier proto-*Prelude* of 1798. A 'Five-Book *Prelude*' dating from early spring 1804 was reconstructed by J. Wordsworth (1977) and published by Wu (1997).

Gill's 'Wordsworth's Poems: The Question of Text' reminds us that currently 'there is no authoritative edition of the poems'. Stillinger (1989) challenges the 'primitivist' ideals of the Cornell Series and Norton *Prelude*, and Leader calls for editors to respect Wordsworth's 'authorial agency'. Three essays by Parrish (1976, 1983, 1988) defend the Cornell edition. Jarvis (1981) questions the reconstruction of a 'Five-Book *Prelude*'; Baker rejects editorial preference for the 1805 *Prelude* over 1850. 'Waiting for the Palfreys: The Great *Prelude* Debate' (1986) is a sprightly forum discussion of *Prelude* texts. Wu (1991) is sceptical of editors' claims to fulfil Wordsworth's intentions. For Wordsworth's revisions in wider cultural contexts see Hanley, Barron and Johnston, Roe (1992b), and J. Wordsworth (1992). Sykes Davies treats revision and Wordsworth's distinctive vocabulary; Galperin links revisions to formulations of poetic 'authority'. The ordering of poems in *Lyrical Ballads* and later collections is treated well by Fraistat, Liu, and Leader.

Two selections are recommended. Gill (W. Wordsworth 1984*d*) includes the 1805 *Prelude*, and some of the prose; poems are ordered by composition 'as nearly as possible [in] their earliest completed state'. Roe (W. Wordsworth 1992) similarly arranges his Penguin selection, printing 'from the earliest text published in a Wordsworth volume' and including the 'Two-Part *Prelude*'. Duncan Wu's splendid *Romanticism: An Anthology* (1998) has complete texts of *Lyrical Ballads* (1798) plus *The Ruined Cottage*, *The Pedlar*, the 'Two-Part *Prelude*', *Michael*, and *The Brothers*. Matlak's and Mellor's *British Literature 1780–1830* follows 'Sonnet on Seeing Miss Helen Maria Williams Weep at a Tale of Distress' (Wordsworth's first published poem) with selections from *Lyrical Ballads*, the 'Two-Part *Prelude*', and extracts from *The Prelude* (1805 and 1850). Lane Cooper's concordance treats a full range of poems; McEahern and Beckwith focus on *Lyrical Ballads* 1798 and 1800 (poems and prose).

Owen and Smyser is the standard edition of Wordsworth's prose (1974), supplemented by Curtis's edition (1993) of the autobiographical 'Fenwick Notes' of 1843. The best edition of the *Guide to the Lakes* is Bicknell's illustrated text (1984). *The Letters of William and Dorothy Wordsworth*, second edition (1967–93), is the standard text. Darlington printed newly discovered love letters between William and Mary Wordsworth (1982), providing evidence for reassessing their relationship.

BIBLIOGRAPHIES

For modern scholarship and criticism in a historical perspective see Hanley and Barron and Kroeber (1985). Both list further bibliographic sources which should also be consulted. For reviews of Wordsworth's poetry during his lifetime see John O. Hayden (1969, 1971), and Reiman.

BIOGRAPHIES

Christopher Wordsworth's *Memoirs of William Wordsworth* (1851) was authorized by the poet's family and, although a highly selective account, represents Wordsworth as perceived by the Victorians. Hitherto unpublished material was made available in Knight's biography of 1889 as a 'quarry' for future biographies. Of these, Legouis (1896) was the first scholarly and critical account, using *The Prelude* as a guide to Wordsworth's development to 1798; his analysis of literary influences and narrative of the poet's experiences in revolutionary France deserve attention. Harper (1916) also concentrated on the early years, supplementing this in 1921 with a first announcement of Wordsworth's love affair with Annette Vallon, further elaborated in Legouis (1922). Moorman (1957, 1965) is the most extensive twentieth-century life, useful on the later years. The standard biography is by Gill (1989): richly informed, alert to Wordsworth's self-fashioning as poet, Gill draws on the long tradition of Wordsworth studies as well as up-to-date critical methods. Hamilton and Williams (1996) are succinct appraisals of Wordsworth's literary career, life, and times.

Reed's chronologies of Wordsworth's early (1770–99) and middle years (1800–15) are indispensable references, as are Wu's catalogues of Wordsworth's reading (1993, 1995). T. W. Thompson gathers material on Wordsworth's schooldays at Hawkshead; Schneider investigates Wordsworth's Cambridge education.

For backgrounds to Wordsworth and the French Revolution see Abrams (1971) and 'Prometheus Rising' in Bloom (1961). E. P. Thompson's compelling polemic 'Disenchantment or Default? A Lay Sermon' traces withdrawal and 'apostasy' in Wordsworth and his contemporaries; his two later essays (1988, 1994) link Wordsworth with Godwin and Thelwall. In essays (1978, 1981, 1987, 1988) and in his major study *Commerce des lumières* (1986) Erdman presents authoritative conjectures about how Wordsworth's participation in revolutionary France reverberated in his imaginative life. Johnston (1986) brings forward Wordsworth as 'active partisan' in Eaton's *Philanthropist* magazine (see also E. P. Thompson 1988). Roe (1988) illuminates Wordsworth's and Coleridge's 'radical years', exploring in detail how their revolutionary activities and creative lives were related. The same author's *Politics of Nature* includes Wordsworth in closely interwoven studies of politics and poetry in the 1790s. Todd (1957) surveys the political life, arguing that Wordsworth's early liberalism was 'essentially conservative' (compare Chandler 1984). On Wordsworth and revolution generally see essays by Janowitz, Johnston, and J. Wordsworth in Hanley and Selden. Chard and Williams (1989) relate Wordsworth to traditions of English dissent (see also Bloom's 'Prometheus Rising'). Friedman and Chandler (1984) argue for conservative, Burkian themes in Wordsworth from the middle of the revolutionary decade. Jaye et al. (1987) place Wordsworth in an illustrated survey of the 'age of English Romanticism'.

For the poet's day-to-day life and composition of many poems Dorothy Wordsworth's journals are the unrivalled source. The only full edition is de Selincourt (D. Wordsworth 1941); Darbishire and Moorman reprint the 'Alfoxden Journal' of 1798 (1971); the standard edition of the 'Grasmere Journals', is edited by Pamela Woof (1991). Life at Alfoxden during 1798, when many *Lyrical Ballads* were written, is evoked in Hazlitt's 'My First Acquaintance with Poets' (1823), and in Mayberry's engaging illustrated account of Wordsworth's West Country years. McCracken places the poems in relation to the

Lake District landscape, with illustrations and maps. Blanshard catalogues portraits and busts of Wordsworth.

CRITICISM

According to Hazlitt (1825) the French Revolution was the model for Wordsworth's early 'poetical experiments' but his later poems were 'artificial', 'classical', and 'courtly'. Arnold (W. Wordsworth 1879) reinforced this judgement, claiming that Wordsworth's achievement was in earlier, short poems communicating 'the joy offered to us in nature [and] in the simple elementary affections and duties'. Nineteenth-century readers held *The Excursion* in high esteem, but Arnold helped establish *The Prelude* as Wordsworth's greatest work. The Wordsworth Society (founded 1880) and massive editions by Knight (1882–9) and Dowden (1892–3) promoted Wordsworth's reputation as the 'High-Priest' of nature whose poetry was a guide to life. For a survey of 'Wordsworth and the Victorians' see Woodring (1987), and for a similarly helpful account Simpson's 'Wordsworth in America' (1987*a*).

In *Oxford Lectures on Poetry* (1909) Bradley acknowledged 'reverential' criticism of Wordsworth but pointed to 'strangeness and paradoxes' in the poems. 'Everything here is natural', Bradley observed, 'but everything is apocalyptic'. With the acknowledgement that Wordsworth is troubled by 'something illimitable' behind ' "reality" ', twentieth-century criticism of him begins. F. R. Leavis (1936) accepted Arnold's importance but quarrelled with his stress on 'joy', arguing that, although Wordsworth was a poet of humane wisdom, his 'convincingly expository tone' masked a lack of intellectual rigour. Beatty, in contrast, found empirical 'philosophic substance' in Wordsworth's 'doctrine and art', whereas Stallknecht (reacting against Beatty) and Rader foregrounded Wordsworth's bold 'mystical excitement'—a 'transcendental' ambition seemingly in conflict with naturalism. Ferry similarly reads the poems as metaphysical narratives of the 'hostility' between Wordsworth's 'passion for eternity' and human worldly experience. John Jones traced Wordsworth's 'decline' in the gradual tempering of 'possible sublimity' into a conventional 'Christian maturity'. Perceived divisions between materialist and ideal aspects of Wordsworth have persisted throughout twentieth-century criticism.

Bloom (1961) and Hartman (1964) identify Wordsworth with the prophetic tradition, a poet for whom the apocalyptic collaboration of nature and imagination succeeded revolution as 'our only way to God'. For Hartman, Wordsworthian nature fosters self-consciousness but ultimately leads (as Bradley indicated) to the visionary country 'from which imagination comes and to which it seeks to return'. Parallels between revolutionary events in the 1960s and 1790s made Wordsworth—like Blake—seem 'intensely contemporary'

(Hartman 1996). M. H. Abrams's monumental study of tradition and revolution in the Romantic period, *Natural Supernaturalism*, identified Wordsworth as 'exemplary poet of the age'—a pioneer of modern, secular consciousness.

Modern critical approaches to Wordsworth have presented successive reconfigurations of imagination, nature, and history. Nature and imagination were explored 'mainly through [poetic] style' by Hartman (1964), who shared the Yale School's preoccupation with text and rhetoric. From the late 1970s, the historical pressures of politics, society, and economics on Wordsworth's poetry have received close attention. In arguing that 'artistic strategies are responses to problems set . . . by history', Marilyn Butler (1981) placed Wordsworth in the cultural mainstream of the Enlightenment, 'the greatest writer' of his times in realizing the potential of established tradition. Further representative examples of historicist criticism are Heinzelman (1980), Simpson (1987b), McGann, Johnston (1983), Levinson, Liu, and Harrison. Some critics, associated with Romantic new historicism, combine Marxist politics, Freudian psychology, and deconstructive reading to reveal historical trauma in Wordsworth's imagination. The introduction to Levinson offers a critical genealogy of Romantic new historicism, while her 'Insight and Oversight; Reading "Tintern Abbey"' (in 1986) is a challenging demonstration of new historicist methodology, arguing that *Tintern Abbey*'s idealization of nature was a calculated and guilty 'erasure' of social/political contexts. Nature 'masks' history in Liu's reading of the Simplon Pass episode in *The Prelude*, Book 6; whereas for Hartman this passage disclosed the transcendental courtship of nature and imagination, for Liu the poem betrayed Wordsworth's 'climactic veiling' of history represented by Napoleon's imperial progress through the Alps.

New historicist criticism, aptly described by Liu as 'deflected or denied positivism able to discriminate absence', has in turn been questioned. Manning (1986) and Abrams (1990) warn against the perils of ideological predetermination. Grob argues that Wordsworth's poetry 'kept faith' with revolutionary idealism. Roe (1992a) questions the coercive tenor of some new historicist criticism, and Vendler affirms the lyric impulse of *Tintern Abbey* against 'the discrete material public events which we call "history"'. McFarland's 'The Clamour of Absence: Reading and Misreading in Wordsworthian Criticism' (in 1992) identifies in new historical criticism an 'arbitrariness and lack of connection' arising from the growth in and fragmentation of English studies. The debate has at times been acrimonious, but indicates a healthy vigour in Wordsworth studies. This is also apparent in psychoanalytic and feminist readings by Ellis, Homans, Mellor, Ross and Barrell, and the essays on *The Prelude* in Jacobus (1989). Page, wary of ideological constraints in some feminist approaches to Wordsworth, offers a perceptive restoration of women 'in the history of Wordsworth's career'. Donald Hayden and, more recently, Kroeber (1974, 1994) and Bate (1991) assert Wordsworth's significance as proto-ecologist—a development anticipated by Hartman's observation (1971) that 'the slower trauma of industrialization' had contributed to 'Wordsworth's anxiety for nature'.

Less preoccupied with theory than with textual minutiae are studies foregrounding manuscript and archival research, close reading, and contextual elucidation. This approach characterized Legouis (1896), in which *The Prelude* was taken as a reliable guide to Wordsworth's early career. In the same tradition is Jonathan Wordsworth (1982), where the detailed knowledge of biography, chronology, and patterns of creativity which informed the same author's ground-breaking study *The Music of Humanity* (1969) is brought to bear on the evolution of *The Prelude*, *The Recluse*, and related poems. Wordsworth's achievements 1797–1807 have attracted numerous critics, although his earlier poems such as *The Vale of Esthwaite*, *An Evening Walk*, and *Descriptive Sketches* are treated well in Legouis (1896), Darbishire, Sharrock, Jacobus (1976), Wu (1994), and, with social/political emphases, in Liu and Williams (1989). Sheats's *The Making of Wordsworth's Poetry* is a fine comprehensive analysis of Wordsworth's development to 1798.

Wordsworth's productions after his return from France (Dec. 1792) included his pamphlet *A Letter to the Bishop of Llandaff* (see text and discussion in W. Wordsworth 1974), and social protest in the *Salisbury Plain* poems of 1793–5, first treated in Welsford. Gill's Cornell edition (1975) reproduced with commentary successive versions of *Salisbury Plain* down to the published text of 1842. Protest and Wordsworth's poetry are explored by Gill (1972) and by Roe (1988) who also (1995) presents a first account of 'lost' sections of Wordsworth's and Wrangham's collaborative Juvenalian satire of summer 1795. Osborn's Cornell *Borderers* (1982) boosted the play's critical reputation. McFarland (1992) memorably describes it as 'dramatically undramatic', packed with the intellectual 'debris' Wordsworth jettisoned before assuming his unique lyrical 'intensity'. For essays in reassessment of *The Borderers*, see the special issue of *Studies in Romanticism* (Fall 1988). For Wordsworth's characters, especially the 'villain-hero' Rivers/Oswald, see G. Wilson Knight, Hartman (1963) on Oswald's modernity as advocate of 'intellectual murder', Thorslev on Wordsworth's Gothicism, Osborn on Rivers's literary and philosophical antecedents, Erdman (1981) on the Scottish Jacobin John Oswald as the model for Rivers, Parker's explorations of Mortimer's roles (1987, 1988), and John Kerrigan (1996) on how 'the energies of retribution' work in *The Borderers* to innovative and uncanny effect. For the play's literary and dramatic contexts see Owen (1975), Jacobus (1976), and Bate (1986), and Richardson for the play as 'mental theatre'. The play's relation to political and social issues is explored in Woodring, Roe (1988), Liu, and McFarland (1992).

Wordsworth's claim for the 'experimental' qualities of *Lyrical Ballads* (1798) was challenged by Coleridge in *Biographia Literaria* (1817), reasserted by Hazlitt (1823 and 1825), and has remained a focus for controversy (for an account see

Jordan 1976). Mayo claimed that the poems conformed to contemporary fashion, whereas Danby argued for the originality of Wordsworth's hard-earned
'simplicity'. Jordan (1970) points out that in 1798 claims for poetic 'novelty'
were commonplace. Parrish (1973), Jacobus (1976), and Glen are valuable on
the origins of *Lyrical Ballads* (1798) and the interweaving of traditional and
innovative strands in the poems. Johnston (1987) relates the ballads' composition to failure to progress with *The Recluse*. Bialostosky (1984), drawing on
Bakhtin, argues for the success of Wordsworth's narrative experiments in dramatic, pastoral, and ballad poetry. Rewarding studies of humanitarian themes
in *Lyrical Ballads* include Averill, Beer (1978, 1979), 'The Significant Group' in
McFarland (1981), Pirie (1982), Blank, and, with political emphases, Thompson
(1969), Spiegelman, Levinson, Turner, Roe (1988, 1992a), Williams (1989), and
McFarland (1992). The Casebook *Wordsworth: Lyrical Ballads* and Campbell are
useful references, including Wordsworth's and Coleridge's views of *Lyrical
Ballads*, plus contemporary, Victorian, and modern assessments.

Wordsworth's and Coleridge's creative interaction preoccupied both poets
in later life. For their accounts see Wordsworth's 'Fenwick Note' to 'We are
Seven', *Biographia Literaria*, and for a recent survey Reed (1965). On the origins of *Lyrical Ballads* see also J. Wordsworth (1969, 1982), Woof's 'Wordsworth
and Coleridge: Some Early Matters', the first chapter in Newlyn (1986) and,
with reference to the poets' early radical commitments, Thompson (1969),
Watson, Beer (1977), and Roe (1988). Heath's study of creative tension in 1801–
2 is useful, and so is McFarland (1981), who presents a formidable argument
for their 'symbiotic' relationship. Parrish (1973), in focusing on Wordsworth
as the 'major partner', sees 'differences of personality, of taste, of ambition, of
poetic philosophy' as fundamental to the relationship. Gravil argues for Coleridge's 'destructive dominance' over Wordsworth. Newlyn (1986), in a brilliant
account of allusive and echoic play between Wordsworth and Coleridge, dates
the poets' awareness of 'radical difference' to spring 1802. Curtis (1971) treats
Wordsworth's creativity in spring 1802, including texts of poems written at
this time. For Wordsworth's interaction with Coleridge during this spring see
Pirie (1970), the introduction to Parrish's edition of Coleridge's *Dejection*, and
Eilenberg's study of property, propriety, and possession in the relationship.
Magnuson finds 'identity and opposition' initiating the poets' complex lyrical
dialogue. For intertextual analysis of Wordsworth's and Coleridge's lyrics
1802–4 see Ruoff, and Paley for later phases of the relationship.

The scheme for a philosophical poem titled *The Recluse* dated from March
1798 and preoccupied Wordsworth until the end of his life (see the *Prelude*
Casebook for a chronology). The first book of *The Recluse* (now titled *Home
at Grasmere*) was published in 1888, eliciting 'Wordsworth's Great Failure' from
William Minto (1889). For *Home at Grasmere*, see Darlington's Cornell edition
(1977). Major studies of *The Recluse* include Bloom (1961) on Wordsworth's

'defiant humanism', J. Wordsworth (1982) on the millenarian background, and Johnston (1984) arguing that *The Recluse* exists in poems completed between 1797–1814. Bewell is a fine study of intellectual and anthropological backgrounds to Wordsworthian themes, including those of the *Recluse*. See also James Butler's essay on 'The Tuft of Primroses' of 1808 and the impossibility of completing *The Recluse*; Lefebure on Coleridge's idea of *The Recluse* as 'an opium eater's fantasy'; Johnston (1990*b*) for Wordsworth's late, feminized, return to *The Recluse* in 1826, and McFarland's exposition (1992) of the 'five blocking factors' which broke Wordsworth's aspirations for the poem.

For Wordsworth's response to Milton see Bloom (1961, 1973, 1976) and Rieger arguing, *contra* Bloom, for Wordsworth's 'unanxious' response to Milton. For Wordsworth, the Romantics, and Milton see Newlyn (1993), the most substantial modern study; see also Peterfreund, MacNally, McFarland (1982), J. Wordsworth (1982), Brinkley (1985), Erdman (1988), Roe (1989), and Jarvis (1991). For Wordsworth and Shakespeare see Bate (1986) and for allusions to English poetry more generally see Stein.

The various texts of *The Prelude*, 1798–1850, have generated a corresponding variety of comment. The *Prelude* Casebook (1972) conveniently gathers Victorian (1852–97) and modern (1926–1967) assessments. Bloom (1986) reprints commentaries from 1951 onwards; Wood contains four essays reflecting modern critical and theoretical positions. Appropriate volumes in the Cornell Series represent current editorial and scholarly views. A landmark in *Prelude* studies was Lindenberger (1963), whose many-faceted readings of the 1805 poem include its language, versification, organization, concern with time, social dimensions, and place in literary history. J. Wordsworth (1982) traces phases of composition between 1798 and 1805, emphasizing the poem's formal and thematic coherence. Gill (1991) is the best short introduction to *The Prelude*. For deconstructive readings of *The Prelude* see Chase on Book 5 as 'the book of accidents'; de Man on autobiography as defined, and disfigured, by text; and Jacobus (1989) exploring the relationship between writing, anxiety, and literary priority in *Prelude*, Book 5. Other notable critical developments are represented by Spivak's 'Sex and History in "The Prelude" ', on illegitimate paternity and revolutionary history, and more generally by the poststructural, psychoanalytic, and feminist approaches in Jacobus (1989).

According to McFarland (1992), 'the melancholy quantity of desiccated verse' Wordsworth wrote in later life was unequalled by any other great poet. In comparing two poems, 'Surprised by Joy' and 'The Triad', McFarland defines the texture of Wordsworth's desiccation, concentrating aspects of his earlier analysis (1981) of Wordsworth's egotism and growing 'rigidity'. Sperry analysed causes of Wordsworth's 'anti-climax', while Groom saw the later poems as continuous with earlier achievements. Positive accounts of Wordsworth's later poetry are to be found in Manning's 'Wordsworth at St. Bees' (1985), in Lyon's study of *The Excursion*, and in Johnston (1984). Johnson traces Wordsworth's preoccupation with sonnets, and Kerrigan (1985) reads the sonnets as the formal equivalent of the 'rooted' worldliness of the young Wordsworth's imagination. Wordsworth's responses to Waterloo are treated by Walker, Chandler (1987), Shaw, and Bainbridge. Wordsworth's prosody is excellently analysed by O'Donnell, and by Sykes Davies. For the complexity of Wordsworth's thinking about aesthetics see the study by Theresa Kelley (1988), and related discussion of the sublime and beautiful in Owen (1973 and 1976). Wordsworth's literary criticism was the subject of Owen (1969), who also edited the critical writings (1974). For Wordsworth's prose more generally (including the *Essays upon Epitaphs*) see Devlin (1980, 1983).

Wordsworth features prominently in debate about the Romantic canon and the nature of Romanticism itself. For 'Romanticism' as a 'posthumous movement' which may have 'cramped' twentieth-century understandings of Wordsworth, see Butler (1981). Bourke seeks to show how the reception of Wordsworth as literary ideal represents the process through which literature comes to 'substitute for, rather than to instigate, political modernity'. For sceptical, gendered questioning of Wordsworth's self-constitution as a poet see Spivak and Jacobus (1989). Butler's and Chandler's essays (1990) interrogate Wordsworth's status as uniquely representative Romantic poet, questioning the 'enthusiastic empathizing with William of . . . otherwise sophisticated Wordsworthians'.

A rewarding first supplement to this essay is John Williams's *Wordsworth: Contemporary Critical Essays* (1993), which collects nine essays and extracts representing the diversity of current approaches. For other eclectic gatherings see Johnston's and Ruoff's *The Age of William Wordsworth* and Gilpin. First published in 1970, *Wordsworth Circle* is a quarterly journal devoted to the poet and his contemporaries, a valuable guide to the evolution of Wordsworth studies in the later twentieth century.

REFERENCES

TEXTS

Wordsworth, Dorothy, *Journals of Dorothy Wordsworth*, ed. Ernest de Selincourt, 2 vols. (London, 1941).
—— *Journals of Dorothy Wordsworth: The Alfoxden Journal, 1798; The Grasmere Journals, 1800–1803*, ed. Helen Darbishire, rev. Mary Moorman (2nd edn., London, 1971).
—— *Dorothy Wordsworth: The Grasmere Journals*, ed. Pamela Woof (Oxford, 1991).
Wordsworth, William, *Poems of Wordsworth*, ed. Matthew Arnold (London, 1879).
—— *The Poetical Works of William Wordsworth*, ed. William Knight, 11 vols. (Edinburgh, 1882–9).

Wordsworth, William, *The Poetical Works of William Wordsworth*, ed. Edward Dowden, 7 vols. (London, 1892–3).

—— *The Recluse* (London, 1888).

—— *The Prelude, or Growth of a Poet's Mind by William Wordsworth*, ed. Ernest de Selincourt (Oxford, 1926).

—— *The Poetical Works of William Wordsworth Edited from the Manuscripts, with Textual and Critical Notes*, ed. Ernest de Selincourt and Helen Darbishire, 5 vols. (Oxford, 1941–9; rev. edn., 1952–9).

—— *The Prose Works of William Wordsworth*, ed. W. J. B. Owen and Jane Worthington Smyser, 3 vols. (Oxford, 1974).

—— *The Salisbury Plain Poems of William Wordsworth*, ed. Stephen Gill, Cornell Wordsworth Series (Ithaca, NY, 1975).

—— *Home at Grasmere*, ed. Beth Darlington, Cornell Wordsworth Series (Ithaca, NY, 1977a).

—— *The Prelude, 1798–9, by William Wordsworth*, ed. Stephen Parrish, Cornell Wordsworth Series (Ithaca, NY, 1977b).

—— *The Prelude, 1799, 1805, 1850*, ed. J. Wordsworth, M. H. Abrams, and S. Gill, Norton Critical Edition (New York, 1979a).

—— *The Ruined Cottage and The Pedlar*, ed. James Butler, Cornell Wordsworth Series (Ithaca, 1979b).

—— *Benjamin, the Waggoner*, ed. Paul F. Betz, Cornell Wordsworth Series (Ithaca, NY, 1981).

—— *The Borderers*, ed. Robert Osborn, Cornell Wordsworth Series (Ithaca, NY, 1982).

—— *Poems, in Two Volumes, and Other Poems, 1800–1807*, ed. Jared Curtis, Cornell Wordsworth Series (Ithaca, NY, 1983).

—— *An Evening Walk*, ed. James Averill, Cornell Wordsworth Series (Ithaca, NY, 1984a).

—— *Descriptive Sketches*, ed. Eric Birdsall and Paul Zall, Cornell Wordsworth Series (Ithaca, NY, 1984b).

—— *The Illustrated Wordsworth's Guide to the Lakes*, ed. Peter Bicknell (Exeter, 1984c).

—— *William Wordsworth*, ed. Stephen Gill, Oxford Authors Series (Oxford, 1984d).

—— *The Fourteen-Book Prelude*, ed. W. J. B. Owen, Cornell Wordsworth Series (Ithaca, NY, 1985a).

—— *Peter Bell*, ed. John E. Jordan, Cornell Wordsworth Series (Ithaca, NY, 1985b).

—— *The Tuft of Primroses with Other Late Poems for The Recluse*, ed. Joseph Kishel, Cornell Wordsworth Series (Ithaca, NY, 1986).

—— *The White Doe of Rylestone; or, The Fate of the Nortons*, ed. Kristine Dugas, Cornell Wordsworth Series (Ithaca, NY, 1988).

—— *Shorter Poems, 1807–1820*, ed. Carl H. Ketcham, Cornell Wordsworth Series (Ithaca, NY, 1989).

—— *The Thirteen-Book Prelude*, ed. Mark Reed, Cornell Wordsworth Series, 2 vols. (Ithaca, NY, 1991).

—— *William Wordsworth: Selected Poetry*, ed. Nicholas Roe, Penguin Poetry Library (London, 1992).

—— *The Fenwick Notes of William Wordsworth*, ed. Jared Curtis (London, 1993).

—— *The Prelude: The Four Texts 1798, 1799, 1805, 1850*, ed. J. Wordsworth (London, 1995).

—— *The Five-Book Prelude*, ed. Duncan Wu (Oxford, 1997).

—— and Wordsworth, Dorothy, *The Letters of William and Dorothy Wordsworth*, ed. Ernest de Selincourt, 6 vols. (Oxford, 1935–9), rev. Alan G. Hill, 8 vols. (Oxford, 1967–93).

—— and Wordsworth, Mary, *The Love Letters of William and Mary Wordsworth*, ed. Beth Darlington (London, 1982).

CRITICISM

Abrams, M. H., *Natural Supernaturalism: Tradition and Revolution in Romantic Literature* (New York, 1971).

—— 'On Political Readings of *Lyrical Ballads*', in K. R. Johnston et al. (eds.), *Romantic Revolutions: Criticism and Theory* (Bloomington, Ind., 1990), 320–49.

Averill, James, *Wordsworth and the Poetry of Human Suffering* (Ithaca, NY, 1980).

Bainbridge, Simon, 'To "Sing it Rather Better": Byron, the Bards, and Waterloo', *Romanticism*, 1/1 (1995), 68–81.

Baker, Jeffrey, 'Prelude and Prejudice', *Wordsworth Circle*, 13/2 (Spring 1982), 79–86.

Barrell, John, 'The Uses of Dorothy: "The Language of the Sense" in "Tintern Abbey"', in J. Williams (ed.), *Wordsworth: Contemporary Critical Essays*, New Casebooks Series (Basingstoke, 1993), 142–71.

Barron, Jonathan, and Johnston, Kenneth, '"A Power to Virtue Friendly": The Pedlar's Guilt in Wordsworth's "Ruined Cottage"', in R. Brinkley and K. Hanley (eds.), *Romantic Revisions* (Cambridge, 1992), 64–86.

Bate, Jonathan, *Shakespeare and the English Romantic Imagination* (Oxford, 1986).

—— *Romantic Ecology: Wordsworth and the Environmental Tradition* (London, 1991).

Beatty, Arthur, *William Wordsworth: His Doctrine and Art in their Historical Relations* (Madison, 1922).

Beer, John, 'The "Revolutionary Youth" of Wordsworth and Coleridge: Another View', *Critical Quarterly*, 19/2 (Summer 1977), 79–87.

—— *Wordsworth and the Human Heart* (Basingstoke, 1978).

—— *Wordsworth in Time* (London, 1979).

Bewell, Alan, *Wordsworth and the Enlightenment: Nature, Man and Society in the Experimental Poetry* (New Haven, 1989).

Bialostosky, Donald, *Making Tales: The Poetics of Wordsworth's Narrative Experiments* (Chicago, 1984).

—— *Wordsworth, Dialogics and the Practice of Criticism* (Cambridge, 1992).

Blank, G. Kim, *Wordsworth and Feeling: The Poetry of an Adult Child* (Cranbury, NJ, 1995).

Blanshard, Frances, *Portraits of Wordsworth* (London, 1959).

Bloom, Harold, *The Visionary Company: A Reading of English Romantic Poetry* (New York, 1961; rev. edn., Ithaca, NY, 1971).

—— *The Anxiety of Influence: A Theory of Poetry* (Oxford, 1973).

—— *Poetry and Repression: Revisionism from Blake to Stevens* (New Haven, 1976).

Bloom, Harold, (ed.) *William Wordsworth's 'The Prelude'* (New York, 1986).

'The Borderers: A Forum', *Studies in Romanticism* (Fall 1988).

Bourke, Richard, *Romantic Discourse and Political Modernity: Wordsworth, the Intellectual and Cultural Critique* (Hemel Hempstead, 1993).

Bradley, A. C., *Oxford Lectures on Poetry* (London, 1909).

Brinkley, Robert A., 'Vagrant and Hermit: Milton and the Politics of "Tintern Abbey"', *Wordsworth Circle*, 16/3 (Summer 1985), 126–35.

—— and Hanley, Keith (eds.), *Romantic Revisions* (Cambridge, 1992).

Butler, James, 'Wordsworth's *Tuft of Primroses*: "An Unrelenting Doom"', *Studies in Romanticism*, 14/3 (Summer 1975), 237–48.

Butler, Marilyn, *Romantics, Rebels and Reactionaries: English Literature and its Background 1760–1830* (London, 1981).

—— 'Plotting the Revolution: The Political Narratives of Romantic Poetry and Criticism', in K. R. Johnston et al. (eds.), *Romantic Revolutions: Criticism and Theory* (Bloomington, Ind., 1990), 133–57.

Campbell, Patrick (ed.), *Wordsworth and Coleridge: 'Lyrical Ballads'*, Critical Perspectives Series (London, 1991).

Chandler, James K., *Wordsworth's Second Nature: A Study of the Poetry and the Politics* (Chicago, 1984).

—— ' "Wordsworth" after "Waterloo" ', in K. R. Johnston and G. W. Ruoff (eds.), *The Age of William Wordsworth* (New Brunswick, NJ, 1987), 84–111.

—— 'Representative Men, Spirits of the Age, and Other Romantic Types', in K. R. Johnston et al. (eds.), *Romantic Revolutions: Criticism and Theory* (Bloomington, Ind., 1990), 104–32.

Chard, Leslie F., *Dissenting Republican: Wordsworth's Early Life and Thought in their Political Context* (The Hague, 1972).

Chase, Cynthia, 'The Accidents of Disfiguration: Limits to Literal and Rhetorical Reading in Book 5 of *The Prelude*', *Studies in Romanticism*, 18/4 (Winter 1979), 547–65.

Coleridge, Samuel Taylor, *Biographia Literaria*, ed. James Engell and W. J. Bate, Bollingen Collected Coleridge Series 7, 2 vols. (Princeton, 1983).

—— *Coleridge's Dejection: The Earliest Manuscripts and the Earliest Printings*, ed. Stephen Parrish (Ithaca, NY, 1988).

Cooper, Lane, *A Concordance to the Poems of William Wordsworth* (London, 1911).

Curran, Stuart, 'Wordsworth and the Forms of Poetry', in K. R. Johnston and Gene W. Ruoff (eds.), *The Age of William Wordsworth* (New Brunswick, NJ, 1987), 115–32.

Curtis, Jared, *Wordsworth's Experiments with Tradition: The Lyric Poems of 1802, with Texts of the Poems Based on Early Manuscripts* (Ithaca, NY, 1971).

Danby, John, *The Simple Wordsworth: Studies in the Poems 1797–1807* (London, 1960).

Darbishire, Helen, *The Poet Wordsworth* (Oxford, 1950).

Darlington, Beth, 'Two Early Texts: "A Night-Piece" and "The Discharged Soldier"', in J. Wordsworth and B. Darlington (eds.), *Bicentenary Wordsworth Studies in Memory of John Alban Finch* (Ithaca, NY, 1970), 425–48.

de Man, Paul, 'Autobiography as De-facement', *Modern Language Notes*, 94/5 (Dec. 1979), 919–30.

Devlin, D. D., *Wordsworth and the Poetry of Epitaphs* (London, 1980).

—— De Quincey, Wordsworth and the Art of Prose (London, 1983).

Dickstein, Morris, ' "The Very Culture of the Feelings": Wordsworth and Solitude', in K. R. Johnston and G. W. Ruoff (eds.), The Age of William Wordsworth (New Brunswick, NJ, 1987), 315–43.

Eilenberg, Susan, Strange Power of Speech: Wordsworth, Coleridge, and Literary Possession (New York, 1992).

Ellis, David, Wordsworth, Freud and the Spots of Time: Interpretation in 'The Prelude' (Cambridge, 1985).

Erdman, David V., 'Wordsworth as Heartsworth; or, Was Regicide the Prophetic Ground of Those "Moral Questions"?', in D. H. Reiman, M. C. Jaye, and B. T. Bennett (eds.), The Evidence of the Imagination: Studies of Interactions between Life and Art in English Romantic Literature (New York, 1978), 12–41.

—— 'The Man who was not Napoleon', Wordsworth Circle, 12/1 (Winter 1981), 92–6.

—— Commerce des lumières: John Oswald and the British in Paris, 1790–1793 (Columbia, Mo., 1986).

—— 'The Dawn of Universal Patriotism: William Wordsworth among the British in Revolutionary France', in K. R. Johnston and G. W. Ruoff (eds.), The Age of William Wordsworth (New Brunswick, NJ, 1987), 3–20.

—— ' "Milton! Thou Shouldst be Living" ', Wordsworth Circle, 19/1 (Winter 1988), 2–8.

Ferry, David, The Limits of Mortality: An Essay on Wordsworth's Major Poems (Middleton, Conn., 1959).

Finch, John Alban, 'Wordsworth's Two-Handed Engine', in J. Wordsworth and B. Darlington (eds.), Bicentenary Wordsworth Studies in Memory of John Alban Finch (Ithaca, NY, 1970a), 1–13.

—— 'On the Dating of Home at Grasmere: A New Approach', in J. Wordsworth and B. Darlington (eds.), Bicentenary Wordsworth Studies in Memory of John Alban Finch (Ithaca, NY, 1970b), 14–28.

—— 'The Ruined Cottage Restored: Three Stages of Composition', in J. Wordsworth and B. Darlington (eds.), Bicentenary Wordsworth Studies in Memory of John Alban Finch (Ithaca NY, 1970c), 29–49.

Fraistat, Neil, 'The "Field" of Lyrical Ballads (1798)', in The Poem and the Book: Interpreting Collections of Romantic Poetry (Chapel Hill, NC, 1985), 47–94.

Friedman, Michael H., The Making of a Tory Humanist: William Wordsworth and the Idea of Community (New York, 1979).

Fruman, Norman, Coleridge: The Damaged Archangel (London, 1971).

Galperin, William H., Revision and Authority in Wordsworth: The Interpretation of a Career (Philadelphia, 1989).

Gill, Stephen, 'The Original Salisbury Plain: Introduction and Text', in J. Wordsworth and B. Darlington (eds.), Bicentenary Wordsworth Studies in Memory of John Alban Finch (Ithaca, NY, 1970), 142–79.

—— 'Adventures on Salisbury Plain and Wordsworth's Poetry of Protest 1795–7', Studies in Romanticism, 11/1 (Winter 1972), 48–65.

—— William Wordsworth: A Life (Oxford, 1989).

—— William Wordsworth: 'The Prelude', Landmarks of World Literature Series (Cambridge, 1991).

Gill, Stephen, 'Wordsworth's Poems: The Question of Text', in R. A. Brinkley and K. Hanley (eds.), *Romantic Revisions* (Cambridge, 1992), 43–63.

Gilpin, George H. (ed.), *Critical Essays on William Wordsworth* (Boston, 1990).

Glen, Heather, *Vision and Disenchantment: Blake's 'Songs' and Wordsworth's 'Lyrical Ballads'* (Cambridge, 1983).

Gravil, Richard, 'Imagining Wordsworth: 1797–1807–1817', in R. Gravil, L. Newlyn, and N. Roe (eds.), *Coleridge's Imagination: Essays in Memory of Peter Laver* (Cambridge, 1985), 129–42.

Grob, Alan, 'Afterword: Wordsworth and the Politics of Consciousness', in G. H. Gilpin (ed.), *Critical Essays on William Wordsworth* (Boston, 1990), 339–56.

Groom, Bernard, *The Unity of Wordsworth's Poetry* (London, 1966).

Hamilton, Paul, *Wordsworth*, Harvester New Readings Series (Atlantic Highlands, NJ, 1986).

Hanley, Keith, 'Crossings Out: The Problem of Textual Passage in *The Prelude*', in R. Brinkley and K. Hanley (eds.), *Romantic Revisions* (Cambridge, 1992), 103–35.

—— and Barron, David, *An Annotated Critical Bibliography of William Wordsworth* (Hemel Hempstead, 1995).

—— and Selden, Raman (eds.), *Revolution and English Romanticism: Politics and Rhetoric* (Hemel Hempstead, 1990).

Harper, George McLean, *William Wordsworth: His Life, Works, and Influence*, 2 vols. (London, 1916).

—— *Wordsworth's French Daughter: The Story of her Birth, with the Certificates of her Baptism and Marriage* (Princeton, 1921).

Harrison, Gary, *Wordsworth's Vagrant Muse: Poetry, Poverty and Power* (Detroit, 1994).

Hartman, Geoffrey H., 'Wordsworth, *The Borderers*, and "Intellectual Murder"', *Journal of English and Germanic Philology*, 62/4 (Oct. 1963), 761–8.

—— *Wordsworth's Poetry 1787–1814* (New Haven, 1964; 2nd edn., 1971).

—— *The Unremarkable Wordsworth* (London, 1987).

—— 'The Fate of Reading Once More', *Publications of the Modern Language Association of America*, 111/3 (May 1996), 383–9.

Hayden, Donald, 'William Wordsworth: Early Ecologist', in T. M. Harwell (ed.), *Studies in Relevance: Romantic and Victorian Writers in 1972* (Salzburg, 1973), 36–52.

Hayden, John O., *The Romantic Reviewers 1802–1824* (Chicago, 1969).

—— *Romantic Bards and British Reviewers* (London, 1971).

—— 'Substantive Errors in the Standard Edition of Wordsworth's Poetry', *Library*, 29 (1974), 454–9.

Hazlitt, William, 'My First Acquaintance with Poets', in *The Liberal: Verse and Prose from the South* (1823); repr. *William Hazlitt: Selected Writings*, ed. Ronald Blythe (Harmondsworth, 1970), 43–65.

—— 'Mr. Wordsworth', in *Spirit of the Age* (1825); repr. *William Hazlitt: Selected Writings*, ed. Ronald Blythe (Harmondsworth, 1970), 219–31.

Heath, William, *Wordsworth and Coleridge: A Study of their Literary Relations in 1801–2* (Oxford, 1970).

Heinzelman, Kurt, *The Economics of the Imagination* (Amherst, Mass., 1980).

Homans, Margaret, *Bearing the Word: Language and Female Experience in Nineteenth-Century Women's Writing* (Chicago, 1986).

Jacobus, Mary, *Tradition and Experiment in Wordsworth's Lyrical Ballads, 1798* (Oxford, 1976).

—— *Romanticism, Writing and Sexual Difference: Essays on 'The Prelude'* (Oxford, 1989).

Janowitz, Anne, ' "A Night on Salisbury Plain": A Dreadful, Ruined Nature', in K. Hanley and R. Selden (eds.), *Revolution and English Romanticism: Politics and Rhetoric* (Hemel Hempstead, 1990), 225–40.

Jarvis, Robin, 'The Five-Book *Prelude*: A Reconsideration', *Journal of English and Germanic Philology*, 80/4 (Oct. 1981), 528–51.

—— *Wordsworth, Milton and the Theory of Poetic Relations* (Basingstoke, 1991).

Jaye, Michael C., 'William Wordsworth's Alfoxden Notebook: 1798', in D. H. Reiman, M. C. Jaye, and B. T. Bennett (eds.), *The Evidence of the Imagination: Studies of Interactions between Life and Art in English Romantic Literature* (New York, 1978), 42–85.

—— Woof, Robert, and Wordsworth, Jonathan, *William Wordsworth and the Age of English Romanticism* (New Brunswick, NJ, 1987).

Johnson, Lee, *Wordsworth and the Sonnet* (Copenhagen, 1973).

Johnston, Kenneth R., 'The Politics of "Tintern Abbey" ', *Wordsworth Circle*, 14/1 (Winter 1983), 6–14.

—— *Wordsworth and 'The Recluse'* (New Haven, 1984).

—— 'Philanthropy or Treason? Wordsworth as "Active Partisan" ', *Studies in Romanticism*, 25/3 (Fall 1986), 371–409.

—— 'The Triumphs of Failure: Wordsworth's *Lyrical Ballads* of 1798', in K. R. Johnston and G. W. Ruoff (eds.), *The Age of William Wordsworth* (New Brunswick, NJ, 1987), 133–59.

—— 'Wordsworth's Revolutions, 1793–1798', in K. Hanley and R. Selden (eds.), *Revolution and English Romanticism: Politics and Rhetoric* (Hemel Hempstead, 1990*a*), 169–204.

—— 'Narcissus and Joan: Wordsworth's Feminist Recluse?', *Studies in Romanticism*, 29/2 (Summer 1990*b*), 197–221.

—— and Ruoff, Gene W. (eds.), *The Age of William Wordsworth: Critical Essays on the Romantic Tradition* (New Brunswick, NJ, 1987).

—— Chaitin, G., Hanson, K., and Marks, H., *Romantic Revolutions: Criticism and Theory* (Bloomington, Ind., 1990).

Jones, John, *The Egotistical Sublime: A History of Wordsworth's Imagination* (London, 1954).

Jordan, John E., 'The Novelty of the *Lyrical Ballads*', in J. Wordsworth and B. Darlington (eds.), *Bicentenary Wordsworth Studies in Memory of John Alban Finch* (Ithaca, NY, 1970), 340–58.

—— *Why the 'Lyrical Ballads'? The Background, Writing and Character of Wordsworth's 1798 'Lyrical Ballads'* (Berkeley, 1976).

Kelley, Theresa M., *Wordsworth's Revisionary Aesthetics* (Cambridge, 1988).

Kerrigan, John, 'Wordsworth and the Sonnet: Building, Dwelling, Thinking', *Essays in Criticism*, 35/1 (Jan. 1985), 45–75.

—— *Revenge Tragedy: From Aeschylus to Armageddon* (Oxford, 1996).

Knight, G. Wilson, 'The Wordsworthian Profundity', in *The Starlit Dome: Studies in the Poetry of Vision* (London, 1941; repr. 1959), 1–82.

Knight, William, *The Life of William Wordsworth*, 3 vols. (Edinburgh, 1889), vols. ix–xi in *The Poetical Works of William Wordsworth*, ed. W. Knight, 11 vols. (Edinburgh, 1882–9).

Kroeber, Karl, ' "Home at Grasmere": Ecological Holiness', *Publications of the Modern Language Association of America*, 89 (1974); repr. in G. H. Gilpin *Critical Essays on William Wordsworth* (Boston, 1990), 179–96.

—— 'William Wordsworth', in F. Jordan (ed.), *The English Romantic Poets: A Review of Research and Criticism*, Modern Language Association (4th edn., New York, 1985), 255–339.

—— 'Beyond the Imaginable: Wordsworth and Turner', in K. R. Johnston and G. W. Ruoff (eds.), *The Age of William Wordsworth* (New Brunswick, NJ, 1987), 196–213.

—— *Ecological Literary Criticism: Romantic Imagining and the Biology of Mind* (New York, 1994).

Leader, Zachary, *Revision and Romantic Authorship* (Oxford, 1996).

Leavis, F. R., 'Wordsworth', in *Revaluation: Tradition and Development in English Poetry* (London, 1936; repr. Harmondsworth, 1972), 145–90.

Lefebure, Molly, 'Consolations in Opium: The Expanding Universe of Coleridge, Humphry Davy and *The Recluse*', *Wordsworth Circle*, 17/2 (Spring 1986), 51–60.

Legouis, Émile, *The Early Life of William Wordsworth 1770–1798: A Study of 'The Prelude'* (Paris, 1896), trans. J. W. Matthews (London, 1897; repr. 1921), reissued with introduction and index by Nicholas Roe (London, 1988).

—— *William Wordsworth and Annette Vallon* (London, 1922).

Levinson, Marjorie, *Wordsworth's Great Period Poems: Four Essays* (Cambridge, 1986).

Lindenberger, Herbert, *On Wordsworth's 'Prelude'* (Princeton, 1963).

Liu, Alan, *Wordsworth: The Sense of History* (Stanford, Calif., 1988).

Lyon, Judson Stanley, *'The Excursion': A Study* (New Haven, 1950).

McCracken, David, *Wordsworth and the Lake District: A Guide to the Poems and their Places* (Oxford, 1984).

McEahern, Patricia, and Beckwith, Thomas F., *A Complete Concordance to the 'Lyrical Ballads' of Samuel Taylor Coleridge and William Wordsworth, 1798 and 1800 Editions* (New York, 1987).

McFarland, Thomas, *Romanticism and the Forms of Ruin: Wordsworth, Coleridge, and Modalities of Fragmentation* (Princeton, 1981).

—— 'Wordsworth on Man, on Nature, and on Human Life', *Studies in Romanticism*, 21/4 (Winter 1982), 601–18.

—— *William Wordsworth: Intensity and Achievement* (Oxford, 1992).

McGann, Jerome J., *The Romantic Ideology: A Critical Investigation* (Chicago, 1983).

MacNally, Paul, 'Milton and the Immortality Ode', *Wordsworth Circle*, 11/1 (Winter 1980), 28–33.

Magnuson, Paul, *Coleridge and Wordsworth: A Lyrical Dialogue* (Princeton, 1988).

Manning, Peter, 'Wordsworth at St. Bees: Scandals, Sisterhoods, and Wordsworth's Later Poetry', *English Literary History*, 52 (1985), 33–58; repr. in Manning's *Reading Romantics: Texts and Contexts* (New York, 1990), 273–99.

—— 'Placing Poor Susan: Wordsworth and the New Historicism', *Studies in Romanticism*, 25/3 (Fall 1986), 351–69; repr. in Manning's *Reading Romantics: Texts and Contexts* (New York, 1990), 300–20.

Matlak, Richard E., and Mellor, Anne K. (eds.), 'William Wordsworth (1770–1850)', in *British Literature 1780–1830* (Fort Worth, 1996a), 560–657.

—— —— (eds.), *British Literature 1780–1830* (Fort Worth, 1996b).

Mayberry, Tom, *Coleridge and Wordsworth in the West Country* (Stroud, 1992).

Mayo, Robert, 'The Contemporaneity of the *Lyrical Ballads*', *Publications of the Modern Language Association of America*, 69 (June 1954), 486–522.

Mellor, Anne K., 'Writing the Self/Self Writing', in *Romanticism and Gender* (New York, 1993), 144–69.

Minto, William, 'Wordsworth's Great Failure', *Nineteenth Century*, 26 (Sept. 1889), 435–51.

Moorman, Mary, *William Wordsworth. A Biography: The Early Years 1770–1803* (Oxford, 1957).

—— *William Wordsworth. A Biography: The Later Years 1803–1850* (Oxford, 1965).

Newlyn, Lucy, *Coleridge, Wordsworth and the Language of Allusion* (Oxford, 1986).

—— *'Paradise Lost' and the Romantic Reader* (Oxford, 1993).

O'Donnell, Brennan, *The Passion of Meter: A Study of Wordsworth's Metrical Art* (Kent, Oh., 1995).

Osborn, Robert, 'Meaningful Obscurity: The Antecedents and Character of Rivers', in J. Wordsworth and B. Darlington (eds.), *Bicentenary Wordsworth Studies in Memory of John Alban Finch* (Ithaca, NY, 1970), 393–424.

Owen, W. J. B., *Wordsworth as Critic* (Toronto, 1969).

—— 'The Sublime and the Beautiful in *The Prelude*', *Wordsworth Circle*, 4/2 (Spring 1973), 67–86.

—— (ed.) *Wordsworth's Literary Criticism* (London, 1974).

—— '*The Borderers* and the Aesthetics of Drama', *Wordsworth Circle*, 6/4 (Autumn 1975), 227–39.

—— 'Wordsworth's Aesthetics of Landscape', *Wordsworth Circle*, 7/2 (Spring 1976), 70–82.

Page, Judith, *Wordsworth and the Cultivation of Women* (Berkeley and Los Angeles, 1994).

Paley, Morton, *Coleridge's Later Poetry* (Oxford, 1996).

—— '"In some sort seeing with my proper eyes": Wordsworth and the Spectacles of Paris', *Studies in Romanticism*, 27/3 (Fall 1988), 369–90.

Parker, Reeve, 'Reading Wordsworth's Power: Narrative and Usurpation in *The Borderers*', *English Literary History*, 54/2 (Summer 1987), 299–331.

Parrish, Stephen, *The Art of the 'Lyrical Ballads'* (Cambridge, Mass., 1973).

—— 'The Worst of Wordsworth', *Wordsworth Circle*, 7 (1976), 89–91.

—— 'The Editor as Archaeologist', *Kentucky Review*, 4 (1983), 3–14.

—— 'Wordsworth as Satirist of his Age', in K. R. Johnston and G. W. Ruoff (eds.), *The Age of William Wordsworth* (New Brunswick, NJ, 1987), 21–38.

—— 'The Whig Interpretation of Literature', *Text*, 4 (1988), 343–50.

Peterfreund, Stuart, 'Wordsworth, Milton, and the End of Adam's Dream', *Milton and the Romantics*, 3 (1977), 14–21.

Pirie, David, 'A Letter to [Asra]', in J. Wordsworth and B. Darlington (eds.), *Bicentenary Wordsworth Studies in Memory of John Alban Finch* (Ithaca, NY, 1970), 294–339.

—— *William Wordsworth: The Poetry of Grandeur and Tenderness* (New York, 1982).

The Prelude, ed. W. J. Harvey and R. Gravil, Casebook Series (London, 1972).

Rader, Melvin, *Wordsworth: A Philosophical Approach* (Kent, Oh., 1967).

Reed, Mark, 'Wordsworth, Coleridge, and the "Plan" of the *Lyrical Ballads*', *University of Toronto Quarterly*, 34/3 (Apr. 1965), 238–53.

—— *Wordsworth: The Chronology of the Early Years, 1770–1799* (Cambridge, Mass., 1967).

—— *Wordsworth: The Chronology of the Middle Years, 1800–1815* (Cambridge, Mass., 1975).

Reiman, Donald (ed.), *The Romantics Reviewed. Part A: The Lake Poets*, 2 vols. (New York, 1972).

Richardson, Alan, *A Mental Theater: Poetic Drama and Consciousness in the Romantic Age* (University Park, Pa., 1988).

Rieger, James, 'Wordsworth Unalarm'd', in Joseph Wittreich (ed.), *Milton and the Line of Vision* (Madison, 1975), 185–208.

Roe, Nicholas, *Wordsworth and Coleridge: The Radical Years* (Oxford, 1988).

—— 'Wordsworth, Milton, and the Politics of Poetic Influence', MHRA *Yearbook of English Studies*, 19 (1989), 112–26.

—— *The Politics of Nature: Wordsworth and Some Contemporaries* (Basingstoke, 1992a).

—— 'Revising the Revolution: History and Imagination in *The Prelude*, 1799, 1805, 1850', in R. Brinkley and K. Hanley (eds.), *Romantic Revisions* (Cambridge, 1992b), 103–35.

—— 'Wordsworth's Lost Satire', *London Review of Books* (6 July 1995), 21.

Ross, Marlon, 'Naturalizing Gender: Woman's Place in Wordsworth's Ideological Landscape', *English Literary History*, 53/2 (Summer 1986), 391–410.

Ruoff, Gene W., *Wordsworth and Coleridge: The Making of the Major Lyrics, 1802–1804* (New Brunswick, NJ, 1989).

Schneider, Ben Ross, *Wordsworth's Cambridge Education* (Cambridge, 1957).

Sharrock, Roger, 'The Figure in a Landscape: Wordsworth's Early Poetry', *Proceedings of the British Academy*, 58 (1972), 313–33.

Shaw, Philip, 'Commemorating Waterloo: Wordsworth, Southey and the "Muses' Page of State"', *Romanticism*, 1/1 (1995), 50–67.

Sheats, Paul, *The Making of Wordsworth's Poetry* (Cambridge, Mass., 1973).

Simpson, David, 'Wordsworth in America', in K. R. Johnston and G. W. Ruoff (eds.), *The Age of William Wordsworth* (New Brunswick, NJ, 1987a), 276–90.

—— *Wordsworth's Historical Imagination: The Poetry of Displacement* (New York, 1987b).

Sperry, Willard, *Wordsworth's Anti-Climax* (Cambridge, Mass., 1935).

Spiegelman, Willard, *Wordsworth's Heroes* (Berkeley, 1985).

Spivak, Gayatri Chakravorty, 'Sex and History in "The Prelude" (1805): Books IX to XIII', in John Williams (ed.), *Wordsworth: Contemporary Critical Essays*, New Casebooks Series (Basingstoke, 1993), 172–87.

Stallknecht, Newton P., *Strange Seas of Thought: Studies in William Wordsworth's Philosophy of Man and Nature* (1945; repr. Bloomington, Ind., 1958).

Stein, Edwin, *Wordsworth's Art of Allusion* (University Park, Pa., 1988).

Stillinger, Jack, 'Wordsworth and Keats', in K. R. Johnston and G. W. Ruoff (eds.), *The Age of William Wordsworth* (New Brunswick, NJ, 1987), 173–95.

—— 'Textual Primitivism and the Editing of Wordsworth', *Studies in Romanticism*, 28/1 (Spring 1989), 3–28.

Sykes Davies, Hugh, *Wordsworth and the Worth of Words*, ed. J. Kerrigan and J. Wordsworth (Cambridge, 1986).

Thompson, E. P., 'Disenchantment or Default? A Lay Sermon', in *Power and Consciousness*, ed. C. C. O'Brien and W. D. Vanech (New York, 1969), 149–81.

—— 'Wordsworth's Crisis', *London Review of Books* (8 Dec. 1988), 3–6.

—— 'Hunting the Jacobin Fox', *Past and Present* (Feb. 1994), 94–140.

Thompson, T. W., *Wordsworth's Hawkshead*, ed. Robert Woof (Oxford, 1970).

Thorslev, Peter, 'Wordsworth's *Borderers* and the Romantic Villain-Hero', *Studies in Romanticism*, 5/2 (Winter 1966), 84–103.

Todd, F. M., *Politics and the Poet: A Study of Wordsworth* (London, 1957).

Turner, John, *Wordsworth: Play and Politics. A Study of Wordsworth's Poetry 1787–1800* (Basingstoke, 1986).

Vendler, Helen, '*Tintern Abbey:* Two Assaults', in P. Fletcher and J. Murphy (eds.), 'Wordsworth in Context', *Bucknell Review*, 36/1 (Lewisburg, Pa., 1992), 173–90.

'Waiting for the Palfreys: The Great *Prelude* Debate', *Wordsworth Circle*, 17/1 (Winter 1986), 2–38.

Walker, Eric, 'Wordsworth, Wellington, and Myth', in S. Behrendt (ed.), *History and Myth: Essays on English Romantic Literature* (Detroit, 1990), 100–15.

Watson, George, 'The Revolutionary Youth of Wordsworth and Coleridge', *Critical Quarterly*, 18/3 (Autumn 1976), 49–66.

Welsford, Enid, *Salisbury Plain: A Study in the Development of Wordsworth's Mind and Art* (Oxford, 1966).

Williams, John, *Wordsworth: Romantic Poetry and Revolution Politics* (Manchester, 1989).

—— (ed.), *Wordsworth: Contemporary Critical Essays*, New Casebooks Series (Basingstoke, 1993).

—— *William Wordsworth: A Literary Life*, Literary Lives Series (Basingstoke, 1996).

Wood, Nigel (ed.), *'The Prelude': Theory in Practice* (Buckingham, 1993).

Woodring, Carl, 'Wordsworth and the Victorians', in K. R. Johnston and G. W. Ruoff (eds.), *The Age of William Wordsworth* (New Brunswick, NJ, 1987), 261–75.

Woof, Robert, 'Wordsworth and Coleridge: Some Early Matters', in J. Wordsworth and B. Darlington (eds.), *Bicentenary Wordsworth Studies in Memory of John Alban Finch* (Ithaca, NY, 1970), 76–91.

Wordsworth: Lyrical Ballads, ed. A. Jones and W. Tydeman, Casebook Series (Basingstoke, 1972).

Wordsworth, Christopher, *Memoirs of William Wordsworth*, 2 vols. (London, 1851).

Wordsworth, Jonathan, *The Music of Humanity: A Critical Study of Wordsworth's 'Ruined Cottage' Incorporating Texts from a Manuscript of 1799–1800* (London, 1969).

—— '"The Climbing of Snowdon"', in J. Wordsworth and B. Darlington (eds.), *Bicentenary Wordsworth Studies in Memory of John Alban Finch* (Ithaca, NY, 1970), 449–74.

—— 'The Five-Book *Prelude* of Early Spring 1804', *Journal of English and Germanic Philology*, 76/1 (1977), 1–25.

—— *William Wordsworth: The Borders of Vision* (Oxford, 1982).

—— 'Two Dark Interpreters: Wordsworth and De Quincey', in K. R. Johnston and G. W. Ruoff (eds.), *The Age of William Wordsworth* (New Brunswick, NJ, 1987), 214–38.

Wordsworth, Jonathan, 'Wordsworth's Dim and Perilous Way', in K. Hanley and R. Selden (eds.), *Revolution and English Romanticism: Politics and Rhetoric* (Hemel Hempstead, 1990), 205–23.

—— 'Revision as Making: *The Prelude* and its Peers', in R. Brinkley and K. Hanley (eds.), *Romantic Revisions* (Cambridge, 1992), 103–35.

—— and Darlington, Beth (eds.), *Bicentenary Wordsworth Studies in Memory of John Alban Finch* (Ithaca, NY, 1970).

—— and Gill, Stephen, 'The Two-Part *Prelude* of 1798–99', *Journal of English and Germanic Philology*, 72/4 (1973), 503–25.

Wu, Duncan, 'Editing Intentions', *Essays in Criticism*, 41/1 (Jan. 1991), 1–10.

—— *Wordsworth's Reading 1770–1799* (Cambridge, 1993).

—— 'Wordsworth and Helvellyn's Womb', *Essays in Criticism*, 49/1 (Jan. 1994), 6–25.

—— *Wordsworth's Reading 1800–1815* (Cambridge, 1995).

—— (ed.), *Romanticism: An Anthology* (2nd edn., Oxford, 1998).

4. *Samuel Taylor Coleridge*

NICOLA TROTT

TEXTS

The standard edition is the *Collected Works*, though 'standard' seems too bland a term for what is one of the grandest editorial projects of the century, the near accomplishment of which has dramatically and permanently altered the conception of its subject. (For a sense of how it looked to some of the editors on setting out, see the special issue in *Review of English Literature*, 7 (1966), 6–90.) The Bollingen Series has vastly enlarged both the quantity and the kind of material that is now considered as going to the making of 'STC'. Things rarely or never available have been brought to prominence: the 1795 *Lectures*, the *Watchman*, the *Logic*, and the *Essays on his Times* (where masterly detective work has yielded many new attributions). Things commonly known have been substantially reconfigured: the *Friend*, the *Lectures on Literature*, *The Statesman's Manual*, *Table Talk*, *Aids to Reflection*, *Biographia* (an especially contentious text: Fruman 1989, a long-time controversialist in Coleridge studies, has traced the editorial roads not taken); and the essays 'On Poesy and Art', 'The Principles of Genial Criticism', as well as 'The Soul and its Organs of Sense' (from *Omniana*), all to be found among the *Shorter Works and Fragments*. Most important of all, perhaps, things never before printed are now lavishly and comprehensively given: the *Marginalia*, which for Coleridge was a form of composition in itself, has reached the letter 'O'. And a parallel Bollingen Series is producing the astounding *Notebooks*, currently in their fourth twin-volume set of Text and Notes, taking us up to 1826.

Thus far lacking an index, the *Notebooks* remain somewhat impenetrable to the non-specialist; but an invaluable, and fascinating, introduction is at hand, in Coburn's thematically arranged anthology *Inquiring Spirit*. By contrast, students should not be put off by the formidable appearance of the *Collected Works*: here, abundant indices mean that, however unwieldy, the volumes are easy, and wholly absorbing, to use. Moreover, each work in the series, excepting no. xi, offers a lengthy introduction, essential reading for the serious Coleridgian.

Of things yet to come, the most eagerly awaited are the MSS of the *Opus Maximum*, Coleridge's never-completed logosophic masterpiece, and the *Poetical Works*—shortly to supersede E. H. Coleridge and promising much new quarried material, including, apparently, an 'Autograph on an Autopergamene', a poem Coleridge claims to have written in his own blood on a piece of his own skin! The existing *Concordance* is bound to need revising in the light of these developments.

For those wishing to consult first editions, of the poetry especially, no fewer than nine are available in facsimile through the Woodstock Books imprint, introduced by J. Wordsworth, and providing a welcome résumé of Coleridge's publishing career, all the way from 1794 to 1817. Specialist editions include Parrish's *Dejection* (1988) and Wallen's 'Experimental' *Ancient Mariner* (1993), with its (rather disconcerting) triple text of 1798, 1800, and 1817. A variorum printing of seven of the major poems, from *1834*, plus the verse 'Letter', is available in Stillinger.

The standard edition of the *Letters* is by Griggs (1956–71). For anyone starting on Coleridge, the first two volumes are immensely engaging. A handy sample of the whole is available in H. J. Jackson's one-volume edition (1987); and, for the specialist, James Engell (1994) presents new evidence of Coleridge's family background.

For student purposes especially, one selection of the poems stands out: Beer's twice-revised Everyman (1963/1993), chronologically arranged (the format preferred by Coleridge himself), with a full introduction, informative biographical-cum-critical headnotes to each of the eleven sections, and appendices on the revisions of *The Ancient Mariner* and on 'Coleridge and his Critics'. An interesting supplement to Beer is Holmes's new selection (1996) of 101 poems, organized by genre and theme into eight sections, each with a short preface, together with endnotes on every entry, giving a publishing history and brief commentary. Holmes's selection is based on the edition of 1834 (the last overseen by the poet); Beer takes 1828 as a guide, though he also prints the first, 1796, collection, as well as parallel texts of the MS and 1816 versions of 'Kubla Khan', of the 1798 and 1828 *Ancient Mariner*, and *Dejection* in its 'Letter' and 'Ode' forms.

Coleridge's literary criticism is perhaps the best place for students to start familiarizing themselves with the *Collected Works*. Not only are his Lectures remarkable for their insights into Milton and Shakespeare, the two great poles around which his criticism revolves; they are also of fundamental importance in the history of Anglo-American literary theory. The Bollingen *Lectures on Literature* is exemplary in its scrupulosity and completeness, reproducing all versions of the Lecture notes by divers hands. Foakes has also collected Collier's original transcripts of the 1811–12 series, on Shakespeare, into a single volume (1971). There are many editions of Coleridge's Shakespeare criticism, including a theme- and play-based selection, again by Foakes (1989). Much the best way to read selectively on Coleridge and Milton is in Wittreich. Of older collections, Brinkley's (1955) (on the seventeenth century) is still useful, if rare-ish.

Select prose: a vital anthology is Hill's *Imagination* (1978), of fifty-one annotated extracts in chronological sequence (also to be found on his Internet Home Page). H. J. Jackson's Oxford Authors presents all of *Biographia* (1985), together with generous helpings from a wide range of writings, and a separate 'prose' index, and is probably best for getting a sense of the whole. Finally, in what promises to be a user-friendly series, Macmillan is producing thematic anthologies of *Coleridge's Writings*, the first two of which are already out (though their comparative brevity does run the risk of leaving the reader stranded between arcana and gobbets).

CRITICISM

BIBLIOGRAPHIES

There is a full and fully annotated bibliography in three volumes: the first, covering 1793–1899, under R. and J. Haven and M. Adams; the second and third, for 1900–39 and 1940–92, under W. and A. Crawford and E. S. Lauterbach. This is an heroic *omnium gatherum*; more digestible lists for the modern period are to be found in Erdman (1979–) and Elkins and Forstner (1936–70). For accounts in continuous prose, consult the annual *Year's Work in English Studies*, and, for a survey of criticism up to 1984, the long and judicious essay by Schulz (1985). Evidence of Coleridge's own reading is presented in Coffman.

BIOGRAPHIES

Ashton's meticulous Life (1996) looks set to become the standard work. The newcomer should begin with Holmes's portrait of the mesmerizing early visionary: all the best anecdotes are there, but not, it should be said, the early radical Coleridge, an important figure, who is instead to be found in Cornwell. W. J. Bate (1969) has the disadvantage of preceding the *Collected Works*, but the distinct advantages of relative brevity, and elucidatory power. Lefebure has told the story from the addict's perspective. Lastly, Gillman's nineteenth-century account is still of value, since the author's subject (and long-term houseguest) provided much of the material himself.

CHRONOLOGY

Limited chronologies are to be found amongst the preliminaries to each of the *Collected Works*. See Brett (1971) for a brief tabulation; and, for much fuller evidence, Purton.

NICOLA TROTT

Although the consequences of the Bollingen Series are only just beginning to emerge, the best of current work on Coleridge is editorially led, in the sense that it is responsive to the conditions laid down by the *Collected Works*. And here, several trends may be discerned. There are new and notable concentrations in the fields of politics, language, and philosophy, and in the arenas of the very early (Jacobin-Unitarian) and very late (sagacious-logosophical) Coleridges.

Another consequence of the ever-increasing corpus has been a marked shift away from the poetry. This movement reflects the fact that, over the last four decades, all the major publications have been prose works. Having said this, the poet is almost certainly about to make a comeback, thanks to Mays's forthcoming edition; and his advent has already been proclaimed by Stillinger and Paley (1996). One area currently receiving a good deal of attention is the drama, the more welcome since it has been relatively neglected in the past.

That the bulk of criticism is weighted towards the prose marks a departure from what has, in a sense, been a hostile conception of Coleridge's life and work. This conception has understandably drawn sustenance from the *annus mirabilis* with Wordsworth in 1797–8, and from the poets' mutual mythologizing, both of its intensity and promise, and of Coleridge's withdrawal into incapacity compounded by metaphysics. A negative tradition threads back, via T. S. Eliot and Chambers (whose adversarial biography (1938) backhandedly cherished 'a handful of golden poems' among a plethora of lost causes), to the many prejudicial nineteenth-century accounts. That this image has had such compulsive sway is ironically a testimony to Coleridge himself, who at once initiated and resented the charge of having 'dreamed away [his] life to no purpose', and gave to the world his colourful self-caricature as an 'omni-pregnant, nihili-parturient genius'.

But the age of apology, both confessional and defensive, may well be coming to a close. For a start, there is the sheer volume of the evidence now occupying library shelves. Further, there is the related probability of critics' ceasing to be quite so exercised by two of the most long-standing and damaging complaints against Coleridge: the double disgrace of non-originality and non-completion—less politely, of theft and sloth. The originality debate has raged on and off for 150 years, and been especially hot in relation to German philosophy. Accusations of plagiarism were started by De Quincey, among other Germanists, systematized by James Ferrier (*Blackwood's*, Mar. 1840), and courageously investigated by Coleridge's daughter Sara, in a posthumous edition of *Biographia* (1847). The most serious flare-up in recent times was occasioned by Fruman. More forensic than arsonist in method, Fruman's prosecutory life (1972) confronted the academy, not just with the extent of Coleridge's 'borrowings', but also with the deliberate pains he took to conceal them. Since then, editors have sought to ensure that the Coleridge they (and we) present is candidness itself: Engell and Bate's *Biographia* (1983) reproduces the relevant data at length; while the debts to Schelling, which in 'On Poesy and Art' amount to straight transcription, are fully accounted for by Coburn (*Notebooks*, iii. 4397).

For those keen to read up on it, the history of the controversy as far as Fruman is recorded by McFarland (1969: ch. 1); and Fruman himself is answered by the same critic (McFarland 1974). See also the final chapter in Engell (1981), and Christensen's clever deconstructionist argument that the borrowings attest to an awareness of the non-coincidence of any given position with itself. What was lately so hotly contested has now more or less burnt itself out. This would seem to be an effect, partly of the evidence being out in the open, partly of the centre of interest shifting elsewhere. Nevertheless, a conviction of plagiarist guilt lingers on, even among pro-Coleridgians, in the more subtly internalized form which seeks to explain Coleridge's thinking in Germanist terms. As yet, perhaps, no entirely satisfactory study exists of the critique he could be said to have made of his sources.

The second reason for scepticism about Coleridge has been the non-completion or fragmentary nature of the work. This has not so much died out as it has been redefined by modern interests into more of a 'good' than a 'bad' thing: McFarland on Romanticism's 'Forms of Ruin' (1981) is a cardinal case in point. That the concept of the 'Romantic fragment' has been developed with Coleridge in mind (e.g. Janowitz) may be seen as a pragmatic response to his compulsively marginalist and annotative habits of writing; and to the fact that his aesthetic criterion of wholeness or unity is everywhere insisted upon, yet invariably supposes its own negation. It has also been associated with poststructural attitudes (towards the self-undoing nature of language), with the extension of a (German) Romantic irony to the behaviour of texts (Wheeler 1981), and with the new historical critique of form (Levinson).

Coleridge's significance as a figure in literary history is undoubted. Anyone wishing to demonstrate his centrality to the contemporary scene would probably refer to the metacritical elements of criticism. Just as Coleridge is at, even constitutes, the theoretical centre of British Romanticism, so theoretical developments often find their paradigmatic instances in his writings. Indeed, the story of theory could be told as a Coleridgian narrative, both in the general sense that Coleridge is an acknowledged 'father' of theory itself (Christensen), and in the local sense, that his works have tended admirably to confirm, or exemplarily to complement, the theses of particular critics. It was Coleridge who provided Bloom with an early case of the anxiety of influence (1972); de Man with his most influential act of rhetorical analysis; Hartman with a leading instance of Romantic 'self-consciousness' (1970), and McGann with the centrepiece of his cultural-materialist polemic (1983). De Man's famous dissolution of the Coleridgian antithesis between symbol and allegory led to the deconstructive arguments of Rajan, Christensen, and Mileur.

With the advent of McGann, Coleridge emerged as the thinking person's Romantic ideologist, whose theorizing had enabled the idealizations in the culture of his own time, and whose bad faith was being perpetuated by formalist and idealist critics in our own. This historical impetus to criticism was confirmed, and in many cases occasioned, by the bicentenary of the French Revolution. Beginning in the early 1980s, historicism new and old is still in many ways the dominant practice, though there is considerable interest in hermeneutics (see, in the context of the Higher Criticism, Shaffer 1975, and Prickett 1996), as well as more sporadic evidence of a return to rhetoric.

Coleridge is also now at the forefront of a debate surrounding modern editing. In his stimulating discussion of developments in this area, Stillinger has argued for what he calls 'textual pluralism', as against the 'textual primitivism' prominent in Wordsworth studies throughout the 1970s and 1980s. Where the 'primitivist' technique seeks to present the earliest recoverable versions of texts, the 'pluralist' respects the existence, and validity, of multiple versions. For Stillinger, indeed, *all* 'texts' are constructed fixities in a sea of actual textual instability (by his most conservative estimate, there are 94 versions of Coleridge's major poems alone!). As Leader has suggested, this risks exchanging one 'Romantic ideology' about the writing of poetry (spontaneity) for another (process). Still, the work of editing makes it probable that future readers, of the poems especially, will have a greater awareness of textual histories and variants, even if some versions are practically bound to be more equal than others: see, for example, Mays's sense of the decisive editorial cruces in a 'genetic' presentation of versions (1992).

Predictions are hazardous, but it seems safe to assume that the editorial revolution will continue to be a defining force in criticism. And there would seem to be at least two likely consequences of the Bollingen Series. First, a tendency to greater specialization, in areas, arcane or otherwise, newly opened to view. (A less sanguine way of putting this would be to say that comprehensiveness is becoming well-nigh impossible.) Second, an increased conviction of Coleridge's being 'rescuable', as it were, from his detractors. For along with the new textual munificence has come a new advocacy of the work and even of the life: Stillinger's relatively bullish assessment may well be a taste of things to come.

POETRY

INTRODUCTORY AND GENERAL STUDIES

For those starting out on the poetry, House is still the best and most enjoyable integrative survey, and may be supplemented with Cooke. Other useful studies include Schulz—provided the schema is not taken too rigidly—for the plurality of the conversationalist idiom; Watson (for a lively formalist rebuttal of the notion of the Romantics as 'vital barbarians'); Adair (for Coleridge's dreamy coherencies); Crawford (1979: for a compilation of approaches), J. Bate (ch. 3: for the 'Shakespearean Voices in Coleridge's Poetry'); Beer (1959 and 1971: for bizarre and richly suggestive scholarship); Bloom (1971: for a power-fully comprehensive reading of the 'visionary'); Magnuson (1974: for the rhetorical strategies which are used to contain a threat of unbridled imagina-tion); Dekker (for literary-historical investigations); Wheeler (1981: for a read-ing of the poems in relation to the—often negative—interpretative models provided by their prose prefaces, marginalia, and addenda). In addition, the later poetry has now received the book-length attention it deserves in Paley (1996). The vital heritage of nineteenth-century responses may be gathered from J. R. de J. Jackson (1970 and 1991).

THE ANCIENT MARINER

A 'Dutch attempt at German sublimity', in Southey's calculated insult; a 'poet's reverie' in the Wordsworthian subtitle of 1800; having an effect 'like Tom Piper's magic Whistle' to a defensive Lamb; and, (in)famously, a work of 'pure imagination' to its author. Ironically enough, Coleridge's reversal of the complaint lodged by Mrs Barbauld—that the poem 'had no moral' (*Table Talk*)—started a whole school of criticism dedicated to revealing its moral coherence. The classic instance of this symbolic interpretation (Haven 1972 traces its emergence to the nineteenth century) is found in Warren, whose elaborate reading appeals to ideas of the 'One Life' and 'Imagination'. A succession of critics (Auden and Bowra, to name but two) have looked to the work's religious affiliations, in the doctrine of the Fall, or a myth of guilt and redemption. The pantheist variation on this theme is given by Piper; and the poem's search after a unity of both structure and perception is affirmed by Abrams (1971).

Of the many non-Christian readings, Bostetter heads those who oppose Warren, by emphasizing the contrary evidence, of an arbitrary universe, and of irrational, nightmarish, or anarchic forces. Schulz and D. W. Harding instig-ate a psychological approach: the former detects 'a dramatic study in abnor-mal psychology'; the latter is sensitive to the mental significance of the crime, and to the fortuitousness and incompleteness of the recovery. Further note-worthy accounts are Hartman's (1970), of 'the travail of a soul passing from self-consciousness to imagination', and Reed's bleakly thoroughgoing decon-struction of the Mariner's identity. Finally, a quite different, historical route has been struck out, in two main directions: one, by Wylie, in pursuit of natural science; the other, initially by Ebbatson, in the context of the slave trade, which

71

has since been given extended study, of an intelligently cultural-materialist kind, by Keane.

Attention to Coleridge's 'framing' devices (that of the 'tale' itself and, especially, of the marginal 'gloss', added to the poem some time before its 1817 incarnation) has brought about further, divergent lines of interpretation. The presence of an 'editor' in the text was first mooted by Brown (who saw the gloss as a choric device for setting the tone); and a large and sophisticated commentary on the interaction of poetry and prose has followed (much of which sees the marginalia as a streamlining or over-determination of the verse: e.g. Wheeler 1981). In Empson's robustly anti-Christian view, the gloss is the deleterious act of a later, pious Coleridge, revising his text into orthodoxy (and out of Empson's sympathies). In an important essay by McGann (1985), Coleridge is poet-in-charge of a multiple interpretative layering, after the example of biblical Higher Criticism—to all of which readers should bear a properly sceptical and historical relation. A more extreme, poststructuralist case is made by Ferguson, who sees all conventional criticism as a gloss-like editorializing of the poem into 'linear' patterns of 'cause-and-effect'. Wolfson, meanwhile, relates both gloss and 'Rime' to the 'action of circling about a center that defies final understanding' (1986); and Eilenberg reinvigorates the powers of the uncanny by placing the old notions of 'voice' and 'ventriloquy' in the new context of 'our interpretive helplessness' before 'one of the most deeply and elaborately anonymous poems ever written'. Certainly, the questions it poses are unresolved, and unlikely to go away. In A. J. Harding's 1995 study, the narrative is a work of 'pure conjecture', within which the Mariner as primitive mythographer constructs a tale of revenge and redemption.

CHRISTABEL

Nineteenth-century writers were responsive to the eerie quality of the poem: to Hazlitt, it was 'like moon-beams playing on a charnel-house'; to H. N. Coleridge, it was 'witchery by daylight'. Modern critics have struggled with the multiple ambiguities surrounding the status of 'innocence' and 'evil' in the poem, and cohering principally around the vexed questions of sexuality, power, and the significance of the diverse conclusions Coleridge later proposed for his 'fragment' (dealt with by House). Attitudes towards Geraldine are especially divided, ranging all the way from her act of 'sexual desecration' (Knight), to her triumphant embodiment of daemonic and chthonian forces (Paglia). She has also been seen as a form of necessary and disguised evil (in Fogle's chapter-length study), as an instigator of psychological change or maturation, a figure of the unconscious, a mark of poststructuralist inscrutability, and, rather more colourfully, as 'lesbian vampire' (Paglia again), as the serpent of Egyptian myth (Beer 1959), and, by way of the ingenious anagram 'Dire Angel', as a study in Satanic and immanent evil (Peterfreund).

Generic approaches appeal to three main categories: the novelistic or narrative (after the example of Gothic romance (Cooper on parody), or Coleridge's own nomination of 'Faery Tale' (Tomlinson on the 'tale of terror')); the parabolic or allegorical (often by reference to the poet's own psycho-sexual anxieties: Bostetter, Spatz); and the symbolic or 'mythopoeic' (be it Egyptian (Beer 1959) or biblical (Nelson; Harding 1995)). Nelson's structuralist reading has interesting things to say of the poem's generation of opposites and hence the problem of 'the re-union of what in this world is divided'. Swann uses feminist and psychoanalytic theory to question the constructions of genre and gender. Fruman (1972) has emphasized the fratricidal (Cain and Abel) theme, while for Newlyn (1993) the apposite pairing is Miltonic, and the sexual ambiguities of Satan and Eve.

'CONVERSATION POEMS'

Harper's christening of this diverse group of blank verse poems (after Coleridge's subtitle to *The Nightingale*) has stuck as a label of convenience; though much criticism has centred on one or more of the different generic strands it gathers together, among them hymnal, philosophical, loco-descriptive, and seventeenth-century-meditative verse, as well as Miltonic epic and Theocritan pastoral: for references, see Engell, 'Imagining into Nature' (1994). Comprehensive studies are offered by Parker and Dekker; and two excellent later works are Newlyn's (1986: for exact biographical and textual information, as well as a vivid sense of the personal context) and Everest's (for wider, political and historical, contexts). Matheson discusses the important model of Cowper. The conversational structure has been variously analysed as combining ascent with systolic rhythm (Gérard); as passing between the general and the particular (Watson); and as tracing 'two calm–exaltation–calm parabolas' (Schulz). The oft-noted circularity of form and content, meanwhile, has an important confirmation in Beer (1986), who refers to Coleridge's marginalium to *Frost at Midnight*, which gives as his reason for cutting the original 'coda' of 1798 his wish to have the poem make 'a rondo upon itself'. Newlyn (1986) shows how the same poem is foundational for *Tintern Abbey*. Abrams ('Coleridge's "A Light in Sound"', 1984) discusses *The Eolian Harp* and its revisions. Kirkham elucidates the symbolic properties of the landscape of *This Lime-Tree Bower*; while Mellor identifies its relation to contemporary aesthetic categories. For the terminus of the form, in the *Hymn before Sun-Rise*, see Hartman (1972).

NICOLA TROTT

Most recent developments in interpretation have centred around the different texts, which have been deftly summarized and elucidated by Pirie. The Verse *Letter*, in particular, has come a long way since Watson found it 'almost indecently private', and is now securely canonical. The essential modern study of the poem in all its versions, and its part-parentage in Wordsworth's *Ode*, is by Ruoff. Further discussion may be found in Newlyn (1986), who considers the *Letter* at length, and Dekker (though he erroneously reverses the compositional order of *Letter* and *Ode*). That the poem concerns Coleridge's complex and ambivalent feelings 'about the failure of imagination' (Schulz) is generally agreed. Opinions vary greatly as to the quality and significance of the mood, however: Dorothy Wordsworth's *Journal* records the distress it evoked in the immediate circle; but House discovers 'a paeon to her [Sara's] happiness, not a wail over his misery'. The philosophical issues at stake are suggested by Abrams (1953), who (loosely) relates the poem to Kant's 'Copernican revolution in epistemology'; and the Kantian implications are thought-provokingly updated by Tyler.

KUBLA KHAN

This poem was the heart of a large body of pre-Bollingen criticism, cloned from J. L. Lowes's massive archaeological source study (a lacklustre though informative spin-off was A. H. Nethercote's *Road to Tryermaine*, on *Christabel*). Lowes's work had great influence, and is still of interest, if only for its vast accumulations of Coleridge's still vaster reading; but its methodology, associative in structure and rambling in effect, now seems outmoded.

One line of reading, developed by Schneider out of Lowes, treats the poem as a non-meaningful opium dream, presenting 'oscillation' rather than reconciliation. A deservedly more dominant line reads the poem as profoundly meant, and depends upon a variety of symbolic interpretations, often bearing on its reflexivity: House's insight, that it is 'a poem about the act of poetic creation', licensed Watson's, that it is 'a poem about poetry' and, further, 'about two kinds of poem', Kubla's and the poet's—an interpretation that puts the important Platonic context in place. A (Jungian) treatment of the archetypal structure, and the poet's 'ecstasy in imaginative fulfilment', is found in Bodkin. House's idealistic treatment of the work, as a 'triumphant positive statement of the potentialities of poetry', is countered by the subtle and fruitful discriminations of Beer (1959), based on Coleridge's own distinction between 'absolute' and 'commanding' genius.

One important and enduring debate has centred around the prose preface, introducing the poem's self-declared status as 'fragment', and the notorious 'person from Porlock'. Both were additions made with publication in mind, and both meet with scepticism from most critics (though Beer 1971 offers a notable exception). An influential discussion of the poem and its prefatory material is found in Wheeler (1981). Another bone of critical contention concerns the poem's stanzaic form. The tradition of using Coleridge's much later theorizing, his definitions of imagination especially, as an interpretative key to the different 'sections' seems to originate in Watson; but more scrupulous and up-to-date applications of the 'primary' and 'secondary' distinction are available in Wheeler (1991) and Newlyn (1993), who also elaborates the vital relationship to *Paradise Lost*. A recasting of this debate, in terms of modern speech-act theory, is offered by Esterhammer.

POEMS (1796)

The felicitousness of Lamb's injunction—'cultivate simplicity . . . or rather . . . banish elaborateness' (1796 letter)—will strike any new reader of the early poetry. However, the estimation of the epic verse, especially, has undergone significant revision since Watson judged it 'embarrassingly cosmic'. The definitive example of this more indulgent—or culturally aware—outlook is by Wylie, to which may be added Paley's restoration of the millennial framework (1992), and David Collings's (mildly deconstructive) reading of Coleridge's discursive practice in *Religious Musings*. An older work, still useful for Priestleian-Unitarian matters, is by Piper.

VERSE DRAMA

There are chapters in both Cooke and Watson. Fletcher gives an informative if old-fashioned historical account of both Wordsworth and Coleridge. General studies by Donohue, Richardson (1988), and Heller all consider the Romantic preference for closet or mental drama. Carlson's feminist-historical approach is more questionable, but specific to Coleridge (dealing for instance with *Zapolya* in the context of Burke and Schiller).

PROSE

INTRODUCTORY AND GENERAL STUDIES

Coburn (1974 and 1979), writing on the *Notebooks*, offers an excellent introduction to Coleridge's prose speculations and coinages (from 'psycho-analytical' and 'psycho-somatic' to 'cosmopolite'). Among 'pre-Bollingen' critics, Willey's informed historical account (1949) is representative, as well as valuable, in its concern with Coleridge's place in native intellectual traditions. Another very important tradition, established by those who look to the Germans to make

NICOLA TROTT

sense of Coleridge, takes off from Muirhead. Something of the range of prose
currently under consideration is witnessed in the collection edited by Kitson
and Corns. Among more specialized studies, much interesting material is to
be gleaned from Harding's scholarly work on the subject of love (1974). Shaffer
(1975) takes up the topic of Orientalism from the perspective of nineteenth-
century hermeneutics; Leask (1988) and Richardson (1996) investigate its politics. *The Friend* is analysed by Christensen; and there is a full-length historical
study by Coleman. Landscape in the *Notebooks* has drawn the attention of
Baker, and Dugas (in Gravil et al. 1985).

The subject headings introduced below are arranged alphabetically, and
intended to guide readers quickly to the relevant work in a particular area.

IMAGINATION AND FANCY

The single paragraph of definitions in *Biographia*, ch. 13, has produced a vast
and disputatious exegesis. A plain and simple introduction is available in Brett
(1949). In recent times, the imagination controversy has centred in two main
areas: the *Einbildungskraft* debate; and an argument over the status of the 'primary' and 'secondary' forms (see introduction to Coleridge 1969– : vol. vii).
A subsidiary controversy revolves around the imagination–fancy distinction:
see Wheeler (1980), Barfield (1972), and Hardy's witty, colloquial account of
its practical difficulties (1951).

The hostile witnesses to Coleridgian imagination are headed by Warnock.
An important early book by Richards (whose materialist convictions lead him
to overstate Coleridge's idealist position) views the 'primary' imagination as
ordinary perception. A paradigmatic instance of the modern continuation of
this view, in McFarland (1972), adduces the example of Tetens. J. Wordsworth
sketches the history of this interpretation, and seeks to reverse it, by establishing the continuity of the *Biographia* definition with Coleridge's thinking in
the 1790s. Another critic who takes issue with a German-dominated line of
reading, Brisman, opposes the tendency to identify the primary imagination
with Kantian Reason. Linking Reason with the Holy Spirit, he makes a learned
case for the primary's involvement 'in the religious sense of the unity of things
rather than the philosophical category of the universals' (this last being a phenomenological extension of the 'ordinary perception' theory, propounded for
instance by J. R. de J. Jackson 1969).

Two important and wide-ranging collections on the theory and practice of
imagination are edited by Gallant, and by Gravil, Newlyn, and Roe.

LANGUAGE

Coleridge's way with words was legendary: it might 'create a soul under the ribs
of death', remarked Hazlitt. A good place to start is with Barfield's excellent

essay on Coleridge's enjoyment of words (1974). McKusick's valuable book covers the philosophical ground of his developing theories of language, all the way from the Berkeleian 'alphabet' to the discourses of the *Logic*. The most accomplished historical scholarship currently being written is by Fulford, who, together with Paley, has also edited a diverse volume of essays. Kessler's unusual study, especially of the late 'fragments', analyses the tropes by which Coleridge hoped 'to reach beyond conventional metaphor . . . into the mystery of Being'. There are chapters concerning Coleridge on poetic language in Marks and Wallace; while Cole's (difficult) article seeks to return Coleridge's analysis to a public forum.

LITERARY CRITICISM

There is an excellent general study of the criticism by Fogle (who examines how Coleridge's criterion of unity also takes account of particularities). For short pieces, see Beer (in Kitson and Corns), and Lipkowitz's excellent study of Coleridge's scriptural poetics, in which poets of imagination are seen as the modern avatars of biblical prophets. For longer works, see J. R. de J. Jackson (1969), on Coleridge's methodology; Leask's materialist critique of the 'totemic power of Imagination' (1988); and Corrigan's siting of the criticism as a 'product' of Coleridge's historical situation and reading practice.

Badawi's is the standard account of the Shakespeare criticism (applying the idea of organic unity, and making distinctions between Coleridge and his eighteenth-century predecessors). More recent, historicist considerations of his supposed 'anti-theatricality' are found in Galperin. The concept of organic unity, sketched by Abrams (1953), is further elucidated in two historical articles, by Benziger (on its derivation from Leibniz) and Stempel (via Kames and Hume). Bloom (1972) takes up Pater's 'assault upon the Organic principle' and its New Critical applications; while Krieger places the dialogue with modern criticism in a more positive light. Coleridge's dependence on Schlegel has long been recognized: see Helmholtz, and Burwick (1991), who sorts out the Schlegelian influence on the idea of dramatic illusion, while adding new material on Payne Knight. Burwick's 1990 essay, meanwhile, is useful for its clear exposition of Schelling's theory of art (a subject treated at length in Engell 1981) and its account of the relatively neglected distinction between 'imitation' and 'copy'.

Biographia Literaria, Coleridge's most important prose work, has also been his least appreciated. It has an unenviable reputation for obscurity (see 'Philosophy and Religion', below) and disorderliness ('put together with a pitchfork', was Stephen's summary verdict). Typically, Coleridge was his own hostage to fortune, calling it an 'immethodical . . . miscellany'. There is an excellent introduction in Wallace; its compositional history and rationale is recounted by Fogel.

At bottom, complaints about the work rest on a disagreement about the relation between the first and second volume, or the philosopher and the critic. One response has been to rescue literary insight or practice from 'pseudo'-thought or theory. The question of form has been an enduring preoccupation, from Pater ('bundles of notes') to McFarland (1981), who classes *Biographia* among 'rubble-heap works'. Contrary arguments have emerged, in Whalley, for its 'integrity', in Wallace, for its 'design', and in Abrams ('Coleridge and the Romantic Vision', 1984), for an epic *Bildungsgeschichte*. But a tendency to emphasize the 'heterogeneity' rather than the whole (namely Buell on the virtues of digression and 'deformalization', and Christensen's de-Manian variation) has grown in recent work: see Eilenberg's interesting chapters on Coleridge's 'possession' by, and imaginative 'alienation' of, his sources.

Finally, there are the controversies raised by the literary-critical second volume: in respect of Coleridge's criticism of Wordsworth's preface, see Parrish, Bialostosky, McKusick (ch. 4), and Hamilton (a politico-rhetorical argument about the elitism of Coleridge's rejection of 'ordinary' language). In respect of the criticism of Wordsworth's poetry, see Park, Christensen again (on Coleridge's construction, and appropriation, of 'Wordsworthian' genius), Leask (1988), Simpson, H. J. Jackson (on how Coleridge's Wordsworth resembles Johnson's Milton), and Ellison.

PHILOSOPHY AND RELIGION

Coleridge's assertion that 'true metaphysics are nothing else but true divinity' (*Biographia*, ch. 12) has not endeared him to philosophers. His methods of thought have been the subject of inordinate controversy, enormous mockery, and heroic attempts to bring them into coherence. Short introductions to the philosophy are found in Emmet and Abrams ('Coleridge and the Romantic Vision', 1984); a book-length approach, in Appleyard. The prevailing narrative, of Coleridge's transition from materialism to idealism, has had many interpreters, amongst the best and most learned being McFarland's 1969 study, which uses Coleridge's own Schelling-derived division between 'it is' and 'I am' systems of thought. For readings against this consensual grain, see Christensen (who seeks to get beyond epistemological terms, yet argues that Coleridge himself never escaped his Hartleian origins) and Wheeler (1981: introd.; who argues to the contrary that he was never in thrall to associationism). Haven (1959), meanwhile, uses the mystic tradition to show why Hartley was so attractive to the young Coleridge; and the early empiricist and theological contexts are well presented in the introduction to *Lectures 1795*.

Biographia is the *locus classicus* of the debate surrounding Coleridge's obscurity. Byron's response to his 'Explaining metaphysics to the nation' is wickedly apt: 'I wish he would explain his Explanation' (*Don Juan*, dedication). Some of those who have recently tried to do it for him have been collected together by Burwick (1989). Hamilton has argued for the integrity of the theory to the 'practical' criticism; Wheeler (1980) suggests the disorganization is an ironic feint to inculcate a unifying reading practice.

Still more contentious is Coleridge's dependency on, and garbling of, German idealism: the image of his 'transcendental life-preservers' was indelibly fixed by Carlyle; and modern neo-Kantians, headed by Wellek, have generally been hardest on Coleridge. Shawcross provides a clear way in to the subject; Kipperman offers a rapid overview; Orsini a more specialized and erudite account; and there is also a useful short piece by Engell (1990). MacKinnon's essay is the best introduction to Coleridge and Kant and their (important) differences; further information is available in Ashton (1980: ch. 1); and Ann Loades has a good essay on Coleridge's theodicy vis-à-vis Kant's. The notorious presence of Schelling in *Biographia* is dealt with by Burwick (1989) and Ferris. In aesthetics, Modiano documents Coleridge's relation to German *Naturphilosophie* and British traditions (Shaffer 1969–70 too is useful here).

The essential work on Coleridge's religion is by Boulger. A new book by Wendling charts the 'progress' of the whole career; and there is an older version of this spiritual biography by Willey (1972). The seriously theologically-minded should turn to Happel's three-volume study.

The late philosophy is ably covered by Barfield (1972) and Perkins; while Snyder is still useful for the *Opus Maximum*. Prickett (1976) traces the path into the Victorian Church; and Barth explicates the later religious thought—though for those to whom this subject is of real interest, the nearest thing to the horse's mouth is found in Coleridge's disciple Green.

POLITICS AND SOCIETY

A politicized Coleridge has emerged relatively recently (under the auspices of Woodring (see the special number of *Studies in Romanticism*, 21 (1981), 447–74)). Being the representative of both leftist and conservative constituencies, he was, and is, divided against himself. Roe makes an important case for a 'radical' Coleridge, in touch with the dissenting societies of the 1790s reform movement. Butler's tendentious account, of Coleridge the reactionary, states the opposite position clearly. The publication of the political journalism has been a spur to all sides (the most extreme views—that Coleridge is an apostate, and that he was never a Jacobin—are held by E. P. Thompson and McFarland respectively (see the latter's essay in Burwick 1989)).

Specialized studies include Morrow on Coleridge's political writings in the context of political theory. Questions of society, the state, and social reform are considered by Colmer, Calleo, and De Paolo (1987), respectively.

NICOLA TROTT

SCIENCE

The best and most comprehensive study is Levere's, which also shows how integral science was to Coleridge's thinking. Wylie is useful for the early period; Lefebure discusses the important relationship with Davy (see Gravil et al. 1990).

WORDSWORTH

An introduction to the relationship of 'Coleridge and Wordsworth' is available in Brett (1971). Modern studies are divided according to the degree of harmony or disharmony detected, and the direction of their sympathy towards either party. Among those who see antagonism are Parrish and Newlyn (1986: a Bloom-influenced literary study). In the opposite camp are McFarland (1981: symbiosis), Beer (1981: a counter-Bloomian study of influence, interestingly metaphorical rather than biographical); Prickett (1970: ennobling interchange, partnership), and Magnuson (1988: dialogism).

REFERENCES

TEXTS

Coleridge, S. T., *The Complete Poetical Works of Samuel Taylor Coleridge*, ed. Ernest Hartley Coleridge, 2 vols. (Oxford, 1912).
—— *Coleridge's Shakespearean Criticism*, ed. Thomas Middleton Raysor, 2 vols. (1930; London, 1960).
—— *Coleridge's Miscellaneous Criticism*, ed. Thomas Middleton Raysor (Cambridge, Mass., 1936).
—— *The Philosophical Lectures of Samuel Taylor Coleridge*, ed. Kathleen Coburn (London, 1949).
—— *The Portable Coleridge*, ed. I. A. Richards (New York, 1950).
—— *Inquiring Spirit: A New Presentation of Coleridge from his Published and Unpublished Prose Writings*, ed. Kathleen Coburn (London, 1951).
—— *Coleridge on the Seventeenth Century*, ed. Roberta Florence Brinkley (Durham, NC, 1955).
—— *Collected Letters of Samuel Taylor Coleridge*, ed. E. L. Griggs, 6 vols. (Oxford, 1956–71).
—— *The Notebooks of Samuel Taylor Coleridge*, Bollingen Series 50, 4 vols. to date: vols. i, ii, and iii (covering 1794–1804, 1804–8, and 1808–19), ed. Kathleen Coburn (London, 1957, 1961, 1973), vol. iv (covering 1819–26), ed. Kathleen Coburn and Merton Christensen (London, 1990).
—— *Samuel Taylor Coleridge: Poems*, ed. John Beer (1963; rev. 1986; rev. London, 1993).

—— *The Collected Works of Samuel Taylor Coleridge*, gen. ed. Kathleen Coburn, assoc. ed. Bart Winer, Bollingen Series 75 (London, 1969– : square brackets indicate the work is yet to be published): i: *Lectures 1795: On Politics and Religion*, ed. Lewis Patton and Peter Mann (1971); ii: *The Watchman*, ed. Lewis Patton (1970); iii: *Essays on his Times*, ed. David V. Erdman, 3 vols. (1978); iv: *The Friend*, ed. Barbara E. Rooke, 2 vols. (1969); v: *Lectures 1808–1819: On Literature*, ed. R. A. Foakes, 2 vols. (1987); vi: *Lay Sermons*, ed. R. J. White (1972); vii: *Biographia Literaria; or, Biographical Sketches of my Literary Life and Opinions*, ed. James Engell and W. Jackson Bate, 2 vols. (1983); [viii: *Lectures 1818–1819: On the History of Philosophy*, ed. J. R. de J. Jackson]; ix: *Aids to Reflection*, ed. John Beer (1993); x: *On the Constitution of the Church and State*, ed. John Colmer (1976); xi: *Shorter Works and Fragments*, ed. H. J. Jackson and J. R. de J. Jackson, 2 vols. (1995); xii: *Marginalia*, 3 vols. to date: vols. i and ii (A to B and C to H), ed. George Whalley (1980 and 1984), vol. iii (I to O), ed. George Whalley and H. J. Jackson (1992); xiii: *Logic*, ed. J. R. de J. Jackson (1981); xiv: *Table Talk*, ed. Carl R. Woodring, 2 vols. (1990); [xv: *Opus Maximum*, ed. Thomas McFarland]; [xvi: *Poetical Works*, ed. J. C. C. Mays].

—— *Coleridge on Shakespeare: The Text of the Lectures of 1811–12*, ed. R. A. Foakes (London, 1971).

—— *Imagination in Coleridge*, ed. John Spencer Hill (London, 1978).

—— *Samuel Taylor Coleridge*, ed. H. J. Jackson (Oxford, 1985).

—— *Selected Letters*, ed. H. J. Jackson (Oxford, 1987).

—— *Coleridge's 'Dejection': The Earliest Manuscripts and the Earliest Printings*, ed. Stephen Maxfield Parrish (Ithaca, NY, 1988).

—— *'Fears in Solitude' 1798*, with *France: An Ode* and *Frost at Midnight* (Oxford, 1989a).

—— *'Remorse' 1813* (Oxford, 1989b).

—— *'Lyrical Ballads' 1798* (Oxford, 1990a).

—— *'Poems on Various Subjects' 1796* (Oxford, 1990b).

—— *'Sibylline Leaves' 1817* (Oxford, 1990c).

—— *Coleridge's Writings*, gen. ed. John Beer (Basingstoke, 1990– d): i: *On Politics and Society*, ed. John Morrow (1990); ii: *On Humanity*, ed. Anya Taylor (1995).

—— *'Christabel' 1816* (Oxford, 1991).

—— *'Conciones ad Populum' 1795* (Oxford, 1992).

—— *Coleridge's 'Ancient Mariner': An Experimental Edition of Texts and Revisions 1798–1828*, ed. Martin Wallen (New York, 1993).

—— *Coleridge: The Early Family Letters*, ed. James Engell (Oxford, 1994).

—— *Coleridge: Selected Poems*, ed. Richard Holmes (London, 1996).

—— —— and Southey, R., *'The Fall of Robespierre' 1794* (Oxford, 1991).

—— —— *'Joan of Arc' 1796* (Oxford, 1993).

Foakes, R. A. (ed.), *Coleridge's Criticism of Shakespeare: A Selection* (London, 1989).

Wittreich, Joseph Anthony, Jr. (ed.), *The Romantics on Milton: Formal Essays and Critical Asides* (Cleveland, 1970).

CRITICISM

Abrams, M. H., *The Mirror and the Lamp: Romantic Theory and the Critical Tradition* (Oxford, 1953).

Abrams, M. H., *Natural Supernaturalism: Tradition and Revolution in Romantic Literature* (London, 1971).

—— 'Structure and Style in the Greater Romantic Lyric', 'Coleridge's "A Light in Sound": Science, Metascience, and Poetic Imagination"', and 'Coleridge and the Romantic Vision of the World', in *The Correspondent Breeze: Essays on English Romanticism*, foreword by Jack Stillinger (New York, 1984), 76–108, 158–91, 192–224.

Adair, Patricia M., *The Waking Dream: A Study of Coleridge's Poetry* (London, 1967).

Appleyard, J. A., *Coleridge's Philosophy of Literature: The Development of a Concept of Poetry 1791–1819* (Cambridge, Mass., 1965).

Ashton, Rosemary, *The German Idea: Four English Writers and the Reception of German Thought 1800–1860* (Cambridge, 1980).

—— *The Life of Samuel Taylor Coleridge* (Oxford, 1996).

Badawi, M. M., *Coleridge: Critic of Shakespeare* (Cambridge, 1973).

Baker, Harold D., 'Landscape as Textual Practice in Coleridge's *Notebooks*', *English Literary History*, 59 (1992), 651–70.

Barfield, Owen, *What Coleridge Thought* (1971; London, 1972).

—— 'Coleridge's Enjoyment of Words', in John Beer (ed.), L. C. Knights (introd.), *Coleridge's Variety: Bicentenary Studies* (London, 1974), 204–18.

Barth, J. Robert, SJ, *Coleridge and Christian Doctrine* (Cambridge, Mass., 1969).

Bate, Jonathan, *Shakespeare and the English Romantic Imagination* (Oxford, 1986).

Bate, Walter Jackson, *Coleridge* (London, 1969).

Beer, John, *Coleridge the Visionary* (London, 1959).

—— 'Coleridge and Poetry: I. Poems of the Supernatural', in R. L. Brett (ed.), *Writers and their Background: Coleridge* (London, 1971), 45–90.

—— *Coleridge's Poetic Intelligence* (1977; Basingstoke, 1986).

—— 'Coleridge and Wordsworth: Influence and Confluence', in Donald Sultana (ed.), *New Approaches to Coleridge: Biographical and Critical Essays* (London, 1981), 192–211.

Benziger, James, 'Organic Unity: Leibniz to Coleridge', *Publications of the Modern Language Association*, 66 (1951), 24–48.

Bialostosky, Don H., 'Coleridge's Interpretation of Wordsworth's Preface to *Lyrical Ballads*', *Publications of the Modern Language Association*, 93 (1978), 912–24.

Bloom, Harold, *The Visionary Company: A Reading of English Romantic Poetry* (1961; rev. edn., Ithaca, NY, 1971).

—— 'Coleridge: The Anxiety of Influence', in Geoffrey Hartman (ed.), *New Perspectives on Coleridge and Wordsworth: Selected Papers from the English Institute* (New York, 1972), 247–67.

Bodkin, Maud, *Archetypal Patterns in Poetry* (Oxford, 1934).

Bostetter, Edward E., 'The Nightmare World of *The Ancient Mariner*', *Studies in Romanticism*, 1 (1962), 241–54.

Boulger, James D., *Coleridge as Religious Thinker* (New Haven, 1961).

Brett, R. L., 'Coleridge's Theory of the Imagination', in Sir Philip Magnus (ed.), *English Studies 1949: Being Volume Two of the New Series of Essays and Studies* (London, 1949), 75–90.

—— (ed.), *Writers and their Background: Coleridge* (London, 1971).

Brisman, Leslie, 'Coleridge and the Supernatural', *Studies in Romanticism*, 21 (1982), 123–59.

Brown, Huntington, 'The Gloss to *The Rime of the Ancient Mariner'*, *Modern Language Quarterly*, 6 (1945), 319–24.

Buell, L., 'The Question of Form in Coleridge's *Biographia Literaria'*, *English Literary History*, 46 (1979), 399–417.

Burwick, Frederick (ed.), *Coleridge's 'Biographia Literaria': Text and Meaning* (Columbus, Oh., 1989).

—— 'Coleridge and Schelling on Mimesis', in Richard Gravil and Molly Lefebure (eds.), *The Coleridge Connection: Essays for Thomas McFarland* (Basingstoke, 1990), 179–99.

—— 'Illusion and the Poetic Imagination: Coleridge', in *Illusion and the Drama: Critical Theory of the Enlightenment and Romantic Era* (University Park, Pa., 1991), 191–229.

Butler, Marilyn, *Romantics, Rebels and Reactionaries: English Literature and its Background 1760–1830* (Oxford, 1981).

Calleo, David, *Coleridge and the Idea of the Modern State* (New Haven, 1966).

Carlyle, Thomas, *The Life of John Sterling* (1851), excerpted in S. T. Coleridge, *Table Talk*, vol. xiv of *Collected Works*.

Carlson, Julie A., *In the Theatre of Romanticism: Coleridge, Nationalism, Women* (Cambridge, 1994).

Christensen, Jerome, *Coleridge's Blessed Machine of Language* (Ithaca, NY, 1981).

Coburn, Kathleen, *The Self Conscious Imagination: A Study of the Coleridge Notebooks in Celebration of the Bi-centenary of his Birth 21 October 1772* (London, 1974).

—— *Experience into Thought: Perspectives in the Coleridge Notebooks* (Toronto, 1979).

Coffman, Ralph J., *Coleridge's Library: A Bibliography of Books Owned or Read by Samuel Taylor Coleridge* (Boston, 1987).

Cole, Steven E., 'Coleridge, Language, and the Production of Agency', *Modern Philology*, 88 (1990), 109–25.

Coleman, Deirdre, *Coleridge and 'The Friend' (1809–1810)* (Oxford, 1988).

Collings, David, 'Coleridge Beginning a Career: Desultory Authorship in *Religious Musings'*, *English Literary History*, 58 (1991), 167–93.

Colmer, John, *Coleridge, Critic of Society* (Oxford, 1959).

Cooke, Katharine, *Coleridge* (London, 1979).

Cooper, Andrew M., 'Who's Afraid of the Mastiff Bitch? Gothic Parody and Original Sin', in Leonard Orr (ed.), *'Christabel': Critical Essays on Samuel Taylor Coleridge* (New York, 1994), 81–107.

Cornwell, John, *Coleridge: Poet and Revolutionary 1772–1804. A Critical Biography* (London, 1973).

Corrigan, Matthew, *Coleridge, Language, and Criticism* (Athens, Ga., 1982).

Cottle, Joseph, *Reminiscences of Samuel Taylor Coleridge and Robert Southey* (1847; Highgate, 1970).

Crawford, Walter B. (ed.), *Reading Coleridge: Approaches and Applications* (Ithaca, NY, 1979).

—— and Lauterbach, Edward S., with the assistance of Crawford, Ann M., *Samuel Taylor Coleridge: An Annotated Bibliography of Criticism and Scholarship*, ii. *1900–1939* (Boston, 1983); iii: *1940–1992* (1996).

Deen, Leonard W., 'Coleridge and the Sources of Pantisocracy: Godwin, the Bible, and Hartley', *Boston University Studies in English*, 5 (1961), 232–45.

Dekker, George, *Coleridge and the Literature of Sensibility* (London, 1978).

de Man, Paul, 'The Rhetoric of Temporality', in *Blindness and Insight: Essays in the Rhetoric of Contemporary Criticism*, introd. Wlad Godzich (2nd edn., 1983; repr. London, 1989), 187–228.

De Paolo, Charles, *Coleridge's Philosophy of Social Reform* (New York, 1987).

—— *Coleridge: Historian of Ideas* (Victoria, 1992).

De Quincey, Thomas, 'Samuel Taylor Coleridge', in *Recollections of the Lakes and the Lake Poets*, ed. David Wright (Harmondsworth, 1970).

Donohue, Joseph W., Jr., *Dramatic Character in the English Romantic Age* (Princeton, NJ, 1970).

Ebbatson, J. R., 'Coleridge's Mariner and the Rights of Man', *Studies in Romanticism*, 11 (1972), 171–206.

Eilenberg, Susan, *Strange Power of Speech: Wordsworth, Coleridge, and Literary Possession* (New York, 1992).

Eliot, T. S., 'Wordsworth and Coleridge', in *The Use of Poetry and the Use of Criticism: Studies in the Relation of Criticism to Poetry in England* (London, 1933), 67–85.

Elkins, A. C., Jr., and Forstner, L. J., *The Romantic Movement Bibliography 1936–70: A Master Cumulation from ELH, Philological Quarterly, and English Language Notes*, 7 vols. (Ann Arbor, 1973).

Ellison, Julie, *Delicate Subjects: Romanticism, Gender, and the Ethics of Understanding* (Ithaca, NY, 1990).

Emmet, Dorothy, 'Coleridge as Philosopher', in R. L. Brett (ed.), *Writers and their Background: Coleridge* (London, 1971), 195–220.

Empson, William, ' "The Ancient Mariner" ', in *Argufying: Essays on Literature and Culture*, ed. John Haffenden (London, 1987), 297–319.

Engell, James, *The Creative Imagination: Enlightenment to Romanticism* (Cambridge, Mass., 1981).

—— 'Coleridge and German Idealism: First Postulates and Final Causes', in Richard Gravil and Molly Lefebure (eds.), *The Coleridge Connection: Essays for Thomas McFarland* (Basingstoke, 1990), 153–77.

—— 'Imagining into Nature: "This Lime-Tree Bower My Prison" ', in Leonard Orr (ed.), *Critical Essays on Samuel Taylor Coleridge* (New York, 1994), 108–23.

Erdman, David V., et al., *The Romantic Movement: A Selective and Critical Bibliography: 1979–1986* (New York, 1980–7); *1987–* (West Cornwall, Conn. 1988–).

Esterhammer, Angela, 'Speech Acts and Living Words: On Performative Language in Coleridge's 1798 Poems', *Wordsworth Circle*, 24 (1993), 79–83.

Everest, Kelvin, *Coleridge's Secret Ministry: The Context of the Conversation Poems 1795–1798* (Hassocks, 1979).

Ferguson, Frances, 'Coleridge and the Deluded Reader: "The Rime of the Ancient Mariner" ', in Richard Machin and Christopher Norris (eds.), *Post-Structuralist Readings of English Poetry* (Cambridge, 1987), 248–63.

Ferris, David S., 'Coleridge's Ventriloquy: The Abduction from the *Biographia*', *Studies in Romanticism*, 24 (1985), 41–84.

Fletcher, Richard M., *English Romantic Drama 1795–1843: A Critical History* (New York, 1966).

Fogel, Daniel Mark, 'A Compositional History of the *Biographia Literaria*', *Studies in Bibliography*, 30 (1977), 219–34.

Fogle, Richard Harter, *The Idea of Coleridge's Criticism* (Westport, Conn., 1962).

Forster, E. M., 'Silas Tomkyn Comberbache', in *Abinger Harvest* (London, 1936).

Fruman, Norman, *Coleridge: The Damaged Archangel* (1971; London, 1972).

—— 'Coleridge's Rejection of Nature and the Natural Man', in Richard Gravil, Lucy Newlyn, and Nicholas Roe (eds.), *Coleridge's Imagination: Essays in Memory of Pete Laver* (Cambridge, 1985), 69–78.

—— 'Editing and Annotating the *Biographia Literaria*', in Frederick Burwick (ed.), *Coleridge's 'Biographia Literaria': Text and Meaning* (Columbus, Oh., 1989), 1–19.

Fulford, Tim, *Coleridge's Figurative Language* (Basingstoke, 1991).

—— and Paley, Morton D. (eds.), *Coleridge's Visionary Languages: Essays in Honour of J. B. Beer* (Cambridge, 1993).

Gallant, Christine, *Coleridge's Theory of Imagination Today* (New York, 1989).

Galperin, William H., *The Return of the Visible in British Romanticism* (Baltimore, 1993).

Gérard, Albert S., 'The Systolic Rhythm: The Structure of Coleridge's Conversation Poems', *Essays in Criticism*, 10 (1960), 307–19.

Gillman, James, *The Life of Samuel Taylor Coleridge*, 1 vol. only pub. (London, 1838).

Gravil, Richard, Newlyn, Lucy, and Roe, Nicholas (eds.), *Coleridge's Imagination: Essays in Memory of Pete Laver* (Cambridge, 1985).

—— —— —— and Lefebure, Molly (eds.), *The Coleridge Connection: Essays for Thomas McFarland* (Basingstoke, 1990).

Green, Joseph Henry, *Spiritual Philosophy: Founded on the Teaching of the Late Samuel Taylor Coleridge* (London, 1865).

Hamilton, Paul, *Coleridge's Poetics* (Oxford, 1983).

Happel, Stephen, *Coleridge's Religious Imagination*, 3 vols. (Salzburg, 1983).

Harding, Anthony John, *Coleridge and the Idea of Love: Aspects of Relationship in Coleridge's Thought and Writing* (Cambridge, 1974).

—— *The Reception of Myth in English Romanticism* (Columbia, Mo., 1995).

Harding, D. W., *Experience into Words: Essays on Poetry* (London, 1963), 53–71.

Hardy, Barbara, 'Distinction without Difference: Coleridge's Fancy and Imagination', *Essays in Criticism*, 1 (1951), 336–44.

—— ' "I have a smack of Hamlet": Coleridge and Shakespeare's Characters', *Essays in Criticism*, 8 (1958), 252–64.

Harper, George McLean, 'Coleridge's Conversation Poems', in M. H. Abrams (ed.), *English Romantic Poets: Modern Essays in Criticism* (2nd edn., Oxford, 1975), 188–201.

Hartman, Geoffrey H., 'Romanticism and Anti-Self-Consciousness', in *Beyond Formalism: Literary Essays 1958–1971* (New Haven, 1970), 298–310.

—— 'Reflections on the Evening Star: Akenside to Coleridge', in Geoffrey H. Hartman (ed.), *New Perspectives on Coleridge and Wordsworth: Selected Papers from the English Institute* (New York, 1972), 85–131.

Haven, Richard, 'Coleridge, Hartley, and the Mystics', *Journal in the History of Ideas*, 20 (1959), 477–94.

—— 'The Ancient Mariner in the Nineteenth Century', *Studies in Romanticism*, 11 (1972), 364–74.

Haven, Richard, Haven, Josephine, and Adams, Maurianne, *Samuel Taylor Coleridge: An Annotated Bibliography of Criticism and Scholarship*, i: *1793–1899* (Boston, Mass., 1976).

Hazlitt, William, 'My First Acquaintance with Poets' (1823), in *The Complete Works of William Hazlitt*, ed. P. P Howe, 21 vols. (London, 1930–4), xvii. 106–22.

—— 'Mr. Coleridge', in *The Spirit of the Age* (1825), ed. E. D. Mackerness (London, 1969).

Heller, Janet Ruth, *Coleridge, Lamb, Hazlitt, and the Reader of Drama* (Columbia, Mo., 1990).

Helmholtz, A. A., *The Indebtedness of Coleridge to A. W. Schlegel* (Madison, 1907).

Holmes, Richard, *Coleridge: Early Visions* (London, 1989).

House, Humphry, *Coleridge: The Clark Lectures 1951–52* (London, 1953).

Hunt, Leigh, *The Autobiography of Leigh Hunt with Reminiscences of Friends and Contemporaries*, 3 vols. (London, 1850), ch. 16.

Jackson, H. J., 'Johnson's Milton and Coleridge's Wordsworth', *Studies in Romanticism*, 28 (1989), 29–47.

Jackson, J. R. de J., *Method and Imagination in Coleridge's Criticism* (Cambridge, Mass., 1969).

—— (ed.), *Coleridge: The Critical Heritage*, i: *1794–1834* (London, 1970); ii: *1834–1900* (London, 1991).

Janowitz, Anne, 'Coleridge's 1816 Volume: Fragment as Rubric', *Studies in Romanticism*, 24 (1985), 21–39.

Keane, Patrick K., *Coleridge's Submerged Politics: 'The Ancient Mariner' and 'Robinson Crusoe'* (Columbia, Mo., 1994).

Kessler, Edward, *Coleridge's Metaphors of Being* (Princeton, 1979).

Kipperman, Mark, *Beyond Enchantment: German Idealism and English Romantic Poetry* (Philadelphia, 1986).

Kirkham, Michael, 'Metaphor and the Unitary World: Coleridge and Henry Vaughan', *Essays in Criticism*, 37 (1987), 121–34.

Kitson, Peter J., and Corns, Thomas N. (eds.), *Coleridge and the Armoury of the Human Mind: Essays on his Prose Writings* (London, 1991).

Knight, G. W., 'Coleridge's Divine Comedy', in M. H. Abrams (ed.), *English Romantic Poets: Modern Essays in Criticism* (2nd edn., Oxford, 1975), 202–13.

Krieger, Murray, *A Reopening of Closure: Organicism against Itself* (New York, 1989).

Lamb, Charles, 'Christ's Hospital Five and Thirty Years Ago', in *Essays of Elia* (1823).

Leader, Zachary, *Revision and Romantic Authorship* (Oxford, 1996).

Leask, Nigel, *The Politics of Imagination in Coleridge's Critical Thought* (Basingstoke, 1988).

—— *British Romantic Writers and the East: Anxieties of Empire* (Cambridge, 1992).

Lefebure, Molly, *Samuel Taylor Coleridge: A Bondage of Opium* (London, 1974).

Levere, Trevor H., *Poetry Realized in Nature: Samuel Taylor Coleridge and Early Nineteenth-Century Science* (Cambridge, 1981).

Levinson, Marjorie, *The Romantic Fragment Poem: A Critique of a Form* (Chapel Hill, NC, 1986).

Lipkowitz, Ina, 'Inspiration and the Poetic Imagination: Samuel Taylor Coleridge', *Studies in Romanticism*, 30 (1991), 605–32.

Loades, Ann, 'No Consoling Vision: Coleridge's Discovery of Kant's "Authentic" Theodicy', in J. R. Watson (ed.), *An Infinite Complexity: Essays in Romanticism* (Edinburgh, 1983), 95–124.

Lockridge, Laurence S., *Coleridge the Moralist* (Ithaca, NY, 1977).

Logan, Eugenia, *A Concordance to the Poetry of Samuel Taylor Coleridge* (Gloucester, Mass., 1967).

Lowes, John Livingstone, *The Road to Xanadu: A Study in the Ways of the Imagination* (Boston, 1927).

McFarland, Thomas, *Coleridge and the Pantheist Tradition* (Oxford, 1969).

—— 'The Origin and Significance of Coleridge's Theory of Secondary Imagination', in Geoffrey Hartman (ed.), *New Perspectives on Coleridge and Wordsworth: Selected Papers from the English Institute* (New York, 1972), 195–246.

—— 'Coleridge's Plagiarisms Once More: A Review Essay', *Yale Review*, 63 (1974), 252–86.

—— 'The Symbiosis of Wordsworth and Coleridge' and 'Coleridge's Anxiety', in *Romanticism and the Forms of Ruin: Wordsworth, Coleridge, and Modalities of Fragmentation* (Princeton, 1981), 56–103, 104–36.

McGann, Jerome J., *The Romantic Ideology: A Critical Investigation* (Chicago, 1983).

—— 'The Ancient Mariner: The Meaning of the Meanings', in *The Beauty of Inflections: Literary Investigations in Historical Method and Theory* (Oxford, 1985), 135–72.

MacKinnon, D. M., 'Coleridge and Kant', in John Beer (ed.), L. C. Knights (introd.), *Coleridge's Variety: Bicentenary Studies* (London, 1974), 183–203.

McKusick, James C., *Coleridge's Philosophy of Language* (New Haven, 1986).

Magnuson, Paul, *Coleridge's Nightmare Poetry* (Charlottesville, Va., 1974).

—— *Coleridge and Wordsworth: A Lyrical Dialogue* (Princeton, 1988).

Marks, Emerson R., *Coleridge on the Language of Verse* (Princeton, 1981).

Matheson, Ann, 'The Influence of Cowper's *The Task* on Coleridge's Conversation Poems', in Donald Sultana (ed.), *New Approaches to Coleridge: Biographical and Critical Essays* (London, 1981), 137–50.

Mays, J. C. C., 'Reflections on Having Edited Coleridge's Poems', in Robert Brinkley and Keith Hanley (eds.), *Romantic Revisions* (Cambridge, 1992), 136–53.

Mellor, Anne K., 'Coleridge's "This Lime-Tree Bower my Prison" and the Categories of English Landscape', *Studies in Romanticism*, 18 (1979), 253–70.

Mileur, Jean-Pierre, *Vision and Revision: Coleridge's Art of Immanence* (Berkeley and Los Angeles, 1982).

[Mill, John Stuart], *Mill on Bentham and Coleridge* (1840), introd. F. R. Leavis (1950; Cambridge, 1980).

Modiano, Raimonda, *Coleridge and the Concept of Nature* (London, 1985).

Morrow, John, *Coleridge's Political Thought: Property, Morality, and the Limits of Traditional Discourse* (Basingstoke, 1990).

Muirhead, John H., *Coleridge as Philosopher* (London, 1930).

Nelson, Jane A., 'Entelechy and Structure in "Christabel"', *Studies in Romanticism*, 19 (1980), 375–93.

Newlyn, Lucy, *Coleridge, Wordsworth, and the Language of Allusion* (Oxford, 1986).

—— *'Paradise Lost' and the Romantic Reader* (Oxford, 1993).

Orsini, G. N. G., *Coleridge and German Idealism: A Study in the History of Philosophy with Unpublished Materials from Coleridge's Manuscripts* (Carbondale, Ill., 1969).

Paglia, Camille, 'The Daemon as Lesbian Vampire: Coleridge', in *Sexual Personae: Art and Decadence from Nefertiti to Emily Dickinson* (London, 1990), 317–46.

Paley, Morton D., 'Apocalypse and Millennium', *Wordsworth Circle*, 23 (1992), 24–35.

Paley, Morton D., *Coleridge's Later Poetry* (Oxford, 1996).

Park, Roy, 'Coleridge's Two Voices as a Critic of Wordsworth', *English Literary History*, 36 (1969), 361–81.

Parker, Reeve, *Coleridge's Meditative Art* (Ithaca, NY, 1975).

Parrish, Stephen Maxfield, *The Art of the 'Lyrical Ballads'* (Cambridge, Mass., 1973).

Pater, Walter, 'Coleridge', in *Appreciations: With an Essay in Style* (1889; London, 1910), 65–104.

Peacock, Thomas Love, *Nightmare Abbey* (1818).

Perkins, Mary Anne, *Coleridge's Philosophy: The Logos as Unifying Principle* (Oxford, 1994).

Peterfreund, Stuart, 'The Way of Immanence, Coleridge, and the Problem of Evil', *English Literary History*, 55 (1988), 125–58.

Piper, H. W., *The Active Universe: Pantheism and the Concept of Imagination in the English Romantic Poets* (London, 1962).

Pirie, David, 'A Letter to [Asra]', in Jonathan Wordsworth (ed.), assisted by Beth Darlington, *Bicentenary Wordsworth Studies in Memory of John Alban Finch* (Ithaca, NY, 1970), 294–339.

Prickett, Stephen, *Coleridge and Wordsworth: The Poetry of Growth* (Cambridge, 1970).

—— *Romanticism and Religion: The Tradition of Coleridge and Wordsworth in the Victorian Church* (Cambridge, 1976).

—— *Origins of Narrative: The Romantic Appropriation of the Bible* (Cambridge, 1996).

Purton, Valerie, *A Coleridge Chronology* (Basingstoke, 1993).

Rajan, Tilottama, *Dark Interpreter: The Discourse of Romanticism* (Ithaca, NY, 1980).

Reed, Arden, *Romantic Weather: The Climates of Coleridge and Baudelaire* (Hanover, NH, 1984).

Richards, I. A., *Coleridge on Imagination* (London, 1934).

Richardson, Alan, *A Mental Theater: Poetic Drama and Consciousness in the Romantic Age* (University Park, Pa. 1988).

—— *Romanticism, Race, and Imperial Culture, 1780–1834* (Bloomington, Ind., 1996).

Roe, Nicholas, *Wordsworth and Coleridge: The Radical Years* (1988; Oxford, 1990).

Ruoff, Gene W., *Wordsworth and Coleridge: The Making of the Major Lyrics 1802–1804* (London, 1989).

Schneider, Elisabeth, *Coleridge, Opium, and 'Kubla Khan'* (Chicago, 1953).

Schulz, Max F., *The Poetic Voices of Coleridge: A Study of his Desire for Spontaneity and Passion for Order* (Detroit, 1963).

—— 'Coleridge', in Frank Jordan (ed.), *The English Romantic Poets: A Review of Research and Criticism* (4th edn., New York, 1985), 342–462.

Shaffer, Elinor S., 'Coleridge's Revolution in the Standard of Taste', *Journal of Aesthetics and Art Criticism*, 28 (1969–70), 213–21.

—— *'Kubla Khan' and the Fall of Jerusalem: The Mythological School in Biblical Criticism and Secular Literature 1770–1880* (Cambridge, 1975).

Shawcross, John, introduction to *Biographia Literaria by S. T. Coleridge [. . .] with his Aesthetical Essays*, ed. John Shawcross, 2 vols. (Oxford, 1907).

Simpson, David, 'Coleridge on Wordsworth and the Form of Poetry', in Christine Gallant (ed.), *Coleridge's Theory of Imagination Today* (New York, 1989), 211–25.

Snyder, Alice D., *Coleridge on Logic and Learning with Selections from the Unpublished Manuscripts* (New Haven, 1929).

Spatz, Jonas, 'The Mystery of Eros: Sexual Initiation in Coleridge's "Christabel"', *Publications of the Modern Language Association*, 90 (1975), 107–16.

Stempel, Daniel, 'Coleridge and Organic Form: The English Tradition', *Studies in Romanticism*, 6 (1966–7), 89–97.

Stephen, Leslie, 'Coleridge', in *Hours in a Library*, 3 vols. (1892; 2nd edn., London, 1991), vol. iii.

Stillinger, Jack, *Coleridge and Textual Instability: The Multiple Versions of the Poems* (New York, 1994).

Swann, Karen, ' "Christabel": The Wandering Mother and the Enigma of Form', *Studies in Romanticism*, 23 (1984), 533–53.

Swinburne, Algernon, *Essays and Studies* (London, 1875).

Tomlinson, Charles, 'Christabel', in John Wain (ed.), *Interpretations: Essays on Twelve English Poems* (London, 1955), 86–112.

Tyler, Luther, 'Losing "A Letter": The Contexts of Coleridge's "Dejection"', *English Literary History*, 52 (1985), 419–45.

Wallace, Catherine Miles, *The Design of 'Biographia Literaria'* (London, 1983).

Warnock, Mary, *Imagination* (1976; London, 1980).

Warren, Robert Penn, 'A Poem of Pure Imagination: An Experiment in Reading', in *Selected Essays* (New York, 1951), 198–305.

Watson, George, *Coleridge the Poet* (London, 1966).

Wellek, René, *A History of Modern Criticism: 1750–1950*, ii: *The Romantic Age* (1955; London, 1970).

Wendling, Ronald C., *Coleridge's Progress to Christianity: Experience and Authority in Religious Faith* (Lewisburg, Pa., 1995).

Whalley, George, 'The Integrity of *Biographia Literaria*', in Geoffrey Bullough (ed.), *Essays and Studies 1953* (London, 1953), 87–101.

Wheeler, Kathleen, *Sources, Processes, and Methods in Coleridge's 'Biographia Literaria'* (Cambridge, 1980).

—— *The Creative Mind in Coleridge's Poetry* (London, 1981).

—— ' "Kubla Khan" and Eighteenth Century Aesthetic Theories', *Wordsworth Circle*, 22 (1991), 15–24.

Willey, Basil, *The Eighteenth Century Background: Studies on the Idea of Nature in the Thought of the Period* (London, 1949).

—— *Samuel Taylor Coleridge* (London, 1972).

Wolfson, Susan J., 'The Language of Interpretation', in Harold Bloom (ed. and introd.), *Modern Critical Views: Samuel Taylor Coleridge* (New York, 1986), 210–18.

—— ' "Comparing Power": Coleridge and Simile', in Christine Gallant (ed.), *Coleridge's Theory of Imagination Today* (New York, 1989), 167–95.

Woolf, Virginia, 'The Man at the Gate', in *The Death of the Moth, and Other Essays* (1942; Harmondsworth, 1961), 92–7.

Wordsworth, Jonathan, 'The Infinite I AM: Coleridge and the Ascent of Being', in Richard Gravil, Lucy Newlyn, and Nicholas Roe (eds.), *Coleridge's Imagination: Essays in Memory of Pete Laver* (Cambridge, 1985), 22–52.

Wylie, Ian, *Young Coleridge and the Philosophers of Nature* (Oxford, 1989).

5. *Lord Byron*

ANDREW NICHOLSON

In memory of Michael G. Cooke

TEXTS

The first major edition of Byron's collected works to appear after his death
was *The Works of Lord Byron*, edited by John Wright, and published by John
Murray in seventeen volumes in 1832 and 1833. This included Moore's life
of Byron (first published in two volumes in 1830), much of Byron's prose
writings, and many of the poems and remaining cantos of *Don Juan* originally
published by John Hunt. Although Murray issued single or multiple volumes
of collections thereafter throughout the nineteenth century, the next major edition to appear under his imprint was *The Works of Lord Byron*, edited by E. H.
Coleridge (*Poetry*) and Rowland E. Prothero (*Letters and Journals*), published in
thirteen volumes at the turn of the century (1898–1904). This remained the
standard edition until well into the latter half of this century and is still of
inestimable value. A single volume of Coleridge's edition of the poetry, *The
Poetical Works of Lord Byron*, was published by Murray in 1905. Almost simultaneously, Oxford issued a one-volume collection, *Byron: The Poetical Works*,
edited by Frederick Page (1904; rev. edn. by John Jump, 1970), as did Houghton
Mifflin, *The Complete Poetical Works of Lord Byron*, edited by Paul Elmer More
(1905; rev. edn. by Robert Gleckner, 1975). These are still in circulation and
remain serviceable up to a point, though they distinctly lack notes and critical apparatus.

The standard edition of the poetry is now *Lord Byron: The Complete Poetical
Works*, edited by Jerome J. McGann, and published in seven volumes by the
Clarendon Press, Oxford (1980–93).

Selections of the poetry (occasionally with some prose) have been made by
W. H. Auden (1963), Douglas Dunn (1974), A. S. B. Glover (1954), John Jump
(1975), Donald A. Low (1995), Frank D. McConnell (1978), Jerome J. McGann
(1986 and 1994), Robin Skelton (1964), and Susan J. Wolfson and Peter J.
Manning (1996). Of these by far the best is McGann's *Byron: A Critical Edition
of the Major Works* (1986), which contains in full the texts of *Childe Harold, The*

Giaour, Ode to Napoleon Buonaparte, Manfred, Beppo, Mazeppa, Cain, The Vision of Judgment, and *Don Juan,* besides other poems and extracts. However, if taken in conjunction with the Penguin *Don Juan* (see below), Wolfson's and Manning's selection for the Penguin English Poets series (1996) offers an extremely strong alternative. Their text is based on John Wright's edition of 1832–3, and includes in full, and in sequence of composition and/or publication, *English Bards and Scotch Reviewers, Childe Harold,* all five Turkish Tales, *Ode to Napoleon Buonaparte, The Prisoner of Chillon, Manfred, Beppo, Mazeppa, Sardanapalus, The Vision of Judgment,* and other complete poems.

As for single works, *Don Juan* has been edited by Leslie A. Marchand for Houghton Mifflin's Riverside Editions (1958), with a text based principally on Coleridge's; and by T. G. and E. Steffan and W. W. Pratt for the Penguin English Poets series (1973; rev. edns., 1977 and 1982), with a text based on their revised edition of *Byron's Don Juan: A Variorum Edition,* 4 vols. (1957; rev. edn., 1971). This last was the first publication of *Don Juan* to incorporate a thorough critical apparatus, with manuscript variants and cancellations, as well as providing an exhaustive commentary and copious notes. It remains a crucially important work. The same may be said of Steffan's *Lord Byron's Cain* (1968) and Ashton's *Byron's Hebrew Melodies* (1972), both of which are variorum editions with detailed discussions, commentaries, and annotations. I would also urge readers to familiarize themselves with the facsimile editions of much of the poetry, in *The Manuscripts of the Younger Romantics* series published by Garland, which not only reproduce Byron's manuscripts (in many cases with facing transcriptions as well), but also provide further information, documentation, annotation, and commentary supplementing, correcting, or expanding that supplied by McGann (1980–93).

For full details of the publishing history of editions and collections of Byron's works, the reader should consult Coleridge (1898–1904: vii. 89–136), McGann (1980–93: i, pp. xxix–xxxiv), Oscar José Santucho's and Clement Tyson Goode's *A Comprehensive Bibliography,* 177–208, and Thomas James Wise, *A Bibliography of The Writings in Verse and Prose of George Gordon Noel, Baron Byron* (1932–3).

The standard edition of the letters and journals is now *Byron's Letters and Journals,* edited by Leslie A. Marchand, and published in thirteen volumes by John Murray (1973–94). From this Marchand himself made a selection, *Lord Byron: Selected Letters and Journals,* which was published by John Murray in 1982, and has since been reprinted in paperback and most recently published by Pimlico (1993).

The standard edition of the prose writings is now *Lord Byron: The Complete Miscellaneous Prose,* edited by Andrew Nicholson, and published by the Clarendon Press, Oxford (1991). This includes Byron's speeches, reviews, tales, translations from the Armenian, sketches, and reminiscences, as well as other fragmentary pieces, and his important contributions to the Bowles/Pope controversy which contain his views on the current state of literature (and politics).

Thomas Moore's biography, *Letters and Journals of Lord Byron: With Notices of his Life* (1830), remains to some extent canonical. The first biography of value to be written in this century was by Ethel Colburn Mayne, *Byron* (1912; rev. edn., 1924), who later went on to write *The Life of Lady Byron* (1929). These are fair, shrewd, and scholarly accounts, containing certain details and information upon which succeeding biographers have had to rely. André Maurois's *Byron* (1930) and Peter Quennell's *Byron: The Years of Fame* (1935) and *Byron in Italy* (1941), revised editions of both of which were published together in a single volume in 1974, make lively reading, but are not altogether reliable.

The standard biography at present is Leslie A. Marchand's *Byron: A Biography* (1957), a dispassionate, detailed, and thoroughly scholarly work, of which Marchand made an abridgement with additional material, *Byron: A Portrait*, which was published by John Murray in 1971, and has since appeared under various imprints in paperback, the most recent being Pimlico (1993). This is to be strongly recommended.

Byron's family, and his relationship with Lady Byron, have been carefully researched by Malcolm Elwin in *Lord Byron's Family* (1975) and *Lord Byron's Wife* (1962); while his Pisan period has been well documented by C. L. Cline in *Byron, Shelley and their Pisan Circle* (1952). Iris Origo also deals with Byron's period in Italy, from the moment of his meeting Teresa to his final embarkation for Greece, in *The Last Attachment* (1949) which draws on unpublished material in the Italian archives and elsewhere. Harold Nicolson's *Byron: The Last Journey* (1924; new edn. with a supplementary chapter, 1940), is a factual and informative, though thoroughly unsympathetic, account of Byron's final year in Greece; which period has been more evenly addressed by William St Clair in *That Greece Might Still Be Free* (1972), who discusses Byron's involvement in the Greek cause within the context of the whole Philhellenic movement of the time. In *The Late Lord Byron* (1960), Doris Langley Moore details the crises, problems, and attendant issues of sorting out Byron's affairs in the aftermath of his death; while in *Lord Byron: Accounts Rendered* (1974) the complexities of his finances, debts, expenditures, and generosities during his lifetime are examined and unravelled. Ernest J. Lovell's three fine editions, *His Very Self and Voice* (1954), *Medwin's Conversations of Lord Byron* (1966), and *Lady Blessington's Conversations of Lord Byron* (1969), are invaluable sources for contemporary reminiscences and anecdotes about Byron, and for views and opinions expressed by Byron himself. The same path is pursued, in a greatly abbreviated way, by Norman Page in *Byron: Interviews and Recollections* (1985); while in *A Byron Chronology* (1988) he provides a useful and detailed chronology of Byron's life and works, and the principal events of the day, with brief biographical notices of those of his circle. Kenneth Neill Cameron's and

studies thus complement rather than compete with each other. Frederick Shilstone's *Approaches to Teaching Byron's Poetry* (1991) is, as its title suggests, intended more for teachers than students, though it is valuable in grouping together contributions from Byronists who discuss their individual teaching methodologies (historicist, gender, irony, etc.), and is therefore illuminating for the student to see just *what*, and *by whom* and *how*, he or she is being fed.

The most important major studies of Byron remain M. K. Joseph's *Byron the Poet* (1964), Robert Gleckner's *Byron and the Ruins of Paradise* (1967), Jerome J. McGann's *Fiery Dust: Byron's Poetic Development* (1968), and Bernard Blackstone's *Byron: A Survey* (1975). Joseph provides a comprehensive overview of Byron's output, setting each poem he discusses within the context of its sources, revisions, style, verse form, and so forth, which serves as a solid basis for his critical investigation. He is particularly strong on *Childe Harold*, *Cain*, and *Don Juan*, Byron's use of persona, and his role as narrator. Gleckner is mainly concerned with Byron's personae and his struggle for form and the appropriate vehicles and voices for self-expression. The 'Ruins' of the title represent 'the hell of human existence'—the graceless state of 'eternal fall' and damnation to which man has been gratuitously condemned by a God who demonstrates his love by inflicting pain and punishment. Gleckner pursues the recurring motif of 'fall' from *Hours of Idleness* to *Don Juan*, registering an ever-deepening sense of despair and negation from which there is no escape—the only response to which lies in creating (imposing *form* upon the 'Ruins') or in laughter (which Gleckner finds hollow, merely the 'mask of despair'). McGann monitors the various stages of Byron's poetic career from *Hours of Idleness*, *Childe Harold*, the tales and dramas, to *Beppo* (*Don Juan* is deliberately excluded), illustrating how through the very act of writing the poet creates himself and thereby discovers a meaning to life which is as valid for him as it is for mankind as a whole (the thrust behind *Childe Harold*). Crucial to McGann's argument is Byron's mode of self-dramatization: how, for example, through his appointed role as *improvvisatore* narrator in *Beppo*, he dominates not only his poetical materials but his audience as well with the palpable controlling presence of himself as poet. At the same time, McGann registers Byron's concern with the spiritual and material condition of man's nature (the 'Fiery Dust' of the title), the duality of which is shown to be reconciled yet again in *Beppo*: the worldly poet-narrator being the epitome or exemplum of the whole man who recognizes the spiritual *in* the material, the ideal *in* the real, the infinite *in* the present. McGann is particularly informative in matters relating to manuscripts and texts; and his discussion of *Childe Harold*, which forms the core of his study, is outstanding. Bernard Blackstone offers an impressive survey of Byron's entire *œuvre* from the point of what he calls 'topocriticism': that is, 'to approach Byron, to understand him and ultimately to interpret him within his basic "ground", which was, by his own repeated confession, that of the Eastern Mediterranean'.

Hence the poetry is related to the various topoi—the sites and countries (and cultures)—through which Byron journeyed and in which he lived and wrote (especially Greece and his encounter with Islam). Thus, for example, in *Childe Harold*, Canto I, Byron moves 'between the nodes of wisdom (Delphi), power (Seville), and love (Cadiz)', which 'nodes', indeed, form the nucleus of his thought, which Blackstone traces back to the earlier formative works and pursues in those of Byron's maturity. As part of his critical endeavour to address Byron's work as a unified organic whole, Blackstone gives an unusually strong profile to many of the lesser-known pieces, and is particularly suggestive in his readings of the poetry in the light of Blake and Eliot.

Coming now to studies of individual works or genres, the best full-length discussion of Byron as a satirist is Frederick L. Beaty's *Byron the Satirist* (1985). Beaty provides a comprehensive and detailed survey of the satires from *English Bards and Scotch Reviewers* to *Don Juan*, examining their sources, origins, genesis, and nature, and setting each within its historical context. The focus yields interconnections between the satires as a body, and Beaty is especially illuminating in his treatment of *The Vision of Judgment* and *Don Juan*. In this same field, Claude M. Fuess's *Byron as a Satirist in Verse* (1912) remains valuable, as does Alvin Kernan's chapter on *Don Juan* in his broader study, *The Plot of Satire* (1965), and as does Leavis's essay, 'Byron's Satire', in *Revaluation* (1936).

On *Don Juan* itself, Elizabeth French Boyd's *Byron's Don Juan: A Critical Study* (1945) is still seminal for its study of sources and influences, and for providing much of the critical groundwork upon which subsequent scholarship has built. However, the most recent and comprehensive introduction to the poem as a whole, and the one with which to begin, is Anne Barton's *Byron: Don Juan* in the Cambridge University Press Landmarks of World Literature series (1992). In a remarkably concise and lucid account which draws with discrimination on the work of contemporary and earlier critics, Barton addresses almost every aspect of the poem—from its style, structure, genesis, and formative influences, to its hidden ironies, layered meanings, and variety of narrative voices—discussing each of its salient themes within an episodic framework.

In *Don Juan in Context* (1976), Jerome McGann traces the dominating presences of Homer, Horace, Juvenal, and Milton at various stages in Byron's poetic career in order to demonstrate what Byron discarded and what he retained of each of them in *Don Juan*. By analysing the poem's relations to its historical origins and immediate background (its 'shifting contexts'), McGann seeks to illuminate what goes on in the poem itself and to further our awareness of what changes within it (and how), and what remains constant. McGann's essentially positive and affirmatory (historicist) perspective is challenged by Rolf Lessenich in *Lord Byron and the Nature of Man* (1978), in which what is regarded as Byron's profoundly pessimistic view of human nature is claimed as the key to understanding the apparent paradoxes and inconsistencies in *Don Juan*.

In her study *Byron and Joyce through Homer* (1981), Hermione de Almeida examines the comparative indebtedness of Byron's *Don Juan* and Joyce's *Ulysses* to Homer's *Odyssey*, arguing that in both cases 'if Homer is touchstone he is also punching-bag, if he is point of direction he is also point of divergence, if he is authority he is also reason for rebellion'.

A. B. England, in *Byron's Don Juan and Eighteenth-Century Literature* (1975b), pursues the continuities and discontinuities of the rhetorical forms and structures of such eighteenth-century writers as Swift, Pope, Sterne, and Fielding in Byron's verse, illustrating through a series of rigorous textual readings how the burlesque tradition of Butler and Swift is the more vitalizing influence on the satirical mode of *Don Juan*.

Byron's relationship to Regency England is explored by Peter Graham in *Don Juan and Regency England* (1990), who argues that *Don Juan* is in dialogue with Lady Caroline Lamb's thinly veiled fictional account of her stormy affair with Byron in 1812, *Glenarvon* (1816). While both writers sought to expose the vices and hypocrisies of Regency society, Graham suggests that Lamb offered Byron 'an English version of the Don Juan myth . . . from the female point of view', to which *Don Juan* was his 'rebuttal', yet also his acknowledgement of women as 'potent complex beings'.

In *Byron's Don Juan* (1985), Bernard Beatty interrogates the processes of *Don Juan* to see what *kind* of a poem it is and *how* it proceeds. Arguing that it is essentially a comedy elaborated by a series of survivals, playing between *eros* and *thanatos* with the narrator exploiting the 'gaps' as part of the procedural function of the narrative, Beatty gives particular prominence to the spiritual or religious dimension of the poem (a novel perspective in this connection), in which Aurora is seen as the agent of redemption towards which Juan is aspiring. In the course of his discussion Beatty registers the numerous instances of 'gazing' in the poem (the narrator's 'gaze', Aurora's 'gaze'), which figure becomes the central concern in Mark Storey's *Byron and the Eye of Appetite* (1986). The 'Eye' of the title is the hungry, all-consuming eye that desires whatever it gazes upon. Storey monitors the recurrent images reflecting this (of which the most striking is that of one figure stooping over another) in the verse tales, *Childe Harold*, and *Don Juan*, in order to illustrate Byron's testing the limits of passion and feeling in his search for the 'fitting medium of desire'. The 'Eye' is once again crucial to Eric Meyer (1991). Concentrating on *The Giaour* and Cantos 5–8 of *Don Juan*, Meyer pursues those moments where gazes *confront* each other, arguing that they represent (by way of synecdoche) the struggle for power between two cultures, and more particularly the conflict between the colonial-imperialist venture and its colonized and oppressed peoples.

Psychoanalytical studies of *Don Juan* have been pursued by Laura Claridge and David Punter in their contributions to Nigel Wood's *Don Juan* in the Open University Press Theory in Practice Series (1993). Employing the theories of the French psychoanalyst Jacques Lacan, Claridge addresses the poem in order to reveal how language works as a surrogate for the satisfaction of needs. Given 'the inability of language ever to complete a circuit of meaning without referring to yet another signifier—we readily grasp how desire generated from this substitution is infinite in nature. The gap between need and demand initiates desire—an insatiable drive towards completing a lack actually constitutive of the social human being'. Claridge offers a similar, more spacious reading in part III of her book *Romantic Potency: The Paradox of Desire* (1992)—which deals with *Childe Harold*, the dramas, and again *Don Juan*—though here the emphasis seems to be more on how language liberates, how through writing 'one masters life'. David Punter, in a wide-ranging essay which draws on the psychoanalytical theories of Freud, Otto Rank, Jung and his revisionist disciple James Hillman, and Melanie Klein (besides a host of other literary references), offers an analysis of *Don Juan* in the light of various psychological interpretations of its mythic and legendary progenitors, in order to demonstrate the primacy of language in the assertion of self; how 'Language is essential for survival'. Throughout his discussion Punter deliberately seeks to avoid the pitfalls of what he terms 'psychobiography'—the animus here being directed without malice at Peter Manning's inaugurating Freudian 'psychobiography' *Byron and his Fictions* (1978). In this study, which covers the early poems, *Childe Harold*, the dramas, and *Don Juan*, Manning regards Byron's work as concealed self-confession whose 'oedipal content' is governed by the shift from the biographical 'tensions of mother and son', to the poetical 'triangular situation of hero, important woman, and dominating older man', and in which Byron's 'fantasy of perfect self-sufficiency' is ultimately exposed by his 'refusal to portray a successful resolution of the oedipal conflict'.

Frederick Shilstone's *Byron and the Myth of Tradition* (1989) might also be seen in this category. Charting a course through the poetry, letters, journals, conversations, and biography (the last of which is treated with studied caution), Shilstone argues that Byron's entire *œuvre* can be read as a spiritual autobiography, the principal drive of which is an existential quest for an ethics of self. This takes shape as a dialectical struggle in Byron's consciousness between the imperatives of tradition and the will to self-autonomy, which is finally resolved by a synthesis of self and tradition wherein the self appropriates, adapts, or modulates the tradition to its own demands and desires.

In *Self, Text and Romantic Irony: The Example of Byron* (1988), Frederick Garber also sees the 'ambivalent attitude toward the self's autonomy' as being crucial to the Romantic conception of what the self is and does. For the Romantic consciousness, he argues, 'self-making and text-making imply and implicate each other'. Yet pursuing this in the opposite direction he finds that the same relationship may obtain between 'self and text-*unmaking*'. Addressing himself to Byron and the movements and procedures of irony in the verse tales, *Childe*

Harold, and *Manfred*, Garber follows their transformation into satire in *Don Juan*, where junctures of competing narrative voices and poetic attitudes continually interrupt, revise, contradict, or subvert one another, to illustrate how the 'mutual emergence of "self order" and "text order" can be competitive as well as supportive . . . such paradoxical mutuality being one of the defining characteristics of romantic irony'.

Whilst Caroline Franklin's contribution to Wood's *Don Juan* may also be said to be a psychoanalytical study—drawing on the theories of Althusser, Foucault, Kristeva, Lacan, Macherey, and, in particular, Cora Kaplan—its thrust is more a 'socialist-feminist' investigation into 'the ideological premises of the poem, with regard to class, race and gender' which Franklin elucidates by contrasting the various representations of women or female gendered roles it embodies. This she has dealt with far more extensively in her important book *Byron's Heroines* (1992), which provides a historicist-cultural analysis contextualizing Byron's concern with and interest in the nature of women, their rights, and their status in society. Opening with an introduction on eighteenth-century ideas of gender and gender expectations, Franklin proceeds to relate Byron's representations of women to contemporary ideologies of sexual difference and, through a succession of revelatory readings of his texts, identifies a number of female types—the passive, the heroic, the active, the stoical—with which Byron is constantly experimenting in his sustained interrogation of the patriarchal ideology to which they are bound. Thus his heroines range 'from the eroticized passive victim of patriarchal force to masculinized woman-warrior, from the romantic heroine of sentiment to the sexually voracious virago or the chaste republican matron'. Implicit in this is a sexual politics wherein 'male' and 'female' roles are seen as conveniently contrived models or artificial constructs, not biologically but *culturally* determined. Hence Byron exposes the ever-present threat to the prevailing hierarchy that roles may be transgressed, appropriated, reversed; that women may become the salutary potent force of revolutionary change (Neuha in *The Island* is the example here). Such a fine study invites us to look in a fresh direction for the solution to Byron's ideal fusion of liberalism, humanism, and republican freedom.

Gender-oriented, feminist, sexual politics approaches are a relatively recent departure in Byron studies and have been admirably pursued in relation to the Turkish tales, *Sardanapalus*, and *Don Juan* by such critics as Jenni Calder, Cheryl Fallon Guiliano, Sonia Hofkosh, Malcolm Kelsall, Alan Richardson, Nicola J. Watson, and Susan Wolfson in their respective chapters or articles (itemized below). Louis Crompton's *Byron and Greek Love* (1985) also belongs in this genre, dealing as it does with the question of Byron's 'homoeroticism'. What emerges most painfully from Crompton's profoundly sensitive analysis is contemporary society's utterly irrational attitude towards homosexuality (a crime at the time) and its morbid victimization and prejudice against suspects. Crompton also documents the remarkable unpublished papers of Jeremy Bentham which reveal his level-headed and sympathetic treatment of the subject at a period when the issue was still taboo.

Philip Martin's contribution to Wood's *Don Juan*, 'Reading *Don Juan* with Bakhtin', inaugurates another new area in Byron criticism, which has been similarly explored by Suzanne Ferriss and Michael Macovski in their contributions to Alice Levine's and Robert Keane's *Rereading Byron* (1993). In an entertaining discussion, engagingly aware of theorizing a poem that refuses systematic theorization, Martin offers a dialogical reading of *Don Juan* according to Bakhtin's criteria of '*carnivalized literature*': that is, literature whose 'carnival sense of the world possesses a mighty life-creating and transforming power, an indestructible vitality'. Situating the poem within the historical and geographical context of its genesis—Venice 1818—and its generic context of the serio-comic tradition of Italian literature, and acknowledging Byron's self-conscious exposure of its productive processes, Martin registers its polyphony of voices and plurality of modes of discourse which deliberately evade being brought into a consistent and harmonious whole, to justify his claim that *Don Juan* is a 'carnival poem whose discourse is full of its author's presence but whose mobility never allows that author a settled position of authority'. One of the advantages of this approach, it seems to me, is that it allows for a deeper and subtler appreciation of the full scope of Byron's ludic sense of humour.

The mention of Italian literature here brings us within the purview of Peter Vassallo's *Byron: The Italian Literary Influence* (1984), in which the extent of Byron's reading of such poets as Alfieri, Ariosto, Casti, Dante, Petrarch, Pulci, and Tasso is documented and analysed from *Parisina* onwards. In particular, Vassallo focuses on Byron's indebtedness to the Italian burlesque tradition of Casti and Pulci for the satirical mode of *Beppo*, *Don Juan*, and *The Vision of Judgment* (all written in Italy) and on how that influence, especially Pulci's, served him 'in his crusade against the moral cant of the day'. What becomes apparent from this study is how Byron's encounter with Italian literature and with Italy itself helped to release latent energies which might otherwise and elsewhere have remained dormant. In an important way his exposure to Italian literature on Italian soil made him the *English* satirist *par excellence*.

Philip Martin's *Byron: A Poet before his Public* (1982) is a rather different matter from his Bakhtin essay, being largely concerned with how Byron's relationship to his public 'determines his competitive and anxious relation to his contemporaries, and governs the nature of his poetry'. Martin gives a provocatively abrasive account of Byron's attitude to his own works—which is characterized as 'irresponsible' (*Childe Harold*, the tales, and the dramas being seen as insincere and confused outpourings, whilst *Don Juan* relies on shock tactics)—and to his readers, whose applause he at once solicited and yet held in contempt.

This last attitude is shared by the Byron of Jerome Christensen's *Lord Byron's Strength: Romantic Writing and Commercial Society* (1993). This is a dense and recondite study whose vast canvas is deeply involved with and animated by poststructuralist, historicist-materialist criticism. Through a series of socio-economic engagements with virtually the entire corpus of Byron's works, Christensen monitors Byron's protean relationship to the rising consumer-capitalist society and his strategic exploitation and manipulation of 'Lord Byron' as a commodity-product in a market he created yet despised, arguing that Byron's 'Strength' (of the title) lies in his overcoming that very 'Byronism' which commercial society sought to impose upon *him*, Byron (the use or non-use of inverted commas is crucial here and throughout the volume). That is, as I see it, Byron constantly dodges his own projected marketable image of 'Lord Byron' and is always one step ahead of his public who, once it has thought to fix him and labelled the 'Byronic', finds he has moved on and assumed another guise. Hence he remains disconcertingly elusive, indefinable, continually evading capture, reducibility, a finite public shape—which is precisely the strength and 'privilege' of '*Lord*' Byron. In Christensen's words: 'If his evasion of reference identifies Lord Byron's Romanticism, his contempt expresses his strength. However expressed, that strength . . . is irreducible; . . . *Lord* marks Byron's privilege, and in part it is a privilege to confound reference.'

From a very different perspective, William St Clair is also concerned with Byron's readership and the marketing of his works. In his exemplary essay 'The Impact of Byron's Writings: An Evaluative Approach', contributed to Andrew Rutherford's *Byron: Augustan and Romantic* (1990), St Clair draws on statistics in the Treasury archive and the records of sales in the Murray archives in order to provide a quantifiable assessment of Byron's impact on the con-temporary market. What emerges from his analysis is that there were *two* con-stituencies amongst Byron's readers: one consisting of members of the upper echelons of society who enjoyed *Childe Harold* and the tales and with whom Byron remained popular up until 1816; the other consisting of those belong-ing to the lower, middle, and upper working classes with whom Byron became increasingly popular after 1816, who 'read *Don Juan* with enthusiasm but were largely indifferent to *Childe Harold* and the *Tales*'.

From yet another point of view Byron and his readership is the critical focus of Andrew Elfenbein's *Byron and the Victorians* (1995), which is the first study to devote itself to that subject and is both a reassessment of Byron and 'Byronism' and an important reinterpretation of Victorianism. Questioning various assumptions he feels Christensen and others have overlooked or taken for granted, Elfenbein sets out to explore the answer as to why Byron should have become so readily and immediately identified with his heroes during his lifetime: 'My overall concern is not with how Byron revealed himself in his heroes but with what in his writing made his first readers certain that he did.'

This distinction is crucial and operative. Taking us through *The Corsair, Childe Harold, Manfred,* and *Don Juan,* Elfenbein argues that the very 'abstractness' of their descriptions promotes a 'curiosity about the origins of the hero's situation' which Byron refuses to gratify. This leads to an eroticized reading of the texts wherein desire and expectation are never satisfied, until, in *Don Juan,* Byron 'jettisons this language' and 'foregrounds his impatience with the mysteriousness of his earlier representations'. So successful was his own attack on 'Byronism', indeed, 'that it closed off satire as a genre through which Victorian writers could define themselves against Byronism: Byron had done it first'. Hence 'Byronism' had to be created (or recreated) by the literary institutions of the nineteenth century such as the periodical press. This sets the ground for the subsequent chapters which examine how 'Victorian authors created themselves in relation to a past associated with Byron'. The choice of authors is selective but highly representative. Concentrating on specific texts of Carlyle, the Brontës, Tennyson, Bulwer-Lytton, Disraeli, and Wilde, Elfenbein illustrates how they engaged either with Byron's own works or with 'Byronism' as at that moment conceptualized.

The notion of 'Byronism' is challenged from another angle by Malcolm Kelsall in *Byron's Politics* (1987). This study seeks to demythologize Byron and to define his political position against the background of a contemporary opposition. That background, Kelsall argues, was provided initially by the Holland House circle into whose orbit of influence Byron was drawn in 1812, and whose political heritage was rooted in the ideology of the revolutionaries of 1688. Thus, in his discussion of the Frame Work Bill Speech (1812), Kelsall locates Byron working within the Whig patrician tradition, deploying its policy of liberal aristocratic 'resistance' and sharing its discourse of wearied, ineffectual opposition. In his subsequent chapters, dealing successively with *Childe Harold,* IV, *Marino Faliero, The Two Foscari, The Vision of Judgment,* and *Don Juan,* Kelsall finds Byron still locked within this discourse, unable to adapt it to fruitful opposition or to translate it into effective political action. In the mean time he has become an isolated figure, clinging to the obsolete tradition of the 'buff and blue' whose cause had been deserted by his fellow peers, yet dissociating himself from the radical reformers. As such, 'Byron's role is that of a kind of political gadfly, one who attacks when the *estro* is upon him. Because he has no political base, he has no effective role.' His rhetorical outbursts remain vague and bombastic; his gestures towards 'freedom' and 'the people' mere hyperbole and humbug. In the end Byron can offer no practical strategy for political progress.

Following Kelsall's lead, similar such syllables of dolour have been expressed by David Craig and Andrew Noble in their contributions to Angus Calder's *Byron and Scotland: Radical or Dandy?* (1989b). The case for the defence, however, has been vigorously championed by Michael Foot in his racily written and eminently readable *The Politics of Paradise: A Vindication of Byron* (1988): 'I disagree so profoundly with almost every conclusion Professor Kelsall reaches that no profitable argument between us is possible.' For Foot, Byron's life, works, and politics cannot be divorced from one another. Hence his study takes the form of a fusion of salient biographical detail, significant moments of political *action*, and generous quotations from Byron's poetry, letters, journals, speeches, and other prose writings—held together and interwoven by Foot's own commentary and narrative (he is especially strong on *Sardanapalus* and *Cain*, and on Byron's relation to Swift). The overall result is a down-to-earth, undogmatic, though not uncritical presentation of Byron, who is allowed to speak to us and act before us in his own person, which enlists the sympathy and intelligence of the reader in a collaborative effort to establish just what made Byron 'the poet of the Revolution'. The answer for Foot, which we are invited to share, lies in 'the combination of word and deed which he fashioned' and which 'made his faith more potent than that of any of his great contemporaries'.

Forming no part in this debate, but still concerned with politics, is Daniel Watkins's *Social Relations in Byron's Eastern Tales* (1987). Watkins reads the tales both as political allegories and as complexes of social relations and inter-actions, which in turn reveal the political conditions and cultural climate in which they were written: 'Collectively, the Eastern Tales dramatize powerfully the world into which Byron awoke to find himself famous in 1812.' Engag-ing with each of the tales individually, Watkins argues that 'While not every episode can be traced to a specific contemporary event and while not every tyrant is meant to represent the Prince Regent in simple allegorical fashion', none the less the tales project 'in a general yet systematic way a full array of social relations that dominated Byron's world'. Amongst other things, Watkins has some valuable comments to make about Byron's attitude to Napoleon— which is well documented—which might profitably be read in conjunction with James Hogg's equally well-documented, exhaustive essay 'Byron's Vacillat-ing Attitude towards Napoleon' (1981).

The tales have, naturally enough, become the focus of one of the major new areas in Byron criticism: Orientalism. This is a province whose borders were opened up specifically by Edward Said in his highly influential *Orientalism* (1978), and more recently expanded by him in *Culture and Imperialism* (1993). Sadly, however, Said has little to say about Byron individually (there are scat-tered references to him in the former work; none in the latter); and to lump him together indiscriminately with Beckford, Moore, Scott, Goethe, and others, whose treatment of the East is regarded as naive, lacking in experience, and merely exploitative, is, I fear, a grave misrepresentation. Indeed, this is precisely Mohammed Sharafuddin's point of departure in *Islam and Romantic Orientalism: Literary Encounters with the Orient* (1994), which revises and corrects many of Said's dismissive judgements and over-determined generalizations (though without seeking to overthrow Said's underlying thesis). Analysing the perceptions and representations of the East in the works of Beckford, Southey, Landor, Moore, and Byron, Sharafuddin illustrates how each of them in their own way acknowledged Islam as a 'radically foreign' yet legitimate form of life: an *alternative* culture to that of the West, possessing its own distinctive and self-validating moral values, customs, and traditions. If Beckford is seen as the pioneering figure, then Byron is shown as bringing Orientalism to its most sophisticated level of maturity. Through a series of remarkably fresh close readings which concentrate exclusively on the tales, Sharafuddin reveals Byron's deeply sympathetic and positive engagement with the East, and the realism with which he captures its local colour and presents its native character and identity.

Nigel Leask's important historicist study *British Romantic Writers and the East: Anxieties of Empire* (1992) is also concerned with representations of the East in the work of Byron, Shelley, De Quincey, and Coleridge. Again, concentrating exclusively on the tales, Leask demonstrates how each engages with the social and political implications of the patriarchal imperialist colonizing venture, and how they reveal Byron's indignation at (yet anxiety over his own tacit complicity in) its exploitative and manipulative strategies. 'The pathos of the *Tales* lies in Byron's discovery of the extent to which English (and European) culture had become permeated and corroded by what he regarded as the pernicious influence of imperialism, consistently figured as the abandonment of an aristocratic, republican, civic humanist heritage. On a wider scale, Byron sought to elegize the loss of contact of modern European civilization with its classical, Hellenistic source.'

If the weight falls on politics in Leask's account, it falls more on religion in Marilyn Butler's revisionist-historicist chapters 'The Orientalism of Byron's *Giaour*', contributed to Bernard Beatty's and Vincent Newey's *Byron and the Limits of Fiction* (1988), and 'Byron and the Empire of the East', contributed to Andrew Rutherford's *Byron: Augustan and Romantic* (1990). Focusing specifically on *The Giaour* and *Sardanapalus*, Butler sets Byron's liberal-humanist perception and experience of the East against the background of contemporary English missionizing and empire-building in Greece (*The Giaour*) and India (*Sardanapalus*). In both, Butler argues, Byron questions the civilizing, liberating, and progressive claims of Christianity and its evangelists and reveals how Christian orthodoxy is just as backward and tyrannical as Islam. With regard to the Greek movement for independence, *The Giaour* registers Byron's view that intervention by the European powers 'would be to exchange one alien despotism for another'. In *Sardanapalus*, which Butler finds 'preoccupied with issues of religious belief', Byron is seen as 'satirizing the new notion that the British have a God-given mission to colonise and govern other nations, or that killing people may become in the right circumstances a religious activity'.

Byron's *own* religious beliefs and attitudes have been examined by John Clubbe in *English Romanticism: The Grounds of Belief* (1983), who regards Byron as belonging to that second generation of Romantic poets, including Shelley and Keats, who were thoroughly imbued with Milton, the Bible, and patristic writings, yet remained sceptical and intellectually unsystematic in outlook. Much the same general conclusion is reached by the contributors to Wolf Hirst's *Byron, the Bible, and Religion* (1991b), who discuss Byron's knowledge of and allusions to the Bible, his use of biblical imagery and sources, his adaptation of biblical episodes, and his ambivalent attitude towards Christianity, with particular reference to his biblical dramas *Cain* and *Heaven and Earth*.

Which brings us finally to the dramas themselves. Over the last twenty years or so these have steadily begun to receive the serious critical attention and recognition they deserve, providing a corrective perhaps to the view that the Romantic period was essentially a non-dramatic one. Although Samuel Chew's *The Dramas of Lord Byron* (1915) remains valuable as a carefully researched and well-documented general introduction, more recent studies have approached the dramas from a number of different perspectives.

In *Byron Tonight* (1982), Margaret Howell discusses their productions on the English and American stage during the nineteenth century. From an examination of their prompt-copies she shows how—quite contrary to Byron's express desire—they were adapted to suit the taste and emotional demands and expectations of the audience of the day, with elaborate scenery and striking stage effects. Howell also registers that of all the plays producers were most drawn to *Werner*—the actor-manager William Macready making it his own in virtuoso performances that captivated audiences—while *Cain* and *The Deformed Transformed* were almost universally avoided.

Boleslaw Taborski also studies the productions and performance history of the plays, principally on the English and European stage, in his book *Byron and the Theatre* (1972), and the stage mechanics and practicalities of the productions of *Cain* by Constantin Stanislavsky in 1920, and Jerzy Grotowski in 1960, in his contribution to Edwin Stürzl's and James Hogg's *Byron: Poetry and Politics* (1981).

B. G. Tandon's *The Imagery of Lord Byron's Plays* (1976) explores the distinctive images Byron deploys in each of the dramas, in order to identify the individual atmosphere they each inhabit and the ambivalences and contradictions they present.

In *The Metaphysics of Byron* (1976), John Ehrstine follows the recurring patterns of thought in the poetry to illustrate how Byron's concern with the positive and negative aspects of man's condition is similarly developed and dramatized in the plays.

The work of G. Wilson Knight, *Byron and Shakespeare* (1966), Paulino Lim, *The Style of Lord Byron's Plays* (1973), Marjean Purinton, *Romantic Ideology*

Unmasked (1994), Kavita Sharma, *Byron's Plays: A Reassessment* (1982), and Allen Perry Whitmore, *The Major Characters of Lord Byron's Plays* (1974), as well as the articles by Thomas Ashton (1974), Anne Barton (1975, 1990), Murray Biggs (1992), D. M. De Silva (1981), Francis Doherty (1988), David Erdman (1939), Wolf Hirst (1980, 1981), E. D. H. Johnson (1942), Malcolm Kelsall (1978), Robert Ryan (1990), Daniel Watkins (1981), and Susan Wolfson (1991), have all added significantly to our understanding and appreciation of the political, philosophical, ideological, formal, and stylistic dimensions of the plays.

However, within the last eight years two especially fine studies have appeared: Martyn Corbett's *Byron and Tragedy* (1988), and Richard Lansdown's *Byron's Historical Dramas* (1992). Corbett challenges the notion that the dramas are 'essentially undramatic', and therefore examines them *as dramas* in the light of what he perceives as Byron's 'tragic vision': that is, an outlook which combines, though does not resolve, such contradictions as pessimism, yet stoical affirmation; a malignant force of destiny, yet man's courageous (if hopeless) defiance; social or political oppression, yet the individual's self-assertive will. Corbett traces the evolution of this 'tragic vision' from its first appearance in *Manfred* (itself an offspring of the lyric 'Prometheus'), through the historical tragedies and biblical mysteries, to *Werner* and *The Deformed Transformed*. Byron's entire dramatic output is thus presented as a prolonged meditation on the condition of man; each of the dramas addressing this theme in its own particular way, exploring man's relationship to the cosmos, to his community, and to his own self and the roles he is obliged to play, and in so playing must learn to distinguish between. The historical (or Venetian) dramas, for instance, dramatize the conflicting interests of the state and the individual. Moreover, Corbett finds that their intellectual concerns 'evince a striking, symmetrical relationship' with the biblical mysteries, so that '*Marino Faliero* complements *Cain*, whilst *Heaven and Earth* forms an opposing, but equally complementary group with *The Two Foscari*'. Here too a valuable parallel is drawn between the form of *Heaven and Earth*—the 'most experimental in style' of all Byron's dramas—and that of Shelley's *Prometheus Unbound*; while in *Werner* and *The Deformed Transformed* (in which Byron learned 'to adapt the style of *Don Juan* to dramatic purposes'), Corbett observes Byron exploring 'the possibility of integrating the comic with the tragic'. This volume is a happy conflation of interpretation, elucidation, and analysis, and for the first-time reader there is the bonus of a synopsis of each play—the mere mechanics of plot—before the defter tools of criticism are brought to bear. It is the best starting point for the dramas as a whole.

Richard Lansdown concentrates specifically on the historical dramas—*Marino Faliero*, *Sardanapalus*, and *The Two Foscari*—arguing that Byron's idea of the theatre 'was bound up with other, predominantly neo-classical ideas of the political uses and the historical aspects of drama' which, in turn, 'were inexorably bound up with his attitudes to Shakespeare'. Those attitudes, Lansdown claims, were crucially defined in opposition to the 'critical *ideas* of Shakespeare promulgated during the Romantic era' and elaborated in the writings of such commentators as Madame de Staël, the brothers Schlegel, Coleridge, Hunt, and Hazlitt. Hence the three plays are seen as allusive rereadings or remodellings of a Shakespearian paradigm (respectively, *Julius Caesar*, *Antony and Cleopatra*, and *Coriolanus*), whose subtextual corollaries and thematic parallels provide the enabling force or initiating influence for the intellectual and historical preoccupations and representations Byron seeks to dramatize. The initiating text for Lansdown's own discussion is 'Churchill's Grave' (*Hamlet* is the paradigm here), in which Byron is shown as dramatizing himself as an echo, or 'transposition', of Churchill, as a means of reading, or engaging with, his *own* history and fate, and the perplexities they raise, which notion is more fully explored in connection with the dramas themselves. Lansdown's whole debate is preceded by a fascinating account of the state of Regency theatre at the time, and Byron's involvement with it as a member of the subcommittee of the Drury Lane Theatre, which reveals such details as the management and decision policies, the selection processes and political intriguing behind the production of performances, and the nature, taste, and influence of the theatre-going public, thus providing a defined backdrop against which Byron's dramas were written.

On a final note, special mention should be made of the articles and other work I have not touched on here by Drummond Bone, Michael G. Cooke, Malcolm Kelsall, and Jerome J. McGann; also, the two superb collections of original essays, *Byron and the Limits of Fiction*, edited by Bernard Beatty and Vincent Newey (1988), and *Byron: Augustan and Romantic*, edited by Andrew Rutherford (1990). The principal locations for continuing criticism on Byron are *Byron Journal*, *Keats–Shelley Journal*, *Keats–Shelley Review*, the recently founded, biannual *Romanticism*, and *Studies in Romanticism*. Of the last, two recent issues have devoted themselves exclusively to Byron, and to *Sardanapalus: Studies in Romanticism*, 27 (Winter 1988), and 31 (Fall 1992), respectively.

CODA

Byron has had, and continues to have, an enormous influence on the other arts—especially music and painting. Amongst painters, the two outstanding examples are Turner and Delacroix. David Blayney Brown's *Turner and Byron* (1992) provides a splendidly illustrated catalogue of Turner's works on Byronic subjects and the places associated with him, as well as a detailed introduction and commentary. See also Lindsay Stainton's *Turner's Venice* (1985); and, for

Delacroix, Martin Meisel's article 'Pictorial Engagements: Byron, Delacroix, Ford Madox Brown' (1988).

Amongst musicians, the catalogue of examples comprises virtually every major (and many minor) composer of the nineteenth and early twentieth centuries, from Beethoven to Virgil Thomson. In this instance, see the articles by Walter Bernhart (1987), F. W. Brownlow (1978), Paul Chancellor (1960), Glyn Court (1956), Paul Douglass (1986), Alice Levine (1982), and Ronald Stevenson (1983).

Byron's *Hebrew Melodies*, with their original settings by Isaac Nathan, have recently been reproduced with an excellent introduction and commentary by Frederick Burwick and Paul Douglass (1988).

To mark the bicentenary of Byron's birth, a fine recording of a selection of his poetry—set to music by Nathan, Schumann, Mendelssohn, Mussorgsky, Rimsky-Korsakov, Hugo Wolf, Busoni, Nietzsche, and Charles Ives, amongst others—was produced by the British Council in Austria, with Wolfgang Holzmair (baritone) and Thomas Palm (piano): *Two Centuries of Byron in Song*, Preiser Records: 150048–1 (1988).

Schoenberg's truly remarkable *Ode to Napoleon Buonaparte*—a setting of Byron's poem for speaker, piano, and string quartet, Op. 41a (1942), later arranged for speaker, piano, and string orchestra, Op. 41b (1944)—has been recorded on various occasions, and as variously. The best to date of Op. 41a is that by Pierre Boulez and the Ensemble Intercontemporain, with Alain Neveux (piano) and David Wilson-Johnson as a first-rate speaker: CBS Records: 74025 (1982). Thereafter is that by the LaSalle Quartet, with Stefan Litwin (piano) and Kenneth Griffiths (speaker): Deutsche Grammophon: 437 036–2 (1986). The programme notes for this last include Schoenberg's preface 'How I came to compose the Ode to Napoleon' (written in his delightfully quirky English), and his own translation of the *Ode* into German—though, significantly, it is Byron's *English* text that he sets to music. A recent recording of Op. 41b has been made by Yuli Torovsky and I Musici de Montréal, with Marc-André Hamelin (piano) and Kevin McMillan (speaker): Chandos Records: 9116 (1992).

REFERENCES

LIFE, LETTERS, AND RELATED MATERIAL

Cameron, Kenneth Neill, and Reiman, Donald H. (eds.), *Shelley and his Circle, 1773–1822*, 8 vols. (Cambridge, Mass., 1961–86).
Cline, C. L., *Byron, Shelley and their Pisan Circle* (London, 1952).
Elwin, Malcolm, *Lord Byron's Wife* (London, 1962).

Elwin, Malcolm, *Lord Byron's Family* (London, 1975).

Graham, Peter W. (ed.), *Byron's Bulldog: The Letters of John Cam Hobhouse to Lord Byron* (Columbus, Oh., 1984).

Grosskurth, Phyllis, *Byron: The Flawed Angel* (London, 1997).

Lovell, Ernest J., Jr. (ed.), *His Very Self and Voice: Collected Conversations of Lord Byron* (New York, 1954).

—— (ed.), *Medwin's Conversations of Lord Byron* (Princeton, 1966).

—— (ed.), *Lady Blessington's Conversations of Lord Byron* (Princeton, 1969).

Marchand, Leslie A., *Byron: A Biography*, 3 vols. (London, 1957).

—— *Byron: A Portrait* (London, 1971; paperback edn., 1993).

—— (ed.), *Byron's Letters and Journals*, 13 vols. (London, 1973–94).

—— (ed.), *Lord Byron: Selected Letters and Journals* (London, 1982; paperback edn., 1993).

Maurois, André, *Byron* (New York, 1930).

Mayne, Ethel Colburn, *Byron*, 2 vols. (London, 1912; rev. edn. in 1 vol., 1924).

—— *The Life of Lady Byron* (London, 1929).

Moore, Doris Langley, *The Late Lord Byron: Posthumous Dramas* (London, 1961).

—— *Lord Byron: Accounts Rendered* (London, 1974).

Moore, Thomas, *Letters and Journals of Lord Byron: With Notices of his Life*, 2 vols. (London, 1830).

Nicolson, Harold, *Byron: The Last Journey* (London, 1924; new edn. with suppl. ch., 1940).

Origo, Iris, *The Last Attachment* (London, 1949).

Page, Norman (ed.), *Byron: Interviews and Recollections* (London, 1985).

—— *A Byron Chronology* (London, 1988).

Paston, George, and Quennell, Peter, *'To Lord Byron': Feminine Profiles* (London, 1939).

Prothero, Rowland E. (ed.), *The Works of Lord Byron: A New, Revised and Enlarged Edition, with Illustrations. Letters and Journals*, 6 vols. (London, 1898–1901).

Quennell, Peter, *Byron: The Years of Fame* (London, 1935).

—— *Byron in Italy* (London, 1941).

—— *Byron: The Years of Fame; Byron in Italy* (rev. edns. In 1 vol. of 1935 and 1941; London, 1974).

St Clair, William, *That Greece Might Still be Free: The Philhellenes in the War of Independence* (Oxford, 1972).

—— *Trelawny: The Incurable Romancer* (London, 1977).

—— *The Godwins and the Shelleys: The Biography of a Family* (London, 1989).

Trelawny, Edward John, *Records of Shelley, Byron, and the Author*, ed. David Wright (Harmondsworth, 1973).

TEXTS

Ashton, Thomas L., *Byron's Hebrew Melodies* (London, 1972).

Auden, W. H. (ed.), *Byron: Selected Poetry and Prose* (New York, 1963).

Burnett, T. A. J. (ed.), *Lord Byron*, vii: *Childe Harold's Pilgrimage Canto III*, The Manuscripts of the Younger Romantics (New York, 1988).

Burwick, Frederick, and Douglass, Paul (eds.), *A Selection of Hebrew Melodies, Ancient and Modern, by Isaac Nathan and Lord Byron* (Tuscaloosa, Ala., 1988).

Cochran, Peter (ed.), *Lord Byron*, xiii: *The Prisoner of Chillon and Don Juan, Canto IX*, The Manuscripts of the Younger Romantics (New York, 1995).

Coleridge, Ernest Hartley (ed.), *The Works of Lord Byron: A New, Revised and Enlarged Edition, with Illustrations. Poetry*, 7 vols. (London, 1898–1904).

—— (ed.), *The Poetical Works of Lord Byron: The Only Complete and Copyright Text in One Volume* (London, 1905).

Dunn, Douglas (ed.), *A Choice of Byron's Verse* (London, 1974).

Erdman, David V., and Worrall, David (eds.), *Lord Byron*, vi: *Childe Harold's Pilgrimage*, The Manuscripts of the Younger Romantics (New York, 1991).

Glover, A. S. B. (ed.), *Byron: Selected Poetry* (Harmondsworth, 1954).

Jump, John D. (ed.), *Byron: Childe Harold's Pilgrimage and Other Romantic Poems* (London, 1975).

Levine, Alice, and McGann, Jerome J. (eds.), *Lord Byron*, ii: *Don Juan: Cantos I–V*, The Manuscripts of the Younger Romantics (New York, 1985).

—— —— (eds.), *Lord Byron*, i: *Poems 1807–1818*, The Manuscripts of the Younger Romantics (New York, 1986).

—— —— (eds.), *Lord Byron*, iii: *Poems 1819–1822*, The Manuscripts of the Younger Romantics (New York, 1988*a*).

—— —— (eds.), *Lord Byron*, iv: *Miscellaneous Poems*, The Manuscripts of the Younger Romantics (New York, 1988*b*).

Low, Donald A. (ed.), *Byron: Selected Poetry and Prose*, Routledge English Texts (London, 1995).

McConnell, Frank D. (ed.), *Byron's Poetry*, Norton Critical Editions (New York, 1978).

McGann, Jerome J. (ed.), *Lord Byron: The Complete Poetical Works*, 7 vols. (Oxford, 1980–93).

—— (ed.), *Byron: A Critical Edition of the Major Works*, The Oxford Authors (Oxford, 1986).

—— (ed.), *Byron: A Selection of his Finest Poems*, Oxford Poetry Library (Oxford, 1994).

Marchand, Leslie A. (ed.), *Don Juan, by Lord Byron* (Boston, 1958).

More, Paul Elmer (ed.), *The Complete Poetical Works of Lord Byron* (Boston, 1905; rev. edn. by Robert Gleckner, 1975).

Nicholson, Andrew (ed.), *Lord Byron*, v: *Don Juan: Cantos VI–VII*, The Manuscripts of the Younger Romantics (New York, 1989).

—— (ed.), *Lord Byron: The Complete Miscellaneous Prose* (Oxford, 1991).

—— (ed.), *Lord Byron*, viii: *Don Juan: Cantos III–IV*, The Manuscripts of the Younger Romantics (New York, 1992).

—— (ed.), *Lord Byron*, ix: *Don Juan: Cantos X, XI, XII and XVII*, The Manuscripts of the Younger Romantics (New York, 1993).

—— (ed.), *Lord Byron*, x: *Don Juan: Cantos XIV and XV*, The Manuscripts of the Younger Romantics (New York, 1995).

Page, Frederick (ed.), *Byron: The Poetical Works*, Oxford Standard Authors (Oxford, 1904; rev. edn. by John Jump, 1970).

Skelton, Robin (ed.), *Selected Poems of Byron* (London, 1964).

Steffan, Truman Guy, *Lord Byron's Cain: Twelve Essays and a Text with Variants and Annotations* (Austin, Tex., 1968).

Steffan, Truman Guy, and W. W. Pratt (eds.), *Byron's Don Juan: A Variorum Edition*, 4 vols. (Austin, Tex., 1957; rev. edn., 1971).

—— Steffan, E., and Pratt, W. W. (eds.), *Lord Byron: Don Juan* (Harmondsworth, 1973; rev. edns., 1977 and 1982).

Wolfson, Susan J., and Manning, Peter J. (eds.), *Lord Byron: Selected Poems* (Harmondsworth, 1996).

[Wright, John (ed.)], *The Works of Lord Byron with his Letters and Journals and his Life by Thomas Moore*, 17 vols. (London, 1832–3).

BIBLIOGRAPHIES AND REFERENCE

Clubbe, John, 'Byron', in Frank Jordan (ed.), *The English Romantic Poets: A Review of Research and Criticism* (4th edn., New York, 1985).

Hagelman, Charles W., Jr., and Barnes, Robert J., *A Concordance to Byron's Don Juan* (New York, 1967) [cued to Steffan and Pratt 1957].

Looper, Travis, *Byron and the Bible: A Compendium of Biblical Usage in the Poetry of Lord Byron* (Metuchen, NJ, 1978).

Santucho, Oscar José, and Goode, Clement Tyson, Jr., *George Gordon, Lord Byron: A Comprehensive Bibliography of Secondary Materials in English, 1807–1974, with a Critical Review of Research* (Metuchen, NJ, 1977) [An updated edition to 1990 has recently been published (1997)].

Wise, Thomas James, *A Bibliography of the Writings in Verse and Prose of George Gordon Noel, Baron Byron*, 2 vols. (London [Printed for Private Circulation Only], 1932–3).

Yo, Yu Jin, 'A Select Bibliography for *Sardanapalus*', *Studies in Romanticism*, 31 (Fall 1992), 387–90.

Young, Ione Dodson, *A Concordance to the Poetry of Byron* (Austin, Tex., 1965) [cued to More (ed.) 1905].

CRITICISM

Almeida, Hermione de, *Byron and Joyce through Homer* (London, 1981).

Ashton, Thomas L., '*Marino Faliero*: Byron's "Poetry of Politics"', *Studies in Romanticism*, 13 (Winter 1974), 1–13.

Bainbridge, Simon, 'To "Sing it Rather Better": Byron, the Bards, and Waterloo', *Romanticism*, 1/1 (1995), 68–81.

Barton, Anne, '"A Light to lesson ages": Byron's Political Plays', in Jump (1975: 138–62).

—— '*Don Juan* Transformed', in Rutherford (1990: 199–220).

—— *Byron: Don Juan* (Cambridge, 1992).

Beatty, Bernard, *Byron's Don Juan* (London, 1985).

—— *Byron: Don Juan and Other Poems. A Critical Study* (Harmondsworth, 1987).

—— 'Fiction's Limit and Eden's Door', in Beatty and Newey (1988: 1–38).

—— 'Continuities and Discontinuities of Language and Voice in Dryden, Pope, and Byron', in Rutherford (1990: 117–35).

—— and Newey, Vincent (eds.), *Byron and the Limits of Fiction* (Liverpool, 1988).

Beaty, Frederick L., *Byron the Satirist* (De Kalb, Ill., 1985).

Bernhart, Walter, 'Examples of Byron's Impact on 19th Century German and Austrian Music', *Byron Journal*, 15 (1987), 38–54.

Biggs, Murray, 'Notes on Performing *Sardanapalus*', *Studies in Romanticism*, 31 (Fall 1992), 373–85.

Blackstone, Bernard, *Byron: A Survey* (London, 1975).

—— 'Byron & the *Republic*: The Platonic Background to Byron's Political Ideas', in Stürzl and Hogg (1981: 1–41).

Bloom, Harold (ed.), *George Gordon, Lord Byron: Modern Critical Views* (New York, 1986).

Bold, Alan (ed.), *Byron: Wrath and Rhyme* (London, 1983).

Bone, J. Drummond, 'Byron's Ravenna Diary Entry: What is Poetry?', *Byron Journal*, 6 (1978), 78–89.

—— 'Political Choices: *The Prophecy of Dante* and *Werner*' (1981*a*), in Stürzl and Hogg (1981: 152–65).

—— 'On "Influence", and on Byron's and Shelley's Use of *Terza Rima* in 1819', *Keats–Shelley Memorial Bulletin*, 22 (1981*b*), 38–48.

—— 'The Rhetoric of Freedom', in Bold (1983: 166–85).

—— 'Byron, Shelley and Contemporary Poetry 1820–1822' (1988*a*), in Curreli and Johnson (1988: 69–77).

—— '*Beppo*: The Liberation of Fiction' (1988*b*), in Beatty and Newey (1988: 97–125).

—— 'Byron, Scott, and Nostalgia' (1989), in Calder (1989*b*: 119–31).

—— 'First Look at Exile: Byron's Art in 1816', *Byron Journal*, 19 (1991), 69–79.

Boyd, Elizabeth French, *Byron's Don Juan: A Critical Study* (New Brunswick, NJ, 1945).

Brown, David Blayney, *Turner and Byron*, Tate Gallery Exhibition Publication (London, 1992).

Brownlow, F. W., 'Byron and the Musicians of his Time', *Byron Journal*, 6 (1978), 102–4.

Butler, E. M., *Byron and Goethe* (London, 1956).

Butler, Marilyn, 'The Orientalism of Byron's *Giaour*', in Beatty and Newey (1988: 78–96).

—— 'Byron and the Empire of the East', in Rutherford (1990: 63–81).

—— 'John Bull's Other Kingdom: Byron's Intellectual Comedy', *Studies in Romanticism*, 31 (Fall 1992), 281–94.

Calder, Angus, *Byron* (Milton Keynes, 1987).

—— ' "The Island": Scotland, Greece and Romantic Savagery' (1989*a*), in Calder (1989*b*: 132–50).

—— (ed.), *Byron and Scotland: Radical or Dandy?* (Edinburgh, 1989*b*).

Calder, Jenni, 'The Hero as Lover: Byron and Women', in Bold (1983: 103–24).

Carnall, Geoffrey, 'Byron as Unacknowledged Legislator', in Bold (1983: 125–41).

Chancellor, Paul, 'British Bards and Continental Composers', *Musical Quarterly*, 46 (Jan. 1960), 1–11.

Chandler, James, ' "Man fell with apples": The Moral Mechanics of *Don Juan*', in Levine and Keane (1993: 67–85).

Chew, Samuel C., *The Dramas of Lord Byron* (Göttingen, 1915).

—— *Byron in England: His Fame and after Fame* (London, 1924).

Christensen, Jerome, *Lord Byron's Strength: Romantic Writing and Commercial Society* (Baltimore, 1993).

Claridge, Laura, *Romantic Potency: The Paradox of Desire* (New York, 1992).

—— 'Love and Self-Knowledge, Identity in the Cracks: A Lacanian Reading of *Don Juan*', in Wood (1993: 26–55).

Clark, Philip F., 'Charles Baudelaire: Facets of Byron's French Legacy', in Stürzl and Hogg (1981: 265–300).

Clubbe, John, 'Byron as a Romantic Poet', in John Clubbe and Ernest J. Lovell, Jr., *English Romanticism: The Grounds of Belief* (London, 1983), ch. 6.

Cooke, M. G., *The Blind Man Traces the Circle: On the Patterns and Philosophy of Byron's Poetry* (Princeton, 1969).

—— 'Byron and Wordsworth: The Complementarity of a Rock and the Sea', in Robinson (1982: 19– 42).

—— 'Byron, Pope, and the Grand Tour', in Rutherford (1990: 165–80).

Cooper, Andrew M., 'Chains, Pains, and Tentative Gains: The Byronic Prometheus in the Summer of 1816', *Studies in Romanticism*, 27 (Winter 1988), 529–50.

Corbett, Martyn, *Byron and Tragedy* (New York, 1988).

—— 'Lugging Byron out of the Library', *Studies in Romanticism*, 31 (Fall 1992), 361–72.

Court, Glyn, 'Berlioz and Byron and *Harold in Italy*', *Music Review*, 17 (1956), 229–36.

Craig, David, 'Byron the Radical' (1989), in Calder (1989*b*: 7–22).

Crompton, Louis, *Byron and Greek Love* (Berkeley and Los Angeles, 1985).

Cronin, Richard, 'Mapping *Childe Harold* I and II', *Byron Journal*, 22 (1994), 14–30.

Curreli, Mario, and Johnson, Anthony L. (eds.), *Paradise of Exiles: Shelley and Byron In Pisa* (Salzburg, 1988; new, illus. edn., Pisa, 1993).

Davis, Philip, ' "I leave the thing a problem, like all things": On Trying to Catch up with Byron', in Beatty and Newey (1988: 242– 84).

De Silva, D. M., 'Byron's Politics and the History Plays', in Stürzl and Hogg (1981: 113–36).

Diakonova, Nina, 'Byron and Lermontov: Notes on Pechorin's "Journal" ', in Robinson (1982: 144–65).

—— 'Heine as an Interpreter of Byron', *Byron Journal*, 22 (1994), 63–9.

—— and Vacuro, Vadim, 'Byron and Russia: Byron and Nineteenth-Century Russian Literature', in Trueblood (1981: 143–59).

Doherty, Francis M., 'Byron and the Sense of the Dramatic', in Beatty and Newey (1988: 226– 41).

Douglass, Paul, 'Hebrew Melodies as Songs', *Byron Journal*, 14 (1986), 12–21.

Ehrstine, John W., *The Metaphysics of Byron* (The Hague, 1976).

Elfenbein, Andrew, *Byron and the Victorians* (Cambridge, 1995).

Eliot, T. S., 'Byron', in Bonamy Dobrée (ed.), *From Anne to Victoria* (London, 1937), 601–19; repr. in T. S. Eliot, *On Poetry and Poets* (London, 1957), 193–206, and in M. H. Abrams (ed.), *English Romantic Poets: Modern Essays in Criticism* (Oxford, 1960), 196–209.

England, A. B., 'The Style of *Don Juan* and Augustan Poetry' (1975*a*), in Jump (1975: 94–112).

—— *Byron's Don Juan and Eighteenth-Century Literature* (Lewisburg, Pa., 1975*b*).

Erdman, David V., 'Byron's Stage Fright: The History of his Ambition and Fear of Writing for the Stage', *English Literary History*, 6 (Sept. 1939), 219–43.

Escarpit, Robert, 'Byron and France: Byron as a Political Figure', in Trueblood (1981: 48–58).

Ferriss, Suzanne, 'Romantic Carnivalesque: Byron's *The Tale of Calil, Beppo*, and *Don Juan*', in Levine and Keane (1993: 133–49).

Fisch, Harold, 'Byron's Cain as Sacred Executioner' (1991), in Hirst (1991*b*: 25–38).

Fischer, Hermann, 'Byron's "Wrong Revolutionary Poetical System" and Romanticism', in Rutherford (1990: 221–39).

Foot, Michael, *The Politics of Paradise: A Vindication of Byron* (London, 1988).

Franklin, Caroline, *Byron's Heroines* (Oxford, 1992).

—— 'Juan's Sea Changes: Class, Race and Gender in Byron's *Don Juan*', in Wood (1993: 56–89).

Fuess, Claude M., *Byron as a Satirist in Verse* (New York, 1912).

Galperin, William H., *The Return of the Visible in British Romanticism* (Baltimore, 1993), ch. 8, 'The Postmodernism of *Childe Harold*', and 'Postscript: The Feminization of *Don Juan*'.

Garber, Frederick, *Self, Text and Romantic Irony: The Example of Byron* (Princeton, 1988).

Gassenmeier, Michael, 'Augustan Satires and Panegyrics on London and Byron's Image of the City', in Rutherford (1990: 136–64).

Giddey, Ernest, 'Byron and Switzerland: Byron's Political Dimension' (1981*a*), in Trueblood (1981: 179–90).

—— 'Aspects of the Myth of Natural Liberty in Byron's Poetry' (1981*b*), in Stürzl and Hogg (1981: 42–56).

Gleckner, Robert F., *Byron and the Ruins of Paradise* (Baltimore, 1967).

—— (ed.), *Critical Essays on Byron* (New York, 1991).

Goldberg, Leonard S., 'Byron and the Place of Religion' (1991), in Hirst (1991*b*: 153–68).

Graham, Peter W., *Don Juan and Regency England* (Charlottesville, Va., 1990).

—— 'Byron, Hobhouse, and Editorial Symbiosis', *Byron Journal*, 23 (1995), 14–21.

Guiliano, Cheryl Fallon, 'Marginal Discourse: The Authority of Gossip in *Beppo*' (1993*a*), in Levine and Keane (1993: 151–63).

—— 'Gulnare/Kaled's "Untold" Feminization of Byron's Oriental Tales', *Studies in English Literature*, 33 (1993*b*), 785–807.

Hayden, John O., *Romantic Bards and British Reviewers* (London, 1971).

Heinzelman, Kurt, 'Politics, Memory, and the Lyric: Collaboration as Style in Byron's *Hebrew Melodies*', *Studies in Romanticism*, 27 (Winter 1988), 515–27.

Hentschel, Cedric, 'Byron and Germany: The Shadow of Euphorion', in Trueblood (1981: 59–90).

Hirst, Wolf Z., 'Byron's Lapse into Orthodoxy: Au Unorthodox Reading of *Cain*', *Keats–Shelley Journal*, 29 (1980), 151–72.

—— ' "The Politics of Paradise," "Transcendental Cosmopolitics," and Plain Politics in Byron's *Cain* and Keats's *Hyperion*', in Stürzl and Hogg (1981: 243–64).

—— 'Byron's Revisionary Struggle with the Bible' (1991*a*), in Hirst (1991*b*: 77–100).

—— (ed.), *Byron, the Bible, and Religion* (London, 1991*b*).

Hoagwood, Terence Allan, 'Historicity and Scepticism in the Lake Geneva Summer', *Byron Journal*, 19 (1991), 90–103.

—— *Byron's Dialectic: Skepticism and the Critique of Culture* (London, 1993).

Hobsbaum, Philip, 'Byron and the English Tradition', in Bold (1983: 37–56).

Hofkosh, Sonia, 'The Writer's Ravishment: Woman and the Romantic Author—The Example of Byron', in Anne K. Mellor (ed.), *Romanticism and Feminism* (Bloomington, Ind., 1988), 93–114.

Hogg, James, 'Byron's Vacillating Attitude towards Napoleon', in Stürzl and Hogg (1981: 380–427).

Howell, Margaret, *Byron Tonight: A Poet's Plays on the Nineteenth Century Stage* (London, 1982).

Jack, Ian, *The Poet and his Audience* (Cambridge, 1984), ch. III, 'Byron: Too Sincere a Poet'.

Johnson, E. D. H., 'A Political Interpretation of Byron's *Marino Faliero*', *Modern Language Quarterly*, 3 (Sept. 1942), 417–25.

Jones, Steven E., 'Intertextual Influences in Byron's Juvenalian Satire', *Studies in English Literature*, 33 (1993), 771–83.

Joseph, M. K., *Byron the Poet* (London, 1964).

Jump, John D., *Byron* (London, 1972).

—— (ed.), *Byron: A Symposium* (London, 1975).

Keach, William, 'Political Inflection in Byron's *Ottava Rima*', *Studies in Romanticism*, 27 (Winter 1988), 551–62.

Kelsall, Malcolm, 'Goethe, Byron, Ibsen: The Faustian Idea on Stage', *Byron Journal*, 6 (1978), 66–76.

—— 'The Byronic Hero and Revolution in Ireland: The Politics of *Glenarvon*', *Byron Journal*, 9 (1981), 4–19 (also in Stürzl and Hogg 1981: 137–51).

—— *Byron's Politics* (Brighton, 1987).

—— 'Byron and the Romantic Heroine', in Rutherford (1990: 52–62).

—— 'The Slave-Woman in the Harem', *Studies in Romanticism*, 31 (Fall 1992), 315–31.

—— 'Byron and the Women of the Harem', in Levine and Keane (1993: 165–73).

—— 'Lord Byron', in *The Penguin History of Literature*, v: *The Romantic Period*, ed. David B. Pirie (Harmondsworth, 1994), 289–310.

Kernan, Alvin, *The Plot of Satire* (New Haven, 1965), 171–221.

Klein, Jürgen, 'Byron's Idea of Democracy: An Investigation into the Relationship between Literature and Politics', in Stürzl and Hogg (1981: 57–87).

Knight, G. Wilson, *Lord Byron: Christian Virtues* (London, 1952).

—— *Byron and Shakespeare* (London, 1966).

Lansdown, Richard, *Byron's Historical Dramas* (Oxford, 1992).

Leask, Nigel, *British Romantic Writers and the East: Anxieties of Empire* (Cambridge, 1992).

Leavis, F. R., 'Byron's Satire', in *Revaluation* (1936; Harmondsworth, 1972), 139–44.

Lessenich, Rolf P., *Lord Byron and the Nature of Man* (Vienna, 1978).

Levine, Alice, 'Byron and the Romantic Composer', in Robinson (1982: 178–203).

—— and Keane, Robert N. (eds.), *Rereading Byron* (New York, 1993).

Levinson, Marjorie, 'A Question of Taste: Keats and Byron', in Levine and Keane (1993: 187–204).

Lim, Paulino M., *The Style of Lord Byron's Plays* (Salzburg, 1973).

Lovell, Ernest J., Jr., *Byron: The Record of a Quest. Studies in a Poet's Concept and Treatment of Nature* (Austin, Tex., 1949).

—— 'Irony and Image in *Don Juan*', in Clarence C. Thorpe, Carlos Baker, and Bennett Weaver (eds.), *The Major English Romantic Poets: A Symposium in Reappraisal* (Carbondale, Ill., 1957), 129–48; repr. in M. H. Abrams (ed.), *English Romantic Poets: Modern Essays in Criticism* (Oxford, 1960), 228–46.

McGann, Jerome J., *Fiery Dust: Byron's Poetic Development* (Chicago, 1968).

—— *Don Juan in Context* (London, 1976).

—— *The Romantic Ideology* (Chicago, 1983).

—— *The Beauty of Inflections* (Oxford, 1985).

—— *Towards a Literature of Knowledge* (Chicago, 1989).

—— ' "My Brain is Feminine": Byron and the Poetry of Deception', in Rutherford (1990: 26–51).

—— 'Hero with a Thousand Faces: The Rhetoric of Byronism', *Studies in Romanticism*, 31 (Fall 1992*a*), 295–313.

—— 'Byron and the Anonymous Lyric', *Byron Journal*, 20 (1992*b*), 27–45.

—— 'Lord Byron and "The Truth in Masquerade" ', in Levine and Keane (1993: 1–19).

Macovski, Michael, 'Byron, Bakhtin, and the Translation of History', in Levine and Keane (1993: 21–42).

Manning, Peter J., *Byron and his Fictions* (Detroit, 1978).

—— 'Tales and Politics: *The Corsair*, *Lara*, and *The White Doe of Rylestone*', in Stürzl and Hogg (1981: 204–30).

—— *Reading Romantics: Texts and Contexts* (Oxford, 1990).

Marchand, Leslie A., *Byron: A Critical Introduction* (Boston, 1965).

Martin, Philip W., *Byron: A Poet before his Public* (Cambridge, 1982).

—— 'Reading *Don Juan* with Bakhtin', in Wood (1993: 90–121).

Meisel, Martin, 'Pictorial Engagements: Byron, Delacroix, Ford Madox Brown', *Studies in Romanticism*, 27 (Winter 1988), 579–603.

Melchiori, Giorgio, 'Byron and Italy: Catalyst of the *Risorgimento*', in Trueblood (1981: 108–21).

Meyer, Eric, ' "I Know Thee Not, I Loathe Thy Race": Romantic Orientalism in the Eye of the Other', *English Literary History*, 58 (1991), 657–99.

Morgan, Edwin, 'Voice, Tone, and Transition in *Don Juan*', in Bold (1983: 57–77).

Moser, F. de Mello, 'Byron and Portugal: The Progress of an Offending Pilgrim', in Trueblood (1981: 132–42).

Nellist, Brian, 'Lyric Presence in Byron from the *Tales* to *Don Juan*', in Beatty and Newey (1988: 39–77).

Newey, Vincent, 'Authoring the Self: *Childe Harold* III and IV', in Beatty and Newey (1988: 148–90).

Noble, Andrew, 'Byron: Radical, Scottish Aristocrat' (1989), in Calder (1989*b*: 23–43).

Paley, Morton D., 'Envisioning Lastness: Byron's "Darkness", Campbell's "The Last Man", and the Critical Aftermath', *Romanticism*, 1/1 (1995), 1–14.

Protopsaltis, E. G., 'Byron and Greece: Byron's Love of Classical Greece and his Role in the Greek Revolution', in Trueblood (1981: 91–107).

ANDREW NICHOLSON

Pujals, Estaban, 'Byron and Spain: Byron's Poetic Vision of Spain', in Trueblood (1981: 160–78).

Punter, David, '*Don Juan*, or, the Deferral of Decapitation: Some Psychological Approaches', in Wood (1993: 122–53).

Purinton, Marjean D., *Romantic Ideology Unmasked: The Mentally Constructed Tyrannies in Dramas of William Wordsworth, Lord Byron, Percy Shelley, and Joanna Baillie* (London, 1994).

Quinones, Ricardo J., 'Byron's Cain: Between History and Theology' (1991), in Hirst (1991*b*: 39–57).

Redpath, Theodore, *The Young Romantics and Critical Opinion 1807–1824* (London, 1973).

Reiman, Donald H. (ed.), *The Romantics Reviewed, Part B: Byron and Regency Society Poets*, 5 vols. (New York, 1972).

—— *Romantic Texts and Contexts* (Columbia, Mo., 1987).

—— 'Byron in Italy: The Return of Augustus', in Rutherford (1990: 181–98).

—— 'Byron and the Uses of Refamiliarization', in Levine and Keane (1993: 101–17).

Richardson, Alan, 'Escape from the Seraglio: Cultural Transvestism in *Don Juan*', in Levine and Keane (1993: 175–85).

Robinson, Charles E. (ed.), *Lord Byron and his Contemporaries* (London, 1982).

Rutherford, Andrew (ed.), *Byron: The Critical Heritage* (London, 1970).

—— (ed.), *Byron: Augustan and Romantic* (London, 1990).

Ryan, Robert, 'Byron's *Cain*: The Ironies of Belief', *Wordsworth Circle*, 21 (1990), 41–5.

St Clair, William, 'The Impact of Byron's Writings: An Evaluative Approach', in Rutherford (1990: 1–25).

Seed, David, ' "The Platitude of Prose": Byron's Vampire Fragment in the Context of his Verse Narratives', in Beatty and Newey (1988: 126–47).

Sharafuddin, Mohammed, *Islam and Romantic Orientalism: Literary Encounters with the Orient* (London, 1994).

Sharma, Kavita A., *Byron's Plays: A Reassessment* (Salzburg, 1982).

Shilstone, Frederick W., *Byron and the Myth of Tradition* (London, 1988).

—— (ed.), *Approaches to Teaching Byron's Poetry* (New York, 1991).

Stabler, Jane, 'Pit-bull Poetics: One Battle in Byron's "War in Words"', *Romanticism*, 1/1 (1995), 82–9.

Stainton, Lindsay, *Turner's Venice*, British Museum Publications (London, 1985).

Stevens, Ray, 'Scripture and the Literary Imagination: Biblical Allusions in Byron's *Heaven and Earth*' (1991), in Hirst (1991*b*: 118–35).

Stevenson, Ronald, 'Byron as Lyricist: The Poet amongst the Musicians', in Bold (1983: 78–99).

Stevenson, Warren, 'Hebraism and Hellenism in the Poetry of Byron' (1991), in Hirst (1991*b*: 136–52).

Storey, Mark, *Byron and the Eye of Appetite* (London, 1986).

Stürzl, Edwin A., 'Byron and the Poets of the Austrian Vormärz', in Stürzl and Hogg (1981: 88–112).

—— 'Byron and Grillparzer', in Robinson (1982: 105–29).

—— and Hogg, James (eds.), *Byron: Poetry and Politics* (Salzburg, 1981).

Taborski, Boleslaw, *Byron and the Theatre* (Salzburg, 1972).

—— 'Byron's Theatre: Private Spleen or Cosmic Revolt. Theatrical Solutions—Stanislavsky to Grotowski', in Stürzl and Hogg (1981: 356–79).

Tandon, B. G., *The Imagery of Lord Byron's Plays* (Salzburg, 1976).

Thomas, Gordon K., 'Eros and Christianity: Byron in the Underground Resistance-Movement' (1991), in Hirst (1991b: 101–17).

Thorslev, Peter L., Jr., *The Byronic Hero: Types and Prototypes* (Minneapolis, 1962).

—— 'Post-Waterloo Liberalism: The Second Generation', *Studies in Romanticism*, 28 (Fall 1989), 437–61.

—— 'Byron and Bayle: Biblical Skepticism and Romantic Irony' (1991), in Hirst (1991: 58–76).

Treugutt, Stefan, 'Byron and Napoleon in Polish Romantic Myth', in Robinson (1982: 130–43).

Trueblood, Paul Graham (ed.), *Byron's Political and Cultural Influence in Nineteenth-Century Europe: A Symposium* (London, 1981).

Vassallo, Peter, *Byron: The Italian Literary Influence* (New York, 1984).

Wallace, Jennifer, ' "We are all Greeks"?: National Identity and the Greek War of Independence', *Byron Journal*, 23 (1995), 36–49.

Ward, Geoffrey, 'Byron's Artistry in Deep and Layered Space', in Beatty and Newey (1988: 191–225).

Watkins, Daniel P., 'Violence, Class-Consciousness and Ideology in Byron's History Plays', *English Literary History*, 48 (Winter 1981), 799–816.

—— *Social Relations in Byron's Eastern Tales* (London, 1987).

Watson, Nicola J., 'Trans-figuring Byronic Identity', in Mary A. Favret and Nicola J. Watson (eds.), *At the Limits of Romanticism: Essays in Cultural, Feminist, and Materialist Criticism* (Bloomington, Ind., 1994), 185–206.

Webb, Timothy, 'Byron and the Heroic Syllables', *Keats–Shelley Review*, 5 (1990), 41–74.

Whitmore, Allen Perry, *The Major Characters of Lord Byron's Plays* (Salzburg, 1974).

Whittler, Henry S., *Echoes in the Mirror: Facets of Reflection in Don Juan* (New York, 1990).

Wolfson, Susan, ' "Their She Condition": Cross-Dressing and the Politics of Gender in *Don Juan*', *English Literary History*, 54 (1987), 585–617.

—— 'Couplets, Self, and *The Corsair*', *Studies in Romanticism*, 27 (Winter 1988), 491–513.

—— ' "A Problem Few Dare Imitate": *Sardanapalus* and "Effeminate Character" ', *English Literary History*, 58 (1991), 867–902.

Wood, Nigel (ed.), *Don Juan*, Theory in Practice Series (Buckingham, 1993).

Zulawski, Juliusz, 'Byron and Poland: Byron and Polish Romantic Revolt', in Trueblood (1981: 122–31).

6. *Percy Bysshe Shelley*

JERROLD E. HOGLE

To turn to the history of scholarly work on Shelley is to confront a succession of fervid disagreements, sometimes wildly divergent interpretations of his works, and sudden changes of opinion about him in short spans of time. These conflicts, for the most part, point to the very different assumptions by which he and his writing have often been perceived. The reactions of contemporaries to what he actually published from 1810 to 1821, given his unmistakable political and anti-orthodox stances, vary across a wide continuum depending on each reviewer's social and religious affiliations, as we can see in what is reprinted from those years in White (1938), Hayden, Reiman (1972), Redpath, and Barcus. Moreover, the rehabilitation of both his personal reputation and the aims of his writing after his sudden death have been heavily determined, though there have been exceptions, by where his interpreters have placed themselves between those who would turn him into the ethereal 'pure poet' safe for developing middle-class tastes (including Mary Shelley, the first of his posthumous editors) and those who would retain him as a voice for radical social reform (from Horace Smith to Bernard Shaw). This split is best recounted by Fraistat (1994) and continues through much of the later nineteenth century (see Barcus and Engelberg), and it is only exacerbated by the way Shelley is eroticized in some of the commentary on him over that time (see Clarke). So great does this division over him become—and so distorted the 'Shelley myth', too often that of the 'ineffectual angel' suggested in the deceptive biography by T. J. Hogg—that much of the scholarship on Shelley since, beginning with the work of H. Buxton Forman in the 1880s, has been an effort to 'make Shelley whole', to reconstruct the 'actual' texts, literary contexts and sources, political connections, deliberate art, biographical facts, and overarching 'orientations' or 'schemes of thought' (and the relations of both to Shelley's medium, language) that are most basic to his writing in verse and prose.

This reconstruction of Shelley, though, has never been free of conflicting biases that have their own ideological orientations and thus their own class or group affiliations. If the nineteenth-century reaction to him was too neatly divided, and certainly too inclined to divorce the aesthetic and idealistic from the political and realistic in his works, the first half of the twentieth century, while it did start with a rise in Shelley's stock as a major 'Romantic' author (see Kipperman 1992), has seen a curious oscillation of attacks on and defences of him that say as much about the parties to the debate as they do about the different sides of Shelley that each respondent emphasizes so as to place him in a certain hierarchy of values. Nearly all the work on him since about 1950, it turns out, has been a *second* reconstruction of Shelley because of the vehement battle over him prior to and just after the Second World War that leaves him either in or out of sanctioned canons (now highly debatable constructs, as they should be) in circles connected with universities or elite organs of criticism. Among Shelley's works, T. S. Eliot finds only the Dantesque and unfinished *Triumph of Life* to be 'precise' poetic art by his standards. The rest of Shelley's poetry is too unaesthetically infected by 'creeds outworn, tyrants and priests' repugnant to Eliot's own Catholicism and his dissociation of the 'true' poetic tradition from direct political invective. C. S. Lewis answers Eliot in the 1930s by valuing the essentially Christian 'remaking of man' in Shelley's recasting of classical myths (see Hogle 1993). After all, even if Shelley is ostensibly anti-Christian, he at least continues an 'aristocratic tradition' peculiar to England that for Lewis obeys an English 'code of honour' which the American Eliot would not understand. F. R. Leavis, leader of the *Scrutiny* group at Cambridge by the mid-1930s, counters that defence—and helps establish the credentials of his mainly bourgeois colleagues for deciding what 'The Great Tradition' is—by pronouncing Shelley both morally decadent and hampered by a 'weak grasp upon the actual' in his excessively allusive and aristocratically abstract, rather than 'concrete', words and images. This typing of Shelley, combined with Eliot's, soon reappears among some American 'New Critics' seeking to establish the autonomy of poetry as an aesthetic concord of discords (see Barton) and thus as the quintessence of western culture's purity at the time of the Cold War against Communism (to which Marx's daughter, Eleanor Marx Aveling, was pleased to attach Shelley). Allen Tate helps cement this placement of Shelley in the 1940s when he finds the latter's rapid shifting among the vehicles and tenors of different metaphors to be evidence of, again, excessive 'abstraction' inclined to sweep past a *concordia discors* wrought from concrete particulars. Donald Davie must defend Shelley *for* the harmonic and disinterested irony valued by the 'new' criticism by pointing in the early 1950s to 'Shelley's Urbanity', his rapid movement between ethereal and earthly verbal registers for the sake of suggesting how much these different levels really do impinge on each other. Yet even here a social agenda (supposedly anathema to the 'New Criticism') is not far from view. Davie ends up echoing Lewis by saying that Shelley can combine what he does only because he 'had the birth and breeding'—and thus the education—of 'a gentleman'. One way or another in the earlier twentieth century, Shelley must be either exiled from or saved for 'high culture' within the assumptions that all these different aspirants use to attach themselves to it.

The more recent history of Shelley criticism, in turn, is my subject here. The second long-term reconstruction of Shelley is still very much under way. Even so, the range of assessments of him has generally remained as wide and diverse as ever. For devoted readers and interpreters, Shelley cannot inspire neutrality and cannot help but arouse reactions tied to definite ideological commitments, even if certain aspects of his work (or life) have to be emphasized or muted depending on what different lenses of perception urge us to see in him. Indeed, if there is an overall development in Shelley scholarship over the last half-century, it is one that 'makes Shelley whole' in its early stages by demonstrating his artistic, symbolic, myth-making, and/or philosophical integrity, though not always on the same grounds. Yet it is also a movement which, starting in the late 1970s, comes to view Shelley's thought and writing as more genuinely conflicted and 'heteroglossic' than any 'New Critical' irony would allow it to be, though some keep trying to save Shelley for that harmony of differences. The closer we have come to confronting the different assumptions by which we read Shelley in our time, the more we have come to see him *and* his texts as pulled between contending drives culturally, psychologically, artistically, and textually.

TEXTS AND TEXTUAL STUDIES

Shelley was able to see so few of his texts through authorized printings before his drowning in 1822 (and even had so many problems with the few printings he *did* affect) that the establishing of 'definitive' texts of his work remains a problem after over a century and a half of editorial efforts. Within the criteria for accurate Shelley texts so thoroughly presented by Donald Reiman in 1974, the most reliable (and best annotated) one-volume edition of Shelley is the 1977 Norton Critical Edition, rightly the source most often cited in professional criticism today, even in the face of the good one-volume selection published by Everyman's Library and recently revised and expanded (Shelley 1995). For those texts not fully or even partially presented in 1977 (*Queen Mab* with all its notes, *Laon and Cythna* (later retitled *The Revolt of Islam*), *Rosalind and Helen*, several lyrics and fragments, the letters, and all the prose except 'On Love', 'On Life', and the *Defence of Poetry*), the current reader must look for the most scholarly texts in very different places. *Laon and Cythna* (the original) is best presented in the second volume of Shelley (1973–5), the start of an otherwise problematic 'complete poetry' that was abandoned after the death of its editor, Neville Rogers. The other poetic works not in the Norton (at least until it is revised) can be satisfactorily cited from Shelley (1970a), the last revision of the Oxford Standard Authors volume on the poet; or, in the case of the shorter lyrics, from the meticulously edited texts (with variants) included in Chernaik; or, in the case of all the verse works written prior to 1818, from the fine first volume of Shelley (1989). Sadly, the only concordance to Shelley's poetry there is (F. S. Ellis's) is not keyed to these later editions, though it does remain helpful in tracing his most repeated allusions and word-patterns. As for the poet's many letters, they are being re-edited as I write, so the best edition for consulting these remains Shelley (1964b), partly because of its appendix on 'Shelley's Reading' that locates evidence of what the poet read in his individual letters and Mary Shelley's journal. Meanwhile, Shelley's prose up to 1817, except for his Gothic novels of 1810, has been beauti-fully edited in Shelley (1993) (with a second volume to come). Those novels, *Zastrozzi* and *St Irvyne*, have been edited and annotated well in Shelley (1986). And if the prose after 1817 has to be cited from editions of the works other than the Norton, the prose volumes (v–vii) of Shelley (1926–30) are at least more reliable, despite how antiquated this edition has become, than the very erratic and often misdated Shelley (1954) (corrected, but not enough, in 1966). The poet's political prose, in any case, is fairly well collected in Shelley (1970b); only his major (if unfinished) 'Philosophical View of Reform' is less complete there than it is in Shelley (1990), which gathers the political prose and verse of 1819 in a paperback designed for non-academics. The important *Defence of Poetry* and his shorter critical writings and reviews (along with Thomas Love Peacock's 'The Four Ages of Poetry', to which the *Defence* responds) are con-veniently put together in Shelley (1967), although the most fully annotated text of the *Defence* is the thorough study of it by Delisle. Shelley's translations of Plato are best collated in Notopoulos (at least until the second volume of Shelley 1993, which will include all his prose translations edited by Timothy Webb), and the dates of his prose compositions, so complicated because many of them were unpublished notebook entries, are most fully and accurately listed in one place in an appendix to Dawson, who has consulted all the best editors of Shelley's prose.

So much remains unsettled about Shelley's texts for two principal reasons: (1) the rediscovery and recent reprinting of Shelley manuscripts, an extensive project still under way, and (2) the ongoing debate over how much Shelley's texts should be 'fixed', given his own processes of incessant revision, the delib-erately sceptical and shifting nature of his thinking, and the incompleteness in so much that he left unpublished, not just *The Triumph of Life*. Zillman's 1959 Variorum Edition of *Prometheus Unbound*, while still helpful as a survey of crit-ical statements on that work through the late 1950s, has had to be superseded as a textual study by Zillman's own 1968 revision, by Goslee (1985a), and by Neil Fraistat's volume on the *Prometheus* notebooks in the *Bodleian Shelley Manuscripts* series (Shelley 1986– : vol. ix), all because of the many partial drafts that have become increasingly available. True, there have been catalogues and scattered reproductions of Shelley manuscripts and notebooks since the later nineteenth century, but these have been consolidated and surpassed since 1960 by three massive efforts. First, there are the Pforzheimer Library *Shelley and his Circle* volumes full of transcribed manuscripts, many (though not all) of them Shelley's. These invaluable books, also replete with useful biographical and interpretative commentary, include definitive renderings of his early poems in *The Esdaile Notebook* (Pforzheimer, vol. ii, which is even more reliable than Shelley 1964a or 1966) and the notebook drafting of the 'Philosophical View' (Pforzheimer, vol. vi), right now the best available annotated text of that piece. Then there are *all* the newly photocopied and transcribed *Shelley Manuscripts* from the Bodleian Library, Oxford (again, Shelley 1986–   ), each volume of which includes introductions and commentary by experts, either on the holograph(s) of a single work or on notebooks where Shelley drafted several different pieces. Finally, we have Reiman's fine series *The Manuscripts of the Younger Romantics*. A full eight of these volumes offer annotated copies and transcriptions of Shelley holographs and notebooks from collections other than those at the Bodleian or the Pforzheimer. Now even non-editorial interpretations can take account of evidence visible in Shelley's manuscripts, especially as they make us see relations between his texts that may not have been visible before. Recent critics are thus citing manuscripts of this poet's texts more and more (see the essays on Shelley in Brinkley and Hanley), some with the aim of showing how Shelley's revisions help us settle his meanings (Goslee 1985a and Reiman in Brinkley and Hanley) and others with the claim that the variants show important indecisions stemming from irresolvable quandaries basic to Shelley's writing (Rajan 1990, where the author uses manuscript evidence to revise her own reading of *The Triumph of Life* in Rajan 1980).

After all, the 'decidability' of the meanings in Shelley's texts is now hotly debated. The increased availability of the manuscripts has coincided with the rise of—and resistances to—'deconstructive' and 'new historicist' approaches to interpretation. Behrendt, for example, somewhat affiliated with the latter movement, has accelerated this debate by presenting many of Shelley's texts as calculated appeals to conflicting ideological agendas among different groups of readers at Shelley's time and since. The continuing struggle over 'how we know what Shelley means' given the state of his texts has even led to Curran (1993), a group of essays on the textual and intertextual conditions of Shelley's works first presented at the Keats–Shelley Association Conference in New York held, along with other events, to celebrate the poet's bicentenary (1792–1992). Indeed, this debate has so invigorated Shelley studies that the forthcoming *Complete Poetical Works* of Shelley from the Johns Hopkins University Press, perhaps the 'definitive edition' still being sought by many, is editing the verse works unpublished by Shelley, which make up most of his 'corpus', as very much texts-in-process, as decidedly unsettled 'poetry' to be presented with all knowable variants, indecisions, and gaps on the printed page and 'on line' (an agenda explained by Donald Reiman, co-editor of this edition with Neil Frais-tat, in his essay for Clark and Hogle). Even renderings of apparently 'settled' texts, as in Knerr's edition of *Adonais* with its interpretative conclusions supposedly buoyed by the poet's satisfaction with the first printing, are put in some question by this adventure into the finished *unfinishing* of Shelley's dynamic writings.

CRITICISM AND COMMENTARY

Despite the multiplicity of interpretations of him in the course of the last two centuries, good comprehensive bibliographies of criticism focused on Shelley and his circle are fairly easy to find. Dunbar (1976) provides the fullest listing available for work on Shelley from 1823 to 1950, and he has augmented this undertaking first with a more annotated (if not complete) cataloguing of work published from 1950 to 1984 (Dunbar 1986) and then with his editing, even now, of the 'Current Bibliography' at the end of each annual issue of the *Keats–Shelley Journal*, which always contains an annotated section on 'Books and Articles Relating to the Shelleys and their Circle'. Large collections of these Keats–Shelley Association bibliographies have been put together in volumes encompassing Shelley studies from 1950 to 1962 (Green and Wilson) and 1962 to 1974 (Hartley), with every year since 1974 being reliably covered in each *Keats–Shelley Journal*. The best essay evaluating work on Shelley up to 1984 (including more good articles on single works than I can treat) is Curran (1985). For a more detailed sense of how Shelley has been read this century, the serious student can find several one-volume collections of valuable essays and book chapters (in addition to those gathered at the end of Shelley 1977). Indeed, a good sense of how such criticism has progressed can be derived from reading these anthologies, including the editors' introductions, in this roughly chronological order: Barcus, Ridenour,* Woodings, Swinden,* Wagenknecht (1978), Allott, Everest (1983),* Wagenknecht (1984), Bloom (1986),* Spencer Hall (1990) (an 'Approaches to Teaching' volume), Blank (1991),* Everest (1992), O'Neill (1993a and 1993b, particularly the Longman Critical Reader*), Curran (1993), Bennett and Curran,* and Clark and Hogle; the asterisked ones offer a 'short course' in the most influential material and the last several offer revisions of essays first written for Shelley's bicentenary. For thoroughly worked-out interpretations, however—particularly ones that allow readers to establish the all-important assumptions of each critic—there is still no substitute for reading the best-developed books or major essays on Shelley. Which ones a student of the poet should choose first after reading several of his works, of course, depends on the level or area of study the student wants to pursue. I therefore offer the following suggestions about the most helpful commentary on Shelley by separating the forms it takes over the last seventy years into several large categories of interest.

For those advanced scholars just starting to move beyond first perusals of Shelley's texts, I suggest the following progression of readings: O'Neill (1989b) (a good 'literary life' that stays close to the texts); the whole of Shelley (1977) (including all introductions and footnotes); Reiman (1969) in its 1988 revision (which will help tie the Norton commentary together); Ferber; and Webb (1977) (which starts with an assessment of the critical controversy over Shelley and responds by showing his main orientations in classical, Christian, and contemporary reading, politics, philosophy, poetic styles, and visionary hopes as they are tempered by counter-realizations). Those who plan to press beyond these beginnings to emphasize Shelley's lyric poetry should proceed from here to Chernaik, then Hughes and Keach; those who want to concentrate on the longer verse and dramatic works should now turn to Baker (mainly for sources and context), then Wilson and Sperry; those who want to stress the political Shelley should read Dawson, then Cameron (1950, 1974), then Scrivener; and those who seek more orientation to Shelley's philosophical and theoretical predilections (keeping in mind that they changed) should read Pulos and the first chapter of Reiman (1965), then Hogle on the *Defence* in Spencer Hall (1990), before turning to the Cameron books too, starting with *The Young Shelley*. Whatever itinerary the student follows at this stage, it is vital that he or she keep returning to the texts (poetry, plays, prose, *and* letters), partly to avoid accepting too quickly every aspect of the interpretations read thus far. After all, this opening course of reading will show sensitive students some of the range of disagreement that Shelley has long provoked and so leave them inclined to reserve judgement until they have more textual, material, philosophical, and interpretative evidence. Some of that evidence, before further steps are taken, should come from more reading in the history of Shelley's time and in the pre-texts (or 'sources') for his work, English and non-English, ancient and contemporary, esoteric and journalistic, to which students are most drawn by their initial reading. Three 'period' histories that cut through some of the cant in others to place Shelley in a wide socio-political context are Butler (1981), Everest (1990), and Simpson (1993), though these surveys should be augmented by the other general books on 'Romantic' social, economic, political, and literary history recommended in this volume.

For getting at the relations of Shelley's life to his works, readings, associates, and contemporaries beyond what the above efforts provide, scholars can still find much valid information in White's massive 1940 tomes (preferable to condensed versions of them) and in the vibrant Holmes biography of 1974, which is also more speculative, so much so that it should not be used as a sole authority in controversial matters—especially since Holmes's assumptions about what 'counts' in biography differ from White's, as do White's assumptions from O'Neill's, and so on. The Cameron books can also be read in chronological order as a rich two-volume literary biography, though Cameron (1974) structurally separates lived events from the work more than the 1950 book does, signalling some changes over the years in how he views life in relation to writing. St Clair uses still different assumptions in his informative look at Shelley's relation to all the Godwins. Other studies that persuasively relate segments of Shelley's life, including personal tendencies, to aspects of his works include Brewer, Brown, Clark (1989), Dawson, Foot, Hodgart, Hogle (1988), King-Hele, Morton, Reiman (1965, 1969), Rieger, Robinson, Rogers, Sperry, and Weinberg, with these last two being especially helpful in relating the life to several major works. Suggestive and (for some) controversial studies of Shelley's personal psychology in connection with his writing include Gallant at one extreme and Crook and Guiton at another. A great deal of reason is restored by Gelpi, though, in her careful re-examination of Shelley's early relationship to his mother and the cultural positioning of mothers at his time. Good cautions, too, against overemphasizing biography at the expense of Shelley's stated efforts to transcend the excessively personal in his writing are provided by Slater and the later chapters of Keach. The most concise assessment of the various early biographies, one with which I generally agree, appears in Curran (1985).

SHELLEY'S NEOPLATONISM

Given Shelley's attention to and translations of Plato (as shown most in Notopoulos) and Thomas Medwin's emphasis in his early Shelley biography, it has been tempting for some, especially among his pre-1950 defenders against Eliot and Leavis, to 'ground' his work in metaphysical assumptions rooted in Plato's dialogues, or at least in Neoplatonic visions of 'absolute, transcendent Unities' derived from such semi-Platonists as Plotinus and his Christian followers. The most overwhelming proponent of this position is Carl Grabo, whose various readings of Shelley are best put together in his big book of 1936 and are reinforced by Melvin Solve's slightly earlier explication of Shelley's basic theory of poetry. Grabo's claims are then powerfully reinforced, despite some very different emphases, not just by the thoroughness of Notopoulos, but by such highly accomplished critics as Baker, Butter, Fogle (esp. 1949), Knight (up to a point), Pottle, Wilson, and Perkins, so much so that the influential Abrams book of 1953 on Romantic literary theory confidently makes Shelley the most fully Platonic of the best-known English Romantic writers.

125

This view has therefore continued well beyond its peak in the 1950s, as we can see in Woodman (1964), Rogers, Shelley (1984), and the Hodgart volume offered in 1985 as a standard introduction to Shelley. Even C. E. Pulos, when he helps launch the countering view of the poet as a sceptic in the empiricist tradition in 1954, strives to base Shelley's scepticism on the kind articulated by Socrates in Plato's dialogues so that the poet's Platonism and scepticism can be asserted as one and the same. For more revisionist views since the 1950s and 1960s on Shelley's use of Plato, see Wasserman, Cameron (1974), Webb (1977), Sperry, Hogle (1988), Ulmer, and Kabitoglou.

SHELLEY'S SCEPTICISM: FROM THE HISTORY OF IDEAS TO DECONSTRUCTION

Since Pulos's effort and those that have most vividly extended it over the next three decades (Reiman 1965, Wasserman, Curran 1975, Steinman 1978, Hoagwood 1988), the understanding of Shelley as an empirically based sceptic—and an idealist only as a sceptic—has become the most accepted sense of his 'intellectual position' among experts on his writing and reading. Today, on one hand, we can hardly deny Shelley's extensive study of Bacon, Locke, Berkeley, David Hume, William Godwin, their Greek and Roman forebears, and Sir William Drummond's *Academical Questions* (which Shelley cites as indicative of his favoured 'intellectual philosophy' in the essay 'On Life', an unabashed statement of scepticism drafted as an addendum to the 'Philosophical View' in 1819). On the other hand, what it means for Shelley to believe from this reading that 'all things exist only as they are perceived, at least in relation to the percipient' (as he puts it in the *Defence*), and what *that* means for his construction of poems, essays on metaphysics, or visions of political reform have proven to be highly debatable matters despite the agreement on his 'sceptical' base. Although the best experts on his liberal-to-radical social views (Cameron 1974, Dawson, Scrivener, Foot, Hogle 1988, Hoagwood 1988, Behrendt) all see connections between his gradualist itinerary for change by 1819 and his sceptical manner of questioning fixed absolutes enforced by the doctrines of Church and State, they frequently disagree on what that direction means and on Shelley's sources for specific passages in his political writing.

Readers of his poetry as 'sceptically idealist' are even more divided, though often quite insightful in their particular interpretations. When Earl Wasserman collects all his previous and later readings of Shelley texts, with certain glaring omissions (no 'Witch of Atlas' nor *Triumph of Life*), in his learned and detailed book of 1971, he claims an overriding consistency of thought throughout all the works he treats. For him the Shelleyan interplay of entirely mental impressions (the association of ideas) keeps approaching, yet failing to reach, a complete union of thoughts with each other; hence Shelley's quest for ultimate 'Ones' and unities, the 'idealism' in his scepticism. But few other proponents of the 'sceptical Shelley' have found such a philosophical consistency in his writing, perhaps because they have been less influenced than Wasserman was by the older Johns Hopkins 'History of Ideas'. For some of these others (Abbey, Clark, McGann 1966, Quinney, Rieger, Weisman, Welburn), albeit in different ways, Shelley's earlier idealism (Platonic for a few) gradually and painfully confronts the inadequacy of perceptions and words to attain the objects of desire that mental idealizations dimly suggest, particularly if perceptions and words keep being pulled back, as parts of empiricism demand, to very earthly, disunified experience or the alienation of the individual psyche from the physical and social worlds. For others writing in this general vein, by contrast (Armstrong, Cooke 1976 and 1979, Cronin, Curran 1975, Jean Hall 1980 and 1991, Spencer Hall 1983, Keach, O'Malley, O'Neill 1989a, Reiman 1965 and 1988, Rieder 1981, Steinman 1983, and Wright), Shelley's poetry generally moves towards viewing the incompleteness of thought and the desires that thought arouses as positive liberations from excessively fixed constructs of myth or experience. This joyful irony becomes the catalyst, for these critics, of a Shelleyan dialectic among possibly contrary thoughts and words whereby Janus-faced images and complex metaphors or new myths are formed in poetic works that at least suggest the power of, or the need for, imagination to remake the world we perceive towards a more open array of possible reconceptions. These renderings of Shelley as sceptical idealist, while being as different among themselves as other kinds are, generally carry the main direction of Wasserman's static mind-set back towards a 'new critical' interplay of contradictory, yet ultimately harmonized, thoughts-in-language that appear most fully for readers, we are told, in the workings of Shelley's best poems. When they do not do precisely this (which can sometimes be said of Jean Hall, Wright, parts of Welburn, Schulze, and Leo's reading of Shelley's *Defence*), such efforts lean towards a phenomenological union of contraries at the core of thought like the one applied to other Romantic writers by Georges Poulet.

Beginning in the 1970s and accelerating most in the 1980s, however, for reasons persuasively suggested by Arac, a 'deconstructive' strain of critical reading comes to join and transform these visions of 'sceptical' Shelley, and the very diverse results—based on no more agreement than we usually find—have greatly complicated the senses of his works and assumptions that have developed out of the 'sceptical turn' in Shelley studies. This change is forecast quite clearly in the 1970s by the Shelley segments of Armstrong and Simpson (1979) (their only sustained writing on Shelley as a poet), but it becomes most pronounced among those writers directly affected by the poststructuralist essays of Jacques Derrida and/or the 'Yale School' transformations of him, especially after four Yale scholars plus Derrida himself published a collection sporadically focused on Shelley's *The Triumph of Life* (Bloom et al. 1979), which contains the first appearance of Paul de Man's 'Shelley Disfigured' (also included in de

Man's *Rhetoric of Romanticism*). In this perspective, generally speaking, the incompleteness of the thought or impression in the sceptical or phenomeno-logical sense of Shelley becomes bound up with the tendency of 'signifiers' (of which words are but one form) to differ from and defer to other signifiers, inside or outside thinking, before they can be said to constitute meanings or generate focused desires. For some in this line, who generally follow de Man—though rarely accepting the meaningless shift from figure to figure that he sees as the basis of writing—Shelley's pursuits of idealized and final meanings are both aroused and undercut by the continual movement between metaphors on which such projections actually depend (Hodgson, Leighton, Miller, Ulmer, Rajan 1980 and 1990, and the essay by Ferguson in Reed). In most of these cases, this conflict of impulses takes Shelley somewhat by surprise and becomes more pronounced and painfully acknowledged the closer he gets to *The Triumph of Life*. For others, however (Tetreault, Hogle 1982 and 1988, Jacobs), this interdependence of thought and the constantly unsettled movement of language, a condition which Shelley comes wilfully to accept, is what allows the poet to open up the most fixed and oppressive texts of western culture and turn their elements towards more liberated figural, hence mental and social, combinations. All these efforts help us deal much better than we could before with Shelley's intertextuality and the 'veil upon veil' process of his ever-shifting tropes (that quality detailed in Hughes and McGann 1971). Yet, in their increasing disagreements with each other, the most sophisticated of these critics feel the need to bring in other theoretical vocabularies (associationist, psychoanalytic, feminist, and Marxist primarily) to deal with the texts they try to explain. Sheerly word-based 'deconstruction', as even its most helpful users find, cannot account on its own for the appeals in Shelley's writing to the many psychological contradictions and socio-cultural quandaries overwhelm-ing both his readers and himself (as we have been reminded best, in the midst of all this, by Behrendt, Bruhm, Claridge, Clark 1989, Fry 1980, Gallant, Gelpi, Levinson, Morton, O'Neill 1989b, Weisman, and several of the essays in both Bennett and Curran and Clark and Hogle).

SHELLEY AND LANGUAGE

Happily, though, the 'deconstructive turn' in the mainly 'sceptical' Shelley has helped refocus scholarly attention on this poet's approach to his medium. Cronin and Keach have done the most in the 1980s, even as they proceed from more 'New Critical' than deconstructive assumptions, to assess Shelley's philo-sophy of language, his conflicted sources for that philosophy (especially Locke and Horne Tooke), the effects of that philosophy on the structures of his works, and the relation of all this to the particulars of his poetic style. This much-needed effort has been ably assisted by the work of Stuart

Peterfreund, Fry's major essay on Shelley's *Defence* (1983), and moments in Armstrong, Behrendt, Blank (1991), Chernaik, Curran (1993), Dawson, de Man, Delisle, Everest (1983), Jean Hall (1980), Hogle (1988), Leighton, Miller, Quinney, Rajan (1990), Reed, Schulze, Simpson (1979), Tetreault, Ulmer, Webb (1977), Weisman, Wright, and the Worton essay in Allott. Leighton is especially helpful in connecting Shelley to earlier traditions of 'sublime' language and some of the ironies endemic to verbal sublimity. Still, the more one reads all this work, the more one finds very different senses of how Shelley viewed words, even to the point (particularly in Cronin, Fry, and Leighton) where the Shelley scholar can find him at odds with himself in working out a philosophy of language.

SHELLEY AS AN ARTIST, TRANSFORMER OF GENRES, AND ICONOCLASTIC REMYTHOLOGIZER (OR DEMYTHOLOGIZER)

The refocus on language, extending 'New Critical' tendencies once inimical to Shelley in some circles, has also helped continue (and sometimes reorient) the important post-Leavis emphasis on showing how much and in what ways Shelley is an artful craftsman in verse. Now aided by the availability of his manuscripts and consequently more insight into his revisions, there has been a steady output of close readings that draw out his ingenious uses of poetic devices and imagery, from Fogle (1949, 1974), Pottle, Davie, and Bloom (1959) to Reiman (1965, 1969), Behrendt, Chernaik, Jean Hall (1980), Hogle (1988), Jacobs, Jones, O'Malley, O'Neill (1989a), Sacks, Sperry, Tetreault, Ulmer, Weisman, and especially Cronin and Keach—though what Shelley's stylistic brilliance indicates is far from the same for most of these scholars. Along the way, this interest in Shelley the verbal artist has attracted helpful attention to relations and parallels between his works and painting (Colwell, Twitchell), sculpture (Goslee 1985b), and, not so surprisingly, music (Anderson, Kramer). It has also led critics to examine the ways he makes parts of single works or books of his poems relate to each other across his corpus (see Wilson, Bloom 1959 and 1961, Chernaik, Wasserman, Steinman 1983, Curran 1975, and especially Fraistat 1985).

At the same time, our greater orientation to Shelley as a deliberate writer has led us to appreciate his reworking and knowledge of established genres, a subject only fitfully dealt with (except in Baker, Reiman, and Wasserman) until the 1970s. Stuart Curran has been a major force in re-establishing Shelley's genre-based foundations *and* transformations in dramatic tragedy (the 1970 book on *The Cenci*), epic and the epic strains in other genres (Curran 1975, along with Wilkie), and numerous other forms from hymn to romance (see Curran's vital *Poetic Form* volume of 1986). Attention to genre is also prominent, often under Curran's influence, in Behrendt, Cronin, Hogle (1988), and, with more specific focal points, in Chernaik (on lyric), Fraistat (1985) (on the book of poems), Fry (1980) (on the ode), Jost and Wagner (on the sonnet), Hoagwood (1985) (on prophecy), Paley and Goldsmith (on apocalyptic poetry), Jones (in the first thorough study of Shelley's satires, also helpful on genre in general), King-Hele (on the 'scientific' epic-romance à la Erasmus Darwin), Levinson (on the 'fragment poem', which for her means *Julian and Maddalo* more than *The Triumph of Life*), McNiece (on the hymn, ode, and epic as modified by the French Revolution), Sacks and Speigelman (on the elegy and pastoral), Scrivener (on the occasional poem), Fischer (on verse narrative), and Webb (1976, 1977) (on the Greek song and dialogue, the Dantean-Petrarchan *trionfi*, the Goethean closet drama, and Calderonian *autos* and tragedies). The relation of Shelley's dramatic works (*Prometheus Unbound* and *The Cenci* espe-cially) to the wider context of Romantic drama has been best presented, albeit quite differently, not only in Curran (in all three books), but in Donohue, Richardson, Bate, Purinton, and Carlson. A strong 'new historicist' advance in genre study that richly complicates the early nineteenth-century uses of 'romance', as well as Shelley's variations on those uses, is provided in the recent book by Duff. And there are very informative studies on Shelley's ways of reworking the several generic proclivities of certain authors highly influential on him, particularly Dante (Webb 1976 and 1977, Pite, Steve Ellis), Spenser (Kucich), Shakespeare (Curran 1970, Bate), Milton (Wittreich, Brisman 1973, Curran 1975, Goslee 1985*b*), Rousseau (Duffy), Byron (Brewer, Robinson), Keats (Cox, Curran in Everest 1983), and Wordsworth (Blank 1989, Bloom 1976). Even the 'Gothic' strain in Shelley's adolescent *and* later writing, seen with early clarity by Bertrand Evans as basic to *The Cenci*, has been receiving increased attention, just as the Gothic has, notably in Shelley (1986), Aers et al., Bruhm, Hogle (1981), Murphy, and Reiman (1987), though more can certainly be made of this generic influence.

Throughout studies of Shelley's artistry with genres, however, a question keeps being raised only to receive a plethora of conflicting answers: how much does Shelley accept the frames of existing forms or how much—and to what ends—does he use them radically to destroy and reconfigure older modes? This question has been posed especially in relation to Shelley's frequent uses of Graeco-Roman, biblical, 'Oriental', and Christianized *myths*, uses often inter-mingled with the poet's wide scientific knowledge (see Grabo 1930, King-Hele, and Jeffrey). Yeats certainly raised this question when he faced Shelley's in-fluence on him (see also Bornstein) and saw his predecessor dipping into a vast, fragmented collective unconscious, a 'Great Memory', both like and unlike Jung's. With the information provided in such later studies of Shelley's allu-sions as the ones by Grabo (1930), Bush, Baker, Bloom (1959), Rieger, Wasserman, and Curran (1975), post-1940s critics have ranged across several possibilities: (1) Shelley seeing his recast myths as among his ways of reconstructing the objectified world with a unifying subjective will (Bloom 1959, O'Malley, Frye, Abrams 1971, Cantor, Wright, Cooke 1976, Jean Hall 1980 and 1991, Harding); (2) Shelley attempting to create a new 'syncretic' mythology by combining different systems in a fashion that casts down all outside authorities to show the supremacy of the sympathetic imagination (Wasserman, Curran 1975, Cooke 1979, Korshin, Hoagwood 1985); (3) Shelley being *anti*-syncretic with his fragmenting and reconnecting of mythic *figures* so as to achieve either a counter-religion of freedom or a continual disruption of possibly confining absolutes (Webb 1977, Tetreault, Hogle 1988, Jacobs); or (4) Shelley being forced to confront, in his mixing of myths and metaphors from the West and East, the conflicting drives and ideologies he is actually caught between (Rieder 1985, Cantor, Waldoff, Quint, Sperry, Hogle 1988, Behrendt, Clark 1989, O'Neill 1989*a*, Rajan 1980 and 1990, Jacobs, Gelpi, Janowitz, Leask, Duff). Yet another alternative, the one that makes Shelley the most extreme of iconoclasts (or 'breaker of vessels' for the later Harold Bloom), is the view that takes him to be repeating the ancient gnostics in their mythic and tropic counterings of orthodox Christianity. This reading of him, much criticized after the advancements of it in Rieger and Bloom 1976, has recently found attractive new life in Bryan Shelley's explanation for the way the poet employs and reorients Judeo-Christian scripture. We are also gaining an increased sense of how myths came to Shelley already politicized (as in Cameron 1974, Scrivener, Curran 1986*b*, Hogle 1988, Linda Lewis, and Janowitz). Clearly the debate over Shelley as myth-maker will continue to depend on each interpreter's particular view of the main and real foundations behind his 'mythopoeic' or 'iconoclastic' process.

SHELLEY AND FORMS OF PSYCHOANALYSIS

Given Shelley's fairly explicit moments of anticipating the interests of Freud, Jacques Lacan, and even Julia Kristeva (see Hogle 1988), it is no surprise that there have been several kinds of psychoanalytic approaches to his life and work, especially since 1950. The biographical efforts of Holmes, Crook and Guiton, and Gallant employ Freudian thinking to greater and greater degrees, though Gallant makes even more suggestive use of Jungian and Kleinian variations on Freud. In readings of Shelley's works, the most intriguing and unabashed Freudian approaches, though some are *quite* different from the others, include Waldoff, Schapiro, Rapaport, Sacks, and portions of Sperry, along with Weiskel's placement of Shelley within his very Freudian sense of the sublime. The later Harold Bloom and his progeny (Bloom 1976, Brisman 1973 and 1978, Blank 1989) have read Shelley's responses to his precursors within a neo-Freudian 'anxiety of influence' which is consequently more 'Father'-fixated than some find him to be. Suggestive Lacanian readings of Shelley appear in Fry (1980), Claridge, and portions of Hogle (1988), while Hogle (1988) and

Ulmer do the most to interface psychoanalytic and deconstructive theory, along with other perspectives, to articulate the nature of Shelleyan *desire*. After all, the nature and processes of love in Shelley are major themes and problems in his work addressed quite provocatively, though not exclusively (nor should they be), by forms of psychoanalytic theory. Indeed, provided there is due attention to Morton's new insights on Shelley's sense of 'the body', no explorations of Shelleyan desire should proceed further without taking account of the recent work of Gelpi, who combines social history, feminist critique, plus Freudian, Kleinian, Lacanian, and Kristevan psychoanalysis to deal with the biographical, psychological, and textual levels of Shelley's *eros* (see also Gelpi's Kristevan piece in Blank 1991 and her highly Lacanian essay in Clark and Hogle). The reasons why Shelley is so at odds with himself about love and love's projections, Gelpi reveals, stem from conflicts in his basic drives and the ideologies of his culture that only a combination of perspectives can explain.

SHELLEY, WOMAN, AND QUESTIONS OF GENDER

Among Gelpi's contributions, too, is the information she offers (also in Blank 1991) on the positioning of women in the middle- to upper-class home at Shelley's time, as well as in his work. By doing that, she helps bring to an important climax—a vital point of departure for future study—the recent scholarly scrutiny of Shelley on 'woman' and of the mobility of gender distinctions in his writing. Since the growth of feminist criticism after the 1960s, Shelley's relationship to women (personal and literary) has provoked wide disagreement. On the one hand, there is Nathaniel Brown's evidence-laden argument that Shelley is very much a proto-feminist in many poems and in his vision of love's androgynous ideal, a view given some support by Woodman (1981). On the other hand, there is the highly provable argument, most succinctly made by Anne Mellor, that female love-objects in Shelley (as in other male Romantics) are narcissistic self-projections from a very male point of view constructed to serve continuations of male supremacy in western culture. Ranged between these views are the extensive reflections on Shelley, his constructions of woman, and his ways of gendering states and levels of being in Sperry, Hogle (1988), Ulmer, and especially Marlon Ross, who both contextualizes Shelley within the increased writing of poetry and prose by women at his time and shows the more and more conflicted nature of the figure of woman in Shelley's writing. A powerful explanation for such conflicts, particularly in Shelley's use of female 'Liberty' figures, is offered in Janowitz's essay on how women become different for Shelley depending on his different ideological perspectives at different times. The effect on all this of the poet's complex relations with Mary Shelley (looked at closely in Cameron 1974) has been recently addressed by many key writers, including Mellor, Betty Bennett,

William Veeder, and Emily Sunstein, cited in the 'Mary Shelley' chapter of this book. Gelpi brings coherence and great fairness to this ongoing debate by all the information she has recovered about it and by her careful readings of Shelley's work. At the same time, she leaves us a Shelley more conflicted on women and gender than we have ever known and so one who remains quite open for further examination on these issues, provided we consider the range of historical information that a Gelpi, Ross, or Janowitz, as well as a Brown, can bring to bear.

SHELLEY AND HISTORY (MARXISM, POLITICS, 'NEW HISTORICISM', AND CULTURAL STUDIES)

There is little question that the most important revelations in the immediate future of Shelley criticism are going to come from new and revived forms of historical—and *cultural*-historical—study that reassess what we do and do not know already about Shelley as a poet inundated by multiple social, economic, and political forces permeating his awareness (consciously or unconsciously) and inhabiting the very words and genres with which he writes. There is, of course, a basic battery of vital readings that one must complete, roughly in the following order, to know the political (and perhaps proto-Marxist) Shelley that 'newer historicism' is now and will be addressing: Cameron (1950, 1974), McNiece, Woodring, Guinn, Matthews, Dawson, Scrivener, Hoagwood (1988), Hogle (1988), Behrendt, and much of what appears in Bennett and Curran. Then, too, the reading of Shelley (sometimes positively, sometimes negatively) through the sorts of Marxist lenses that have helped, in part, to establish 'new historicism' and cultural studies can be found most forcefully in Aveling and Aveling, Williams's sense of Shelley's contribution to the definition of 'culture', Cameron (1974), Foot, the Aers–Cook–Punter collection, Quint, McGann (1983), Levinson, Purinton, Everest's major essay in his 1983 volume (also in O'Neill 1993*a*), several of the pieces in Bennett and Curran, and Keach's essay in Clark and Hogle. We should also keep returning to the pre-'new historicism' provided by Butler, not just in 1981 but in 1979, where she provides the most historicist account there is of Peacock's relation to Shelley and the confluence of historical factors basic to the *Defence of Poetry*. But if we are to continue probing the ideologically leftist or (more often) divided Shelley that these studies expose, we must consider the more recent efforts that see him struggle with the contraries tearing at him as he attempts to redefine particular 'hot topics' of his moment: the nature and efficacy of 'sensibility' and 'sentiment' (Clark), the politics and art of pain and torture (Bruhm), the position, again, of woman (Gelpi, Janowitz), the rise of bourgeois nationalism (Kipperman 1991, Simpson 1993), the cultural levels and politics of 'taste' (Morton), the relation of poetry to concepts of 'high' or 'low' culture (Simpson

1993), the British conquest and construction of the 'East' and thus Shelley's kind of 'Orientalism' (Leask), the consequent historical changes in what 'romance' includes (Duff), and this poet's relationship to the discussion and iconography, not to mention the reality, of slavery and racism (Baum).

This progression, as it accelerates in future studies, may increase our sense of Shelley as a very multi-levelled and contradictory person, thinker, and writer, living and working in the midst of conflicts we have only begun to recover. But that will continue the post-nineteenth-century project of recovering the 'true Shelley', as much as that is possible, even if the result is not the unified mind or artistic career that has so often been sought. We need not set aside the poet so highly attuned to the possibilities of language, poetic artifice, classical and biblical allusions, cross-personal and even some cross-cultural understanding, or particular social changes and moral reforms; we must understand these aspects of and desires in him *even more* as their roots, qualities, and implications prove more complicated than they once seemed. Above all, this history of Shelley criticism, in the light of 'new historicism', should make us acutely aware that the way we edit, read, and use Shelley in this and the next century is governed by our own and our predecessors' ideological and thus political assumptions. The study of Shelley should, among other things, make us confront and re-examine these assumptions, even as we keep looking at the ways and reasons by which *he* strove to be an 'unacknowledged legislator of the world'.

REFERENCES

TEXTS AND TEXTUAL STUDIES

Delisle, Fanny, *A Study of Shelley's* A Defence of Poetry: *A Textual and Critical Evaluation*, 2 vols. (Salzburg, 1974).

Forman, H. Buxton, *The Shelley Library: An Essay in Bibliography* (London, 1886; repr. New York, 1975).

Pforzheimer Library, The Carl H., *Shelley and his Circle, 1773–1822*, vols. i–iv ed. Kenneth Neill Cameron, vols. v–viii ed. Donald H. Reiman (Cambridge, Mass., 1973–86).

Reiman, Donald H. (gen. ed.), *The Manuscripts of the Younger Romantics*, 20 vols. (New York, 1985–   ).

Shelley, Percy Bysshe, *The Complete Works of Percy Bysshe Shelley*, ed. Roger Ingpen and Walter E. Peck, Julian Edition, 10 vols. (New York, 1926–30).

—— *Shelley's Prose; or, The Trumpet of a Prophecy*, ed. David Lee Clark (Albuquerque, N. Mex., 1954; corr. 1966).

—— *Shelley's* Prometheus Unbound: *A Variorum Edition,* ed. Lawrence J. Zillman (Seattle, 1959).

—— *The Esdaile Notebook,* ed. Kenneth Neill Cameron (London, 1964a).

—— *The Letters of Percy Bysshe Shelley,* ed. Frederick L. Jones, 2 vols. (Oxford, 1964b).

—— *The Esdaile Poems,* ed. Neville Rogers (Oxford, 1966).

—— *Shelley's Critical Prose,* ed. Bruce R. McElderry, Jr. (Lincoln, Nebr., 1967).

—— *Shelley's* Prometheus Unbound: *The Text and Drafts,* ed. Lawrence J. Zillman (New Haven, 1968).

—— *Poetical Works,* ed. Thomas Hutchinson, rev. G. M. Matthews, Oxford Standard Authors (Oxford, 1970a).

—— *Shelley: Political Writings,* ed. Roland A. Duerkson (New York, 1970b).

—— *The Complete Poetical Works of Percy Bysshe Shelley,* ed. Neville Rogers, Oxford English Texts, 2 vols. (Oxford, 1973–5).

—— *Shelley's Poetry and Prose,* ed. Donald H. Reiman and Sharon B. Powers, Norton Critical Edition (New York, 1977).

—— *Shelley's* Adonais: *A Critical Edition,* ed. Anthony Knerr (New York, 1984).

—— *Zastrozzi and St. Irvyne,* ed. Stephen C. Behrendt, Oxford World's Classics (Oxford, 1986).

—— *The Bodleian Shelley Manuscripts,* gen. ed. Donald H. Reiman, 23 vols. (New York, 1986–   ).

—— *The Poems of Shelley,* vol. i, ed. Geoffrey M. Matthews and Kelvin Everest (London, 1989).

—— *Shelley's Revolutionary Year: Shelley's Political Poems and the Essay 'A Philosophical View of Reform',* ed. Paul Foot (London, 1990).

—— *The Prose Works of Percy Bysshe Shelley,* vol. i, ed. E. B. Murray (Oxford, 1993).

—— *Shelley: Poems and Prose,* ed. Timothy Webb, Everyman's Library (rev. edn., London, 1995).

CRITICISM AND COMMENTARY

Abbey, Lloyd, *Destroyer and Preserver: Shelley's Poetic Skepticism* (Lincoln, Nebr., 1979).

Abrams, Meyer H., *The Mirror and the Lamp: Romantic Theory and the Critical Tradition* (New York, 1953; repr. New York, 1962).

—— *Natural Supernaturalism: Tradition and Revolution in Romantic Literature* (New York, 1971).

Aers, David, Cook, Jonathan, and Punter, David, *Romanticism and Ideology: Studies in English Writing, 1765–1830* (London, 1981).

Allott, Miriam (ed.), *Essays on Shelley* (Liverpool, 1982).

Anderson, Erland, *Harmonious Madness: A Study of Musical Metaphors in the Poetry of Coleridge, Shelley, and Keats* (Wolfeboro, NY, 1975).

Arac, Jonathan, 'Shelley, Deconstruction, History', in his *Critical Genealogies: Historical Situations for Postmodern Literary Studies* (New York, 1987), 97–113.

Armstrong, Isobel, *Language as Living Form in Nineteenth-Century Poetry* (Brighton, 1982).

Aveling, Eleanor Marx, and Aveling, Edward, *Shelley's Socialism: Two Lectures* (London, 1888).

Baker, Carlos, *Shelley's Major Poetry: The Fabric of a Vision* (Princeton, 1948).

Barcus, James E. (ed.), *Shelley: The Critical Heritage* (London, 1975).

Barton, Wilfrid Converse, *Shelley and the New Criticism: The Anatomy of a Critical Misevaluation* (Salzburg, 1973).

Bate, Jonathan, *Shakespeare and the English Romantic Imagination* (Oxford, 1986).

Baum, Joan, *Mind-Forg'd Manacles: Slavery and the English Romantic Poets* (Hamden, Conn., 1994).

Behrendt, Stephen C., *Shelley and his Audiences* (Lincoln, Nebr., 1989).

Bennett, Betty T., and Curran, Stuart (eds.), *Shelley: Poet and Legislator of the World* (Baltimore, 1995).

Blank, G. Kim, *Wordsworth's Influence on Shelley: A Study of Poetic Authority* (London, 1989).

—— (ed.), *The New Shelley: Late Twentieth-Century Views* (London, 1991).

Bloom, Harold, *Shelley's Mythmaking* (New Haven, 1959).

—— *The Visionary Company: A Reading of English Romantic Poetry* (Ithaca, NY, 1961; rev. edn., 1971).

—— *Poetry and Repression: Revisionism from Blake to Stevens* (New Haven, 1976).

—— et al., *Deconstruction and Criticism* (New York, 1979).

—— (ed.), *Percy Bysshe Shelley*, Modern Critical Views (New York, 1986).

Bornstein, George, *Yeats and Shelley* (Chicago, 1970).

Brewer, William D., *The Shelley–Byron Conversation* (Gainesville, Fla., 1994).

Brinkley, Robert, and Hanley, Keith (eds.), *Romantic Revisions* (Cambridge, 1992).

Brisman, Leslie, *Milton's Poetry of Choice and its Romantic Heirs* (Ithaca, NY, 1973).

—— *Romantic Origins* (Ithaca, NY, 1978).

Brown, Nathaniel, *Sexuality and Feminism in Shelley* (Cambridge, Mass. 1979).

Bruhm, Steven, *Gothic Bodies: The Politics of Pain in Romantic Fiction* (Philadelphia, 1994).

Bush, Douglas, *Mythology and the Romantic Tradition in English Poetry* (London, 1937; repr. New York, 1969).

Butler, Marilyn, *Peacock Displayed: A Satirist in his Context* (London, 1979).

—— *Romantics, Rebels and Reactionaries: English Literature and its Background 1760–1830* (Oxford, 1981).

Butter, Peter, *Shelley's Idols of the Cave* (London, 1954; repr. New York, 1969).

Cameron, Kenneth Neill, *The Young Shelley: Genesis of a Radical* (London, 1950; repr. New York, 1962).

—— *Shelley: The Golden Years* (Cambridge, Mass., 1974).

Cantor, Paul, *Creature and Creator: Myth-Making and English Romanticism* (Cambridge, 1984).

Carlson, Julie, *In the Theater of Romanticism: Coleridge, Nationalism, Women* (Cambridge, 1994).

Chernaik, Judith, *The Lyrics of Shelley* (Cleveland, 1972).

Claridge, Laura, *Romantic Potency: The Paradox of Desire* (Ithaca, NY, 1992).

Clark, Timothy, *Embodying Revolution: The Figure of the Poet in Shelley* (Oxford, 1989).

—— and Hogle, Jerrold E. (eds.), *Evaluating Shelley* (Edinburgh, 1996).

Clarke, Eric O., 'Shelley's Heart: Sexual Politics and Cultural Value', *Yale Journal of Criticism*, 8 (1995), 187–208.

Colwell, Frederic S., 'Shelley and Italian Painting', *Keats–Shelley Journal*, 29 (1980), 43–66.

Cooke, Michael G., *The Romantic Will* (New Haven, 1976).

—— *Acts of Inclusion: Studies Bearing on an Elementary Theory of Romanticism* (New Haven, 1979).

Cox, Jeffrey N., 'Keats, Shelley, and the Wealth of Imagination', *Studies in Romanticism*, 34 (1995), 365–400.

Cronin, Richard, *Shelley's Poetic Thoughts* (New York, 1981).

Crook, Nora, and Guiton, Derek, *Shelley's Venomed Melody* (Cambridge, 1986).

Curran, Stuart, *Shelley's* Cenci: *Scorpions Ringed with Fire* (Princeton, 1970).

—— *Shelley's Annus Mirabilis: The Maturing of an Epic Vision* (San Marino, Calif., 1975).

—— 'Percy Bysshe Shelley', in Frank Jordan (ed.), *The English Romantic Poets: A Review of Research and Criticism* (4th edn., New York, 1985), 593–663.

—— *Poetic Form and British Romanticism* (Oxford, 1986a).

—— 'The Political Prometheus', *Studies in Romanticism*, 25 (1986b), 430–55.

—— (ed.), Special Shelley Bicentenary Issue, *Keats–Shelley Journal*, 42 (1993).

Davie, Donald, 'Shelley's Urbanity', in his *Purity of Diction in English Verse* (London, 1953), 133–59.

Dawson, P. M. S., *The Unacknowledged Legislator: Shelley and Politics* (Oxford, 1980).

de Man, Paul, *The Rhetoric of Romanticism* (New York, 1984).

Donohue, Joseph W., Jr., *Dramatic Character in the English Romantic Age* (Princeton, 1970).

Duff, David, *Romance and Revolution: Shelley and the Politics of a Genre* (Cambridge, 1994).

Duffy, Edward, *Rousseau in England: The Context of Shelley's Critique of the Enlightenment* (Berkeley, 1979).

Dunbar, Clement (ed.), *A Bibliography of Shelley Studies: 1823–1950* (New York, 1976).

—— (ed.), *Shelley Studies, 1950–1984: An Annotated Bibliography* (New York, 1986).

Eliot, T. S., *The Use of Poetry and the Use of Criticism: Studies in the Relation of Criticism to Poetry in England* (London, 1933).

Ellis, F. S., *A Lexical Concordance to the Poetical Works of Percy Bysshe Shelley* (London, 1892; repr. New York, 1968).

Ellis, Steve, *Dante and English Poetry: Shelley to T. S. Eliot* (Cambridge, 1983).

Engelberg, Kartsten Klegs, *The Making of the Shelley Myth: An Annotated Bibliography of Criticism of Percy Bysshe Shelley* (London, 1988).

Evans, Bertrand, *Gothic Drama from Walpole to Shelley* (Berkeley, 1947).

Everest, Kelvin (ed.), *Shelley Revalued: Essays from the Gregynog Conference* (Leicester, 1983).

—— *English Romantic Poetry: An Introduction to the Historical Context and the Literary Scene* (London, 1990).

—— (ed.), Percy Bysshe Shelley Bicentenary Issue, *Essays and Studies*, 45 (1992).

Ferber, Michael, *The Poetry of Shelley* (London, 1993).

Fischer, Hermann, *Romantic Verse Narrative: The History of a Genre*, trans. Sue Bollans (Cambridge, 1991).

Fogle, Richard Harter, *The Imagery of Keats and Shelley: A Comparative Study* (Chapel Hill, NC, 1949).

—— *The Permanent Pleasure: Essays on the Classics of Romanticism* (Athens, Ga, 1974).

Foot, Paul, *Red Shelley* (London, 1980).

Fraistat, Neil, *The Poem and the Book: Interpreting Collections of Romantic Poetry* (Chapel Hill, NC, 1985).

—— 'Illegitimate Shelley: Radical Piracy and the Textual Edition as Cultural Performance', *Publications of the Modern Language Association*, 85 (1994), 409–23.

Fry, Paul H. *The Poet's Calling in the English Ode* (New Haven, 1980).

—— *The Reach of Criticism: Method and Perception in Literary Theory* (New Haven, 1983).

Frye, Northrop, *A Study of English Romanticism* (New York, 1968).

Gallant, Christine, *Shelley's Ambivalence* (London, 1989).

Gelpi, Barbara Charlesworth, *Shelley's Goddess: Maternity, Language, Subjectivity* (Oxford, 1992).

Goldsmith, Steven, *Unbuilding Jerusalem: Apocalypse and Romantic Imagination* (Ithaca, NY, 1993).

Goslee, Nancy Moore, 'Shelley at Play: A Study of Text and Sketch in his *Prometheus Notebooks*', *Huntington Library Quarterly*, 48 (1985*a*), 210–55.

—— '*Uriel's Eye*': Miltonic Stationing and Statuary in Blake, Keats, and Shelley (University, Ala., 1985*b*).

Grabo, Carl, *A Newton among Poets: Shelley's Use of Science in* Prometheus Unbound (Chapel Hill, NC, 1930).

—— *The Magic Plant: The Growth of Shelley's Thought* (Chapel Hill, NC, 1936).

Green, David Bonnell, and Wilson, Edwin Graves (eds.), *Keats, Shelley, Byron, Hunt, and their Circles. A Bibliography: July 1, 1950–June 30, 1962* (Lincoln, Nebr., 1964).

Guinn, John Pollard, *Shelley's Political Thought* (The Hague, 1969).

Hall, Jean, *The Transforming Image: A Study of Shelley's Major Poetry* (Urbana, Ill. 1980).

—— *A Mind that Feeds upon Infinity: The Deep Self in English Romantic Poetry* (Rutherford, NJ, 1991).

Hall, Spencer, 'Power and the Poet: Religious Mythmaking in Shelley's "Hymn to Intellectual Beauty"', *Keats–Shelley Journal*, 32 (1983), 123–49.

—— (ed.), *Approaches to Teaching Shelley's Poetry* (New York, 1990).

Harding, Anthony John, *The Reception of Myth in English Romanticism* (Columbia, Mo., 1995).

Hartley, Robert A. (ed.), *Keats, Shelley, Byron, Hunt, and their Circles. A Bibliography: July 1, 1962–December 31, 1974* (Lincoln, Nebr., 1978).

Hayden, John O. (ed.), *Romantic Bards and British Reviewers* (Lincoln, Nebr., 1971).

Hoagwood, Terence Allan, *Prophecy and the Philosophy of Mind: Traditions of Blake and Shelley* (University, Ala., 1985).

—— *Skepticism and Ideology: Shelley's Political Prose and its Philosophical Context from Bacon to Marx* (Iowa City, 1988).

Hodgart, Patricia, *A Preface to Shelley* (London, 1985).

Hodgson, John, *Coleridge, Shelley, and Transcendental Inquiry: Rhetoric, Argument, Metapsychology* (Lincoln, Nebr., 1989).

Hogg, Thomas Jefferson, *The Life of Percy Bysshe Shelley* (London, 1858).

Hogle, Jerrold E., 'Shelley's Fiction: The "Stream of Fate"', *Keats–Shelley Journal*, 30 (1981), 78–99.

—— 'Shelley's Poetics: The Power as Metaphor', *Keats–Shelley Journal*, 31 (1982), 159–97.

—— *Shelley's Process: Radical Transference and the Development of his Major Works* (Oxford, 1988).

—— 'Shelley's Texts and the Premises of Criticism', *Keats–Shelley Journal*, 42 (1993), 66–79.

Holmes, Richard, *Shelley: The Pursuit* (London, 1974).

Hughes, Daniel J., 'Coherence and Collapse in Shelley, with Particular Reference to *Epipsychidion*', *English Literary History*, 28 (1961), 260–83.

Jacobs, Carol, *Uncontainable Romanticism: Shelley, Bronte, Kleist* (Baltimore, 1990).

Janowitz, Anne, ' "A Voice from across the Sea": Communitarianism at the Limits of Romanticism', in Mary A. Favret and Nicola J. Watson (eds.), *At the Limits of Romanticism: Essays in Cultural, Feminist, and Materialist Criticism* (Bloomington, Ind., 1994), 83–100.

Jeffrey, Lloyd, *Shelley's Knowledge and Use of Natural History* (Salzburg, 1976).

Jones, Steven E., *Shelley's Satire: Violence, Exhortation, and Authority* (De Kalb, Ill., 1994).

Jost, François, 'Anatomy of an Ode: Shelley and the Sonnet Tradition', *Comparative Literature*, 34 (1982), 223–46.

Kabitoglou, E. Douka, *Plato and the English Romantics: Dialogi* (London, 1990).

Keach, William, *Shelley's Style* (London, 1985).

King-Hele, Desmond, *Shelley: His Thought and Work* (3rd edn., Rutherford, NJ, 1984).

Kipperman, Mark, 'Macropolitics of Utopia: Shelley's *Hellas* in Context', in Jonathan Arac and Harriet Ritvo (eds.), *Macropolitics of Nineteenth-Century Literature: Nationalism, Exoticism, Imperialism* (Philadelphia, 1991), 86–101.

—— 'Absorbing a Revolution: Shelley Becomes a Romantic, 1889–1903', *Nineteenth-Century Literature*, 47 (1992), 187–211.

Knight, G. Wilson, *The Starlit Dome: Studies in the Poetry of Vision* (London, 1941; repr. Oxford, 1971).

Korshin, Paul, *Typologies in England, 1650–1820* (Princeton, 1982).

Kramer, Lawrence, *Music and Poetry: The Nineteenth Century and After* (Berkeley, 1985).

Kucich, Greg, *Keats, Shelley, and Romantic Spenserianism* (University Park, Pa., 1991).

Leask, Nigel, *British Romantic Writers and the East: Anxieties of Empire* (Cambridge, 1992).

Leavis, F. R., 'Shelley', in his *Revaluation: Tradition and Development in English Poetry* (London, 1936; repr. New York, 1947).

Leighton, Angela, *Shelley and the Sublime: An Interpretation of the Major Poems* (Cambridge, 1984).

Leo, John Robert, 'Criticism of Consciousness in Shelley's *A Defence of Poetry*', *Philosophy and Literature*, 2 (1978), 42–57.

Levinson, Marjorie, *The Romantic Fragment Poem: A Critique of a Form* (Chapel Hill, NC, 1986).

Lewis, C. S., 'Shelley, Dryden, and Mr. Eliot', in his *Rehabilitations and Other Essays* (London, 1939), 3–34.

Lewis, Linda M., *The Promethean Politics of Milton, Blake, and Shelley* (Columbia, Mo., 1992).

McGann, Jerome, 'The Secrets of an Elder Day: Shelley after *Hellas*', *Keats–Shelley Journal*, 15 (1966), 28–41.

—— 'Shelley's Veils: A Thousand Images of Loveliness', in W. Paul Elledge and Richard L. Hoffman (eds.), *Romantic and Victorian* (Cranbury, NJ, 1971), 198–218.

McGann, Jerome, *The Romantic Ideology: A Critical Investigation* (Chicago, 1983).

McNiece, Gerald, *Shelley and the Revolutionary Idea* (Cambridge, Mass., 1969).

Matthews, Geoffrey M., 'A Volcano's Voice in Shelley', *English Literary History*, 24 (1957), 191–228.

Medwin, Thomas, *The Life of Percy Bysshe Shelley* (rev. edn., London, 1847; repr. London, 1913).

Mellor, Anne K., *Romanticism and Gender* (London, 1993).

Miller, J. Hillis, *The Linguistic Moment: From Wordsworth to Stevens* (Princeton, 1985).

Morton, Timothy, *Shelley and the Revolution in Taste: The Body and the Natural World* (Cambridge, 1994).

Murphy, John, *The Dark Angel: Gothic Elements in Shelley's Works* (Cranbury, NJ, 1975).

Notopoulos, James A., *The Platonism of Shelley: A Study of Platonism and the Poetic Mind* (Durham, NC, 1949).

O'Malley, Glenn, *Shelley and Synaesthesia* (Evanston, Ill., 1964).

O'Neill, Michael, *The Human Mind's Imaginings: Conflict and Achievement in Shelley's Poetry* (Oxford, 1989a).

—— *Percy Bysshe Shelley: A Literary Life* (London, 1989b).

—— (ed.), *Shelley*, Longman Critical Readers (London, 1993a).

—— (ed.), Shelley Special Issue, *Durham University Journal*, 85 (July 1993b).

Paley, Morton D., 'Apocapolitics: Allusion and Structure in Shelley's *Mask of Anarchy*', *Huntington Library Quarterly*, 54 (1991), 91–109.

Perkins, David, *The Quest for Permanence: The Symbolism of Wordsworth, Shelley, and Keats* (Cambridge, Mass., 1959).

Peterfreund, Stuart, 'Shelley, Monboddo, Vico, and the Language of Poetry', *Style*, 15 (1981), 382–400.

Pite, Ralph, *The Circle of our Vision: Dante's Presence in English Romantic Poetry* (Oxford, 1994).

Pottle, Frederick A., 'The Case of Shelley', *Publications of the Modern Language Association*, 67 (1952), 589–608.

Poulet, Georges, 'Romanticism', in his *The Metamorphoses of the Circle*, trans. Carley Dawson, Eliot Coleman, and G. Poulet (Baltimore, 1966), 91–118.

Pulos, C. E., *The Deep Truth: A Study of Shelley's Scepticism* (Lincoln, Nebr., 1954).

Purinton, Marjean D., *Romantic Ideology Unmasked: The Mentally Constructed Tyrannies in Dramas of William Wordsworth, Lord Byron, Percy Shelley, and Joanna Baillie* (Newark, Del., 1994).

Quinney, Laura, *Literary Power and the Criteria of Truth* (Gainesville, Fla., 1995).

Quint, David, 'Representation and Ideology in *The Triumph of Life*', *Studies in English Literature*, 18 (1978), 640–54.

Rajan, Tilottama, *Dark Interpreter: The Discourse of Romanticism* (Ithaca, NY, 1980).

—— *The Supplement of Reading: Figures of Understanding in Romantic Theory and Practice* (Ithaca, NY, 1990).

Rapaport, Herman, 'Staging *Mont Blanc*', in Marc Krupnik (ed.), *Displacement: Derrida and After* (Bloomington Ind., 1983), 54–73.

Redpath, Theodore (ed.), *The Young Romantics and Critical Opinion 1807–1824* (London, 1973).

Reed, Arden (ed.), *Romanticism and Language* (Ithaca, NY, 1984).

Reiman, Donald H., *Shelley's 'The Triumph of Life': A Critical Study, Based on a Text Newly Edited from the Bodleian Manuscript* (Urbana, Ill., 1965).

—— *Percy Bysshe Shelley*, Twayne English Authors (Boston, 1969; rev. edn., Boston, 1988).

—— (ed.), *The Romantics Reviewed: Contemporary Reviews of English Romantic Writers, 1793–1830*, vols. viii–ix (New York, 1972).

—— 'The Complete Poetical Works of Percy Bysshe Shelley, edited by Neville Rogers', *Journal of English and Germanic Philology*, 73 (1974), 251–6.

—— *Romantic Texts and Contexts* (Columbia, Mo., 1987).

—— *Intervals of Inspiration: The Skeptical Tradition and the Psychology of Romanticism* (Greenwood, Ill., 1988).

Richardson, Alan, *A Mental Theater: Poetic Drama and Consciousness in the Romantic Age* (University Park, Pa., 1988).

Ridenour, George E. (ed.), *Shelley: A Collection of Critical Essays*, Twentieth Century Views (Englewood Cliffs, NJ, 1965).

Rieder, John, 'Shelley's "Mont Blanc": Landscape and the Ideology of the Sacred Text', *English Literary History*, 48 (1981), 778–98.

—— 'The "One" in *Prometheus Unbound*', *Studies in English Literature*, 25 (1985), 775–800.

Rieger, James, *The Mutiny Within: The Heresies of Percy Bysshe Shelley* (New York, 1967).

Robinson, Charles E., *Shelley and Byron: The Snake and Eagle Wreathed in Fight* (Baltimore, 1976).

Rogers, Neville, *Shelley at Work* (2nd edn., Oxford, 1967).

Ross, Marlon B., *The Contours of Masculine Desire: Romanticism and the Rise of Women's Poetry* (Oxford, 1989).

Sacks, Peter, *The English Elegy: Studies in the Genre from Spenser to Yeats* (Baltimore, 1985).

St Clair, William, *The Godwins and the Shelleys: The Biography of a Family* (London, 1989).

Schapiro, Barbara, *The Romantic Mother: Narcissistic Patterns in Romantic Poetry* (Baltimore, 1983).

Schulze, Earl J., *Shelley's Theory of Poetry: A Reappraisal* (The Hague, 1966).

Scrivener, Michael Henry, *Radical Shelley: The Philosophical Anarchism and Utopian Thought of Percy Bysshe Shelley* (Princeton, 1982).

Shelley, Bryan, *Shelley and Scripture: The Interpreting Angel* (Oxford, 1994).

Simpson, David, *Irony and Authority in Romantic Poetry* (New York, 1979).

—— *Romanticism, Nationalism and the Revolt against Theory* (Chicago, 1993).

Slater, John F., 'Self-Concealment and Self-Revelation in Shelley's "Epipsychidion"', *Papers on Language and Literature*, 11 (1975), 279–92.

Solve, Melvin, *Shelley: His Theory of Poetry* (New York, 1927; repr. New York, 1964).

Sperry, Stuart, *Shelley's Major Verse: The Narrative and Dramatic Poetry* (Cambridge, Mass., 1988).

Spiegelman, Willard, *Majestic Indolence: English Romantic Poetry and the Work of Art* (New York, 1995).

Steinman, Lisa M., 'Shelley's Skepticism: Allegory in "Alastor"', *English Literary History*, 45 (1978), 255–69.

JERROLD E. HOGLE

Steinman, Lisa M., 'From "Alastor" to "The Triumph of Life": Shelley on the Nature and Source of Linguistic Pleasure', *Romanticism Past and Present*, 7 (1983), 23–36.

Swinden, Patrick (ed.), *Shelley: Shorter Poems and Lyrics*, A Casebook (London, 1976).

Tate, Allen, *Reason in Madness: Critical Essays* (New York, 1941).

Tetreault, Ronald, *The Poetry of Life: Shelley and Literary Form* (Toronto, 1987).

Twitchell, James, *Romantic Horizons: Aspects of the Sublime in English Poetry and Painting, 1770–1850* (Columbia, Mo., 1983).

Ulmer, William, *Shelleyan Eros: The Rhetoric of Romantic Love* (Princeton, 1990).

Wagenknecht, David (ed.), Articles on Shelley issue, *Studies in Romanticism*, 17 (1978).

—— Shelley Special Issue, *Studies in Romanticism*, 23 (1984).

Wagner, Jennifer Ann, *A Moment's Monument: Revisionary Poetics and the Nineteenth Century English Sonnet* (Madison, 1996).

Waldoff, Leon, 'The Father–Son Conflict in *Prometheus Unbound*: The Psychology of a Vision', *Psychoanalytic Review*, 62 (1975), 79–96.

Wasserman, Earl R., *Shelley: A Critical Reading* (Baltimore, 1971).

Webb, Timothy, *The Violet in the Crucible: Shelley and Translation* (Oxford, 1976).

—— *Shelley: A Voice Not Understood* (Manchester, 1977).

Weinberg, Alan, *Shelley's Italian Experience* (London, 1991).

Weiskel, Thomas, *The Romantic Sublime: Studies in the Structure and Psychology of Transcendence* (Baltimore, 1976).

Weisman, Karen A., *Imageless Truths: Shelley's Poetic Fictions* (Philadelphia, 1994).

Welburn, Andrew, *Power and Self-Consciousness in the Poetry of Shelley* (New York, 1986).

White, Newman Ivey, (ed.), *The Unextinguished Hearth: Shelley and his Contemporary Critics* (New York, 1938).

—— *Shelley*, 2 vols. (New York, 1940).

Wilkie, Brian, *Romantic Poets and Epic Tradition* (Madison, 1965).

Williams, Raymond, *Culture and Society 1780–1950* (London, 1958; repr. New York, 1966).

Wilson, Milton, *Shelley's Later Poetry: A Study of his Prophetic Imagination* (New York, 1959).

Wittreich, Joseph A. (ed.), *The Romantics on Milton: Formal Essays and Critical Asides* (Cleveland, 1970).

Woodings, R. B. (ed.), *Shelley*, A Casebook (London, 1968).

Woodman, Ross G., *The Apocalyptic Vision in the Poetry of Shelley* (Toronto, 1964).

—— 'The Androgyne in *Prometheus Unbound*', *Studies in Romanticism*, 20 (1981), 225–47.

Woodring, Carl, *Politics in English Romantic Poetry* (Cambridge, Mass., 1970).

Wright, John W., *Shelley's Myth of Metaphor* (Athens, Ga., 1970).

Yeats, William Butler, 'The Philosophy of Shelley's Poetry' (1900), in his *Essays and Introductions* (New York, 1961), 73–92.

7. John Keats

GREG KUCICH

Upon the one hundredth anniversary of the publication of Keats's first volume of poems in 1817, Sidney Colvin gasped at the enormous 'load' of scholarly work on Keats that had accumulated and wondered if 'all this labour' had left anything new to discuss. It is a testament of Keats's remarkable achievement in such a short span of poetic activity that his life and writings have inspired the generations succeeding Colvin to find plenty to say. Keats is the only major Romantic writer whose reputation among critics and poets has remained continuously strong throughout the last two centuries, especially during the recent boom of reappraisals provoked by the 1995 bicentennial of his birth. This latest outpouring of critical energy—which includes special issues on Keats in five journals of Romantic studies, a new biography, fresh editions of the poetry, and two major collections of revisionary essays—makes the present an exhilarating, transitional moment in studies of Keats. He has emerged from all this recent activity in a plethora of new looks, particularly marked by the social and political dynamics of his time. These reassessments grow out of previous critical traditions, however, and broaden areas of inquiry developed by generations of earlier Keats critics. Tracing new trajectories in such a relation to the long, distinguished history of writings on Keats constitutes the basic pattern of this bibliography.

The model and inspiration for this plan is the superb bibliographical essay by Jack Stillinger, which 'Present, Past & Future sees' of Keats studies (1985). Published slightly over a decade ago, Stillinger's essay comprehensively summarizes the history of Keats criticism to that date and presciently anticipates many of the recent developments. Readers of this bibliography should use it in tandem with Stillinger's, regarding it as a condensed, freshly refined, and updated complement to his seminal work.

BIBLIOGRAPHIES, TEXTS, AND CONCORDANCES

Stillinger's bibliographical essay does not claim to be exhaustive, and additional as well as updated direction can be found in a variety of more specialized

I wish to express my gratitude to Julie Schuetz, whose insightful and energetic assistance made an invaluable contribution to this project.

checklists and bibliographies. Evert and Rhodes provide a more recent though not heavily annotated introduction to Keats bibliography. MacGillivray offers an informative introductory essay on Keats's reception history from his own time up to the 1940s, followed by a detailed, annotated listing of criticism during this period. Hearn's checklist of criticism between 1945 and 1981 is less useful because it provides no annotations and no thematic organization. More specialized in his focus, Rhodes annotates criticism on the major odes from Keats's time to 1980. In response to the mounting tradition of Japanese scholarship on Keats, Okada examines the reasons for Keats's popularity in Japan and furnishes a summary of Japanese reactions over the last hundred years. In addition to these specialized bibliographies, comprehensive checklists of Keats criticism, with short annotations, are published annually in the *Keats–Shelley Journal*. Green and Wilson, and Hartley, have collected the bibliographies for 1950–74 in two convenient volumes. Keats sections are also included annually in the *MLA International Bibliography* and in the standard bibliographies of Romanticism.

The authoritative edition of Keats's poetry, certain to remain so for some time, is Stillinger's (1978). It presents the most accurate texts of Keats's poems available complemented by a detailed editorial apparatus that lists manuscript emendations and traces the publication history of each poem through all of its transcriptions and manuscript versions. A 'reading' edition of the same texts is also available (1982), which reduces the textual machinery and provides more interpretative commentary on the poems. Allott's edition of the complete poems is less authoritative textually, but it supplies the best annotations currently available. The committed Keats scholar will have both Stillinger's and Allott's editions at hand.

Several reliable, less expensive editions of the poems and prose are available in paperback. Barnard, though working before Stillinger's edition appeared, prints a textually sound collection of the complete poems with extensive annotations and helpful appendices featuring Keats's Milton marginalia and his review of Edmund Kean's acting (1973). Cook, benefiting from while also adjusting Stillinger's editorial work, provides what has become the most useful selection of poems and prose. It offers significantly more letters than the previous standard selection of letters and poems edited by Bush (1959), and it also contains examples of Keats's Shakespeare and Milton marginalia as well as his Kean review. Roe gives an innovative selection of the poetry that highlights its political dimensions, followed by a useful sampling of critical responses from the nineteenth century to the present (1995 edn.).

Several more specialized editions of Keats's writings can be particularly helpful for those working on individual poems, the status of the poetry manuscripts, the publication and reception history of the poetry, and Keats's annotations of other writers. The Woodstock series of reprints includes facsimiles of the three volumes of poetry Keats published during his life (Wordsworth). Steinhoff offers a critical edition of *Endymion*, featuring detailed criticism on the poem's themes, structures, sources, and reception history. Harry Buxton Forman's eight-volume 'Hampstead Edition' of Keats's works (1938–9; rev. Maurice Buxton Forman) is still important because it reprints contemporary reviews of Keats's poetry, poems written to Keats, Keats's own periodical reviews, and his marginalia on Shakespeare, Milton, Hazlitt, and Burton. Considerable recent work has made facsimiles of Keats's poetry holographs available for study. Stillinger's seven-volume contribution to *The Manuscripts of the Younger Romantics* series includes facsimile holographs of *Endymion* and *Hyperion* (1985–8). His edition of the poetry manuscripts at Harvard (1990), which houses the largest collection of Keats materials and ranks with Keats House, Hampstead, as the two main Keats archives, provides a reader-friendly arrangement of thirty-seven poetry holographs, printed transcriptions of the manuscripts, and final textual versions all grouped together on facing pages so that readers can trace the complex movement from first composition through manuscript revision to printed text. Vendler's introductory essay to this volume (1990) conveys the spirit of charged compositional excitement revealed by the manuscripts and suggests how their physical shape can illuminate important stylistic and thematic dimensions of the poetry. Gittings prints manuscript facsimiles of the five major odes published in the *Lamia volume* (1970*b*). The availability of so much carefully edited manuscript material raises a host of stimulating questions about Keats's compositional practices, the often problematic role of editors and transcribers in the production of his texts, and the immense difficulties of establishing stable texts and determining authorial intentions—issues that are succinctly discussed by Stillinger (1974).

The standard edition of Keats's letters remains Rollins's two-volume work (1958). This textually scrupulous edition has not been superseded in the four decades since its publication, although there have been minor corrections of the text and expansions of the commentary. Gittings provides a fresh set of interpretative notes in his substantial and reliable selection of the letters (1970*a*), which is less expensive and more readily available than Rollins's edition.

Additional manuscript and textual materials of importance for studies of Keats and his circle have been assembled in Rollins's *The Keats Circle* (1948), which contains an invaluable collection of letters and papers on Keats produced by members of his circle. Stillinger assembles a wealth of facsimile material on Keats, most of it produced by Richard Woodhouse and Charles Brown, in his volumes for *The Manuscripts of the Younger Romantics*. A particularly important item in this collection is the facsimile of Woodhouse's annotated copy of Keats's 1817 volume, *Poems*, which had been previously transcribed and discussed by Sperry (1967). Maurice Buxton Forman prints a transcription of Keats's lecture notes from his student period at Guy's Hospital (1934).

..
GREG KUCICH

Reproductions of Keats's marginalia on other writers are scattered through-out a wide body of texts including the editions mentioned above as well as works by Spurgeon, Wittreich, Haworth, Gittings (1956), and Lowell. Errors in Lowell's transcriptions have been corrected by Anderson and Lau (1986). Although Owings provides a descriptive catalogue of all the existing books that Keats owned, we still need a comprehensive work that collects all of the avail-able marginalia in a single edition. Keats scholars now enjoy the benefits of modern concordances of the poems and letters (Pollard; Becker, Dilligan, and Bender) keyed to the standard editions of Stillinger and Rollins.

CRITICISM

The history of biographical writing on Keats constitutes an intriguing topic in itself, intelligently discussed by Marquess, partly because the mass of surviv-ing letters and documents made it possible to construct a detailed record (almost day-to-day at times) of Keats's poignant experiences throughout his adult years, and partly because the stratagems of his biographers in the nine-teenth century created in themselves various forms of high drama. The stand-ard biographies that continue to function as essential research tools were all produced in the 1960s. W. J. Bate's monumental study (1963) is arguably the best single book on Keats in its depth of insight, amplitude of concerns, and technical mastery of the details of Keats's life. Ward's biography of the same year offers more information on the political conditions of Keats's time and presents a new though not always convincing psychoanalytic account of the emotional traumas of his boyhood and their effect on his mature attitudes toward art, women, and experience. Gittings's biography (1968), culminating a series of critical works on Keats's backgrounds (1954, 1956, 1964), supplies important details about the English places, institutions, and customs that helped condition his thought and writing. Each of these biographies is valu-able in its own way, and committed students of Keats will be familiar with them all. Lowell's 1925 life is still engaging because of its passionate champion-ship of Keats and its sustained record of a female poet's response to him. The production of nineteenth-century biographies by Milnes and Rossetti discloses fascinating records of the quarrels among Keats's friends over his reputation, well documented in Rollins (1948), and the gendered disputes about his courage and maturity that consumed many of his early critics.

Three decades of research since the major biographies of the 1960s, along with the imminence of the bicentennial, made the production of new bio-graphical efforts inevitable. What has appeared in the last few years, however, is of mixed quality. Pinion's chronology of Keats's life, designed as a quick ref-erence guide, is flawed by factual errors, textual inaccuracies, and a general unfamiliarity with recent Keats criticism. More successful is Walker's photo-graphic re-creation of Keats's 1818 northern walking tour with Brown, which includes introductory notes on the details of the trip, the characteristics of local regions, and the political climate of the time. Walker also gives texts of the letters Keats and Brown wrote on their travels as well as Brown's journ-alistic record of the trip. A non-scholarly but engaging work of biographical interest is Clark's poetic novel on Keats's life, which is particularly rich in Keatsian phrasings and insights. As stimulating as these various efforts can be, they have not fulfilled the emerging need for a new biography in the wake of recent materialist and feminist revaluations of Keats studies. Coote's recent biography does place a strong emphasis on the socio-political conditions of early nineteenth-century Europe, but his study is light in its scholarship and provides few additions to the biographical works of the 1960s. The time is ripe for a major new scholarly biography.

Helpful starting points in Keats criticism are furnished by the introductory studies of Hirst (1981), Watson, and Barnard (1987), the last of which is most abreast of recent critical innovations. Each of these introductions builds funda-mentally on the developing tradition of Keats criticism, whose evolutionary shifts all serious students of Keats need to comprehend. Indeed, the historical development of critical and biographical studies of Keats has become an important issue for critics interested in the ways our current perceptions may be implicated in the ideological investments of past writings. Although it can be critically reductive to map out rigidly demarcated phases of Keats com-mentary, it is possible and useful to formulate a brief sketch of this developing critical tradition, which will be followed by a more detailed section on special flashpoints of critical interest.

The earliest published reactions to Keats appeared in the periodical press and were frequently negative, their hostility motivated, as in the notorious 'Cockney School' reviews of Lockhart and Croker (Matthews), by political biases against Keats's class background, liberal politics, and stylistic eroticism. His supporters defended him in the press but also stressed his sufferings on the rack of hostile reviews, which created the myth best known through Shelley's *Adonais* of a hypersensitive Keats crushed by a mean-spirited world. The ground was thus set for debates about his masculinity, which Milnes took up in his 1848 biography celebrating Keats's courage and creative vigour, examples of which he identified in extensive reproductions of the poems and letters. From this point on Keats's reputation steadily improved, although controversies about his manliness persisted, flamed by Harry Buxton Forman's 1878 publication of his love letters to Fanny Brawne, and estimations of the extent of his greatness remained divided. Later Victorian sympathizers were split between Arnold's qualified praise of his striking but still immature gift for Shakespearian felicity of expression (Matthews) and Rossetti's admiration of his otherworldly, feminized beauty, which inspired many Pre-Raphaelite paintings of his works.

By the early twentieth century, a new generation of scholars shifted the focus to Keats's intellectual depth, his political and philosophical investments, his mature use of literary sources, and his rigorous programme of creative development (Colvin, Thorpe 1926, Lowell, de Selincourt, Finney). We are still deeply indebted to these pioneering scholars, who remain worth consulting especially for work on Keats's ideas and sources. New Criticism found in Keats one of the few compelling exemplars among all the Romantics of condensed poetic expression, paradox, and irony. The Keats of the odes received special emphasis, honoured representatively by Brooks for his textual density. The New Critical emphasis on Keatsian paradox helped set an agenda for increasingly sophisticated studies of irony in the poems and letters, which became one of the leading concerns for Keats scholars from the 1950s to the 1980s, especially in relation to his conflicts between imagination and reality (Stillinger 1971). Philosophically oriented critics like de Man found such ironic dynamics highly conducive to deconstructive readings. About the same time, the subject of Keats's sources became energized by the advent of influence theory in the works of Bate (1970) and Bloom (1971, 1973, 1976), who took Keats as a stunning model for the post-Miltonic poet's Oedipal struggles with the giants of literary tradition. The psychoanalytic strain of Bloom's theorizing was complemented, moreover, by a series of brilliant if sometimes eccentric studies of Keats's emotional life and its impact on his stylistic formulations (Bayley 1962, John Jones, Ricks).

This combined work on irony, deconstructive poetics, psychology, style, and influences, along with the great biographical efforts of the 1960s, placed Keats at the centre of Romantic studies for several decades. However, the emergence of new historicism and feminist theory in Romantic criticism of the 1980s called for radically modified approaches to Keats, which were initiated by McGann's materialist readings of Keats and Ross's pioneering investigations of Keats and gender issues. Important work in these areas proceeded throughout the 1980s and 1990s, yet Keats studies did not always seem to keep pace with the advance of feminist/historicist work that drove Romantic criticism throughout much of this period. Growing concerns about this gap coincided with the imminence of the bicentennial, however, to generate a surge of historicist and feminist readings in the last few years, best represented by the work of Roe, Mellor (1993), and Wolfson (1990, 1991, 1995a).

The most effective way to become familiar with these developing traditions is to consult the various collections of critical essays on Keats. Numerous compilations of nineteenth-century commentary are available. Schwartz and Reiman (1972) reproduce the largest selections of contemporary reviews, while Redpath and Hayden locate such responses within the literary and political conditions of early nineteenth-century periodical reviewing. Matthews gives a broader selection of Keats commentary in letters, essays, prefaces, and reviews dating from 1816 to 1863. Harwell reprints numerous Victorian responses from 1848 to 1900, and Rollins (1946) traces Keats's growing reputation in America up to the publication of Milnes's biography in 1848. *The John Keats Memorial Volume* contains a fascinating array of turn-of-the-century critical and poetic responses by such figures as Shaw, Hardy, Yeats, and Bridges.

Twentieth-century criticism has been collected in a variety of sources, many of which prioritize specific areas of interest in the developing tradition. Bate (1964) offers a rich sampling of critical approaches from the 1920s to the 1960s, which broadly emphasize the range of Keats's poetic experimentation and trace his unique significance for poets from the nineteenth century on. Muir represents mid-twentieth-century critical interest in Keatsian duality, as do Danzig and Stillinger (1968) in their more specialized collections of essays on *The Eve of St Agnes* and the major odes. Bloom's grouping of essays from the 1960s to the 1980s highlights the deconstructive work of the Yale School (1985). De Almeida's collection (1990*a*) marks developments in Keats studies from the 1960s up to its publication in 1990, complementing mid-century essays with newly commissioned work on Keats in relation to politics, science, medicine, and gender. Evert and Rhodes's volume characterizes the priorities of Keats scholars and teachers at the start of the 1990s. The more immediately recent spate of work on Keats, politics, and gender is well represented in Roe (1995*a*) and the special bicentennial issues on Keats published in 1995–6 by *Keats–Shelley Journal*, *European Romantic Review*, *Studies in Romanticism*, *Romanticism*, and the *Keats–Shelley Review*.

The most helpful gatherings of critical reactions for those tracing Keats's overall reception history can be found in Hill and Roe (1995 edn.), both of which provide a range of commentary from the nineteenth and twentieth centuries. Hill's substantial collection of essays is somewhat limited by its specialized focus on the narrative poems and its termination in the 1960s. Roe's edition of selected poems concludes with a section of critical extracts from Hunt in 1816 to Mellor in 1993, which offers a concise history of the entire critical tradition. For recent discussions of the ways this developing tradition has affected the latest trajectories in Keats studies, see Scott (1995) and Kucich (1996).

The following, more detailed consideration of specialized topics begins with critical developments at the cutting edge of Keats studies today, but this arrangement is designed to show how recent innovations derive from distinguished critical genealogies and serve ultimately to reassess and renew the impressive traditions of Keats criticism. Many of the newest developments emanate from historicist revaluations of Keats's experience and writings, yet these reconsiderations of his immediate social and political circumstances build on important precedents throughout the history of Keats scholarship.

Contemporary reviewers like Lockhart were motivated fundamentally by political biases, and though many of Keats's earlier critics ignored his political investments completely there were some, like Shaw, who celebrated his opposition to the hegemonic political, religious, and economic values of his time. Shaw's delightfully iconoclastic essay, which claims that Keats would have become a 'fullblooded modern revolutionist', is required reading for anyone working on Keats and politics. Of a more scholarly bent, Garrod's early twentieth-century book examines Keats's firm commitment to liberal political causes (1926). Thorpe's essay of several years later provides an informative record of Keats's sustained involvement with the politics of his time (1931). Finney details the important influence of the liberal political education that Keats received at Enfield School, Guy's Hospital, and within Hunt's literary circle, backgrounds which also receive treatment in the major biographies of the 1960s, especially in Ward's. More recently, Hartman considers the nationalistic ideology informing 'To Autumn', and Koch finds the attacks on political retrenchment in Hunt's *Examiner* conditioning the narrative and thematic structures of major works like *Endymion* and *Hyperion*. When McGann's seminal essay on Keats's politics encouraged a new wave of historicist readings in the 1980s, there was thus a well-established though not always highly visible tradition of scholarship on which to build.

The first major development of this background appeared in the 1986 *Studies in Romanticism* special issue on 'Keats and Politics', edited by Wolfson and containing a series of essays on the interconnection of politics, gender, and style in Keats's poetry (Bewell 1986, Bromwich 1986, Dickstein 1986, Fry, Keach). Major books soon followed, with Levinson producing an aggressively polemical study of Keats's class anxieties (1988) and Watkins formulating a more controlled though equally challenging Marxist analysis of the conditioning impact of capitalist ideology on Keats's poetic structures, themes, and characterizations (1989). Some Keats scholars feel that work of this sort temporarily stalled in the 1990s—there were no more related books until Roe's 1995 *Keats and History* and his 1997 *John Keats and the Culture of Dissent*—but we can trace a steady proliferation of historicist articles throughout the last decade.

Keats's theories of history and their political implications are examined by Reed, Newey (1989, 1995), and Kucich (1995b) in studies that expand on the previous work of Eggers. The economic pressures that impinge on much of Keats's literary experience are analysed by Heinzelman, Cooper, Kelley (1987), Hoagwood (1995), and Elizabeth Jones, all of whom build on Ruthven's earlier work. While most of these historicist readings focus on Keats's open engagement with specific historical events, particular market-place issues, and direct political influences like Hunt's *Examiner*, Watkins (1987) and Hoagwood (1989) explain how social networks of relations condition the symbolic order of poems that do not deal on the surface with economic or political concerns.

This type of investigation of symbolic structures has been particularly fruitful in studies of the poem that until recently has been considered the most transcendentally detached of all Keats's works, 'To Autumn' (Bennett 1990*b*, 1991; Roe 1995*b*).

Much as this corpus of historicist work has invigorated Keats criticism, it has not been welcomed unconditionally. Though few would now question the importance of studying Keats's social contexts, some critics have wondered if in our rush to politicize his writings we have distorted his overall creative accomplishment. De Almeida (1990*b*) and O'Neill (1995), for example, warn against naive forms of historical critique. Such reservations about the materialist emphases of recent criticism are probably responsible for those impressions of a temporary decline in historicist work. Meanwhile, others have ventured to integrate aesthetic and historicist modes of appreciating Keats (Vendler 1987, Phinney, Kandl). This increasingly urgent search for ways to evaluate Keatsian poetic formulations within materialist frames constitutes one of the strongest challenges for future Keats criticism.

Work on Keats and gender has profited the most from recent historicist criticism. Here, too, there is a lively though not always recognized tradition. The earliest reviewers of Keats were troubled by his gender instabilities, and controversies about his masculinity swirled throughout the nineteenth century. Twentieth-century readings of his divided attitudes toward sexuality and gender began to develop seriously in the 1960s and 1970s with the studies of John Jones, D'Avanzo, Enscoe, Van Ghent, and Ricks. These books still provide an important foundation for the more recent proliferation of work on Keats and gender. The many new studies in this area examine Keats's interactions with women and his representations of female characters, but they often focus more subtly on his tendency to work out his creative aspirations and divisions in problematically gendered terms. Where Homans and Swann find his form of negative capability antagonistic to feminine experience, Mellor sees a more redemptive embrace of feminine positions in his poetic theory and practice (1993). Wolfson traces his various swerves between masculinist and feminist forms of subjectivity (1990, 1991, 1995*a*, 1995*b*). Hilton and Lau (1984) analyse his ways of expressing his conflict about imagination and realism in divided attitudes toward women. Alwes makes this the central concern of her book on Keats's female characters, but she does not provide much commentary on the social and political conditions of gender relations in the early nineteenth century. Ross (1989, 1990), Levinson (1988), Bewell (1992), and Watkins (1996) are more effective in this regard. Ross also provides the fullest account of Keats's interactions with women writers (1989), a topic that Whiting and Kucich (1995*a*) explore in more specific relation to Charlotte Smith and Mary Tighe. Among the most illuminating of all the fine work on Keats and gender now available are studies by Friedman and Philip Cox that investigate his self-conscious ways of performing and testing the boundaries of gender identity. Significant, provocative, yet still largely exploratory, this body of scholarship pinpoints one of the most stimulating areas of Keats studies open to future, more nuanced development, especially in relation to the homosocial and homoerotic dynamics of the Keats circle.

Because so many of these political and gender issues were first worried over by nineteenth-century readers, it was inevitable that recent criticism should focus on such particular aspects of Keats's reception history. Aske (1995), Roe (1992), and Wolfson (1986*a*, 1990, 1995*a*, 1995*b*) provide excellent analyses of the intersecting roles of politics, class, and gender in nineteenth-century reactions to Keats. The early poetry that provoked many of those negative responses has been reconsidered as well in terms of its strategic combination of stylistic and political subversiveness (Keach, Levinson 1988, Roe 1992). Renewed interest in Keats's political contexts has also inspired fresh studies of the social and intellectual environments he entered at Enfield School and Guy's Hospital. Scholarly work on his medical background has been going on for some time, with Smith, Gittings (1968, 1971), and Wells documenting the gruesome medical conditions in which he trained. More recently the impact of this background on his poetic creations has been explored by Holstein and Lisa Perkins. The major studies of the social, scientific, and political milieu of his medical experience remain those of Goellnicht and de Almeida (1991). Both works are valuable in their own right, with Goellnicht focusing more substantially on Keats's experience at Guy's and its impact on his poetry and de Almeida furnishing a broader analysis of the interconnections among medical, scientific, philosophical, and political discourses in the early nineteenth century. Keats's critics have always been interested in the Enfield School environment and its liberal political atmosphere (Marples, Sperry 1979), but we are still just beginning to explore the exact nature of the political training he received there (Barnard 1995, Roe 1997).

Many of the issues that have centrally preoccupied Keats critics throughout much of the twentieth century remain alive and vital today. Keats's theories of the creative imagination and negative capability, for instance, figure prominently in nearly every major study of this century, though particularly useful and contrasting treatments of his divided allegiances to imagination and reality are gathered in debates among Wasserman, Stillinger (1971), and Waldoff (1985). W. J. Bate (1939), Wigod, Starr, and Fraustino provide a variety of specialized treatments of negative capability. Both topics have taken on a new urgency for feminist readers like Homans and Mellor (1993), who find them deeply implicated in Keats's problematic experiences of gender. In a related pattern, Keats's mythologizing has engaged critics throughout the twentieth century and continues to receive innovative treatment. Bush's major work on mythology and Romanticism remains foundational (1937), but it has been extended in a variety of illuminating ways by Goldberg (in relation to eighteenth-century forms of classicism), Aske (1985; connected to Bloomian theories of influence anxiety), Van Ghent (in relation to Keats's notion of the poet hero), and Evert (in terms of secularizations of Christian institutions). Most recently, Bewell has called our attention to the significant political implications of Keats's classicism (1986).

The philosophical, scientific, and religious backgrounds to which Keats responded have similarly interested critics throughout the twentieth century. Following the early work of Thorpe (1926) and Finney, numerous studies on Keats's engagement with eighteenth-century philosophy and psychology, including theories of the sublime, have appeared (Caldwell; Ende; Sperry 1963, 1973; Ryan 1976a, 1976b; Lau 1983). Platonic influences are traced, at times quite inventively, by Blackstone and, in a more controlled fashion, by Kabitoglou. Keats's involvement with the science of his time receives extensive treatment in studies of his medical experience, but the best single work in this area is by Sperry (1973). Blackstone, Bewell (1992), and Barnard (1980) provide more specialized studies of Keats's interests in botany and astronomy. His vexed interactions with the religious thought and institutions of his time have generated ongoing disputes about his religious beliefs, best encapsulated by the different positions on this subject taken by Sharp (1979) and Ryan (1976a). Both agree that Keats grappled with religious concerns and disparaged mainstream Christianity throughout his life, but where Sharp finds him completely abandoning organized religion for a secularized form of spiritual beauty Ryan locates his thought within liberal traditions of deism and natural religion. Both studies are valuable, and Ryan follows up on his with a recent essay on the links between religious and political dissent (1990).

Keats's ironic modes and their relation to various philosophical traditions have fascinated generations of readers, provoking a rich variety of theoretical approaches. In addition to the previously mentioned New Critical work and the mid-twentieth-century studies on imagination, major Keats critics like David Perkins (1959), Bush (1966), and Dickstein (1971) have all explored the complex workings of Keatsian contrariety, especially in relation to the split between imagination and reality. Sperry examines the eighteenth-century philosophical backgrounds to Keatsian irony (1973), and Mellor (1980) situates Keats's doubling modes of writing and thinking within the context of nineteenth-century German philosophy. Wolfson offers substantial discussions of the formal and rhetorical strategies of Keats's duality (1985, 1986b), which she associates with deconstructive frames in a critical move extensively developed by de Man, Rajan (1980, 1991), and Woodman. Reader response theory is represented by Spiller, and Schmid presents a lively Bakhtinian analysis. Feminist critics sometimes find such studies of irony inattentive to gender issues, but Baker demostrates how Keats's indeterminacy is closely related to his gender divisions.

These studies of Keatsian irony, especially in its formal dimensions, build on a rich tradition of criticism of Keats's poetic craftsmanship that begins with Finney and Ridley, develops through W. J. Bate (1945) and the mid-century biographers, figures prominently in the criticism of the 1960s, and continues to engage critics today. Where this type of criticism focused at first on formal details, more recent critics attend to the various narrative devices that structure the poems. Stillinger demonstrates the usefulness of examining narrative techniques in the poems (1990*b*), an approach followed by Little and, in a more theoretically sophisticated consideration of narrative and audience reception, by Bennett (1994). The ordering of Keats's poems, both in independent groups and within published volumes, has concerned many critics (Stillinger 1971, Fraistat), but Vendler's detailed study of the odes (1983) remains the major work in this area and the best sustained reading of the odes. Keats's experiments with the generic forms and traditions of sonnet writing and epic are treated by Zillman and Wilkie. His fascination with the theatre and dramatic writing was first examined in depth by Slote, but it has become a more compelling topic in light of recent reconsiderations of the material conditions of Romantic drama (Burroughs, Watkins 1986). Keats's poetic dialogues with the themes and structures of painting are thoroughly discussed in Jack's seminal book, but many perceptive studies have expanded on this foundation. Goslee and Cummings analyse Keatsian poetic metaphors in relation to theories of painting and architecture that he studied. Kelley (1995) and Scott (1994) reconsider the poems on art in relation to political and gender pressures. The impact of nineteenth-century musical practice and theory on Keats's poetry has been examined recently by Minahan, Brown, Becker, and Schneider, but additional work is needed on this intriguing topic.

Keats's letters are often considered as a unique genre in themselves, teeming with the kinds of ideas, energies, structural patterns, and divisions that inform the poetry. Nearly every major book on Keats deals in some manner with the enduring fascination of these letters, although Ricks and Hirst (1981) are especially insightful. Several more specialized studies of the letters are particularly worth consulting. Eliot and Trilling both offer memorable accounts of the wise, heroic consciousness that emerges from these writings. David Perkins draws connections between recurrent patterns of diction and imagery in poems and letters (1953). Wolfson shows how poems and letters participate in shared acts of ironic doubling (1982), and Michael makes an original argument for the later letters as a kind of sustained poem written after Keats had abandoned formal poetic composition. Pack celebrates the redemptive comic spirit that runs throughout the letters. Keats's humour, manifested in both poems and letters, has always endeared readers to him, and his genius for comedy is the subject of spirited essays by Dunbar and Bayley (1993). Gittings provides a revealing appendix on Keats's sexual slang (1968), which Bennett finds to be an important vehicle of political dissent (1990*a*). The uproar of Keatsian humour was facilitated by and usually circulated within his special circle of friends, about which much has been written (Richardson 1963, 1980). Of special interest is Sharp's use of gift exchange theory to examine the admirable reciprocity of Keats's interactions with friends, colleagues, and the literary spirits of the past (1989). Stillinger makes an important argument for the collaborative process among friends and associates through which many of Keats's poems underwent a form of multiple authorship (1991).

Keats's personal and literary relations with contemporary writers have received extensive critical treatment and continue to provoke innovative readings. His conflicted interactions with Wordsworth have attracted the most attention, starting with Balslev and developing in the work of Stillinger (1987), Wolfson (1986*b*), and Waldoff (1989). Roe (1990) stresses Keats's disappointment with Wordsworth's political conservatism. Stillinger provides the best condensed account of Keats's dealings with Coleridge (1990*a*). Bromwich gives the fullest discussion of his involvement with Hazlitt (1984). The details of his extended contact with Shelley are outlined by Reiman (1961–86). Fogle presents a sustained analysis of the stylistic differences between Keats and Shelley, while Curran makes a strong case for Shelley's subtle critiques of Keats in *Adonais*. Jeffrey N. Cox and Roe (1992) offer revisionary assessments of the political significance of the interactions between Keats and Shelley within the Hunt circle. Byron always put Keats on edge, and the class and sexual jealousies motivating this reaction have been explored by Hirst (1985), Lau (1990), and Levinson (1993). Lau also provides an excellent study of Keats's specific readings of contemporary poets (1991), which is an indispensable research tool for anyone working on Keats's relations with contemporary writers. His dealings with the women writers of his time have been discussed in the section above on gender, but there is much room for new work in this area.

Keats's intense engagements with his literary predecessors have inspired a staggering range of critical studies, but it is possible to distinguish several key emphases. Since the early twentieth-century studies of Murry, Spurgeon, Finney, and Priestley, critics have celebrated Keats's passionate attachments to Spenser, Shakespeare, Milton, Chaucer, and Dante while carefully tracing his readings and adaptations of their works. These kinds of source studies have continued through the work of Gittings (1956), White, Jonathan Bate, and Williams. Scholarship on Keats's eighteenth-century literary sources has similarly proceeded (Biggs, Gittings 1955, King, Sheats), though not so prolifically. But the practice of source studies became radically changed with the growth of influence theory in the last several decades, which prioritizes the conflicted nature of Keats's relations with overpowering predecessors. In addition to the pioneering work of W. J. Bate and Bloom in this field, Brisman (1978) and Sherwin conduct representative arguments for Keats's revisionary contention with the spirits of the past. Several critics have attempted in recent years to adjust the terms of these analyses by arguing that Keats's creative inhibitions were balanced by a more redemptive, creatively enabling sense of involvement with his forebears (Harding, Edmundson, Kucich 1991). Newlyn and Kucich (1995b) have extended this entire debate about belatedness into new considerations of its links to political pressures and gender conflicts.

Keats's impact on following writers has been so constant and profound that more may have been written on this topic than on any other issue in Keats studies. It is only possible to give a representative selection here, but the wide range of this condensed sample should illustrate the unique character of his afterlife among the poets. His influence on Victorian writers was outlined some time ago by Ford, whose general study has been extended by more specialized readings of his influence on Tennyson, Browning, Hallam, Hopkins, Morris, and Dickinson (Brisman 1992, Gurney, Kolb, Bump, Kerrigan, Short, Fontana). Bornstein discusses his broad impact on modernism, particularly on Stevens. There are numerous, more detailed treatments of his influence on Yeats, Joyce, Owen, Eliot, and Williams (James Jones, Bayley 1962, Stallworthy, Murphy, Finklestein). Birk provides a useful summary of the many articles written on Keats and Faulkner. A growing number of essays are appearing on Keats's relation to more recent poets like Olson, Larkin, and Clampitt (Spanos, Bayley 1984, O'Neill 1988), and to non-English-speaking poets like Rilke and Mallarmé (Fitzgerald, Cohn). Important work could be done on Keats's relation to the colonial institutions of his time and to postcolonial poets like Walcott. Gender concerns have been raised in some of these influence studies, such as Brisman's, but one of the most intriguing opportunities for future work on Keats among the poets entails a more substantial consideration of his special appeal for women poets like Lowell and Clampitt. Such a challenge, along with the many other opportunities for new work identified in this essay, confirms that in continuing the best traditions of the past the revisionary criticism of recent years has pointed the way for much more to be said as Keats enters his third century.

REFERENCES

TEXTS AND TEXTUAL STUDIES

Allott, Miriam (ed.), *The Poems of John Keats* (London, 1970).

Barnard, John (ed.), *John Keats: The Complete Poems* (Harmondsworth, 1973).

Becker, Michael G., Dilligan, Robert J., and Bender, Todd K. (eds.), *A Concordance to the Poems of John Keats* (New York, 1981).

Bush, Douglas (ed.), *John Keats: Selected Poems and Letters* (Boston, 1959).

Cook, Elizabeth (ed.), *John Keats* (Oxford, 1990).

Forman, Harry Buxton (ed.), *Letters of John Keats to Fanny Brawne* (London, 1878).

—— (ed.), *The Poetical Works and Other Writings of John Keats*, rev. Maurice Buxton Forman, 8 vols. (New York, 1938–9).

Forman, Maurice Buxton (ed.), *John Keats's Anatomical and Physiological Note Book* (1934; New York, 1970).

Gittings, Robert (ed.), *The Letters of John Keats* (Oxford, 1970a).

—— (ed.), *The Odes of Keats and their Earliest Known Manuscripts* (London, 1970b).

Pollard, David (ed.), *A KWIC Concordance to the Letters of John Keats* (Hove, 1989).

Roe, Nicholas (ed.), *John Keats: Selected Poems* (London, 1995).

Rollins, Hyder Edward (ed.), *The Keats Circle*, 2 vols. (Cambridge, Mass., 1948).

—— (ed.), *The Letters of John Keats 1814–1821*, 2 vols. (Cambridge, Mass., 1958).

Sperry, Stuart M., 'Richard Woodhouse's Interleaved and Annotated Copy of Keats's *Poems* (1817)', *Literary Monographs*, 1 (1967), 101–64, 308–11.

Steinhoff, Stephen T. (ed.), *Keats's Endymion: A Critical Edition* (New York, 1987).

Stillinger, Jack, *The Texts of Keats's Poems* (Cambridge, Mass., 1974).

—— (ed.), *The Poems of John Keats* (Cambridge, Mass., 1978).

—— (ed.), *John Keats: Complete Poems* (Cambridge, Mass., 1982).

—— (ed.), *The Manuscripts of the Younger Romantics: John Keats*, 7 vols. (New York, 1985–8).

—— (ed.), *John Keats: Poetry Manuscripts at Harvard* (Cambridge, Mass., 1990).

Wittreich, Joseph Anthony (ed.), *The Romantics on Milton* (Cleveland, 1970).

Wordsworth, Jonathan (ed.), *John Keats: Poems* (Oxford, 1989).

—— (ed.), *John Keats: Lamia 1820* (Oxford, 1990)

—— (ed.), *John Keats: Endymion* (Oxford, 1991).

CRITICISM AND COMMENTARY

Alwes, Karla, *Imagination Transformed: The Evolution of the Female Character in Keats's Poetry* (Carbondale, Ill., 1993).

Anderson, Norman A., 'Corrections to Amy Lowell's Reading of Keats's Marginalia', *Keats–Shelley Journal*, 23 (1974), 24–31.

Aske, Martin, *Keats and Hellenism* (Cambridge, 1985).

—— 'Keats, the Critics, and the Politics of Envy' (1995), in Roe (1995a: 46–64).

Baker, Jeffrey, *John Keats and Symbolism* (Brighton, 1986).

Balslev, Thora, *Keats and Wordsworth: A Comparative Study* (Copenhagen, 1962).

Barnard, John, 'Sun-Spots in Keats's Epistle "To My Brother George"', *Keats–Shelley Memorial Bulletin*, 31 (1980), 57–60.

—— *John Keats* (Cambridge, 1987).

—— 'Charles Cowden Clark's "Cockney" Commonplace Book' (1995), in Roe (1995a: 65–87).

Bate, Jonathan, *Shakespeare and the English Romantic Imagination* (Oxford, 1986).

Bate, W. J., *Negative Capability: The Intuitive Approach in Keats* (Cambridge, Mass., 1939).

—— *The Stylistic Development of Keats* (Cambridge, Mass., 1945).

—— *John Keats* (London, 1963).

Bate, W. J., (ed.), *Keats: A Collection of Essays* (Englewood Cliffs, NJ, 1964).

—— *The Burden of the Past and the English Poet* (New York, 1970).

Bayley, John, 'Keats and Reality', *Proceedings of the British Academy*, 48 (1962), 91–125.

—— 'Larkin and the Romantic Tradition', *Critical Quarterly*, 26 (1984), 61–6.

—— 'Keats and the Genius of Parody', *Essays in Criticism*, 43 (1993), 112–22.

Becker, Michael G., 'Keats's Fantasia: The "Ode on Melancholy," Sonata Form and Mozart's "Fantasia in C Minor" for Piano, K 475', *Comparatist*, 17 (1993), 18–37.

Bennett, Andrew J., '"Fragment of Castle-Builder" and Keats's Use of Sexual Slang', *English Language Notes*, 28 (1990*a*), 39–50.

—— 'The Politics of Gleaning in Keats's "Ode to a Nightingale" and "To Autumn"', *Keats–Shelley Journal*, 39 (1990*b*), 34–8.

—— 'Agrarian Politics and the Economics of Writing: Keats's "To Autumn"', *Criticism*, 33 (1991), 333–51.

—— *Keats, Narrative, and Audience* (Cambridge, 1994).

Bewell, Alan J., 'The Political Implication of Keats's Classicist Aesthetics', *Studies in Romanticism*, 25 (1986), 220–9.

—— 'Keats's "Realm of Flora"', *Studies in Romanticism*, 31 (1992), 71–98.

Biggs, H. E., 'Swift and Keats', *Publications of the Modern Language Association*, 61 (1946), 1101–8.

Birk, John F., 'Tryst beyond Time: Faulkner's "Emily" and Keats', *Studies in Short Fiction*, 28 (1991), 203–13.

Blackstone, Bernard, *The Consecrated Urn: An Interpretation of Keats in Terms of Growth and Form* (London, 1959).

Bloom, Harold, 'Keats and the Embarrassments of Poetic Tradition', in his *The Ringers in the Tower: Studies in Romantic Tradition* (Chicago, 1971), 131–42.

—— *The Anxiety of Influence* (London, 1973).

—— *Poetry and Repression* (New Haven, 1976).

—— (ed.), *John Keats* (New York, 1985).

Bornstein, George, *Transformations of Romanticism in Yeats, Eliot, and Stevens* (Chicago, 1976).

Brisman, Leslie, *Romantic Origins* (Ithaca, NY, 1978).

—— '*Maud*: The Feminine as the Crux of Influence', *Studies in Romanticism*, 31 (1992), 21–43.

Bromwich, David, *Hazlitt: The Mind of a Critic* (London, 1983).

—— 'Keats's Radicalism', *Studies in Romanticism*, 25 (1986), 197–210.

Brooks, Cleanth, 'Keats's Sylvan Historian: History without Footnotes', in his *The Well Wrought Urn: Studies in the Structure of Poetry* (New York, 1947), 139–52.

Brown, Marshall, 'Unheard Melodies: The Force of Form', *Publications of the Modern Language Association*, 107 (1992), 465–81.

Bump, Jerome, 'Hopkins and Keats', *Victorian Poetry*, 77 (1974), 33–43.

Burroughs, Catherine, 'Acting in the Closet: A Feminist Performance of Hazlitt's *Liber Amoris* and Keats's *Otho the Great*', *European Romantic Review*, 2 (1992), 125–44.

Bush, Douglas, *Mythology and the Romantic Tradition in English Poetry* (Cambridge, Mass., 1937).

—— *John Keats: His Life and Writings* (New York, 1966).

Caldwell, James Ralston, *John Keats' Fancy: The Effect on Keats of the Psychology of his Day* (Ithaca, NY, 1945).

Clark, Tom, *Junkets on a Sad Planet: Scenes from the Life of John Keats* (Santa Rosa, Calif., 1994).

Cohn, Robert G., 'Keats and Mallarmé', *Comparative Literature Studies*, 7 (1970), 195–203.

Colvin, Sidney, *John Keats* (New York, 1917).

Cooper, Andrew, 'The Apian Way: Virgil's Bees and Keats's Honeyed Verse', *Texas Studies in Literature and Language*, 33 (1991), 160–81.

Coote, Stephen, *John Keats: A Life* (London, 1995).

Cox, Jeffrey N., 'Keats, Shelley, and the Wealth of Imagination', *Studies in Romanticism*, 34 (1995), 365–400.

Cox, Philip, 'Keats and the Performance of Gender', *Keats–Shelley Journal*, 44 (1995), 40–65.

Cummings, Robert, 'Keats's Melancholy in the Temple of Delight', *Keats–Shelley Journal*, 36 (1987), 50–62.

Curran, Stuart, '*Adonais* in Context', in Kelvin Everest (ed.), *Shelley Revalued: Essays from the Gregynog Conference* (Totowa, NJ, 1983), 165–82.

Danzig, Allan (ed.), *Twentieth-Century Interpretations of* The Eve of St. Agnes (Englewood Cliffs, NJ, 1971).

D'Avanzo, Mario, *Keats's Metaphors for the Poetic Imagination* (Durham, NC, 1967).

de Almeida, Hermione (ed.), *Critical Essays on John Keats* (Boston, 1990a).

—— 'Introduction: Intellectual Keats' (1990b), in de Almeida (1990a: 1–9).

—— *Romantic Medicine and John Keats* (Oxford, 1991).

de Man, Paul, 'Introduction' to his *The Selected Poetry of Keats* (New York, 1966).

de Selincourt, Ernest, 'Introduction' to his *The Poems of John Keats* (New York, 1921), pp. xix–xlviii.

Dickstein, Morris, *Keats and his Poetry: A Study in Development* (Chicago, 1971).

—— 'Keats and Politics', *Studies in Romanticism*, 25 (1986), 175–81.

Dunbar, Georgia S., 'The Significance of the Humor in "Lamia" ', *Keats–Shelley Journal*, 8 (1959), 17–26.

Edmundson, Mark, 'Keats's Mortal Stance', *Studies in Romanticism*, 26 (1987), 86–104.

Eggers, J. Philip, 'Memory in Mankind: Keats's Historical Imagination', *Publications of the Modern Language Association*, 88 (1971), 990–8.

Eliot, T. S., *The Use of Poetry and the Use of Criticism* (Cambridge, Mass., 1933).

Ende, Stuart, *Keats and the Sublime* (New Haven, 1976).

Enscoe, Gerald, *Eros and the Romantics: Sexual Love as a Theme in Coleridge, Shelley, and Keats* (The Hague, 1967).

Evert, Walter H., *Aesthetic and Myth in the Poetry of Keats* (Princeton, 1965).

—— and Rhodes, Jack W. (eds.), *Approaches to Teaching Keats's Poetry* (New York, 1991).

Finkelstein, Norman, 'Beauty, Truth and *The Wanderer*', in Carroll F. Terrell (ed.), *William Carlos Williams: Man and Poet* (Orono, Me., 1983), 233–42.

Finney, Claude Lee, *The Evolution of Keats's Poetry*, 2 vols. (Cambridge, Mass., 1936).

Fitzgerald, William, 'Articulating the Unarticulated: Form, Death, and Other in Keats and Rilke', *Modern Language Notes*, 100 (1985), 949–67.

Fogle, Richard Harter, *The Imagery of Keats and Shelley: A Comparative Study* (Chapel Hill, NC, 1949).

Fontana, Ernest, 'Dickinson's "Go not too near a House of Rose" (Poem 1434) and Keats' ODE ON MELANCHOLY', *Dickinson Studies*, 68 (1988), 26–9.

Ford, George H., *Keats and the Victorians: A Study of his Influence and Rise to Fame* (New Haven, 1944).

Fraistat, Neil, '"Lamia" Progressing: Keats's 1820 Volume', in his *The Poem and the Book: Interpreting Collections of Romantic Poetry* (Chapel Hill, NC, 1985), 95–140.

Fraustino, Daniel V., 'Negative Capability: The Ethics of Esthetics', *Research Studies*, 50 (1982), 62–8.

Friedman, Geraldine, 'The Erotics of Interpretation in Keats's "Ode on a Grecian Urn": Pursuing the Feminine', *Studies in Romanticism*, 32 (1993), 225–43.

Fry, Paul H., 'History, Existence, and "To Autumn"', *Studies in Romanticism*, 25 (1986), 211–19.

Garrod, H. W., *Keats* (Oxford, 1926).

Gittings, Robert, *John Keats: The Living Year* (Cambridge, Mass., 1954).

—— 'Keats and Chatterton', *Keats–Shelley Journal*, 4 (1955), 47–54.

—— *The Mask of Keats: A Study of Problems* (Cambridge, Mass., 1956).

—— *The Keats Inheritance* (London, 1964).

—— *John Keats* (London, 1968).

—— 'Keats and Medicine', *Contemporary Review*, 219 (1971), 138–42.

Goellnicht, Donald, *The Poet-Physician: Keats and Medical Science* (Pittsburgh, 1984).

Goldberg, M. A., *The Poetics of Romanticism: Toward a Reading of John Keats* (Yellow Springs, Oh., 1969).

Goslee, Nancy M., 'Plastic to Picturesque: Schlegel's Analogy and Keats's *Hyperion* Poems', *Keats–Shelley Journal*, 30 (1981), 118–52.

Green, David Bonnell, and Wilson, Edwin Graves (eds.), *Keats, Shelley, Byron, Hunt, and their Circles. A Bibliography: July 1, 1950–June 30, 1962* (Lincoln, Nebr., 1964).

Gurney, Stephen, 'Between Two Worlds: Keats's "Hyperion" and Browning's "Saul"', *Studies in Browning and his Circle*, 8 (1980), 53–74.

Harding, Anthony John, 'Speech, Silence, and the Self-Doubting Interpreter in Keats's Poetry', *Keats–Shelley Journal*, 35 (1986), 83–103.

Hartley, Robert A. (ed.), *Keats, Shelley, Byron, Hunt, and their Circles. A Bibliography: July 1, 1962–December 31, 1974* (Lincoln, Nebr., 1978).

Hartman, Geoffrey, *The Fate of Reading* (Chicago, 1975).

Harwell, Thomas Meade, *Keats and the Critics, 1848–1900* (Salzburg, 1972).

Haworth, Helen E., 'Keats's Copy of Lamb's *Specimens of English Dramatic Poets*', *Bulletin of the New York Public Library*, 74 (1970), 419–27.

Hayden, John O., *The Romantic Reviewers 1802–1824* (Chicago, 1969).

Hearn, Ronald, *Keats Criticism since 1954: A Bibliography* (Salzburg, 1981).

Heinzelman, Kurt, 'Self-Interest and the Politics of Composition in Keats's *Isabella*', *English Literary History*, 55 (1988), 159–93.

Hill, John Spencer (ed.), *Keats: The Narrative Poems* (London, 1983).

Hilton, Nelson, 'Keats, Teats, and the Fane of Poesy', in Deirdre Coleman and Peter Otto (eds.), *Imagining Romanticism: Essays on English and Australian Romanticisms* (West Cornwall, Conn., 1992), 49–71.

Hirst, Wolf Z., *John Keats* (Boston, 1981).

—— 'Lord Byron Cuts a Figure: The Keatsian View', *Byron Journal*, 13 (1985), 36–48.

Hoagwood, Terence Allan, 'Keats and Social Contexts: *Lamia*', *Victorian Poetry*, 29 (1989), 675–97.

—— 'Keats, Fictionality, and Finance: *The Fall of Hyperion*' (1995), in Roe (1995a: 127–42).

Holstein, Michael E., 'Keats: The Poet-Healer and the Problem of Pain', *Keats–Shelley Journal*, 36 (1987), 32–49.

Homans, Margaret, 'Keats Reading Women: Women Reading Keats', *Studies in Romanticism*, 29 (1990), 341–70.

Jack, Ian, *Keats and the Mirror of Art* (Oxford, 1967).

The John Keats Memorial Volume (London, 1921).

Jones, Elizabeth, 'Writing for the Market: Keats's Odes as Commodities', *Studies in Romanticism*, 34 (1995), 343–64.

Jones, James Land, *Adam's Dream: Mythic Consciousness in Keats and Yeats* (Athens, Ga. 1975).

Jones, John, *John Keats's Dream of Truth* (London, 1969).

Kabitoglou, E. Douka, 'Adapting Philosophy to Literature: The Case of John Keats', *Studies in Philology*, 89 (1992), 115–36.

Kandl, John, 'Private Lyrics in the Public Sphere: Leigh Hunt's *Examiner* and the Construction of a Public "John Keats" ', *Keats–Shelley Journal*, 44 (1995), 84–101.

Keach, William, 'Cockney Couplets: Keats and the Politics of Style', *Studies in Romanticism*, 25 (1986), 182–96.

Kelley, Theresa M., 'Poetics and the Politics of Reception: Keats's "La Belle Dame Sans Merci" ', *English Literary History*, 54 (1987), 332–62.

—— 'Keats, Ekphrasis, and History' (1995), in Roe (1995a: 212–37).

Kerrigan, John, 'Writing Numbers: Keats, Hopkins, and the History of Chance' (1995), in Roe (1995a: 280–308).

King, E. H., 'Beattie and Keats: The Progress of the Romantic Minstrel', *English Studies in Canada*, 3 (1977), 176–93.

Koch, June Q., 'Politics in Keats's Poetry', *Journal of English and Germanic Philology*, 71 (1972), 491–501.

Kolb, Jack, ' "On First Looking into Pope's Iliad": Hallam's Keatsian Sonnet', *Victorian Poetry*, 29 (1991), 89–92.

Kucich, Greg, *Keats, Shelley, and Romantic Spenserianism* (University Park, Pa., 1991).

—— 'Gender Crossings: Keats and Tighe', *Keats–Shelley Journal*, 44 (1995a), 29–39.

—— 'Keats's Literary Tradition and the Politics of Historiographical Invention' (1995b), in Roe (1995a: 238–61).

—— 'Keats in Transition: The Bicentennial and its Provocations', *Romanticism*, 2 (1996), 1–8.

Lau, Beth, 'Keats, Associationism, and "Ode to a Nightingale" ', *Keats–Shelley Journal*, 32 (1983), 46–62.

—— 'Keats's Mature Goddesses', *Philological Quarterly*, 63 (1984), 323–41.

—— 'Further Corrections to Amy Lowell's Transcriptions of Keats's Marginalia', *Keats–Shelley Journal*, 35 (1986), 30–9.

—— 'Keats and Byron' (1990), in de Almeida (1990a: 206–22).

—— *Keats's Reading of the Romantic Poets* (Ann Arbor, 1991).

Levinson, Marjorie, *Keats's Life of Allegory* (Oxford, 1988).

—— 'A Question of Taste: Keats and Byron', in Alice Levine and Robert N. Keane (eds.), *Rereading Byron: Essays Selected from Hofstra University's Byron Bicentennial Conference* (New York, 1993), 187–204.

Little, Judy, *Keats as a Narrative Poet: A Test of Invention* (Lincoln, Nebr., 1975).

Lowell, Amy, *John Keats*, 2 vols. (Boston, 1925).

McGann, Jerome J., 'Keats and the Historical Method in Literary Criticism', *Modern Language Notes*, 94 (1979), 988–1032.

MacGillivray, J. R., *Keats: A Bibliography and Reference Guide with an Essay on Keats's Reputation* (Toronto, 1949).

Marples, Morris, *Romantics at School* (London, 1967).

Marquess, William Henry, *Lives of the Poet: The First Century of Keats Biography* (University Park, Pa., 1985).

Matthews, G. M. (ed.), *Keats: The Critical Heritage* (New York, 1971).

Mellor, Anne K., *English Romantic Irony* (Cambridge, Mass., 1980).

—— *Romanticism and Gender* (New York, 1993).

Michael, Jennifer Davis, 'Pectoriloquy: The Narrative of Consumption in the Letters of Keats', *European Romantic Review*, 6 (1995), 38–56.

Milnes, Richard Monckton, *Life, Letters, and Literary Remains of John Keats*, 2 vols. (London, 1848).

Minahan, John A., *Word like a Bell: John Keats, Music and the Romantic Poet* (Kent, Oh., 1992).

Muir, Kenneth (ed.), *John Keats: A Reassessment* (Liverpool, 1969).

Murphy, Patrick, 'Eliot's Polemic with Keats in *The Waste Land*', *Papers on Language and Literature*, 24 (1988), 91–3.

Murry, John Middleton, *Keats and Shakespeare* (London, 1926).

Newey, Vincent, ' "Alternate uproar and sad peace": Keats, Politics, and the Idea of Revolution', *Yearbook of English Studies*, 19 (1989), 265–89.

—— 'Keats, History, and the Poets' (1995), in Roe (1995a: 165–93).

Newlyn, Lucy, *'Paradise Lost' and the Romantic Reader* (Oxford, 1993).

Okada, Akiko, 'Japanese Scholarship on Keats', *Keats–Shelley Journal*, 39 (1990), 166–79.

O'Neill, Michael, ' "The Knowledge of Contrast, Feeling for Light and Shade": Amy Clampitt's "Voyages: A Homage to John Keats" ', *Keats–Shelley Review*, 3 (1988), 47–61.

—— ' "When this warm scribe my hand": Writing and History in *Hyperion* and *The Fall of Hyperion*' (1995), in Roe (1995a: 143–64).

—— (ed.), *Keats: Bicentenary Readings* (Edinburgh, 1997).

Owings, Frank N., Jr., *The Keats Library: A Descriptive Catalogue* (Hampstead, n.d.).

Pack, Robert, 'Keats's Letters: Laughter as Autobiography', in his *Affirming Limits: Essays on Morality, Choice, and Poetic Form* (Amherst, Mass., 1985), 131–50.

Perkins, David, 'Keats's Odes and Letters: Recurrent Diction and Imagery', *Keats–Shelley Journal*, 2 (1953), 51–60.

—— *The Quest for Permanence: The Symbolism of Wordsworth, Shelley, and Keats* (Cambridge, Mass., 1959).

Perkins, Lisa Heiserman, 'Keats's Mere Speculations', *Keats–Shelley Journal*, 43 (1994), 56–74.

Phinney, A. W, 'Keats in the Museum: Between Aesthetics and History', *Journal of English and Germanic Philology*, 90 (1991), 208–29.

Pinion, F. B., *A Keats Chronology* (London, 1992).

Priestley, F. E. L., 'Keats and Chaucer', *Modern Language Quarterly*, 5 (1944), 439–77.

Rajan, Tilottama, *Dark Interpreter: The Discourse of Romanticism* (Ithaca, NY, 1980).

—— 'Teaching Keats from the Standpoint of a Deconstructive Phenomenology', in Evert and Rhodes (1991: 70–6).

Redpath, Theodore, *The Young Romantics and Critical Opinion 1807–1824* (London, 1973).

Reed, Thomas A., 'Keats and the Gregarious Advance of Intellect in *Hyperion*', *English Literary History*, 55 (1988), 195–232.

Reiman, Donald, H., 'Keats and Shelley', in his *Shelley and his Circle*, 8 vols. (Cambridge, Mass., 1961–86), v. 399–427.

—— (ed.), *Shelley, Keats, and London Radical Writers*, in his *The Romantics Reviewed: Contemporary Reviews of British Romantic Writers*, 9 vols. (New York, 1972), part C, vols. i–ii.

Rhodes, Jack Wright, *Keats's Major Odes: An Annotated Bibliography of Criticism* (Westport, Conn., 1984).

Richardson, Joanna, *The Everlasting Spell* (London, 1963).

—— *Keats and his Circle* (London, 1980).

Ricks, Christopher, *Keats and Embarrassment* (Oxford, 1974).

Ridley, M. R., *Keats' Craftsmanship: A Study in Poetic Development* (Oxford, 1933).

Roe, Nicholas, ' "Bright Star, Sweet Unrest": Image and Consolation in Wordsworth, Shelley, and Keats', in Stephen C. Behrendt (ed.), *History and Myth: Essays on English Romantic Literature* (Detroit, 1990), 130–48.

—— 'Keats's Lisping Sedition', *Essays in Criticism*, 42 (1992), 36–55.

—— (ed.), *Keats and History* (Cambridge, 1995a).

—— 'Keats's Commonwealth' (1995b), in Roe (1995a: 194–211).

—— *John Keats and the Culture of Dissent* (Oxford, 1997).

Rollins, Hyder Edward, *Keats' Reputation in America to 1848* (Cambridge, Mass., 1946).

Ross, Marlon B., *The Contours of Masculine Desire: Romanticism and the Rise of Women's Poetry* (Oxford, 1989).

—— 'Beyond the Fragmented Word: Keats at the Limits of Patrilineal Language', in Laura Claridge and Elizabeth Langland (eds.), *Out of Bounds: Male Writers and Gender(ed) Criticism* (Amherst, Mass., 1990), 110–31.

Rossetti, William Michael, *Life of John Keats* (London, 1887).

Ruthven, K. K., 'Keats and *Dea Moneta*', *Studies in Romanticism*, 15 (1976), 445–59.

Ryan, Robert M., *Keats: The Religious Sense* (Princeton, 1976a).

—— 'Keats's "Hymn to Pan": A Debt to Shaftesbury?', *Keats–Shelley Journal*, 26 (1976b), 31–4.

—— 'The Politics of Greek Religion' (1990), in de Almeida (1990a: 261–79).

Schmid, Thomas H., 'Silence and Celebration: Pastoral Dialogism in Keats's "Ode on a Grecian Urn" ', *Keats–Shelley Journal*, 44 (1995), 66–83.

Schneider, Matthew, 'Romantic Bards and English Composers: The Case of Keats and Holst', *European Romantic Review*, 6 (1995), 57–74.

Schwartz, Lewis M. (ed.), *Keats Reviewed by his Contemporaries: A Collection of Notices for the Years 1816–1821* (Metuchen, NJ, 1973).

Scott, Grant F., *The Sculpted Word: Keats, Ekphrasis, and the Visual Arts* (Hanover, NH, 1994).

—— 'Introduction: Tabloid Keats', *European Romantic Review*, 6 (1995), pp. i–xii.

Sharp, Ronald A., *Keats, Skepticism, and the Religion of Beauty* (Athens, Ga., 1979).

—— 'Keats and the Spiritual Economies of Gift Exchange', *Keats–Shelley Journal*, 38 (1989), 66–81.

Shaw, George Bernard, 'Keats', in *The John Keats Memorial Volume* (London, 1921), 173–6.

Sheats, Paul D., 'Keats, the Greater Ode, and the Trial of Imagination', in J. Robert Barth, SJ, and John L. Mahoney (eds.), *Coleridge, Keats, and the Imagination: Romanticism and Adam's Dream* (Columbia, Mo., 1990), 174–200.

Sherwin, Paul, 'Dying into Life: Keats's Struggle with Milton in *Hyperion*', *Publications of the Modern Language Association*, 93 (1978), 383–95.

Short, Clarice, 'William Morris and Keats', *Publications of the Modern Language Association*, 59 (1944), 513–23.

Slote, Bernice, *Keats and the Dramatic Principle* (Lincoln, Nebr., 1958).

Smith, Hillas, *Keats and Medicine* (Newport, RI, 1995).

Spanos, William V., 'Charles Olson and Negative Capability: A Phenomenological Interpretation', *Contemporary Literature*, 21 (1980), 38–80.

Sperry, Stuart M., 'Keats's Skepticism and Voltaire', *Keats–Shelley Journal*, 12 (1963), 75–93.

—— *Keats the Poet* (Princeton, 1973).

—— 'Isabella Jane Towers, John Towers, and Keats', *Keats–Shelley Journal*, 28 (1979), 35–58.

Spiller, M. R. G., 'Circularity and Silence on the *Grecian Urn*', *Durham University Journal*, 80 (1987), 53–8.

Spurgeon, Caroline, *Keats's Shakespeare: A Descriptive Study Based on New Material* (London, 1928).

Stallworthy, Jon, *Wilfred Owen: A Biography* (Oxford, 1977).

Starr, Nathan Comfort, 'Negative Capability in Keats's Diction', *Keats–Shelley Journal*, 15 (1966), 59–68.

Stillinger, Jack (ed.), *Twentieth-Century Interpretations of Keats's Odes* (Englewood Cliffs, NJ, 1968).

—— *The Hoodwinking of Madeline and Other Essays on Keats's Poems* (Urbana, Ill., 1971).

—— 'John Keats', in Frank Jordan (ed.), *The English Romantic Poets: A Review of Research and Criticism* (New York, 1985), 665–718.

—— 'Wordsworth and Keats', in Kenneth R. Johnston and Gene W. Ruoff (eds.), *The Age of William Wordsworth: Critical Essays on the Romantic Tradition* (New Brunswick, NJ, 1987), 173–95.

—— 'Keats and Coleridge', in J. Robert Barth, SJ, and John L. Mahoney (eds.), *Coleridge, Keats, and the Imagination: Romanticism and Adam's Dream* (Columbia, Mo., 1990*a*), 7–28.

—— 'Reading Keats's Plots' (1990*b*), in de Almeida (1990*a*: 88–102).

—— 'Keats and his Helpers: The Multiple Authorship of *Isabella*', in his *Multiple Authorship and the Myth of Solitary Genius* (Oxford, 1991), 25–49.

Swann, Karen, 'Harassing the Muse', in Anne K. Mellor (ed.), *Romanticism and Feminism* (Bloomington, Ind., 1988), 81–92.

Thorpe, Clarence DeWitt, *The Mind of John Keats* (New York, 1926).

—— 'Keats's Interest in Politics and World Affairs', *Publications of the Modern Language Association*, 46 (1931), 1228–45.

Trilling, Lionel, 'Introduction' to his *The Selected Letters of John Keats* (New York, 1951), 3–41.

Van Ghent, Dorothy, *Keats: The Myth of the Hero*, rev. and ed. Jeffrey Cane Robinson (Princeton, 1983).

Vendler, Helen, *The Odes of John Keats* (Cambridge, Mass., 1983).

—— 'Keats and the Use of Poetry', in Hank Lazar (ed.), *What is a Poet?* (Tuscaloosa, Ala., 1987), 66–83.

—— 'The Living Hand of Keats', in Stillinger (ed.), (1990: pp. xiv–xxii).

Waldoff, Leon, *Keats and the Silent Work of Imagination* (Urbana, Ill., 1985).

—— 'Keats's Identification with Wordsworth: Selective Affinities', *Keats–Shelley Journal*, 38 (1989), 47–65.

Walker, Carol Kyros, *Walking North with Keats* (New Haven, 1992).

Ward, Aileen, *John Keats: The Making of a Poet* (New York, 1963).

Wasserman, Earl R., *The Finer Tone: Keats' Major Poems* (Baltimore, 1953).

Watkins, Daniel P., 'A Reassessment of Keats's *Otho the Great*', *Clio*, 16 (1986), 49–66.

—— 'Personal Life and Social Authority in Keats's *Isabella*', *Nineteenth-Century Contexts*, 11 (1987), 33–49.

—— *Keats's Poetry and the Politics of the Imagination* (Rutherford, NJ, 1989).

—— *Sexual Power in British Romantic Poetry* (Gainesville, Fla., 1996).

Watson, J. R., 'Keats', in his *English Poetry of the Romantic Period 1789–1830* (London, 1985), 259–91.

Wells, Walter A., *A Doctor's Life of John Keats* (New York, 1959).

White, R. S., *Keats as a Reader of Shakespeare* (Norman, Okla., 1987).

Whiting, George W., 'Charlotte Smith, Keats, and the Nightingale', *Keats–Shelley Journal*, 12 (1963), 4–8.

Wigod, Jacob D., 'Negative Capability and Wise Passiveness', *Publications of the Modern Language Association*, 67 (1952), 383–90.

Wilkie, Brian, 'Keats and the Mortal Taste', in his *Romantic Poets and Epic Tradition* (Madison, 1965), 145–87.

Williams, Meg Harris, *Inspiration in Milton and Keats* (Totowa, NJ, 1982).

Wolfson, Susan, J., 'Keats the Letter-Writer: Epistolary Poetics', *Romanticism Past and Present*, 6 (1982), 43–61.

—— 'Composition and "Unrest": The Dynamics of Form in Keats's Last Lyrics', *Keats–Shelley Journal*, 34 (1985), 53–82.

—— 'Introduction. Keats and Politics: A Forum', *Studies in Romanticism*, 25 (1986a), 171–74.

—— *The Questioning Presence: Wordsworth, Keats, and the Interrogative Mode in Romantic Poetry* (Ithaca, 1986b).

—— 'Feminizing Keats' (1990), in de Almeida (1990a: 317–56).

—— 'Keats's "Gordian Complication" of Women', in Evert and Rhodes (1991: 77–85).

Wolfson, Susan, J., 'Keats and the Manhood of the Poet', *European Romantic Review*, 6 (1995*a*), 1–37.

—— 'Keats Enters History: Autopsy, *Adonais*, and the Fame of Keats' (1995*b*), in Roe (1995*a*: 17–45).

Woodman, Ross, 'Nietzsche, Blake, Keats, and Shelley: The Making of a Metaphorical Body', *Studies in Romanticism*, 29 (1990), 115–49.

Zillman, Lawrence John, *John Keats and the Sonnet Tradition* (Los Angeles, 1939).

These principles have guided the preparation of the first complete edition of all of Clare's surviving poetry, the Oxford English Texts edition, under the general editorship of Eric Robinson, which replaces the two-volume *Poems of John Clare*, edited by J. W. Tibble (1935), as well as previous partial editions. Of the OET edition six volumes have appeared to date, *The Later Poems of John Clare 1837–1864* (2 vols., 1984a) and *The Early Poems of John Clare 1804–1822* (2 vols., 1989), edited by Eric Robinson and David Powell, and *Poems of the Middle Period*, vols. i–ii (1996), edited by Eric Robinson, David Powell, and P. M. S. Dawson. A further three volumes will follow, two more devoted to poems of the middle period (including *The Midsummer Cushion*), and a final volume containing the poems of the Northborough period (as well as additions and corrections to the previous volumes), all edited by the same team. This complete critical edition of all the poetry with textual variants probably goes beyond the needs and the pockets of students and general readers. Readers who want a selection of Clare's work in a reliable modern text are advised to turn to the Oxford Authors *John Clare*, edited by Eric Robinson and David Powell (1984b), which contains some prose (including the 'Journey out of Essex') as well as a generous selection of the verse. A more restricted and slightly modernized but still reliable selection is Geoffrey Summerfield's edition of *John Clare: Selected Poetry* (1990b) for the Penguin Poetry Library. The Methuen English Texts selection of *Selected Poetry and Prose*, edited by Merryn and Raymond Williams, is short but textually reliable and has a useful introduction. The Everyman *Selected Poems*, edited by J. W. and Anne Tibble (1965), offers a very full selection (including the only accessible version of 'The Village Minstrel'), but its text must now be considered as unacceptably editorialized. The Wordsworth Poetry edition of *The Works of John Clare* (1995), a reprint of Arthur Symons's selection of *Poems by John Clare* (1908), is both restricted and textually unreliable, and is of only historical interest, despite its tempting price. The selections of Clare's work can be supplemented by textually reliable modern editions of *The Parish*, edited by Eric Robinson (1985); *The Shepherd's Calendar* (the poems devoted to the different months), edited by Eric Robinson, Geoffrey Summerfield, and David Powell (1993a); *Cottage Tales*, edited by Eric Robinson, David Powell, and P. M. S. Dawson (1993b) (containing the narrative poems published in Clare's 1827 volume and others); *The Midsummer Cushion* (the volume as originally prepared by Clare, from which a selection was published in 1835), edited by Anne Tibble and R. K. R. Thornton (1979); *The Rural Muse*, edited by R. K. R. Thornton (1982) (reproducing Clare's press-copy for the 1835 volume); and *Northborough Sonnets*, edited by Eric Robinson, David Powell, and P. M. S. Dawson (1995). Substantial selections of Clare's prose are also available, including his writings on natural history, collected as *The Natural History Prose Writings of John Clare*, edited by Margaret Grainger (including Clare's 1824–5 journal) (1984c). Some of his miscellaneous prose is included in *The*

Journal, Essays, The Journey from Essex, edited by Anne Tibble (1980), but it is still necessary to consult *The Prose of John Clare*, edited by J. W. and Anne Tibble (1951), which is neither complete nor totally reliable. Clare's correspondence is available as *The Letters of John Clare*, ed. Mark Storey (1985), and a paperback selection from this standard edition is also available (1988).

The richest manuscript sources for Clare's poetry and prose are the collections in the Peterborough Museum and the Northampton Central Library, which are available on microfilm (ten and eleven reels respectively) from EP Microform Ltd., Bradford Road, East Ardsley, Wakefield, Yorkshire.

THE LIFE

The main sources of information about Clare's life are his own auto-biographical accounts, particularly his 'Sketches in the Life of John Clare Written by Himself', written in 1821 largely for the benefit of his publisher John Taylor, and the subsequent autobiographical fragments, which, along with his 'Journey out of Essex' of 1841, have been published as *John Clare's Autobiographical Writings* and in a revised and expanded version as *John Clare by Himself*; his letters, available in a collected edition (see above); the letters to him, particularly the six volumes in the British Library (MSS Egerton 2245–50); and accounts by those who knew him (many of which are reproduced in Storey 1973). Readers are advised where possible to consult this primary material before turning to the biographies. Crossan in his useful critical survey of the available accounts of Clare's life (including Clare's own) claims with reason that 'no one has told Clare's story better than he tells it himself' (Crossan 1986). There is no reason to think that Clare fabricated any significant events or details, but his evident concern over his self-presentation to the world and perhaps to himself means that his account should not be accepted uncritically. His biographers have however all too often contented themselves with reproducing his account of events and supplementing it with their own embroidery. His first biographer, Frederick Martin, is notorious for his exercise of the novelizing imagination, but the tendency towards unfounded conjecture is still to be detected in his latest, Edward Storey. While the early biographers, J. L. Cherry and Martin, have to be approached with particular caution, it has to be remembered that they may have had access to information from those who knew Clare. Martin has an evident admiration and a keen sympathy for Clare which does him credit, but leads him to overstress his naivety and otherworld-liness, and to regard with a rather jaundiced eye the conduct of his patrons. The reprinted edition of 1964 has notes by Eric Robinson and Geoffrey Summerfield which correct at least some of his more obvious errors, and later biographers have been rightly cautious in their use of him. June Wilson calls him 'colourful but unreliable', but her own 1951 biography (which makes particularly effective use of the letters to Clare preserved in the British Library) cannot avoid reproducing some of his anecdotes, with due caution. The Tibbles' biography of 1932 (rev. 1972) has for long been the standard account of the life, and makes generous use of Clare's autobiographical writings and journal and of the letters to him. Their familiarity with his writings, both published and unpublished, is impressive, though their tendency to draw biographical inferences from the poetry should be regarded with suspicion. Edward Storey's account, despite its tendency to romance beyond the ascertainable facts, is the most accessible, because the most recent, and incorporates research into local records and Storey's own knowledge of the local area. But the definitive modern biography, making a properly critical use of the available materials and treating the poetry more precisely and knowledgeably than any of the previous biographers has managed to do, remains to be written.

CRITICISM

For a poet who can still justly be considered as neglected, the amount of available critical comment on Clare is surprisingly extensive, and there has been an increasing amount of attention paid to him in recent years which has generated some notable work. Useful introductory studies of his poetic career as a whole are Mark Storey (1974), Howard (1981) and Chilcott (1985a). However, it can hardly be said that there is as yet a clear critical consensus regarding his work. The variety of views that have been offered of Clare's poetry is well illustrated in the Critical Heritage volume edited by Mark Storey (1973), which carries the story on into the twentieth century; Storey also offers an account of the critical tradition (1994). One reason for the lack of consensus is the fact that Clare was an unusually undogmatic personality. In an age awash with systems (to the disgust of Byron, not surprisingly the one great contemporary with whom Clare felt an affinity, to the point of identification in the early asylum years) Clare preferred to appeal to a deliberately undefined 'common sense'. This can lead him to be, or to appear, self-contradictory, both as a man and a writer. One consequence is that critics who pursue too tenaciously a single line of interpretation (such as Crossan 1976 or Todd 1973) are in danger of providing an account that is at best only partial. Another problem in bringing Clare into critical focus is the difficulty of deciding just where to place him in the literary tradition. As Greg Crossan has observed (1976), he can be plausibly connected with the poetry characteristic of no less than five centuries. The danger of defining him as a Romantic poet (as his birth date might encourage us to do) is that he is seen as a derivative or imitative figure (as in Bloom). Howard (1981) applies Romantic criteria perhaps too consistently, but he offers a persuasive reconstruction of what he sees as the Romantic poetics underlying his practice, and shows that Clare certainly qualifies as a Romantic poet some of the time. Swingle (1975) and McKusick (1994) argue persuasively for an *anti*-Romantic strain in Clare, and the present writer would agree that Clare is often a deliberate critic of his famous contemporaries, so that to judge him by their standards is to prejudge the critical points at issue. Critics have more habitually stressed Clare's kinship with the descriptive poetry of the eighteenth century, though often noting the essential differences as much as the similarities. These differences are discussed in what can be regarded as the founding work of contemporary Clare studies, Barrell (1972), which is cited in virtually all subsequent critical discussions. Barrell directed attention particularly to the ideological implications of the differences between the practice of leading eighteenth-century poets of landscape such as Thomson and Cowper and that of Clare, with his focus on the local and near-at-hand and his avoidance of a hierarchizing and dominating point of view over the things described. Barrell's account in effect revived the old debate as to the value of Clare's 'purely descriptive' poetry, as it was taken to be, in comparison with the more 'thoughtful' or 'philosophic' poetry of poets such as Wordsworth or Keats; but at the same time it performed the valuable service of reminding us that more than merely literary values are at stake, and that the lack of certain supposedly desirable qualities in Clare might in itself be a valuable quality of another kind. The arguments over the value of Clare's descriptive poetry are a distant echo of Schiller's distinction between the 'naive' (ancient, unreflective) and the 'sentimental' (modern, philosophic), a distinction that Sychrava has explicitly applied to Clare, though she does not endorse the usual preference for the latter. Barrell's discussion of just how Clare describes landscape is extended in Brownlow (1983), and the general issue of the ways of seeing embodied in his poetry is tackled in Chilcott (1985a).

As Barrell showed, Clare's literary qualities are inseparable from social values, and Clare has become of increasing interest to historians as well as literary scholars as a representative of those labouring classes who were rarely able to find a voice; though the very fact that Clare did find his voice also makes him unrepresentative. Raymond Williams situated Clare's work in an account of general cultural development, while Thompson and Neeson have both shown the contribution that Clare's work can make to our historical understanding of working-class experience. Johanne Clare (1987a) shows how Clare's class situation and experience shaped his work. The volume edited by Goodridge (1994) tries to connect him with other members of the 'self-taught' tradition. Clare's own social and political views are as complex as any other aspect of him, and while it is tempting for moderns to find a properly radical consciousness in his work (Lucas 1986, 1990, 1994a, 1994b) such an identification is probably overstating the case (see Dawson 1992, 1996). New historicism is

—— 'The John Clare Collection in Northampton Public Library', *Library World*, 65 (May 1964*b*).

Rosenbaum, Barbara, and White, Pamela, *Index of English Literary Manuscripts*, vol. iv, part 1 (London, 1982).

EDITIONS

The following listing concentrates on editions currently available, excluding those which have now been superseded.

Chilcott, Tim, *A Publisher and his Circle: The Life and Work of John Taylor, Keats's Publisher* (London, 1972).

Clare, John, *Poems by John Clare*, ed. Arthur Symons (1908); reissued as *The Works of John Clare* (Ware, 1995).

—— *The Poems of John Clare*, ed. J. W. Tibble 2 vols. (London, 1935).

—— *The Prose of John Clare*, ed. J. W. and Anne Tibble (London, 1951).

—— *John Clare: Selected Poems*, ed. J. W. Tibble and Anne Tibble (London, 1965).

—— *Selected Poems and Prose of John Clare*, ed. Eric Robinson and Geoffrey Summerfield (London, 1967).

—— *The Midsummer Cushion*, ed. Anne Tibble and R. K. R. Thornton (Ashington, 1979).

—— *The Journal, Essays, The Journey from Essex*, ed. Anne Tibble (Manchester, 1980).

—— *The Rural Muse*, ed. R. K. R. Thornton (Ashington, 1982*a*).

—— *John Clare's Birds*, ed. Eric Robinson and Richard Fitter (Oxford, 1982*b*).

—— *The Later Poems of John Clare 1837–1864*, ed. Eric Robinson and David Powell, 2 vols. (Oxford, 1984*a*).

—— *John Clare*, ed. Eric Robinson and David Powell (London, 1984*b*).

—— *The Natural History Prose Writings of John Clare*, ed. Margaret Grainger (London, 1984*c*).

—— *The Letters of John Clare*, ed. Mark Storey (Oxford, 1985*a*).

—— *The Parish*, ed. Eric Robinson and David Powell (Harmondsworth, 1985*b*).

—— *Poems Descriptive of Rural Life and Scenery* (reprint of 1st edn., 1820; Bury St Edmunds, 1986*a*).

—— *Selected Poetry and Prose*, ed. Merryn and Raymond Williams (London, 1986*b*).

—— *John Clare: Selected Letters*, ed. Mark Storey (Oxford, 1988).

—— *The Early Poems of John Clare 1804–1822*, ed. Eric Robinson and David Powell, 2 vols. (Oxford, 1989*a*).

—— *The Summons*, ed. Eric Robinson (Market Drayton, 1989*b*).

—— *The Hue & Cry: A Tale of the Times*, ed. Eric Robinson (Market Drayton, 1990*a*).

—— *John Clare: Selected Poetry*, ed. Geoffrey Summerfield (London, 1990*b*).

—— *The Shepherd's Calendar 1827* (facsimile edn.; Oxford, 1991).

—— *The Shepherd's Calendar*, ed. Eric Robinson, Geoffrey Summerfield, and David Powell (London, 1993*a*).

—— *Cottage Tales*, ed. Eric Robinson, David Powell, and P. M. S. Dawson (Ashington, 1993*b*).

—— *Northborough Sonnets*, ed. Eric Robinson, David Powell, and P. M. S. Dawson (Ashington, 1995).

Clare, John, *Poems of the Middle Period 1822–1837*, vols. i–ii, ed. Eric Robinson, David Powell, and P. M. S. Dawson (Oxford, 1996).

Robinson, Eric, and Summerfield, Geoffrey, 'John Taylor's Editing of Clare's *The Shepherd's Calendar*', *Review of English Studies*, 14 (1963), 359–69.

BIOGRAPHIES

Cherry, J. L., *The Life and Remains of John Clare, the 'Northamptonshire Peasant Poet'* (London, 1873).

Clare, John, *John Clare's Autobiographical Writings*, ed. Eric Robinson (Oxford, 1983).

——*John Clare by Himself*, ed. Eric Robinson and David Powell (Ashington, 1996).

Crossan, Greg, 'The Nine "Lives" of John Clare', *John Clare Society Journal*, 5 (1986), 37–46.

Martin, Frederick W., *The Life of John Clare* (1865), introd. and notes by Eric Robinson and Geoffrey Summerfield (London, 1964).

Storey, Edward, *A Right to Song: The Life of John Clare* (London, 1982).

Tibble, J. W., and Tibble, Anne, *John Clare: A Life* (London, 1932; 2nd rev. edn. with introd. by Geoffrey Grigson, London, 1972).

—— ——*John Clare: His Life and Poetry* (London, 1956).

Wilson, June, *Green Shadows: The Life of John Clare* (London, 1951).

CRITICAL STUDIES

Banfield-Pearce, Lynne, 'John Clare and Peter De Wint', *John Clare Society Journal*, 3 (1984), 40–7.

Barker, Jonathan, ' "The Songs of our Land are Like Ancient Landmarks": The Poetry of John Clare', *Agenda*, 22 (1984–5), 78–89.

Barrell, John, *The Idea of Landscape and the Sense of Place 1730–1840: An Approach to the Poetry of John Clare* (Cambridge, 1972).

—— 'John Clare, William Cobbett and the Changing Landscape', in Boris Ford (ed.), *From Blake to Byron*, vol. v of *The New Pelican Guide to English Literature* (Harmondsworth, 1982), 226–43.

—— 'John Clare's "The Lane" ', *John Clare Society Journal*, 2 (1983), 3–8.

Bate, Jonathan, 'The Rights of Nature', *John Clare Society Journal*, 14 (1995), 7–15.

Bates, Tom, 'Notes on "Maying or Love & Flowers" ', *John Clare Society Journal*, 10 (1991), 43–6.

—— 'John Clare and "Boximania" ', *John Clare Society Journal*, 13 (1994), 5–17.

Birns, Nicholas, ' "The riddle nature could not prove": Hidden Landscapes in Clare's Poetry', in Haughton et al. (1994: 189–220).

Blackmore, Evan, 'John Clare's Psychiatric Disorder and its Influence on his Poetry', *Victorian Poetry*, 24 (1986), 209–28.

Blamires, David, 'Chapbooks, Fairytales and Children's Books in the Writings of John Clare: Part I', *John Clare Society Journal*, 15 (1996), 27–53.

Bloom, Harold, 'John Clare: The Wordsworthian Shadow', in *The Visionary Company: A Reading of English Romantic Poetry* (1961; rev. edn., Ithaca, NY, 1971), 444–60.

Blythe, Ronald, 'An Inherited Perspective: Landscape and the Indigenous Eye', in Paul Hallberg (ed.), *The Feeling for Nature and the Landscape of Man* (Gotheburg, 1980), 12–25.

—— '"The Best of Thee Is Still Unknown": Kindred Spirits' (1994), in Goodridge (1994a: 181–92).

—— 'Solvitur Ambulando: John Clare and Footpath Walking', *John Clare Society Journal*, 14 (1995), 17–27.

Boden, Helen, 'Clare, Gender and Art' (1994), in Goodridge (1994a: 198–208).

Brewer, William D., 'John Clare and Lord Byron', *John Clare Society Journal*, 11 (1992), 43–56.

—— 'Clare's Struggle for Poetic Identity in "The Village Minstrel"', *John Clare Society Journal*, 13 (1994), 73–80.

Brownlow, Timothy, 'A Molehill for Parnassus: John Clare and Prospect Poetry', *University of Toronto Quarterly*, 48 (1978), 23–40.

—— *John Clare and Picturesque Landscape* (Oxford, 1983).

—— 'A Moment's Monument', *John Clare Society Journal*, 3 (1984), 34–7.

Caddel, Richard, 'Things Held in Common', *John Clare Society Journal*, 7 (1988), 41–8.

Campbell, Bruce, 'The Birds of John Clare', *Folio* (Summer 1980).

Cannell, Mary, 'John Clare and George Green'(1994), in Goodridge (1994a: 193–7).

Chambers, Douglas, '"A love for every simple weed": Clare, Botany and the Poetic Language of Lost Eden', in Haughton et al. (1994: 238–58).

Chilcott, Tim, *'A Real World & Doubting Mind': A Critical Study of the Poetry of John Clare* (Hull, 1985a).

—— 'Indeterminacy in Clare's "The Landrail"', *John Clare Society Journal*, 4 (1985b), 5–11.

—— 'The Circumference of Knowledge: John Clare's "Stone Pit"', *John Clare Society Journal*, 7 (1988), 4–9.

—— 'An Article on Articles', *John Clare Society Journal*, 9 (1990), 31–43.

Chirico, Paul, 'Writing Misreadings: Clare and the Real World' (1994), in Goodridge (1994a: 125–38).

Clare, Johanne, *John Clare and the Bounds of Circumstance* (Kingston, 1987a).

—— 'The "English Truth" of John Clare', *John Clare Society Journal*, 6 (1987b), 21–33.

Coletta, W. John, 'Ecological Aesthetics and the Natural History Poetry of John Clare', *John Clare Society Journal*, 14 (1995), 29–46.

Constantine, David, 'Outside Eden: John Clare's Descriptive Poetry', in J. R. Watson (ed.), *An Infinite Complexity: Essays in Romanticism* (Edinburgh, 1983), 181–201.

Counsel, June, 'Coming to Clare', *John Clare Society Journal*, 5 (1986), 5–8.

Cox, Peter, '"The Hearts Hid Anguish": Clare and Tennyson in Epping Forest', *John Clare Society Journal*, 13 (1994), 33–9.

Crossan, Greg, *A Relish for Eternity: The Process of Divinization in the Poetry of John Clare* (Salzburg, 1976).

—— 'John Clare's Poetry: An Examination of the Textual Accuracy of Some Recent Editions', *Studies in Romanticism*, 23 (1984a), 581–98.

—— 'The Godfrey Collection of Clare Items in the Peterborough Museum', *John Clare Society Journal*, 3 (1984b), 17–25.

—— 'Clare and Enfield's "Speaker"', *Notes and Queries*, NS 34 (1987), 27–8.

Crossan, Greg, 'Clare's "Aching(?) Sight" ', *John Clare Society Journal*, 7 (1988), 50–1.

—— 'Clare's Debt to the Poets in his Library', *John Clare Society Journal*, 10 (1991*a*), 41.

—— 'John Clare's Last Letter', *Notes and Queries*, NS 38 (1991*b*), 319.

—— 'John Clare: Our Contemporary', in Foulkes (1994: 57–68).

Dawson, P. M. S., 'John Clare—Radical?', *John Clare Society Journal*, 11 (1992), 17–27.

—— 'Common Sense or Radicalism? Some Reflections on Clare's Politics', *Romanticism*, 2/1 (1996), 81–97.

Deacon, George, *John Clare and the Folk Tradition* (London, 1983).

Dean, E. Barbara, 'John Clare at Lolham Bridges', *John Clare Society Journal*, 2 (1983), 24–7.

Dixon, George E., 'Clare and Religion', *John Clare Society Journal*, 1 (1982), 47–50.

Engels, William C., 'Clare's Mocking Tone in "An Invite to Eternity" ', *John Clare Society Journal*, 15 (1996), 57–67.

Foulkes, Richard (ed.), *John Clare: A Bicentenary Celebration* (Leicester, 1994).

Fraser, Angus M., 'John Clare's Gypsies', *Journal of the Gipsy Lore Society*, 50 (1971), 85–100 (repr. from *Northamptonshire Past and Present*, 4 (1965), 259–67).

Frosch, Thomas R., 'The Descriptive Style of John Clare', *Studies in Romanticism*, 10 (1971), 137–49.

Fulford, Tim, 'Cowper, Wordsworth, Clare: The Politics of Trees', *John Clare Society Journal*, 14 (1995), 47–59.

Gaull, Marilyn, 'Clare and "the Dark System" ', in Haughton et al. (1994: 279–94).

Gillin, Richard L., 'Minute Particulars and Imaginative Forms', *John Clare Society Journal*, 5 (1986), 22–9.

Goddard, Joe, 'A Formative Influence of John Clare', *John Clare Society Journal*, 3 (1984). 49–52.

Goodridge, John (ed.), *The Independent Spirit: John Clare and the Self-Taught Tradition* (Helpston, 1994*a*).

—— 'Pastoral and Popular Modes in Clare's Enclosure Elegies' (1994*b*), in Goodridge (1994*a*: 139–55).

—— and Thornton, Kelsey, 'John Clare: The Trespasser', in Haughton et al. (1994: 87–129).

Grainger, Margaret, *John Clare: Collector of Ballads* (Peterborough, 1964).

—— and Chandler, John, 'From Helpston to Burghley: A Reading of Clare's "Narrative Verses" ', *John Clare Society Journal*, 7 (1988), 26–40.

Green, David Bonnell, 'John Clare, John Savage, and "The Scientific Receptacle" ', *Review of English Literature*, 7 (1966), 87–98.

—— 'Three Early American Admirers of John Clare', *Bulletin of the John Rylands Library*, 50 (1967–8), 365–86.

Gregory, Horace, 'On John Clare, and the Sight of Nature in his Poetry', in *The Shield of Achilles: Essays on Beliefs in Poetry* (New York, 1944), 21–32.

Groves, David, 'John Clare: "To a Lair at Noon" ', *Notes and Queries*, NS 32 (1985), 356.

—— 'John Clare and James Hogg: Two Peasant Poets in the *Athenaeum*', *Bulletin of Research in the Humanities*, 87 (1986–7), 225–9.

—— 'A Poem in "The Englishman's Magazine" ', *John Clare Society Journal*, 7 (1988), 51–2.

Hand, R. J., 'Anthologized Clare and the Problem of Death Date', *Notes and Queries*, NS 36 (1989), 181–2.

Harrison, Thomas P., *Birds in the Poetry of John Clare* (Peterborough, 1957).

Hatley, Victor A., 'The Poet and the Railway Surveyors: An Incident in the Life of John Clare', *Northamptonshire Past and Present*, 5 (1974), 101–6.

Haughton, Hugh, 'Progress and Rhyme: "The Nightingale's Nest" and Romantic Poetry', in Haughton et al. (1994: 51–86).

—— and Phillips, Adam, 'Introduction: Relocating John Clare', in Haughton et al. (1994: 1–27).

—— —— and Summerfield, Geoffrey (eds.), *John Clare in Context* (Cambridge, 1994).

Heaney, Seamus, 'John Clare: A Bi-centenary Lecture', in Haughton et al. (1994: 130–47).

Heath-Stubbs, John, *The Darkling Plain: A Study of the Later Fortunes of Romanticism in English Poetry from George Darley to W. B. Yeats* (London, 1950), 65–75.

Helsinger, Elizabeth, 'Clare and the Place of the Peasant Poet', *Critical Inquiry*, 13 (1987), 509–31.

Herman, Vimala, 'How to See Things with Words: Language Use and Descriptive Art in John Clare's "Signs of Winter" ', *Language and Style*, 20 (1987), 91–109.

Heyes, Bob, 'John Clare and the Militia', *John Clare Society Journal*, 4 (1985), 48–54.

—— 'Clare and Enclosure', *John Clare Society Journal*, 6 (1987), 10–19.

—— 'A Neglected Account of Clare in the Asylum', *John Clare Society Journal*, 13 (1994), 59–60.

—— 'Some Friends of John Clare: The Poet and the Scientists', *Romanticism*, 2/1 (1996), 98–109.

Höhne, Horst, 'John Clare's Rural Poetry and the Romantic Concept of Nature', *Wissenschaftliche Zeitschrift der Wilhelm-Pieck-Universität Rostock*, 31 (1982), 57–61.

Hold, Trevor, 'The Composer's Debt to John Clare', *John Clare Society Journal*, 1 (1982), 25–9.

Hooker, I. M. F., and Hunt, N. Dermott, 'John Clare: Some Unpublished Documents of the Asylum Period', *Northamptonshire Past and Present*, 3 (1964), 190–8.

Howard, William, *John Clare* (Boston, 1981).

—— 'John Clare's Passionate Shepherd', *John Clare Society Journal*, 4 (1985), 12–22.

I[sham], G[yles], 'John Clare: The Northampton Years', *Northamptonshire Past and Present*, 3 (1964), 185–9.

—— 'Some Clare Manuscripts at Stratfield Saye', *Northamptonshire Past and Present*, 3 (1964), 199–200.

Jack, Ian, 'Poems of John Clare's Sanity', in James V. Logan, John Jordan, and Northrop Frye (eds.), *Some British Romantics* (Columbus, Oh., 1966), 191–232.

Keegan, Bridget, 'Broadsides, Ballads and Books: The Landscape of Cultural Literacy in "The Village Minstrel" ', *John Clare Society Journal*, 15 (1996), 11–18.

Keith, W. J., 'John Clare', in *The Poetry of Nature: Rural Perspectives in Poetry from Wordsworth to the Present* (Toronto, 1980), 39–66.

Kirkup, James, 'John Clare the Bird Watcher', *Eige Seinen*, 118 (1973), 634–7.

Lamont, Claire, 'John Clare and the Gipsies', *John Clare Society Journal*, 13 (1994), 19–31.

Lessa, Richard, 'Time and John Clare's "Calendar" ', *Critical Quarterly*, 24/1 (Spring 1982), 59–71.

—— 'John Clare's Voice, and Two Sonnets', *John Clare Society Journal*, 3 (1984), 26–33.

Levi, Peter, *John Clare and Thomas Hardy* (London, 1975).

Lewis, C. Day, 'Country Lyrics', in *The Lyric Impulse* (London, 1965), 103–29.

Lines, Rodney, 'John Clare's "The Skylark"', *John Clare Society Journal*, 1 (1982), 53–6.

—— 'John Clare and Herbal Medicine', *John Clare Society Journal*, 5 (1986), 16–21.

—— 'Clare's "Rough Country Sonnets"' (1994), in Goodridge (1994a: 156–63).

Lucas, John, '"The Flitting"', *John Clare Society Journal*, 5 (1986), 9–13.

—— 'Places and Dwellings: Wordsworth, Clare and the Anti-picturesque', in Denis Cosgrove and Stephen Daniels (eds.), *The Iconography of Landscape* (Cambridge, 1988), 83–97.

—— 'Peasants and Outlaws: John Clare', in *England and Englishness: Ideas of Nationhood in English Poetry 1688–1900* (London, 1990), 135–60.

—— 'England in 1830: Wordsworth, Clare, and the Question of Poetic Authority', *Critical Survey*, 2 (1992a), 62–6.

—— 'Revising Clare', in Robert Brinkley and Keith Hanley (eds.), *Romantic Revisions* (Cambridge, 1992b), 339–53.

—— *John Clare* (Plymouth, 1994a).

—— 'Clare's Politics' (1994b), in Haughton et al. (1994: 148–77).

—— 'Bloomfield and Clare' (1994c), in Goodridge (1994a: 55–68).

Luckin, Bill, 'The Pathography of the Past', *Times Literary Supplement* (22 Mar. 1974), 294.

Lupini, Barbara, '"An Open and Simple Eye": The Influence of Landscape in the Work of John Clare and Vincent van Gogh', *English*, 23 (1974), 58–62.

McKusick, James C., '"A language that is ever green": The Ecological Vision of John Clare', *University of Toronto Quarterly*, 61 (1991–2), 226–49.

—— 'John Clare's London Journal: A Peasant Poet Encounters the Metropolis', *Wordsworth Circle*, 23 (1992), 172–5.

—— 'Beyond the Visionary Company: John Clare's Resistance to Romanticism', in Haughton et al. (1994: 221–38).

Minor, Mark, 'John Clare and the Methodists: A Reconsideration', *Studies in Romanticism*, 19 (1980), 31–50.

—— 'Clare, Byron, and the Bible: Additional Evidence from the Asylum Manuscripts', *Bulletin of Research in the Humanities*, 85 (1982), 104–26.

Murry, John Middleton, 'The Poetry of John Clare' and 'The Case of John Clare', in *John Clare and Other Studies* (London, 1950), 7–18, 19–24.

—— 'Clare Revisited', in *Unprofessional Essays* (London, 1956), 53–111.

Nattrass, Leonora, 'John Clare and William Cobbett: The Personal and The Political' (1994), in Goodridge (1994a: 44–54).

Neeson, J. M., *Commoners: Common Right, Enclosure and Social Change in England, 1700–1820* (Cambridge, 1993).

Paira-Pemberton, Jean, 'From Anon. to a Name: The "Case" of John Clare', *Recherches anglaises et américaines*, 14 (1981), 39–61.

Paulin, Tom, 'John Clare in Babylon', in *Minotaur: Poetry and the Nation State* (London, 1992), 47–55.

—— 'John Clare: A Bicentennial Celebration', in Foulkes (1994: 69–78).

Pearce, Lynne, 'John Clare's "Child Harold": A Polyphonic Reading', *Criticism: A Quarterly for Literature and the Arts*, 31 (1989), 139–57; rev. and repr. in Lynne Pearce, *Reading Dialogics* (London, 1994), 135–48.

Pedlar, Valerie, ' "No Place Like Home": Reconsidering Matthew Allen and his "Mild System" of Treatment', *John Clare Society Journal*, 13 (1994), 41–57.

Phillips, Adam, 'The Exposure of John Clare', in Haughton et al. (1994: 178–88).

Pinsky, Robert, 'That Sweet Man, John Clare', in Alan Cheuse and Richard Kaffler (eds.), *The Rarer Action: Essays in Honour of Francis Fergusson* (New Brunswick, NJ, 1970); rev. and repr. in Robert Pinsky, *The Situation of Poetry: Contemporary Poetry and its Traditions* (Princeton, 1976), 118–133.

Porter, Roy, ' "All madness for writing": John Clare and the Asylum', in Haughton et al. (1994: 259–78).

Powell, David, 'John Clare: Getting into Print', in Foulkes (1994: 1–26).

Powell, Margaret A., 'Clare and his Patrons in 1820: Some Unpublished Papers', *John Clare Society Journal*, 6 (1987), 4–9.

Raimond, Rosine, 'John Clare et la hantise de l'ailleurs', in *Images de l'ailleurs dans la littérature anglo-américaine* (Reims, 1981), 49–63.

—— 'Le Moi et l'autre ou la quête de soi chez John Clare', in *L'Autre dans la sensibilité anglo-saxonne* (Reims, 1983), 63–75.

Rayment, Nigel, 'The Failure of John Clare's "Natural History of Helpstone": A Problem of Privilege', *Critical Survey*, 2 (1990), 36–41.

Robinson, Eric, 'Clare and Nature', *John Clare Society Journal*, 1 (1982), 7–24.

—— 'Editorial Problems in John Clare', *John Clare Society Journal*, 2 (1983), 9–23.

—— 'Early Poems: The Biographical Evidence', *John Clare Society Journal*, 4 (1985), 31–47.

—— 'John Clare and the Newspapers: Reader and Contributor', *John Clare Society Journal*, 6 (1987a), 37–47.

—— ' "To an Oaken Stem": John Clare's Poem Recovered and Reconsidered', *Review of English Studies*, 38 (1987b), 483–91.

—— 'John Clare's Learning', *John Clare Society Journal*, 7 (1988), 10–25.

—— 'John Clare: Passing the Time of Day', *John Clare Society Journal*, 10 (1991), 17–26.

—— 'John Clare and Weather-Lore', *John Clare Society Journal*, 14 (1995), 61–79.

Rowbotham, Judith, 'An Exercise in Nostalgia? Clare and Enclosure', in Goodridge (1994a: 164–77).

Rush, Phil, 'John Clare: Village Fiddler', *English Dance and Song*, 45 (1983), 10–12.

Sale, Roger, 'John Clare', in *Closer to Home: Writers and Places in England, 1780–1830* (Cambridge, Mass., 1986), 87–111.

Sales, Roger, 'The Politics of Pastoral', in Kathleen Parkinson and Martin Priestman (eds.), *Peasants and Countrymen in Literature* (London, 1982), 91–104.

—— *English Literature in History 1780–1830: Pastoral and Politics* (London, 1983).

Schulz, Max F., 'Crabbe's and Clare's Enclosured Vales', in *Paradise Preserved: Recreation of Eden in Eighteenth and Nineteenth Century England* (Cambridge, 1986), 137–51.

Scrimgeour, Cecil, 'John Clare and the Price of Experience', *John Clare Society Journal*, 2 (1983), 28–39.

Shaw, Clare MacDonald, 'Some Contemporary Women Poets in Clare's Library', in Goodridge (1994a: 87–122).

Shepherd, Valerie, 'Anne Elizabeth Baker's *Glossary of Northamptonshire Words and Phrases* and John Clare's "Rustic Idiom" ', *John Clare Society Journal*, 15 (1996), 69–75.

Smith, Matthew, 'The "Peasant Poet" Replies: *Sketches in the Life of John Clare* as a Response to Taylor's Introduction to *Poems Descriptive*', *John Clare Society Journal*, 15 (1996), 21–5.

Storey, Mark, 'Clare's "Love and Beauty" ', *Explicator*, 28 (1969–70), 60.

—— (ed.), *Clare: The Critical Heritage* (London, 1973).

—— *The Poetry of John Clare: A Critical Introduction* (London, 1974).

—— 'Clare in his Letters', *John Clare Society Journal*, 3 (1984), 5–16.

—— 'The Poet Overheard', *John Clare Society Journal*, 10 (1991), 5–16.

—— 'Clare and the Critics', in Haughton et al. (1994: 28–50).

Strang, Barbara M. H., 'John Clare's Language', in John Clare, *The Rural Muse*, ed. R. K. R. Thornton (Ashington, 1982), 159–73.

Strickland, Edward, 'Conventions and their Subversion in John Clare's "An Invite to Eternity" ', *Criticism*, 24 (1982), 1–15.

—— 'Approaching "A Vision" ', *Victorian Poetry*, 22 (1984), 229–45.

—— 'John Clare and the Sublime', *Criticism*, 29 (1987), 141–61.

—— 'Boxer Byron: A Clare Obsession', *Byron Journal*, 17 (1989), 57–76.

Swingle, L. J., 'Stalking the Essential John Clare: Clare in Relation to his Romantic Contemporaries', *Studies in Romanticism*, 14 (1975), 273–84.

—— 'John Clare and the Heedless Beetle', *John Clare Society Journal*, 14 (1995), 81–7.

Sychrava, Juliet, *Schiller to Derrida: Idealism in Aesthetics* (Cambridge, 1989).

Thompson, E. P., *Customs in Common* (London, 1991).

Thornton, R. K. R., 'The Flower and the Book: The Gardens of John Clare', *John Clare Society Journal*, 1 (1982), 31–45.

—— 'The Nature of "The Parish" ', *John Clare Society Journal*, 5 (1986), 30–5.

—— 'The Complexity of Clare', in Foulkes (1994: 41–56).

Tibble, Anne, 'John Clare and his Doctors', *Charles Lamb Bulletin*, 4 (1973), 77–81.

Todd, Janet M., 'Mary Joyce in the Poetry of John Clare', *Mary Wollstonecraft Newsletter*, 1 (July 1972), 12–18.

—— *In Adam's Garden: A Study of John Clare's Pre-asylum Poetry* (Gainesville, Ha., 1973).

—— ' "Very Copys of Nature": John Clare's Descriptive Poetry', *Philological Quarterly*, 53 (1974), 84–99.

Tomlinson, Steven, 'The Antiquary and the Poet: Edmund Artis and John Clare', *Durobrivae*, 6 (1978), 6–8.

Trick, Kerith, 'Clare's Asylum Experience', in Foulkes (1994: 27–40).

Wade, Stephen, 'John Clare's Use of Dialect', *Contemporary Review*, 223 (Aug. 1973), 81–4.

Wallace, Anne D., 'Farming on Foot: Tracking Georgic in Clare and Wordsworth', *Texas Studies in Literature and Language*, 34 (1992), 509–40.

—— *Walking, Literature, and English Culture: The Origins and Uses of Peripatetic in the Nineteenth Century* (Oxford, 1993).

Waller, Robert, 'Enclosures: The Ecological Significance of a Poem by John Clare', *Mother Earth: Journal of the Soil Association*, 13 (July 1964), 231–7.

Weedon, Margaret, 'John Clare's Early Acquaintance with Literature', *Notes and Queries*, NS 32 (1985), 356–7.

Williams, Anne, 'Clare's "Gypsies" ', *Explicator*, 39 (1981), 9–11.

Williams, Raymond, *The Country and the City* (London, 1973).

9. *Women Poets of the Romantic Period*

JENNIFER BREEN

The cultural status and aesthetic merit of a few women poets in the Romantic period have been discussed in a variety of ways, depending on each critic's theoretical viewpoint as well as on the availability of each woman author's texts. The task of discovering the works of these women poets has been facilitated by J. R. de J. Jackson's *Romantic Poetry by Women: A Bibliography, 1770–1835* (1993), in which is recorded bibliographical and biographical details of 900 women poets who published between 1770 and 1835. He lists 2,325 volumes of women's poetry in order of date of publication. R. C. Alston's *A Checklist of Women Writers, 1801–1900: Fiction, Verse, Drama* (1990) lists all the poetry, fiction, and drama of women authors of the nineteenth century held by the British Library. Works of poetry in Alston's bibliography are usually identifiable from individual reference numbers.

TEXTS

Most of the women's poetry that was published between 1785 and 1832 was available only in specialist libraries until the publication of Roger Lonsdale's *Eighteenth-Century Women Poets: An Oxford Anthology* in 1989. Lonsdale reprinted a wide-ranging selection of women's poetry published up to 1800. My subsequent *Women Romantic Poets, 1785–1832: An Anthology* reprints an innovative selection from the work of twenty-five competent and interesting women poets from the entire Romantic period. My anthology contains biographical and historical notes as well as a useful 'Introduction'. Andrew Ashfield's *Romantic Women Poets* extends the Romantic period from 1770 to 1838. He provides annotated selections that represent his version of 'Romanticism' from thirty-four women poets, but he has reprinted only excerpts from most of his chosen longer poems. Jerome McGann also includes a few poems by twenty-one women poets in his historically organized *The New Oxford Book of Romantic Period Verse* (1993).

Editions of the collected works of women Romantic poets are as yet few in number, although Jonathan Wordsworth's 'Revolution and Romanticism' series has reprinted selected volumes by Anna Barbauld, Felicia Hemans, Charlotte Smith, Mary Tighe, and Helen Maria Williams. The problem with these facsimile reprints is that there is no modern annotation that might assist in the explication of biographical, historical, or typological obscurities. Stuart Curran's *The Collected Poems of Charlotte Smith* (1993) is a variorum edition with informative notes about topical allusions and Smith's contemporary scene. This edition has emerged from the Brown Women Writers' project at Brown University in the USA, whose researchers aim to computerize women's writing in English from 1350 to 1850. William McCarthy's and Elizabeth Kraft's *The Poems of Anna Letitia Barbauld* (1994) is an annotated edition of all her extant poems.

CRITICISM AND COMMENTARY

Mary Wollstonecraft, who is herself now seen as central to 'Romanticism' (Mellor 1995), reviewed some women's poetry of the day in Joseph Johnson's *Analytical Review* (1788–97). Wollstonecraft trenchantly criticized some of these female poets, such as Ann Yearsley, whose 'stale allusions obscure her poems', and praised others, such as Helen Maria Williams, whose 'poems are ingenious and harmonious'. In the eighteenth century, according to Robert W. Uphaus and Gretchen M. Foster, a female 'canon' of poets was recognized. The notion of a 'canon' of women poets survived into the nineteenth century, if we are to judge by Frederic Rowton's anthology *The Female Poets of Great Britain* (1853), in which he includes brief biographies with his selection of poetry. But the notion of a 'canon' of women's poetry seems to have disappeared in the early to mid-twentieth century. Tayler and Luria, for example, in an influential essay, concluded that there were no major women poets between 1785 and 1832 because women preferred to experiment with the newer art form—the novel. This putative shift in emphasis to the novel as an art form, according to Tayler and Luria, is demonstrated by the work of 'important women writers such as Austen, the Brontë sisters, and even Mrs Radcliffe and Mary Shelley'. But Tayler and Luria's judgement seems to have been formed before they had access to the poetry of important women writers of the Romantic period such as Joanna Baillie, Mary Robinson, Anna Seward, Charlotte Smith, and others.

Tayler and Luria's dismissal of women poets is linked to their hypothesis that, because middle-class women authors did not usually learn Latin, they could not write poetry similar to men's. Tayler and Luria also held the view that women who managed to learn Latin, which gave them direct access to classical poetry, then wrote their own poetry as crypto-men. These kinds of assertion, however, do not take into account the most original of the women Romantic poets. These women poets have tended to be discounted because their poetry is somewhat different from poetry by men of that period.

The notion of a 'canon' of women Romantic poets has been revived in the 1980s by a few critics who see this women's poetry either as an interesting separate canon, or as an important part of the 'traditional' male-dominated 'Romantic canon'. Kathleen Hickok, who writes from a sociological angle, is one of the first critics to attempt an analysis of a women's nineteenth-century poetic 'canon', but she is mainly concerned with poets after 1830. In an early article (1982), Germaine Greer, in relation to her thesis that 'it is only by correct interpretation of individual cases that we can grasp what we have in common with the women who have gone our chosen way before us', discusses the poetry of Letitia Elizabeth Landon. But Greer explores questions of biography rather than interpreting and assessing Landon's poetry; for example, Greer reads Landon's poem 'Lines of Life' as 'a strong appeal to posterity to plead her case'.

Stuart Curran, in his seminal article 'Romantic Poetry: The "I" Altered' in *Romanticism and Feminism* (1988), deplores the dismissive attitude among some of his contemporaries to women Romantic poets: 'by the 1790s in Great Britain there were many more women than men novelists and . . . the theater was actually dominated by women . . . In the arena of poetry, . . . the place of women was likewise, at least for a time, predominant, and it is here that the distortions of our received history are the most glaring. Its chronology has been written wholly, and arbitrarily, along a masculine gender line.' Curran identifies the importance of the work of Letitia Elizabeth Landon and Felicia Hemans in the history of popular verse: 'in the writings of the two most famous women poets of this generation, Felicia Hemans and Letitia Landon, who died respectively in 1835 and 1838, we can discern what is otherwise almost strikingly absent in the male Romantic universe, an actual transition into the characteristic preoccupations of Victorian verse.' Curran also lists other women poets of the Romantic period, and discusses in some detail a sample of poems by Mary Robinson, Jane Taylor, Anna Letitia Barbauld, Ann Yearsley, and Charlotte Smith. He distinguishes differences between women and men poets of the Romantic period, concluding, for example, that women poets celebrate 'quotidian values' whereas men poets demonstrate a 'continual urge for visionary flight, an investment in symbols'.

A spate of writing about Landon and Hemans has succeeded Curran's initial assertion of their historical significance, and these two writers of popular verse are now often held to be, rightly or wrongly, leaders in a women's poetic canon. Angela Leighton and Isobel Armstrong, for example, follow Curran in arguing that Landon and Hemans inaugurated aspects of Victorian poetry.

Leighton in particular categorizes Landon and Hemans as early Victorians because she sees these two poets as 'the true originators of a line of poetry which can be distinguished from the Romantics, on the one hand, and the modernists, on the other'. Leighton devotes a chapter each to their poetry, and she gives details of the author's life in relation to her writing. Armstrong, in her attempt to begin to create what she terms a 'feminine poetics' of the Victorian period, places Landon and Hemans, as 'late Romantic writers', firmly at the centre of such a poetics. She discusses Landon's and Hemans's longer narratives in relation to 'woman as traveller through the imagination' as well as discussing these women poets' uses of masks in dramatic monologues. Armstrong's discussion of Landon and Hemans is thus partly geared to arguing their links with later women poets such as the Brontë sisters.

Both Marlon B. Ross and Anne K. Mellor include discussion of the work of Letitia Elizabeth Landon and Felicia Hemans in their theoretical approaches to women's Romantic poetry as a separate canon. Ross (1989) places Landon and Hemans, along with Hannah More, Anna Barbauld, and Mary Tighe, in 'the early nineteenth-century tradition of feminine poetry', instead of making 'our literary history according to the contours of romantic masculine desire'. In his account of some of the escapist literary romances by Hemans and Landon, he outlines differences between male and female 'desire' as represented in those works. But, as Ross realizes, 'desire' emanates from the individual psyche, and he has to make an assessment of the individual in relation to his or her poetry in order to relate 'desire' to art.

Ross thus gives biographical interpretations of women's Romantic poetry in order to construct the historical and social milieu from which each of these poets has emerged: 'Women poets are so sensitive to the potential conflict between domesticity and the wider world of public fame because the conflict is so palpable in their private lives and in their poetic careers. For Felicia Hemans, each major poem becomes a reworking of this troublesome conflict, each time resolving the conflict with a persistence that demonstrates how unsettling the conflict itself is to her psyche.' Hemans's long poem *The Forest Sanctuary* (1825), for example, becomes for Ross a representation of 'the scene of domestic affection that Hemans anticipates and actually experiences with her mother and sister'. Ross contrasts Hemans's domestic life with Landon's: 'The stress and strain of a woman's public life show in her [Landon's] poetry.' Sigmund Freud used the 'Oedipus' legend as represented in Greek drama in order to label certain behaviour that he claimed that he had discovered in male patients. Ross is reversing this process in using facts about women authors' lives in order to explain psychological conflicts that he finds in their poems.

Germaine Greer (1995a) also uses a biographical approach when she suggests that women's art is 'traditionally biodegradable, and women's poetry may be no exception. In the women's aesthetic, "life" is a higher value than "art".' Greer continues this line in her subsequent book on women's poetry (1995b), in which, *inter alia*, she gives further details of Letitia Elizabeth Landon's life in relation to her verse narratives such as *The Improvisatrice* (1824).

Susan J. Wolfson, rather than attempting to assess the aesthetic quality of Felicia Hemans's poems, gives a selective thematic account of Hemans's large output of popular verse. Nanora Sweet also, in relation to theories of the aesthetic of the 'beautiful', explores Hemans's thematic contribution rather than the aesthetic quality of her work. In addition, Sweet places some of Hemans's 'international' poetry in the context of similar works by Byron and Shelley. Peter Cochran, however, tries to buck this current critical trend of ignoring the question about whether much of Felicia Hemans's historically interesting verse is of an indifferent quality. And Jerome McGann, in a literary spoof (1993), queries whether Felicia Hemans should be restored to the literary 'canon' of the Romantic period.

Anne K. Mellor, in *Romanticism and Gender* (1993), in a similar fashion to Marlon Ross, attempts to remedy some of the critical neglect of women Romantic poets. She concentrates on the work of twenty women authors of the Romantic period, ten of whom are poets: Joanna Baillie (her dramas in blank verse), Anna Barbauld, Felicia Hemans, Letitia Elizabeth Landon, Hannah More, Amelia Opie, Mary Robinson, Charlotte Smith, Helen Maria Williams, and Dorothy Wordsworth. Mellor emphasizes distinctions between men's and women's literary engagement with themes, genres, and forms in the Romantic period. This approach leads to her assertion that men and women authors are essentially different in their employment of poetic subjects:

women writers of the Romantic period for the most part foreswore the concern of their male peers with the capacities of the creative imagination, with the limitations of language, with the possibility of transcendence or 'unity of being', with the development of an autonomous self, with political (as opposed to social) revolution, with the role of the creative writer as political leader or religious savior. Instead, women Romantic writers tended to celebrate, not the achievements of the imagination nor the overflow of powerful feelings, but rather the workings of the rational mind, a mind relocated—in a gesture of revolutionary gender implications—in the female as well as the male body.

But here she is using the male Romantics' definitions of 'creative imagination' and 'transcendence'. Moreover, Mellor's emphasis on differences in the use of language that are seen as arising from differences in gender leads to a kind of socio-biographical interpretation of women's poetry, which does not encourage readers to try to assess women's skills in the use of language or metaphor or other poetic devices. As Cole and Swartz point out, Mellor has been influenced by Carol Gilligan's 'Self-in-Relation-to-Others' school of psychology in that she attempts to reveal women poets as celebrators of domesticity and community values.

Cole and Swartz also argue that Mellor mistakenly supposes that women poets usually eschewed the 'sublime' in favour of a 'preoccupation with domesticity, community, the material, the near at hand, and the literal'. Cole and Swartz suggest, in relation to Ann Yearsley's and Dorothy Wordsworth's writings, that an inability to articulate the 'sublime' is, paradoxically, intrinsically 'Romantic', since it is difficult to express in language that which is held in awe. Cole and Swartz show that, although Yearsley's membership of the working class militates against her ability to express herself, her very apostrophizing of her 'wish for words' implies a Romantic desire to encapsulate the sublime in language. In the case of Dorothy Wordsworth, they claim, her consciousness of her gender prevented her following her vocation to become fully a poet. But Dorothy Wordsworth was able to discount this prohibition to some extent, and wrote twenty or so poems that have been recently printed, often for the first time, by Susan Levin in the context of a work of criticism about her writing.

Moira Ferguson has also published, with a cogent introduction, a few hitherto unpublished poems by Ann Yearsley, some of which throw light on Yearsley's dispute with her erstwhile patron Hannah More. Patricia Demers also, in re-examining this public argument between Yearsley, 'the poetical milkwoman', and More, her middle-class patron, attempts 'to understand the contexts and personalities of both combatants'. Donna Landry contextualizes Yearsley's poems and gives detailed *explications de texte* for some of them. Landry also places the poetry of Elizabeth Hands and Elizabeth Bentley firmly in an eighteenth-century mode, suggesting that both poets imitate the 'pastoral', with Hands occasionally subverting eighteenth-century literary conventions. Readers might claim that none of these 'laboring-class poets' is 'Romantic', but perhaps the fact that these women from the working classes wrote poetry at all might in itself be considered 'Romantic' in the sense of breaking the confines of readers' usual expectations.

Dorothy Wordsworth's prose, and, more recently, her poems, have invariably received attention because, in choosing to become her brother William's companion and amanuensis, she placed herself at the hub of the 'Romantic' movement. Alexander (1989) gives a biographical account of Dorothy Wordsworth's prose and poetry, placing her work in the context of William Wordsworth's. Homans, however, interprets much of Dorothy Wordsworth's poetry in its own right (1980), and explores the question of whether Dorothy Wordsworth felt that she was excluded, because she was a woman, from following the vocation of poet. In a subsequent work (1986), Homans expands on this theme in relation to Dorothy Wordsworth: 'romantic [*sic*] poetry also states most compellingly the traditional myth, as transmitted through literature, of woman's place in language as the silent or vanished object of male representation and quest. . . . For a living woman only the role of unthanked handmaiden remains.' Dorothy Wordsworth is represented by Homans as one such handmaiden who worked for her brother William as his amanuensis and also became for him an 'object of representation'.

Thus, although the poetry of Letitia Landon, Felicia Hemans, and Dorothy Wordsworth has received major critical attention, we do not yet have critical exegeses of the majority of the important texts that make up women's Romantic poetry, nor do we have systematic studies of the characteristic forms in which women poets wrote, nor their characteristic uses of metaphor. The few biographical studies of women poets that were published during the first half of this century are out of print as well as out of date: Henderson's on Caroline Nairne (1906); Carhart's on Joanna Baillie (1923); Enfield's on Landon (1928); Ashmun's on Anna Seward (1931); and Rodgers's on Anna Barbauld (1958). Scholarly studies of individual women poets might serve to fill in the gaps in our knowledge of the literary history of the Romantic period.

Nor do we have much history of women's poetry in relation to political events in the Romantic period. The literary history of women's poetry in connection with historical accounts of the abolition of the slave trade is a case in point. Vincent Newey gives an account of the abolition of the slave trade in relation to poetry by William Cowper, William Blake, Robert Southey, William Wordsworth, and Lord Byron without any reference to women's poetry at that time on the theme of slavery. Conversely, Moira Ferguson's historical study discusses a range of poems by Hannah More, Helen Maria Williams, and Ann Yearsley in support of abolition. Ferguson argues that these women authors also subconsciously in their works hinted at dissenters' and women's rights to a full existence in civil law. In relation to Hannah More's poem 'Slavery', for example, she claims, 'More's sentimental approach echoes that of William Cowper . . . [but] sentimentalism as expounded in and by males was tainted as a woman's thing.' A history that takes account of both men's and women's Romantic poetry is beginning to emerge in essays rather than in longer works of literary historical criticism. Roger Simpson, for example, relates Arthurian legend to both Tennyson and Landon; and Marlon B. Ross (1994) discusses Anna Barbauld's 'Eighteen Hundred and Eleven' in the context of dissenting politics. Stuart Curran (1994) places Mary Robinson's *Lyrical Tales* (1800) in the context of the publication of William Wordsworth's and Samuel Taylor Coleridge's *Lyrical Ballads* (1798) as well as of Robert Southey's 'English Eclogues' (1799).

The relationship between some women's poems and William Wordsworth's is at the heart of a few contributions in recent journals. David Chandler demonstrates that William Wordsworth's 'A Night-Piece' is in part a response to Anna Barbauld's 'A Summer Evening's Meditation'. Chandler also gives a brief publishing history of Barbauld's poem. And Paul Kelley shows how William Wordsworth quotes a passage from Charlotte Smith's 'To the South Downs' in his early poem 'An Evening Walk'. Pamela Woof comments on Dorothy Wordsworth's and Mary Lamb's comparable authorship in relation to their more famous brothers. Jane Aaron reports the lack of critical attention paid to Mary Lamb, but Aaron, rather than making an assessment of Mary Lamb's poetry, tends to acclaim her as a sister on whom Charles Lamb could rely.

Karina Williamson, in 'The Eighteenth Century and the Sister Choir', rehearses the prohibitions against writing poetry that seventeenth- and eighteenth-century women from all classes experienced. Williamson also reflects on the quality, quantity, and nature of women's poetry, making some reference to women poets of the early Romantic period. Jerome McGann (1995) restores Mary Robinson's sonnet series *Sappho and Phaon* (1813) to a position of importance in literary history. McGann at first courageously explores 'the formal and rhetorical conventions' of this sonnet series in relation to Sappho, but then he reverts to biographical criticism when he concludes, 'Throughout *Sappho and Phaon*, Robinson builds a shrewd retort to the facile slanders regularly directed at her.' But nevertheless McGann's kind of intellectual appraisal of a significant woman poet of the Romantic period is essential for current literary studies. An integration of criticism of women Romantic poets within the traditional literary histories of Romanticism—as these recent articles in their own various ways attempt—seems the most feasible as well as the most useful way of giving these women poets their due aesthetic, cultural, and historical status.

REFERENCES

BIBLIOGRAPHIES, CHECKLISTS, AND DICTIONARIES

Alston, R. C. (comp.), *A Checklist of Women Writers, 1801–1900: Fiction, Verse, Drama* (London, 1990).

Blain, Virginia, Clements, Patricia, and Grundy, Isobel (eds.), *The Feminist Companion to Literature in English: Women Writers from the Middle Ages to the Present* (London, 1990).

Jackson, J. R. de J. (comp.), *Romantic Poetry by Women: A Bibliography, 1770–1835* (Oxford, 1993).

Todd, Janet (ed.), *A Dictionary of Women Writers* (London, 1989).

TEXTS

Anthologies

Ashfield, Andrew (ed.), *Romantic Women Poets, 1770–1838* (Manchester, 1995).

Breen, Jennifer (ed.), *Women Romantic Poets, 1785–1832: An Anthology* (London, 1992; new edn., 1994).

Leighton, Angela, and Reynolds, Margaret (eds.), *Victorian Women's Poetry: An Anthology* (Oxford, 1995).

Lonsdale, Roger (ed.), *Eighteenth-Century Women Poets: An Oxford Anthology* (Oxford, 1989).

McGann, Jerome J. (ed.), *The New Oxford Book of Romantic Period Verse* (Oxford, 1993).

Individual Authors

Barbauld, Anna Letitia, *Poems, 1792*, facsimile edn., Revolution and Romanticism Series (Spelsbury, 1993).

—— *The Poems*, ed. William McCarthy and Elizabeth Kraft (Athens, Ga., 1994).

Hemans, Felicia, *Records of Woman, 1828*, facsimile edn., Revolution and Romanticism Series (Spelsbury, 1991).

Landon, Letitia Elizabeth, *Poetical Works: A Facsimile Reproduction of the 1873 Edition*, ed. F. J. Sypher (Delmar, 1990).

—— *The Fate of Adelaide, a Swiss Romantic Tale; and Other Poems: A Facsimile Reproduction*, ed. F. J. Sypher (Delmar, 1990).

Smith, Charlotte, *Elegiac Sonnets, 1789*, facsimile edn., Revolution and Romanticism Series (Spelsbury, 1992).

—— *The Poems of Charlotte Smith*, ed. Stuart Curran (New York, 1993).

Tighe, Mary, *Psyche, with Other Poems, 1811*, facsimile edn., Revolution and Romanticism Series (Spelsbury, 1992).

Weller, Earle V. (ed.), *Keats and Mary Tighe* (New York, 1928; repr. 1966).

Williams, Helen Maria, *Poems, 1786*, facsimile edn., Revolution and Romanticism Series (Spelsbury, 1994).

Yearsley, Ann, 'The Unpublished Poems of Ann Yearsley', ed. and introd. Moira Ferguson, *Tulsa Studies in Women's Literature*, 12/1 (1993), 13–46.

CRITICISM AND COMMENTARY

Aaron, Jane, 'Charles and Mary Lamb: The Critical Heritage', *Charles Lamb Bulletin*, 59 (1987), 73–85.

Alexander, Meena, *Women in Romanticism: Mary Wollstonecraft, Dorothy Wordsworth and Mary Shelley* (London, 1989).

Armstrong, Isobel, ' "A Music of Thine Own": Women's Poetry—an Expressive Tradition?', in *Victorian Poetry: Poetry, Poetics, and Politics* (London, 1993), 318–77.

Ashmun, Margaret, *The Singing Swan: An Account of Anna Seward* (New Haven, 1931).

Carhart, Margaret S., *The Life and Work of Joanna Baillie* (New Haven, 1923).

Chandler, David, 'Wordsworth's "A Night Piece" and Mrs Barbauld', *Notes and Queries*, 40/1 (1993), 40–1.

Clarke, Norma, *Ambitious Heights: Writing, Friendship, Love. The Jewsbury Sisters, Felicia Hemans and Jane Carlyle* (London, 1990).

Cochran, Peter, 'Fatal Fluency, Fruitless Dower: The Eminently Marketable Felicia Hemans', *Times Literary Supplement* (21 July 1995), 13.

Cole, Lucinda, and Swartz, Richard G., ' "Why Should I Wish for Words?": Literacy, Articulation, and the Borders of Literary Culture', in Mary A. Favret and Nicola J. Watson (eds.), *At the Limits of Romanticism* (Bloomington, Ind., 1994), 143–70.

Curran, Stuart, 'Romantic Poetry: The "I" Altered', in Anne K. Mellor (ed.), *Romanticism and Feminism* (Bloomington, Ind., 1988), 185–207.

Curran, Stuart, 'Mary Robinson's *Lyrical Tales* in Context', in Carol Shiner Wilson and Joel Haefner (eds.), *Re-visioning Romanticism: British Women Writers, 1776–1837* (Philadelphia, 1994), 17–35.

Demers, Patricia, ' "For Mine's a Stubborn and Savage Will": "Lactilla" (Ann Yearsley) and "Stella" (Hannah More) Reconsidered', *Huntington Library Quarterly: Studies in English and American History and Literature,* 56/2 (1993), 135–50.

Ellison, Julie, 'The Politics of Fancy in the Age of Sensibility', in Carol Shiner Wilson and Joel Haefner (eds.), *Re-visioning Romanticism: British Women Writers, 1776–1837* (Philadelphia, 1994), 228–55.

Enfield, Doris E., *L. E. L.: A Mystery of the Thirties* (London, 1928).

Ferguson, Moira, *Subject to Others: British Women Writers and Colonial Slavery, 1670–1834* (London, 1993).

Greer, Germaine, 'The Tulsa Center for the Study of Women's Literature: What We Are Doing and Why We Are Doing It', *Tulsa Studies in Women's Literature*, 1/1 (1982), 5–26.

—— 'A Biodegradable Art: Changing Fashions in Anthologies of Women's Poetry', *Times Literary Supplement* (30 June 1995*a*), 7–8.

—— *Slip-Shod Sibyls: Recognition, Rejection and the Woman Poet* (London, 1995*b*).

Haefner, Joel, 'The Romantic Scene(s) of Writing', in Carol Shiner Wilson and Joel Haefner (eds.), *Re-visioning Romanticism: British Women Writers, 1776–1837* (Philadelphia, 1994), 256–73.

Henderson, George, *Lady Nairne and her Songs* (Paisley, 1899; 4th edn., 1906).

Hickok, Kathleen, *Representations of Women: Nineteenth-Century British Women's Poetry* (Westport, Conn., 1984).

Homans, Margaret, *Women Writers and Poetic Identity: Dorothy Wordsworth, Emily Brontë, and Emily Dickinson* (Princeton, 1980).

—— *Bearing the Word: Language and Female Experience in Nineteenth-Century Women's Writing* (Chicago, 1986).

Kelley, Paul, 'Charlotte Smith and "An Evening Walk" ', *Notes and Queries* 29 (227)/3 (1982), 220.

Landry, Donna, *The Muses of Resistance: Laboring-Class Women's Poetry in Britain, 1739–1796* (Cambridge, 1990).

Leighton, Angela, *Victorian Women Poets: Writing against the Heart* (Hemel Hempstead, 1992).

Levin, Susan M., *Dorothy Wordsworth and Romanticism* (New Brunswick, NJ, 1987).

Lootens, Tricia, 'Hemans and Home: Victorianism, Feminine "Internal Enemies", and the Domestication of National Identity', *Publications of the Modern Language Association*, 109 (1994), 234–53.

McGann, Jerome J., 'Literary History, Romanticism, and Felicia Hemans', *Modern Language Quarterly*, 54/2 (1993), 215–35.

—— 'Mary Robinson and the Myth of Sappho', *Modern Language Quarterly*, 56/1 (1995), 55–76.

McKerrow, Mary, 'Joanna Baillie and Mary Brunton: Women of the Manse', in Dale Spender (ed.), *Living by the Pen: Early British Women Writers* (New York, 1992), 160–74.

Mellor, Anne K., *Romanticism and Gender* (New York, 1993).

—— 'A Revolution in Female Manners', in Duncan Wu (ed.), *Romanticism: A Critical Reader* (Oxford, 1995), 408–16.

Newey, Vincent, 'The Abolition of the Slave Trade', in Jean Raimond and J. R. Watson (eds.), *A Handbook to English Romanticism* (New York, 1992), 1–4.

Pascoe, Judith, 'Female Botanists and the Poetry of Charlotte Smith', in Carol Shiner Wilson and Joel Haefner (eds.), *Re-visioning Romanticism: British Women Writers, 1776–1837* (Philadelphia, 1994), 193–209.

Rodgers, Betsy, *Georgian Chronicle: Mrs. Barbauld and her Family* (London, 1958).

Ross, Marlon B., *The Contours of Masculine Desire: Romanticism and the Rise of Women's Poetry* (New York, 1989).

—— 'Configurations of Feminine Reform: The Woman Writer and the Tradition of Dissent', in Carol Shiner Wilson and Joel Haefner (eds.), *Re-visioning Romanticism: British Women Writers, 1776–1837* (Philadelphia, 1994), 91–110.

Rowton, Frederic, *The Female Poets of Great Britain: A Facsimile of the 1853 Edition*, ed. Marilyn L. Williamson (Detroit, 1982).

Simpson, Roger, 'Landon's "A Legend of Tintagel Castle": Another Analogue of Tennyson's "The Lady of Shallott" ', *Tennyson Research Bulletin*, 4/4 (1985), 179–85.

Sweet, Nanora, 'History, Imperialism, and the Aesthetics of the Beautiful: Hemans and the Post-Napoleonic Moment', in Mary A. Favret and Nicola J. Watson (eds.), *At the Limits of Romanticism* (Bloomington, Ind., 1994), 170–84.

Tayler, Irene, and Luria, Gina, 'Gender and Genre: Women in British Romantic Literature', in Marlene Springer (ed.), *What Manner of Woman: Essays on English and American Life and Literature* (New York, 1977), 98–123.

Uphaus, Robert W., and Foster, Gretchen M. (eds.), *The 'Other' Eighteenth Century: English Women of Letters, 1660–1800* (East Lansing, Mich., 1991).

Watson, J. R., 'Dorothy Wordsworth', in Jean Raimond and J. R. Watson (eds.), *A Handbook to English Romanticism* (New York, 1992), 288–90.

Williamson, Karina, 'The Eighteenth Century and the Sister Choir', *Essays in Criticism*, 40/4 (1990), 271–86.

Wolfson, Susan J., ' "Domestic Affections" and "the spear of Minerva": Felicia Hemans and the Dilemma of Gender', in Carol Shiner Wilson and Joel Haefner (eds.), *Re-visioning Romanticism: British Women Writers, 1776–1837* (Philadelphia, 1994), 128–66.

Wollstonecraft, Mary, *The Works of Mary Wollstonecraft*, ed. Janet Todd and Marilyn Butler, vol. vii (London, 1989).

Woof, Pamela, 'Dorothy Wordsworth and Mary Lamb, Writers', *Charles Lamb Bulletin* 67 (1989), 69–82.

Wordsworth, Jonathan, 'Ann Yearsley to Caroline Norton: Women Poets of the Romantic Period', *Wordsworth Circle*, 26/3 (1995), 114–24.

10. *Poetry by Burns, Cowper, Crabbe, Southey, and Other Male Authors*

MICHAEL ROSSINGTON

This chapter is concerned with poetry by men which contributed significantly to the literary culture of the Romantic period in England and Scotland at the time but has subsequently, with some notable exceptions, been given less attention both textually and critically than that bestowed upon the seven male poets to whom individual chapters are devoted in this volume. For current purposes, it has been convenient to discuss male, non-canonical poetry in one chapter. But it must be acknowledged immediately that such a categorization, which groups together so many obviously different poets, is arbitrary except in the sense (crucial for this volume) that it derives largely from familiar critical taxonomies. Despite such problems of definition, however, there are gains as well as shortfalls in the perspective afforded here. To study these poets, and their female peers, is to gain a heightened awareness of the discrepancy between the still fairly inflexible hierarchy of poetic status amongst the 'Romantics' which has prevailed in the late twentieth century and the more fluid, embattled state of poetic reputations in the period itself. Furthermore, the modern reader is forced to question the often paradoxically exclusive orthodoxies at work within current definitions of writing at the margins. The chapter's potential scope has necessitated discrimination of various kinds. Literally dozens of published poets—many of whom were well known in their day—are given no space at all, and four very different poets—Burns, Cowper, Crabbe, and Southey—are given more space than the rest (a kind of canon of the non-canonical), primarily because of their significance for authors and readers in

I would like to acknowledge the support of the following in preparing this chapter: the Department of English Literary and Linguistic Studies and the staff of the Robinson Library, University of Newcastle upon Tyne; the staff of the Literary and Philosophical Society, Newcastle upon Tyne.

the period. A list of the poets mentioned, with their dates, is provided below (before the section headed 'References').

In a chapter unavoidably preoccupied with inclusiveness, expediency has dictated a three-part division. The introduction deals with the vexed question of categorizing the poetry considered and with established reference works of relevance. 'Texts' deals with the currently available forms in which the poems may be read. The 'Criticism' section is divided into three parts which address contemporary reception, author-centred approaches, and thematic approaches in contemporary Romantic studies. The need to address the question of the availability and reliability of texts for a significant number of poets, combined with the view that some of the most revealing and pertinent criticism and comment is made by their contemporaries, results in a relatively small amount of space being given over to twentieth-century criticism. It should be noted that, for reasons of space, this chapter observes the volume's chronological delimitation, 1785–1830, fairly strictly. Thus, regrettably, notwithstanding one or two exceptions, reference is not made to work published by the poets under consideration before the earlier and after the later date (this particularly affects treatment of the *œuvres* of Beddoes, Hartley Coleridge, Crabbe, Cowper, Darley, Elliott, Hood, Hunt, and Landor). Reference to translations, drama, and prose (including letters) is usually excluded. The poetry of Scott and Peacock is considered in the relevant chapter devoted to each.

INTRODUCTION

'MINOR', 'OTHER', 'LESSER', 'SECONDARY', AND OTHER LABELS

It is worth at the outset examining how the work of the poets treated in this chapter has come to be comparatively neglected in editorial and critical terms. Any assertion of the significance of the poetry of the writers addressed here must necessarily confront the question of the way that a 'canon' of poetry of the Romantic period has been posited over the past fifty years or so. Words like 'minor', 'other', 'lesser-known', 'secondary', 'transitional', all of which have been readily employed to categorize some of the poets discussed below (see Bloom and Trilling, Reiman, and J. R. Watson 1992), confess to, even encourage, a view of poetry in the English Romantic period as divisible between the work of those writers who are in some sense 'central' and the work of a mass of justifiably neglected figures whose work is only retrieved from oblivion in order to prove its instrinsic marginality. But the questions 'central to what?' and 'marginal to what?' have been asked with increasing urgency in recent years, and for a variety of reasons a consensus about who is at the 'centre' and who at the 'margins' no longer pertains (witness Clare). Whatever the enduring richness of critical endeavour in respect of the 'major' Romantic poets, a hierarchical and deselective approach to poetry of the period is at least questionable for several reasons.

First, as is made clear in the introduction to this volume, the post-1945 Anglo-American view of the Romantic 'canon' as centring on six major authors has been interrogated repeatedly and systematically in recent decades. The case for a more open literary history of the Romantic period, which is recept-ive to how poets whose work has come to be neglected were read and criti-cized in the period itself, has been argued eloquently by Butler (see especially 1989 but also 1987 and 1988). The premiss of this chapter is that the de-familiarizing experience of reading poetry which has defied twentieth-century associations of the label 'Romantic' is both necessary for a properly literary-historical understanding of the literature of the period c.1785–c.1830, and instructive as a means of promoting awareness of the prescriptive definitions of 'Romantic' writing which have pervaded critical discourse. In other words, the generic, technical, and thematic diversity of the poetic output examined below testifies not to aberrant writing but rather to the limitations of defini-tions of 'Romanticism' itself as it has been taught, written about, and read in English literature syllabuses (on this topic, see McGann 1993). An aware-ness that literary 'value' is, in part, a culturally and historically delimited concept enables a reader to be at least receptive to Byron's ranking of his contemporaries:

He [Scott] is undoubtedly the Monarch of Parnassus, and the most *English* of bards. I should place Rogers next in the living list—(I value him more as the last of the *best* school)—Moore and Campbell both *third*—Southey and Wordsworth and Coleridge—the rest όι πολλοι [hoi polloi]—thus:—

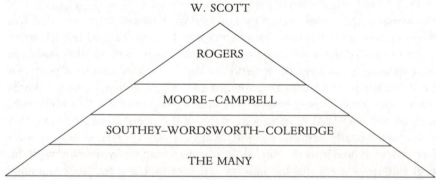

W. SCOTT

ROGERS

MOORE–CAMPBELL

SOUTHEY–WORDSWORTH–COLERIDGE

THE MANY

There is a triangular 'Gradus ad Parnassum!'—the names are too numerous for the base of the triangle. Poor Thurlow has gone wild about the poetry of Queen Bess's reign—*c'est dommage*. I have ranked the names upon my triangle more upon what I believe popular opinion, than any decided opinion of my own. (Byron 1973–82: iii. 219–20)

Second, an exclusively canonical approach to poetry in the period runs the risk of ignoring the ways in which modern definitions of 'major' and 'minor' Romantic poetry conceal a literary culture which in reality appears to have been far less neatly sifted, and in which poetical and critical hierarchies variously competed or overlapped with one another simultaneously. Reading Hunt's *Story of Rimini* (1816) alongside Keats's *Poems* (1817) or Southey's *Thalaba* (1801) alongside Shelley's *Alastor and Other Poems* (1816) may not help the reader to resolve abiding interpretative doubts. But in such cases the way that poetry which has come to be valued as canonical can be seen to define itself, in part, by means of a critical absorption of other contemporary poetry, suggests the perils of regarding the Romantic poetic canon as a kind of fortressed enclosure. Finally, current critical and editorial activity suggests that the conventional literary history of the Romantic period has been, and is being, challenged most forcefully by research and scholarship concerned to recover the contemporary profile of poetry by women. The need to investigate the work of marginalized male poets may be seen not so much in competition with scholarly endeavour in relation to women writers as consonant with it, part of a broad project which seeks to reflect more deeply about the variety of poetry in the Romantic period.

STANDARD BIBLIOGRAPHICAL AND REFERENCE WORKS

This chapter does not seek to duplicate standard information about editions, bibliographies, and criticism of many lesser-known individual poets of the period which may be found in established reference works. Though published over thirty years ago, there are three reference works which are still of great value for bibliographical information on primary and secondary materials up to the early 1960s: the *New Cambridge Bibliography of English Literature (NCBEL)*, Jack, and Houtchens and Houtchens. The first two remain the standard starting points, especially useful for information on editions of the works of individual poets. Houtchens and Houtchens contains particularly helpful descriptive bibliographical essays on the work of Campbell, Hunt, Landor, Moore, and Southey. From the same era, the 'individual author' bibliographies in Renwick are rather sketchy. The sections on Cowper and Crabbe in Mell, and the chapter entitled 'Secondary and Minor Poets' in Reiman (on Beddoes, Campbell, Hogg, Hood, Hunt, Landor, Moore, Rogers, and Southey), are far from comprehensive but fulfil a useful function as preliminary bibliographical guides. For criticism, especially recent work, the usual sources apply, such as the Modern Language Association annual bibliography, the annual bibliographical listings of the *Keats–Shelley Journal* (for poets associated with Keats, Shelley, Byron, and their circles such as Hunt, Reynolds, and Horace Smith), *The Romantic Movement: A Selective and Critical Bibliography*, and the *Year's Work in English Studies*. The quick-reference entries on Burns, Campbell, Cowper, Crabbe, Hogg, Hunt, Lamb, Landor, Moore, Rogers, and Southey in Raimond and Watson serve a useful summary purpose. In addition to the above there are single-author bibliographies or reference guides, dealing mainly with secondary material, to Cowper (Hartley), Crabbe (Bareham and Gatrell, Peterson), Hunt (Lulofs and Ostrom, which is preferable to Waltman and McDaniel), Jones (Cannon 1979), and Southey (Curry 1977). Egerer, Russell, and the second volume of Landré contain thorough bibliographical descriptions of the early editions of the poetical works of Burns, Cowper, and Hunt respectively. Those interested in pursuing manuscript studies will find two reference works of immense value. Sutton's location register details manuscripts in publicly available collections in the British Isles while Margaret Smith's *Index* lists the extant manuscripts of Burns, Cowper, and Crabbe in repositories outside, as well as within, the UK. Smith's introductions, which survey the literary manuscripts of the latter three poets, should be consulted.

TEXTS

Most of the poets referred to here have not received anything like the sustained textual and editorial treatment given in recent decades to the work of the seven accorded individual chapters in this volume. The only 'collected' or 'complete' editions of the works of many poets considered here date from between the early nineteenth and the mid-twentieth centuries, and relatively few poems, and certainly not the *œuvres* of individual authors (with the important exceptions of Burns, Cowper, and Crabbe), have been edited systematically according to modern editorial principles involving the full collation of manuscript sources and other witnesses. These older editions, often impressive feats of scholarship in their time, may still be consulted in libraries or acquired through second-hand bookshops, but it should be remembered that they do not always contain reliable texts of poems nor a reliable 'canon' of the poet's works. This is partly because scholarly endeavour has brought, and continues to bring, to light evidence concerning attribution, manuscripts, authorial intentions, and relations between authors and publishers, of which the earlier editor was unaware. But there are additional reasons as to why the texts of poems in these older editions cannot be regarded as 'authoritative'. In contemporary Romantic literary studies, there has been much debate recently about what exactly constitutes an 'authoritative' text, or even whether the concept is viable (see McGann 1991). In preparing an edition of the poetical works of a poet of the Romantic period for a late twentieth-century readership, which should the editor use as 'copy text', the text of a poem as approved by the author for publication in a first edition, or the text of the same poem revised by the author for publication later in his life? Each choice may be defended because each text may be regarded as having authorial sanction, though at different points in time. Ideally, therefore, older 'collected' editions of a poet's works are best consulted in conjunction with early editions of particular poems, some of which are reprinted in the 'facsimile' series discussed below. The basis of the scholarly annotation necessary to draw out the textual, literary, and cultural significance of these poems for today's readership is sometimes partially available in older editions but may also be gleaned, in a form that is obviously more dispersed than for canonical poets, from books and articles discussed in the 'Criticism' section below.

Burns

The most scholarly modern edition of the poems and songs is Burns (1968), the Oxford English Texts edition in three volumes, the final volume of which contains a textual introduction, commentary, and a full glossary. Burns (1969), the Oxford Standard Authors edition, is based on Burns (1968) but it omits the apparatus criticus and the textual introduction and is 'reduced' in respect of the chronology, bibliography, and glossary. Kinsley's acknowledgement in his preface that 'The canon of Burns's work will probably never be fully established' (Burns 1968, 1969) has been borne out by recurrent controversies about the scope and content of the Burns canon. On textual matters too, Kinsley cannot be regarded as uncontroversial, let alone definitive. The texts in his editions are 'based on Burns's holographs, and transcripts revised in his hand; the authoritative Kilmarnock (1786) and Edinburgh (1787–94) editions of his *Poems, chiefly in the Scottish Dialect* (some copies with autograph corrections and additions); Johnson's *Scots Musical Museum* (1787–1803) and *Thomson's Select Collection of Original Scotish Airs* (1793–1818); transcripts of manuscripts which are not at present accessible; and early printings in newspapers, periodicals, and tracts' (Burns 1968, 1969). For considered and detailed criticism of the editorial methods of Burns (1968), see G. Ross Roy who draws attention to several instances of incompletely documented variants and other deficiencies. While Burns (1969) states that it 'provides material only for an elementary study of Burns's craft', it does offer a basic reading text to its intended audience of 'the student and the general reader' although it is unannotated. More accessible and useful for those seeking an initial encounter with Burns is the selected edition by Calder and Donnelly with its good, concentrated annotation and a chronology, bibliography, and brief but lucid glossary. Calder and Donnelly follow Kinsley's text most of the time but they offer several interesting and considered departures from it. For example in 'Tam O'Shanter', where Kinsley follows the Edinburgh edition of 1793 in omitting the lines 'Three Lawyers' tongues, turn'd inside out, | Wi' lies seam'd like a beggar's clout; | And Priests' hearts, rotten, black as muck, | Lay stinking, vile, in every neuk.

—', justifying his decision on aesthetic grounds as well as those of editorial principle (Burns 1968: iii. 1362), Calder and Donnelly restore them to their state in the earliest printed edition, the second volume of Grose's *Antiquities of Scotland* (1791), and thereby provide a measure of Burns's uncompromising satirical acuity in its undiluted form before, bowing to Alexander Fraser Tytler's suggestion, Burns agreed to cut out 'the hit at the lawyer and priest' (Burns 1985*a*: ii. 85). McGuirk offers another good, modern Penguin edition of Burns's poems. Glossaries of the kind provided in the above editions are likely to be essential for most readers who will be unfamiliar with eighteenth-century Lowland Scots, in which Burns wrote much of his best work, and it should be remembered that Burns himself supplied glossaries to the various editions of *Poems, Chiefly in the Scottish Dialect* published in his lifetime. Burns (1985*b*), an edition of *Poems, Chiefly in the Scottish Dialect* (1786), is entitled *The Kilmarnock Poems* (duly emphasizing the significance of its non-metropolitan place of publication), and offers an introduction, particularly useful on the poet's use of Lowland Scots, as well as notes. It goes further than the above editions in assisting the reader by incorporating detailed marginal glosses in the reading text itself. Burns (1993*a*) is a revised and expanded edition of Burns (1985) containing 'Holy Willie's Prayer' and 'Tam o'Shanter' as well as *The Kilmarnock Poems*. Burns (1993*b*) is the first modern edition of 'all discoverable songs by Burns'.

Cowper

The recent scholarly edition of the complete poetical works of Cowper by Baird and Ryskamp is executed to very high standards. It contains reliable texts, accompanying textual notes, a biographical and textual introduction, a substantial commentary, and a particularly useful section in the 'Textual Introduction' to the third volume on 'The Development of the Canon' in which the early editions of Cowper's poems are analysed. The best possible starting point for the reader who seeks an informed introduction to Cowper's poetry, however, is to be found in Sambrook's Longman Annotated Texts edition of Cowper's *The Task* and 'Selected Other Poems'. Apart from its judicious selection of the poems likely to be of most interest to the general reader and its up-to-date bibliography of criticism, Sambrook's edition is the best reading text of Cowper's poems on at least three counts. It contains a substantial introduction, in which the intellectual and biographical contexts of Cowper's work are debated thoroughly. The reader gains enormously from the generous and detailed annotation on the page which draws out the significance of biographical, historical, literary, and textual matters. Finally, Sambrook has edited the poems afresh. His editorial procedures and therefore the texts offered are, in certain respects, independent of those to be found in other editions including Baird and Ryskamp, the final two volumes of which were, anyway, published after his own. Though dated and wanting by comparison with the above, Milford's fourth edition of Cowper's poetical works, originally published in 1934 and reprinted in a new impression in 1967 with the most salient of its textual and bibliographical errors corrected and new explanatory notes by Russell, is widely available and remains of some value.

Crabbe

The edition of the complete poetical works of Crabbe by Dalrymple-Champneys and Pollard constitutes a major contribution to contemporary Romantic studies. Its primary significance (discussed in Edwards 1989) is that it draws on recently discovered manuscript material, and pays particularly close attention to the complex evolution of his poems from draft forms to finally printed versions. It supplies a wealth of detailed information of interest to the reader and scholar of Crabbe through its introduction, 'Commentary' (containing introductions to individual poems and explanatory notes), textual notes, and appendices which contain, amongst other things, variant readings of poems in manuscript and proof versions, alterations in capitalization, punctuation, and orthography made in editions published in the poet's lifetime, a descriptive bibliography of early editions, and a note of additions to the canon after 1834. It addresses in particularly welcome detail the problem of the status of 'accidentals' (that is, such questions as capitalization, orthography, and punctuation) for an editor offering a text of Crabbe's poems, an issue of interest to all editors of literary texts in the period. However, while Dalrymple-Champneys and Pollard is always worth consulting, the best reading text of Crabbe's poems, and the best selection, is Gavin Edwards's compelling edition for the Penguin Selected English Poets series which includes the complete *Tales* of 1812 (Crabbe 1991). The quality of Edwards's edition far surpasses that of the several other post-war selected editions of Crabbe's poetry. Though he is not afforded very much space with which to introduce and annotate, the depth of his engagement with the textual and contextual features of Crabbe's work (particularly evident in his notes) is enough to make one wonder at the continued comparative neglect of this extraordinary poet whose work, as Edwards points out, has been fated to disappear between the labels of convenience 'Augustan' and 'Romantic' bequeathed by modern literary history. Edwards's edition is also of major editorial and textual significance in its own right. While acknowledging the impact of Dalrymple-Champneys and Pollard on his own work, his edition 'is based on independent study of early printed editions and of copies of most of the relevant known manuscripts', and his texts differ 'in certain respects' from those offered by them. Both editions are significant for their refusal to 'regularize' the texts of the poems, that is, to subject them to standardized editorial treatment in respect of 'accidentals'. This can be seen, in part, as a mark of editorial fidelity to the often crucially irregular way in

which the poems themselves are registered by their readers, but it also signals
a proper recognition of how the verse, as it was printed in Crabbe's lifetime,
straddles distinct eras in the history of the printing and publication of poetry.
Dalrymple-Champneys's defence of the significance of her editorial practice
puts the issue well:

Since [Crabbe's] literary career spanned a period of fifty years, during which there
were considerable changes in printing practice and in the use of accidentals, the choice
of the first (or second) editions as copy-text means that the poems are printed here in
successively differing styles. This variety of approach, while it emphasizes the role of
the printer, is in keeping with the character and development of Crabbe's verse, which
altered radically over the years and is not well suited to uniform treatment. The rough
texture of *Inebriety*, the dignified late Augustan style of the London printed quartos,
the unconventional, irregular style of the works of his middle period printed by Brettell,
and the near modernity of *Tales of the Hall* are in each case appropriate. To preserve
the contemporary dress in which they severally appeared is to contribute to their effect
and to point the differences between them. (Crabbe 1988: vol. i)

The significance of this non-uniform editorial practice is developed by Edwards
in respect of Crabbe's deployment of the initial capital letter in his poems.
With reference to manuscripts and proofs as well as printed versions of poems,
he argues convincingly that Crabbe's use of initial capital letters is often pur-
poseful rather than arbitrary (Edwards 1987, 1989; Crabbe 1991). A further
important addition to the Crabbe canon, *The Voluntary Insane*, has recently
been edited by Felix Pryor (Crabbe 1995), and is helpfully reviewed by Wells.
It is one of four previously unpublished verse tales discovered in a manuscript
notebook of Crabbe's which came to light in 1989, and therefore too late for
inclusion in either of the editions discussed above.

Southey

The lack of a modern scholarly edition of the complete poetical works of
Southey makes for a profoundly frustrating state of affairs for the reader who
seeks to understand the significance of the work in its time. More debate about
the most desirable basis on which to produce reliable texts of the poems is
necessary, as is co-ordinated work on the complete poetical canon. *The Poetical
Works of Southey, Collected by Himself* (1837–8) is grossly inadequate in several
respects. There are deliberate exclusions in the case of early poems, and many
texts are substantially revised from their first published form. Southey's political tergiversation motivated many of these excisions and alterations, as the
example of his epic narrative *Joan of Arc* (to which Coleridge contributed)
demonstrates. The full impact of its idiosyncratic form and politically charged
content is best understood through reading the first edition of 1796 in conjunction with the significantly revised second edition of 1798 (which contains

numerous additional notes) rather than the subsequently revised version of 1837–8. Fitzgerald's substantial selected edition of 1909 (widely available though out of print) cannot be recommended. Textually it is based on Southey's collected edition, the canon it offers is virtually unaltered from that of 1837–8, and it almost entirely omits the copious notes to the epic narratives which provide an important measure of their cultural and historical significance. The only other twentieth-century selection, by Grigson, is likewise of no textual significance, and contains almost exclusively shorter lyric poems. Any assessment of Southey's poetic canon must now acknowledge the poems he contributed to newspapers and magazines, especially those published in the *Morning Post* between 1798 and 1803, reprinted and edited in Southey (1984). The publication of facsimile reprints of *The Fall of Robespierre* (1794), *Poems* (1797), *Joan of Arc: An Epic Poem* (1796), *Thalaba the Destroyer* (1801), and *Wat Tyler: A Dramatic Poem* (1817) in the Revolution and Romanticism series (discussed below) is to be welcomed. It is to be hoped that eventually reprints of the three later long narrative poems, *Madoc* (1805), *The Curse of Kehama* (1810), and *Roderick, the Last of the Goths* (1814), will be available, thereby enabling the modern reader to gain a fuller understanding of Southey's poetry.

Other poets, and further sources of texts

For most of the rest of the poets considered here, information concerning preferred editions of their work may be found in the standard bibliographical and reference works referred to above, particularly Jack and Renwick. A few editions, some selected, of the works of individual poets merit special notice. Higgens's selection of Beddoes's verse is interesting but Beddoes (1950), which derives from the same editor's standard edition of 1935, remains the best and most substantial selection. Pite's edition of the influential translation of Dante's *Divina Commedia* by Cary is very useful. The selection of poems by Darley introduced and annotated by Anne Ridler is commendable. The Stirling/South Carolina Research Edition of the collected works of Hogg under the general editorship of Douglas S. Mack, projected to run to thirty-one volumes, constitutes a major ongoing editorial project in Romantic studies. Recently published is Garside's edition of *A Queer Book*, the fascinating textual complexity of which is elegantly unravelled in a thorough and clear introduction. A commentary to the poems and a glossary are also provided. The best starting point for the interested reader unfamiliar with Hogg's verse is Mack (1970) but some of the several selections of Hogg's poems published since, such as Groves's broad selection of 1986, the same author's more specialized edition of some of the parodies of 1990, and Petrie's edition of *Scottish Pastorals*, take into account more recent textual scholarship. Rickword's edition of the satirical verse of Hone reprints the pamphlets with the illustrations by Cruikshank, along with some of the ripostes. Hood is well served in the substantial and thoroughly annotated selection by Clubbe and in Flint's briefer sampling. Milford's 1923 edition of the poetical works of Hunt is incomplete and wanting by modern editorial standards, but nevertheless remains the only twentieth-century edition of his poems. The poetry of Jones, long recognized as influencing the way India is represented in poetry of the period, is well served in two recent selections of his works by Pachori and Franklin (Jones 1995). Franklin's handsomely produced edition is the more substantial in every respect and represents a major advance in providing a modern readership with the means to understand Jones's work and its significance. Though often somewhat prolix, the editorial commentary in the headnotes and notes to individual poems is designed to fulfil the ambitious overall aim of the volume, 'to enable a university audience of readers of English literature to access the central texts of Jones with a knowledge of their place in eighteenth- and nineteenth-century English and European culture'. Hanley's selection of the writings of Landor, with its helpful introduction and notes, is an essential starting point for those seeking to engage with the unique demands of his poetry. In contrast to the editorial policy of Wheeler's standard edition of the collected poems (which usually favours the first published version of a text), Hanley's edition seeks to reflect the author's final intentions, thus generally providing the last printed version of texts revised by Landor before his death. There are excerpts only in Hanley of one of Landor's poems likely to be of most interest to a modern reader, *Gebir*; a modern facsimile reprint of the first edition is available, but the text of the second, revised, edition of 1803 in Wheeler is preferable. Though its annotation is light, Beckwith's edition of the poems and other works of White contains a useful introduction and substantial selection.

Although mostly priced for library purchase, facsimile reprint series provide, in many cases, not only the most readily available means for a present-day reader to gain access to a text of a particular poem, but the only means of gaining an albeit reprographically mediated sense of the embodied form in which the early editions of volumes of poetry were read. However, while a facsimile reprint version of a poem will be welcome as a reading text for some readers, for others it will have its drawbacks. Those who seek, or require, orientation will find that the introduction to a modern reprint will usually, for reasons of economy, contain little information about textual matters, while bibliographical and contextual detail as well as annotation is usually scant or non-existent. It should also be remembered that even the most ambitious series so far (Reiman's) has produced reprints of but a small proportion of the total amount of poetry published in the period covered by this volume. Notwithstanding such generic qualifications, three recent series (the first two of which are no longer in print) are worthy of note. The Scolar Press Facsimile

(1971–3) series contains facsimiles of: Burns's *Poems, Chiefly in the Scottish Dialect* (1786), including the poems added in the 1787 edition published in Edinburgh; Cowper's *Poems* (1782) and *The Task* (1785); Crabbe's *The Borough* (1810); Darwin's *The Botanic Garden* (1791) and *The Temple of Nature* (1803). The Romantic Context: Poetry series (1976–8), selected and arranged by Donald Reiman, contains 128 volumes of 'significant minor poetry' published between 1789 and 1830 including reprints of volumes by Bloomfield, Bowles, Canning and Gifford, Cary, Darley, Darwin, Dyer, Elliott, Frere, Hayley, Lloyd, Mant, Procter, Reynolds, Horace Smith, James Smith, Thelwall, and White (in some cases the reprint contains more than one volume of poems by the author or authors concerned). 'Revolution and Romanticism 1789–1834' is an ongoing series (1989–) of facsimile reprints chosen and introduced by Jonathan Wordsworth. Thus far reprints of volumes of poems by Bowles, Burns, Campbell, Canning and Frere, Hartley Coleridge, Crowe, Darwin, Frere, Gilbert, Hogg, Hunt, Landor, Mant, Moore, Rogers, Southey, and Thelwall have been published. In keeping with the dominant strain in contemporary Romantic textual scholarship, 'Revolution and Romanticism' provides 'early or unusual versions (normally the first) of some texts, reinforcing an underlying purpose of the series in reminding us how publication was seen at the time when reputations were made and the original critical judgements formed'. In its provision of good-quality reprints, handsomely produced, 'Revolution and Romanticism' undoubtedly makes an important contribution to current Romantic studies. In addition to these series, it is worth mentioning the facsimile reprint of the 1807 edition of Sir William Jones's *Works*, including his poetry, introduced by Garland Cannon (Jones 1993*a*).

Many of the advantages and disadvantages of facsimile versions of texts of poems apply to *The English Poetry Full-Text Database*, available on CD-ROM and magnetic tape, currently the readiest collection of the published works of poets of the period available. Apart from its applications for various kinds of research (see the introduction to Karlin), its primary use is to enable relatively speedy access to the texts of the published poems of all authors in the period under consideration here. While it would be improper to quibble with an achievement of this magnitude, it is worth emphasizing that the bibliographical basis of the database is *NCBEL*, currently in the process of being revised and updated. The bibliographical details of the source-text for any poem may be readily consulted both on screen and in printed form (see Karlin). But because most of the texts on *The English Poetry Full-Text Database* are taken from nineteenth-century editions (now out of copyright), the discoveries and achievements of recent editors and textual scholars in respect of an author's canon, and the texts within that canon, cannot be represented. The *Database* provides the text alone (i.e. no annotation).

Anthologies are a helpful (though obviously limited) means of gaining a cursory familiarity with the work of some of the poets. In several cases, however,
they provide a ready means of drawing attention to the reshaping of the poetic
landscape that comes about when canonical poetry is not seen in splendid isolation but as part of the literary current of the era. The explicit rationale of
two recent anthologies (McGann 1993 and Wu) has been to offer reconstruct-
ive accounts of poetry of the Romantic period through variously representing
the traditionally unrepresented. The selection of poetry published between
1785 and 1799 in Lonsdale, however, is the most original and compelling
available for this part of the period known as 'Romantic'. Each of these three
distinctive anthologies is characterized by a common purpose: to redress the
approach of such modern anthologies as Bloom and Trilling, one of the most
exclusive yet influential statements of the Romantic poetic canon. Earlier
anthologies in fact have provided generous samplings of some of the work
of poets 'recovered' by McGann and Wu (see, particularly, Milford 1928 but
also Hayward and Wright). Reeves's selection, which includes poetry from
the 1820s and beyond by Beddoes, Hartley Coleridge, Darley, and Hood, is
sufficiently generous to be of use to the reader who seeks a preliminary
engagement with the work of these poets of the latter part of the period.
Similarly useful is Auden's interesting selection of poems by Beddoes, Campbell, Hartley Coleridge, Darley, Elliott, Hood, Hunt, Lamb, Landor, Moore,
and Southey. There are also a number of specialized anthologies of interest.
Particularly recommended is the selection by Kent and Ewen of parodies published between 1797 and 1831 which entertains hugely even as it demonstrates
the extraordinary level of stylistic intimacy amongst poets of the period. Mostly
well-known examples of parodic poems by, amongst others, Canning, Frere,
Hogg, Hone, Hood, Reynolds, and the Smith brothers are included along with
very informative headnotes and up-to-date bibliographical information. Barrell
and Bull provide a good selection of pastoral verse from the period (including poems or excerpts from poems by Bloomfield, Burns, Cowper, Crabbe,
Elliott, Hood, Landor, and Southey). Two noteworthy anthologies of Scottish
verse which contain poems by Burns, Hogg, and others, are MacQueen and
Scott, and Watson's *The Poetry of Scotland* (Roderick Watson 1995), which
includes generous selections and on-page glossaries. No anthology dedicated
to working-class poetry in the period yet exists but some work published before
1830 by 'self-taught' poets, such as Bamford and Rodger, is represented by
Maidment. Leonard's inspiring example of the possibilities of research at local
level yields work by poets—many without formal education—in Renfrewshire
from the French Revolution to the First World War. Bennett's selection of 350
poems on the theme of war published between 1793 and 1815, taken mainly
from journals and magazines, is a useful research tool though it is only lightly
annotated.

The best guide to the contemporary reception of the poetry of Burns is Low's *Critical Heritage* volume (Low 1974a), which contains the most important contemporary reviews of the volumes of Burns's poetry published in his lifetime and details the reception of his work among contemporary writers including Coleridge, Cowper, Charles Lamb, Scott, and Dorothy and William Wordsworth. The assessment of the contexts and scope of the early criticism of Burns offered in the introduction to Low (1974a) is invaluable. Henry Mackenzie's reference, in his review of *Poems, Chiefly in the Scottish Dialect* (1786), to 'this Heaven-taught ploughman' (Low 1974a) captures the willingness of critics to juxtapose as apparent paradox the genius of the poet with his non-metropolitan, 'peasant' roots. This vein of fascination with a critically imposed contrast between Burns's brilliance as a poet and the obscurity of his social origins (a contrast captured in the image offered by Cowper of a bright candle shut up in a dark lantern, quoted below) is continued, most famously, in the seventh stanza of Wordsworth's 'Resolution and Independence', published in *Poems in Two Volumes* (1807):

> I thought of Chatterton, the marvellous Boy,
> The sleepless Soul that perished in its pride;
> Of Him who walked in glory and in joy
> Behind his plough, upon the mountain-side:
> By our own spirits are we deified;
> We Poets in our youth begin in gladness;
> But thereof comes in the end despondency and madness.

While his poetic abilities were widely recognized, the less than respectful views of morality and religion espoused in many of Burns's poems attracted censure even from those such as Jeffrey who readily appreciated his prodigious talents. In seeking to establish a more reasoned basis for the critical assessment of Burns's poetry than mere wonder at the phenomenon of the 'ploughman poet', Jeffrey's lengthy review of R. H. Cromek's *Reliques of Robert Burns* (1808) attacks the poet, using biographical sources on account of 'faults for which the defects of his education afford an obvious cause' (Low 1974a). In Jeffrey's view these deficiencies include 'the undisciplined harshness and acrimony of his invective' and 'his contempt, or affectation of contempt, for prudence, decency and regularity'. In short, Jeffrey takes exception to the respects in which Burns's poetry may be seen as 'uncivilized', where for many readers the satirical methods employed by the poet to expose or ridicule what passes for 'civilization' are both profound and liberating. Finally, it is worth quoting Cowper on the demands of reading Burns for the first time:

MICHAEL ROSSINGTON

Poor Burns loses much of his deserved praise in this country through our ignorance of his language. I despair of meeting with any Englishman who will take the pains that I have taken to understand him. His candle is bright, but shut up in a dark lantern. I lent him to a very sensible neighbour of mine; but his uncouth dialect spoiled all; and before he had half read him through he was quite *ram-feezled* [exhausted]. (Letter to Samuel Rose, 27 Aug. 1787, cited in Low 1974*a*)

These sentences say less, perhaps, about Anglo-Scottish literary relations than about prejudice towards poetry written in 'non-standard' language. In this context, Angus Calder's comments on the enduring reputation of Burns are apposite: 'His dialect had no terrors for working people in England. It is twentieth-century ideology that has marginalized Burns as a "regional" exception in "English" literature and has made him seem, to nationalistic Scots like MacDiarmid, charming but brainless, like a nice old dog' (Burns 1991).

Russell's point that *The Task* 'was the most popular poem of its day with the reading public' may be seen in conjunction with Byron's remark that Cowper 'lived at a fortunate time for his works' (letter to John Murray, 7 Feb. 1821, Byron 1991: 147). Byron's view is that the popularity of Cowper's poetry after the publication of *Poems* (1782) and *The Task* (1785), and posthumously (at least in the early decades of the nineteenth century), can be ascribed to the appeal of its religious content at a period of evangelical revival. In the absence of a *Critical Heritage* volume, bibliographical information about, and summaries of, the contemporary critical reception of Cowper's poetry have to be gleaned from several sources. Hartley and Russell contain relevant information but the first chapter of Newey (1982) provides the best economical survey of his poetic reputation, starting with his contemporaries. Austen, Blake, Bowles, Burns, Coleridge, Lamb, Scott, and Southey were amongst his admirers, but he fared less well with Byron, Hazlitt, and Hunt. Modern readers may find Coleridge's praise, Hazlitt's criticism, and Jeffrey's even-handed account all useful in taking initial critical bearings. Jeffrey's attempt to 'proclaim the balance' of his 'defects and excellencies' includes praise for a poet 'who reclaimed the natural liberty of invention' (Jeffrey 1983) but reproach for stylistic defects. As Morgan notes (Jeffrey 1983), a running-title in the later printing of the review in Jeffrey (1844) refers to Cowper as 'the modern liberator of our poetry'. Like Jeffrey, Coleridge responds favourably to what might be called Cowper's modernity, his incipient 'Romantic' tendencies, when he comments in *Biographia Literaria* that 'Bowles and Cowper were, to the best of my knowledge, the first who combined natural thoughts with natural diction; the first who reconciled the heart with the head' (Coleridge 1983). The sense that Cowper showed how a poetic domain regarded as hitherto constricted could be opened up to introspection, accessibly expressed, appears to underlie Coleridge's marvellously compact appreciation, 'the divine Chit chat of Cowper' (letter to John Thelwall, 17 Dec. 1796, repr. in Coleridge 1987), a phrase which seems to have been earlier communicated to Lamb (letter to Coleridge, 5 Dec. 1796, repr. in Lamb 1912). Cowper's detractors could be expected to be hostile to the reflective, homiletic cast of his poetry, particularly *The Task*. Byron's reference to 'that maniacal Calvinist & coddled poet' (letter to John Murray, 20 May 1820, Byron 1973–82: vii. 101), along with his splenetic aside (which he contradicts elsewhere) 'Cowper was no Poet' (letter to Annabella Milbanke, 29 Nov. 1813, Byron 1973–82: iii. 179), perhaps say as much about his sensitivity to religious sentiment in poetry as they do about Cowper's work. Hazlitt's dissatisfaction with what he sees as 'the finicalness of the private gentleman' derives from a view of Cowper's poetry as solipsistic in its self-protective fastidiousness, while his complaint that 'he seldom launches out into general descriptions of nature: he looks at her over his clipped hedges, and from his well-swept garden-walks', protests at what he sees as mere affectation to 'simplicity and plainness' (Hazlitt).

Pollard's point that 'the Romantic reaction to Crabbe might well be summed up as Hazlitt v. Jeffrey' suggests that contemporary criticism of the poetry of Crabbe offers not just insights into his *œuvre* but a convenient means of gauging the conflict between traditional and modern critical schools in the early decades of the nineteenth century. The notable defenders of Crabbe's poetry, Byron, Scott, Austen, and Jeffrey, all praised the commitment to tradition, both poetical and moral, in his work. Byron commended him as 'Nature's sternest Painter, yet the best' (*English Bards and Scotch Reviewers*, 858) and, though mistaken in his prediction, distinguished Crabbe favourably from himself and his contemporaries: 'With regard to poetry in general I am convinced the more I think of it—that he and *all* of us—Scott—Southey—Wordsworth—Moore —Campbell—I—are all in the wrong—one as much as another—that we are upon a wrong revolutionary poetical system—or systems—not worth a damn in itself—& from which none but Rogers and Crabbe are free—and that the present & next generations will finally be of this opinion . . . Crabbe's the man—but he has got a coarse and impracticable subject' (letter to Murray, 15 Sept. 1817, Byron 1973–82: v. 265–6). But it was Jeffrey, in particular in his review of *Poems* (1807), who initiated the still prevalent view that Crabbe offers his readers, both contemporary and modern, a means of challenging 'Romantic', in particular Wordsworthian, aesthetic values from within. At the end of this, the first of his reviews of Crabbe's four volumes published between 1807 and 1819, Jeffrey expressed relief that a recognizably traditional theory and practice of poetry, recently challenged by Wordsworth and the Lake School, was still alive in the work of Crabbe: 'we trust . . . that he will soon appear again among the worthy supporters of the old poetical establishment, and come in time to surpass the revolutionists in fast firing as well as in weight of metal' (Jeffrey 1808). He would later, in reviewing *Tales* (1812), acknowledge Crabbe as, 'upon the whole, the most original writer who has ever come before us' (Pollard). Jeffrey was, however, by no means uncritical of Crabbe, expressing particular offence at being presented 'with spectacles which it is purely painful and degrading to contemplate' (Pollard) in what are now regarded as some of the best poems in *The Borough*, the sequence entitled 'The Poor of the Borough' including 'The Parish-Clerk', 'Ellen Orford', 'Abel Keene', and 'Peter Grimes'. It was also Jeffrey who, in commenting that 'There is, of course, no unity or method in [*The Borough*],—which consists altogether of a succession of unconnected descriptions' (Pollard), arguably elicited Crabbe's most important public defence of the deliberately disconnected structure of his longer poems, the preface to *Tales* (1812) which is reprinted in Edwards (1991) and Pollard. But Jeffrey's most signal legacy to subsequent criticism is to promote and defend the now commonplace view of Crabbe as a 'realist', though this label is questioned in Edwards (1987, 1990) (discussed below). Jeffrey contrasts 'the manly sense and correct picturing of Mr. Crabbe' with 'the elaborate raptures and obscure originalities of these new artists', Wordsworth in particular; 'Mr Crabbe exhibits the common people of England pretty much as they are' whereas 'Mr Wordsworth and his associates show us something that mere observation never yet suggested to anyone' (Pollard). The features of Crabbe's work which Jeffrey values as sound in their fidelity to a putatively 'real' world are precisely those which, for Wordsworth and Hazlitt, impoverish his work, even threatening to disqualify him from the title 'poet'. The former complained that 'nineteen out of 20 of Crabbe's Pictures are mere matters of fact; with which the Muses have just about as much to do as they have with a Collection of medical reports, or of Law cases' (to Samuel Rogers, 29 Sept. 1808, in Wordsworth 1969: 268) and the latter that 'Literal fidelity serves him in the place of invention' (Pollard). Notwithstanding his acknowledgement that 'Mr. Crabbe is a *fascinating* writer', Hazlitt argues that his lack of transcendent or imaginative sympathies yields only narrow literal-mindedness: 'His Muse is not one of the daughters of Memory, but the old toothless, mumbling, dame herself' (Pollard), hence the charge of him being 'of all poets the least poetical':

He sets out with professing to overturn the theory which had hallowed a shepherd's life, and made the names of grove and valley music to our ears, in order to give us truth in its stead; but why not lay aside the fool's cap and bells at once, why not insist on the unwelcome reality in plain prose? If our author is a poet, why trouble himself with statistics? If he is a statistic writer, why set his ill news to harsh and grating verse? The philosopher in painting the dark side of human nature may have reason on his side, and a moral lesson or a remedy in view. The tragic poet, who shows the sad vicissitudes of things and the disappointments of the passions, at least strengthens our yearnings after imaginary good, and lends wings to our desires, by which we, 'at one bound, high overleap all bound' of actual suffering. But Mr. Crabbe does neither. He gives us discoloured paintings of things—helpless, repining, unprofitable, unedifying distress. (Pollard)

In fact, these comments appear to derive, in part, from a rather superficial reading of *The Village* (1783) and ignore the supernatural, even 'Gothic', elements of poems such as 'Sir Eustace Grey' and 'Peter Grimes'. The views of Hazlitt and Jeffrey, antithetical in their evaluation though actually similar in what they see as distinctive about the poetry, remain the best starting point for critical reflections on Crabbe. Pollard's *Critical Heritage* volume offers the best available selection of contemporary critical reviews and comments on Crabbe's published volumes, but many of the reviews including those by Jeffrey are, frustratingly, abridged. The chapter on Crabbe in Hodgart and Redpath contains a judicious selection of the critical perspectives of his contemporaries.

Probably the most notorious contemporary assessment of the poetry of Southey is Jeffrey's criticism of *Thalaba* in a review primarily devoted to a denunciation of the poetical principles of Wordsworth and the 'Lake School', a guilt by association which was to haunt Southey subsequently and which he regarded as both inaccurate and unjust. Jeffrey takes issue with what he sees as the lamentable versification of *Thalaba*, 'a jumble of all the measures that are known in English poetry, (and a few more), without rhyme, and without any sort of regularity in their arrangement'; with the poem's subject, 'almost as ill chosen as the diction; and the conduct of the fable as disorderly as the versification'; and, finally, with its unwieldy method of *bricolage*, 'the book is entirely composed of scraps, borrowed from the oriental tale books, and travels into the Mahometan countries seasoned up for the English reader with some fragments of our own ballads, and shreds of our older sermons' (Madden). Coleridge's defence of Southey in *Biographia* includes eulogies for 'the pastoral charms and wild streaming lights of the "*Thalaba*," ' and for *The Curse of Kehama*, 'a gallery of finished pictures in one splendid fancy piece' (Coleridge 1983), two poems which, as Shelley's letters and early poetry testify, had a particular impact on a younger, ideologically antipathetical poet. Hazlitt's judgement of the unevenness of Southey's verse in *Spirit of the Age* however singles out for praise the republican poems of the 1790s including *Joan of Arc* and *Wat Tyler*, but also acknowledges of the later epic narratives, 'the spirit, the scope, the splendid imagery, the hurried and startling interest that pervades them' (Hazlitt). Madden's *Critical Heritage* volume is the best resource for a preliminary overview of the reception of Southey's poetic volumes both by reviewers and by contemporary writers (it includes some of the best-known satires and parodies by Canning, Frere, James Smith, and Byron), though there are important omissions (for example, it does not contain all Jeffrey's reviews of Southey's verse). For other poets of the period, Hazlitt and Jeffrey are especially useful both in their acuteness as readers of poetry and in the strong judgements they offer. Hazlitt's *Spirit of the Age* contains sketches of Campbell, Gifford, Moore, and Hunt, and his *Lectures on the English Poets* refer to Bloomfield, Campbell, Moore, and Rogers. Jeffrey (1844) contains a selection of criticism originally published in the *Edinburgh Review* including slightly revised texts of reviews of volumes by Campbell, Moore, and Rogers. Hayden provides useful summary accounts of the reception of the work of Hunt and Moore (as well as Southey and Crabbe) in contemporary reviews.

Burns has attracted a vast and varied range of critical approaches. Crawford offers a thorough and detailed assessment of the poems and songs. Two individually published essays, Kinsley (1974) on Burns and the peasantry, and Roe (1996) on Burns's posthumous reputation, literary and cultural, offer brief accounts of enduringly interesting features of his work. The following three collections of essays, published over the past twenty-five years, offer wide-ranging scholarly and critical evaluations: Low (1974*b*), Jack and Noble, and Simpson. Bold and Lindsay supply entertaining companions for those who seek to savour all aspects of Burns and his work. The major modern critical reassessment of Cowper is by Newey (1982). In offering trenchant close readings of all the major poems with relevant reference to Cowper's religious views and his engagement with eighteenth-century poetry and criticism, Newey goes boldly beyond earlier, somewhat incapacitating twentieth-century readings of Cowper's poetry as 'transitional'. Though less rigorous than Newey in its readings, Hutchings (1983) provides an approachable critical introduction, while Priestman confronts in useful detail a topic too often evaded in relation to *The Task*, 'the baffling nature of the poem's structure'. Briefer accounts which provide valuable insights deriving from close readings include Davie's comments on Cowper's poetic methods, Spacks's chapter on 'heightened perception' in his poetry, and the discriminating assessment of his politics in Newey (1991). With regard to Cowper's relationship to the Romantics, the influence of his 'poetry of introspection' on *Lyrical Ballads* (1798), especially *Tintern Abbey*, and Coleridge's 'Conversation Poems', is examined in Jacobus; Priestman's final chapter offers a detailed, structural comparison of *The Task* and *The Prelude*; and Barrell contrasts rewardingly his poetic observations of landscape with those of Clare. Edwards (1990) offers the most refreshing of the several book-length studies of Crabbe published in recent decades, while Bareham, Chamberlain, Haddakin, and New offer interesting critical accounts. Through close readings of a range of Crabbe's poems, especially the 'Tales', Edwards's book (which contains his 1987 essay) seeks to rescue Crabbe's poetry both from the sterile and, as it turns out in his view, suspect critical label 'realist', and to redeem Crabbe's awkward status in literary history from Hazlitt to Leavis and beyond by seeing him not as 'a belated pre-Romantic but [as] an anti-Romantic'. Edwards's method is historicizing but his readings are scrupulously attentive and open-minded. The phrase 'on border land' in his book's title (from 'Delay has Danger' (1819)) emphasizes Crabbe's preoccupation with the marginal, in terms of both the social status of the central characters of his narrative poems and the liminal physical worlds they inhabit. Both Hatch and McGann are also preoccupied with the unsynthesized, un-Romantic, quality of Crabbe's poetry. In his book, Hatch examines Crabbe's 'manner of handling conflicting social, moral, and religious questions in terms of a drama where the ideas can rarely be subsumed into an integrated theory, but are introduced as independent entities, each with its own degree of truth'. Such a view is developed in McGann (1985) ('the truths to which [Crabbe] is devoted institute a critique of the Truth which Romanticism sought to sustain') and, in relation to Crabbe's avoidance of poetic forms conventionally associated with the longer poem, in McGann (1989); 'The apparently rambling, even random structure of *The Borough*, anticipated in the similarly organized "The Parish Register", is a mirror of Crabbe's vision of truth.' Swingle's rewarding examination of *Tales* as depicting 'a "state" of temporality, a labyrinth of temporal sequences, that captures Crabbe's complex vision of time's dominion over man', may be usefully seen in conjunction with McGann (1985) and Edwards's exploration of Crabbe's attentiveness to capitalization, in its assertion that 'Crabbe draws us into a lower-case view of the world, one which can only be captured in the artistic net of an indefinite series of individual, diverging tales, no one of which can be writ as large as The Tale'. Hillis Miller offers, *inter alia*, a rhetorical reading of 'The Parting Hour' by which the poem 'deconstructs two of those cherished certainties of humanist literary study, the continuity of the self and the organic continuity of narrative from beginning to middle to end'. Ricks's acute essay 'George Crabbe's Thoughts of Confinement' (Ricks 1996) explores the poetic possibilities of restriction in his work. Butler, in several essays (1987, 1988, 1989, 1990), seeks to recover the significance of the religious and oriental themes of Southey's epic poems (particularly *Thalaba*) in their time, especially for now more celebrated poets such as Shelley, and in so doing demonstrates—perhaps better than any other recent critic—the rewards of exploring neglected poems, and their contexts, in the period. Raimond (1968) (in French) and Bernhardt-Kabisch each contain chapters which deal in detail with all the major epic poems and the early lyrical verse of Southey. Curry (1975) is merely cursory on the poetry though useful as a biographical introduction and for its critical assessment of Southey's complete *œuvre*. Carnall has some interesting remarks particularly about the republican poetry of the 1790s in the course of his study of the development of Southey's political ideas.

There are book-length biographical and critical introductions to the work of Beddoes (Thompson 1985), Bloomfield (Lawson), Campbell (Mary Miller),

Darwin (Hassler, King-Hele 1968), Hogg (Nelson Smith), Hood (Lloyd Jeffrey), Hunt (Thompson 1977), Jones (Franklin 1995), Landor (Dilworth), and White (McGhee). In addition, there are discriminating critical essays on Beddoes by Heath-Stubbs (who treats him along with Darley and Hood in a chapter entitled 'The Defeat of Romanticism'), Frye, and Ricks (1984) (who examines 'the vitality of [Beddoes's] language in relation to the celebration of death'). King-Hele (1986) examines the impact of the poetry of Darwin on his contemporaries. Gilbert's extraordinary poem *The Hurricane* (1796), and the theosophy of its author, are usefully introduced by Kaufman. Manning's textual history of Hone's piracy of Byron's *Corsair* offers fascinating insights into Hone's methods and interests. Kucich offers a reassessment of the 'Spenserianism' of Hunt, of particular importance to students of Keats's early poems. The significance of Jones's work as a whole for eighteenth-century culture is related helpfully by Mukherjee while Hewitt and Moussa-Mahmoud offer critical accounts especially of his poetical interests, and assess the impact of his work on poetry of the Romantic period. Vitoux's essay on Landor's *Gebir* provides an economical account of the poem and its contexts useful for those bewildered on an initial encounter. Gittings and, more especially, Barnard offer important accounts of the significance of the poetry of Reynolds, particularly in relation to Keats's career. J. R. Watson (1978) addresses the difficulty of categorizing the poetry of Rogers in an introductory way. Though largely biographical, Curran (1977) supplies a helpful evaluation of the significance of Horace Smith in Regency literary circles.

THEMATIC APPROACHES

Curran (1986), primarily concerned with poetic form, offers one of the best critical introductions, both in its breadth and detail, to the variety of poetic experiment in the period. J. R. Watson (1989), on 'Pre-Romanticism', includes selections from some of the best-known literary criticism of Cowper and Crabbe. Though primarily concerned with Dante's presence in the poetry of the major Romantic poets, Pite's discussion (1994) both of Cary's translations of the *Divina Commedia*, and of such well-known poems of the period as Hunt's *Story of Rimini*, is invaluable. McGann's book (1996) on the poetry of sensibility in the latter decades of the eighteenth century promotes renewed awareness of the significance of the poetry of Jones and the Della Cruscans including Robert Merry. The impact of the French Revolution and its aftermath on Cowper, Crabbe, and Southey is assessed in fresh and useful ways in Hutchings (1989), Edwards (1993) and Raimond (1989), and useful accounts of politically aware poetry of the 1790s by Dyer, Lamb, and Southey are offered by Roe

(1992). Butler's introduction to Romantic Orientalism (Butler 1994) is a highly commendable starting point for those interested in the oriental poetry and interests of such figures as Jones, Landor, and Southey while Brown's survey article includes reference to lesser-known poems set in the Orient. In terms of their scholarly detail and thoroughness Majeed's chapters on Jones, Southey, and Moore are valuable, while Leask's chapters on Byron and Shelley are enriched through judicious reference to the poetry of their contemporaries also drawn to the East. Methodologically problematical in its assertion of the way the work of his chosen poets demonstrates a 'realistic' rather than, as Said would have it, a purely discursive 'Orientalism', Sharafuddin nevertheless offers the interesting argument that Landor's *Gebir*, Southey's *Thalaba*, and Moore's *Lalla Rookh* 'mark an advance in the understanding of and sympathy with the Orient'. Drew's predisposition to locate Platonizing tendencies in English Romantic writing about India has a somewhat obscuring effect on his chapter on Jones. Roderick Watson (1984: chs. 5, 6), provides a useful outline of the historical and cultural contexts of Scottish poetry in the period. Poetry by those variously categorized as working-class or without formal education is introduced by Sales, who comments cursorily on Bloomfield, Hone, and White. McCalman and Worrall are worthy successors to Thompson in offering the fruits of original research into, amongst other kinds of text, songs, pamphlet verse, and ballads produced within urban, politically radical popular culture in the period.

LIST OF POETS MENTIONED

William Cowper (1731–1800); Erasmus Darwin (1731–1802); William Crowe (1745–1829); Sir William Jones (1746–94); Richard Payne Knight (1750–1824); George Crabbe (1754–1832); George Dyer (1755–1841); Robert Merry (1755–98); William Gifford (1756–1826); Robert Burns (1759–96); William Gilbert (?1760–?1825); William Lisle Bowles (1762–1850); Samuel Rogers (1763–1855); John Thelwall (1764–1834); Robert Bloomfield (1766–1823); John Hookham Frere (1769–1846); George Canning (1770–1827); James Hogg (1770–1835); Robert Southey (1774–1843); Henry Francis Cary (1775–1844); Charles Lloyd (1775–1839); James Smith (1775–1839); Charles Lamb (1775–1834); Walter Savage Landor (1775–1864); Richard Mant (1776–1848); Thomas Campbell (1777–1844); Horatio [Horace] Smith (1779–1849); Thomas Moore (1779–1852); William Hone (1780–1842); Ebenezer Elliott (1781–1849); Alexander Rodger (1784–1846); Leigh Hunt (1784–1859); Henry Kirke White (1785–1836); Bryan Waller Procter ('Barry Cornwall') (1787–1874); Samuel Bamford (1788–1872); George Darley (1795–1846); John Hamilton Reynolds (1796–1852); Hartley Coleridge (1796–1849); Thomas Hood (1799–1845); Thomas Lovell Beddoes (1803–49).

REFERENCES

EDITIONS

Auden, W. H. (ed.), *Nineteenth-Century Minor Poets*, notes by George R. Greeger (London, 1967).

Barrell, John and Bull, John (eds.), *The Penguin Book of English Pastoral Verse* (Harmondsworth, 1982).

Beddoes, Thomas Lovell, *The Works of Thomas Lovell Beddoes*, ed. H. W. Donner (London, 1935).

—— *Plays and Poems of Thomas Lovell Beddoes*, ed. H. W. Donner (London, 1950).

—— *Selected Poems*, ed. Judith Higgens (Manchester, 1976).

Bennett, Betty T. (ed.), *British War Poetry in the Age of Romanticism: 1793–1815* (New York, 1976).

Bloom, Harold, and Trilling, Lionel (eds.), *Romantic Poetry and Prose* (New York, 1973).

Burns, Robert, *The Poems and Songs of Robert Burns*, ed. James Kinsley, 3 vols. (Oxford, 1968).

—— *Poems and Songs*, ed. James Kinsley (Oxford, 1969).

—— *The Letters of Robert Burns*, ed. J. De Lancey Ferguson, 2nd edn. by G. Ross Roy, 2 vols. (Oxford, 1985a).

—— *The Kilmarnock Poems (Poems, Chiefly in the Scottish Dialect, 1786)*, ed. Donald A. Low (London, 1985b).

—— *Selected Poetry*, ed. Angus Calder and William Donnelly, Penguin Poetry Library (Harmondsworth, 1991).

—— *Poems in Scots and English (The Kilmarnock Poems, 'Holy Willie's Prayer', Tam o'Shanter')*, ed. Donald A. Low (London, 1993a).

—— *The Songs of Robert Burns*, ed. Donald A. Low (London, 1993b).

—— *Robert Burns: Selected Poems*, ed. Carol McGuirk, Penguin English Poets. (Harmondsworth, 1993c).

Cary, H. F. (tr.), *The Divine Comedy*, ed. Ralph Pite (London, 1994).

Coleridge, Samuel Taylor, and Southey, Robert, *The Fall of Robespierre 1794* (Oxford, 1991).

Cowper, William, *Poetical Works*, ed. H. S. Milford, Oxford Standard Authors, 4th edn., with corrections and additions by Norma Russell (London, 1967).

—— *The Poems of William Cowper*, ed. John D. Baird and Charles Ryskamp, 3 vols., i: *1748–82*, ii: *1782–5*, iii: *1785–1800* (Oxford, 1980–95).

—— *William Cowper: The Task and Selected Other Poems*, ed. James Sambrook, Longman Annotated Texts (Harlow, 1994).

Crabbe, George, *The Complete Poetical Works*, ed. Norma Dalrymple-Champneys and Arthur Pollard (gen. ed. Norma Dalrymple-Champneys), 3 vols. (Oxford, 1988).

—— *Selected Poems*, ed. Gavin Edwards, Penguin English Poets (Harmondsworth, 1991).

—— *The Voluntary Insane*, ed. Felix Pryor (London, 1995).

Darley, George, *Selected Poems of George Darley*, ed. Anne Ridler (London, 1979).

Groves, David (ed.), *Selected Poems and Songs*, The Association for Scottish Literary Studies (Edinburgh, 1986).

The English Poetry Full-Text Database, Software Version 4.0 (Cambridge, 1995).

Hayward, John (ed.), *The Oxford Book of Nineteenth-Century English Verse* (Oxford, 1964).

Hogg, James, *Selected Poems*, ed. Douglas S. Mack (Oxford, 1970).

—— *James Hogg: Scottish Pastorals*, ed. Elaine Petrie (Stirling, 1988).

—— *Poetic Mirrors. Comprising The Poetic Mirror (1816) and New Poetic Mirror (1829–31)*, ed. David Groves (Frankfurt am Main, 1990).

—— *A Queer Book*, ed. P. D. Garside (Edinburgh, 1995).

Hood, Thomas, *Selected Poems of Thomas Hood*, ed. John Clubbe (Cambridge, Mass., 1970).

—— *Selected Poems*, ed. Joy Flint (Manchester, 1992).

Hunt, J. H. Leigh, *The Poetical Works of Leigh Hunt*, ed. H. S. Milford (London, 1923).

Jones, Sir William, *The Collected Works of Sir William Jones*, introd. Garland Cannon, 13 vols. (Richmond, 1993a) [a facsimile reprint, with additional material, of the 1807 edn.].

—— *A Reader*, ed. Satya S. Pachori (Delhi, 1993b).

—— *Selected Poetical and Prose Works*, ed. Michael J. Franklin (Cardiff, 1995).

Kent, David A., and Ewen, D. R. (eds.), *Romantic Parodies, 1797–1831* (Cranbury, NJ, 1992).

Lamb, Charles, *The Works of Charles and Mary Lamb*, ed. E. V. Lucas, 6 vols. (London, 1912).

Landor, Walter Savage, *The Poetical Works of Walter Savage Landor*, ed. Stephen Wheeler, 3 vols. (Oxford, 1937).

—— *Selected Poetry and Prose*, ed. Keith Hanley (Manchester, 1981).

—— *Gebir 1798* (Oxford, 1993).

Leonard, Tom (ed.), *Radical Renfrew: Poetry from the French Revolution to the First World War by Poets Born, or Sometime Resident in, the County of Renfrewshire* (Edinburgh, 1990).

Lonsdale, Roger (ed.), *The New Oxford Book of Eighteenth-Century Verse* (Oxford, 1984).

McGann, Jerome J. (ed.), *The New Oxford Book of Romantic Period Verse* (Oxford, 1993).

MacQueen, John, and Scott, Tom (eds.), *The Oxford Book of Scottish Verse* (London, 1966).

Maidment, Brian (ed.), *The Poorhouse Fugitives: Self-Taught Poets and Poetry in Victorian Britain* (Manchester, 1987).

Milford, H. S. (ed.), *The Oxford Book of Regency Verse 1798–1837* (London, 1928).

Reeves, James (ed.), *Five Late Romantic Poets: George Darley, Hartley Coleridge, Thomas Hood, Thomas Lovell Beddoes, Emily Brontë* (London, 1974).

Reiman, D. H. (ed.), *The Romantic Context: Poetry*, 128 vols. (New York, 1976–8).

Rickword, Edgell (ed.), *Radical Squibs and Loyal Ripostes: Satirical Pamphlets of the Regency Period, 1819–1821*, illustrated by George Cruikshank and others (Bath, 1971).

Southey, Robert, *Joan of Arc: An Epic Poem* (Bristol, 1796).

—— *Joan of Arc*, 2 vols. (2nd edn., Bristol, 1798).

—— *Thalaba the Destroyer: A Metrical Romance*, 2 vols. (London, 1801).

—— *Madoc* (London, 1805).

—— *The Curse of Kehama* (London, 1810).

—— *Roderick, the Last of the Goths* (London, 1814).

—— *The Poetical Works of Southey, Collected by Himself*, 10 vols. (London, 1837–8).

Southey, Robert, *Poems of Robert Southey Containing Thalaba, The Curse of Kehama, Roderick, Madoc, A Tale of Paraguay, and Selected Minor Poems*, ed. M. H. Fitzgerald (London, 1909).

—— *A Choice of Robert Southey's Verse*, ed. Geoffrey Grigson (London, 1970).

—— *The Contributions of Robert Southey to the* Morning Post, ed. Kenneth Curry (Huntsville, Ala. 1984).

—— *Poems 1797* (Oxford, 1989a).

—— *Wat Tyler: A Dramatic Poem 1817* (Oxford, 1989b).

—— *Thalaba the Destroyer 1801* (Oxford, 1991).

—— and Coleridge, Samuel Taylor, *Joan of Arc 1796* (Oxford, 1993).

Watson, Roderick (ed.), *The Poetry of Scotland: Gaelic, Scots and English 1380–1980* (Edinburgh, 1995).

White, Henry Kirke, *Poems, Hymns and Prose Writings by Henry Kirke White*, ed. R. T. Beckwith (Oxford, 1985).

Wordsworth, Jonathan (ed.), *Revolution and Romanticism, 1789–1834*, 132 vols. to date (Oxford, 1989–).

Wright, David (ed.), *English Romantic Verse* (Harmondsworth, 1968).

Wu, Duncan (ed.), *Romanticism: An Anthology* (Oxford, 1994).

CRITICISM

Bareham, Terence, *George Crabbe* (London, 1977).

—— and Gatrell, S., *A Bibliography of George Crabbe* (Folkestone, 1978).

Barnard, John, 'Keats's "Robin Hood", John Hamilton Reynolds, and the "Old Poets"', *Proceedings of the British Academy*, 75 (1989), 181–200.

Barrell, John, *The Idea of Landscape and the Sense of Place: An Approach to the Poetry of John Clare* (Cambridge, 1972).

Bernhardt-Kabisch, Ernest, *Robert Southey*, Twayne's English Authors Series (Boston, 1977).

Bold, Alan, *A Burns Companion* (Basingstoke, 1991).

Brown, W. C., 'English Travel Books and Minor Poetry about the Near East, 1775–1825', *Philological Quarterly*, 16 (1937), 249–71.

Butler, Marilyn, 'Revising the Canon', *Times Literary Supplement* (4–10 Dec. 1987), 1349 and 1359–60.

—— *Literature as a Heritage; or, Reading Other Ways* (Cambridge, 1988).

—— 'Repossessing the Past: The Case for an Open Literary History', in Marjorie Levinson (ed.), *Rethinking Historicism: Critical Readings in Romantic History* (Oxford, 1989), 64–84.

—— 'Plotting the Revolution: The Political Narratives of Romantic Poetry and Criticism', in Kenneth R. Johnston et al. (eds.), *Romantic Revolutions: Criticism and Theory* (Bloomington, Ind., 1990), 133–57.

—— 'Orientalism', in David B. Pirie (ed.), *The Penguin History of Literature, v: The Romantic Period* (Harmondsworth, 1994), 395–447.

Byron, Lord, *Byron's Letters and Journals*, ed. Leslie A. Marchand, 12 vols. (London, 1973–82).

—— *The Complete Miscellaneous Prose*, ed. Andrew Nicholson (Oxford, 1991).

Cannon, Garland, *Sir William Jones: A Bibliography of Primary and Secondary Sources* (Amsterdam, 1979).

Carnall, Geoffrey, *Robert Southey and his Age: The Development of a Conservative Mind* (Oxford, 1960).

Chamberlain, Robert L., *George Crabbe*, Twayne's English Authors Series (New York, 1965).

Coleridge, Samuel Taylor, *Biographia Literaria or Biographical Sketches of my Literary Life and Opinions*, ed. James Engell and W. Jackson Bate, *The Collected Works of Samuel Taylor Coleridge*, vol. vii (Princeton, 1983).

—— *Selected Letters*, ed. H. J. Jackson (Oxford, 1987).

Crawford, Thomas, *Burns: A Study of the Poems and Songs* (Edinburgh, 1960).

Curran, Stuart, 'The View from Versailles: Horace Smith on the Literary Scene of 1822', *Huntington Library Quarterly*, 40 (1977), 357–71.

—— *Poetic Form and British Romanticism* (New York, 1986).

Curry, Kenneth, *Southey*, Routledge Author Guides (London, 1975).

—— *Robert Southey: A Reference Guide* (Boston, 1977).

Davie, Donald, *Purity of Diction in English Verse* (2nd edn., London, 1967).

Dilworth, Ernest, *Walter Savage Landor*, Twayne's English Authors Series (New York, 1971).

Drew, John, *India and the Romantic Imagination* (Delhi, 1987).

Edwards, Gavin, 'Crabbe's So-Called Realism', *Essays in Criticism*, 37 (1987), 303–20.

—— 'The Essential Crabbe', *Essays in Criticism*, 39 (1989), 84–91.

—— *George Crabbe's Poetry on Border Land* (Lampeter, 1990).

—— 'Crabbe's Regicide Households', in Alison Yarrington and Kelvin Everest (eds.), *Reflections on Revolution: Images of Romanticism* (London, 1993), 83–95.

Egerer, J. W., *A Bibliography of Robert Burns* (Edinburgh, 1964).

Franklin, Michael J., *Sir William Jones*, Writers of Wales (Cardiff, 1995).

Frye, Northrop, 'Yorick: The Romantic Macabre', in *A Study of English Romanticism* (1968; repr. Brighton, 1983), 51–85.

Gittings, Robert, 'The Poetry of John Hamilton Reynolds', *Ariel*, 1 (1970), 7–17.

Haddakin, Lilian, *The Poetry of Crabbe* (London, 1955).

Hartley, Lodwick, *William Cowper: The Continuing Revaluation. An Essay and a Bibliography of Cowperian Studies from 1895 to 1960* (Chapel Hill, NC, 1961).

Hassler, Donald M., *Erasmus Darwin*, Twayne's English Authors Series (New York, 1973).

Hatch, Ronald B., *Crabbe's Arabesque: Social Drama in the Poetry of George Crabbe* (Montreal, 1976).

Hayden, John O., *The Romantic Reviewers 1802–1824* (London, 1969).

Hazlitt, William, *Lectures on the English Poets* and *The Spirit of the Age; or Contemporary Portraits*, ed. C. M. Maclean (London, 1910).

Heath-Stubbs, John, 'The Defeat of Romanticism', in *The Darkling Plain: A Study of the Later Fortunes of Romanticism in English Poetry from George Darley to W. B. Yeats* (London, 1950).

Hewitt, R. M., 'Harmonious Jones', *Essays and Studies*, 28 (1942), 42–59.

Hodgart, Patricia, and Redpath, Theodore (eds.), *Romantic Perspectives: The Work of Crabbe, Blake, Wordsworth, and Coleridge as Seen by their Contemporaries and by Themselves* (London, 1964).

Houtchens, C. W., and Houtchens, L. H. (eds.), *The English Romantic Poets & Essayists: A Review of Research and Criticism* (rev. edn., New York, 1966).

Hutchings, W. B., *The Poetry of William Cowper* (London, 1983).

—— 'William Cowper and 1789', *Year's Work in English Studies*, 19 (1989), 71–93.

Jack, Ian, *English Literature 1815–1832*, vol. x of *The Oxford History of English Literature* (Oxford, 1963).

Jack, R. D. S., and Noble, Andrew (eds.), *The Art of Robert Burns* (London, 1982).

Jacobus, Mary, *Tradition and Experiment in Wordsworth's Lyrical Ballads, 1798* (Oxford, 1976).

Jeffrey, Francis, review of Crabbe's *Poems* (1807) in *Edinburgh Review*, 12 (Apr. 1808), 131–51.

—— *Contributions to the Edinburgh Review*, 4 vols. (London, 1844).

——*Jeffrey's Criticism: A Selection*, ed. Peter F. Morgan (Edinburgh, 1983).

Jeffrey, Lloyd N., *Thomas Hood*, Twayne's English Authors Series (New York, 1972).

Jordan, Frank, (ed.), *The English Romantic Poets: A Review of Research and Criticism* (4th edn., New York, 1985).

Karlin, Daniel (introd.), *English Poetry: A Bibliography of the English Poetry Full-Text Database* (Cambridge, 1995).

Kaufman, Paul, ' "The Hurricane" and the Romantic Poets', *English Miscellany*, 21 (1970), 99–115.

King-Hele, Desmond, *The Essential Writings of Erasmus Darwin* (London, 1968).

—— *Erasmus Darwin and the Romantic Poets* (Basingstoke, 1986).

Kinsley, James, 'Burns and the Peasantry, 1785', *Proceedings of the British Academy*, 60 (1974), 135–53.

Kucich, Greg, 'Leigh Hunt and Romantic Spenserianism', *Keats–Shelley Journal*, 37 (1988), 110–35.

Landré, Louis, *Leigh Hunt (1784–1859): Contribution à l'histoire du Romantisme anglais*, 2 vols. (Paris, 1936).

Lawson, Jonathan, *Robert Bloomfield*, Twayne's English Authors Series (Boston, 1980).

Leask, Nigel, *British Romantic Writers and the East: Anxieties of Empire* (Cambridge, 1992).

Lindsay, Maurice, *The Burns Encyclopaedia* (London, 1980).

Low, Donald A. (ed.), *Robert Burns: The Critical Heritage* (London, 1974a).

—— *Critical Essays on Robert Burns* (London, 1974b).

Lulofs, Timothy, J., and Ostrom, Hans, *Leigh Hunt: A Reference Guide* (Boston, 1985).

McCalman, Iain, *Radical Underworld: Prophets, Revolutionaries and Pornographers in London, 1795–1840* (Cambridge, 1988).

McGann, Jerome J., 'The Anachronism of George Crabbe', *English Literary History*, 48 (1981), 555–72; repr. in revised form in *The Beauty of Inflections: Literary Investigations in Historical Method and Theory* (Oxford, 1985), 294–312.

—— 'George Crabbe: Poetry and Truth', *London Review of Books*, 11/6 (16 Mar. 1989), 16–17.

—— *The Textual Condition* (Princeton, 1991).

—— *The Poetics of Sensibility: A Revolution in Literary Style* (Oxford, 1996).

McGhee, Richard D., *Henry Kirke White*, Twayne's English Authors Series (Boston, 1981).

Madden, Lionel (ed.), *Robert Southey: The Critical Heritage* (London, 1972).

Majeed, Javed, *Ungoverned Imaginings: James Mill's* The History of British India *and Orientalism* (Oxford, 1992).

Manning, Peter J., 'The Hone-ing of Byron's Corsair', in Jerome J. McGann (ed.), *Textual Criticism and Literary Interpretation* (Chicago, 1985), 107–26; repr. in *Reading Romantics: Texts and Contexts* (New York, 1990), 216–37.

Mell, Donald C., Jr. (ed.), *English Poetry 1660–1800: A Guide to Information Sources*, American Literature, English Literature, and World Literatures in English Information Guide 40 (Detroit, 1982).

Miller, J. Hillis, 'The Ethics of Reading: Vast Gaps and Parting Hours', in Ira Konigsberg (ed.), *American Criticism in the Poststructuralist Age* (Ann Arbor, 1981), 19–41.

Miller, Mary Ruth, *Thomas Campbell*, Twayne's English Authors Series (Boston, 1978).

Moussa-Mahmoud, Fatma, *Sir William Jones and the Romantics* (Cairo, 1962).

Mukherjee, S. N., *Sir William Jones: A Study in Eighteenth-Century British Attitudes to India* (2nd edn., London, 1987).

New, Peter, *George Crabbe's Poetry* (London, 1976).

The New Cambridge Bibliography of English Literature (Cambridge, 1969).

Newey, Vincent, *Cowper's Poetry: A Critical Study and Reassessment* (Liverpool, 1982).

—— 'William Cowper and the Condition of England', in Vincent Newey and Ann Thompson (eds.), *Literature and Nationalism* (Liverpool, 1991), 120–39.

Peterson, Ann, 'A Secondary Bibliography of George Crabbe: 1975–1989', *Bulletin of Bibliography*, 51 (1994), 269–72.

Pite, Ralph, *The Circle of our Vision: Dante's Presence in English Romantic Poetry* (Oxford, 1994).

Pollard, Arthur (ed.), *Crabbe: The Critical Heritage* (London, 1972).

Priestman, Martin, *Cowper's Task: Structure and Influence* (Cambridge, 1983).

Raimond, Jean, *Robert Southey: L'Homme et son temps. L'œuvre—le rôle* (Paris, 1968).

—— 'Southey's Early Writings and the Revolution', *Year's Work in English Studies*, 19 (1989), 181–96.

—— and Watson, J. R. (eds.), *A Handbook to English Romanticism* (New York, 1992).

Reiman, D. H. (ed.), *English Romantic Poetry 1800–1835: A Guide to Information Resources*, American Literature, English Literature, and World Literatures in English Information Guide 27 (Detroit, 1979).

Renwick, W. L., *English Literature 1789–1815*, vol. ix of *The Oxford History of English Literature* (Oxford, 1963).

Ricks, Christopher, 'Thomas Lovell Beddoes: "A Dying Start"', in *The Force of Poetry* (Oxford, 1984), 135–62.

—— 'George Crabbe's Thoughts of Confinement', in *Essays in Appreciation* (Oxford, 1996), 67–89.

Roe, Nicholas, *The Politics of Nature: Wordsworth and Some Contemporaries* (Basingstoke, 1992).

—— 'Authenticating Robert Burns', *Essays in Criticism*, 46 (1996), 195–218.

MICHAEL ROSSINGTON

The Romantic Movement: A Selective and Critical Bibliography, in *English Literary History* (1937–49); *Philological Quarterly* (1950–64); *English Language Notes* (1965–78); published as *The Romantic Movement*, ed. David V. Erdman (New York, 1980–   ).

Roy, G. Ross, Review of Kinsley (1968), *Modern Philology*, 70 (1972–3), 73–6.

Russell, Norma, *A Bibliography of William Cowper to 1837* (Oxford, 1963).

Sales, Roger, 'Poor Relations: Writing in the Working Class 1770–1835', in David B. Pirie (ed.), *The Penguin History of Literature, v: The Romantic Period* (Harmondsworth, 1994), 257–88.

Sharafuddin, Mohammed, *Islam and Romantic Orientalism: Literary Encounters with the Orient* (London, 1994).

Simpson, Kenneth (ed.), *Burns Now* (Edinburgh, 1994).

Smith, Margaret M. (ed.), with contributions by Penny Boumelha, *Index of English Literary Manuscripts, iii: 1700–1800, Part I: Addison to Fielding* (London, 1986).

Smith, Nelson C., *James Hogg*, Twayne's English Authors Series (Boston, 1980).

Spacks, Patricia Meyer, *The Poetry of Vision: Five Eighteenth-Century Poets* (Cambridge, Mass., 1967).

Sutton, David C. (ed.), *Location Register of English Literary Manuscripts and Letters: Eighteenth and Nineteenth Centuries*, 2 vols. (London, 1995).

Swingle, L. J., 'Later Crabbe in Relation to the Augustans and Romantics: The Temporal Labyrinth of his *Tales in Verse, 1812*', *English Literary History*, 42 (1975), 580–94.

Thompson, E. P., *The Making of the English Working Class* (London, 1963).

Thompson, James R., *Leigh Hunt*, Twayne's English Authors Series (Boston, 1977).

—— *Thomas Lovell Beddoes*, Twayne's English Authors Series (Boston, 1985).

Vitoux, Pierre, '*Gebir* as an Heroic Poem', *Wordsworth Circle*, 7 (1976), 51–7.

Waltman, John L., and McDaniel, Gerald G., *Leigh Hunt: A Comprehensive Bibliography* (New York, 1985).

Watson, J. R., 'Samuel Rogers: The Last Augustan', in J. C. Hilson et al. (eds.), *Augustan Worlds* (Leicester, 1978), 281–97.

—— (ed.), *Pre-Romanticism in English Poetry of the Eighteenth Century: The Poetic Art and Significance of Thomson, Gray, Collins, Goldsmith, Cowper & Crabbe* (Basingstoke, 1989).

—— *English Poetry of the Romantic Period 1789–1830* (1985; 2nd edn., Harlow, 1992).

Watson, Roderick, *The Literature of Scotland* (Basingstoke, 1984).

Wells, Robert, 'The Authority of the Damned' (review of Crabbe 1995), *Times Literary Supplement*, 4852 (29 Mar. 1996), 26.

Wordsworth, William, and Wordsworth, Dorothy, *Letters of William and Dorothy Wordsworth, The Middle Years, Part I: 1806–1811*, ed. E. de Selincourt, rev. Mary Moorman (Oxford, 1969).

Worrall, David, *Radical Culture: Discourse, Resistance, and Surveillance, 1790–1820* (Hemel Hempstead, 1992).

11. *Walter Scott*

FIONA ROBERTSON

GENERAL

As the most prolific author of his day and the most influential novelist of the nineteenth century, Scott attracted extensive critical commentary for many decades. At the end of the Victorian period, however, his critical fortunes went into apparently irreversible decline. Their recent revival, stimulated by new developments in criticism and theory, has made Scott the focus of some of the most innovative and most illuminating scholarship in contemporary Romantic studies; and this revaluation has important implications for the study of the Romantic period as a whole. The range of Scott's writing is in itself a challenge to narrower notions of Romanticism. He was prolific in all the major modern literary forms: famous first as a poet and ballad collector; a respected literary reviewer and editor; an influential supporter of Scottish theatre and a less influential dramatist; a letter-writer of very high quality and the keeper of one of literature's greatest personal journals; a historian and biographer, most notably of Napoleon; the author of a highly successful series of historical works for children; and, most importantly of all, an innovative writer of historical fiction. The most central of marginalized figures, Scott requires critics to reconsider traditional configurations of the period and its characteristic literary modes.

TEXTS

Current Scott scholarship is crucially engaged in establishing texts. This is inseparable from the shift in Scott's critical reputation. When he was considered careless, 'a great novelist with a weak aesthetic conscience' (Gordon 1969), few readers were concerned with the accuracy of the version in which they read his works. In 1978 Philip Gaskell's analysis of *The Heart of Midlothian* highlighted Scott's revisions and—at that time an almost unheard-of suggestion—attention to precise verbal detail. Since then, the world of the Scott text has turned upside down. Editions, of the novels at least, now presuppose a high level of authorial engagement, and readers have access to a wealth of editorial help which was unknown even ten years ago.

Several factors have influenced the current excitement over Scott's texts. First, the way in which Scott and an array of amanuenses, transcribers, compositors, and editors physically produced the published texts of the Waverley Novels is of compelling scholarly interest in the current climate of research into the collaborative nature of textual production. Second, Scott's texts exist in different versions, corresponding roughly to the early and the later years of his novelistic career: debate is guaranteed. Third, critical revaluation has drawn attention to a conscious craftsmanship and a complex literary self-consciousness which demand editorial precision. Finally, 1985 saw one of those rare moments in literary history at which manuscript treasure unexpectedly comes to light. The estate of a New York collector was found to include the interleaved set of novels which Scott used to make his revisions for the Magnum Opus (the last collected edition of the novels to be published under his direction). The interleaved set was purchased by the National Library of Scotland in 1986, a major acquisition which added to the excitement already generated by plans to produce the first ever complete scholarly edition of Scott's novels, now under way as the Edinburgh Edition of the Waverley Novels (several volumes already published: completion projected, in thirty volumes, for 2003). An introduction to these matters can be found in the volume of essays published to accompany the National Library of Scotland's microfiches of the interleaved set (I. G. Brown).

No single text offers readers an entirely untroubled route through the complex compositional and publication history of Scott's novels. First edition texts of individual works require correction from manuscript and proof readings; this is the work undertaken by the Edinburgh Edition. Of the collected editions, a special status has always been accorded to the Magnum Opus (48 vols., 1829–33, with additional collections of the poetical and non-fictional prose appended in the years following Scott's death). The Magnum Opus too, however, requires correction from its manuscript base, the interleaved set, and its cumulative position in Scott's career exposes it to the accretions of textual error from previous states of each novel. Later collected editions (such as the Centenary, 1870–1, the Dryburgh, 1892–4, and the Border, 1892–4, with its notes by Andrew Lang) are based on the Magnum Opus. The seven currently available volumes of the Edinburgh Edition are a new departure in that they seek to restore what they call the 'initial creative process' of Scott's novels, going back to manuscript, proof, and first edition readings, and rejecting the material (much of it new introductions and notes) written for the Magnum Opus. An article by Alexander and Garside sets forth the significance of this decision. The Edinburgh Edition will be the standard collected library edition for the next generation of readers, but it has aroused some controversy. Two substantial review articles assess its textual policy and the new view of Scott it presents (Inglis, Robertson 1996).

Those reading single novels by Scott will find helpful critical editions in the Oxford World's Classics, Everyman, and Penguin series. In general, the World's Classics editions are the best available, containing particularly good critical introductions and full explanatory notes. The Everyman Classics have unrevised texts, prefaced by new critical introductions, and provide extracts from relevant criticism as well as notes. B. & W. Publishing have reprinted in paperback some volumes from the Dryburgh edition, with brief new introductions but no new notes. With the exception of Lamont's *Waverley* (a revised version of her ground-breaking 1981 edition) all these paperback editions are based on Magnum Opus rather than on first edition texts; their texts will differ in places from those of the Edinburgh Edition, therefore, and include the late introductions and notes. This apparently specialized question is crucial to the understanding of Scott's frame narratives, which have received a great deal of attention in recent criticism (Gaston, Jordan 1980, Klepetar, Orr, Robertson 1994, Wilt).

By contrast, the modern textual state of Scott's poetry is a reminder that writers may be barred from canonicity for reasons other than gender, class, or political persuasion. The fullest modern reprint, produced for the Wordsworth Poetry Library series in 1995, includes all the long narrative poems, lyrics, and poems written for the Waverley Novels; while the standard complete edition remains the Oxford collection first edited by J. Logie Robertson in 1894. Older collections are usually incomplete and textually unreliable, although again the Magnum Opus edition (edited by J. G. Lockhart) is of special interest. As a result, the poems which outsold all others before the advent of Byron are now most commonly sampled in necessarily limited selections such as Carcanet's *Selected Poetry* (Reed); among these selections, Crawford's edition is the most useful. The Woodstock facsimile series includes a reprint of *The Lay of the Last Minstrel*; and Bridge Studios have published a paperback reprint of *The Lady of the Lake*. T. F. Henderson's four-volume edition of *Minstrelsy of the Scottish Border* remains the standard text of that work, and includes the important late 'Essay on Imitations of the Ancient Ballad'. Scott's five plays likewise await textual attention, but can be read together in the twelfth volume of the 1833–4 *Poetical Works* (Lockhart), or, with the exception of the first play (*The House of Aspen*), in the Wordsworth Poetry Library volume.

The standard text of Scott's wide range of non-fictional prose remains the twenty-eight volumes edited by Lockhart in 1834–6. Of particular interest are the essays on 'Chivalry', 'Romance', and 'Drama', originally written for the *Encyclopaedia Britannica*, the reviews of Austen and *Frankenstein*, the collection of introductions to Ballantyne's Novelist's Library known as *Lives of the Novelists*, and the *Letters on Demonology and Witchcraft*. Ioan Williams has edited a collection of Scott's views on other novelists; while Garside's facsimile edition of *The Visionary* makes available Scott's journalistic intervention in the political controversies of 1819, and P. H. Scott's edition of the *Letters of Malachi Malagrowther* sets forth his successful campaign to preserve the Scottish currency. Curry's edition of the *Edinburgh Annual Register* re-presents Scott's articles for this short-lived Tory magazine; the anonymous 'Of the Living Poets of Great Britain' (1810) is interesting for its evaluation of his own poetry, as well as for its criticisms of Coleridge and Wordsworth. Recent editorial work on *Tales of a Grandfather*, the stories from Scottish and French history which Scott wrote for his invalid grandson, John Hugh Lockhart, offers the opportunity for a reassessment of Scott's contribution to children's literature.

Of Scott's private writings, the *Letters* are in an unsatisfactory state of extended half-life. No edition has appeared to replace Grierson's twelve volumes of 1932–7, although the incompleteness and intermittent inaccuracy of this collection are widely recognized. Bell's 1979 article on the subject calculates that between 4,000 and 5,000 letters await inclusion. Grierson's collection remains the standard, however, and is adequate for non-specialized scholarly use. Its lack of an index prompted the separate publication of J. C. Corson's invaluable *Notes and Index to . . . [Grierson's Edition]*. Further material can be found in Partington's two collections of letters; and both sides of Scott's correspondence with the flamboyant Irish Gothicist C. R. Maturin have been edited by Ratchford and McCarthy. Corrected texts of some of Scott's more personal letters are included in Hewitt's collection of Scott's autobiographical writings, along with selections from the *Journal* and a newly edited text of Scott's memoirs, the so-called 'Ashestiel Autobiography' begun in 1808. The celebrated *Journal* itself is best read in Anderson's edition, which replaces earlier editions by Douglas (1890) and Tait and Parker (1939–46). Rubenstein (1978*a*) discusses changing critical responses to the three editions.

CRITICISM

Scott studies are served by a few excellent guides to criticism. Corson's bibliography guides readers deftly through the Scott craze at its peak and covers the period up to 1940. Hayden (1969) surveys early reviews of Scott. Rubenstein's invaluable *Reference Guide*, which gives details of criticism published between 1932 and 1977, is continued in her *Annotated Bibliography of Scholarship and Criticism*, covering the years 1975 to 1990. Ford and Bolton (1992) catalogue dramatizations of Scott's novels. Scholarly articles about Scott appear most regularly in the *Scottish Literary Journal* and *Studies in Scottish Literature*, and there is a *Scott Newsletter* for shorter notes and enquiries. The annual 'year's work' issue of the *Scottish Literary Journal* is the best source of information about new studies of Scott. Scott's own studies can be traced in Cochrane's *Catalogue of the Library at Abbotsford*.

Scott's critical reputation has an unsettled history. Accused by Mark Twain of creating the cultural climate which caused the American Civil War, celebrated by Ruskin as the only books fit for the sickroom, linked by Newman to the revival of interest in the Roman Catholic Church, the Waverley Novels were never far from the centre of nineteenth-century socio-literary debate. And the critical slump, when it came, was severe. In this situation, early accounts of Scott's importance for his contemporaries are an especially valuable resource. Hayden's representative selection for the *Critical Heritage* series is the best starting point. The most stimulating early commentaries are Hazlitt's essay on Scott in *The Spirit of the Age* and Jeffrey's reviews of *Marmion* and *Waverley* (see Hayden's *Critical Heritage*). Coleridge's more scattered comments are primarily to be found in his marginalia on the novels (included in Raysor's edition of his *Miscellaneous Criticism*) and in his letters, one of which (1821) contains one of the most frequently quoted of all remarks about Scott, that his novels encompass 'the two great moving principles of social humanity' (adherence to the past and the passion for progress). Nobody working on Scott's poetry should miss Coleridge's aspersions on *The Lay of the Last Minstrel*, cast in a letter to Wordsworth included in Hayden's *Critical Heritage*. James Hogg's imitation Scott poem 'Wat o' the Cleuch', from his *Poetic Mirror* (1816: recently edited by Groves), is a telling combination of affection and resistance. Hogg's informal memoirs of Scott, the varying texts of which have been edited by Mack, provide a shrewd character assessment and especially thought-provoking material on *Old Mortality*. As might be expected, Scott's influence makes him an implicit or explicit presence in much Romantic-period writing. For example, his re-creations of medieval times are discussed by Mr Chainmail in Peacock's *Crotchet Castle*. In 1850, Thackeray took his dispute with *Ivanhoe* to the lengths of a corrective sequel, *Rebecca and Rowena*.

From the Victorian period, when direct influence from Scott—on the Brontës, George Eliot, Thackeray, Hardy, Stevenson, historical novelists such as Bulwer-Lytton—was at its height, three pieces of criticism are outstanding. The first is Carlyle's review of the first six volumes of Lockhart's *Life*. Here, some of the most lasting charges against Scott are levelled with memorable directness: 'His life was worldly; his ambitions were worldly. There is nothing spiritual in him; all is economical, material, of the earth earthy.' For Carlyle he is 'one of the *healthiest* of men', but 'unconscious of an aim in speaking', a writer with no moral purpose. An abridged version of Carlyle's review is included in Hayden's *Critical Heritage*. The second key item is Nassau Senior's judgement on the novels, reprinted in his *Essays on Fiction*. The third is Mark Twain's assessment of Scott's impact on the culture of the American South, made in *Life on the Mississippi*. Twain accuses Scott of undoing all the good of the French Revolution and of setting back the course of progress in politics, religion, and social justice. The case against Scott as a promoter of cultural regression is nowhere else so combatively expressed. Twain returns to the theme in more oblique fashion when describing the foundered steamboat, the *Walter Scott*, in *The Adventures of Huckleberry Finn*. Critical reaction to Scott has recently been analysed in terms of the cultural preoccupations it reveals: Wilt (ch. 1), Ferris (1991: *passim*), Robertson (1994: ch. 1).

Before moving to twentieth-century criticism, separate attention must be given to the tradition of biographical criticism of Scott. Despite, or because of, his decision to publish his novels anonymously, literary appreciation of Scott has lingered long over questions of personality and sentimental evocations of lifestyle. This is partly the result of one biographer's talent. *Memoirs of the Life of Sir Walter Scott*, by Scott's son-in-law J. G. Lockhart, remains one of the greatest of all literary biographies. Several of Scott's friends and acquaintances wrote memoirs after his death: the most interesting are those by James Hogg, William Laidlaw, Basil Hall, and Washington Irving. Robertson (1997) collects nineteen of these memoirs and provides new assessment of their authors. Lockhart's *Life*, however, created an icon for the Victorian period. Aided by Scott's own reflections on the events of his life (a key factor in the appeal of the Magnum Opus), Lockhart produced a moralistic tale of success, disaster, and self-sacrificing redemption, which enjoyed numerous retellings. After Lockhart, the life rivalled the works as a narrative construct. Lockhart is still essential reading for anyone seriously interested in Scott, but modern biographies have certain advantages. The fullest and most scholarly is Johnson's two-volume work of 1970; Buchan is interesting as a writer's life of a writer and a Scottish novelist's reflections on a defining presence in Scottish fiction; while Wilson provides an informal, affectionate account interspersed with criticism of the novels. The other major biographical studies—Grierson, Pearson, Cecil—remain readable and informative. The most recent critical biography, by John Sutherland, follows a sharply sceptical line through the myths which have grown up around Scott. Sutherland provides reinterpretation rather than new evidence, but he is helpful in highlighting the political charge of Scott's thinking and the reasons for Lockhart's inventions and embroideries. Among specialist accounts of particular aspects of Scott's career, Clark anatomizes Scott's early life; MacNalty casts a historian of medicine's eye over Scott's ailments; and Quayle, a descendant of the maligned Ballantynes, reinterprets Scott's finances. Sultana's studies of Scott's last journey (1986) complement his editorial work (1977) on the troubled text of the final, unfinished, novel, *The Siege of Malta*; while his investigations into Scott's visit to Belgium and France in 1815 illuminate a formative episode (1993). Garside (1982) provides a telling account of the means by which Scott acquired his baronetcy, while Prebble amasses curious material on Scott's role in stage-managing George IV's visit to Edinburgh in 1822 (also the subject of excellent analysis in Manning's introduction to her edition of *Quentin Durward*).

The dip in Scott's reputation in the early years of the twentieth century is closely related to Jamesian ideas about the lowly rank of story in the art of the novel, best expressed by E. M. Forster ('Scott's fame rests upon one genuine basis. He could tell a story'). Nothing affected Scott's reputation more than the debased standing of what Forster regarded as the 'primitive power' of maintaining readers' curiosity. Writers whose interest in the historical particularity of cultures—especially, as in Joyce, national culture—was traceable in large part to Scott silently ceased to discuss him. Yet, as Virginia Woolf notes, his neglect by 'high' literary culture made no difference to his continuing popularity with readers. Scott's importance to Woolf's father Leslie Stephen, who wrote one of the most considered of Victorian assessments of his novels, produces a constant subtext of critical questioning in *To the Lighthouse*; while two of Woolf's essays in *The Moment* ponder Scott's mixture of modernity and antiquarianism, his affiliations with the 'ventriloquist' and 'playwright' schools of fiction, and memorably pronounce on his vapid central figures. Woolf and E. M. Forster are united in deploring the effect of Scott's style in moments of passion. The most eloquent modern defence of the qualities of feeling in Scott's prose is Alexander (1979).

In all the notable critical developments of the first two-thirds of the twentieth century, Scott is conspicuous by his absence. He had his place in the more dutiful surveys of literature, but he was consigned to a single footnote in the most influential critical work on the novel, Leavis's *Great Tradition*. This was the period in which Scott's popularity, facility, and range met with their most gifted detractors. Carlyle, who had based his doubts about Scott on a secure public confidence in his worth, would have been intrigued by the logical extension of his comments about 'want of purpose'. Scott was effectively barred from critical revaluation by an assumed lack of moral or artistic seriousness; and in a critical climate dominated by a faith in verbal icons his supposed lack of interest in the precise words on the page led to a profound and lasting critical indifference.

Critical revaluation began with Lukács's comments in *The Historical Novel*, the first attempt to examine Scott's techniques in relation to the wider cultural and intellectual preoccupations of his times. Lukács set out to examine why Scott's historical fiction should have arisen when it did; to explore its links with revolutionary ferment and the defeat of Napoleon; and to determine the key elements in Scott's historical realism as a literary construct. Central to the case was the claim that 'historical faithfulness in Scott is the authenticity of the historical psychology of his characters'; and nobody has described this quite so sharply. Much subsequent criticism relies fundamentally on Lukács's identification of Scott with the early form of the historical novel. A less happy outcome was the apparent confirmation of an old lurking suspicion that Scott had been a great artist in spite of himself: that his works have depths which he could not understand and to which he would have been ideologically opposed. Lukács also reinitiated what has become a particularly hoary concern of subsequent criticism: was Scott a Romantic writer or fundamentally anti-Romantic? Despite Lukács, Scott rarely figures prominently in Marxist literary histories; those which have most to offer him, such as Jameson, pay him little attention.

After Lukács, the greatest single stimulus to the critical revaluation of Scott came in a two-part essay by Daiches (1951), which remains one of the best accounts of Scott's historical techniques and their significance. Many subsequent studies explore aspects of Scott's historicism and its interaction with fiction (David Brown, Fleishman, Lascelles, Kerr, Shaw 1983, Waswo). Of these, Shaw's is the most sophisticated and ambitious, and Waswo's article the most stimulating short account. Brown gives a sensible and accessible survey of Scott's major historical fiction; it may be supplemented by the more questioning discussion by Kerr, which emphasizes the interrelationship of history and fiction as 'verbal worlds' and 'forms of understanding'. Kerr's account also leads into more concentratedly political readings of Scott by emphasizing the polemical force of historical selection and the process by which historical crisis, translated into literary conventions and granted the transformational causality of plot, is simultaneously concealed and exposed. As this suggests, Scott studies benefited greatly from the reconsideration of history's status as narrative which began with Hayden White's study *Metahistory*. Garside (1975) is the best account of the grounding of Scott's historicism in the work of the Scottish 'philosophical' historians.

The 1960s and 1970s saw a steady but modest flow of critical work. Studies of particular aspects of Scott's work from this period continue to be highly valuable. Parsons remains the best assessor of Scott's use of traditional materials concerning demonology and witchcraft; Kestner restarts serious interest in Scott's use of oral tradition; Colby's chapter and Hennelly's article on *Waverley* are still the most accessible accounts of this novel's engagement with the romance fiction of its day. More typical of this period, however, are the full-length general studies. The essential work on Scott's heroes remains Welsh (1963), recently reprinted with the addition of three extra essays (1992), one of which ('Patriarchy, Contract, and Repression in Scott's Novels') is an important development of his original ideas. Welsh considers the mediocrity of the hero as part of Scott's concern with property, restraint, and the anxieties of repressed desire. Of the few studies of Scott's entire novelistic *œuvre*, the most helpful place to begin remains Hart (1966). Many of his views about individual novels have been disputed by later critics, but this remains a reliable overview and is particularly useful on the novels set in medieval and Renaissance times, which are still underrepresented in more recent criticism. Gordon's account (1969) contains still-useful guidance on its central theme,

Scott's contradictory loyalties, but later critics have convincingly shown that we need not take at face value Scott's constant depreciations of his art. Furthering the assumption that Scott wrote much that can be discarded, Cockshut's study seeks to demonstrate that sharp discrimination between novels is essential if Scott is to be valued as he deserves; his interpretation of the battle scene at Drumclog in *Old Mortality* is one of the few genuinely close readings of the workings of Scott's historical method in a single episode.

While some critics were developing the investigation of Scott the historicist, others furthered the revaluation of Scott the story-teller. The late 1960s saw a number of studies of the narrative structure of Scott's novels, the most thorough by Cusac. Kroeber examines the narrative art of Scott's poetry as well as the novels, although he assumes too lowly a status for both. Most significantly of all, in 1976 Frye acknowledged Scott as the moving force behind his study of the structure of romance, *The Secular Scripture*. Growing interest in what Frye calls the 'building blocks' and the formulaic nature of romance— interacting with the reassessment of other popular forms of literature, such as Gothic fiction, detective stories, and romance's reinvention as science fiction— was part of a thoroughgoing reassessment of narrative form which led many to look afresh at Scott. Scott's combination of the modes of romance and novel is the subject of a lucid article by Nellist; while among more recent studies, Orr evaluates Scott's roles as novelist and story-teller. Weinstein stimulated a new wave of interest in the prefaces by printing a collection of them, with a critical introduction, in 1978. All these developments testified to a growing conviction of Scott's narratorial sophistication. Much subsequent debate about Scott can be traced to an incisive reading of Waverley Novel endings and fictions of authority in an article by Hart (1978*b*). To complement this article on endings, Ferris (1988) reflects on the techniques and purposes of the beginnings of Scott's novels, focusing on *A Legend of Montrose*.

The start of the 1980s saw one highly significant attempt to place Scott in a larger history of the novel. Levine includes two provocative chapters on Scott in his study of 'the realistic imagination', but refuses to accept any degree of conscious artistry on Scott's part. The chapters focus, as Scott criticism was increasingly to focus, on secrecy, defensiveness, strategies of distance and deferral, but they are unable to concede that Scott had more than a superficial interest in such things. Morse (1982), in contrast, is attentive to the use of superstition, madness, and instability in Scott's novels, and discusses the more neglected novels with a predisposition to accept 'unprecedented virtuosity and complexity' where he finds it (as he does in *Kenilworth* and *The Fair Maid of Perth*). Also attentive to Scott's place in the wider realm of Romantic-period fiction, Cottom considers his novels alongside those of Radcliffe and Austen in terms of 'the civilized imagination'. He emphasizes their romance elements, which he discusses in terms of 'borderlines' between competing cultural and generic forms; and the importance of superstition, law, and violence. The publication, in 1980, of Tulloch's important study of Scott's language also opened up the range of novels on which critics were prepared to comment, with its analysis of the artifices of Scott's creation of convincing Scottish and 'period' language.

The 1980s also saw the consolidation of studies primarily concerned with Scott's relationship to the social and political events of his own times. Farrell (1980) considers elements of tragedy in Scott's novels as the response to revolutionary anxiety; while the argument that Scott's historical novels are not about the past but about contemporary society is most extensively analysed by McMaster (1981). McMaster relates particular incidents and controversies in Scott's times to issues registered in the novels: for example, Scott's fictional depictions of monarchy in the novels of the early 1820s are examined in the context of the politicized controversy surrounding Caroline, Princess of Wales. The involvement of Scott's art in contemporary politics is succinctly demonstrated by Hewitt (1983). Increasingly, the trend in this type of criticism has been to question Scott's supposed moderation and neutrality, as in Dickson's article on *Old Mortality*.

The movement towards more carefully nuanced social and political readings accompanied an interest in distinct stages in Scott's career. The most suggestive and thoughtful readings of the first phase of Scott's novelistic output are to be found in Millgate (1984). Ending with the publication of the Third Series of *Tales of my Landlord* in 1819, Millgate's study examines the early novels as an interconnected series and demonstrates the significance of Scott's manipulation of the mysterious identity of the 'Author of *Waverley*'. The chapters work well as studies of individual novels, but Millgate's fascination with the larger shapes of the career as a whole inaugurates a continuing concern in the best studies of Scott. Moves to reassess Scott's works as a series and as a cumulative cultural phenomenon prove much more sensitive than the 'single great novel' approach to the ways in which he worked on contemporary readers' imaginations. A year after Millgate's study, Wilt's *Secret Leaves* contributed in a rather different way to this reorientation. Its title reconfirming critics' interest in Scott's secrecy and implicitly taking up Frye's evocation of a 'secular scripture', this is the most stimulating full-length critical interpretation of Scott's novels. Wilt's continually provocative readings highlight the techniques of 'kidnapped romance', personal and cultural modes of secrecy, and the ways in which the Waverley Novels became the environment of later nineteenth-century fiction. It is significant in the history of Scott criticism for re-swivelling Scott's career around *Ivanhoe* and for drawing attention to questions of gender in many of the novels. Those following up Wilt's rereading of *Ivanhoe* will find interesting comments on this novel in Simmons (1990b), a study of nineteenth-century representations of the Norman Conquest.

The question of Scott's relationship to the literary traditions of his own land has been a constant generator of debate, much of it recalling the socio-literary concerns of the best Victorian commentators. Opinion on his role in Scottish literature and in nationalist politics is divided. Craig argues that Scott was too insensitive to the social turmoil of the present to have even a sense of what had mattered in the past; his failure to deal with the pressing concerns of contemporary Scotland led to Scottish literature's limiting pre-occupation with the past. Nairn's analysis of 'the three dreams of Scottish nationalism' reaches similar conclusions. Muir places Scott at a particular stage in Scottish writers' relationship to their native language, while P. H. Scott presents the case for Scott's nationalist sympathies. Hart's (1978a) survey of two centuries of Scottish fiction includes an interesting perspective on Scott's novels as part of a Scottish type of Gothic fiction, and is one of the best available considerations of Scott's relationship to his contemporaries Hogg and Galt. MacQueen also considers Scott in relation to other Scottish writers and to Enlightenment ideas. A rather different angle on the subject of Scottishness and Scott's part in creating it can be found in Trevor-Roper's contribution to a series of essays on 'the invention of tradition'. Discussion of Scott in the context of Scottish and North American 'provincialism', with particularly acute readings of *The Heart of Midlothian* and *Redgauntlet*, is to be found in Manning's important book (1990). Crawford's 1992 study explicitly engages with these aspects of Scottish cultural identity, and examines what he calls the 'proto-Modernist' elements in Scott's work.

Throughout this period, Scott has been more frequently invoked in theoretically oriented studies. There are also several works which pay him special attention, although he has avoided becoming the mascot of any particular school of theory. Among reader-response studies, Iser includes a chapter on *Waverley* in his study of the 'implied reader', confirming the trend among scholars choosing just one Scott novel to fix upon *Waverley*. A detailed response to Iser's treatment of Scott is given by Stein. New historicism in its various inflections has had much to offer Scott; but although the upsurge of interest in Scott and the academic interest in cultural materialist and new historicist methods broadly coincide, new historicisms have been a facilitating climate rather than a dominant methodology in recent Scott criticism. With the exception of Butler, none of the most prominent historicist critics takes Scott as a particular focus of interest. Those interested in the engagement of new historicist critics with particular Scott novels might sample Bann (1989). One of the aims of the 1991 International Scott Conference was to explore the impact of various forms of critical theory on the reading of Scott: accordingly, several short papers included in the proceedings of that conference (Alexander and Hewitt 1993), especially those by Punter, Findlay, Diedrick, and Politi, offer useful points of departure for a consideration of the possible fruitfulness of interpretative models drawn from Derrida, Foucault, Klein, and others. The volume's title, *Scott in Carnival*, pays tribute to the ideas which proved most consistently stimulating, those of Bakhtin. The collection also deserves attention for the essays on Meg Merrilies and India (Garside) and the continuing impact of feminist ideas (Anderson, Dale, McCracken-Flesher). Among other studies, Elam's interpretation of romance in postmodernism brings Scott's 'welter of textuality' into contact with Umberto Eco, Kathy Acker, and Italo Calvino, not to mention Derrida and theories of gender; Bann (1984: 93–111) offers a Kleinian reading of Scott's desires; and Fielding examines questions of orality and literacy in relation to selected works by Scott, including the neglected *Monastery*.

Feminist studies have proved particularly propitious for Scott. Separate attention is given below to their impact on readings of the poetry. The best accounts use feminist and poststructuralist theories to illuminate the conditions into which Scott's novels sprang: most ambitiously of all, Ferris (1991) addresses the questions of gender and genre in historical fiction up to and including Scott. Ferris examines the impact of Scott's fictions on early nineteenth-century taxonomies of genre and traces the assumption of authority by which the Waverley Novels distinguished themselves from competing fictions, especially from the conventions of 'female reading' and 'feminine writing' (illustrated by the reception of works by Maria Edgeworth, Lady Morgan, and others). It is the best account to date of Scott's intervention in the market for fiction and of the critical climate which helped to create his success.

Critical interest in postcolonial literatures has, with a few exceptions, been rather slow to recognize Scott, although Scott was, with Byron, the British writer of the period who made the most dramatic impact on world literatures, and he is referred to frequently in Said's influential *Orientalism*. Since a writer's impact on other cultures is essentially an act of translation (even a Bloomian misprision), it is neither surprising nor limiting that the accounts which do exist tend to be hostile (for example, Green's argument that Scott promotes the ideology of 'the aristomilitary caste' and produces works which support British imperialism). But as Kerr reminds us by invoking Michael Hechter's claims for Celtic 'internal colonialism' in his reading of Scott, the Waverley Novels are constructions of national identity written from within the experience of cultural assimilation by another nation, which makes them potent models for historical fiction in colonial and postcolonial countries. Recent analysis of the construction of national identities, particularly by Benedict Anderson and Linda Colley, is full of significance for readings of Scott. Trumpener's wide-ranging article on national tales and historicism in the age of *Waverley* is an important contribution and characteristic of recent studies in refusing to isolate Scott's experiments in national history from those of Irish and Scottish contemporaries. Scott's relationship to the politics of colonialism and nationalism is considered in McCracken-Flesher's thought-provoking essay (1991); while Rignall's article (1991) on Scott's importance for a range of later novelists of empire pays particular attention to *The Surgeon's Daughter*.

All these works draw on Scott's variety and imaginative range in ways which stimulate broader studies. In an innovative and influential article, Kathryn Sutherland (1987) explores Scott's 'economics of the imagination', working from the ideas of Adam Smith to Scott's development of a model of art which is intricately related to the modes of production and speculation. Recent articles increasingly open up the study of previously neglected novels: of particular note are Alexander (1990) (*Kenilworth*), Gamerschlag and Simmons (1990*a*) (*Count Robert of Paris*), Harkin (*The Monastery*), McCracken-Flesher (1994) ('The Highland Widow'), and Sroka (1987) (*Woodstock*). Beiderwell, meanwhile, develops a particular thematic concern with justice and law, as it operates in a range of Waverley Novels. And although Scott studies are perhaps best seen as productively fragmented in the past few years, there have been more general theses which attempt to engage with the fractures induced by any effort to see Scott whole. Of the two most recent full-length studies, Duncan brilliantly extends previous discussion of the relationship between the romance and the novel, and provides detailed discussions of four Scott novels in particular (*Waverley, Guy Mannering, The Bride of Lammermoor, The Heart of Midlothian*); while Robertson (1994) uses Scott's indebtedness to Gothic techniques of suspense and deferral to draw in a wide range of previously neglected novels. Both studies build with discernible new certainty on the re-establishment of Scott's literary reputation in the 1980s.

Criticism of Scott's poetry, plays, and non-fictional prose has been rarer, but does not fundamentally diverge from the history given above. The most interesting work has been provoked by the poetry. Davie's (1961*b*) evaluation is an exception in a low period for appreciation of Scott's verse. Eller (1978) gives a thematic reading of *The Lay of the Last Minstrel*. Alexander (1975) gathers together a great deal of significant information about the ways in which Scott's poems were reviewed; a standard of historical investigation maintained in his later collections of essays on *The Lay of the Last Minstrel* (1978) and *Marmion* (1981). Manning's 1982 article on Scott's use of Ossian pays particular attention to *The Lady of the Lake*, and provides useful orientation for study of that poem; from an entirely different angle, McMaster (1983) provides a rare structuralist reading of the same work. Ross (1986) considers the function of metrical romance in the Romantic period, with special reference to Scott, while his later study of the model of the organic development of the nation-state (1991) includes an important discussion of the neglected *Rokeby* in relation to texts by Burke, Hazlitt, and Wordsworth. The 1833–4 *Poetical Works* (the edition designed to follow on from the Magnum Opus texts of the novels) is analysed by Millgate (1989). The best interpretative work on the poetry (such as

Millgate 1990) emphasizes narrative technique and a sophistication of historical presentation more fully documented in criticism of the Waverley Novels.
Although it resists the artistic as opposed to the merely commercial value of
Scott's poetry, Murphy's chapter elucidates the ways in which Scott targeted
the poetical tastes of his times. Scott's importance among the period's imitations and evocations of poetic romance is considered by Curran in his study
of the poetic forms of Romanticism. The poems' high incidence of enchant-
ments, witches, and cross-dressing have attracted revisionist feminist criticism
(Goslee 1988); criticism of the novels alongside the poetry (Wilt, Ferris 1991)
likewise focuses on Scott's use of the feminized forms of romance and the
degree to which all his work can be seen as a move to incorporate to masculine literary traditions forms and subjects commonly read as feminine. In
this, there are parallels to be drawn with gendered readings of the genre experiments of other writers of the period, most notably Keats. Goslee (1988) is the
only full study of Scott's poetry, bringing feminist theory and narrative theory
to bear on each of the long narrative poems.

There are few studies of Scott as critic. The most extensive, by Ball, is now
somewhat out of date. Morgan provides the most satisfying account of the
principles underlying Scott's literary criticism, and his affiliations with other
critics of his time. Berland provides a useful reading of Scott's edition of
Dryden. Robertson (1994) includes a section on Scott as critic of Gothic fiction
and tales of the supernatural. Rubenstein (Alexander and Hewitt 1983) considers Scott as literary biographer. The *Lives of the Novelists* receive welcome
attention in Cafarelli's more general study, while Friedman evaluates the *Life
of Napoleon* in the context of other British writings on the same subject.
Assessments of Scott the dramatist are rarer still. Evans includes Scott (somewhat dismissively) in his broader study of Gothic drama; while the account of
all Scott's plays given by Purkayastha works from the conviction that his
talents were incompatible with good writing for the stage. Worth develops the
implications of a particular period of Scott's involvement with the Edinburgh
stage, a subject treated more generally by Bell (Alexander and Hewitt 1993).
Robertson (Alexander and Hewitt 1993) examines the plays in relation to
Gothic drama of the 1790s, and argues for the significance of some of the plays
as intertexts of the novels.

Finally, a brief account of Scott's position in more general studies of the
Romantic period and his interrelationships with other literatures and art forms.
Attention to Scott in recent surveys of the Romantic period remains patchy.
The fullest and most interesting account is given in Kelly's guide to the fiction
of the period. Garside (1994) is a useful brief introduction to the course of Scott's
publishing career, although it only considers three novels. More ambitious
and more suggestive is Butler's chapter on Scott and Austen as conservative

novelists. The fullest account of Scott's indebtedness to Chaucer and to medieval romance is Mitchell (1987), although the superficially more special-ized chapter in Johnston's study of medievalist scholarship in the eighteenth and nineteenth centuries raises more interesting questions about the purposes of Scott's medievalism.

There is of course an extensive literature devoted to Scott's influence on other writers. Various aspects of Scott's importance for other literatures are considered in the course of *Scott and his Influence* (Alexander and Hewitt 1983). This huge subject is outside the scope of the present guide; but there have been many studies of Scott's impact on other European writers, notably Alexis, Almeida Garrett, Andersen, Balzac, Dumas, Feval, Hugo, Ingemann, Manzoni, Pushkin, Sand, Soler, Stifter, and Tolstoy. Of shorter pieces tracing influence on a whole culture, Lyons gives a revealing account of Scott's impact on France; while those seeking a general overview of Scott's impact on European literature should consult the helpful article by Massie. The effect of the poetry and Waverley Novels on later nineteenth-century British writing is best traced in studies of individual writers: the bibliography below gives as samples essays by Rignall (1984) (on Gaskell and Hardy), Farrell (1984) (on Emily Brontë, Tennyson, Hardy), and C. Stephen Finley (on Ruskin). Stone's interpretation of Victorian writing in the context of Romanticism provides a more general discussion. Twain's attacks have helped to ensure that Scott's importance for American literature has never gone unnoticed; there are accounts in Chase, Fiedler (an especially brisk and provocative account), and Hook (which includes details of sales figures and American reviews as well as some interesting mater-ial rebutting Twain). Most impressive of all is Dekker's specialized account of Scott's impact on American historical romance.

Scott has had a wide influence on non-literary arts, and his hold on nineteenth-century culture is not easily disentangled from them. On the visual arts, Gerald Finley discusses Turner as illustrator to Scott; Errington examines Scott in the context of contemporary artists, especially Raeburn and Wilkie; Altick examines the popularity of paintings inspired by Scott; and Meisel assesses Scott's novels in the context of paintings and plays based on them. Of these accounts, Altick and Meisel are the most generally useful. Scott and music, a potentially expansive subject, has inspired relatively few studies. Fiske provides information in the course of a more general account, while Mitchell (1977) studies the operas based on Scott. Scott and film, likewise, has attracted few commentators, but Tait has compiled a list of relevant material, and Chandler (1990) considers the cinematography of D. W. Griffith in relation to Scott's historical techniques. Already separately mentioned, Bolton (1992) is a general study of dramatizations of Scott; a shorter piece, Bolton (1988), lists BBC radio and television plays based on the Waverley Novels.

REFERENCES

TEXTS

Alexander, J. H. (ed.), *Kenilworth: A Romance*, Edinburgh Edition of the Waverley Novels 11 (Edinburgh, 1993).

—— (ed.), *The Bride of Lammermoor*, Edinburgh Edition of the Waverley Novels 7a (Edinburgh, 1995).

—— (ed.), *A Legend of the Wars of Montrose*, Edinburgh Edition of the Waverley Novels 7b (Edinburgh, 1995).

Anderson, W. E. K. (ed.), *The Journal of Sir Walter Scott* (Oxford, 1972).

The Antiquary, introd. James Robertson (text repr. from Dryburgh edn., 1892–4) (Edinburgh, 1993).

Baker, William, and Alexander, J. H. (eds.), *Tales of a Grandfather: The History of France (Second Series)* (De Kalb, Ill., 1997).

Calder, Angus (ed.), *Old Mortality* (Harmondsworth, 1975).

Crawford, Thomas (ed.), *Sir Walter Scott: Selected Poems* (Oxford, 1972).

Curry, Kenneth (ed.), *Sir Walter Scott's Edinburgh Annual Register* (Knoxville, Tenn., 1977).

Duncan, Ian (ed.), *Ivanhoe*, Oxford World's Classics (Oxford, 1996).

The Fair Maid of Perth, introd. James Robertson (text repr. from Dryburgh edn., 1892–4) (Edinburgh, 1995).

Garside, Peter D. (ed.), *The Visionary*, Regency Reprints 1 (Cardiff, 1984).

—— (ed.), *The Black Dwarf*, Edinburgh Edition of the Waverley Novels 4a (Edinburgh, 1993).

Grierson, H. J. C., et al. (eds.), *The Letters of Sir Walter Scott*, 12 vols. (London, 1932–7).

Henderson, T. F. (ed.), *Minstrelsy of the Scottish Border*, 4 vols. (Edinburgh, 1902; rev. edn., 1932).

Hewitt, David (ed.), *The Antiquary*, Edinburgh Edition of the Waverley Novels 3 (Edinburgh, 1995).

The Lady of the Lake (Berwick upon Tweed, 1990).

Lamont, Claire (ed.), *Waverley* (Oxford, 1981), rev. edn., Oxford World's Classics (Oxford, 1986).

—— (ed.), *The Heart of Midlothian*, Oxford World's Classics (Oxford, 1982).

The Lay of the Last Minstrel, introd. Jonathan Wordsworth, Revolution and Romanticism, 1789–1834 (Oxford, 1992).

Lockhart, J. G. (ed.), *The Poetical Works of Sir Walter Scott, Bart.*, 12 vols. (Edinburgh, 1833–4).

—— (ed.), *The Miscellaneous Prose Works of Sir Walter Scott, Bart.*, 28 vols. (Edinburgh, 1834–6).

Mack, Douglas S. (ed.), *The Tale of Old Mortality*, Edinburgh Edition of the Waverley Novels 4b (Edinburgh, 1993).

Manning, Susan (ed.), *Quentin Durward*, Oxford World's Classics (Oxford, 1992).

Partington, Wilfred (ed.), *The Private Letter-Books of Sir Walter Scott: Selections from the Abbotsford Manuscripts. With a Letter to the Reader from Hugh Walpole* (London, 1930).

—— (ed.), *Sir Walter's Post-Bag: More Stories and Sidelights from his Unpublished Letter-Books*, foreword by Hugh Walpole (London, 1932).

Ratchford, Fannie E., and McCarthy, William H., Jr. (eds.), *The Correspondence of Sir Walter Scott and Charles Robert Maturin with a Few Other Allied Letters* (Austin, Tex., 1937).

Reed, James (ed.), *Sir Walter Scott: Selected Poems* (Manchester, 1992).

Robertson, Fiona (ed.), *The Bride of Lammermoor*, Oxford World's Classics (Oxford, 1991).

Scott, Paul Henderson (ed.), *The Letters of Malachi Malagrowther* (London, 1981).

Sutherland, John (ed.), *Rob Roy*, Everyman Classics (London, 1995).

Sutherland, Kathryn (ed.), *Redgauntlet*, Oxford World's Classics (Oxford, 1985).

Tulloch, Graham (ed.), *The Two Drovers and Other Stories*, introd. Lord David Cecil, Oxford World's Classics (Oxford, 1987).

The Waverley Novels, 48 vols. (known as the 'Magnum Opus' edn.) (Edinburgh, 1829–33).

Weinstein, Mark (ed.), *Saint Ronan's Well*, Edinburgh Edition of the Waverley Novels 16 (Edinburgh, 1995).

Williams, Ioan (ed.), *Sir Walter Scott on Novelists and Fiction* (London, 1968).

Wilson, A. N. (ed.), *Ivanhoe*, Penguin Classics (London, 1984).

The Works of Sir Walter Scott, Wordsworth Poetry Library (Ware, 1995).

CRITICISM

Alexander, J. H., *Two Studies in Romantic Reviewing: Edinburgh Reviewers and the English Tradition; The Reviewing of Walter Scott's Poetry: 1805–1817*, Salzburg Studies in English Literature: Romantic Reassessment 49, 2 vols. (Salzburg, 1975).

—— *The Lay of the Last Minstrel: Three Essays*, Salzburg Studies in English Literature: Romantic Reassessment 77 (Salzburg, 1978).

—— ' "Only Connect": The Passionate Style of Walter Scott', *Scottish Literary Journal*, 6/2 (1979), 37–54.

—— *Marmion: Studies in Interpretation and Composition*, Salzburg Studies in English Literature: Romantic Reassessment 30 (Salzburg, 1981).

—— 'The Major Images in *Kenilworth*', *Scottish Literary Journal*, 17/2 (1990), 27–35.

—— and Garside, Peter, 'Editing the Waverley Novels', in Philip W. Martin and Robin Jarvis (eds.), *Reviewing Romanticism* (New York, 1992), 14–31.

—— and Hewitt, David S. (eds.), *Scott and his Influence: The Papers of the Aberdeen Scott Conference, 1982*, Association for Scottish Literary Studies Occasional Papers 6 (Aberdeen, 1983).

Altick, Richard D., *Paintings from Books: Art and Literature in Britain, 1760–1900* (Columbus, Oh., 1985).

Anderson, Benedict, *Imagined Communities: Reflections on the Origin and Spread of Nationalism* (London, 1983).

Anderson, James, 'Sir Walter Scott as Historical Novelist', *Studies in Scottish Literature*, 4 (1966–7), 29–41, 63–78, 155–78; 5 (1967–8), 14–27, 83–97, 143–66; repr. in his *Sir Walter Scott and History: With Other Papers* (Edinburgh, 1981).

Ball, Margaret, *Sir Walter Scott as a Critic of Literature* (1907; Port Washington, NY, 1966).

Bann, Stephen, *The Clothing of Clio: A Study of the Representation of History in Nineteenth-Century Britain and France* (Cambridge, 1984).

—— 'The Sense of the Past: Image, Text, and Object in the Formation of Historical Consciousness in Nineteenth-Century Britain', in H. Aram Veeser (ed.), *The New Historicism* (New York, 1989), 102–15.

Beiderwell, Bruce, *Power and Punishment in Scott's Novels* (Athens, Ga., 1992).

Bell, Alan (ed.), *Scott Bicentenary Essays: Selected Papers Read at the Sir Walter Scott Bicentenary Conference* (Edinburgh, 1973).

—— 'The Letters of Sir Walter Scott: Problems and Opportunities', in J. A. Dainard (ed.), *Editing Correspondence: Papers Given at the 14th Annual Conference on Editorial Problems* (New York, 1979), 63–80.

Berland, K. J. H., 'Scott's Dryden: The Whig Interpretation of Literary History', *Restoration*, 9/1 (1985), 2–8.

Bolton, H. Philip, 'Sir Walter Scott on BBC', *Scott Newsletter*, 12 (1988), 2–9.

—— *Scott Dramatized* (London, 1992).

Brown, David, *Walter Scott and the Historical Imagination* (London, 1979).

Brown, Iain Gordon (ed.), *Scott's Interleaved Waverley Novels (The 'Magnum Opus': National Library of Scotland MSS. 23001–41) An Introduction and Commentary* (Aberdeen, 1987).

Buchan, John, *Sir Walter Scott* (London, 1932).

Butler, Marilyn, *Romantics, Rebels and Reactionaries: English Literature and its Background 1760–1830* (Oxford, 1981).

Cafarelli, Annette Wheeler, *Prose in the Age of Poets: Romanticism and Biographical Narrative from Johnson to De Quincey* (Philadelphia, 1990).

Cecil, Lord David, *Sir Walter Scott*, The Raven Miscellany (London, 1933).

Chandler, James K., 'The Historical Novel Goes to Hollywood: Scott, Griffith, and Film Epic Today', in Gene W. Ruoff (ed.), *The Romantics and Us: Essays on Literature and Culture* (New Brunswick, NJ, 1990), 237–73.

—— 'Scott and the Scene of Explanation: Framing Contextuality in *The Bride of Lammermoor*', *Studies in the Novel*, 26 (1994), 69–98.

Chase, Richard, *The American Novel and its Tradition* (Garden City, NY, 1957).

Clark, Arthur Melville, *Sir Walter Scott: The Formative Years* (Edinburgh, 1969).

Cochrane, John George, *Catalogue of the Library at Abbotsford* (Edinburgh, 1838).

Cockshut, A. O. J., *The Achievement of Walter Scott* (London, 1969).

Colby, Robert A., *Fiction with a Purpose: Major and Minor Nineteenth-Century Novels* (Bloomington, Ind., 1967).

Coleridge, Samuel Taylor, *Coleridge's Miscellaneous Criticism*, ed. Thomas Middleton Raysor (London, 1936).

Colley, Linda, *Britons: Forging the Nation 1707–1837* (London, 1992).

Corson, James C., *A Bibliography of Sir Walter Scott: A Classified and Annotated List of Books and Articles Relating to his Life and Works 1797–1940* (Edinburgh, 1943).

—— *Notes and Index to Sir Herbert Grierson's Edition of the Letters of Sir Walter Scott* (Oxford, 1979).

Cottom, Daniel, *The Civilized Imagination: A Study of Ann Radcliffe, Jane Austen, and Sir Walter Scott* (Cambridge, 1985).

Craig, David, *Scottish Literature and the Scottish People 1680–1830* (London, 1961).

Crawford, Robert, *Devolving English Literature* (Oxford, 1992).

Criscuola, Margaret Movshin, 'The Porteus Mob: Fact and Truth in *The Heart of Midlothian*', *English Language Notes*, 22 (1984), 43–50.

Cullinan, Mary P., 'History and Language in Scott's *Redgauntlet*', *Studies in English Literature*, 18 (1978), 659–75.

Curran, Stuart, *Poetic Form and British Romanticism* (New York, 1986).

Cusac, Marian H., *Narrative Structure in the Novels of Sir Walter Scott*, De Proprietatibus Litterarum, edenda curat C. H. Van Schooneveld, Series Practica 6 (The Hague, 1969).

Daiches, David, 'Scott's Achievement as a Novelist' (1951); repr. in his *Literary Essays* (Edinburgh, 1956), 88–121.

—— 'Scott's *Redgauntlet*', in Robert C. Rathburn and Martin Steinmann, Jr. (eds.), *From Jane Austen to Joseph Conrad: Essays Collected in Memory of James T. Hillhouse* (Minneapolis, 1958), 46–59.

—— 'Sir Walter Scott and History', *Études anglaises*, 24 (Oct.–Dec. 1971), 458–77.

—— 'Scott's *Waverley*: The Presence of the Author', in Ian Campbell (ed.), *Nineteenth-Century Scottish Fiction: Critical Essays* (Manchester, 1979), 6–17.

Davie, Donald, *The Heyday of Sir Walter Scott* (London, 1961*a*).

—— 'The Poetry of Sir Walter Scott', *Proceedings of the British Academy*, 47 (1961*b*), 61–75.

Dekker, George, *The American Historical Romance*, Cambridge Studies in American Literature and Culture (Cambridge, 1987).

Dickson, Beth, 'Sir Walter Scott and the Limits of Toleration', *Scottish Literary Journal*, 18/2 (1991), 46–62.

Duncan, Ian, *Modern Romance and Transformations of the Novel: The Gothic, Scott, Dickens* (Cambridge, 1992).

Elam, Diane, *Romancing the Postmodern* (London, 1992).

Elbers, Joan S., 'Isolation and Community in *The Antiquary*', *Nineteenth-Century Fiction*, 27 (1973), 405–23.

Eller, Ruth, 'Themes of Time and Art in *The Lay of the Last Minstrel*', *Studies in Scottish Literature*, 13 (1978), 111–24.

Errington, Lindsay, 'Sir Walter Scott and Nineteenth-Century Painting in Scotland', in Wendy Kaplan (ed.), *Scotland Creates: 5000 Years of Art and Design* (London, 1990), 121–35.

Evans, Bertrand, *Gothic Drama from Walpole to Shelley*, Univ. of California Publications in English 18 (Berkeley and Los Angeles, 1947).

Farrell, John P., *Revolution as Tragedy: The Dilemma of the Moderate from Scott to Arnold* (Ithaca, NY, 1980).

—— '*The Bride of Lammermoor* as Oracular Text in Emily Brontë, Tennyson, and Hardy', *South Central Review*, 1 (1984), 53–63.

Ferris, Ina, 'The Historical Novel and the Problem of Beginning: The Model of Scott', *Journal of Narrative Technique*, 18 (1988), 73–82.

—— *The Achievement of Literary Authority: Gender, History, and the Waverley Novels* (New York, 1991).

Fiedler, Leslie A., *Love and Death in the American Novel* (1960; rev. edn., London, 1967).

Fielding, Penny, *Writing and Orality: Nationality, Culture, and Nineteenth-Century Scottish Writing* (Oxford, 1996).

Finley, C. Stephen, 'Scott, Ruskin, and the Landscape of Autobiography', *Studies in Romanticism*, 26 (1987), 549–72.

Finley, Gerald, *Landscapes of Memory: Turner as Illustrator to Scott* (Berkeley and Los Angeles, 1980).

Fiske, Roger, *Scotland in Music: A European Enthusiasm* (Cambridge, 1983).

Fleishman, Avrom, *The English Historical Novel: Walter Scott to Virginia Woolf* (Baltimore, 1971).

Ford, Richard, *Dramatisations of Scott's Novels: A Catalogue*, Oxford Bibliographical Society Occasional Publications 12 (Oxford, 1979).

Forster, E. M., *Aspects of the Novel* (London, 1927).

Franklin, Caroline, 'Feud and Faction in *The Bride of Lammermoor*', *Scottish Literary Journal*, 14/2 (1987), 18–31.

Friedman, Barton, *Fabricating History: English Writers on the French Revolution* (Princeton, 1988).

Frye, Northrop, *The Secular Scripture: A Study of the Structure of Romance*, The Charles Eliot Norton Lectures, 1974–5 (Cambridge, Mass., 1976).

Gamerschlag, Kurt, 'The Making and Unmaking of Sir Walter Scott's *Count Robert of Paris*', *Studies in Scottish Literature*, 15 (1980), 95–123.

Garside, Peter D., 'Scott and the "Philosophical" Historians', *Journal of the History of Ideas*, 36 (1975), 497–512.

—— 'Redgauntlet and the Topography of Progress', *Southern Review*, 10 (1977a), 155–73.

—— 'Waverley's Pictures of the Past', *English Literary History*, 44 (1977b), 659–82.

—— 'Patriotism and Patronage: New Light on Scott's Baronetcy', *Modern Language Review*, 77 (1982), 16–28.

—— 'Rob's Last Raid: Scott and the Publication of the Waverley Novels', in Robin Myers and Michael Harris (eds.), *Author/Publisher Relations during the Eighteenth and Nineteenth Centuries* (Oxford, 1983), 88–118.

—— 'Union and *The Bride of Lammermoor*', *Studies in Scottish Literature*, 19 (1984), 72–93.

—— 'Politics and the Novel 1780–1830', in David B. Pirie (ed.), *The Romantic Period*, vol. v of *Penguin History of Literature* (London, 1994), 49–85.

Gaskell, Philip, *From Writer to Reader: Studies in Editorial Method* (Oxford, 1978), 101–17.

Gaston, Patricia S., *Prefacing the Waverley Prefaces: A Reading of Sir Walter Scott's Prefaces to the Waverley Novels*, American University Studies Series 4: English Language and Literature 130 (New York, 1991).

Gordon, Robert C., '*The Bride of Lammermoor*: A Novel of Tory Pessimism', *Nineteenth-Century Fiction*, 12 (1957), 110–24.

—— *Under Which King? A Study of the Scottish Waverley Novels* (Edinburgh, 1969).

—— 'The Marksman of Ravenswood: Power and Legitimacy in *The Bride of Lammermoor*', *Nineteenth Century Literature*, 41 (1986), 49–71.

Goslee, Nancy Moore, 'Witch or Pawn: Women in Scott's Narrative Poetry', in Anne K. Mellor (ed.), *Romanticism and Feminism* (Bloomington, Ind., 1988), 115–36.

—— *Scott the Rhymer* (Lexington, Ky., 1988).

Green, Martin, *Dreams of Adventure, Deeds of Empire* (London, 1980).

Grierson, H. J. C., *Sir Walter Scott, Bart: A New Life Supplementary to, and Corrective of, Lockhart's Biography* (London, 1938).

Harkin, Patricia, 'The Fop, the Fairy, and the Genres of Scott's *Monastery*', *Studies in Scottish Literature*, 19 (1984), 177–93.

Hart, Francis Russell, *Scott's Novels: The Plotting of Historic Survival* (Charlottesville, Va., 1966).

—— *The Scottish Novel: A Critical Survey* (London, 1978a).

—— 'Scott's Endings: The Fictions of Authority', *Nineteenth-Century Fiction*, 33 (1978b), 48–68.

Hayden, John O., 'The Satanic School, Sir Walter Scott', in his *The Romantic Reviewers 1802–1824* (Chicago, 1969), 125–34.

—— (ed.), *Scott: The Critical Heritage* (London, 1970).

Hazlitt, William, *Lectures on the English Poets; The Spirit of the Age*, introd. Catherine Macdonald Maclean (London, 1910).

Hechter, Michael, *Internal Colonialism: The Celtic Fringe in British National Development* (Berkeley and Los Angeles, 1975).

Hennelly, Mark M. '*Waverley* and Romanticism', *Nineteenth-Century Fiction*, 28/2 (1973), 194–209.

Hewitt, David S. (ed.), *Scott on Himself: A Selection of the Autobiographical Writings of Sir Walter Scott*, Association for Scottish Literary Studies 10 (Edinburgh, 1981).

—— 'Scott's Art and Politics', in Alan Bold (ed.), *Sir Walter Scott: The Long-Forgotten Melody* (London, 1983), 43–64.

—— 'Walter Scott', in Douglas Gifford (ed.), *The History of Scottish Literature*, iii (Aberdeen, 1988), 65–87.

Hillhouse, James T., *The Waverley Novels and their Critics* (London, 1936).

Hogg, James, *Memoir of the Author's Life* and *Familiar Anecdotes of Sir Walter Scott*, ed. Douglas S. Mack (Edinburgh, 1972).

—— *Anecdotes of Sir W. Scott*, ed. Douglas S. Mack (Edinburgh, 1983).

—— 'Wat o' the Cleugh', repr. in *James Hogg: 'Poetic Mirrors'*, ed. David Groves, Scottish Studies Centre of the Johannes Gutenberg Universität Mainz in Germersheim 11 (Frankfurt am Main, 1990), 16–46.

Honour, Hugh, *Romanticism* (New York, 1979).

Hook, Andrew, *Scotland and America: A Study of Cultural Relations* (Glasgow, 1975).

Inglis, A. A. H., 'All Change for Edinburgh Waverley: The First Fruits of the New Scott Edition' (review of *The Edinburgh Edition of the Waverley Novels*, 4a, 4b, 11), *Scottish Literary Journal*, supp. 41 (1994), 1–11.

Iser, Wolfgang, *The Implied Reader: Patterns of Communication in Prose Fiction from Bunyan to Beckett* (1972), trans. anon. (Baltimore, 1974).

Jameson, Fredric, *The Political Unconscious: Narrative as a Socially Symbolic Act* (London, 1981).

Johnson, Edgar, *Sir Walter Scott: The Great Unknown*, 2 vols. (London, 1970).

Johnston, Arthur, *Enchanted Ground: The Study of Medieval Romance in the Eighteenth Century* (London, 1964).

Jordan, Frank, 'Chrystal Croftangry, Scott's Last and Best Mask', *Scottish Literary Journal*, 7/1 (1980), 185–92.

—— 'The Vision of Pandemonium in Scott's Novels', *Scottish Literary Journal*, 19/2 (1992), 24–35.

Kelly, Gary, *English Fiction of the Romantic Period 1789–1830*, Longman Literature in English Series (London, 1989).

Kerr, James, *Fiction against History: Scott as Storyteller* (Cambridge, 1989).

Kestner, Joseph, 'Linguistic Transmission in Scott: *Waverley, Old Mortality, Rob Roy*, and *Redgauntlet*', *Wordsworth Circle*, 8 (1977), 333–48.

Kiely, Robert, *The Romantic Novel in England* (Cambridge, Mass., 1972).

Klepetar, Steven F., 'Levels of Narration in *Old Mortality*', *Wordsworth Circle*, 13 (1982), 38–45.

Kroeber, Karl, *Romantic Narrative Art* (Madison, 1960).

Lamont, Claire, 'Scott as Story-Teller: *The Bride of Lammermoor*', *Scottish Literary Journal*, 7/1 (1980), 113–26.

—— '*Waverley* and the Battle of Culloden', *Essays and Studies*, 44 (1991), 14–26.

Lascelles, Mary, *The Story-Teller Retrieves the Past: Historical Fiction and Fictitious History in the Art of Scott, Stevenson, Kipling and Some Others* (Oxford, 1980).

Levine, George, *The Realistic Imagination: English Fiction from Frankenstein to Lady Chatterley* (Chicago, 1981).

Lockhart, John Gibson, *Memoirs of the Life of Sir Walter Scott, Bart.*, 7 vols. (Edinburgh, 1837–8); 2nd edn., 10 vols. (Edinburgh, 1839).

Lukács, Georg, *The Historical Novel* (1937), trans. Hannah and Stanley Mitchell (London, 1962).

Lyons, Martyn, 'The Audience for Romanticism: Walter Scott in France, 1815–51', *European History Quarterly*, 14 (1984), 21–46.

McCracken-Flesher, Caroline, 'Thinking Nationally/Writing Colonially? Scott, Stevenson and England', *Novel*, 24/2 (1991), 296–318.

—— '*Pro Matria Mori*: Gendered Nationalism and Cultural Death in Scott's "The Highland Widow"', *Scottish Literary Journal*, 21/2 (1994), 69–78.

McMaster, Graham, *Scott and Society* (Cambridge, 1981).

—— 'Lévi-Strauss in the Scottish Highlands: A Structuralist Account of Scott's *Lady of the Lake*', *Studies in English Literature* (Tokyo), 61/1 (1983), 3–25.

MacQueen, John, *The Rise of the Historical Novel*, vol. ii of *The Enlightenment and Scottish Literature* (Edinburgh, 1989).

MacNalty, Sir Arthur S., *Sir Walter Scott: The Wounded Falcon* (London, 1969).

Manning, Susan, 'Ossian, Scott, and Nineteenth-Century Scottish Literary Nationalism', *Studies in Scottish Literature*, 17 (1982), 39–54.

—— *The Puritan-Provincial Vision: Scottish and American Literature in the Nineteenth Century*, Cambridge Studies in American Literature and Culture (Cambridge, 1990).

Massie, Allan, 'Scott and the European Novel', in Alan Bold (ed.), *Sir Walter Scott: The Long-Forgotten Melody* (London, 1983), 91–106.

Meisel, Martin, *Realizations: Narrative, Pictorial, and Theatrical Arts in Nineteenth Century England* (Princeton, 1983).

Millgate, Jane, 'Scott and the Dreaming Boy: A Context for *Waverley*', *Review of English Studies*, NS 32 (1981), 286–93.

—— *Walter Scott: The Making of the Novelist* (Edinburgh, 1984).

—— *Scott's Last Edition: A Study in Publishing History* (Edinburgh, 1987).

—— 'Scott the Cunning Tailor: Refurbishing the *Poetical Works*', *Library*, 11 (1989), 336–51.

—— '"Naught of the Bridal": Narrative Resistance in *The Lay of the Last Minstrel*', *Scottish Literary Journal*, 17/2 (1990), 16–26.

Mitchell, Jerome, *The Walter Scott Operas: An Analysis of Operas Based on the Works of Sir Walter Scott* (Tuscaloosa, Ala., 1978).

—— *Scott, Chaucer, and Medieval Romance: A Study in Sir Walter Scott's Indebtedness to the Literature of the Middle Ages* (Lexington, Ky., 1987).

Morgan, Peter F., *Literary Critics and Reviewers in Early 19th-Century Britain* (London, 1983).

Morse, David, *Perspectives on Romanticism: A Transformational Analysis* (London, 1981).

—— 'Scott and the Historical Novel', in his *Romanticism: A Structural Analysis* (London, 1982), 141–88.

Muir, Edwin, *Scott and Scotland: The Predicament of the Scottish Writer* (London, 1936).

Murphy, Peter, *Poetry as an Occupation and an Art in Britain 1760–1830*, Cambridge Studies in Romanticism 3 (Cambridge, 1993).

Nairn, Tom, 'The Three Dreams of Scottish Nationalism', in *Memoirs of a Modern Scotland*, ed. Karl Miller (London, 1970), 34–54.

Nellist, Brian, 'Narrative Modes in the Waverley Novels', in R. T. Davies and B. G. Beatty (eds.), *Literature of the Romantic Period, 1750–1850*, Liverpool English Texts and Studies (Liverpool, 1976), 56–71.

Orr, Marilyn, 'Voices and Text: Scott the Storyteller, Scott the Novelist', *Scottish Literary Journal*, 16/2 (1989), 41–59.

Parsons, Coleman Oscar, *Witchcraft and Demonology in Scott's Fiction: With Chapters on the Supernatural in Scottish Literature* (Edinburgh, 1964).

Peacock, Thomas Love, *Crotchet Castle*, in *Nightmare Abbey and Crotchet Castle*, ed. Raymond Wright, Penguin Classics (Harmondsworth, 1974).

Pearson, Hesketh, *Walter Scott: His Life and Personality* (1954), introd. Allan Massie (London, 1987).

Polhemus, Robert, 'Fatal Love and Eroticizing History: Walter Scott's *The Bride of Lammermoor* (1819)', in his *Erotic Faith: Being in Love from Jane Austen to D. H. Lawrence* (Chicago, 1990), 55–78.

Politi, Jina, 'Narrative and Historical Transformations in *The Bride of Lammermoor*', *Scottish Literary Journal*, 15/1 (1988), 70–81.

Prebble, John, *The King's Jaunt: George IV in Scotland, 1822* (London, 1988).

Punter, David, *The Literature of Terror: A History of Gothic Fictions from 1765 to the Present Day* (London, 1980).

Purkayastha, Pratyush Ranjan, *The Romantics' Third Voice: A Study of the Dramatic Works of the English Romantic Poets*, Salzburg Studies in English Literature: Poetic Drama and Poetic Theory 41 (Salzburg, 1978).

Quayle, Eric, *The Ruin of Sir Walter Scott* (London, 1968).

Reed, James, *Sir Walter Scott: Landscape and Locality* (London, 1980).

Rignall, J. M., 'The Historical Double: *Waverley, Sylvia's Lovers, The Trumpet-Major*', *Essays in Criticism*, 34 (1984), 14–32.

Rignall, J. M., 'Walter Scott, J. G. Farrell, and the Fictions of Empire', *Essays in Criticism*, 41 (1991), 11–27.

Robertson, Fiona, *Legitimate Histories: Scott, Gothic, and the Authorities of Fiction* (Oxford, 1994).

—— 'Copied-Text: The New Edinburgh Waverleys', *Review of English Studies*, NS 47 (1996), 59–65.

—— *Scott*, in *Lives of the Great Romantics by their Contemporaries*, 2nd ser. vol. iii (London, 1997).

Ross, Marlon B., 'Scott's Chivalric Pose: The Function of Metrical Romance in the Romantic Period', *Genre*, 19 (1986), 267–97.

—— 'Romancing the Nation-State: The Poetics of Romantic Nationalism', in Jonathan Arac and Harriet Ritvo (eds.), *Macropolitics of Nineteenth-Century Literature: Nationalism, Exoticism, Imperialism* (Philadelphia, 1991), 56–85.

Rubenstein, Jill, 'The Dilemma of History: A Reading of Scott's *Bridal of Triermain*', *Studies in English Literature*, 12/4 (1972), 721–34.

—— 'Scott's *Journal* and its Critics', *Wordsworth Circle*, 9 (1978a), 200–8.

—— *Sir Walter Scott: A Reference Guide*, A Reference Publication in Literature, ed. Marilyn Gaull (Boston, 1978b).

—— *Sir Walter Scott: An Annotated Bibliography of Scholarship and Criticism 1975–1990*, Association for Scottish Literary Studies Occasional Papers 11 (Aberdeen, n.d.).

Said, Edward W., *Orientalism* (London, 1978).

Scott, Paul Henderson, *Walter Scott and Scotland* (Edinburgh, 1981).

Senior, Nassau, 'Sir Walter Scott', in his *Essays on Fiction* (London, 1864), 1–188.

Shaw, Harry E., *The Forms of Historical Fiction: Sir Walter Scott and his Successors* (Ithaca, NY, 1983).

—— 'Scott's "Daemon" and the Voices of Historical Narration', *Journal of English and Germanic Philology*, 88 (1989), 21–33.

Simmons, Clare A., 'A Man of Few Words: The Romantic Orang-Outang and Scott's *Count Robert of Paris*', *Scottish Literary Journal*, 17/1 (1990a), 21–34.

—— *Reversing the Conquest: History and Myth in Nineteenth-Century British Literature* (New Brunswick, NJ, 1990b).

Sroka, Kenneth M., 'Wealth and Illth in *St Ronan's Well*', *Scottish Literary Journal*, 7/1 (1980), 167–84.

—— 'Scott's Aesthetic Parable: A Study of *Old Mortality*'s Two-Part Structure', *Essays in Literature* (Maccomb, Ill.), 10 (1983), 183–97.

—— 'Fairy Castles and Character in *Woodstock*', *Essays in Literature*, 14 (1987), 189–205.

Stein, Richard L., 'Historical Fiction and the Implied Reader: Scott and Iser', *Novel*, 14 (1981), 213–31.

Stephen, Sir Leslie, 'Hours in a Library No. 3: Some Words about Sir Walter Scott', *Cornhill Magazine*, 24 (Sept. 1871), 278–93.

Stone, Donald D., *The Romantic Impulse in Victorian Fiction* (Cambridge, Mass., 1980).

Sultana, Donald E., '*The Siege of Malta*' Rediscovered: An Account of Sir Walter Scott's Mediterranean Journey and his Last Novel* (Edinburgh, 1977).

—— *The Journey of Sir Walter Scott to Malta* (New York, 1986).

—— *From Abbotsford to Paris and Back: Sir Walter Scott's Journey of 1815* (Stroud, 1993).

Sutherland, John, *The Life of Walter Scott: A Critical Biography* (Oxford, 1995).

Sutherland, Kathryn, 'Fictional Economies: Adam Smith, Walter Scott and the Nineteenth-Century Novel', *English Literary History*, 54 (1987), 97–127.

Tait, Margaret, 'Film Archaeology: Scott on the Cinema Screen', *Scott Newsletter*, 10 (1987), 16–19.

Thackeray, William Makepeace, *Rebecca and Rowena* (London, 1850).

Trevor-Roper, Hugh, 'The Invention of Tradition: The Highland Tradition of Scotland', in E. Hobsbawm and T. Ranger (eds.), *The Invention of Tradition* (Cambridge, 1983), 15–43.

Trumpener, Katie, 'National Character, Nationalistic Plots, National Tale and Historical Novel in the Age of *Waverley*, 1806–30', *English Literary History*, 60 (1993), 685–731.

Tulloch, Graham, *The Language of Sir Walter Scott: A Study of his Scottish and Period Language* (London, 1980).

Twain, Mark [Samuel Langhorne Clemens], *Life on the Mississippi* (1883), introd. James M. Cox (New York, 1984).

—— *The Adventures of Huckleberry Finn* (1884), ed. and introd. Peter Coveney (Harmondsworth, 1966).

Wallace, Tara Ghoshal, 'Walter Scott and Feminine Discourse: The Case of *St Ronan's Well*', *Journal of Narrative Technique*, 19 (1989), 233–47.

Waswo, Richard, 'Story as Historiography in the Waverley Novels', *English Literary History*, 47 (1980), 304–30.

Weinstein, Mark A. (ed.), *The Prefaces to the Waverley Novels* (Lincoln, Nebr., 1978).

Welsh, Alexander, *The Hero of the Waverley Novels with New Essays on Scott* (Princeton, 1992; 1st pub. New Haven, 1963).

White, Hayden, *Metahistory: The Historical Imagination in Nineteenth-Century Europe* (Baltimore, 1973).

Wilson, A. N., *The Laird of Abbotsford: A View of Sir Walter Scott* (Oxford, 1980).

Wilt, Judith, *Secret Leaves: The Novels of Walter Scott* (Chicago, 1985).

Wittig, Kurt, *The Scottish Tradition in Literature* (Edinburgh, 1958).

Woolf, Virginia, 'Gas at Abbotsford' and 'The Antiquary', from *The Moment*, repr. in her *Collected Essays*, 4 vols. (London, 1966–7), i. 134–43.

Worth, Christopher, ' "A very nice Theatre at Edinr.": Sir Walter Scott and Control of the Theatre Royal', *Theatre Research International*, 17/2 (1992), 86–95.

12. *Jane Austen*

FIONA STAFFORD

TEXTS

Although Jane Austen's earliest surviving writings date from the late 1780s, her first published novel was *Sense and Sensibility*, which appeared in three volumes in 1811. By 1813 all the copies had sold, so Thomas Egerton published a second, revised, edition; the same year also saw the appearance of the first and second editions of *Pride and Prejudice*. *Mansfield Park* followed in 1814, but since Egerton was reluctant to authorize a further edition, the rights were bought by John Murray who published *Emma* late in 1815 (title-page dated 1816) and the second edition of *Mansfield Park* in 1816. After the death of Jane Austen, *Northanger Abbey* and *Persuasion* were published as a four-volume set in 1818, together with a 'Biographical Notice' written by her elder brother, Henry. There were no further English editions until 1833, when Richard Bentley published all the novels in his Standard Novels series. The first scholarly edition was R. W. Chapman's *The Novels of Jane Austen*, which came out in five volumes in 1923 and established the texts, based on collations of the early editions, that were to provide the basis of numerous subsequent editions. Of the recent popular editions, the New Penguin texts have been edited directly from the first editions; this is particularly significant in the cases of *Sense and Sensibility* and *Mansfield Park*, since all previous texts had used the second editions. Many of the twentieth-century editions of Austen's novels retain their value because of the distinguished writers who have contributed introductory essays. (For full details of the original texts, and numerous subsequent editions, see David Gilson, *A Bibliography of Jane Austen* (Oxford, 1982).)

The rapid appearance of Austen's novels has often been attributed to the idea (preserved by Austen's family) of versions of *Pride and Prejudice*, *Sense and Sensibility*, and *Northanger Abbey* having been written in the 1790s; any such early drafts are lost, however, and their form has been disputed. The manuscripts of the published novels, too, were destroyed after typesetting, although two cancelled chapters of *Persuasion* and a draft title-page for *Northanger Abbey* survive in manuscript. There are a number of minor works, not published in Austen's lifetime, which have since appeared in print. In 1868, her verses on Mrs Lefroy appeared in Sir John Henry Lefroy's *Notes and Documents Relating to the Family of Loffroy*, and were also included, together with some other short poems and the 'Plan of a Novel', in James Edward Austen-Leigh's *A Memoir of Jane Austen* of 1870. In the following year, the second edition of the *Memoir* included 'The Mystery', *The Watsons*, *Lady Susan*, parts of *Sanditon*, and the cancelled chapter of *Persuasion*, while William and Richard Arthur Austen-Leigh's *Jane Austen: Her Life and Letters* (1913) published the 'Opinions of *Emma*'. *Sanditon* first appeared in full in 1925 as *Fragment of a Novel*, edited by R. W. Chapman (like the other fragments, and indeed the major novels, it has inspired continuations by other writers which, though hardly conventional criticism, are often interesting responses to the texts).

Apart from 'The Mystery', and an 1895 edition of *Charades*, Austen's juvenilia did not begin to appear until 1922 when *Love and Freindship* was published, with a preface by G. K. Chesterton. The early collections were gradually published in their entirety as *Volume the First* (1933), *Volume the Third* (1951), and *Volume the Second* (1963) (the last edited by B. C. Southam rather than Chapman). *Three Evening Prayers* was published in San Francisco in 1940, while other poems were collected together with the rest of the minor works for the sixth volume of R. W. Chapman's Oxford edition, which appeared in 1954. The unexpected appearance in 1977 of Jane Austen's play *Sir Charles Grandison* led to a new edition, transcribed and edited by Brian Southam in 1980. Various paperback selections from the *Minor Works* have since appeared, but the most useful recent edition is the World's Classics *Catharine and Other Writings*, edited from the manuscripts by Margaret Anne Doody and Douglas Murray. (For details of Austen's manuscripts, see B. C. Southam, *Jane Austen's Literary Manuscripts: A Study of the Novelist's Development through the Surviving Papers*, Oxford, 1964.)

Although Austen was a prolific correspondent, only 161 of her letters survive, and some of these only through copies. Both Henry Austen and James Edward Austen-Leigh used material from the letters for their biographies, but it was not until 1884 that Edward Knatchbull-Hugessen, the first Baron Brabourne (and son of Austen's niece Fanny Knight), produced the two-volume *Letters of Jane Austen*. This was superseded in 1932 by R. W. Chapman's *Jane Austen's Letters to her Sister Cassandra and Others*, which was slightly revised and expanded for the second edition of 1952. Deirdre Le Faye's new edition *Jane Austen's Letters* (1995) includes not only further material that has emerged since 1952, but also full details of the letters, their provenance, and the numerous people and places mentioned in the correspondence. A facsimile edition containing 'reproductions of every known extant letter, fragment, and autograph copy' was prepared by Jo Modert in 1990.

CRITICISM

When Dale Spender published her pioneering study *Mothers of the Novel: 100 Good Women Writers before Jane Austen* in 1986, the implication was plain: Jane Austen's reputation, unlike those of so many of her female predecessors, had suffered no serious decline in the centuries following her death. Spender's title alludes to Austen's curious status as a 'watershed' figure in English literary history; hailed by George Saintsbury as 'the mother of the English novel in the nineteenth century', and subsequently canonized by F. R. Leavis as the first of the 'Great Tradition' of English novelists, Austen has frequently been singled out to mark the point at which the experimental form of the eighteenth century matured into the classic nineteenth-century novel. Her popular standing has also been cemented by film and television adaptations, by mass paperback editions, and by the perennial appearances of her novels as 'set texts' for A level examinations. If some women writers have been unfairly neglected by twentieth-century readers, Jane Austen is not of their number.

Indeed, when Austen *has* inspired defences from twentieth-century critics, they have often been motivated by a desire to rescue her from her admirers rather than from oblivion. Fay Weldon, for example, made a public denunciation of 'England's Jane' on Channel Four's *J'Accuse* programme in November 1991, but despite the standard gibes at Austen's failure to comment on current affairs, it was more the popular image of Jane Austen that came under fire than the novels themselves. The work of Austen, like that of the Society for the Preservation of Rural England, was seen to represent an image of an elegant English past, where anything distasteful (sex, war, poverty, politics) was carefully excluded.

Weldon's iconoclasm has, however, a distinguished critical heritage. Her comments are reminiscent of Henry James's 'dear, everybody's dear, Jane', or Virginia Woolf's desire (1936) to write an essay on Austen's coarseness ('The people who talk of her as a niminy-piminy spinster always annoy me'), or indeed, of a host of critics in the 1940s. Richard Aldington's introduction to the Chawton edition, for example, begins with a dismissal of the 'gushing heroine-worship' of her 'cheer-boys' (Macaulay, Newman, Tennyson, Arnold Bennett, and Saintsbury); but his own preference for Austen's 'epigrammatic disillusionment' and 'deadly comment on human nature' is in fact characteristic of the contemporary critical trend spearheaded by the influential journal *Scrutiny*.

Here Q. D. Leavis developed her 'Critical Theory of Jane Austen' which, in direct response to 'the conventional account of Miss Austen as prim, demure, prudish and so on', presented her as a serious author, whose work represented the culmination of years of writing and rewriting and should be read in terms of its literary achievement. Even more provocative was the psychoanalyst

D. W. Harding's assertion that 'Austen's books are, as she meant them to be, read and enjoyed by precisely the sort of people whom she disliked', especially as he then applied the famous description of Mrs Bennet ('a woman of mean understanding, little information and uncertain temper') to the 'complacent readers' of Austen's novels, from her own acquaintances to the present day.

If Aldington's celebration of Austen's 'epigrammatic disillusion' was aimed at the distinguished enthusiasts who had compared her to Shakespeare or Homer, Harding's exposure of her 'regulated hatred' attempted to counter those who found her novels havens of comic tranquillity (or, as G. K. Chesterton had put it, 'The novels of Jane Austen | Are the ones to get lost in'). Elizabeth Jenkins's otherwise fine *Jane Austen: A Biography* (1938) had opened with a paean of praise for the 'vanished loveliness' of the eighteenth century, while the turn-of-the-century gift sets of the novels, with their attractive Hugh Thomson or C. E. Brock illustrations, all contributed to sealing Austen in a remote rural past of elegant frocks and country strolls. Indeed, Harding's essay takes as its starting point a quotation from Beatrice Kean Seymour's recent *Jane Austen: Study for a Portrait*:

In a society which has enthroned the machine-gun and carried it aloft even into the quiet heavens, there will always be men and women—Escapist or not, as you please—who will turn to her novels with an unending sense of relief and thankfulness.

For Harding, such 'Escapist' attitudes were the source of serious misinterpretations, since readers were being encouraged to gloss over those odd sentences or subclauses that threatened to disturb their perceptions of her reassuring world.

In the context of the Second World War, Harding's rigorous analysis of Austen's less benign aspects was overtly polemical. It was, after all, to *Pride and Prejudice* that Winston Churchill turned to for relief from the Blitz ('What calm lives they had, those people!'). May 1940 had also seen the foundation of the Jane Austen Society, devoted to preserving the author's home at Chawton. Sheila Kaye-Smith and G. B. Stern's hugely popular *Talking of Jane Austen*, printed on wartime paper in 1943, gives some sense of the appeal of Austen to contemporary readers, with its poignant 'there is so little of death, in Jane'. Perhaps this was one of the reasons why H. Brett-Smith, when working in a hospital during the First World War, had recommended the works of Austen for the severely shell-shocked, or why Rudyard Kipling had created his secret society of Austen readers in the trenches, in his extraordinary short story 'The Janeites'.

To publish an article unsympathetic to Jane Austen during the Second World War was thus daring indeed; and the impact of Harding's undeferential approach is obvious from R. W. Chapman's *Jane Austen: A Critical Bibliography*. Chapman, the devoted editor and author of the unassuming, but invaluable, *Jane Austen: Facts and Problems*, refused to allocate individual entries to

D. W. Harding, Reuben Brower, or Marvin Mudrick, observing that 'I group these essays in iconoclasm . . . as seeming to issue from a common view, and that one with which I am so out of sympathy that I do not trust myself to discriminate'. Brower's 'The Controlling Hand: Jane Austen and *Pride and Prejudice*' had also appeared in *Scrutiny*, but it was Marvin Mudrick who (thought Chapman), finding Austen 'as hard-boiled as her Emma', had caused the most distress by publishing an entire book on the subject.

Mudrick's seminal study, *Jane Austen: Irony as Defense and Discovery*, took its epigraph from 'Regulated Hatred' and, like Harding's essay, presented itself as a reaction, this time against the 'mass of cosy family adulation, self-glorifying impressionistic picking-at à la Woolf and Forster, and nostalgic latter-day enshrinements of the author as the gentle-hearted chronicler of the Regency order'. For the post-war American critic, it was not so much the 'Escapist' Jane that aggravated as the saintly Aunt, whose reputation had been fostered in the nineteenth century by the series of memoirs, records, and reminiscences produced by her nephews and nieces. In place of this Victorian view of 'dear Aunt Jane', Mudrick posed a distinctly ungentle-hearted writer, whose irony served as a defence against her society and her own deeper feelings.

Mudrick's polemics in turn provoked comment from those more sympathetic to Austen, such as Lionel Trilling, whose introduction to the Riverside edition of *Emma* raised a polite eyebrow at Professor Mudrick and suggested that the warmth expressed by Austen's admirers might in fact be stimulated by the work itself 'in some unusual promise that it seems to make, in some hope that it holds out'. Trilling was thus defending the notion of Austen's England (and specifically Highbury) as idyllic, but in a thoughtful, learned account that related *Emma* to Schiller's definition of the idyll, and to Shakespeare's pastoral comedy.

Rather less muted was John Bayley's address to the Jane Austen Society in 1967, which followed Trilling's criticism of Mudrick but went on to voice vigorously anti-iconoclastic opinions: 'She bothered Professor Garrod: she got under his skin: in re-reading her he discovered something about his own outlook on life that made it urgently necessary to depreciate hers' (*Jane Austen Society Report for the Year 1967*). By implication, the defensiveness perceived by Marvin Mudrick revealed more about the critic than the subject.

With the recent reassessment of the *Scrutiny* project, too, it is possible, perhaps, to detect in the choice of essays on Austen an editorial desire to set apart the literary critic from the mass of readers who might read their Jane lovingly and voraciously, but not intelligently. The evocation of a popular Austen cult also served as a useful rhetorical device to emphasize the radical nature of the readings about to be presented. But, as Brian Southam points out in the second volume of his *Jane Austen: The Critical Heritage*, the Scrutineers' account of the traditional view of Austen was itself a 'critical fiction', misleading to readers and showing a blatant disregard for the numerous and varied views of Austen that already existed ('Had Mrs Leavis read the *Memoir* reviews . . . she would have seen that her series of articles was not an act of revelation, but of reclamation'). With the publication of the juvenilia in the 1920s, and the (even more startling) *Letters* in 1932, any lingering Victorian notions about Austen's primness had largely been exploded, while 1939 had seen the publication of the book that is now widely regarded as the starting point of serious Austen criticism: Mary Lascelles's *Jane Austen and her Art*. Though written with all the admiration of the most devoted Janeite, Mary Lascelles's work (discussed more fully below) is a brilliant analysis of the writer's art and, as such, did not fit the Harding/Leavis/Mudrick caricatures of existing criticism.

The desire to clear the decks of earlier critics before attempting to write on Austen is, nevertheless, understandable, given the vast secondary literature devoted to her work. The very list of her admirers—Scott, Coleridge, Sheridan, Tennyson, Macaulay, Lewes, Trollope, James, Forster, Woolf, Wharton, Chesterton, Kipling, Auden, Lodge, Drabble—is quite enough to provoke a perverse need to find fault, if only to say something different. Austen has, in a sense, produced a critical 'anxiety of influence', as Walton Litz observed after rereading the entire corpus in preparation for *The Jane Austen Handbook*: 'how difficult it is to say anything startlingly new about her art (most modern criticism plays variations on themes uncovered by her nineteenth-century critics)' (*Jane Austen Society Report for 1985*).

This is, perhaps, unduly pessimistic, given the way in which readings of Austen, as of so many other apparently familiar writers, have been affected by the explosion of new critical approaches in the 1980s and 1990s, but Litz's comment is interesting in that he shares Southam's respect for nineteenth-century critics. Far from consisting merely of 'gushing heroine-worship', the comments of early critics are often perceptive and sensitive to issues that continue to preoccupy readers of today. With the help of the *Critical Heritage* volumes edited by Brian Southam, and the bibliographies compiled by Chapman, Gilson, Roth, and Weinsheimer, it is possible to perceive not only general trends in critical attitudes, but also genealogies for particular critical ideas.

The publication of James Austen-Leigh's *Memoir*, for example, gave rise to both the purple praises of Anne Thackeray ('Dear Anne Elliot!—sweet, impulsive, womanly, tenderhearted—') *and* the most perceptive piece of Austen criticism to emerge from the nineteenth century: Richard Simpson's anonymous review in the *North British Review*. Simpson, a distinguished Renaissance scholar, used his essay to point out Austen's characteristic strengths—her 'manifest irony', her 'critical faculty', her perception of the individual as part of society, and her celebration of 'intelligent love'—and in doing so anticipated many of the points developed by subsequent critics. He also observed that her work 'has all the minute attention to detail of the most accomplished miniature-painter', an idea that may have been influenced by G. H. Lewes's important *Blackwood's* article of 1859 where Austen's 'miniatures' were compared with Scott's 'frescoes', or may have derived from the *Memoir* itself, since James Edward Austen-Leigh had drawn a parallel between the work of Jane Austen and that of Sir William Ross, the great early nineteenth-century miniaturist. Austen-Leigh's own comment probably had its origins in a letter he had received from his aunt in December 1816, in which she made the flattering, if teasing, contrast between his 'strong, manly sketches' and her own 'little bit (two Inches wide) of Ivory'. The notion of Austen the miniaturist has also been explored by twentieth-century readers, such as Herbert Read and Samuel Alexander in the 1920s, and more recently Mark Hennelly, Lance Bertelson, Grant Holly, and John Dussinger, while the more general analogy between her art and that of the painter has inspired not only a long tradition of critical imagery, but also entire articles such as those by Katrin Burlin and Peter Sabor. Whether or not each critic has been aware of earlier responses is perhaps unimportant, but the existence of recurrent motifs in Austen criticism indicates not only the aspects of her work that have most frequently attracted discussion, but also the critical assumptions that have informed the comments.

Although, for a late twentieth-century critic such as Mark Hennelly, Austen's 'bit of Ivory' is complicated by Romantic aesthetics and epistemology, in the nineteenth century the use of the painting analogy generally reveals a more straightforward assumption that Austen's art is mimetic, and that her chief strength lies in the accurate depiction of the world she knew well. This was Scott's main point when he wrote the first major review of her work for the *Quarterly Review*: 'The author's knowledge of the world, and the peculiar tact with which she presents characters that the reader cannot fail to recognize, reminds us something of the Flemish school of painting.' Half a century later, Goldwin Smith, reviewing the *Memoir*, was similarly struck: 'She painted English society as it was, in all its features'; while S. F. Malden, writing one of the earliest books on Austen, praised the 'life-like pictures of human beings who are immortal in their truth to nature'.

As the period represented by Austen became more remote, Scott's approach began to metamorphose into two distinct critical traditions—one that saw Austen's ability to portray convincing characters as evidence of her universal appeal, the other preferring to set her in relation to her age and find in her novels realistic depictions of a distinctive historical period.

The favourite nineteenth-century comparison between Austen and Shakespeare was part of the former response, typified by G. H. Lewes, that admired the writer's 'power of constructing and animating character' and found the novels to be filled with living men and women, whose personalities and experiences afforded endless delight to readers of any age. Closely related is the recurrent emphasis on Austen's moral vision, and when A. C. Bradley addressed the question of her affinities with Shakespeare, he celebrated both her comedy and her morality ('in her justice, she is quite Shakespearian'). This preoccupation with an inherent moral seriousness, which informs not only the nineteenth-century critics but also many of the major twentieth-century comments (notably those of F. R. Leavis, Lionel Trilling, Mark Schorer, Andrew Wright, Edgar Shannon, Ian Watt, Alistair Duckworth, Susan Morgan, Jan Fergus), may be discussed in relation to earlier writers or to eighteenth-century social, religious, and philosophical ideas, but nevertheless retains a sense that the modern reader may somehow be edified by Austen's work: that human nature is essentially unchanging, and that Austen's 'moral vision', emerging through the accurate representation of human nature, must always be relevant.

And this appreciation of her universality has frequently been linked to the admiration of her skill as an artist, as can be seen in Reginald Farrer's fascinating essay of 1917 which, though still emphasizing Austen's reliance on personal observation ('On the feelings of her men, of course, Jane Austen has nothing to say at first hand, is too honest an artist to invent'), nevertheless celebrates *Emma* as the 'culminating figure of English high-comedy' and argues for an Austen whose art transcends history. For Virginia Woolf, too, reviewing W. and R. A. Austen-Leigh's *Jane Austen: The Life and Letters* in 1913, the art of Jane Austen is that of the creator rather than the mere copier: 'she fills every inch of her canvas with observation, fashions every sentence into meaning, stuffs up every chink and cranny of the fabric until each novel is a little living world, from which you cannot break off a scene or even a sentence without bleeding it of some of its life.' The point is made more explicitly by the philosopher Samuel Alexander, whose 1928 lecture on Austen rejected the notion that her art was 'mere faithful description' and argued instead for her powers of design and the transforming power of her humour ('The truth which the artist conveys is not altogether the truth which he discovers, but which he makes').

These were the views that paved the way for Mary Lascelles's extended analysis of *Jane Austen and her Art*, where the only significant context for the novels is that of literary history (although it opens with a brief biography, the real interest in Austen's life is her development as a writer—and her responses to what she read). Her discussions of the structure of the novels, and the complicated interweaving of plot, dialogue, narration, and dramatic effects, set new standards for close reading, and were followed by critics such as Reuben Brower, Andrew Wright, Howard Babb, Wendy Craik, Barbara Hardy, Yasmine Gooneratne, Jane Nardin, and Bruce Stovel, who have variously drawn attention to the formal patterns, rhythms, and oppositions in Austen's novels, as well as to her development of free indirect discourse and irony.

Lascelles's elegant, if sometimes donnish, analysis is also alert to both Austen's debts *and* the ways in which she ironized or excelled her favourite authors ('Fanny Burney takes pains to be ridiculous. Her followers are often merely slovenly. Jane Austen neither strains after grandiloquence nor slips into slovenliness. She practises but one grammatical irregularity which is uncomfortable to the ear now—what may be called the dislocated clause'). The range of literary reference is very extensive and, by revealing Austen's affinities with Burney, Pope, Richardson, and Johnson, Mary Lascelles did much to quash the Jamesian view of Austen as natural genius (i.e. amateur), even as she drew on his aesthetic theory for her own analysis of the narrative.

The emphasis on Austen's reading has also been underlined by numerous subsequent critics. Unlike the combative tone of the dialogue between the iconoclasts and the Janeites, however, the contributions to the general understanding of Austen's literary debts have been more conscious of a team effort, as the work of successive editors has been augmented by short notes and essays on particular allusions. Thus Elizabeth Nollen's essay on the significance for *Sense and Sensibility* of Ann Radcliffe's *A Sicilian Romance* begins by acknowledging the importance of Walton Litz's *Jane Austen: A Study in her Artistic Development* (1965), which had found sources for the same novel in Elizabeth Inchbald's *Nature and Art*, Jane West's *A Gossip's Story*, and Maria Edgeworth's *Letters of Julia and Caroline*. (Ironically, Martin Melander had begun his own 1950 essay on *A Gossip's Story* and *Sense and Sensibility* by acknowledging a hint from Joyce Tompkins's *The Popular Novel in England*, but was apparently unaware of her subsequent expansion of the hint in an article of 1940, 'Elinor and Marianne: A Note on Jane Austen'.)

In addition to the mass of short notes on allusive (and often elusive) phrases, there have also been important studies devoted entirely to Austen's engagement with earlier texts. In 1966, Frank W. Bradbrook attempted to bring some order to the apparently miscellaneous nature of Austen's reading by dividing his invaluable *Jane Austen and her Predecessors* into generically titled chapters ('Periodicals', 'Moralists in Prose', 'The Picturesque' . . .) and linking the novels to a host of eighteenth-century works. Further debts were uncovered in Kenneth Moler's *Jane Austen's Art of Allusion*, which focused more exclusively on the fictional and didactic context to suggest links between Austen's early parodies and the mature novels in their borrowings and inversions of familiar narrative patterns. More recently Jocelyn Harris's *Jane Austen's Art of Memory* has argued that Austen's novels are permeated by her reading, and discusses the ways in which each of them is shaped by earlier texts. Harris's extended discussion of the significance of *A Midsummer Night's Dream* to *Emma* has moved a long way from Macaulay's hearty comparison between Austen and Shakespeare, and the nineteenth-century celebration of their respective abilities to create 'real' characters.

For those who have followed Scott's admiration for Austen's accurate representations of the world, but whose interest is as much attracted by the 'world' as by the representation, the critical literature is also vast. Throughout the twentieth century, readers have been fascinated by Austen's historical surroundings, intrigued at first, perhaps, by the possibility of linking her life with her work, or merely by the notorious charms of Regency England, but informed more recently by the historicist tendency of academic criticism.

The hagiographic publications of the Austen family, despite their pervasive emphasis on the quietness of Aunt Jane's life, encouraged interest in the biographical elements of the novels by providing information that could be related to the texts. Numerous accounts have followed Henry Austen's 'Biographical Notice' and his nephew's *Memoir*, but the evidence has led to very different interpretations. For David Cecil, Austen is the very model for Elizabeth Bennet and Emma: pretty, witty, and wise, and blessed with a respectable family in the south of England. Jane Aiken Hodge, however, adopted a more gloomy, psychological approach to the 'Double Life' of Jane Austen, finding beneath the polished surface of her novels the 'depth and bitterness' of a painful and frustrating personal history ('She had the gift of laughter; and she needed it'). Park Honan's *Jane Austen: Her Life* is a well-balanced, comprehensive account, which uses the biographical information judiciously to shed light on the novels and present a convincing picture of the writer's development, but it is likely to be superseded by David Nokes's forthcoming biography.

Among the earliest readers to move beyond the immediate creation of context through reminiscence and correspondence were Constance and Ellen Hill, who undertook a literary pilgrimage to 'see places where she dwelt, to look upon the scenes that she had looked upon, and to learn all that could be learned of her surroundings'. Their account of the journey, complete with line drawings of Bath, Lyme Regis, and Chawton, started the trend for the study of Austen and place, which has been manifest in the particular (Jean Freeman, *Jane Austen in Bath*; David Waldron Smithers, *Jane Austen in Kent*; Graham Sparkes, *Jane Austen: Her Hampshire Days*) and the more general (Anne-Marie Edwards, *In the Steps of Jane Austen*). Less insistently biographical is Maggie Lane's *Jane Austen's England*, which sets the familiar sites in a larger historical context of Enclosure Acts, picturesque theory, and landscape gardening, illustrating Austen's concerns through carefully selected contemporary engravings and passages of poetry.

The use of contemporary illustrations was, of course, pioneered by R. W. Chapman's edition of the *Novels* with their now rather quaint plates of 'Parisian Head Dresses', 'Fashionable Furniture', or 'The Five Positions of Dancing', which made an interest in the social history of the early nineteenth century part of the reading experience. Numerous books and pamphlets have followed, giving information on the music, menus, clergymen, clothes, education, etiquette, seaside, and stoves of Jane Austen's day, and shedding varying degrees of light on the novels from which they take their subjects.

Despite the steady stream of social-historical material, however, the old view of Austen's art as being untouched by the particular—and in particular, the political—persisted. Austen-Leigh's pronouncement that 'she never touched upon politics, law, or medicine' has been repeated by numerous critics, reaching its most extreme form in David Aers's denunciation of both Austen's ignorance of contemporary events and her uncritical acceptance of the prevailing Tory ideology of the class to which she belonged. Ironically, Aers's attack is itself a reaction to the more sophisticated approaches to the relationship between text and context that had begun to emerge in the 1970s.

Alistair Duckworth's *The Improvement of the Estate*, for example, had not concentrated exclusively on the estates visited by Austen herself, but rather on the eighteenth-century discourse of landscape gardening, in order to ground its discussion of individualism in the images of the estates that 'function not only as the settings of action but as indexes to the character and social responsibility of their owners'. *Mansfield Park* thus becomes a key text, embodying Burkian values of tradition and social responsibility in the face of an alarming new world of false improvements, theatricality, and social disorder. (Although the paperback edition of 1994 warns the reader to beware of one or two outdated attitudes, Duckworth, perhaps appropriately, stands by his original interpretation of Austen as a conservative writer, despite challenges by other critics.)

The political context of Austen's work was also explored thoroughly by Marilyn Butler, whose *Jane Austen and the War of Ideas* follows Duckworth's view of the conservative Austen, but through a discussion of the immediate literary context. Rather than tracing literary allusions, however, Butler approaches the immediate fictional predecessors as political writers, in order to demonstrate the 'partisan' nature of Austen's own novels, where the persistent assimilation of the individual into society is 'expressive of the conservative side in an active war of ideas'.

Butler's work was thus important not only in helping to demolish the old view of Austen as an apolitical writer, but also in its insistence that the fiction of Austen's day was inherently political, thus encouraging a reconciliation between formal and contextual approaches. Her view of Austen's reaction against sentimentality, for example, can be seen in the background of Nicola Watson's later discussion of the abandonment of letter fiction with its dangerous Jacobin associations, in favour of the characteristic Austenian third-person narrative, in *Revolution and the Form of the British Novel, 1785–1825*. Nancy Armstrong and Maaja Stewart, too, though influenced more by Foucault, Bakhtin, and Jameson, have analysed Austen's 'domestic fiction' in relation to the social history of women, and the challenge to traditional male power structures, while Franco Moretti sees *Pride and Prejudice* as a *Bildungsroman*, a form defined by the period in which it emerged: as a literature of process, compelled by the 'accelerated pace of history'.

These developments were anticipated by David Monaghan's collection, *Jane Austen in a Social Context*, which was explicitly influenced by the social criticism of the 1970s and a belief in the 'relationship between literary form and the structure of the social environment in which it is developed', although the theoretical allegiance is modified by an emphasis on the continuing importance of historical detail ('the full complexity of Jane Austen's social vision would be revealed as a result of a cumulative process'). The collection brought together not only literary critics (Nina Auerbach, Ann Banfield, Marilyn Butler, Jan Fergus, Jane Nardin, Leroy Smith, Patricia Spacks, Tony Tanner) each with an individual view of the relationship between text and context, but also included an essay by the historian Christopher Kent, who suggested that the attitudes of literary critics to Austen's 'historical dimensions' has more to do with 'limitations in their conceptions of history . . . than limitations in her art'. Kent's view harks back to the old mimetic tradition, but makes its case not by assertions and pictorial metaphors, but by illuminating tiny details of the text through reference to the 'consumer history' of the Industrial Revolution. It is an approach similar to that of Warren Roberts in *Jane Austen and the French Revolution* and finds a more recent, and rather more sophisticated, proponent in Roger Sales, whose *Jane Austen and Representations of Regency England* is a masterpiece of contextualization.

Among the apparently minor historical details that have gradually come to be seen as major interpretative cruces is Sir Thomas Bertram's visit to Antigua in *Mansfield Park*. In the 1960s, Brian Southam pointed out to the Jane Austen Society that George Austen had been a trustee for a plantation in Antigua, and that Francis Austen had visited the island in June 1805, while Avrom Fleishman devoted a few pages of his *A Reading of Mansfield Park* to the significance for Sir Thomas Bertram of the economic crisis in Antigua in 1805–7 and the contemporary abolition movement. These points were absorbed into Warren Roberts's account of the historical context in 1979, while Selma James also linked Sir Thomas's activities with the slave trade and the subjection of women. But it was not until colonialism became a more urgent critical issue that *Mansfield Park* began to be perceived, in Moira Ferguson's words, as 'a post-abolition narrative'. Although Edward Said has condemned Austen ('who in *Mansfield Park* sublimates the agonies of Caribbean existence to a mere half-dozen passing references to Antigua') others, such as Margaret Kirkham, have celebrated the novel's radical spirit, citing not only Austen's admiration for the abolitionist Thomas Clarkson, but also her title, carefully chosen to evoke the famous 'Mansfield Judgment' of 1772, which upheld the rights of the black slave James Somerset.

Margaret Kirkham's insights into slavery are bound up with her central emphasis on feminism, and her belief that Austen's 'individual talent' must be considered 'in its collective, feminist context'. The notion of Austen as primarily a woman was, of course, not new, given her inclusion in Mrs Elwood's *Memoirs of the Literary Ladies of England*, of 1843. Sarah Tytler's otherwise rather bland, late Victorian, account of Jane Austen is also alert to the position of women in the novels and expresses anxiety that the list of 'distinguished admirers of Miss Austen's books' is predominantly male. In *A Room of one's Own*, Virginia Woolf famously attributed to Jane Austen the invention of a feminine sentence ('a perfectly natural, shapely sentence, proper to her own use'), while Rebecca West linked Austen's 'feminism' to the scepticism of French eighteenth-century thought ('it is surely not a coincidence that a country gentlewoman should sit down and put the institutions of a society regarding women through the most gruelling criticism they ever received, just at the time when Europe was generally following Voltaire and Rousseau').

Half a century later, as feminism became a dominant force in literary studies, Austen criticism turned more and more on the question of her gender. Sandra Gilbert and Susan Gubar included Austen in *The Madwoman in the Attic* and, while arguing for a largely conservative figure limited by her circumstances, also pointed to some of the less overt elements in her novels, where a more resistant female voice could be found. Despite the influential contemporary arguments for the conservative Austen, a more subversive figure began to emerge once more, whose power derived not from her 'regulated hatred' or defensive irony, but from her sceptical attitude towards patriarchy. The 1980s witnessed an explosion of feminist readings, such as Mary Poovey's influential *The Proper Lady and the Woman Writer* which, like the work of Nina Auerbach and Nancy Armstrong, set Austen in the company of women writers working within a restricted situation to develop a distinctive form. Deborah Kaplan, however, is less interested in limitation than in enablement, and argues for the importance for Austen of female friendship, and of a 'women's culture' to resist prevailing ideologies. For Alison Sulloway and Mary Evans, it is the rights of women that are the key to Austen, who is to be seen in the context of late eighteenth-century feminist debate.

Among the most lively, and yet subtle, analyses is that of Claudia Johnson, who sees Austen as a political writer, but also regards gender as a complicating factor, suggesting that contemporary women novelists developed 'stylistic techniques which enabled them to use politically charged material in an exploratory and interrogative, rather than hortatory and prescriptive, manner'. The centrality of the female consciousness, and the use of narrative patterns and themes familiar from more overtly political writers, allows Austen to explore marriage, primogeniture, and patriarchy, but in ways more subtle —and independent—than any of her contemporaries. Through her careful analysis of Austen's political explorations, Johnson also suggests a reordering of the Austen canon by foregrounding the cynicism of *Sense and Sensibility* and suggesting that it is *Pride and Prejudice*, with its 'perfect comedic harmony and extravagant felicity', that is the least characteristic of the novels.

Sense and Sensibility has also attracted the attention of those engaged with the burgeoning critical literature of the Body. Tony Tanner's introduction to the 1969 Penguin edition (later revised for his *Jane Austen*) with its interest in 'secrecy and sickness' was well ahead of its time, and anticipated the more recent critical emphasis on the importance of the physical. John Dussinger, for example, has pointed out that although 'the body is scarcely described at all', it is nevertheless constantly being suggested, not only through crucial scenes of dancing and walking, but also through the metonyms of food and drink ('Austen's novels do reveal by innuendo and symbolic allusion a surprising frankness toward the human body'). If Dussinger sees food as power, John Wiltshire's impressive study *Jane Austen and the Body* argues that 'Emma's health is the enabling basis of her largesse', and Fanny's lack of it 'the ground of her fragile construction of a conservative self'. Wiltshire's view of Austen's epistemological inquiries as being a question of the response to the external world of the 'the bones, the tissues, the nerves' reflects his own interest in early nineteenth-century medical writings, just as Helen Small's reading of *Sense and Sensibility* emerges from a study of the relationship between literary and medical representations of female insanity.

For Tony Tanner, the 'sickness' in the novel is not so much an issue of medicine but of language. The 'muffled scream from Marianne at the heart of the novel' fascinates Tanner (and indeed Angela Leighton, who puts an explicitly feminist slant on her reading of 'Sense and Silences') because he regards communication as the central concern of Austen's writings. His accomplished analysis of the novels in *Jane Austen* thus focuses not only on the way in which characters speak—or fail to speak—but also on the crucial roles played by certain words.

Tanner's attention to language may in part reflect the critical trends of the 1980s, when interest in Saussure and Derrida placed language at the centre of the debates over literary studies, but it also draws on a tradition of Austen criticism that pre-dates poststructuralism. Formal analyses of Austen's work, such as Andrew Wright's study of 1953, had demonstrated the complexities of the narration, even though the desire to uphold a moral Jane Austen led C. S. Lewis to assert only a year later that she used 'the great abstract nouns of the classical English moralists . . . unblushingly and uncompromisingly'. According to Lewis, '*good sense, courage, contentment, fortitude,* "some duty neglected, some failing indulged", *impropriety, generous candour, blamable distrust, just humiliation, vanity, folly, ignorance, reason*' were the Johnsonian concepts 'by which Jane Austen grasps the world', but subsequent decades have seen a host of studies of her use of language, all of which have contributed to a much less clearly defined relationship between Austen's words and her world.

In the early 1970s, Norman Page's *The Language of Jane Austen* and K. C. Phillipps's *Jane Austen's English* did much to reveal the linguistic complexities through their extended discussions of the various meanings of particular words, the importance of grammatical and semantic changes, the social implications of the variations in speech, and the peculiar distinctions between apparent synonyms. Stuart Tave's critical study, which focused on key words in the novels, reflected a similar awareness, arguing that there were in fact 'few "good" or "bad" words', since meaning was determined by 'persons, places, times, circumstances'. George Steiner, too, warned of the deceptive 'openness' of Austen's prose, and argued that readers needed to be aware of the 'cumulative effect of key words and turns of phrase' which carried a great weight of hidden semantic and ethical meaning, while Daniel Cottom, some years later, asserted that it was the 'social and cultural context' that determined the meaning of words, rather than the narrator or the characters.

The growing awareness of the elusiveness of Austen's language has led not only to full-length studies of particular words, such as C. C. Barfoot's investigation of the 'vocabulary of Fate', or to J. F. Burrows's remarkable computer-aided analysis of the usage of the novels' 'common words', but also to a general fascination with the instability of the texts and the ensuing difficulties of interpretation. With the poststructuralist emphasis on the plurality, rather than definition, of meaning, critics of the 1980s began to seize on the puns and puzzles, the letters and lacunae, to reveal a series of texts in which writing, reading, and interpretation were of paramount importance. *Emma*, in particular, lends itself to linguistic analysis, as Grant Holly's mischievous essay on puns or Joseph Litvak's sophisticated reading of 'Self, Society, and Text in *Emma*' demonstrate, and although the meaning of the text can no longer be determined, it is clearly very different from that presented by those critics interested in the moral reformation of the heroine (as Adena Rosmarin has pointed out in terms that do not appear to be uncertain).

One of the most influential and exciting discussions to emerge from the 1980s was D. A. Miller's *Narrative and its Discontents* which not only examined the 'linguistic indicators' in the texts, giving due attention to puns, naming, and chatter, but also considered the implications for the structure of the novels of recent theoretical developments. In Miller's analysis, Austen's novels are not 'fully governed by the end', but generated 'by an underlying instability of desire, language, and society', making closure problematic, and possible only through the exclusion of the 'narratable'. More recently, Michiel Heyns has applied René Girard's notion of the 'scapegoat' to *Mansfield Park*, examining the 'expulsion' of Mary Crawford not only in terms of the novel's necessary closure, but also as the rival of the ostensible heroine, whose final pre-eminence is complicated by her very victory over the 'heroine *manquée*'.

Although recent collections of essays on Austen's novels have foregrounded the late twentieth-century critical shifts, the revolution of the early 1980s was perhaps best conveyed by David Lodge, whose experience as an editor of both *Emma* and a Casebook on *Emma* can be seen in his portrayal, in *Small World*, of the reformation of Morris Zapp:

'I used to be a Jane Austen man. I think I can in all modesty say I was *the* Jane Austen man. I wrote five books on Jane Austen, every one of which was trying to establish what her novels meant—and naturally, to prove that no one had properly understood what they meant before. Then I began a commentary on the works of Jane Austen, the aim of which was to be utterly exhaustive, to examine the novels from every conceivable angle—historical, biographical, rhetorical, mythical, structural, Freudian, Jungian, Marxist, existentialist, Christian, allegorical, ethical, phenomenological, archetypal, you name it. So that when each commentary was written, there would be *nothing further to say* about the novel in question.

Of course, I never finished it. The project was not so much Utopian as self-defeating. By that I don' just mean that if successful it would have eventually put us all out of business. I mean that it couldn't succeed because it isn't possible, and it isn't possible because of the nature of language itself, in which meaning is constantly being transferred from one signifier to another and can never be absolutely possessed.

Although Morris Zapp is defeated by his own conversion to poststructuralism, the irony of the passage plays between a commonsense view of the absurdity of applying literary theory to Austen, and a critical excitement over the inexhaustability of her texts.

REFERENCES

TEXTS

First editions

Jane Austen, *Sense and Sensibility*, 3 vols. (London, 1811).

—— *Pride and Prejudice*, 3 vols. (London, 1813).

—— *Mansfield Park*, 3 vols. (London, 1814).

—— *Emma*, 3 vols. (London, 1816).

—— *Northanger Abbey and Persuasion*, 4 vols. (London, 1818).

—— *Love and Freindship and Other Early Works*, with a preface by G. K. Chesterton (London, 1922).

—— *Fragment of a Novel*, ed. R. W. Chapman (Oxford, 1925).

—— *The Manuscript Chapters of Persuasion*, ed. R. W. Chapman (Oxford, 1926).

FIONA STAFFORD

Jane Austen, *Volume the First by Jane Austen*, ed. R. W. Chapman (Oxford, 1933).
—— *Volume the Third by Jane Austen*, ed. R. W. Chapman (Oxford, 1951).
—— *Volume the Second by Jane Austen*, ed. B. C. Southam (Oxford, 1963).
—— *Jane Austen's Sir Charles Grandison*, ed. Brian Southam (Oxford, 1980).

Collected editions

Austen, Jane, *Novels of Jane Austen: Complete in Five Volumes* (London, 1833).
—— *Jane Austen's Novels*, ed. R. B. Johnson, 10 vols. (London, 1892).
—— *The Novels*, introd. Austin Dobson, illustrations by Hugh Thomson and C. E. Brock (London, 1895–7).
—— *The Temple Edition of the Novels*, illustrated by C. E. Brock (London, 1899).
—— *The Novels of Jane Austen*, ed. R. W. Chapman, 5 vols. (Oxford, 1923). This edition was subsequently revised by Brian Southam and Mary Lascelles, and the *Minor Works* added as vol. vi. in 1954.
—— *Jane Austen's Novels*, the Chawton Edition, with an introduction by Richard Aldington, 6 vols. (London, 1948).
—— the Everyman Editions, introd. Mary Lascelles: *Sense and Sensibility* (London, 1962); *Northanger Abbey and Persuasion* (London, 1962); *Mansfield Park* (London, 1963); *Pride and Prejudice* (London, 1963); *Emma* (London, 1964).
—— the Penguin Editions: *Persuasion*, introd D. W. Harding (Harmondsworth, 1965); *Emma*, introd. Ronald Blythe (Harmondsworth, 1966); *Mansfield Park*, introd. Tony Tanner (Harmondsworth, 1966); *Sense and Sensibility*, introd. Tony Tanner (Harmondsworth, 1969); *Pride and Prejudice*, introd. Tony Tanner (Harmondsworth, 1972); *Northanger Abbey*, introd. Anne Henry Ehrenpreis (Harmondsworth, 1972); *Lady Susan/The Watsons/Sanditon*, ed. and introd. Margaret Drabble (Harmondsworth, 1974).
—— the Oxford English Novels Series, each with textual notes and bibliography by James Kinsley: *Sense and Sensibility*, ed. Claire Lamont (Oxford, 1970); *Pride and Prejudice*, ed. Frank Bradbrook (Oxford, 1970); *Mansfield Park*, ed. John Lucas (Oxford, 1970); *Emma*, ed. David Lodge (Oxford, 1971); *Northanger Abbey* and *Persuasion*, ed. John Davie (Oxford, 1971). These editions were reissued in the World's Classics Series in 1980, and again with new introductions in 1990–5: *Sense and Sensibility*, introd. Margaret Anne Doody (1990); *Pride and Prejudice*, introd. Isobel Armstrong (1990); *Mansfield Park*, introd. Marilyn Butler (1990); *Northanger Abbey, Lady Susan, The Watsons, Sanditon*, introd. Terry Castle (1990); *Persuasion*, introd. Claude Rawson (1990); *Emma*, introd. Terry Castle (1995).
Catharine and Other Writings, ed. Margaret Anne Doody and Douglas Murray was first published in the World's Classics Series (Oxford, 1993).
—— the new Everyman Editions: *Pride and Prejudice*, introd. Peter Conrad (London, 1991); *Emma*, introd. Marilyn Butler (London, 1991); *Sense and Sensibility*, introd. Peter Conrad (London, 1992); *Mansfield Park*, introd. Peter Conrad (London, 1992); *Northanger Abbey*, introd. Claudia Johnson (London, 1992); *Persuasion*, introd. Judith Terry (London, 1992); *Sanditon and Other Stories*, introd. Peter Washington (London, 1996).

—— the new Penguin Edition of the Novels of Jane Austen: *Sense and Sensibility*, ed. Ros Ballaster (Harmondsworth, 1995); *Northanger Abbey*, ed. Marilyn Butler (Harmondsworth, 1995); *Pride and Prejudice*, ed. Vivien Jones (Harmondsworth, 1996); *Mansfield Park*, ed. Kathryn Sutherland (Harmondsworth, 1996); *Emma*, ed. Fiona Stafford (Harmondsworth, 1996).

Letters

Austen, Jane, *The Letters of Jane Austen*, ed. Lord Brabourne, 2 vols. (London, 1884).
—— *Jane Austen's Letters to her Sister Cassandra and Others*, ed. R. W. Chapman (Oxford, 1932; 2nd edn., 1952).
—— *Jane Austen's Manuscript Letters in Facsimile*, ed. Jo Modert (Carbondale, Ill., 1990).
—— *Jane Austen's Letters*, ed. Deirdre Le Faye (Oxford, 1995).

BIBLIOGRAPHY

Chapman, R. W., *Jane Austen: A Critical Bibliography* (Oxford, 1953).
Gilson, David, *A Bibliography of Jane Austen* (Oxford, 1982).
Keynes, Geoffrey, *Jane Austen: A Bibliography* (London, 1929).
Roth, Barry, *An Annotated Bibliography of Jane Austen Studies, 1973–83* (Charlottesville, Va., 1985).
—— and Weinsheimer, Joel, *An Annotated Bibliography of Jane Austen Studies, 1952–72* (Charlottesville, Va., 1973).

CRITICISM

Aers, David, Cook, Jonathan, and Punter, David (eds.), *Romanticism and Ideology: Studies in English Writing, 1765–1830* (London, 1981).
Alexander, S., *The Art of Jane Austen* (Manchester, 1928).
Armstrong, Nancy, *Desire and Domestic Fiction: A Political History of the Novel* (New York, 1987).
Auerbach, Nina, *Communities of Women* (Cambridge, Mass., 1978).
Austen, Caroline, *My Aunt Jane: A Memoir* (Alton, 1952).
Austen-Leigh, J. E., *A Memoir of Jane Austen* (1870; rev. edn., 1871), ed. R. W. Chapman (Oxford, 1926).
Austen-Leigh, R. A. (ed.), *Austen Papers*, privately printed (London, 1942).
Austen-Leigh, W., and Austen-Leigh, R. A., *Jane Austen: Her Life and Letters: A Family Record* (1913), rev. edn., Deirdre Le Faye (London, 1989).
Babb, Howard S., *Jane Austen's Novels: The Fabric of Dialogue* (Cleveland, 1962).
Bailey, J., *Introductions to Jane Austen* (London, 1931).
Ballaster, Ros (ed.), *Sense and Sensibility*, New Penguin Edition (Harmondsworth, 1995).
Banfield, Ann, *Unspeakable Sentences* (London, 1982).
Barfoot, C. C., *The Thread of Connection: Aspects of Fate in the Novels of Jane Austen and Others* (Amsterdam, 1982).
Bayley, John, 'Emma and her Critics', *Jane Austen Society Report for the Year 1967*, 16–29.

Bertelson, Lance, 'Jane Austen's Miniatures: Painting, Drawing and the Novels', *Modern Language Quarterly*, 45 (1984), 350–72.

Bodenheimer, R., 'Looking at Landscape in Jane Austen', *Studies in English Literature*, 21 (1981), 605–24.

Bradbrook, F. W., *Jane Austen and her Predecessors* (Cambridge, 1966).

Bradley, A. C., 'Jane Austen: A Lecture', *Essays and Studies by Members of the English Association*, 2 (1911), 7–36.

Brower, Reuben, 'The Controlling Hand: Jane Austen and *Pride and Prejudice*', *Scrutiny*, 13 (1945–6), 99–111.

—— *Fields of Light* (New York, 1951).

Burlin, Katrin, '"Pictures of Perfection" at Pemberley: Art in *Pride and Prejudice*', in Todd (1983: 155–70).

Burrows, J. F., *Computation into Criticism* (Oxford, 1987).

Butler, M., *Jane Austen and the War of Ideas* (Oxford, 1975).

—— introduction to *Emma*, Everyman edition (London, 1991).

—— (ed.) *Northanger Abbey*, New Penguin edition (Harmondsworth, 1995).

Byrde, P., *A Frivolous Distinction: Fashion and Needlework in the Works of Jane Austen* (Bath, 1979).

Cecil, Lord David, *A Portrait of Jane Austen* (London, 1978).

Chapman, R. W., *Jane Austen: Facts and Problems* (Oxford, 1948).

Churchill, Winston, *The Second World War*, vol. v (London, 1952).

Collins, Irene, *Jane Austen and the Clergy* (London, 1994).

Cornish, F. W., *Jane Austen* (London, 1913).

Cottom, D., *The Civilized Imagination: A Study of Ann Radcliffe, Jane Austen, and Sir Walter Scott* (Cambridge, 1985).

Craik, W. A., *Jane Austen: The Six Novels* (London, 1965).

De Rose, Peter, and McGuire, S. W., *A Concordance to the Works of Jane Austen*, 3 vols. (New York, 1982).

Devlin, D. D., *Jane Austen and Education* (London, 1975).

Doody, M., and Murray, D. (eds.), *Catharine and Other Writings*, World's Classics edition (Oxford, 1993).

Drabble, Margaret, introduction to *Lady Susan, The Watsons, Sanditon*, Penguin edition (Harmondsworth, 1974).

Duckworth, A., *The Improvement of the Estate* (1971; paperback edn., Baltimore, 1994).

Duncan-Jones, E. E., 'Notes on Jane Austen', *Notes and Queries*, 196 (1951), 14–16.

—— 'Jane Austen and Crabbe', *Review of English Studies*, 5 (1954), 174.

Dussinger, J., *In the Pride of the Moment: Encounters in Jane Austen's World* (Columbus, Oh., 1990).

Edwards, Anne-Marie, *In the Steps of Jane Austen* (2nd edn., Southampton, 1985).

Ehrenpreis, A. H., introduction to *Northanger Abbey*, Penguin edition (Harmondsworth, 1972).

Elwood, A. K., *Memoirs of the Literary Ladies of England*, 2 vols. (London, 1843).

Evans, Mary, *Jane Austen and the State* (London, 1987).

Farrer, Reginald, 'Jane Austen, *ob.* July 18 1817', *Quarterly Review*, 228 (1917), 1–30.

Fergus, Jan, *Jane Austen and the Didactic Novel* (London, 1983).

Ferguson, Moira, '*Mansfield Park*: Slavery, Colonialism and Gender' *Oxford Literary Review*, 13 (1991), 118–39.

Finch, C., and Bowen, P., ' "The Tittle-Tattle of Highbury": Gossip and the Free Indirect Style of *Emma*', *Representations*, 31 (1990), 1–18.

Fleishman, A., *A Reading of Mansfield Park* (Minneapolis, 1967).

Freeman, Jean, *Jane Austen in Bath* (Alton, 1969).

Gard, Roger, *Jane Austen's Novels: The Art of Clarity* (New Haven, 1992).

Garrod, H. W., 'Jane Austen: A Depreciation', in *Essays by Divers Hands, Being Transactions of the Royal Society of Literature*, NS 8 (1928), 21–40.

Gilbert, Sandra, and Gubar, Susan, *The Madwoman in the Attic: The Woman Writer and the Nineteenth-Century Literary Imagination* (New Haven, 1979).

Gooneratne, Y., *Jane Austen* (Cambridge, 1970).

Grey, J. D. (ed.), *Jane Austen's Beginnings* (Ann Arbor, 1989).

—— Litz, W., and Southam, B. (eds.), *The Jane Austen Handbook* (London, 1986).

Halperin, J. (ed.), *Jane Austen: Bicentenary Essays* (Cambridge, 1975).

—— *The Life of Jane Austen* (Brighton, 1984).

Harding, D. W., 'Regulated Hatred: An Aspect of the Work of Jane Austen', *Scrutiny*, 8 (1940), 346–62.

—— introduction to *Persuasion*, Penguin edition (Harmondsworth, 1965).

Hardy, B., *A Reading of Jane Austen* (London, 1975).

Harris, J., *Jane Austen's Art of Memory* (Cambridge, 1989).

Hennelly, M., '*Pride and Prejudice*: The Eyes Have It', in Todd (1983: 187–207).

Heyns, M., *Expulsion and the Nineteenth-Century Novel* (Oxford, 1994).

Hickman, Peggy, *A Jane Austen Household Book* (London, 1977).

Hill, C., *Jane Austen: Her Homes and her Friends* (London, 1902).

Hodge, Jane Aiken, *The Double Life of Jane Austen* (London, 1972).

Holly, Grant, 'Emmagrammatology', *Studies in Eighteenth-Century Culture*, 19 (1989), 39–52.

Honan, Park, *Jane Austen: Her Life* (London, 1987).

Hubback, J. H., and Hubback, E. C., *Jane Austen's Sailor Brothers* (London, 1906).

James, Henry, 'The Lesson of Balzac', *Atlantic Monthly*, 96 (1905), 166–80.

James, Selma, *The Ladies and the Mammies: Jane Austen and Jean Rhys* (Bristol, 1983).

Jane Austen Society, *Reports* (1940–).

Jenkins, Elizabeth, *Jane Austen: A Biography* (London, 1938).

Johnson, Claudia L., *Jane Austen: Women, Politics, and the Novel* (Chicago, 1988).

Kaplan, D., *Jane Austen among Women* (Baltimore, 1992).

Kaufmann, D., 'Law and Propriety in *Sense and Sensibility*: Austen on the Cusp of Modernity', *English Literary History*, 59 (1992), 385–408.

Kaye-Smith, S., and Stern, G. B., *Talking of Jane Austen* (London, 1943).

Kipling, Rudyard, 'The Janeites', *Storyteller* (May 1924), 139–50.

Kirkham, M., *Jane Austen: Feminism and Fiction* (Brighton, 1983).

Lane, Maggie, *Jane Austen's England* (London, 1986).

—— *Jane Austen and Food* (London, 1995).

Lascelles, Mary, *Jane Austen and her Art* (Oxford, 1939).

—— introductions to the Everyman editions of the novels (1962–4).

Laski, Marghanita, *Jane Austen and her World* (London, 1969).

Leavis, F. R., *The Great Tradition* (London, 1948).

Leavis, Q. D., 'A Critical Theory of Jane Austen's Writings', *Scrutiny*, 10 (1941–2), 61–87, 114–42, 272–94; 12 (1944–5), 104–19.

Lefroy, Sir John Henry, *Notes and Documents Relating to the Family of Loffroy . . . by a Cadet* (Woolwich, 1868).

Leighton, Angela, 'Sense and Silences', in Todd (1983: 128–41).

Lewes, G. H., 'Recent Novels', *Fraser's Town and Country Magazine*, 36 (1847), 686–95.

—— 'The Novels of Jane Austen', *Blackwood's Edinburgh Magazine*, 86 (1859), 99–113.

Lewis, C. S., 'A Note on Jane Austen', *Essays in Criticism*, 4 (1954), 359–71.

Litvak, Joseph, 'Reading Characters: Self, Society, and Text in *Emma*', *Publications of the Modern Language Association*, 100 (1985), 763–73.

Litz, A. Walton, *Jane Austen: A Study in her Artistic Development* (New York, 1965).

Lodge, David (ed.), *Emma*, A Casebook (London, 1968).

—— *Small World* (London, 1984).

—— introduction to *Emma*, World's Classics (new edn., Oxford, 1990).

Macaulay, Thomas Babington, 'Diary and Letters of Madame D'Arblay', *Edinburgh Review*, 76 (1843), 523–70,

MacDonagh, O., *Jane Austen: Real and Imagined Worlds* (New Haven, 1991).

McMaster, Juliet, (ed.), *Jane Austen's Achievement* (London, 1976).

—— *Jane Austen on Love* (Victoria, 1978).

—— and Stovel, B. (eds.), *Jane Austen's Business* (London, 1996).

Malden, S. F., *Jane Austen* (London, 1889).

Melander, M., 'An Unknown Source of Jane Austen's *Sense and Sensibility*', *Studia Neophilologia*, 22 (1950), 146–70.

Miller, D. A., *Narrative and its Discontents* (Princeton, 1981).

Moler, K., *Jane Austen's Art of Allusion* (Lincoln, Nebr., 1968).

Monaghan, D., *Jane Austen: Structure and Social Vision* (London, 1980).

—— (ed.), *Jane Austen in a Social Context* (Totowa, NJ, 1981).

—— (ed.), *Emma*, New Casebook (London, 1992).

Mooneyham, L., *Romance, Language and Education in Jane Austen's Novels* (London, 1988).

Moretti, Franco, *The Way of the World* (London, 1987).

Morgan, S., *In the Meantime: Character and Perception in Jane Austen's Fiction* (Chicago, 1980).

Mudrick, M., *Jane Austen: Irony as Defense and Discovery* (Princeton, 1952).

Mukherjee, M., *Jane Austen* (London, 1991).

Nardin, J., *Those Elegant Decorums: The Concept of Propriety in Jane Austen's Novels* (Albany, NY, 1973).

Nollen, E., 'Ann Radcliffe's *A Sicilian Romance*: A New Source of Jane Austen's *Sense and Sensibility*', *English Language Notes*, 22 (1984), 30–7.

Page, N., *The Language of Jane Austen* (Oxford, 1972).

Phillipps, K. C., *Jane Austen's English* (London, 1970).

Piggott, P., *The Innocent Diversion: A Study of Music in the Life and Writings of Jane Austen* (London, 1979).

Pinion, F. B., *A Jane Austen Companion* (London, 1979).

Poovey, Mary, *The Proper Lady and the Woman Writer: Ideology as Style in the Works of Mary Wollstonecraft, Mary Shelley, and Jane Austen* (Chicago, 1984).

Read, Herbert, *Reason and Romanticism* (London, 1926).

Roberts, W., *Jane Austen and the French Revolution* (London, 1979).

Rosmarin, A., ' "Misreading" *Emma*: The Powers and Perfidies of Interpretive History', *English Literary History*, 51 (1984), 315–42.

Sabor, Peter, ' "Staring in Astonishment": Portraits and Prints in *Persuasion*', in McMaster and Stovel (1996: 17–29).

Said, Edward, *Culture and Imperialism* (London, 1993).

Saintsbury, George, *A History of Nineteenth Century Literature* (London, 1896).

Sales, Roger, *Jane Austen and Representations of Regency England* (London, 1994).

Schorer, M., 'The Humiliation of Emma Woodhouse', *Literary Review*, 2 (1959), 547–63.

Scott, Walter, '*Emma*', *Quarterly Review*, 14 (1815), 188–201 (actually published Mar. 1816).

Seymour, Beatrice Kean, *Jane Austen: Study for a Portrait* (London, 1937).

Shannon, E., '*Emma*: Character and Construction', *Publications of the Modern Language Association* 71 (1956), 637–50.

Sherry, N., *Jane Austen* (London, 1966).

Simpson, R., 'Jane Austen', *North British Review*, 52 (1870), 129–52.

Small, Helen, *Love's Madness: Medicine, the Novel, and Female Insanity, 1800–1865* (Oxford, 1996).

Smith, Goldwin, *Jane Austen* (London, 1890).

Smith, Leroy, *Jane Austen and the Drama of Women* (New York, 1983).

Smithers, D. W., *Jane Austen in Kent* (Westerham, 1981).

Southam, B. C., *Jane Austen's Literary Manuscripts* (Oxford, 1964).

—— *Jane Austen: The Critical Heritage*, vol. i (London, 1968); vol. ii: *The Critical Heritage, 1870–1940* (London, 1987).

—— 'Jane Austen and Antigua', *Jane Austen Society Report for the Year 1969* (1969), 18–20.

—— 'The Silence of the Bertrams: Slavery and the Chronology of *Mansfield Park*', *Times Literary Supplement*, 17 February, 1995.

Sparkes, G., *Jane Austen: Her Hampshire Days* (Winchester, 1985).

Spender, Dale, *Mothers of the Novel: 100 Good Women Writers Before Jane Austen* (New York, 1986).

Steiner, George, *After Babel: Aspects of Language and Translation* (London, 1975).

Stewart, Maaja, *Domestic Realities and Imperial Fictions: Jane Austen's Novels in Eighteenth-Century Contexts* (Athens, Ga., 1993).

Stokes, Myra, *The Language of Jane Austen* (London, 1991).

Stovel, B., 'Comic Symmetry in *Emma*', *Dalhousie Review*, 57 (1977), 453–64.

Sulloway, A., *Jane Austen and the Province of Womanhood* (Philadelphia, 1989).

Sutherland, Kathryn, 'Jane Austen's Literary History: The Case for *Mansfield Park*', *English Literary History*, 59 (1992), 409–40.

Tanner, Tony, introductions to the Penguin editions of *Mansfield Park* (Harmondsworth, 1966), *Sense and Sensibility* (Harmondsworth, 1967), *Pride and Prejudice* (Harmondsworth, 1972).

FIONA STAFFORD

Tanner, Tony, *Jane Austen* (London, 1986).

Tave, S. *Some Words of Jane Austen* (London, 1973).

Todd, Janet (ed.), *Jane Austen: New Perspectives* (London, 1983).

Tompkins, J. M. S., *The Popular Novel in England 1770–1800* (London, 1932).

—— 'Elinor and Marianne: A Note on Jane Austen', *Review of English Studies*, 14 (1940), 33–43.

Trilling, L., '*Mansfield Park*', in *The Opposing Self* (London, 1955), 181–202.

—— introduction to the Riverside edition of *Emma*, republished as 'Emma and the Legend of Jane Austen', in *Beyond Culture* (London, 1966), 42–61.

Tytler, Sarah (Henrietta Keddie), *Jane Austen and her Works* (London, 1880).

Watson, N., *Revolution and the Form of the British Novel, 1790–1825* (Oxford, 1994).

Watt, Ian (ed.), *Jane Austen: A Collection of Critical Essays* (Englewood Cliffs, NJ, 1963).

West, Rebecca, preface to *Northanger Abbey* (London, 1932).

Williams, M., *Jane Austen: Six Novels and their Methods* (London, 1986).

Williams, R., *The Country and the City* (London, 1973).

Wiltshire, J., *Jane Austen and the Body* (Cambridge, 1992).

Woolf, Virginia, unsigned review of W. and R. A. Austen-Leigh, *Jane Austen: Her Life and Letters: A Family Record*, and Sybil G. Brinton, *Old Friends and New Faces*, *The Times Literary Supplement*, 8 May 1913.

—— 'Jane Austen at Sixty', *Nation and Athenaeum*, 34 (1923), 433–4.

—— *The Common Reader* (London, 1925).

—— *A Room of one's Own* (London, 1929).

—— *The Letters of Virginia Woolf*, 6 vols., ed. N. Nicolson (London, 1975–80).

Wright, A., *Jane Austen's Novels: A Study in Structure* (London, 1953).

13. *Thomas Love Peacock*

J. P. DONOVAN

Although Thomas Love Peacock (1785–1866) produced a substantial quantity of poetry in modes commonly practised by both the major and minor writers of his day—the meditative and loco-descriptive poem, personal lyric, mythological narrative, and verse satire—he is now regarded chiefly as the author of a kind of satirical prose fiction often considered to be peculiar to him and which an early reviewer described as combining the novel, the drama, and the essay. In five novels with contemporary settings—*Headlong Hall* (1816), *Melincourt* (1817), *Nightmare Abbey* (1818), *Crotchet Castle* (1831), and *Gryll Grange* (1860–1)—as well as in the two historical romances *Maid Marian* (1822) and *The Misfortunes of Elphin* (1829), Peacock developed comic and critical perspectives on the fashions and opinions in the arts and public life which were current at various moments in his long career. He also wrote a number of trenchant essays examining the literature, as well as the literary culture and reputations, of the Romantic period. In 1820 Peacock's friend Shelley described his 'fine wit' as 'a strain too learnèd for a shallow age', declaring his proper audience to be 'the chosen spirits of the time'. It has since become a commonplace that his novels could never be widely popular, and his reputation has indeed been marked by the devoted connoisseurship, and occasionally by the sceptical mistrust, which are the usual extremes of response to writers whose afterlife has been both vigorous and persistent, though confined to a set of readers with a taste for intellectual comedy. From his own day until well into the twentieth century his appeal has typically been accounted for on an implicit (and sometimes explicit) analogy with the old Madeira wine so relished by his characters: this makes him out to be at once pungent and mellow, rather cordial and tonic than intoxicating, improving with age and to be regularly savoured in small quantities, above all an acquired taste for the cultivated palate. Most of the criticism considered in this chapter, which concentrates on work published in the last half-century or so, makes an equally appreciative, if more methodical and austere, address to Peacock; its central concern has been to inform understanding of a writer who makes very particular demands on his readers' knowledge of the literary, intellectual, and political conditions out of, and to which, he wrote.

TEXTS

Bibliographies of original and later editions of Peacock's works are given in Brett-Smith and Jones, Read (1959), which provides descriptions and assessments, Read (1963–4), and Nicholes (1969); Madden (1970) briefly evaluates collected, selected, and single-volume modern editions. The article on Peacock by N. Joukovsky in the forthcoming third edition of the *Cambridge Bibliography of English Literature* will contain a considerably expanded list of his writings.

The 'Halliford' edition of Brett-Smith and Jones remains the standard collection of Peacock's fiction, poetry, plays, essays and letters, whether complete or fragmentary, published or unpublished in his lifetime. Significant additions to it, as well as corrections and refinements, are made in the articles by Joukovsky listed in the References section below under 'Texts and textual studies'. Brett-Smith and Jones exclude brief fragments and print selections only from Peacock's opera reviews and from his unpublished writings on cookery (for the latter see Mendelson). Some 'official' writing connected with Peacock's employment in the East India Company is also left out, for which see Cameron and Reiman, and Fain (1970). The letters printed in the Halliford edition need to be supplemented by Scott, which contains eight letters written to T. J. Hogg in 1817–19, by Brett-Smith (1933), and by Green. Gallon (1969) describes the contents of eighty-seven additional letters written between 1839 and 1855 which are now among the papers of Lord Broughton in the British Library. Joukovsky's new edition of Peacock's letters, at this time of writing in the final stages of preparation for Oxford University Press, will include over 200 previously unpublished letters and documents. The eight volumes which have appeared to date of *Shelley and his Circle*, ed. Cameron and Reiman, include transcriptions of manuscripts of letters and of imaginative prose and verse by Peacock as well as of an 'official' essay on Indian affairs: all are furnished with informative commentaries, biographical, literary, and historical, which supply the want of such information in Brett-Smith and Jones. Since the editorial matter in the Halliford edition is largely textual and bibliographical, the student in search of the explanatory annotation that is needed to elucidate a writer so topical, learned, and allusive as Peacock is directed to the editions of single and smaller groups of works listed under 'Texts and textual studies' below. All are useful—David Garnett's especially among older editions. Wright, and especially Joukovsky (1970), and Baron and Slater, have recently established standards of informative annotation that it would be well to see extended to the other novels. Brett-Smith (1921) annotates 'The Four Ages of Poetry' as do Jordan and Bromwich, the last-named sparsely. Mills (1970) conveniently brings together the 'Memoirs of Shelley' and the elegiac 'The Last Day of Windsor Forest', as well as most of Peacock's other important literary and musical essays and reviews, but without annotation. Peacock's poetry has not been widely reprinted; it is best read in the Halliford edition, but Joukovsky (1994) should be consulted for important additions and modifications to the texts of the early poems.

The catalogue of the sale of Peacock's library in 1866, reproduced in Munby, is an informative index to his interests.

CRITICISM

Guides to criticism and commentary can be found in various forms in Brett-Smith and Jones, Read (1959, 1963–4), Ward (supplementing Read for reviews in the years 1805–20), Jack, Nicholes (1969), Madden (1970), Sage, Reiman (1979), Burns (1985a), and Prance. Joukovsky's article on Peacock in the forthcoming third edition of the *Cambridge Bibliography of English Literature* will list reviews and critical articles to 1875 as well as important scholarship and criticism to 1920.

Peacock's reputation both as poet and novelist remained modest, though broadly favourable, during his lifetime and developed slowly thereafter. Read (1963–4) lists the contemporary reviews (to which Ward makes a number of additions) as well as later critical response to 1963; while Read (1959) surveys critical and scholarly work to 1958, with strategic quotation from important items. Sage gathers important nineteenth-century essays and reviews as well as twentieth-century criticism. Prance's odd title conceals what is in effect a reader's guide to Peacock's fiction comprising an annotated bibliography of selected books and articles to 1990, a dictionary of characters in the novels, plays, and fictional fragments, a list of songs in the novels and plays, and an appendix of the most important of Peacock's contemporaries upon whom he is considered to have drawn in creating his characters, together with sources for the attributions in Peacock's biographers and critics.

Most of what is known of Peacock's life can be found in the substantial 'Biographical Introduction' to Brett-Smith and Jones. Nicholes's briefer account (1961) adds some details, while Joukovsky's researches (1985) considerably augment and amend the received view of Peacock's first thirty years. Further minor additions to his biography have been made; for example, by Gallon (1969), Madden (1985), and McKay (1989). The new material that will become available in Joukovsky's edition of the letters will both increase and modify current understanding of Peacock's life. There are two full-length biographies. The accuracy and specificity of Carl Van Doren's humane and cautious book have been much improved upon by discoveries made since its appearance in 1911. Van Doren offers a sober and not uncritical assessment of Peacock the writer as achieving pre-eminence in his age in a satiric vein characterized by a self-conscious singularity and eccentricity of outlook which is held in 'austere restraint' by a 'careful literary craftsmanship'—a combination that ensures him permanent status as a minor classic. Felton's biography aims at a wide rather than a specialized readership; drawing together readily available material on Peacock's life and times, it presents a positive and readable portrait of its subject, but its statements require to be verified against the sources listed above. A new biography that would incorporate recently uncovered information and relate Peacock to current understanding of the Romantic and Victorian periods is clearly desirable.

Several short introductory studies map the contours of Peacock's literary output and provide basic biographical and contextual indications as well as brief bibliographies. Mulvihill's (1987a) is the most up to date in its critical perspectives and references; though Madden's (1967) is also informative and discerning and, like Mulvihill, the author takes a systematic overview of all of Peacock's writings. Campbell's is briefer than either of these, and now appears somewhat slight and dated; it includes a lively appreciation (given in Sage) of Anthelia Melincourt, a character who is remarkable in the fiction of the time for her education and independence. J. I. M. Stewart's stylish pamphlet in the Writers and their Work series makes a number of shrewd and elegant observations on the novels, but functions better as a general critical essay than an introduction, and is perhaps best approached after some acquaintance has been established with Peacock and with writing on him.

No full-length study of Peacock appeared until the twentieth century. Van Doren's biography apart, several of these stand out as of evident interest and value—the first of which, Freeman's, was also the first notable attempt at a comprehensive estimate of Peacock as literary artist to be based upon acquaintance with all of his major writings. Freeman's wide reading enables him to locate Peacock's works tellingly in relation to contemporary imaginative literature and controversy. His post-Victorian criterion for the evaluation of the poetry, its approach to a 'direct personal expression of sentiment', now seems old-fashioned and ill-adapted to the greater part of Peacock's verse; while his confident identification of characters in the novels with their supposed actual counterparts can miss the complexity and nuance of Peacock's satiric methods and intentions. Trenchantly delivered, his judgements sometimes appear quirky or misconceived, but his response to Peacock's fiction is guided by an enthusiastic critical intelligence which commands attention.

J. B. Priestley's book (1927) is organized as a literary biography followed by critical chapters on the various works. Like Van Doren and Freeman, Priestley now needs to be supplemented by later research which has established the course of Peacock's life and the intricacy of his encounter with contemporary opinion and debate in greater detail. It can none the less still profitably be read as an alert and generously appreciative study of Peacock, a mode of criticism in which Priestley's earlier essay on Prince Seithenyn (1925) of *The Misfortunes of Elphin* is an exuberant classic. We may now hesitate to regard Peacock as

quite so simply genial and convivial as Priestley tends to do, while still valuing the aptness of his professional writer's homage to the earlier humourist as
pre-eminent in a 'style of grave banter, wise mischief, salted with irony and
sparkling with fun . . . it is all his own, one of the clear voices of English prose'.

Jean-Jacques Mayoux's book (1933) is a substantial historical and analytic
study of Peacock as writer and critical thinker. Mayoux brings a wide acquaintance with European thought and art, as well as detailed researches into the
intellectual milieu of late eighteenth- and early nineteenth-century England,
to an investigation of Peacock's career. The result is a broad and yet finely
nuanced exposition of the complex and sometimes contradictory strands that
went to the creation of Peacock's outlook and literary practice. The specialist
is more likely than the interested student to pick up a long and demanding
book in French but serious study of Peacock should not pass it by. (Important
extracts are given in translation in Sage.)

Carl Dawson's study (1970) aims to see Peacock complete a century or so
after his death, and to this end devotes much attention—more than half the
book—to his verse and non-fictional prose. Dawson provides the fullest general treatment available of Peacock's poetry, has perceptive remarks to make
about his prose style, and devotes chapters to his political views, musical criticism, and writing on cookery, as well as making a searching examination
of his critical and autobiographical essays. His consideration of the novels is
particularly strong on their structure, analogues, and literary ancestry; but
has less to say on their engagement with contemporary issues and opinion.
Dawson's Peacock is fundamentally a serious artist who operates as a satirist
according to a consistent set of principles. For the student wanting a detailed
overview of Peacock's literary production, methodically set out and conducted
in a deliberate and judicious manner, this book answers the need.

Howard Mills (1969) pursues a more contentiously evaluative inquiry that
discovers a master-pattern of apprenticeship–maturity–decline to be the governing rhythm of Peacock's career. Mills concentrates upon Peacock as a critic
of the Regency period, locating his highest and most characteristic achievement in *Melincourt* (1817) and (especially) *Nightmare Abbey* (1818) which were
written while he enjoyed the close association with Shelley which gave him
an indispensable personal contact with a major figure of the Romantic movement. Thereafter Peacock's fiction loses vitality of response to its age and
recedes into a conservatism of outlook and temper, though some later literary reviews and music criticism retain the sharp critical edge of his earlier
satires. The limitations of such a model adequately to account for the course
of a long writing life, which many have seen as more variously achieved and
appealing, become evident when Mills is dealing with Peacock after about
1820. Dawson, Butler, and Burns offer different conceptions of his artistic and
intellectual evolution which seriously challenge many of Mills's judgements.

Marilyn Butler's study (1979) is an altogether more searching exercise in both its methods and its conclusions. It takes as its point of departure the double obstacle that has been placed in the way of a fully informed reading of Peacock by the passage of time and the accretions of critical opinion— unfamiliarity with the intellectual tradition in which he wrote and with the specifics of contemporary opinion that he appropriated in his novels. Butler therefore sets out to reconstruct more fully and cogently than before both the reading from which Peacock derived his characteristic set of mind and the atmosphere of literary fashion and polemical debate in which he wrote any one of his important texts. These are shown to elucidate both the large historical and philosophical perspectives that are evoked in his fiction and the ample topical notation with which he renders opinion and controversy. The Peacock that emerges from the study is more engaged and incisive, less the merely jovial eccentric, than many readers have taken him to be—rather a major critical intelligence which is consistently exercised in accordance with a set of principles deriving directly from the pagan, republican, and democratic ideals of the Enlightenment. 'Everything Peacock [published] was the genuine, if partial, expression of a coherent philosophy of life and art', a coherence that maintained its essential and unifying humanism and scepticism, whether directed against the Romantic or the mechanistic, to the end of his writing life. This penetrating study of Peacock as above all a critic of the public intellectual life of his times neglects neither his poetic idealism nor his 'characteristic elegance of form'; and it offers a testing example of the historical method of literary study as applied to a Romantic author.

Marilyn Butler's is the last comprehensive treatment of Peacock's work to be published, though the scope and the critical acumen of Brian Burns's study of the novels (1985a) give it the force of a general estimate. Burns's concern to show 'both the uniformity and the variety of Peacock's writing' proceeds by closely detailed readings of the novels which are alive to their larger narrative movements as well as to their local texture and tonal shifts. He regards Peacock as essentially a moralist who trains his gaze on human behaviour in its permanent characteristics as well as the contemporary manifestations stressed by Marilyn Butler. Burns is notably successful in discriminating both the development in Peacock's literary art through the seven novels and the rich particularity of individual texts. Two shorter books, both Swedish academic studies, Kjellin's and McKay's (1992), examine the novels closely from more formalist points of view. Kjellin concentrates upon structural elements of story and dialogue, relating each to the various narrative types that are incorporated into the novels and Peacock's practice to that of the ancient and modern masters who might have served as models for him. McKay charts the course of Peacock's 'technical experimentation' in formal and stylistic terms and finds that it goes hand in hand with an evolution towards depth of characterization and psychological realism.

The most interesting recent articles on Peacock's novels address one (and sometimes both) of two large and related questions which also form a principal concern of the book-length studies: the function of his comedy as a critical perception of his times; and the means by which his texts give significant shape and weight to issues charged with particular meaning for contemporary readers. Each of these lines of investigation provides an indirect response to a strain in Peacock criticism which has judged his peculiar form of satire to be unsatisfactory because it seems to sacrifice moral clarity and seriousness to the production of comic effects. Among recent writers Hewitt, Dyson, and (in part) Mills (1969) most thoroughly represent this view which finds Peacock's humour often a mask for failures of intelligence and his attitude towards the important subjects he treats, at its worst, one of 'frivolous and reactionary complacency' (Hewitt). Garside presents a persuasive corrective to this position supported by a subtly attentive reading of *Headlong Hall*. Linda Brooks, following Frye (1957), points out debts to the Menippean satire of Lucian, the satirist of the second century AD who was a favourite author of Peacock's. Dawson (1985) makes a fertile and suggestive grouping of Jane Austen, Byron, and Peacock as creators of appropriately individual comic languages; while Bate, in a wide-ranging essay, places Peacock in company with Byron and Hazlitt as formulating comic antidotes to the Wordsworthian sublime. Polhemus finds *Nightmare Abbey* a representative Peacockian comic narrative in its creation of an essentially religious image of communal experience involving loss of egotistical attachments. Hoff's formal studies (1972, 1975a, 1975b) of voice and genre gesture at an approach which could profitably be carried further in narratological and linguistic terms, as could Schmid's consideration of *Melincourt* and *Nightmare Abbey* in the light of the modern theorists of comedy Mikhail Bakhtin and Umberto Eco.

Among important studies of Peacock's sources and 'background', Rowland's scholarly account of his researches for *The Misfortunes of Elphin* should be coupled with Butler's demonstration (1985) of the ideological significance of the use of early Welsh myth in the novel. Madden's (1985) is the latest in an interesting series of studies (notably Herbert Wright's and Gallon's (1968)) of Peacock's Welsh associations. Duff's interesting chapter on the chivalric revival of the 1810s improves upon Chandler and adds a pertinent dimension to our understanding of *Melincourt*, which could be extended to include *Maid Marian*. Both these novels, as well as *Crotchet Castle and Gryll Grange*, contain female characters who seem each to personify Claire Clairmont's exclamation in a letter of 1818 to Byron: 'How I delight in a lovely woman of strong and cultivated intellect!' To earlier admirers (Able, Campbell, Wilson) of these active and independent fictional women, which have been largely neglected by recent gender criticism, may be added Crabbe (1978, 1979) who surveys them against contemporary writing on the education and duties of females, and Brown who emphasizes the sources in earlier authors (especially Mary Wollstonecraft) of

J. P. DONOVAN

Peacock's ideal of feminine perfection as well as noting interesting resemblances between it and the presentation of erotic experience in Shelley's poetry. Burns's essay on *Gryll Grange* (1985b) is a good introduction to the larger subject of the significance of classical material in the fiction. Kelly weaves a number of these strands together in an excellent chapter which concludes that it is the novels' 'formal and thematic elements considered in their interrelationships and as a whole' which constitute a significant critical reflection of Romantic culture. The skill with which this hypothesis is pursued through analysis of the dramatic, narrative, and linguistic strategies of the texts allows this essay to perform the office for the end of the twentieth century that Spedding's fine review did for the end of the Romantic period, that of a summing-up in brief compass and in apt and suggestive terms of the characteristic apprehension of Peacock at a given moment in critical history.

Peacock's poetry invites more attention than it has received. Butler (1981) defines his central poetic interests and sympathies as lying squarely in the camp of the second-generation Romantics Shelley, Byron, Keats, Hunt, and Hazlitt inasmuch as they all derived central inspiration from pagan, classical, and Mediterranean sources which they express in poetic modes that carry an important political dimension. She elaborates upon this in a study of his mythological poems (1982) as didactic and polemical vehicles for enforcing a progressive point of view on matters of contemporary intellectual controversy. Brogan makes a preliminary classification and estimate of the verse satires, which await a more searching critical inquiry.

The Four Ages of Poetry has been the most studied of Peacock's critical essays, both because it prompted Shelley's *A Defence of Poetry* and because, dramatically at odds with his general critical position and practice, it is intriguing in itself. Krieger, Mulvihill (1984b), and Butler (1979, 1985) variously elucidate its historical methods and assumptions in the context of related contemporary writings; while Haley, Hall, Fry, and Hogle provide readings that display its intricate links with Shelley's *Defence*.

REFERENCES

TEXTS AND TEXTUAL STUDIES

Baron, Michael, and Slater, Michael (eds.), *Headlong Hall* and *Gryll Grange* (Oxford, 1987).
Brett-Smith, H. F. B. (ed.), *Peacock's Four Ages of Poetry, Shelley's Defence of Poetry, Browning's Essay on Shelley* (Oxford, 1921 and frequently reprinted).
—— 'The L'Estrange–Peacock Correspondence', *Essays and Studies*, 18 (Oxford, 1933), 122–48.

—— and Jones, C. E. (eds.), *The Works of Thomas Love Peacock*, 10 vols. (London, 1924–34; repr. New York, 1967) ['The Halliford Edition'].

Bromwich, David (ed.), 'The Four Ages of Poetry', in *Romantic Critical Essays* (Cambridge, 1987), 199–211.

Cairncross, A. S. (ed.), *Maid Marian* (Edinburgh, 1935).

Cameron, Kenneth Neill, and Reiman, Donald H. (eds.), *Shelley and his Circle 1773–1822*, 8 vols. to date (Cambridge, Mass., 1961–86).

Cole, Henry (ed.), *The Works of Thomas Love Peacock*, 3 vols. (London, 1875) [preface by Lord Houghton; biographical notice by Peacock's grandaughter Edith Nicolls].

Dodson, Charles B. (ed.), *Nightmare Abbey, The Misfortunes of Elphin, Crotchet Castle* (New York, 1971).

Fain, John T., 'Peacock's Essay on Steam Navigation', *South Atlantic Bulletin*, 35 (1970), 11–15.

Garnett, David (ed.), *The Novels of Thomas Love Peacock* (London, 1948; repr. in 2 vols., 1963).

Garnett, Richard (ed.), *Thomas Love Peacock: The Novels, Calidore and Miscellanea*, 10 vols. (London, 1891) [vol. x contains recollections of Peacock by Sir Edward Strachey, the son of Peacock's friend and colleague at India House].

Green, David Bonnell, 'Two Letters of Thomas Love Peacock', *Philological Quarterly*, 40 (1961), 593–6.

Johnson, R. Brimley (ed.), *The Poems of Thomas Love Peacock* (London, 1906).

Jordan, John E. (ed.), *A Defence of Poetry: Percy Bysshe Shelley, The Four Ages of Poetry: Thomas Love Peacock* (Indianapolis, 1965).

Joukovsky, Nicholas A., 'A Critical Edition of Thomas Love Peacock's *Headlong Hall* and *Nightmare Abbey* with Some Material for a Critical Edition of *Melincourt*', D.Phil. thesis (Oxford, 1970).

—— 'Thomas Love Peacock on Sir Robert Peel: An Unpublished Satire', *Modern Philology*, 73 (1975a), 81–4.

—— 'The Composition of Peacock's *Melincourt* and the Date of the "Calidore" Fragment', *English Language Notes*, 13 (1975b), 18–25.

—— 'A Mistaken Peacock Attribution: "A Can of Cream from Devon"', *Notes and Queries*, 22 (1975c), 112–13.

—— 'A Dialogue on Idealities: An Unpublished Manuscript of Thomas Love Peacock', *Yearbook of English Studies*, 7 (1977), 128–40.

—— 'A New "Little Book" by Thomas Love Peacock', *Modern Philology*, 85 (1988), 293–9.

—— 'The Lost Greek Anapests of Thomas Love Peacock', *Modern Philology*, 89 (1991–2), 363–74.

—— 'Thomas Love Peacock's Manuscript "Poems" of 1804', *Studies in Bibliography*, 47 (1994), 196–211.

—— 'Peacock and his "Pet Politician": An Unpublished Latin Squib on the Coalition against Palmerston', *Modern Language Review*, 91/4 (1996), 833–9.

Lloyd-Evans, Barbara (ed.), *Novels of Thomas Love Peacock* (London, 1967) [texts of *Headlong Hall, Nightmare Abbey, Melincourt, Crotchet Castle* with introd. by J. B. Priestley].

Mendelson, Anne, 'The Peacock–Meredith Cookbook Project: Long-Sundered Manuscripts and Unanswered Questions', *Biblion: The Bulletin of the New York Public Library*,
2 (1993), 77–99.

Mills, Howard (ed.), *Memoirs of Shelley and Other Essays and Reviews* (London, 1970).

Moody, H. L. B. (ed.), *A Peacock Selection* (London, 1966).

Scott, W. S. (ed.), *New Shelley Letters* (London, 1948).

Tomkins, A. R., *Nightmare Abbey*, Medallion English Texts (London, 1966).

Wordsworth, Jonathan (ed.), *Nightmare Abbey* [facsimile of 1818 edition] (Oxford, 1992).

Wright, Raymond (ed.), *Nightmare Abbey* and *Crotchet Castle* (Harmondsworth, 1969).

Yarker, P. M. (ed.), *Headlong Hall* and *Nightmare Abbey* (London, 1961).

CRITICISM AND COMMENTARY

Able, Augustus Henry, *George Meredith and Thomas Love Peacock: A Study in Literary
Influence* (Philadelphia, 1933).

Amis, Kingsley, *What Became of Jane Austen? and Other Questions* (London, 1970).

Bate, Jonathan, 'Apeing Romanticism', in Michael Cordner, Peter Holland, and John
Kerrigan (eds.), *English Comedy* (Cambridge, 1994), 221–40.

Bell, Clive, *Potboilers* (London, 1918).

Brogan, Howard O., 'Romantic Classicism in Peacock's Verse Satire', *Studies in English
Literature 1500–1900*, 14 (1974), 525–36.

Brooks, Harold, 'A Song from Mr. Cypress', *Review of English Studies*, 38 (1987), 368–74.

Brooks, Linda M., 'Lucian and Peacock: Peacock's Menippean Romanticism', *Revue
belge de philologie et d'histoire*, 66 (1988), 590–601.

Brown, Nathaniel, 'The "Brightest Colours of Intellectual Beauty": Feminism in
Peacock's Novels', *Keats–Shelley Review*, 2 (1987), 91–104.

Buchanan, Robert, 'Thomas Love Peacock: A Personal Reminiscence', *New Quarterly
Magazine*, 4 (1875), 238–55; repr. in his *A Poet's Sketch-Book* (London, 1883), 93–118
and *A Look Round Literature* (London, 1887), 162–84.

Burns, Bryan, *The Novels of Thomas Love Peacock* (London, 1985a).

—— 'The Classicism of Peacock's *Gryll Grange*', *Keats–Shelley Memorial Bulletin*, 36 (1985b),
89–101.

Bush, Douglas, *Mythology and the Romantic Tradition in English Poetry* (Cambridge, Mass.,
1937; repr. New York, 1963).

Butler, Marilyn, *Peacock Displayed: A Satirist in his Context* (London, 1979).

—— *Romantics, Rebels and Reactionaries: English Literature and its Background 1760–1830*
(Oxford, 1981).

—— 'Myth and Mythmaking in the Shelley Circle', *English Literary History*, 49 (1982),
50–72; repr. in Kelvin Everest (ed.), *Shelley Revalued* (Leicester, 1983), 1–19.

—— 'Druids, Bards and Twice-Born Bacchus: Peacock's Engagement with Primitive
Mythology', *Keats–Shelley Memorial Bulletin*, 36 (1985), 57–76.

Buxton, John, *The Grecian Taste: Literature in the Age of Neo-Classicism 1740–1820* (London,
1978).

Cameron, K. N., 'Shelley and *Ahrimanes*', *Modern Language Quarterly*, 3 (1942), 287–95.

Campbell, Olwen Ward, *Thomas Love Peacock* (London, 1953).

Chandler, Alice, 'The Quarrel of the Ancients and Moderns: Peacock and the Medieval Revival', *Bucknell Review*, 13 (Dec. 1965), 39–50; repr. in her *A Dream of Order: The Medieval Ideal in Nineteenth-Century English Literature* (Lincoln, Nebr., 1970; London, 1971), 115–21.

Chapman, R. W., 'Thomas Love Peacock', in his *Johnsonian and Other Essays and Reviews* (Oxford, 1963), 96–103.

Cole, Sir Henry, *Thomas Love Peacock: Biographical Notes from 1785–1862* (London: privately printed in 10 copies, 1874).

Colmer, John, 'Godwin's *Mandeville* and Peacock's *Nightmare Abbey*', *Review of English Studies*, 21 (1970), 331–6.

Crabbe, John K., 'The Harmony of her Mind: Peacock's Emancipated Women', *Tennessee Studies in Literature*, 23 (1978), 75–86 [practically identical to the following article].

—— 'The Emerging Heroine in the Works of Thomas Love Peacock', *Zeitschrift für Anglistik und Amerikanistik* (A Quarterly of Language, Literature, and Culture), 27 (1979), 121–32 [practically identical to the preceding article].

Cunningham, Mark, ' "Fatout! who am I?": A Model for the Honourable Mr. Listless in Thomas Love Peacock's *Nightmare Abbey*', *English Language Notes*, 30 (1992), 43–5.

Dawson, Carl, *Thomas Love Peacock* (London, 1968).

—— *His Fine Wit: A Study of Thomas Love Peacock* (London, 1970).

—— 'Peacock's Comedy: A Retrospective Glance', *Keats–Shelley Memorial Bulletin*, 36 (1985), 102–13.

de Groot, H. B., 'The Status of the Poet in an Age of Brass: Isaac Disraeli, Peacock, W. J. Fox and Others', *Victorian Periodicals Newsletter*, 10 (1977), 106–22.

Duff, David, *Romance and Revolution: Shelley and the Politics of a Genre* (Cambridge, 1994).

Dyson, A. E., 'Peacock: The Wand of Enchantment', in his *The Crazy Fabric: Essays in Irony* (London, 1965), 57–71.

Fain, John T., 'Peacock on the Spirit of the Age (1809–1860)', in Robert A. Bryan et al. (eds.), *All These to Teach: Essays in Honour of C. A. Robertson* (Gainesville, Fla., 1965), 180–9.

Felton, Felix, *Thomas Love Peacock* (London, 1973).

Freeman, A. Martin, *Thomas Love Peacock: A Critical Study* (London, 1911).

Fry, Paul, 'Shelley's "Defence of Poetry" in our Time', in his *The Reach of Criticism: Method and Perception in Literary Theory* (New Haven, 1983), 125–67.

Frye, Northrop, *Anatomy of Criticism: Four Essays* (Princeton, 1957).

—— *The Critical Path: An Essay on the Social Context of Literary Criticism* (Bloomington, Ind., 1971).

Gallon, David, 'Thomas Love Peacock and Wales: Some Suggestions', *Anglo-Welsh Review*, 17 (1968), 125–34.

—— 'Thomas Love Peacock's Later Years: The Evidence of Unpublished Letters', *Review of English Studies*, 20 (1969), 315–19. See further Peter Hawkins, *Review of English Studies*, 21 (1970), 338.

Garside, Peter, '*Headlong Hall* Revisited', *Trivium*, 14 (May 1979), 107–26.

Haley, Bruce, 'Shelley, Peacock, and the Reading of History', *Studies in Romanticism*, 29 (1990), 439–61.

Hall, Jean, 'The Divine and the Dispassionate Selves: Shelley's *Defence* and Peacock's *The Four Ages of Poetry*', *Keats–Shelley Journal*, 41 (1992), 139–63.

Harrold, William F., 'Keats's "Lamia" and Peacock's "Rhododaphne" ' *Modern Language Review*, 61 (1966), 579–84.

Hewitt, Douglas, 'Entertaining Ideas: A Critique of *Crotchet Castle*', *Essays in Criticism*, 20 (1970), 200–12; repr. in his *The Approach to Fiction: Good and Bad Reading of Novels* (London, 1972), 147–60.

Hinkle, Roger, *Comedy and Culture: England 1820–1900* (Princeton, 1980).

Hoff, Peter Sloat, 'The Voices of *Crotchet Castle*', *Journal of Narrative Technique*, 2 (1972), 186–98.

—— 'Maid Marian and The Misfortunes of Elphin: Peacock's Burlesque Romances', *Genre*, 8 (1975a), 210–32.

—— 'The Paradox of the Fortunate Foible: Thomas Love Peacock's Literary Vision', *Texas Studies in Literature and Language*, 17 (1975b), 481–8.

Hogle, Jerrold E., 'The Poetics of Re-vision: Teaching *A Defence of Poetry*', in Spencer Hall (ed.), *Approaches to Teaching Shelley's Poetry* (New York, 1990), 114–19.

House, Humphrey, 'The Works of Peacock', *Listener*, 42 (1949), 997–8.

Howells, Coral Ann, 'Biographia Literaria and Nightmare Abbey', *Notes and Queries*, 16 (1969), 50–1.

Hunt, John Dixon, 'Sense and Sensibility in the Landscape Designs of Humphrey Repton', *Studies in Burke and his Time*, 19 (1978), 3–28.

Jack, Ian, *English Literature 1815–1832*, vol. x of *The Oxford History of English Literature* (Oxford, 1963).

Johnson, Diane, *The True History of the First Mrs. Meredith and Other Lesser Lives* (London, 1973).

Joukovsky, Nicholas A., 'Peacock's Sir Oran Haut-ton: Byron's Bear or Shelley's Ape?', *Keats–Shelley Journal*, 29 (1980), 173–90.

—— 'Peacock before Headlong Hall: A New Look at his Early Years', *Keats–Shelley Memorial Bulletin*, 36 (1985), 1–40.

Kane, Richard C., 'Bergsonian Comic Theory and *Crotchet Castle*', *Pennsylvania English*, 12 (1986), 39–43.

Kelly, Gary, *English Fiction of the Romantic Period 1789–1830* (London, 1989).

Kennedy, William F., 'Peacock's Economists: Some Mistaken Identities', *Nineteenth-Century Fiction*, 21 (1966), 185–91.

Kiely, Robert, *The Romantic Novel in England* (Cambridge, Mass., 1972).

Kiernan, Robert F., *Frivolity Unbound: Six Masters of the Camp Novel* (New York, 1990).

Kjellin, Håkan, *Talkative Banquets: A Study in the Peacockian Novels of Talk*, Stockholm Studies in the History of Literature 14 (Stockholm, 1974).

Krieger, Murray, 'The Arts and the Idea of Progress', in Marvin Chodorow and Roy Harvey Pearce (eds.), *Progress and its Discontents* (Berkeley and Los Angeles, 1982), 449–69.

Ludwig, Jack Berry, 'The Peacock Tradition in English Prose Fiction', Ph.D. thesis (University of California, Los Angeles, 1953).

McFarland, G. F., 'Shelley and Julius Hare: A Review and a Response', *Bulletin of the John Rylands University Library of Manchester*, 57 (1974–5), 406–29.

McKay, Margaret, 'Thomas Love Peacock in the Diaries of Sir Henry Cole', *Notes and Queries*, 36 (1989), 176–8.

—— *Peacock's Progress: Aspects of Artistic Development in the Novels of Thomas Love Peacock*, Studia Anglistica Upsaliensia 78 (Stockholm, 1992).

Mackerness, E. D., 'Thomas Love Peacock's Musical Criticism', *Wind and the Rain*, 4 (Winter 1948), 177–87.

Madden, Lionel, *Thomas Love Peacock* (London, 1967).

—— 'A Short Guide to Peacock Studies', *Critical Survey*, 4 (1970), 193–7.

—— ' "Terrestrial Paradise": The Welsh Dimension in Peacock's Life and Work', *Keats–Shelley Memorial Bulletin*, 36 (1985), 41–56.

Madden, Mary, and Madden, Lionel, 'Edward Scott, Botdalog and his Literary Circle: Thomas Love Peacock, James Mill and William Owen Pugh', *National Library of Wales Journal*, 24 (1986), 352–7.

Mason, Ronald, 'Notes for an Estimate of Peacock', *Horizon*, 9 (1944), 238–50.

Mayoux, Jean-Jacques, *Un Épicurien anglais: Thomas Love Peacock* (Paris, 1933).

—— preface to *L'Abbaye de Cauchemar, Les Malheurs d'Elphin* [French translation of *Nightmare Abbey* and *The Misfortunes of Elphin*] (Paris, 1936; *L'Abbaye de Cauchemar* repr. Paris, 1993).

Mills, Howard, *Peacock: His Circle and his Age* (Cambridge, 1969).

—— 'The Dirty Boots of the Bourgeoisie: Peacock on Music', *Keats–Shelley Memorial Bulletin*, 36 (1985), 77–88.

Mullet, Charles F., '*The Bee* (1790–94): A Tour of Crotchet Castle', *South Atlantic Quarterly*, 66 (1967), 70–86.

Mulvihill, James D., 'Thomas Love Peacock's *Crotchet Castle*: Reconciling the Spirits of the Age', *Nineteenth-Century Fiction*, 38 (1983), 253–70.

—— 'Peacock and Perfectibility in *Headlong Hall*', *Clio*, 13/3 (1984a), 227–46.

—— ' "The Four Ages of Poetry": Peacock and the Historical Method', *Keats–Shelley Journal*, 33 (1984b), 130–47.

—— 'A New Coleridge Source for Peacock's *Melincourt*', *Notes and Queries*, 32 (1985), 344–5.

—— 'A Tookean Presence in Peacock's *Melincourt*', *English Studies*, 67 (1986), 216–20.

—— *Thomas Love Peacock* (Boston, 1987a).

—— 'A Source for Peacock's Satire on Spiritualism in *Gryll Grange*', *Notes and Queries*, 34 (1987b), 491–2.

—— 'Peacock, Monboddo and the Dialogue', *Notes and Queries*, 35 (1988), 310–11.

Munby, A. N. L. (ed.), *Sale Catalogues of the Libraries of Eminent Persons*, i: *Poets and Men of Letters* (London, 1971).

Nesbitt, G. L., *Benthamite Reviewing: The First Twelve Years of the Westminster Review 1824–1836* (New York, 1934).

Newbolt, Henry, 'Peacock, Scott and Robin Hood', *Transactions of the Royal Society of Literature*, 4 (1924), 87–118; repr. in his *Studies Green and Gray* (London, 1926), 162–92.

Nicholes, Eleanor L., 'Thomas Love Peacock: Life and Works', in Kenneth Neill Cameron (ed.), *Shelley and his Circle 1773–1822*, vol. i (Cambridge, Mass., 1961); repr. in K. N. Cameron (ed.), *Romantic Rebels: Essays on Shelley and his Circle* (Cambridge, Mass., 1973), 90–114.

Nicholes, Eleanor L., 'Thomas Love Peacock', in *The New Cambridge Bibliography of English Literature*, iii: *1800–1900* (Cambridge, 1969), 700–4.

Polhemus, Robert M., *Comic Faith: The Great Tradition from Austen to Joyce* (Chicago, 1981).

Prance, Claude A., *The Characters in the Novels of Thomas Love Peacock 1785–1866: With Bibliographical Lists* (Lewiston, NY, 1992).

Praz, Mario, *The Hero in Eclipse in Victorian Fiction* (London, 1956).

Prickett, Stephen, 'Peacock's Four Ages Recycled', *British Journal of Aesthetics*, 22 (1982), 158–66.

—— *England and the French Revolution*, Macmillan Education Context and Commentary Series (New York, 1989).

Priestley, J. B., *The English Comic Characters* (London, 1925; repr. 1963).

—— *Thomas Love Peacock* (London, 1927; repr. with an introd. by J. I. M. Stewart, 1966).

Quinn, Mary A., ' "Ozymandias" as Shelley's Rejoinder to Peacock's "Palmyra" ', *English Language Notes*, 21/4 (1984), 48–56.

Raleigh, Walter, *On Writing and Writers* (London, 1926).

Read, Bill, 'The Critical Reputation of Thomas Love Peacock with an Annotated Enumerative Bibliography of Works by and about Peacock from February, 1800 to June, 1958', Ph.D. thesis (Boston University, 1959); available as microfilm or xerox from University Microfilms (Ann Arbor).

—— 'Thomas Love Peacock: An Enumerative Bibliography', *Bulletin of Bibliography*, 24 (1963–4), 32–4, 70–2, 88–91.

Reiman, Donald H., *English Romantic Poetry, 1800–1835: A Guide to Information Sources* (Detroit, 1979), 212–16.

Robinson, Eric, 'Thomas Love Peacock: Critic of Scientific Progress', *Annals of Science*, 10 (1954), 69–77.

Robinson, H. M., 'Aristophanes, Coleridge and Peacock', *Notes and Queries*, 26 (1979), 232.

Rodway, Alan, *English Comedy* (Berkeley and Los Angeles, 1975).

Rowland, Jenny, 'The Sources of Thomas Love Peacock's *The Misfortunes of Elphin*', *Anglo-Welsh Review*, 23 (1976), 103–29.

Rudinsky, Norma L., 'The Source of Asterias' Paean to Science in Peacock's *Nightmare Abbey*', *Notes and Queries*, 22 (1975a), 66–8.

—— 'A Second Original of Peacock's Menippean Caricature Asterias in *Nightmare Abbey*: Sir John Sinclair, Bart.', *English Studies: A Journal of Language and Literature*, 56 (1975b), 491–7.

—— 'Satire on Sir John Sinclair before Peacock's Asterias in *Nightmare Abbey*', *Notes and Queries*, 23 (1976), 108–10.

—— 'Contemporary Response to the Caricature Asterias in Peacock's *Nightmare Abbey*', *Notes and Queries*, 24 (1977), 335–6.

Sage, Lorna (ed.), *Peacock: The Satirical Novels. A Casebook* (London, 1976).

Saintsbury, George, *Essays in English Literature, 1780–1860* (London, 1890).

—— *Collected Essays and Papers, 1875–1920*, 4 vols. (London, 1923).

—— *Prefaces and Essays* (London, 1933).

Salz, P. J., 'Peacock's Use of Music in his Novels', *Journal of English and Germanic Philology*, 54 (1955), 370–9.

Schmid, Thomas H., *Humor and Transgression in Peacock, Shelley, and Byron: A Cold Carnival* (Lewiston, NY, 1992).

Schwank, Klaus, 'From Satire to Indeterminacy: Thomas Love Peacock's *Nightmare Abbey*', in Michael Gassenmeier and Norbert H. Platz (eds.), *Beyond the Suburbs of the Mind: Exploring English Romanticism*, Studien zur Englischen Romantik 2 (Essen, 1987), 151–62.

Simpson, Roger, 'A Source of Peacock's *The Misfortunes of Elphin*', *Notes and Queries*, 33 (1984), 165–6.

Slater, Michael, 'Peacock's Victorian Novel', in Joanne Shattuck (ed.), *Dickens and Other Victorians: Essays in Honour of Philip Collins* (Basingstoke, 1990), 172–84.

Smith, George Barnett, 'Thomas Love Peacock', *Fortnightly Review*, 45 (1873), 189–206.

Spedding, J. H., 'Tales by the Author of *Headlong Hall*', *Edinburgh Review*, 68 (1839), 432–59; repr. in his *Reviews and Discussions: Literary, Political and Historical, not Relating to Bacon* (London, 1879), 121–52.

Staines, David, 'King Arthur in Victorian Fiction', in J. J. Buckley (ed.), *The Worlds of Victorian Fiction* (Cambridge, Mass., 1975), 267–93.

Stewart, J. I. M., *Thomas Love Peacock*, Writers and their Work (London, 1964).

Tedford, Barbara, 'A Recipe for Satire and Civilization', *Costerus: Essays in English and American Language and Literature*, 2 (1972), 197–212.

Teyssandier, Hubert, 'T. L. Peacock et le récit satirique', in his *Les Formes de la création romanesque à l'époque de Walter Scott et de Jane Austen 1814–20* (Paris, 1977), 190–250.

Tillyard, E. M. W., *Essays Literary and Educational* (London, 1962).

Tomkinson, N., 'Thomas Love Peacock', *Notes and Queries*, 37 (1990), 26–7.

Van Doren, Carl, *The Life of Thomas Love Peacock* (London, 1911; repr. New York, 1966).

Vidal, Gore, 'Thomas Love Peacock: The Novel of Ideas', in his *United States: Essays 1952–1992* (New York, 1993), 147–62.

Walling, William, ' "On Fishing up the Moon": In Search of Thomas Love Peacock', in Donald H. Reiman et al. (eds.), *The Evidence of the Imagination: Studies of Interactions between Life and Art in English Romantic Literature* (New York, 1978), 334–53.

Ward, William S., 'Contemporary Reviews of Thomas Love Peacock: A Supplementary List for the Years 1805–1820', *Bulletin of Bibliography*, 25 (1967), 35.

Wilson, Edmund, 'The Musical Glasses of Peacock', in his *Classics and Commercials* (New York, 1950), 404–11.

Woolf, Virginia, 'Phases of Fiction: The Satirists and Fantastics', *Bookman*, 69 (1929), 404–12; repr. in her *Granite and Rainbow* (London, 1958), 130–5.

Wright, Herbert, 'The Associations of Thomas Love Peacock with Wales', *Essays and Studies*, 12 (Oxford, 1926), 24–46.

Wright, Julia M., 'Peacock's Early Parody of Thomas Moore in *Nightmare Abbey*', *English Language Notes*, 30/4 (1993), 31–8.

14. *Mary Wollstonecraft Shelley*

PAMELA CLEMIT

GENERAL

Mary Wollstonecraft Shelley has long been celebrated and patronized as the author of *Frankenstein; or, The Modern Prometheus* (1818), a work which has been canonized on university and sixth-form courses, studied exhaustively by scholars of different critical persuasions, and travestied by film-makers. Yet relatively few readers of *Frankenstein* realize that Mary Shelley also wrote five other novels, one novella, two mythological verse dramas, dozens of tales, stories, essays, and reviews, two books of travel writings, and two sets of notes to her editions of P. B. Shelley's works. However, the situation is changing. In the late 1980s, authoritative editions of her letters and journals appeared, which shed new light on her thirty-year career as a professional writer. More recently, the first scholarly edition of her novels and selected writings has been published, and this provides the basis for a critical reassessment of Mary Shelley as a major nineteenth-century writer. The beginnings of this reassessment are already apparent in recent criticism, which has moved beyond *Frankenstein*. Thus, as well as reviewing the most important developments in *Frankenstein* criticism, this survey will evaluate newer and more wide-ranging work.

TEXTS AND TEXTUAL COMMENTARY

The standard scholarly edition of Mary Shelley's writings is published by Pickering & Chatto in eight volumes (gen. ed. Crook with Clemit). This reprints all of her full-length novels: *Frankenstein, Valperga; or, The Life and Adventures of Castruccio, Prince of Lucca* (1823), *The Last Man* (1826), *The Fortunes of Perkin Warbeck* (1830), *Lodore* (1835), and *Falkner* (1837). In addition, there is one volume of shorter writings, which contains her novella *Matilda* (written 1819), two mythological verse dramas *Proserpine* and *Midas* (both written 1820), twelve essays and reviews, and all of the prefaces and notes to her editions of P. B. Shelley's poetry and prose (1839–40). There is also one volume of travel writings, containing *History of a Six Weeks' Tour* (1817) and *Rambles in Germany and Italy, in 1840, 1842, and 1843* (1844). In most cases, the copy text is the first published text of each item, and variants from revised texts are recorded in appendices, a policy which is especially illuminating in the case of *Frankenstein*, where the revised text of 1831 differs significantly from the text of the first edition of 1818. However, there are three instances in which the copy text is the manuscript fair copy: *Matilda* and *Midas*, both of which remained unpublished during Mary Shelley's lifetime, and *Proserpine*, which was published only in a much truncated form in *The Winter's Wreath*, a literary annual. It should be noted that the edition of *Matilda* in the *Novels and Selected Works* marks a significant advance on the two earlier editions (see below), both of which are based on the first published text of 1959 (Nitchie). For the Pickering edition, however, the text has been newly transcribed from the manuscript fair copy, and Mary Shelley's rough draft, 'The Fields of Fancy', is transcribed in full for the first time, enabling readers to compare the two radically different manuscript versions of the novella. Students interested in the manuscripts of *Frankenstein*, *Matilda*, *Proserpine*, and *Midas*, or in Mary Shelley's transcriptions of P. B. Shelley's writings, may wish to consult the relevant volumes in two collections of facsimile reproductions: *Manuscripts of the Younger Romantics* and *The Bodleian Shelley Manuscripts* (both gen. ed. Reiman).

Turning to student texts, both the 1818 and the 1831 *Frankenstein* are readily available in paperback. The 1831 text, the last one corrected by the author and thus the conventional choice, is available in Oxford World's Classics (Joseph), in Penguin Classics (Hindle), which has a valuable critical introduction, and in a Bedford Books edition which includes essays from a range of modern critical perspectives (Smith). However, the 1818 text is fast becoming the standard text for serious students: first published by Rieger in a scholarly edition (reprinted in paperback), it has been preferred by Bennett and Robinson for their *The Mary Shelley Reader*, and has also been edited by Butler for Pickering (reprinted by Oxford), and by Macdonald and Scherf for Broadview. Since Mary Shelley's revisions change the meaning of the text in important ways, students should be aware of the differences between the two editions. The task of comparison is facilitated in the Rieger, Butler, and Macdonald and Scherf editions by appendices which list substantive changes in the 1831 text and reprint the author's 1831 introduction, while Hindle lists variants between 1831 and 1818. Butler also provides a useful commentary on the critical significance of Mary Shelley's revisions, most of which, she says, '*introduce* an element of interpretation into Frankenstein's narrative, where they congregate', by adding new mythic and spiritual resonances. Critics remain divided between the 1818 and the 1831 editions of the novel: some have accepted Mary Shelley's retrospective account of the composition of the novel in the 1831 introduction as authoritative; others have reconstructed the 1818 setting and concerns (see below). This uncertainty about the authoritative text has been compounded by a dispute over authorship. Rieger was the first to argue that P. B. Shelley, the author of the preface to the 1818 edition, played a significant role in the composition of the story; Murray in his study of the manuscripts adopts a compromise position, concluding that P. B. Shelley's 'creative impulse added its own initiative to the novel's effect, though always in keeping with Mary's conception and with her implicit sanction'; Mellor (1988) views P. B. Shelley's revisions as distorting impositions; while Leader argues that Mary Shelley's 'sense of authorship as collaborative' led her to welcome P. B. Shelley's contributions, which 'may have posed less of a test or threat than Mellor thinks'.

The availability of Mary Shelley's other writings in student editions is steadily improving. Bennett and Robinson's *The Mary Shelley Reader* includes *Matilda*, several tales, stories, and reviews, the preface to her edition of *The Poetical Works of Percy Bysshe Shelley* (1839), and a small number of letters. Annotations and commentary are brief, but this is the first student edition to present a view of Mary Shelley as a major nineteenth-century author, rather than as solely the 'Author of *Frankenstein*'. Mary Shelley's short stories, most of which were originally published in *The Keepsake*, one of the most popular literary annuals of the day, are available with a scholarly commentary in Robinson's paperback *Collected Tales and Stories*; *Matilda* may be read alongside *Mary* and *Maria* by Mary Wollstonecraft (Mary Shelley's mother) in Todd's Pickering Women's Classics edition (reprinted in Penguin). There are two unannotated reprints of Luke's 1965 edition of *The Last Man*, but the Oxford World's Classics edition (Paley) and the Broadview Literary Texts edition (McWhir) are to be preferred. In addition, there is a recent Broadview Literary Texts edition of *Lodore*, and work is in progress on two paperback editions of *Valperga*.

BIOGRAPHIES AND LETTERS

Mary Shelley's letters have been authoritatively edited by Bennett, and Mary Shelley's journals, which contain lists of books read by herself and her husband from 1814 to 1822, have been recently re-edited to a high standard by Feldman and Scott-Kilvert. Both of these editorial projects have done much to establish and deepen awareness of Mary Shelley's long career as author and editor. Bennett's edition in particular has made an immense contribution to Mary Shelley scholarship. It presents hundreds of previously unpublished letters which illuminate Mary Shelley's political opinions, intellectual contacts, personal friendships, and, perhaps most important, her 'fundamental consciousness of herself as author' (Bennett 1992). Moreover, Bennett's editorial rationale has important implications for literary critics. By contrast with earlier commentators, who viewed Mary Shelley solely in terms of her relations with P. B. Shelley, the challenge for Bennett was 'to recognize fully Mary Shelley as the source of her own works, and provide annotations that demonstrated her interaction with the influences and interests in her life from which that artistic reality emanated' (Bennett 1993). It remains to be seen how literary critics will respond to the new, complex, politically aware Mary Shelley made visible in this edition. Bennett has published a paperback selection of Mary Shelley's letters, and Feldman and Scott-Kilvert's edition of the journals has been reissued in paperback.

There is no standard biography of Mary Shelley. Though Grylls and Nitchie contain useful material, they give only cursory attention to Mary Shelley's career after the death of her husband. The subtitles of two later biographies, 'Child of Light' (Spark) and 'Moon in Eclipse' (Dunn), betray a recurrent sense of Mary Shelley as a figure overshadowed by her distinguished relations, though Spark in a revised edition of her biography presents her as 'a professional writer of lasting fame'. Sunstein was the first biographer to assimilate and interpret the new editions of the letters and journals, but there is still a need for a study that does justice to Mary Shelley's political awareness, her versatility as a writer, and her wide circle of intellectual and literary contacts. A full-scale biography by Bennett is under way.

CRITICISM

There is a useful bibliography of *Frankenstein* criticism in Spector. For primary texts and criticism of other works, readers should consult Lyles. Sunstein gives a full list of Mary Shelley's writings in an appendix, but readers should note that some of the essays are doubtful attributions. The third edition of the *Cambridge Bibliography of English Literature* (currently in preparation) will contain an authoritative list of primary texts. Early reviews of *Frankenstein*, *Valperga*, and *The Last Man* are available in Reiman's compilation of facsimile reproductions. Useful surveys of twentieth-century criticism are provided by Baldick, who traces the development of the *Frankenstein* myth in later nineteenth-century writings, and by Botting (1991), who analyses the critical tradition, using the theoretical frameworks of Derrida, Foucault, Freud, and Lacan.

Criticism of *Frankenstein* came of age in 1979 with a collection of essays called *The Endurance of Frankenstein* (Levine and Knoepflmacher), which recognized the novel's 'stunning ambivalences' as a positive quality and gave serious attention to its wide range of metaphorical and mythical meanings. Previous critics were on the whole puzzled by the textual and generic instability of *Frankenstein*, and tended to approach the novel with a restrictive, predetermined agenda, which owed much to the interpretative context supplied by Mary Shelley in her retrospective account of the composition of the novel in the introduction to the 1831 edition. Here she set out to answer the question which every reader, then and now, must have asked: 'How I, then a young girl, came to think of, and to dilate upon, so very hideous an idea?' The effect of her account is to establish a new way of reading a work which early reviewers, prompted by the dedication to the author's father William Godwin, had linked with the radical political writings of the 1790s (see Reiman 1972). In 1831, by contrast, Mary Shelley emphasizes biographical, aesthetic, and moral concerns. Her emphasis on the overtly literary genesis of her tale forms an essential part of its remaking as a Romantic text. Setting up an elaborate context for the composition of the novel, she presents herself as the daughter of distinguished literary parents, and as the nearly silent listener to the erudite conversations of P. B. Shelley and Byron while in Switzerland in the summer of 1816. In addition, she describes how the idea for the story came to her in a dream, and presents the process of composition as involuntary and unwilled. She describes the book itself as a 'hideous progeny', thus identifying it with the monster of her tale as a product of transgression against divine order. Mid-twentieth-century critics took this account at face value and read *Frankenstein* largely in terms of Mary Shelley's relations with other people, Godwin, P. B. Shelley, or Byron. Going one step further, Bloom presented the novel in relation to contemporary texts issuing from what he terms 'the archetypal world of the Romantics'. He claims that 'what makes *Frankenstein* an important book, though it is only a strong, flawed novel with frequent clumsiness in its narrative and characterization, is that it contains one of the most vivid representations we have of the Romantic mythology of the self, one that resembles Blake's *Book of Urizen*, Shelley's *Prometheus Unbound*, and Byron's *Manfred*, among other works'. Though Bloom attributes a certain value to *Frankenstein*, it nevertheless remains a lesser work because it lacks 'sophistication and imaginative complexity', qualities which in this account are found only in Romantic poetry. However, other critics did recognize a sophistication and imaginative complexity in *Frankenstein*, and the most useful early readings concerned with literary relations are those which consider the novel as engaging in critical dialogue with works by Godwin, P. B. Shelley, or Byron (Harvey, Fleck, Goldberg), or which study a fuller range of sources (Pollin).

There are two other groups of early interpretations based on restrictive presuppositions. First, some readings emphasize the moral and psychological dimensions of the tale, which has been variously described as a treatment of 'the psychological problem of evil' (Hume), a 'mythology of the mind' (Nelson), or a 'purely mental drama of damnation' (Swingle). In readings such as these the social and historical circumstances of the novel are ignored and the story of *Frankenstein* is reduced, in Baldick's phrase, to 'a parable about

the eternal dilemmas of the human condition'. That this approach is still attractive to modern critics can be seen in Veeder's full-length study, which attributes
to Mary Shelley a 'lifelong concern with the psychological ideal of androgyny',
and is a fund of commonplace remarks about 'enduring' psychic forces. A
second group of limiting interpretations read the novel as a prophecy of dangerous scientific inventions (Florescu, Tropp), with the monster as a 'techno-
logical double' (Tropp) standing in opposition to humanity. However, the view
of the monster as a subhuman automaton involves a serious misreading of
the story, where the monster's exemplary humanity is emphasized. In addition, reading the novel as a cautionary tale of scientific research—whether
computer technology, nuclear power, or genetic engineering—reduces it to a
timelessly reapplicable message and overlooks its specific historical and scientific
context. For informed analyses of *Frankenstein* in relation to the scientific controversies of the day, readers should turn to the more recent studies by Mellor
and Butler.

The Endurance of Frankenstein introduces a larger set of critical perspectives
—psychobiographical, historical, generic, cinematic—which suggest that *Frankenstein* 'belongs to a prophetic tradition open only ... to mature literary
imaginations' (Levine and Knoepflmacher). Yet the collection as a whole
remains curiously unsure about the question posed at the start: 'How much
of the book's complexity is actually the result of Mary Shelley's self-conscious
art and how much is merely the product of the happy circumstances of subject, moment, milieu?' (Levine and Knoepflmacher). This uncertainty concerning the status of Mary Shelley as a self-conscious artist remains a feature
of *Frankenstein* criticism down to the present day. Nevertheless these essays,
taken together, have established a consensus about the meaning of the novel:
that it presents 'a secular myth, with no metaphysical machinery, no gods'
(Levine); that Mary Shelley expresses through the figure of Frankenstein her
responses to Godwin and P. B. Shelley; that the monster, as well as being
Frankenstein's double, is also concerned with issues of female identity; and
that the greatness of the book lies in its 'fusion of the personal and the political, the private and the ideological' (Scott). Two sets of essays in this collection are especially important in shaping the agenda for criticism of the next
fifteen years. 'Biographical Soundings: Of Mothers and Daughters', which
reprints Moers's classic essay 'Female Gothic' (see below), and includes a study
of *Frankenstein* as an expression of Mary Shelley's conflicting emotions towards
her parents (Knoepflmacher), provides a lead for feminist interpretations; while
'Contexts: Society and Self', which contains essays on Mary Shelley's critique
of the bourgeois family (Ellis 1979), her use of literary conventions from conservative political writings on the French Revolution (Sterrenburg 1979), and
her critique of P. B. Shelley's ideological commitments (Scott), forms the starting point for serious consideration of Mary Shelley as a political writer.

PAMELA CLEMIT

The history of feminist readings of *Frankenstein* parallels the history of the development of feminist criticism from the mid-1970s onwards. Early feminist critics, seeking to avoid traditional approaches which claimed the experience of males as universally human, interpreted all women's thought and writing in terms of the function of being a woman. Thus Moers (1976) reads *Frankenstein* as 'a birth myth', which reflects Mary Shelley's 'early and chaotic experience, at the very time she became an author, with motherhood'. In another influential reading, *Frankenstein* is a reflection not of female biological experience but of female experience of patriarchal literary forms: 'a gothic psychodrama reflecting Mary Shelley's own sense of what we might call bibliogenesis . . . a version of the misogynistic story implicit in *Paradise Lost*' (Gilbert and Gubar). This approach has the effect of removing Mary Shelley from the mainstream Romantic canon, and placing her in a selective tradition of women writers who were 'literally and figuratively confined' by 'an overwhelmingly male-dominated society' and by 'male texts' (Gilbert and Gubar). Poovey, who situates Mary Shelley alongside Mary Wollstonecraft and Jane Austen in the wider context of early nineteenth-century bourgeois society, reads *Frankenstein* as a critique of Romantic egotism which violates social obligations, a thesis extended by Mellor into the realms of politics and science. Both Poovey and Mellor have done much to consolidate the prevailing Anglo-American view, first adumbrated by Fleck, of Mary Shelley as a politically conservative writer: Poovey sees her as trapped between the 'masculine' role of authorship and the dominant ideology of feminine propriety, while Mellor views her as an apologist for bourgeois family values.

Other feminist readings interpret *Frankenstein* in the light of poststructuralist theories, highlighting the reduction or exclusion of the female. Jacobus provides an instructive critique of feminists who insist on 'an unbroken continuity between "life" and "text" ', arguing instead for an approach based on the French concept of *écriture féminine*, in which 'the "feminine" . . . is to be located in the gaps, the absences, the unsayable or unrepresentable of discourse and representation'. Thus she interprets *Frankenstein* as a representation of 'oedipal politics', in which there is no place for a female author except as 'a dismembered corpse'. Johnson suggests that the novel focuses on 'the elimination of the mother' as well on 'the fear of somehow affecting the death of one's own parents'. A broader perspective is offered by the postcolonialist critic Spivak, who views *Frankenstein* as a novel which resists the oppositions on which western individualism is based by its refusal of narrative closure. Shifting the discussion to the realm of language, Homans argues that Frankenstein, having circumvented the maternal by his act of solitary creation, comes to resemble the son in Lacanian psychoanalysis, who 'seeks figurations that will at once make restitution for the mother and confirm her death and absence by substituting for her figures that are under his control'. For all the ingenuity of such readings, the question remains: 'Can the prevalent mode of feminist criticism go beyond narrow agendas to see women's diversity rather than insist that women have only one and the same life-experience?' (Bennett 1993).

By contrast with feminist readings which tend to emphasize unconscious meanings, historical critics recognize Mary Shelley as a self-conscious artist for whom fiction is an intervention in the public world. Several critics have read *Frankenstein* as relating back to the polarized political debates of the 1790s. Paulson relates the novel to images of revolutionary terror found not only in contemporary Gothic fiction but also in the revolutionary narratives of Burke and Barruel. Yet the novel is more than an allegory of the upheavals of the 1790s; its elaborate framework of political allusions establishes it as 'a retrospect on the whole process through Waterloo' (Paulson). For Sterrenburg (1979), Mary Shelley is a deeply conservative writer who draws on images of monstrosity in revolutionary polemics to criticize her father's utopian optimism, a view disputed by Clemit, who argues that Mary Shelley is in fact following Godwin in her reworking of these images. Both critics note that the text voices competing political views, but while Sterrenburg sees Mary Shelley as moving away from politics towards 'the quarrel within', Clemit sees her as engaged in a revaluation of political traditions in the manner of Godwin in his later novels, P. B. Shelley, and Byron. For Baldick the contending political positions in *Frankenstein* lead to a 'mythically productive equivocation', and, following Sterrenburg, he surveys the development of the novel itself as a political metaphor in nineteenth-century writings. O'Flinn's lucid account of Mary Shelley's response to events in England at the time of the novel's composition, notably the Luddite disturbances and the Pentridge rising, provides an instructive reminder that *Frankenstein* is not solely concerned with politics in the head, and again reveals a Mary Shelley 'who shared the radicalism of Byron and Shelley'. The politically engaged novelist of ideas found in historical readings is thus very different from the timorous, beleaguered authorial figure uncovered by feminist criticism.

Several other strands in *Frankenstein* criticism deserve brief notice. The novel has been considered from new angles in two monographs that link Mary Shelley with other writers of the period. For Favret, Mary Shelley shares with Mary Wollstonecraft, Helen Maria Williams, and Jane Austen a concern with the forms of public and private expression offered by letter-writing: as 'an interactive combination of tales' with no central narrative authority, *Frankenstein* shows an awareness of the democratizing power of correspondence. Newlyn's discussion of *Frankenstein* as a mythopoeic revision of *Paradise Lost*, a line of argument first sketched by Tannenbaum, offers a useful corrective to Gilbert and Gubar by restoring *Frankenstein* to the mainstream Romantic canon. In addition, there are several accessible studies of the stage and film history of *Frankenstein* (Florescu, Tropp); Lavalley, who begins with Richard Brinsley

Peake's *Presumption; or, The Fate of Frankenstein* (1823) and ends with Jim Sharman's *The Rocky Horror Picture Show* (1975), offers the best survey, but O'Flinn also has some thought-provoking remarks on the Universal and Hammer films. Finally, a New Casebooks volume of essays studying *Frankenstein* in relation to modern critical theory has appeared, the tone of which is set by the editor's assertion: '*Frankenstein* is a product of criticism, not a work of literature' (Botting 1995). Criticism of *Frankenstein* seems to have imploded.

The Last Man is traditionally regarded as Mary Shelley's most important work after *Frankenstein*. While it is generally recognized that the two central male characters, Adrian and Lord Raymond, are fictional counterparts of P. B. Shelley and Byron, criticism on the whole has moved beyond biographical foraging to explore the work's intellectual themes. Serious criticism began with Sterrenburg's (1978) authoritative study of the novel as 'an ambitious, historically significant anatomy of the revolutionary age', in which Mary Shelley not only pursues the critique of Godwinian optimism begun in *Frankenstein* but also undercuts a number of other political positions, from Burke's conservative organicism to P. B. Shelley's idealistic support of the Greek struggle for independence. Some critics have read the novel as predominantly a critique of P. B. Shelley's thought (Blumberg, Mellor, Paley 1993), while feminist critics have linked the feminine personifications of destructive nature and the plague with an authorial desire for revenge on egotistical males (Poovey, Mellor). *The Last Man* has been seen by others as embodying a thoroughgoing pessimism in which 'consciousness itself is seen as contradictory, equivocal, and self-cancelling' (Snyder), or as a denial 'of *all* ideologies' (Mellor 1988), which opens the way to twentieth-century existentialism and nihilism. Such readings surely overlook the novel's insistence on the 'the fundamental importance of everything that is life-affirming' (Stafford). Most interpretations convincingly place the novel as a deliberate contrast to earlier literary treatments of the last man theme which used the trope of the end of civilization to point up ethical or religious concerns, a tradition first documented by Sambrook. Stafford, however, reads *The Last Man* in the wider context of the myth of the last of the race 'from Milton to Darwin', highlighting important continuities with Godwin in the exploration of contemporary issues such as catastrophism and Malthusian theory.

Several studies include discussion of Mary Shelley's other works as well. Of the critical books already mentioned, Poovey discusses *Falkner*, Mellor discusses *Matilda*, and Blumberg and Clemit both discuss *Valperga*. On the whole these studies confirm rather than challenge the directions established by criticism of *Frankenstein*. As already seen in the case of *The Last Man*, Poovey and Mellor view the later novels as direct extensions of the concerns mapped in *Frankenstein*. Thus for Poovey, the conflict between stereotypical feminine propriety and masculine assertiveness in *Frankenstein* is resolved in *Falkner* when the heroine is able to reconcile her father and lover precisely by conforming to nineteenth-century notions of feminine self-denial. Mellor reads *Matilda* as a projection of Mary Shelley's hostility towards her father and husband. Blumberg's study of Mary Shelley's early novels offers a fairly conventional view of Mary Shelley as a critic of the intellectual views of her father and husband, and argues for her affinity with Byron's outlook instead. By contrast, Clemit situates the early novels in the Godwinian tradition of politically engaged fiction, presenting her as a widely read intellectual whose writings show her underlying continuity with Godwin's themes and techniques. This line of argument was first adumbrated in relation to *Valperga* and *Perkin Warbeck* by Bennett, who persuasively contends that both novels offer 'an exploration of historical forces which shape the lives of individuals' (Bennett 1978). Finally, Hill-Miller's lucid and well-researched study explores Godwin's twofold legacy of intellectual support and emotional coldness to his daughter, tracking the motif of father–daughter relations through *Frankenstein*, *Matilda*, *Lodore*, and *Falkner*. Though Hill-Miller tends to reduce novelistic themes to typical patterns of father–daughter relationships, she is also attentive to issues of literary interchange, and her book should by read by everyone interested in the vexed question of Mary Shelley's relationship with Godwin.

There has been one attempt to date to survey the whole of Mary Shelley's career beyond *Frankenstein*. A collection of essays called *The Other Mary Shelley* (Fisch et al.) gives accounts of her editions of her husband's poems, journals, dramas, short stories, travel writings, and longer fiction, notably *Valperga* and *The Last Man*. Yet this 'other' Mary Shelley turns out to be a figure deeply familiar to readers of Mellor and Poovey. While paying lip-service to Mary Shelley's 'intellectual backgrounds and political commitments', the editors present 'a writer whose resistance to Romanticism from within the discursive field we call "Romantic" is in many ways continuous with the insights of contemporary feminist analysis'. Though there are valuable studies of Mary Shelley's literary dialogue with Byron (Cantor), of her revision of classical myth in her verse dramas (Richardson), and of the historical context of *Valperga*, which is read in relation to late eighteenth-century cults involving female prophets (Lew), all of these essays are aligned, more or less explicitly, with Mellor's reading of *Frankenstein* as an unequivocally conservative protest 'in the name of domesticity against the destructive effects of the Romantic heroic ideal' (Cantor). In a lone chapter of dissent, Ellis (1993) argues not only for Mary Shelley's continuity of radical interests throughout her career, but also that her 'radicalism is not necessarily, or even particularly, feminine', and this indicates some of the broader concerns that a more even-handed collection would have included. It is already evident that work at press for the 1997 bicentenary and other work in progress will significantly change critical perceptions of Mary Shelley in the next few years.

REFERENCES

TEXTS AND TEXTUAL STUDIES

Bennett, Betty T., 'Finding Mary Shelley in her Letters', in Robert Brinkley and Keith Hanley (eds.), *Romantic Revisions* (Cambridge, 1992), 291–306.

—— 'Feminism and Editing Mary Wollstonecraft Shelley: The Editor And?/Or? the Text', in George Bornstein and Ralph G. Williams (eds.), *Palimpsest: Editorial Theory in the Humanities* (Ann Arbor, 1993), 67–96.

—— and Robinson, Charles E. (eds.), *The Mary Shelley Reader* (Oxford, 1990).

Butler, Marilyn (ed.), *Frankenstein: or, The Modern Prometheus: The 1818 Text*, Pickering Women's Classics (London, 1993); World's Classics (Oxford, 1994).

Crook, Nora (gen. ed. with Pamela Clemit), *The Novels and Selected Works of Mary Shelley*, 8 vols.: i: *Frankenstein; or, The Modern Prometheus* (1818 edn.), ed. Nora Crook; ii: *Matilda* [retitled from *Mathilda*], *Dramas, Reviews & Essays, Prefaces & Notes*, ed. Pamela Clemit; iii: *Valperga; or, The Life and Adventures of Castruccio, Prince of Lucca*, ed. Nora Crook; iv: *The Last Man*, ed. Jane Blumberg; v: *The Fortunes of Perkin Warbeck*, ed. Doucet Devin Fischer; vi: *Lodore*, ed. Fiona Stafford; vii: *Falkner*, ed. Pamela Clemit; viii: *Travel Writings*, ed. Jeanne Moskal, Pickering Masters (London, 1996).

Hindle, Maurice (ed.), *Frankenstein; or, The Modern Prometheus*, Penguin Classics, (Harmondsworth, 1985; rev. edn., 1992) [1831 edn.].

Joseph, M. K. (ed.), *Frankenstein; or, The Modern Prometheus*, World's Classics (Oxford, 1980) [1831 edn.].

Leader, Zachary, *Revision and Romantic Authorship* (Oxford, 1996).

Luke, Hugh J. (ed.), *The Last Man*, repr. with new introd. by Brian Aldiss (London, 1985); repr. with new introd. by Anne K. Mellor (Lincoln, Nebr., 1993).

Macdonald, D. L., and Scherf, Kathleen (eds.), *Frankenstein; or, The Modern Prometheus: The 1818 Version*, Broadview Literary Texts (Peterborough, 1994).

McWhir, Anne (ed.), *The Last Man*, Broadview Literary Texts (Peterborough, 1996).

Murray, E. B., 'Shelley's Contribution to Mary's *Frankenstein*', *Keats–Shelley Memorial Bulletin*, 29 (1978), 50–68.

Nitchie, Elizabeth, *Mathilda*, Extra Series 3 of *Studies in Philology* (Chapel Hill, NC, 1959).

Paley, Morton D. (ed.), *The Last Man*, World's Classics (Oxford, 1994).

Reiman, Donald H. (gen. ed.), *Manuscripts of the Younger Romantics: Shelley*, 9 vols. in progress (New York, 1985–   ): v: *The Harvard Shelley Manuscripts*, ed. Donald H. Reiman (1991); viii: *Fair-Copy Manuscripts of Shelley's Poems in European and American Libraries*, eds. Donald H. Reiman and Michael O'Neill (1997); ix: *The 'Frankenstein' Manuscripts*, ed. Charles E. Robinson (1996).

—— (gen. ed.), *The Bodleian Shelley Manuscripts*, 23 vols. in progress (New York, 1986–   ): i: *'Peter Bell the Third' and 'The Triumph of Life'*, ed. Donald H. Reiman (1986); ii: *Bodleian MS. Shelley Adds. D. 7*, ed. Irving Massey (1987); iv: *A Facsimile of Bodleian MS. Shelley D. 1*, ed. E. B. Murray, 2 vols. (1988); x: *Mary Shelley's Plays and her Translation of the Cenci Story*, eds. Betty T. Bennett and Charles E. Robinson (1992); xii: *Shelley's 'Charles the First' Notebook*, ed. Nora Crook (1991); xx: *The 'Defence of*

Poetry' Fair Copies, ed. Michael O'Neill (1994); xxii: *Bodleian MS. Shelley Adds. D. 6 and Bodleian MS. Shelley Adds. C. 5*, 2 parts, ed. Alan Weinberg (1997).

Rieger, James (ed.), *Frankenstein; or, The Modern Prometheus: The 1818 Text* (Chicago, 1974; paperback edn., 1982).

Robinson, Charles E. (ed.), *Collected Tales and Stories, with Original Engravings* (Baltimore, 1976; paperback edn., 1990).

Smith, Johanna M. (ed.), *Frankenstein*, Bedford Books (New York, 1992) [1831 edn.].

Todd, Janet (ed.), *Matilda* [retitled from *Mathilda*], in one volume with Mary Wollstonecraft, *Mary and Maria*, Pickering Women's Classics (London, 1991); Penguin Classics (Harmondsworth, 1992).

Vargo, Lisa (ed.), *Lodore*, Broadview Literary Texts (Peterborough, 1997).

BIOGRAPHIES AND LETTERS

Bennett, Betty T. (ed.), *The Letters of Mary Wollstonecraft Shelley*, 3 vols. (Baltimore, 1980–8).

—— (ed.), *Selected Letters of Mary Wollstonecraft Shelley* (Baltimore, 1995).

Dunn, Jane, *Moon in Eclipse: A Life of Mary Shelley* (London, 1978).

Feldman, Paula R., and Scott-Kilvert, Diana (eds.), *The Journals of Mary Shelley, 1814–1844*, 2 vols. (Oxford, 1987).

Grylls, R. Glynn, *Mary Shelley: A Biography* (Oxford, 1938).

Nitchie, Elizabeth, *Mary Shelley: Author of 'Frankenstein'* (New Brunswick, NJ, 1953).

Spark, Muriel, *Child of Light: A Reassessment of Mary Shelley* (Hadleigh, 1951); repr. in revised form as *Mary Shelley* (London, 1987).

Sunstein, Emily W., *Mary Shelley: Romance and Reality* (Boston, 1989; rev. edn., Baltimore, 1991).

CRITICISM

Baldick, Chris, *In Frankenstein's Shadow: Myth, Monstrosity, and Nineteenth-Century Writing* (Oxford, 1987).

Behrendt, Stephen C. (ed.), *Approaches to Teaching Shelley's 'Frankenstein'* (New York, 1990).

Bennett, Betty T., 'The Political Philosophy of Mary Shelley's Historical Novels: *Valperga* and *Perkin Warbeck*', in Donald H. Reiman, Michael C. Jaye, and Betty T. Bennett (eds.), *The Evidence of the Imagination: Studies of Interactions between Life and Art in English Romantic Literature* (New York, 1978), 354–71.

Bloom, Harold, 'Frankenstein, or The New Prometheus', *Partisan Review*, 32 (1965), 611–18; repr. in his *The Ringers in the Tower* (Chicago, 1971), 119–29.

Blumberg, Jane, *Mary Shelley's Early Novels* (Basingstoke, 1993).

Botting, Fred, *Making Monstrous: 'Frankenstein', Criticism, Theory* (Manchester, 1991).

—— (ed.), *Frankenstein*, New Casebooks (Basingstoke, 1995).

Cantor, Paul A., 'Mary Shelley and the Taming of the Byronic Hero: "Transformation" and *The Deformed Transformed*', in Fisch et al. (1993: 89–106).

Clemit, Pamela, *The Godwinian Novel: The Rational Fictions of Godwin, Brockden Brown, Mary Shelley* (Oxford, 1993).

Ellis, Kate Ferguson, 'Monsters in the Garden: Mary Shelley and the Bourgeois Family', in Levine and Knoepflmacher (1979: 123–42).

—— 'Subversive Surfaces: The Limits of Domestic Affection in Mary Shelley's Later Fiction', in Fisch et al. (1993: 220–34).

Favret, Mary A., Romantic Correspondence: Women, Politics, and the Fiction of Letters (Cambridge, 1993).

Fisch, Audrey A., Mellor, Anne K., and Schor, Esther H. (eds.), The Other Mary Shelley: Beyond 'Frankenstein' (New York, 1993).

Fleck, P. D., 'Mary Shelley's Notes to Shelley's Poems and Frankenstein', Studies in Romanticism, 6 (1967), 226–54.

Florescu, Radu, In Search of Frankenstein (London, 1977).

Gilbert, Sandra M., and Gubar, Susan, The Madwoman in the Attic: The Woman Writer and the Nineteenth-Century Literary Imagination (New Haven, 1979).

Goldberg, M. A., 'Moral and Myth in Mrs. Shelley's Frankenstein', Keats–Shelley Journal, 8 (1959), 27–38.

Harvey, A. D., 'Frankenstein and Caleb Williams', Keats–Shelley Journal, 29 (1980), 21–7.

Hill-Miller, Katherine C., 'My Hideous Progeny': Mary Shelley, William Godwin, and the Father–Daughter Relationship (Newark, NJ, 1995).

Homans, Margaret, Bearing the Word: Language and Female Experience in Nineteenth-Century Women's Writing (Chicago, 1986).

Hume, Robert D., 'Gothic versus Romantic: A Revaluation of the Gothic Novel', Publications of the Modern Language Association, 84 (1969), 282–90.

Jacobus, Mary, 'Is There a Woman in this Text?', New Literary History, 14 (1982), 117–41.

Johnson, Barbara, 'My Monster/My Self', Diacritics, 12 (1982), 3–11.

Knoepflmacher, U. C., 'Thoughts on the Aggression of Daughters', in Levine and Knoepflmacher (1979: 88–119).

Lavalley, Albert J., 'The Stage and Film Children of Frankenstein: A Survey', in Levine and Knoepflmacher (1979: 243–89).

Levine, George, 'The Ambiguous Heritage of Frankenstein', in Levine and Knoepflmacher (1979: 3–30).

—— and Knoepflmacher, U. C. (eds.), The Endurance of Frankenstein: Essays on Mary Shelley's Novel (Berkeley and Los Angeles, 1979).

Lew, Joseph W., 'God's Sister: History and Ideology in Valperga', in Fisch et al. (1993: 159–81).

Lyles, W. H., Mary Shelley: An Annotated Bibliography (New York, 1975).

Mellor, Anne K., Mary Shelley: Her Life, her Fiction, her Monsters (London, 1988).

Moers, Ellen, Literary Women (New York, 1976).

—— 'Female Gothic', in Levine and Knoepflmacher (1979: 77–87).

Nelson, Lowry, Jr., 'Night Thoughts on the Gothic Novel', Yale Review, 52 (1963), 236–57.

Newlyn, Lucy, 'Paradise Lost' and the Romantic Reader (Oxford, 1993).

O'Flinn, Paul, 'Production and Reproduction: The Case of Frankenstein', Literature and History, 9 (1983), 194–213; repr. in Peter Humm, Paul Stigant, and Peter Widdowson (eds.), Popular Fictions: Essays in Literature and History (London, 1986), 196–221.

Paley, Morton D., 'Mary Shelley's *The Last Man*: Apocalypse without Millennium', *Keats–Shelley Review*, 4 (1989), 1–25; repr. in Fisch et al. (1993: 107–23).

Paulson, Ronald, 'Gothic Fiction and the French Revolution', *English Literary History*, 48 (1991), 532–54; repr. in his *Representations of Revolution (1789–1820)* (New Haven, 1983), 215–47.

Pollin, Burton R., 'Philosophical and Literary Sources of *Frankenstein*', *Comparative Literature*, 17 (1965), 97–108.

Poovey, Mary, '"My Hideous Progeny": Mary Shelley and the Feminization of Romanticism', *Publications of the Modern Language Association*, 95 (1980), 332–47; repr. in her *The Proper Lady and the Woman Writer: Ideology as Style in the Works of Mary Wollstonecraft, Mary Shelley, and Jane Austen* (Chicago, 1984), 114–42.

Reiman, Donald H. (ed.), *The Romantics Reviewed: Contemporary Reviews of British Romantic Writers*, 8 vols. (New York, 1972), part C.

Richardson, Alan, '*Proserpine* and *Midas*: Gender, Genre, and Mythic Revisionism in Mary Shelley's Dramas', in Fisch et al. (1993: 124–39).

Sambrook, A. J., 'A Romantic Theme: The Last Man', *Forum for Modern Language Studies*, 2 (1966), 25–33.

Scott, Peter Dale, 'Vital Artifice: Mary, Percy, and the Psychopolitical Integrity of *Frankenstein*', in Levine and Knoepflmacher (1979: 172–202).

Snyder, Robert Lance, 'Apocalypse and Indeterminacy in Mary Shelley's *The Last Man*', *Studies in Romanticism*, 17 (1978), 435–52.

Spector, Robert D., *The English Gothic: A Bibliographic Guide to Writers from Horace Walpole to Mary Shelley* (Westport, Conn., 1984).

Spivak, Gayatri Chakravorty, 'Three Women's Texts and a Critique of Imperialism', *Critical Inquiry*, 12 (1985), 243–61.

Stafford, Fiona, *The Last of the Race: The Growth of a Myth from Milton to Darwin* (Oxford, 1994).

Sterrenburg, Lee, '*The Last Man*: Anatomy of Failed Revolutions', *Nineteenth-Century Fiction*, 33 (1978), 324–47.

—— 'Mary Shelley's Monster: Politics and Psyche in *Frankenstein*', in Levine and Knoepflmacher (1979: 143–71).

Swingle, L. J., 'Frankenstein's Monster and its Romantic Relatives: Problems of Knowledge in English Romanticism', *Texas Studies in Literature and Language*, 15 (1973), 51–65.

Tannenbaum, Leslie, 'From Filthy Type to Truth: Miltonic Myth in *Frankenstein*', *Keats–Shelley Journal*, 26 (1977), 101–13.

Tropp, Martin, *Mary Shelley's Monster* (Boston, 1976).

Veeder, William, *Mary Shelley & Frankenstein: The Fate of Androgyny* (Chicago, 1986).

15. *Fiction of the Romantic Period (Godwin, Wollstonecraft, Bage, Edgeworth, Burney, Inchbald, Hays, and Others)*

SUSAN MATTHEWS

The authors grouped together in this chapter would probably have struck a contemporary as a very odd assortment indeed: Edgeworth and Burney are two of the highest-selling, most respected, and highest-earning novelists of the period, whereas other writers such as Hogg would have been seen as minor figures. The modern sense that Austen, Scott, and, perhaps for the last ten years, Mary Shelley are the most important novelists of the period does not (with the exception of Scott) echo how the period itself saw the novel. Moreover, the separate category of the Gothic novel is in some senses hard to sustain when so many novels contain Gothic elements; works such as *Caleb Williams*, *Maria*, or *Confessions of a Justified Sinner* could belong within this category, and many women's novels, including many of Burney's, have strong Gothic elements. This chapter also deals with writers such as Godwin and Wollstonecraft who would not have been thought of primarily as novelists (and who thus also appear in other chapters).

But if these novelists include names that would have been more familiar than Jane Austen's within the period, by the early part of this century they would probably have been viewed as minor and lacking in many cases in literary value. It is only since the mid-1970s that work on a great range of novels within the Romantic period has begun seriously. Until then, minor novelists of the Romantic period might have seemed a distinctly uninteresting subject, surveyed usefully by a few pioneers such as J. M. S. Tompkins but otherwise largely unexplored.

The change in status and intellectual excitement clearly comes from three major new kinds of focus: interest in the politics of the period, especially the political debate of the 1790s, writing associated with nationalism or national identity (the regional novel), and thirdly the new interest in women writers. Although these tendencies could be grouped together under the title of expanding the canon, the interest in novelists other than Austen, Scott, and Shelley does not yet seem to be uniformly spread. A 'minor' novelist has a greater chance of being the subject of a critical study or being reprinted (at least in an accessible paperback version) if female or politically radical. For instance, although Gary Kelly makes a very convincing case for the import-ance of Lamb's *Rosamund Gray* in *English Fiction of the Romantic Period* this text is only available in the useful but expensive Woodstock facsimile series. A num-ber of critics (including Kelly 1990) have recently written on Eaton Stannard Barrett's *The Heroine* but this is another text that remains very much in the hinterland of contemporary maps of the novel in the period. It also seems to be the case that more energy has so far been given to rediscovering novels from the 1790s and that the period after 1815 remains the domain of Austen, Scott, and Shelley. However, the tremendous growth of interest in chil-dren's literature has encouraged work on a number of other writers, especially Maria Edgeworth, William Godwin, and Mary Shelley, as writers or publishers for children.

TEXTS

The position changes rapidly, with new editions coming into print and quickly going out of print again. A ground-breaking project in the late 1980s was the Pandora Press series inspired by Dale Spender's *Mothers of the Novel*. This brought into cheap paperback a large number of novels by women from the Romantic period including Mary Hays's *Memoirs of Emma Courtney*, Edgeworth's *Helen*, and others. The novels were poorly edited, without notes and with usu-ally unhelpful introductions by contemporary novelists. Yet the series had an important function in creating a demand for accessible editions of female novelists of the period: they could more easily be included on undergraduate courses and when the editions (poor as they were) disappeared, their loss was felt. Since then, editions of Edgeworth, Hays, and other writers have begun to reappear slowly, but in much better editions, especially from OUP and Everyman. The Woodstock facsimile series has also been important in repro-ducing a wide range of novels from the period, by men as well as women. These excellent texts have the function of expanding university library hold-ings of the period—being too expensive to affect the setting of the under-graduate syllabus in most cases. The choice of text in this series represents a more acute sense of historical context than is reflected by more mainstream publishers like OUP or Everyman, necessarily guided by commercial pressures and so by critical fashions. Yet the expense of the texts means that they probably appeal to those who might in any case have access to a copyright library. Finally an important publishing project of a rather different kind is represented by new Pickering & Chatto editions, notably of novels by Godwin, Wollstonecraft, and Edgeworth. These editions are superbly edited and annotated and they probably do as much as any other publishing project both to reflect but also to shape the scope of academic study in the period. Important editions include the forthcoming *Works of Maria Edgeworth* (including all the major fiction for adults and most of the best of the juvenile fiction), *The Collected Novels and Memoirs of William Godwin*, *Desmond* by Charlotte Smith, and *Nature and Art* by Elizabeth Inchbald.

GENERAL STUDIES

The first study to look at novel production in the period outside the familiar territory of Austen and Scott was J. M. S. Tompkins, *The Popular Novel in England 1770–1800* (1932, 1961). This is still a useful book, one whose approach seems more in tune with current critical approaches than it probably seemed at any time between the 1930s and the 1980s. Tompkins approaches the novel 'rather as a popular amusement than a literary form'. And despite her unwillingness to make claims for the importance of the material she describes, her mapping of novel production and consumption, her account of the novel market, circulating libraries, reviewing, Sensibility, and didacticism, above all her willingness to investigate novels irrespective of literary criteria of quality remains fascinating and has clearly been influential on more recent accounts. Investigating the novel in the 1790s, it is interesting that Tompkins remarks that 'the novel, then, had for the first time been the arena of a serious war of ideas'. The subjects of Marilyn Butler's ground-breaking study of 1975, *Jane Austen and the War of Ideas*, which takes seriously such novelists as Elizabeth Hamilton, Hannah More, Holcroft, and Godwin, already are part of the picture that Tompkins draws in 1932. Tompkins stops in 1800, and her survey does not attempt to draw the links between literary production and changing political and social patterns in the period that often preoccupy later attempts to survey the period.

By far the most convincing recent attempt to map the novel in the period is Gary Kelly's 1989 *English Fiction of the Romantic Period 1789–1830*, a knowledgeable account which is as good on tracing social and class change as on focusing on specific novels. Kelly traces a story of the changing attitudes of gentry and professional classes to aristocratic and courtly culture through a very wide range of novels, major and minor, keeping always a sharp eye on the influence of the market and of patterns of consumption. The book is consistently alert and, while writing well of Austen and Scott, takes figures such as Holcroft, Charlotte Smith, Jane Porter, or Charles Lamb just as seriously. Kelly sees Austen as 'the representative Romantic novelist', but he also sees her importance as being centred in the 'trash of the circulating library' and as being the ability to identify

the central thematic and formal issues of the novel of the period—the gentrification of the professional classes and the professionalization of the gentry, the place of women in a professionalized culture that denies them any significant role in public or professional life, the establishment of a 'national' culture of distinction and discrimination in the face of fashion and commercialized culture, the resiting of the authentic self in an inward moral and intellectual being so cultivated as to be able to negotiate successfully the varieties of social experience and cultural discriminations, the establishment of a standard speech based on writing, and resolution of the relationship of authoritative narration and detailed representation of subjective experience.

Austen's achievement is therefore seen as inextricable from that of the huge range of other novel writers in the Romantic period, to which this book gives equal prominence. There are useful bibliographies and an excellent chronology of novel production. Kelly's account of the novel in the period, which begins with his *The English Jacobin Novel* in 1976, continues interestingly in a series of books and articles, including a particularly useful discussion of the gendering of novel production in 1990: 'Unbecoming a Heroine: Novel Reading, Romanticism, and Barrett's *The Heroine*'. This identifies a 'split in reading between learned and professional (male) culture on one hand, and entertaining and fanciful (female) culture on the other', tracing perceived links between gender, genre, and class conflict.

Feminist scholarship has done as much as an interest in popular culture to open up the period. Marilyn Butler's 1987 introduction to her earlier *Jane Austen and the War of Ideas* sketches usefully the role of feminist critics and scholars of the late 1970s and early 1980s: writers such as Ellen Moers, Gilbert and Gubar, and Elaine Showalter. In much of their work a stress appears on the idea of women writers forming a tradition and culture of their own, and this focus encourages a range of critics to explore, first the literary antecedents of Jane Austen, but then the richness of the specifically female literary culture from which she emerges. Writers like Burney, Edgeworth, Inchbald, Charlotte Smith, seem no longer to be minor writers, but are treated by critics with a new seriousness. Janet Todd's work has been important in a series of books, from *Women's Friendship in Literature* (1980) to *A Dictionary of British and American Women Writers 1660–1800* (1985), *Sensibility* (1986), and *The Sign of Angellica* (1989), which discusses women writers through the eighteenth century and up to 1800. It seems typical of feminist scholarship to divide the period at 1800 and to focus on the eighteenth century (or nineteenth century) rather than the Romantic period, a form of periodization which often seems to fit women's literary production less well than it does men's. There are now many feminist scholars working mainly on women's fiction in the eighteenth century, the period which following Jane Spencer's *The Rise of the Woman Novelist* seems increasingly to see the domination of women's writing in the novel. Despite its lack of critical sophistication, Dale Spender's *Mothers of the Novel* performed an important function in making strident claims for women's literary productivity in the novel in the eighteenth century. Studies covering female authored fiction in the eighteenth century are still appearing, such as Katherine Sobba Green's *The Courtship Novel 1740–1820: A Feminized Genre* (1991). Green's account traces continuities between eighteenth-century women's novels and later works from the Romantic period including Burney's *Cecilia* and *Camilla*, Jane West, and Mary Brunton, as well as Edgeworth's *Belinda*. Nevertheless, the notion of the courtship novel begins to seem too loose to link so many novels, most of which are dealt with fairly briefly. It seems that by this stage in the 1990s, a primary focus on gender is too narrow to produce complex and rewarding readings. Probably the most satisfying accounts of women's fiction in recent years have drawn as well on the accumulating understanding of cultural movements such as Sensibility, on class conflict and identity, and on the political affiliations of writers.

Important recent studies of women's writing and the novel in the Romantic period include Anne K. Mellor's chapter on 'A Novel of their Own: Romantic Women's Fiction 1790–1830' in *The Columbia History of the British Novel*. This account of women's writing is likely to be as influential as Mellor's previous contributions to the study of women's poetry in the period. It shares her characteristic qualities of ambition, confidence, and an ability to create stirring labels. The tone is often one of affirmation and contains claims that seem challenging but can be surprisingly obvious. For the women's novel in the period, Mellor uses her own concept of 'Romantic Feminism', already identified in her accounts of women's poetry. Like other recent writers on women's texts, she is in essence rebutting Mary Poovey's influential construction of women's writing in the period as constrained within the ideology of the Proper Lady, and she challenges the currently ubiquitous use of conduct literature as a context for women's writing and writing about women which she sees as leading to the perception of women's writing as conservative: 'Even perceptive feminist critics of the novel have asserted that the female-authored fictions of the Romantic period register the triumph of patriarchal ideology.' Instead, she sees a wide range of women novelists as challenging domestic ideology:

While the psychological and rhetorical accommodations noted by critics undoubtedly occurred in writing by women of the Romantic period, I emphasize here the existence of an equally strong Romantic female literary tradition that openly challenged and revised the patriarchal domestic ideology in powerful ways. We can no longer assume that the doctrine of the separate spheres, the sexual division of labor into the public/ male and the private/female realms, was universally accepted during the Romantic period.

Mellor's survey uses non-canonical women novelists, discussing for instance, Charlotte Smith's *The Old Manor House* (1794), Edgeworth's *Belinda*, and Susan Ferrier's *Marriage* before turning to the female Gothic tradition and focusing as is conventional nowadays on 'the finest Gothic novel of the Romantic period, Mary Shelley's *Frankenstein*'. The account is highly selective and simplifying throughout. Her claims are, in a sense, unsurprising, that Romantic women novelists advocated rational rather than erotic love. She sees female Romantic novelists as following on from Wollstonecraft's *Vindication of the Rights of Woman*: 'In the fiction of feminine Romanticism, such egalitarian marriages and the lasting domestic harmony they bring, grow out of rational love rather than sexual passion, especially where the women are concerned.' But what she claims as the 'new feminine Romantic ideology' embodied uniformly in the novels by women she discusses could surely just as well be seen as textbook examples of a continuity with the patriarchal domestic ideology of conduct literature as of a revolutionary new feminine Romantic ideology. This is an account of women's writing that is important but also needs to be argued with. The attempt to isolate one feminine ideology is probably unhelpful, ignoring as it does the lively debates and differences between women novelists of the time. Caroline Gonda's 1996 study *Reading Daughters' Fiction* provides a more complex account of women's fiction in the period.

Gary Kelly's *The English Jacobin Novel* (1976) and Pamela Clemit's *The Godwinian Novel* (1993) are the two most important general studies of politics and the novel (along of course with Marilyn Butler's *Jane Austen and the War of Ideas* which in 1975 did as much as any other book to open up study of novelists other than the famous two or three). Eleanor Ty's *Unsex'd Revolutionaries: Five Women Novelists of the 1790s* (on Wollstonecraft, Williams, Inchbald, Smith, and Hays) focuses on women writers and on the politicization of the novel in the 1790s, looking not just at the obvious examples (she explores Hays's *Victim of Prejudice* as well as the *Memoirs of Emma Courtney*) and choosing as themes issues of subjectivity and identity, mother–daughter relations, and the politics of gender. This kind of scope (the inclusion of non-canonical novels, and a focus on issues suggested by feminist criticism) is now typical of the best work in studies of the novel of the period. A recent attempt to map the distinctive energies of the novel in the 1790s is Patricia Meyer Spacks's 'Novels of the 1790s: Action and Impasse' in *The Columbia History of the British Novel* which looks at form as much as ideology and at a range of texts, not only *Caleb Williams*, *Hermsprong*, and *Anna St Ives*, but also works such as Charlotte Smith's *Desmond* and *The Old Manor House*. Spacks concludes that only Godwin and Inchbald developed 'at least in single novels—expressive structures of novelistic action'.

One of the most stimulating and ambitious recent studies to cover the novel throughout the Romantic period is Nicola Watson's 1994 *Revolution and the Form of the British Novel 1790–1825: Intercepted Letters, Interrupted Seductions*. Drawing together many of the most lively areas of recent investigation (Sensibility, women's writing, politics) but going well beyond any of these discrete areas, Watson's account spans political novelists of the 1790s (such as Godwin, Hays, Smith, and Wollstonecraft), regional novelists—so-called—like Edgeworth, Sydney Owenson, Lady Morgan, and Scott, and later figures like Maturin, Hazlitt, Hogg, and Byron in *Don Juan*. Its formal project is to 'illuminate the hitherto unexplained transformation of the eighteenth century novel into the forms more characteristic of the nineteenth century'. And it does this by tracing how formal innovations are produced in response to cultural anxieties stemming from the French Revolution. The key text for this study, by means of which Watson makes the crucial link between sentimental fiction and politics, is Rousseau's *La Nouvelle Héloïse* (still not available in any inexpensive translation) and it is through this text that she makes her claim that the plot of unfolding revolution was commonly understood by contemporaries as a plot of seduction (frequently across class lines). This claim allows texts such as Hays's *Memoirs of Emma Courtney* and Morgan's *The Wild Irish Girl* to feature in an argument that ends up with Hazlitt's *Liber Amoris*, Hogg's *Confessions of a Justified Sinner*, and Byron's *Don Juan*. While there is perhaps a danger of a strong thesis running wild, the readings of individual texts and sense of historical difference in the succeeding decades of the period make this a fascinating book throughout. The breadth of interest and refusal to stay within the categories of women's writing, or political novel, make this a more rewarding work than many other attempts to map the period.

Edward Copeland's *Women Writing about Money: Women's Fiction in England, 1790–1820* (1995) started as a study of that familiar topic, money in Jane Austen's novels, but has developed into a fascinating investigation of the discourse of money in women's fiction which ranges widely to cover works by Mary Brunton, Hamilton, Edgeworth, Hannah More, Susan Ferrier, and magazine fiction. Copeland's book coincides with another fascinating study that foregrounds the economic, Catherine Gallagher's *Nobody's Story: The Vanishing Acts of Women Writers in the Marketplace, 1670–1820* (1994). Although this has a much longer time span, working out a thesis which addresses the role of women and writing through the eighteenth century, there are chapters on both Burney and Edgeworth which challenge and expand the rather comfortable assumptions of much of the work on these two writers. Gallagher's 'nobodies' are 'literal nobodies: authorial personae, printed books, scandalous allegories, intellectual property rights, literary reputations, incomes, debts, and fictional characters. They are the exchangeable tokens of modern authorship that allowed increasing numbers of women writers to thrive as the eighteenth century wore on.' Gallagher's important book challenges the notion that women authors construct identities in publishing: 'To concentrate on the elusiveness of these authors, instead of bemoaning it and searching for their positive identities, is to practice a different sort of literary history.' Unlike many other writers on women authors, Gallagher does not see women as belonging to a separate tradition, but 'takes them to be special in their extreme typicality'.

STUDIES OF INDIVIDUAL AUTHORS

As must already be clear, much of the most intelligent criticism of non-canonical authors occurs in the context of multi-author studies. Certainly it is hard to find interesting single author studies of writers such as Holcroft, Bage, or Charlotte Smith although each of these writers features in more wide-ranging studies already described. Nevertheless there are some authors, Wollstonecraft, Godwin, Burney, and Edgeworth, who have attracted a considerable number of studies in recent years.

FANNY BURNEY

There have been a series of book-length studies on Fanny (now more often Frances) Burney including Judy Simons, *Fanny Burney* (1987), Margaret Anne Doody, *Frances Burney: The Life in the Works,* Julia Epstein, *The Iron Pen: Frances Burney and the Politics of Women's Writing* (1989), and Katharine Rogers, *Frances Burney: The World of Female Difficulties* (1990). All these four works look at Burney's biography as well as her fiction, taking her as in some ways representative of femininity at a particular historical moment. An argument develops which is in some ways parallel to the attempts to place Austen politically; Burney can be seen either as protesting against the constraints and restrictions imposed on middle-class women, or as a conservative upholder of female propriety. In 1991 *Eighteenth-Century Fiction* published a 'Special *Evelina* Issue' containing six articles and this seems to mark the completion of one phase of Burney criticism. As Margaret Anne Doody notes in her contribution to this issue, 'Beyond *Evelina*: The Individual Novel and the Community of Literature', four of the articles focus (in sophisticated and interesting ways) on the representation of identity in *Evelina*—on names and naming, anonymity and family roles. Burney clearly strikes a powerful chord with a particular generation of (American) critics, focusing questions of individuality, subjectivity, and femininity. But Doody suggests that other kinds of approach are possible. The emphasis of many critics has been on the presentation of the heroine in Burney's fiction, and on her attempts to find and secure her own identity. But in her own time, Burney's fiction was noted rather for her creation of characters and there have also been recent critics who have focused instead on the elements of violence and cruelty in Burney's fiction, or on the portrayal of other classes. Catherine Gallagher in *Nobody's Story* studies Burney's use of the figure of Nobody in a new way that sees Burney as typical of 'what both the talented literary entrepreneur and the serious, self-effacing philosopher were said to do in the eighteenth century'. The four novels, *Evelina*, *Cecilia*, *Camilla*, and *The Wanderer*, are all now available in well-edited and affordable editions from Oxford.

MARY WOLLSTONECRAFT

Wollstonecraft is of course hard to label as a novelist: her works cover politics, feminism, reviewing, travel writing, and only incidentally perhaps novels. The focus of much writing on Wollstonecraft has been biographical, with biographies by Tomalin and Sunstein following on from Godwin's *Memoirs* which did so much to determine Wollstonecraft's early reputation. Probably the greatest interest in recent years has been in the *Vindication of the Rights of Woman*. Her novels have been slower to take central stage. Nevertheless, particularly under the influence of the growing sophistication of studies of Sensibility in the eighteenth century and on into the Romantic period, there have been some fascinating new studies of Wollstonecraft's two novels. Mary Poovey's highly influential 1984 study *The Proper Lady and the Woman Writer* establishes the terms of the argument for many, with her claim that Wollstonecraft critiques romance, but then falls back into its assumptions. Laurie Langbauer, in a sophisticated study of *Women and Romance: The Consolations of Gender in the English Novel*, a study which moves from Charlotte Lennox to look at Dickens and George Eliot, devotes a chapter to Wollstonecraft's *Maria* which is at once part of a longer theoretical argument about the 'traditional connection between women and the literary genre "romance"' and a subtle essay on this particular novel. For Langbauer, it is the figure of the mother, seen to some extent through the lens of French feminists like Kristeva, that allows her to take the argument beyond Poovey, to claim that the mother in Wollstonecraft's writing is 'both outside and inside romance: in command of language even to speaking new terms for her own self-definition, to breaking with the ignorance and immaturity of romance, and at the same time subverting the order and meaning of language, partaking of the romance of the infantile and unutterable'. Langbauer goes on to investigate the tendency towards 'a dangerous essentialism' in her argument. A version of Langbauer's discussion can also be found in 'An Early Romance: Motherhood and Women's Writing in Mary Wollstonecraft's Novels' in Anne K. Mellor's 1988 *Romanticism and Feminism*. A less subtle, but full and useful, account of Wollstonecraft as a novelist occurs in Eleanor Ty's *Unsex'd Revolutionaries: Five Women Novelists of the 1790s*. The other most interesting recent writer on Wollstonecraft as a novelist has been Syndy McMillen Conger who collects two articles on Wollstonecraft and sensibility in *Sensibility in Transformation: Creative Resistance to Sentiment from the Augustans to the Romantics* (1990), but then in a book-length study of 1994, *Mary Wollstonecraft and the Language of Sensibility*, provides probably the most convincing study of this context. Wollstonecraft also appears as a key figure in G. J. Barker-Benfield's *The Culture of Sensibility: Sex and Society in Eighteenth Century Britain* (1992), especially in a final chapter on 'Wollstonecraft and the Crisis over Sensibility' which contains informed and subtle readings of novels by Burney, Edgeworth, and Wollstonecraft.

WILLIAM GODWIN

The most important discussions of Godwin as a novelist come within larger studies of the novels of the 1790s, notably Kelly's *The English Jacobin Novel* and Pamela Clemit's *The Godwinian Novel*, both of which are essential reading. Marilyn Butler has a valuable 1982 discussion of *Caleb Williams*, 'Godwin, Burke, and *Caleb Williams*' (reprinted in Wu's *Romanticism: A Critical Reader*) which argues characteristically for the political force and consistency of Godwin's novel as a response to Burke's thought, in particular arguing against attempts to psychologize the novel and so turn it away from a reference to public events. Much discussion of *Caleb Williams* (easily the most discussed of the novels) focuses on the question of whether it does or does not consistently develop the ideas of *Political Justice*. For Butler, as for Kenneth W. Graham in *The Politics of Narrative: Ideology and Social Change in William Godwin's Caleb Williams* (1990), the two texts work coherently together. All the novels are now available in the superbly edited Pickering edition, but it is perhaps as significant that Godwin's second novel, *St Leon* (1799), his first historical novel, is available in an Oxford paperback with an authoritative introduction by Pamela Clemit. Clemit's introduction argues for the importance of the novel which 'exploits the increased range of historical narrative for a figurative rendering of contemporary concerns'. She also argues that *St Leon* shows how Godwin was won over to Wollstonecraft's 'culture of the heart' and is his most overt tribute to her thought.

MARIA EDGEWORTH

Edgeworth's modern critical reputation begins with Marilyn Butler's 1972 literary biography which is still essential for material on Edgeworth's intellectual background. But in this account, Butler has limited time or respect for some of the novels, particularly those of London life such as *Belinda*. Two new kinds of critical focus have since encouraged interesting work on Edgeworth's novels: feminist criticism and the new interest in nationalism and regionalism. There is a book-length study of Edgeworth by Elizabeth Harden (1971) and Beth Kowaleski-Wallace has written fascinatingly on *Belinda* in a 1988 article 'Home Economics' which focuses on the figure of Lady Delacour and contemporary views of motherhood and breastfeeding, and again in a book-length study *Their Father's Daughters*. Several critics have also written of Edgeworth's fiction in terms of its Irish context, notably Tom Dunne in *Maria Edgeworth and the Colonial Mind*. There is an excellent article from 1988 by Catherine Gallagher, 'Fictional Women and Real Estate in Maria Edgeworth's *Castle Rackrent*', which argues that 'Edgeworth's Anglo-Irishness and her interests as a woman . . . are served by her commodification of a certain kind of "Irish" language: that which she characterizes as a language of dispossession.' Gallagher writes again in a subtle and complex way on Edgeworth in her 1994 study *Nobody's Story*. In a fascinating article of 1989, Michael Ragussis argues that Edgeworth's 1817 novel *Harrington* is the first work in English to inquire into the nature and representation of Jewish identity. The novel, he argues, is prompted by a letter from an American Jew who wrote to complain of an anti-Semitic portrait in Edgeworth's 1812 *The Absentee*.

ELIZABETH INCHBALD

Elizabeth Inchbald's *A Simple Story* of 1791 has for some time been in print edited by J. M. S. Tompkins, but in 1988 was reissued with a useful introduction by Jane Spencer claiming the novel as 'one of the most remarkable of the late eighteenth century'. Challenging the two most influential earlier readings of the novel, by Gary Kelly in the 1976 *The English Jacobin Novel* and by Terry Castle in *Masquerade and Civilization* (1986), Spencer rejects the idea that *A Simple Story* can be read satisfactorily either as 'a kind of Jacobin novel' or as the work of 'an anti-authoritarian writer who makes female desire triumph over masculine authority'. Instead, Spencer analyses Inchbald's use of the literary figure of the coquette and her treatment of the theme of female education, and sees the treatment of female desire as ultimately conforming to 'the infantile fantasy of union with a powerful father'. But if the novel as a whole is not seen as anti-authoritarian, Spencer does recognize the first part of this two-part novel as focusing in a new way on female sexuality. The Oxford edition with Jane Spencer's introduction is now usefully complemented by a Penguin edition with an introduction by Pamela Clemit which is particularly strong on placing *A Simple Story* with a new precision in its historical context. Clemit rightly points out that the novel dates from both the 1770s and the 1790s, and shows that it cannot therefore be read simply or mainly in terms of the political debates of the 1790s. She points to the recognition by contemporaries of Inchbald's innovatory dramatic technique and shows how it contributes to two debates: on the position and responsibilities of the English Catholic community, and on the proper education for women. Unlike Spencer, Clemit sees the novel as telling 'a story of the triumph of transgression'. This edition and introduction add significantly to the debate on Inchbald's novel.

Lady Caroline Lamb's *Glenarvon*, a scandalous success on its first publication but critically scorned since then, is now republished and edited by Frances Wilson with a good introduction, chronology, and section on 'Lady Caroline Lamb and her critics'. Wilson reads *Glenarvon* in the light of recent theoretical discussions of femininity, desire, and fantasy, arguing that *Glenarvon* is 'unreadable' only 'in the same way that femininity and desire have been seen as unreadable'. It is a sophisticated and interesting argument and together with other recent articles, notably by Malcolm Kelsall on 'The Byronic Hero and Revolution in Ireland: The Politics of *Glenarvon*', Peter Graham, and Nicola Watson on 'Trans-Figuring Byronic Identity' suggests that Lamb's much scorned novel is ready for a serious reassesment.

Mary Hays's *Memoirs of Emma Courtney*, issued briefly by Pandora Press in the 1980s but since then out of print, is now available edited by Eleanor Ty with a helpful introduction which focuses on Hays's place within rational dissenting and radical circles in the 1790s, stressing the influence on her thought of Helvetius and Rousseau. Following on from influential readings of the novel by Tilottama Rajan (1993) and Nicola Watson (1994*b*), Ty also writes well of the formal construction of the novel and its use of an epistolary form which is more monologic than dialogic, placing this formally inventive novel in relation both to eighteenth-century novel forms and to later kinds of women's autobiography.

James Hogg has for some time had a unique role in accounts of the novel in the Romantic period, featuring often as the end point of the story, and as the sole Scottish novelist (with the exception of course of Scott). Following on from André Gide's discovery of the novel this century, Hogg's *Confessions of a Justified Sinner* has taken on a key role in many accounts of the novel and Romanticism, a role which is usually quite independent of Hogg's other literary production or of the particular Scottish milieu to which he (uneasily) belonged. There are many readings which focus on the Gothic elements of the story, on the doubling of identities, and on the narrative methods, but one of the most interesting and provocative is Eve Kosofsky Sedgwick's reading in

Between Men, her study of male homosocial desire. Both Gary Kelly (1989) and Nicola Watson (1994*a*) use Hogg's novel interestingly within larger arguments. In Kelly's account, Hogg's novel marks the limits of Romantic fiction, and exposes the false claims of such fiction to speak 'for all parts, regions, classes, and levels of society but in fact only speaking for the professional middle classes who practise this culture, literature and fiction, and who think they have seized the living culture and language of the common people, such as "the Ettrick Shepherd"'. In Kelly's account, Hogg's *Confessions* also works as a political fable, a reading of the French Revolution. Recently, work by David Groves and others is beginning to return Hogg's striking novel to its Scottish context, with the republication of Hogg's other novels, the increase of work on other Scottish novelists such as Ferrier and Galt, and the appearance of a journal, *Studies in Hogg and his Circle*.

REFERENCES

EDITIONS

Bage, Robert, *Hermsprong, or, Man As He is Not*, ed. with introd. Peter Faulkner, World's Classics (Oxford, 1985).

Burney, Fanny, *Evelina, or The History of a Young Lady's Entrance into the World*, ed. with introd. Edward A. Bloom with the assistance of Lillian D. Bloom, World's Classics (Oxford, 1968).

—— *Camilla*, ed. Edward A. Bloom and Lillian D. Bloom, World's Classics (Oxford, 1972).

—— *Cecilia, or Memoirs of an Heiress*, ed. Peter Sabor and Margaret Anne Doody, introd. Margaret Anne Doody (Oxford, 1988).

—— *The Wanderer; or, Female Difficulties*, ed. Margaret Anne Doody, Robert L. Mark, and Peter Sabor, introd. Margaret Anne Doody, World's Classics (Oxford, 1991).

Edgeworth, Maria, *Helen*, introd. Maggie Gee (London, 1987).

——*Castle Rackrent; and Ennui*, ed. Marilyn Butler (London, 1992).

—— *Belinda*, ed. with introd. Kathryn J. Kirkpatrick, World's Classics (Oxford, 1994).

——*The Works of Maria Edgeworth*, gen. ed. Marilyn Butler and W. J. McCormack, Pickering Masters, 12 vols. (London, 1998).

Ferrier, Susan, *Marriage*, ed. Herbert Foltinek, new introd. Kathryn Kirkpatrick, World's Classics (Oxford, 1987).

Galt, John, *Annals of the Parish, or The Chronicle of Dalmailing during the Ministry of the Rev. Micah Balwhidder*, ed. James Kinsley (Oxford, 1967).

Godwin, William, *The Collected Novels and Memoirs of William Godwin*, gen. ed. Mark Philp, introd. Mark Philp and Marilyn Butler, Pickering Masters, 8 vols. (London, 1992).

—— *St Leon*, ed. with introd. Pamela Clemit, World's Classics (Oxford, 1994).

Hays, Mary, *Memoirs of Emma Courtney*, introd. Sally Cline (London, 1987).

—— *Memoirs of Emma Courtney*, ed. with introd. Eleanor Ty, World's Classics (Oxford, 1996).

Hogg, James, *The Private Memoirs and Confessions of a Justified Sinner*, ed. with introd. John Carey, World's Classics (Oxford, 1969).

Holcroft, Thomas, *Anna St. Ives*, ed. Peter Faulkner (Oxford, 1970).

Inchbald, Elizabeth, *A Simple Story*, ed. J. M. S. Tompkins, introd. Jane Spencer, World's Classics (Oxford, 1988).

—— *A Simple Story*, ed. with introd. Pamela Clemit (London, 1996).

—— *'Nature and Art' and 'Emily Herbert; or, Perfidy Punished: A Novel in a Series of Letters'*, ed. Shawn L. Maurer, Pickering Women's Classics (London, 1997).

Lamb, Lady Caroline, *Glenarvon*, ed. Frances Wilson (London, 1995).

Morgan, Lady (Sydney Owenson), *The Wild Irish Girl* (London, 1986).

Smith, Charlotte, *The Old Manor House*, ed. Anne Henry Ehrenpreis (Oxford, 1987).

—— *Desmond*, ed. Antje Blank and Janet Todd, Pickering Women's Classics (London, 1997).

Wollstonecraft, Mary, *The Works of Mary Wollstonecraft*, ed. Janet Todd and Marilyn Butler, Pickering Masters, 7 vols. (London, 1989).

CRITICISM

General

Butler, Marilyn, *Jane Austen and the War of Ideas* (Oxford, 1975; rev. edn. 1987).

—— *Romantics, Rebels and Reactionaries: English Literature and its Background 1760–1830* (Oxford, 1981).

Copeland, Edward, *Women Writing about Money: Women's Fiction in England, 1790–1820* (Cambridge, 1995).

Gallagher, Catherine, *Nobody's Story: The Vanishing Acts of Women Writers in the Market-place, 1670–1820* (Berkeley and Los Angeles, 1994).

Gilbert, Sandra M., and Gubar, Susan, *The Madwoman in the Attic: The Woman Writer and the Nineteenth-Century Literary Imagination* (New Haven, 1979).

Gonda, Caroline, *Reading Daughters' Fiction* (Cambridge, 1996).

Green, Katherine Sobba, *The Courtship Novel 1740–1820: A Feminized Genre* (Lexington, Ky., 1991).

Jones, Ann H. *Ideas and Innovations: Best-Sellers of Jane Austen's Age* (New York, 1986).

Kelly, Gary, *The English Jacobin Novel 1780–1805* (Oxford, 1976).

—— *English Fiction of the Romantic Period 1789–1830* (London, 1989).

—— 'Unbecoming a Heroine: Novel Reading, Romanticism and Barrett's *The Heroine*', *Nineteenth Century Literature*, 45/2 (1990), 220–41.

Mayo, R. D., *The English Novel in the Magazines, 1740–1815* (Evanston, Ill., 1962).

Mellor, Anne K. (ed.), *Romanticism and Gender* (Bloomington, Ind., 1988).

—— 'A Novel of their Own: Romantic Women's Fiction 1790–1830', in John Richetti (ed.), *The Columbia History of the British Novel*, vol. xix (New York, 1994), 327–51.

Moers, Ellen, *Literary Women* (New York, 1976).

Poovey, Mary, *The Proper Lady and the Woman Writer: Ideology as Style in the Works of Mary Wollstonecraft, Mary Shelley, and Jane Austen* (Chicago, 1984).

Showalter, Elaine, *A Literature of their Own: British Women Novelists from Brontë to Lessing* (Princeton, 1977).

Spacks, Patricia Meyer, 'Novels of the 1790s: Action and Impasse', in John Richetti (ed.), *Columbia History of the British Novel*, vol. xix (New York, 1994), 247–74.

Spencer, Jane, *The Rise of the Woman Novelist: From Aphra Behn to Jane Austen* (Oxford, 1986).

Todd, Janet, *Women's Friendship in Literature* (New York, 1980).

—— (ed.), *A Dictionary of British and American Women Writers 1660–1800* (Totowa, NJ, 1985).

—— *Sensibility: An Introduction* (London, 1986).

—— *The Sign of Angellica: Women, Writing, and Fiction, 1660–1800* (London, 1989).

Tompkins, J. M. S., *The Popular Novel in England 1770–1800* (Lincoln, Nebr., 1932; repr. 1961).

Turner, Cheryl, *Living by the Pen: Women Writers in the Eighteenth Century* (London, 1992).

Ty, Eleanor, *Unsex'd Revolutionaries: Five Women Novelists of the 1790s* (Toronto, 1993).

Watson, Nicola, *Revolution and the Form of the British Novel 1790–1825: Intercepted Letters, Interrupted Seductions* (Oxford, 1994a).

WOLLSTONECRAFT

Barker-Benfield, G. J. *The Culture of Sensibility: Sex and Society in Eighteenth Century Britain* (Chicago, 1992).

Conger, Syndy McMillen, *Sensibility in Transformation: Creative Resistance to Sentiment from the Augustans to the Romantics* (London, 1990).

—— *Mary Wollstonecraft and the Language of Sensibility* (London, 1994).

Godwin, William, *Memoirs of the Author of a Vindication of the Rights of Woman*, ed. Richard Holmes (Harmondsworth, 1987).

Jones, Chris, *Radical Sensibility: Literature and Ideas in the 1790s* (London, 1993).

Kelly, Gary, *Revolutionary Feminism: The Mind and Career of Mary Wollstonecraft* (London, 1992).

Langbauer, Laurie, *Women and Romance: The Consolations of Gender in the English Novel* (Ithaca, NY, 1990).

Sunstein, Emily, *A Different Face: The Life of Mary Wollstonecraft* (Baltimore, 1989).

Tomalin, Claire, *The Life and Death of Mary Wollstonecraft* (Harmondsworth, 1974).

GODWIN

Butler, Marilyn, 'Godwin, Burke, and *Caleb Williams*', *Essays in Criticism*, 32 (1982), 237–57; repr. in Duncan Wu (ed.), *Romanticism: A Critical Reader* (Oxford, 1995), 343–58.

Clemit, Pamela, *The Godwinian Novel: The Rational Fictions of Godwin, Brockden Brown, Mary Shelley* (Oxford, 1993).

Graham, Kenneth W., *The Politics of Narrative: Ideology and Social Change in William Godwin's Caleb Williams* (New York, 1990).

Rajan, Tilottama, 'Wollstonecraft and Godwin: Reading the Secrets of the Political Novel', *Studies in Romanticism*, 27/2 (1988), 221–51.

St Clair, William, 'William Godwin as Children's Bookseller', in Gillian Avery and Julia Briggs (eds.), *Children and their Books: A Celebration of the Work of Iona and Peter Opie* (Oxford, 1989), 165–79.

Tysdal, B. J., *William Godwin as Novelist* (London, 1981).

INCHBALD

Castle, Terry, *Masquerade and Civilization: The Carnivalesque in Eighteenth Century English Culture and Fiction* (Stanford, Calif., 1986).

Rogers, K. M. 'Inhibitions on Eighteenth-Century Women Novelists: Elizabeth Inchbald and Charlotte Smith', *Eighteenth-Century Studies*, 11 (1977), 63–78.

LAMB, LADY CAROLINE

Clubbe, John, '*Glenarvon*—Revised and Revisited', *Wordsworth Circle*, 10/2 (1979), 205–17.

Graham, Peter W., *Don Juan and Regency England* (Charlottesville, Va., 1990).

—— 'Fictive Biography in 1816: The Case of *Glenarvon*', *Byron Journal*, 19 (1991), 53–68.

Kelsall, Malcolm, 'The Byronic Hero and Revolution in Ireland: The Politics of *Glenarvon*', *Byron Journal*, 9 (1981), 4–16.

Watson, Nicola, 'Trans-Figuring Byronic Identity', in Mary Favret and Nicola Watson (eds.), *At the Limits of Romanticism: Essays in Cultural, Feminist and Materialist Criticism* (Bloomington, Ind., 1994*b*), 185–206.

EDGEWORTH

Butler, Marilyn, *Maria Edgeworth: A Literary Biography* (Oxford, 1972).

Dunne, Tom, *Maria Edgeworth and the Colonial Mind* (Dublin, 1985).

Ferris, Ina, *The Achievement of Literary Authority: Gender, History, and the Waverley Novels* (New York, 1991).

Gallagher, Catherine, 'Fictional Women and Real Estate in Maria Edgeworth's *Castle Rackrent*', *Nineteenth-Century Contexts*, 12/1 (1988), 11–18.

Harden, O. Elizabeth McWhorter, *Maria Edgeworth's Art of Prose Fiction* (The Hague, 1971).

Hurst, Michael, *Maria Edgeworth and the Public Scene* (London, 1969).

Kowaleski-Wallace, Elizabeth, 'Home Economics', in *Eighteenth Century: Theory and Interpretation* (1988), 242–62.

—— *Their Father's Daughters: Hannah More, Maria Edgeworth, and Patriarchal Complicity* (New York, 1991).

McCormack, W. J., *Ascendancy and Tradition in Anglo-Irish Literary History, 1789–1939* (Oxford, 1989).

Ragussis, Michael, 'Representation, Conversion and Literary Form: *Harrington* and the Novel of Jewish Identity', *Critical Inquiry*, 16/1 (1989), 113–43.

SUSAN MATTHEWS

BURNEY

Campbell, Gina, 'How to Read like a Gentleman: Burney's Instructions to her Critics in *Evelina*', *English Literary History*, 57/3 (1990), 557–83.

Cutting-Gray, Joanna, 'Writing Innocence: Fanny Burney's *Evelina*', *Tulsa Studies in Women's Literature*, 9/1 (1990), 43–57.

Doody, Margaret Anne, *Frances Burney: The Life in the Works* (New Brunswick, NJ, 1988).

—— 'Beyond *Evelina*: The Individual Novel and the Community of Literature' *Eighteenth-Century Fiction*, 13/4 (1991), 359–72.

Epstein, Julia, *The Iron Pen: Frances Burney and the Politics of Women's Writing* (Madison, 1989).

—— 'Burney Criticism: Family Romance, Psychobiography and Social History' *Eighteenth-Century Fiction*, 13/4 (1991), 277–82.

Hutner, Heidi '*Evelina* and the Problem of the Female Grotesque' *Studies in Philology*, 88/2 (1991), 191–204.

Newton, Judith Lowder, *Women, Power and Subversion: Social Strategies in British Fiction 1778–1860* (Athens, Ga., 1981).

Rogers, Katharine M., *Frances Burney: The World of Female Difficulties* (New York, 1990).

Simons, Judy, *Fanny Burney* (London, 1987).

Straub, Kristina, *Divided Fictions: Fanny Burney and Feminine Strategy* (Lexington, Ky., 1987).

HAYS

Rajan, Tilottama, 'Autonarration and Genotext in Mary Hays', *Memoirs of Emma Courtney*', *Studies in Romanticism*, 32/2 (1993), 146–76.

HOGG

Groves, David, *James Hogg: The Growth of a Writer* (Edinburgh, 1988).

Kosofsky Sedgwick, Eve, *Between Men: English Literature and Male Homosocial Desire* (New York, 1985).

BAGE

Faulkner, Peter, *Robert Bage* (Boston, 1979).

16. *Romantic Gothic*

PETER GARSIDE

The Gothic and the Romantic as literary historical terms have rarely stood easily together. When interest in Gothic literature began to revive in the early twentieth century, the mode was largely understood as a subgenre of the novel, at best providing an interesting link between rationalism and Romanticism, though some commentators were more inclined to sense a last gasp of the eighteenth-century sentimental tradition. In the 1960s an influential school of criticism positioned the Gothic rather as a counter-movement to the Romantic, as a kind of obverse or dark side to the latter's optimism and pursuit of the organic and transcendental. More recently, interest in the Gothic has expanded to such an extent that it is sometimes regarded as offering a better site for investigating deep ruptures and divisions underlying the literature of the Romantic period: broadly 'popular' and relatively open to female writers compared with the allegedly 'male' and elitist tradition of the main Romantic poets, while at the same time more diverse and lasting in its cultural effects.

Notwithstanding these shifting perspectives, and the more constant problem of defining such a fluid mode as the Gothic (whether through its motifs, the 'terror' effect, or narrative structure), a number of salient points have remained stable and for the most part unchallenged. After a brief hiatus in the wake of Horace Walpole's *Castle of Otranto* (1764)—a 'Gothic Story' which gave the movement its title as well as establishing a number of leading characteristics—the Gothic became a dominant mode in fiction during the 1790s, accounting (it has been estimated) for at least a third of output, and remained a strong component in that genre until the 1820s. In the adjacent field of drama, Gothic plays caused a sensation on several notable occasions. Nearly all the leading Romantic poets were affected, directly or indirectly, by Gothic influences, and a number of canonical texts of the period resist satisfactory interpretation without an awareness of Gothic conventions. Taking its title to mean mainly 'Gothic literature in the Romantic period' (as opposed to 'Gothic literature of a Romantic nature'), the following account attempts to track modern scholarship and criticism on the Gothic as a general literary movement during its classic 'historical' phase from approximately 1790 to 1820. In the process, it also focuses on a number of key texts, chiefly (though not exclusively) those by three writers who are exceptional in having been primarily associated with the Gothic both by their contemporaries and by modern critics: Ann Radcliffe (1764–1823), Matthew Gregory ('Monk') Lewis (1775–1818), and Charles Robert Maturin (1782–1824).

TEXTS

Our knowledge about the production of Gothic literature in the Romantic period is limited by inadequacies in the current bibliographies, several of which derive from before the Second World War. Andrew Block's *English Novel 1740–1850* contains more than 4,000 titles between 1780 and 1830, amongst which is discernible a large upsurge in fiction (of all types) in the later 1780s, then again during the 1790s, with a level of about 100 new titles annually being reached by the new century. The listings however are often not based on copies seen, so that several entries probably never saw the light of day, and Block's indiscriminate mixing of reprints, miscellanies, chapbooks, etc. alongside standard novels makes for a shaky basis for analysis. Ascertaining Gothic content by title only is at best a hazardous activity (the term 'Gothic' itself is rare in subtitles after Walpole), so at first sight Summers's *A Gothic Bibliography* (1940) seems a promising addition. Unfortunately the 'elastic' policy adopted is taken to bursting point, as Summers obsessively pursues every work by authors with Gothic associations, while taking on board an unwieldy variety of forerunners and successors of the mode. The sheer weight of detail offered (in separate author and title lists) on matters such as subsequent editions and spin-offs still makes it a valuable tool for researchers, though one to be handled carefully. Tarr later managed to locate 609 volumes [*sic*] listed by Summers, though only 306 proved to be Gothic fictions, the remainder being primarily sentimental novels in the epistolary form. Her own end bibliography is consequently more focused, though in breadth and authority it has been superseded by the check-list of titles 1764–1824 supplied by Lévy (1968) as an appendix to his magisterial study of the Gothic novel. A breakdown of some 340 items listed by the latter suggests that the 1790s and 1800s were by far the most fertile decades, followed by a steady falling-off in the 1810s.

These figures are corroborated in their tendency by a number of other specialist bibliographies, invaluable to the student of Gothic fiction. Blakey gives a full account of one of the leading library proprietors and publishers of popular fiction in the early Romantic period, William Lane, who was also a major supplier to other circulating libraries throughout the country. Generally speaking his Minerva Press was *reactive* rather than an originator of trends, and as such its history is especially useful as a barometer of taste. Blakey's exhaustive chronological list of its publications (nearly all fiction) shows that between 1790 and 1820 Lane and his successor, A. K. Newman, regularly published twenty to thirty new novels a year (representing up to about one-third of total output by the trade). Gothic titles overtake domestic-sentimental titles from about 1793, with two main types evident by the end of the decade: a species of 'terror' titles after the pattern of Ann Radcliffe's *Mysteries of Udolpho* (1794), often signalled by key title words such as 'Abbey'; and, later in the decade, a new brand of 'German' fictions, in the fabrication of which Lane appears to have been uncharacteristically innovative. An equivalent picture is provided by the career of J. F. Hughes, who briefly overtook the Minerva as a producer of fiction around 1805–10, and who is now best known as the publisher of some of M. G. Lewis's later works. Of sixty-four titles seen at first hand, Garside (1987) notes an almost equal division between sentimental, Gothic, and scandal fictions. While several of the Gothic titles garishly proclaim their 'horror' credentials and indebtedness to Lewis's *The Monk* (1796), the Radcliffian style is also still evident (T. J. Horsley Curties's *Monk of Udolpho* (1807) through its title claims a joint derivation!).

An alternative view is provided by research on the content of contemporary magazines. Mayo (1943) uses the widely circulating *Lady's Magazine* as an indicator of popular taste. Taking 'Gothic' to mean a tale containing 'one or more scenes of terror in the conventional mode', he traces a rising curve from 1791, with half of the fiction in the magazine containing Gothic elements by 1795; this is followed by a high water mark in 1805 (84 per cent), followed by a drop to 44 per cent 1807–9, spiralling down to total absence of Gothic components in 1813–14. This would suggest that M. G. Lewis in continuing to produce Gothic-style titles in the early 1800s was swimming *with* the tide, and that the common idea of Walter Scott's historical fiction replacing (or assimilating) the Gothic is not inconsistent with trends apparent among the magazine's female readership. Maturin, seen this way, can appear as attempting a revival of the Gothic form with *Melmoth the Wanderer* (1820), but his *Fatal Revenge* (1807) by Mayo's calculations was published at 'the zenith of the general interest in the Gothic'. Mayo's later essay (1950), based on a broader study of periodicals, is somewhat less sanguine in its findings, noting that several magazines eschewed the Gothic, one at least evidently bowing to pressure to exclude it on the grounds of impropriety. This too is reflected in Mayo's massive record (1962) of fiction in the magazines between 1740 and 1815, which nevertheless notes the popularity of the Gothic *tale* or *fragment* in the later eighteenth century, and the invasive influence of Radcliffe from the 1790s. Another product of the period, the short tale (often a distillation of a longer novel) in single-volume form, known as 'shilling shockers' or (from the covers) as blue books, is recorded by Watt, though his account is limited to conventional themes and lacks bibliographical support.

Readers needing quick access to plots and key motifs will find help from two recent surveys. Tracy's *Gothic Novel 1790–1830* (1981) provides plot summaries for 208 texts from the Romantic period, as well as useful indexes of motifs and characters. Unfortunately its choice of texts stems initially from Summers, and as a result several titles included are not, even in the broadest sense, definable as Gothic fictions. More impressive—and in some ways offering the best bibliography of Gothic fiction in the Romantic period—is Frank's *The First Gothics* (1987). This offers useful synopses of 500 Gothic fictions, mostly full-length novels, from 1764 to the late 1820s: it also gives reliable title descriptions, an indication of type (e.g. 'Sentimentalized Gothic'), a record of modern editions, and biographical and research data relating to each item. The end matter includes a wealth of bibliographical information.

Copies of Gothic novels in their original form are extremely rare, and even specialist collections, such as the Sadleir-Black Collection at the University of Virginia, are a long way from offering coverage. Most novels of this type were borrowed rather than purchased by their original readers, and then disposed of by circulating libraries to make room for eagerly sought new stock (see Varma 1972). Apart from a few exceptions (Radcliffe is one) Gothic fictions were not written by named authors of note; and, at a time when the status of the novel was generally low, anonymous or pseudonymous productions of this kind were usually considered as ephemeral, even more so after the backlash in the reviews against Lewis's *Monk* in the late 1790s.

The revival of interest in the Gothic from the 1960s, however, has encouraged a regular flow of reprints—with the result that novels in this mode are probably proportionately better represented than other types of fiction from the period. The year 1968 saw the republication in Penguin (ed. Fairclough) of three classic supernatural tales, Walpole's *Otranto*, William Beckford's *Vathek* (1786), and Mary Shelley's *Frankenstein* (1818), which had hitherto been hard to find. At the other end of the scale of familiarity the Northanger Set of Jane Austen Horrid Novels, under the general editorship of and with introductions by Varma (1968), made available for the first time the 'horrid' novels listed by Isabella Thorpe in Austen's *Northanger Abbey* (1818), which earlier had been regarded as either spoof titles or lost for ever. This collection, with its seven novels published 1793–8—six by the Minerva Press—offers a valuable insight into the pervasive influence of the German *Schauerroman* (shudder novel) at this time: six titles claim German attributes and/or a German provenance, though only two are genuine translations. By far the biggest input in this field was provided by the Arno Press's Collection of Gothic Novels, published in three series between 1972 and 1977, comprising together thirty titles, in the form of facsimile reproductions of early editions and with new introductory material by a variety of hands. The collection ranges between lesser known 'representative' titles and those by relatively well-known authors. It includes all Ann Radcliffe's novels (apart from *Udolpho* and *The Italian* (1797), which were already available in modern editions), Lewis's melodramatic *Bravo of*

Venice (1805), and Maturin's *Fatal Revenge*, as a result making the main Gothic fiction of these three canonical writers generally accessible. Additionally all Charlotte Dacre's four novels are included, along with a number of other eye-catching titles such as *Manfroné; or, The One-Handed Monk* (1809), allegedly by the somewhat shadowy Mary-Anne Radcliffe. The usefulness of this collection is occasionally marred by the use of editions other than the earliest in some instances.

Modern edited texts of Gothic fiction are largely confined to the main authors. All Ann Radcliffe's novels, apart from her first and last, have appeared in the Oxford English Novels Series and/or the paperback World's Classics, with sound critical introductions and useful annotation. A fitting culmination is found in Alison Milbank's (1993) edition of *A Sicilian Romance* (1790), which includes a notably up-to-date introduction. Milbank chooses a later edition (that of 1821, the last in the author's lifetime) as her base text, whereas the previous editors of Radcliffe in the series usually opt for the earliest. Since there appears to be no direct evidence that Radcliffe actively intervened in later editions—most of the (usually) minor changes found between editions are best explained as the product of intermediaries working for the publishers—the choice of text to be followed is not of enormous significance, though the first has the advantage of taking us closest to the author's original copy. Radcliffe's earliest work of fiction, *The Castles of Athlin and Dunbayne* (1789), has recently been reprinted in the Pocket Classics series published by Alan Sutton, but with the briefest of introductions and devoid of textual commentary.

In comparison M. G. Lewis's most famous Gothic work, *The Monk* (1796), has proved a minefield for textual scholars. In addition to a variety of early authorial changes (most obviously in the extensively expurgated fourth edition of 1798, when the title was changed to *Ambrosio; or, The Monk*), the transmission of the text was further complicated by various underhand strategies used by the publisher in marketing his editions—a situation brilliantly unravelled by Todd in 1949. Since then textually alert editions have been been produced by Peck (1952) and Anderson (1973), the first following the first edition of 1796, the second the author's manuscript. Anderson's edition includes a still useful introduction, and, by virtue of being based on an unusually well-prepared autograph manuscript, takes us close to the author's original intentions.

No scholarly edition of Maturin's *Fatal Revenge* is currently available, though the text can be accessed either in the Arno series or through the paperback reprint (1994) in the Pocket Classics series. In the case of *Melmoth the Wanderer*, readers have a better choice between two well-balanced modern editions: Hayter's Penguin edition (1977), with its lively and informative introduction; and the 1968 Oxford English Novels volume edited by Grant, since reissued in World's Classics with a new introduction by Chris Baldick. The texts of both these reproduce the first edition of 1820, making silent correction of obvious errors and misprints. Baldick's anthology of *Gothic Tales* (1992), a valuable record of a form which remained in currency beyond the nineteenth century, includes seven tales published either in magazines or in chapbooks between 1773 and 1802.

Textual studies in the field of drama, the other genre into which the Gothic entered in fairly unmediated form, have generally lagged behind those relating to fiction, though there have been some interesting late developments. Bertrand Evans's *Gothic Drama from Walpole to Shelley* (1947), still useful as a guide, traces the development of an English native tradition from Walpole's *The Mysterious Mother* (1768), through the numerous stage adaptations of Radcliffe and the influx of German elements in the 1790s, and finds a high point in the prominent figure of M. G. Lewis. Evans also highlights the influence of Gothic drama on the Romantic poets, and provides a helpful appendix listing some 130 titles, stretching from the *Mysterious Mother* to adaptations of Maturin's *Melmoth* and Mary Shelley's *Frankenstein* in 1823. Access to texts has recently been enhanced in two ways. Facsimile-based editions of Lewis's *Castle Spectre* (1798) and Maturin's *Bertram; or, The Castle of St Aldobrand* (1816), the most significant Gothic plays of their period, were published by Woodstock Books in 1990 and 1992 respectively, both with helpful introductions by Jonathan Wordsworth. More comprehensive is Jeffrey Cox's *Seven Gothic Dramas*, which includes edited versions of *Castle Spectre* and *Bertram*, as well as other representative plays. Cox's texts take into account both the earliest published edition and the original licensing copies presented to the Lord Chamberlain's censor; his collection shows a commendable awareness of editorial issues and contemporary stage conditions.

Access to texts and bibliographical information are both likely to improve through new technologies and forms of transmission such as the Internet. Of special significance here, as a transmittable source, is the discovery of a major collection of English novels from 1796 to 1834 at Schloss Corvey, in Germany, representing up to 80 per cent of total production (Garside 1992), and unusually rich in Gothic titles. Graham's printed catalogue gives an idea of its extensiveness, while being seriously flawed on matters of detail. A full microfiche edition of English fiction in the collection, including 2,240 novels, has been produced by Belser Knowledge Services, though the take-up by Anglo-American libraries so far has been limited. A full descriptive bibliography of English fiction, 1770–1830, based partly on the Corvey holdings, is currently in preparation (under the general editorship of Garside, Raven, and Schöwerling) and will be published in two volumes by Oxford University Press.

CRITICISM

More than one commentator has pointed to a similarity between traditional Gothic literature and modern criticism on the Gothic, and the parallel is inviting on temporal as on other levels. If the revival of interest in the 1920s and

1930s is reminiscent in some respects of the early Walpolian years, the rapid acceleration of critical interpretation since 1970 seems akin in its intensity to the rapid outpouring of Gothic fiction during the 1790s. Indicative of the increasing perception of the Gothic as a field in its own right, rather than as a curiosity or side issue, are four bibliographical surveys of scholarship and critical responses. McNutt's *Eighteenth-Century Gothic Novel* (1975) offers carefully segmented sections on general studies as well as on editions and commentary (contemporary reviews and modern criticism) relating to six major novelists: Walpole, Clara Reeve, Charlotte Smith, Radcliffe, Lewis, and Beckford. Spector's *English Gothic* (1984) presents its material more discursively, an introduction on Gothicism being followed by individual chapters tracing commentary to date on major practitioners paired as follows: Walpole and Reeve; Smith and Radcliffe; Lewis and Beckford; Maturin and Mary Shelley— each chapter being backed up by extensive bibliographies. Fisher's *The Gothic's Gothic* (1988), which is divided into two parts, on authors and subjects, offers somewhat haphazard 'card-index' type comments on a wide variety of items, with a heavy emphasis on earlier records such as memoirs, matched by a noticeable absence of criticism post-1975. Frank's *Gothic Fiction* (1988) alone eschews commentary, providing instead extensive listings of sources and criticism, with sections on major English and American writers, French and German Gothic, special Gothic themes, and ending with a selective listing of Gothic films.

The earliest critical studies of Gothic literature are largely surveys of writers and their works, with an emphasis on sources and leading motifs. Birkhead's *Tale of Terror* (1921) covers the main ground sensibly and efficiently, differentiating Radcliffe (decorous, discreet) from Lewis ('German', explicit), while pointing to a new level of intensity in Maturin. Railo by contrast is now virtually unreadable, his study of 1927 consisting of long lists of 'themes', motifs, and settings, with the haunted castle professedly central to these. A continual slippage of terms ('horror romanticism', 'the romanticism of horror') makes it impossible to tell where Gothicism is meant to stand in relation to Romanticism. The starting point in Sadleir's pamphlet of the same year is Jane Austen's 'horrid novels', and on one level it records a successful antiquarian chase to locate copies of each. Without ever entirely convincing, Sadleir argues that the titles are not random, but represent rather a deliberate mix of genuine and false German titles, delicate Radcliffian terror and darker Lewisian horror. More interesting, in the light of recent attempts to decode the Gothic ideologically, is Sadleir's association of 'the Gothic romantic epoch' with the French Revolution, the ruined castle in his eyes representing a declining past tyranny.

A fitting conclusion to this first phase of Gothic criticism is Summers's mammoth *Gothic Quest* (1938). Like its bibliographical counterpart, it still serves as a marvellous repository of details about titles, publishers, translations, etc., though its commentary now seems insufficiently guided by a central thesis or sense of discrimination. While the significance of Radcliffe is broadly acknowledged, the greatest emphasis by far is placed on 'Monk' Lewis and his imitators. In concluding, Summers launches into an attack on Sadleir and the French surrealist André Breton for associating the 'romantic Gothic' with revolutionary turmoil, countering somewhat tendentiously that the main English Gothicists were conservatives. Ultimately, however, Summers's main insistence is that Gothic was a form of high nostalgia, essentially aristocratic and idealist in its leanings.

Varma's *The Gothic Flame* (1957), the next full-length study, can now be seen as a transitional document. In its insistence that the Gothic 'arose out of a quest for the numinous' and concern for subcategorization it follows on from the Summers school, sometimes to the point of presenting a pastiche. The main difference lies in an overlayer of Freudian and surrealist phraseology, signalling the presence of more significant psychological undercurrents. This was followed by a more pronounced shift in the 1960s away from influences and motifs to the pursuit of an underlying 'monomyth' or (in Lévy's terms) of 'deep structures'. Fiedler's 1960 study of American fiction includes a number of trenchant and highly influential comments on the socio-psychological nature of English Gothic. Freud's influence is implicit in his observations on the 'self-duplicating nightmare' in Radcliffe's plots, though the spotlight shifts quickly from the fleeing heroine to the male villain-hero, in Fiedler's view the main invention of the Gothic form. He also prioritizes an Oedipal plot of male incest, reflective of the anxieties of a revolutionary age over the destruction of 'the old ego-ideals of Church and State'. Another airing to these ideas was given by Nelson, who like Fiedler elevates Lewis above Radcliffe, placing *The Monk* at the threshold of more profound investigations into the human psyche, such as Melville's *Moby-Dick*. While avoiding direct 'explanation' of the Gothic, Nelson points to a loss of religion as one possible factor (God having been 'secularized out of the graveyard').

One result of this tendency to grant deeper significance to the Gothic was a reappraisal of its relationship with Romanticism generally. Whereas for Praz the 'tale of terror' only penetrated into the 'higher sphere' of literature through Byron and Scott, Hume in a key article of 1969 grants Gothic the status of a distinct literary movement, comparable to Romanticism; though ultimately his argument is to present it as a less coherent (and by implication unsuccessful) form. Romanticism is equated with Coleridge's idea of the Imagination, reaching out from difficulty towards unity and transcendence; the Gothic by contrast, like Fancy, remains locked in paradox and denied any perception of 'high truth'. In his rejoinder of 1971, Platzner questioned the degree to which the Gothic can be extended to include works such as *Wuthering Heights*, while claiming (not unreasonably) that Romanticism is too complex to be interpreted in Coleridgian terms; he also picks out 'a singular quality of evil' as the main Gothic quality. Hume countered with accusations of ontological narrowness, and the encounter brought diminishing returns as it became more personalized. But a potent idea had been established, returning in a fuller form in the influential collection of essays edited by Thompson (1974). For Thompson the 'Dark Romanticism' of the Gothic, while expressing the negative side of Romantic idealism, itself represents a vital, energetic, if ultimately pessimistic, creative field: its practitioners caught between the cosmic optimism of the poets and a more medieval-like notion of sin-ridden humanity.

The accessibility of fresh texts combining with new critical methodologies created a heady mix in the 1970s. Todorov's structural study of the Fantastic (first made available in English in 1973) focuses on the classic Gothic at one point to show how its texts fall primarily into the category of the *marvellous* (supernatural accepted) or the *uncanny* (supernatural explained), yet noting how readers will sometimes experience the effect of the *fantastic*, i.e. uncertainty. Kiely's *Romantic Novel in England* (1972), notwithstanding its title, deals predominantly with Gothic novels, and includes valuable analytic chapters on *Udolpho*, *The Monk*, and *Melmoth*. Mainly textual in his emphasis, Kiely sees paradox, tension, and irreconcilability as the distinguishing features of the period's fiction. A number of articles at this time show a determination to move discussion of the Gothic into new theoretical areas: Keech proposes a shift from 'stock devices' to effective response; Lydenberg (1978), in attempting to open up conventional comparisons between Gothic literature and architecture, highlights elements such as generic uncertainty; Holland and Sherman bring to bear issues relating to gender and reader response in their debate on 'Gothic Possibilities'; Madoff adds a fresh historical/psychological dimension to earlier etymological surveys (Longueil, Kliger) of 'Gothic' as a term.

The end of the decade was marked by three full studies, the first since Varma, all of which extend the generic study of the Gothic. According to Howells (1978), the traditional Gothic brought fiction into contact with the irrational, especially deeper sexual urges, but was unable to integrate this into a cohesive narrative form (through countervailing forces such as moral conservativism). For MacAndrew, rather than representing a set of conventions, the Gothic tradition is best seen as a continuing narrative mode through which the psychology of evil and the dilemma of the human condition can be examined. Unlike MacAndrew, Punter in his seminal *Literature of Terror* (1980) added a historical materialist dimension to formalist and psychological considerations. His brilliant final chapter ('Towards a Theory of the Gothic') locates a deep malaise in the middle classes late in the eighteenth century, under the new pressures of capitalism and urbanization. In his analysis, the continuance of these factors offers the best explanation for the longevity of the Gothic and its survival in other media such as film. No single book on the Gothic has proved so durable as Punter's, and his theoretical chapter is a direct source for the four major approaches (listed below) which have dominated discussion since.

1. *Mythic Gothic.* Punter's 'broad brush' approach, itself reflecting a tendency since Nelson and Hume to expand beyond the conventional 1820s cut-off point, is mirrored in Wilt's book of the same year. This sets out to explore ways in which the 'old Gothic' infused and energized the mainstream novel of the later nineteenth century, including F. R. Leavis's Great Tradition. Wilt echoes Porte and others in claiming a 'theological root' for the Gothic, the imperfectly rationalized forces of the past, religious and political, still having a power to fascinate (as Gothic 'ghosts'); and her first chapter offers critical comment on *The Italian, The Monk,* and *Melmoth,* in an intense, perceptive, but sometimes unfortunately opaque way. Little sense is given of a socio-historical basis: the Sadleir–Summers controversy briefly comes into view, only to be overridden as an irrelevance. Just as ahistorical, though in a different way, is Bayer-Berenbaum, who treats high medieval Gothic architecture and Gothic literature as a single imaginative vision. Day's 1985 study of Gothic fantasy is closer to Punter in mixing Freudian and Marxian insights, but more single-mindedly pursues an all-embracing monomyth, involving the descent of 'divided' protagonists into a Gothic underworld. Day emphasizes unnatural gender roles as a source of division, locating these in the bourgeois family structure of the nineteenth century. His book offers diverse if sometimes diffuse discussion of a wide range of texts, with special attention to those featuring doubling and division, and includes analysis of Radcliffe (as feminine Gothic), Lewis, and Maturin, though none of these is central. One difficulty is that not all texts can be made to fit this mythic pattern; another, that the concept of a constant middle-class society and readership tends to conflate a variegated and complex era. The same pressures towards inclusiveness can be sensed in Botting's 1996 guide *Gothic* (the omission of the definite article is telling), which follows a route from early and Romantic Gothic, through American Gothic (Poe, Hawthorne), Victorian fiction (Brontës, Wilkie Collins), 1890s Gothic (Stevenson, Wilde), modernism (Conrad), and postmodernism (Umberto Eco), onto film (ending with Coppola's 1992 version of Bram Stoker's *Dracula,* as a not-too-convincing dead end).

2. *Political Gothic.* A contrary pull, back to the traditional Gothic, has come through critics reinvestigating a connection between the French Revolution and the flood of Gothic publications in the 1790s. The idea that the romances of Radcliffe and Lewis embodied revolutionary tensions in Europe can be traced back to de Sade (1800), though in Summers and Sadleir this degenerated into an insistence on attributing specific political positions to writers. Paulson (1981, 1983) brilliantly revives the issue by noting a significant overlap between political and fictional metaphors—fortified castles, tyrannical

masters, imperilled heroines—which, he claims, could hardly be missed by contemporary readers. In Lewis's *Monk*, according to this reading, Ambrosio's history reflects two aspects of Revolution: a bursting out from repression, followed by accelerating havoc (most evident in a violent mob scene) in the wake of his self-liberation. Paulson also makes the point that the convoluted plotting of Gothic fiction matches the difficulties contemporaries must have felt in reading the events of the Revolution from England. A similar path is followed by Morse, where the sense of correlation is extended to take in post-Waterloo Britain. Cox similarly picks out two phases in Gothic drama: the first in the wake of the fall of the Bastille, when liberation from confinement is a leading motif; the second paralleling the reactionary political climate after the defeat of Napoleon, and marked by a new species of alienated villain-hero. The overall tendency in the valuable collection of essays edited by Graham (1989) is to emphasize Gothic as a revolutionary aesthetic. Other new historicist critics have placed the Gothic at the interface of conflicting aristocratic and bourgeois values: a line pursued by Cottom, who equates the works of Radcliffe with Austen and Scott; and, more recently, by Kelly (1989), Richter (1989), and Bernstein. Clery (1995) also employs a historical materialist approach to locate the *rise* of supernatural fiction in a context of socio-economic transformations in later eighteenth-century England, with a focus on factors such as the growth of consumerism, the trope of female authorship and readership, and shifting legal positions regarding marriage and inheritance.

Other commentators present the 'Glorious' Revolution of 1688 as an alternative epicentre for the cultural shocks manifested in the Gothic. Following on from the suggestions of Lévy and Porte, Sage (1988) contextualizes Radcliffe, Lewis, and Maturin in terms of problematic anxieties about the Catholic past, revived and exacerbated by current agitation for Catholic emancipation. He also extends the analysis to include the Lutheran-Calvinist tradition of 'self-scrutiny', a main source in his view of the Gothic 'divided self', and finds in opposed views of the nature of testimony a way of approaching narrative complexities in *The Monk* and *The Italian* as well as the labyrinthine nature of Gothic narrative generally. New light is likewise thrown on the topos of the ruined abbey by Charlesworth, who notes a shift in perspective and tonal response as the threat of Jacobitism diminished in the later eighteenth century.

3. *Female Gothic*. The term 'Female Gothic' was coined by Ellen Moers, originally appearing in two articles written for the *New York Review of Books* in 1974, then again as the heading for a chapter (incorporating the same material) in her influential *Literary Women* (1976). At a time when 'Gothics' by contemporary women authors were proliferating, Moers drew a line of female Gothic writing from Radcliffe, through *Frankenstein* (interpreted as a birth myth) and Christina Rossetti's narrative poem *Goblin Market*, to the 'modern female Gothic' of Carson McCullers and others. While her emphasis tends to

be physiological rather than psychological, Moers stands at a head of a school of feminist criticism which has gone on to interpret the Gothic as a form profoundly subversive of patriarchal social norms. Three contributions appearing in 1980 indicate the various strands feeding into this approach. Bette Roberts, expanding hints previously made by Tompkins (1932), argued strongly (albeit in the main deductively) for a predominantly female authorship and readership of Gothic romance in the late eighteenth century. Kahane countered the male critics' accentuation of the Oedipal plot in the Gothic, turning attention instead to the spectral figure of the 'dead-undead mother', briefly analysing Radcliffe's *Udolpho* in Lacanian terms as a search for an ambiguous maternal presence. Sedgwick likewise questioned the validity of Freudian 'depth' psychology in the case of the Gothic. Re-examining its main conventions, in Radcliffe, Lewis, and Maturin, she argues (contrary to earlier claims about 'stage-props' and 'claptrap') that the strongest signification is found in surface qualities, discerning also a pattern of doubling (in set motifs, spatial relations, narrative patterning, etc.) which negates the notion of a coherent inner self. Sedgwick's strict post-structuralist approach (repeated in a classic article of 1981) prevented her from claiming a distinct psychological or historical origin, but her suggestion that the Gothic is about fragmented subjectivity was to have wide-ranging effects.

All these influences funnelled into the important collection of 1983 edited by Fleenor, which more than any previous work helped stake out the Gothic as a territory for feminist literary investigation. Fleenor's introduction pictures the Gothic heroine, in an oppressive patriarchal world, split between a largely socially constructed image of feminine 'purity', on the one hand, and the contrary figure of the passion-dominated 'dark' woman. Following on from Kahane, she also places at the heart of the Gothic 'the conflict with the all-powerful devouring mother'. The sixteen essays in this volume range widely from traditional to modern popular Gothic, with Radcliffe and Mary Shelley the dominant figures in the early historical phase. Three essays centre on Radcliffe in particular, though in each (as in Fleenor's introduction, and the volume as a whole) one also feels a strong pull towards the Brontës as the most central exponents of Female Gothic.

This tendency to 'universalize' the female Gothic is less apparent in two sophisticated overviews by Ellis and Delamotte, both published at the end of the decade. Ellis proposes a definition of 'feminine' and 'masculine' Gothic in terms of the formulation of gender roles amongst the middle classes late in the eighteenth century, and especially in relation to the ideology of female domesticity. Radcliffian Gothic is seen as challenging the notion of the insulated home from within, by displacing its inadequacies into a Gothic setting and framework; Lewis's 'masculine' Gothic, on the other hand, places the protagonist as an outsider, working to subvert the idea of 'separate spheres' from without. While one of the declared aims of the book is to restore an erstwhile marginalized feminine Gothic to the centre, some of Ellis's most persuasive analyses concern the extreme states of alienation found in Lewis and Maturin. Delamotte's study owes a great deal to Sedgwick in concentrating on formal elements such as boundaries and their indeterminacy, but makes a clearer move to relate these to psychoanalytic issues, and more specifically to the actual conditions experienced by women in the 1790s and beyond. The continuing strength of feminist investigations of the Gothic, along psychoanalytic and materialist lines, is well evidenced in the special collection of essays on Female Gothic writing edited by Miles (1994).

4. *Formalist Gothic.* Approaches attempting to read the Gothic synchronically, as embodying certain consistent stylistic or structural features, are relatively less evident in the 1980s. Noteworthy as an early deconstructionist account is Hogle's discussion of the crypt as a metaphor for narrative. Through valuable analyses of Radcliffe, *The Monk*, and *Melmoth*, his 1980 article shows how the search for meaning is frustrated, as narratives are constantly deflected into new narratives, pointing to an emptiness at the heart of the Gothic. Carter provides a full-length discussion of the traditional Gothic in terms of Todorov's three categories, with special attention to formal characteristics such as the mediated narrative (multiple narrators, distancing techniques), and also in the light of reader-response theory. (Another attempt to utilize reader-response theory, Richter 1988, posits a shift from an earlier judgemental approach to a more 'empathic' mode of reading.) Interestingly one of the strongest challenges to the critical upgrading of the Gothic has been mounted along formalist grounds. Napier's *Failure of Gothic* (1987) points to a basic contradiction between two components: (1) the providential, move to closure, moral restraint, etc.; and (2) the desire to create instability, terror, uncertainty. In her view this leads to a fatal disjunction, leaving the reader uncertain, exhausted, and alienated. Haggerty (1985, 1989) to a degree replicates this view, in noting a dichotomy between metonymic writing characteristic of realism and a more metaphorical style (subjective, poetic) characteristic of romanticism. However, in his view a fusion of these elements went on to create a new form of 'affective fiction', finding its apotheosis in tales like Henry James's *Turn of the Screw*, but already adumbrated by the 'early' Gothic, most markedly in the objectification of intense fear in *Melmoth*. Unlike Haggerty, Napier favours a termination at 1820 if the Gothic is to be treated meaningfully in its original form.

To some degree, Napier's objections have been overridden by a new school of criticism in the 1990s which views modal instability and narrative disjunction in a positive light. Miles in his *Gothic Writing* (1993) takes a Foucauldian approach, first, by locating the discourses and discursive structures which habitually compose Gothic texts, and secondly, by taking issue with traditional, teleological approaches to the genre. The Gothic in his eyes does not develop, or progress, but remains a site in which discursively inflected representations of the human subject irresolutely encounter each other. For Miles, complaints about the incoherence of the Gothic are misplaced, for it was such irresolution that signified and appealed. Howard in her book of 1994 argues that Gothic fiction needs to be viewed in terms of the competing discourses of the period, a Bakhtinian 'multivoicedness' characterizing an essentially hybrid form. Howard is especially wary of unitary meanings imposed from a 'committed' modern viewpoint, and herself goes on to offer detailed commentary on key texts with reference to a variety of discourses. It is noticeable, however, that in order to arrive at this point Howard feels compelled to negotiate a number of alterative approaches, theological, psychoanalytical, formalist, and political/historical. A similar procedure is evident in Kilgour's 1995 study, where detailed commentary is enclosed by summaries of critical methodologies at each end. Kilgour's own thrust is eclectically new historicist, with a particular focus on the imagined past, as made present in the Gothic, considered in relation to social and ideological issues in England surrounding the French Revolution. Particular analysis includes a study of contesting narrative patterns through Radcliffe and Lewis, concluding with the reassertion of orderly narrative in *The Italian*.

As this last instance suggests, many of the most interesting commentaries on individual writers and texts will be found in larger generic studies of the Gothic. One striking feature here has been the increasing prominence given to Mary Shelley, whose *Frankenstein* is described by Botting as 'one of the texts now synonymous with Gothic'; though contemporaries are unlikely to have considered the work a direct offshoot of the terror tradition. (For Mary Shelley generally, see Pamela Clemit's entry in this volume.) The availability of the Northanger Novels in print has also fostered interest in the Germanic 'anti-Illuminist' fiction of the 1790s (see Bette Roberts 1989, Carter), as well as broader discussion concerning the degree to which a distinct *Schauerroman* pre-existed and influenced the English Gothic (Hadley is sceptical; Le Tellier more open to possibilities). Among 'minor' indigenous figures, Regina Maria Roche (author of the once immensely popular *Children of the Abbey* (1796)) is unusual in having received both bibliographical and critical attention (Howells 1978; Schroeder 1979, and 1980; Botting). As a whole, however, it is Radcliffe, Lewis, and Maturin who have provided the most common thread. The following paragraphs offer a brief account of more specific scholarship and criticism relating to their work.

ANN RADCLIFFE

The private nature of Radcliffe's life, and the carefully monitored 'facts' disclosed in T. N. Talfourd's memoir (prefaced to the posthumous *Gaston de*

Blondeville (1826))), have allowed little leeway to biographers. Grant's 1951 biography adds some information about her family connections to the bare facts found in studies stemming from the 1920s (McIntyre, Tompkins 1980), but without clearly stating sources. The introductory guide by Murray in the Twayne English Authors Series routinely positions Radcliffe as a transitional figure between rationalism and Romanticism, stressing (like Wieten earlier) her influence on Romantic poetry. Apart from Stoler's thesis-based Arno study, most criticism has come in the form of articles and essays, several before 1980 expressing a sense of limitation (Sypher, Smith, Kelly 1979). Three main strands, sometimes overlapping, have been apparent since: studies concentrating on Radcliffe's relation to the picturesque and the sublime; attempts at fixing her ideological position; and (mostly feminist) psychoanalytic investigations. In the first case, the groundwork was laid by McKillop's positioning of Radcliffe's distinction between 'terror' and 'horror' in contemporary aesthetics; a trail followed further in Ware's somewhat mechanical demonstration of her indebtedness to Burke's *Enquiry*. Later commentators (Hagstrum, Murrah, Flaxman) throw a more positive light on Radcliffe's aesthetic engagements, and recent reappraisal has associated her with a liberating female Sublime (see Milbank). Poovey, in a seminal essay of 1979, places her romances ideologically in relation to a new bourgeois sentimentalism and the uncovering of its acquisitive materialist (and sexually aggressive) underside during the tensions of the 1790s. Other commentators in this area have located overarching 'conservative' (Durant, London, Benedict) and latent radical (Howells 1989, Clery 1992) tendencies. Psychoanalytic critics, following the lead of Sedgwick and Kahane, bring Freudian and Lacanian insights to bear on the recurring motifs, patterns of repetition, and gender relations in the novels, primarily in *Udolpho* (Fawcett, Castle, Macdonald). Other works have received markedly less attention, though Todd's essay on ambivalent attitudes towards the servant figure in *The Italian* and Hennelly's account (1987) of the same work's narrative structure are both useful contributions.

A clear sign of Radcliffe's growing status is Miles's recent book-length study (1995), which in its biographical section works hard to place her in the liberal camp. Miles also offers informed commentary on all the novels published in her lifetime, assimilating in his analysis the major critical approaches listed above. According to Miles, Radcliffe's withdrawal as a public novelist can be connected with the reactionary assault on 'radical' elements in literature, at the end of the 1790s, which made untenable the delicate balance between the proper lady and woman author.

MATTHEW GREGORY LEWIS

In contrast with Radcliffe, Lewis actively courted public attention, though even he can hardly have anticipated the furore that broke out after the publication of *The Monk*. A densely documented account of the critical reaction, including Coleridge's accusation of sexual indecency and irreligion, is given by Parreaux, who also provides an impressive bibliography corrective of Summers and other predecessors. Even when Lewis's works had fallen into relative obscurity, his memory was strong enough to justify the 1839 memoir by Baron-Wilson, which includes several unpublished items and some eighty letters. The authoritative modern biography is Peck's, which uses a wide range of sources, including surviving manuscripts, and corrects while adding to the correspondence in Baron-Wilson. The critical evaluations included, however, are routine and there is a tendency to look down at Lewis's works. Modern interpretation of Lewis owes much to Brooks's article of 1973, which, assimilating the recent promptings of Todorov, argues that *The Monk* is reflective of a post-sacred world where 'terror' has replaced theology. Grudin counters that it is rather placed in an archaic situation where demonology is a real factor, and that Lewis looks back from a confident 'establishment' position. Lewis's conservatism is also argued by Watkins (1986), who traces the story's disruptions to 'violations of social hierarchy'. Brooks's view of the novel as a psychodrama, with disturbingly radical undercurrents, has nevertheless proved lastingly influential, as is evident in two recent contributions by Jones and Macdonald (1992), both of whom compare patterns of desire in the novel with its main narrative trajectories. *Castle Spectre*, which as a performed and published play attracted at least as much attention as the novel, has received scant attention, though Reno usefully discusses the unusual introduction of a 'real' ghost on stage and Cox gives a full account of Lewis's use of Gothic conventions in a variety of theatrical modes.

CHARLES ROBERT MATURIN

A tendency amongst critics to associate Maturin's Gothicism with mainstream Romanticism can be traced back to Walter Scott's *Quarterly* review of *Fatal Revenge* in 1810, in which Maturin's pseudonymous novel is picked out for its striking powers from numerous 'flat imitations of the Castle of Udolpho'. Scott's continuing support helped set Maturin on a career as a 'named' author, and one of the main primary sources for his literary activities is the record of the correspondence between the two writers provided by Ratchford and McCarthy. There are a number of critical biographies, dating back to the 1920s. Idman's, a routine critical biography, offers sound synopses of the main works (clearly deemed necessary when nearly all were out of print); it also characterizes *Fatal Revenge* and *Melmoth* as tales of terror, noting a Radcliffian element in the former and a greater degree of 'supernaturalness' in *Melmoth*. Scholten, by contrast, having established that Maturin worked best as a terror novelist, devotes half his space to *The Albigenses* (1824), as a forgotten historical novel. More modern biographical accounts include Fierobe's wide-ranging, if over-schematic, overview (with an exhaustive bibliography); and two unusually good 'series' volumes by Kramer and Lougy.

Critical voices on Maturin before the 1960s tend to be of the 'lone wolf' variety: Hammond in 1956 claims a pivotal place for *Melmoth* in English literature while lamenting the 'excessive rarity' of copies. Four of the five thesis-based volumes on Maturin in the Arno Press Gothic Studies and Dissertations series stress his connection with Romanticism, Scott (1980) not untypically pointing to a mutual concern for 'expanded consciousness'. At the head of journal criticism stands Dawson's contribution of 1968, which shows the Gothic as reclaimed by Maturin working through paradox to disrupt normative ideas and language, and thus overlapping with the Romantics' urge to unify the discordant. Similarly stressing *Melmoth*'s psychological and metaphysical profundity, Eggenschwiler argues that suffering there in the form of Gothic experience can lead to a higher spiritual state; Hennelly (1981), more bleakly, senses an anticipation of modern existentialism, a 'divided' human consciousness operating in an absurdist universe. Fowler argues that *Melmoth*'s fragmented, multifariously confusing narratives serve as a structural paradigm for the human condition in a fallen world, where nevertheless God's purpose can be darkly glimpsed. The novel's famous 'Chinese-box' structure is also given extensive treatment in a chapter in Bayer-Berenbaum; while Marie Roberts, in her 1990 book, sees aspects of the Rosicrucian novel in both *Fatal Revenge* and *Melmoth*— in the latter case 'transmogrified into a *tour de force* of Romantic consciousness'. Maturin's dramatic output is covered sensibly in the course of Kramer's biography; while the stage popularity of *Bertram* (1816), and, more particularly, Coleridge's assault on its 'jacobinical' qualities, are the subject of an astute and historically alert article by Watkins (1989).

More comprehensive bibliographical information will no doubt lead to fresh insights concerning matters such as the gender balance of authorship. Attention is already turning to authors whose work stands outside the conventional classifications, such as Charlotte Dacre (see Miles 1993). Critical investigations are also likely to consider the Gothic more fully in relation to poetry. A new willingness to bring into view texts by Coleridge and Keats is apparent in Miles's 1993 overview, while Bruhm in his study of physical pain and Romantic transcendence pairs Wordsworth with Radcliffe and Byron with Lewis. Another interesting development has come in the form of fresh reassessment of Walter Scott's Waverley Novels in the light of Gothic fiction. Far from seeing a replacement or displacement of Gothicism, as is conventionally claimed, Duncan and Robertson in major books present Scott as a significant participant in the Gothic phenomenon and as a main conduit for its diffusion into mainstream fiction. If the Gothic and Romantic remain awkward cousins, there can be few remaining doubts about the dynamic nature of their relationship.

PETER GARSIDE

REFERENCES

TEXTS

Bibliographies and publishing history

Blakey, Dorothy, *The Minerva Press 1790–1820* (London, 1939).

Block, Andrew, *The English Novel 1740–1850: A Catalogue Including Prose Romances, Short Stories, and Translations of Foreign Fiction* (London, 1939; rev. edn., 1961; repr. 1968).

Evans, Bertrand, 'A List of Gothic Plays', in his *Gothic Drama from Walpole to Shelley* (Berkeley and Los Angeles, 1947), 239–45.

Frank, Frederick S., *The First Gothics: A Critical Guide to the English Gothic Novel* (New York, 1987).

Garside, Peter, 'J. F. Hughes and the Publication of Popular Fiction, 1803–10', *Library*, 9 (1987), 240–58.

—— 'Collections of English Fiction in the Romantic Period: The Significance of Corvey', in Rainer Schöwerling and Hartmut Steinecke (eds.), *Die fürstliche Bibliothek Corvey* (Munich, 1992), 70–81.

Graham, John, *Novels in English: The Eighteenth- and Nineteenth-Century Holdings at Schloss Corvey, Höxter, Germany* (New York, 1983).

Lévy, Maurice, 'Bibliographie chronologique du roman "gothique" 1764–1824', in his *Le Roman 'gothique' anglais 1764–1824* (Toulouse, 1968), 684–708.

—— 'English Gothic and the French Imagination: A Calendar of Translations, 1767–1828', in G. R. Thompson (ed.), *The Gothic Imagination: Essays in Dark Romanticism* (Pullman, Wash., 1974), 150–70.

Mayo, Robert D., 'How Long was Gothic Fiction in Vogue?', *Modern Language Notes*, 58 (1943), 58–64.

—— 'Gothic Romance in the Magazines', *Publications of the Modern Language Association*, 65 (1950), 762–89.

—— *The English Novel in the Magazines 1740–1815: With a Catalogue of 1375 Magazine Novels and Novelettes* (Evanston, Ill., 1962).

Schroeder, Natalie, 'Regina Maria Roche, Popular Novelist, 1789–1834: The Rochean Canon', *Papers of the Bibliographical Society of America*, 73 (1979), 462–8.

Summers, Montague, *A Gothic Bibliography* (London, 1940).

Todd, William B., 'The Early Editions of *The Monk*, with a Bibliography', *Studies in Bibliography*, 2 (1949), 3–24.

Tracy, Ann B., *The Gothic Novel 1790–1830: Plot Summaries and Index to Motifs* (Lexington, Ky., 1981).

Varma, Devendra P., *The Evergreen Tree of Diabolical Knowledge* (Washington, 1972).

Watt, William W., *Shilling Shockers of the Gothic School: A Study of Chapbook Gothic Romances* (Cambridge, Mass., 1932; repr. New York, 1967).

Selected texts

Baldick, Chris (ed.), *The Oxford Book of Gothic Tales* (Oxford, 1992).

Cox, Jeffrey N. (ed.), *Seven Gothic Dramas 1789–1825* (Athens, Oh., 1992).

Curties, T. J. Horsley, *The Monk of Udolpho; A Romance* (4 vols., 1807), foreword by Devendra P. Varma, introd. Mary Muriel Tarr, 4 vols. (Arno Press, New York, 1977) [facsimile reproduction of the 1st edn. of 1807].

Dacre, Charlotte, *Confessions of the Nun of St. Omer: A Tale* (3 vols., 1805), introd. Devendra P. Varma, 2 vols. (Arno Press, New York, 1972) [facsimile reproduction of the 1st edn. of 1805].

—— *Zofloya; or, The Moor: A Romance of the Fifteenth Century* (3 vols., 1806), foreword by G. Wilson Knight, introd. Devendra P. Varma, 3 vols. (Arno Press, New York, 1974) [facsimile reproduction of the 1st edn. of 1806].

—— *The Libertine* (4 vols., 1807), foreword by John Garrett, introd. Devendra P. Varma, 4 vols. (Arno Press, New York, 1974) [facsimile reproduction of 1st edn. of 1807].

—— *The Passions* (4 vols., 1811), foreword by Sandra Knight-Roth, introd. Devendra P. Varma, 4 vols. (Arno Press, New York, 1974) [facsimile reproduction of 1st edn. of 1811].

Fairclough, Peter (ed.), *Three Gothic Novels*, introd. Mario Praz, Penguin Classics (Harmondsworth, 1968; repr. 1986) [contains Horace Walpole's *Castle of Otranto* (1764), William Beckford's *Vathek* (1786), and Mary Shelley's *Frankenstein* (1818)].

Lewis, Matthew Gregory, *The Monk* (3 vols., 1796), ed. Louis F. Peck, introd. John Berryman (New York, 1952; 1959) [follows the 1st edn. of 1796].

—— *The Monk* (3 vols., 1796), ed. Howard Anderson, Oxford English Novels (London, 1973); World's Classics (1980) [follows the author's manuscript].

—— *The Castle Spectre: A Drama* (1798), introd. Jonathan Wordsworth, Woodstock Books (Oxford, 1990) [facsimile reproduction of the 1st edn. of 1798].

—— *The Castle Spectre* (1798), in *Seven Gothic Dramas 1789–1825*, ed. Jeffrey N. Cox (Athens, Oh., 1992), 149–224 [follows the 1st edn. of 1798, in conjunction with the Larpent licensing version (LA 1187) in the Huntington Library].

—— *Tales of Wonder; Written and Collected by M. G. Lewis*, 2 vols. (London, 1801).

—— *The Bravo of Venice: A Romance* (1805), introd. Devendra P. Varma (Arno Press, New York, 1972) [facsimile reproduction of the 1st edn. of 1805].

Maturin, Charles Robert, *Fatal Revenge; or, The Family of Montorio: A Romance* (3 vols., 1807), foreword by Henry D. Hicks, introd. Maurice Lévy, 3 vols. (Arno Press, New York, 1974) [facsimile reproduction of 1st edn. of 1807].

—— *Fatal Revenge; or, The Family of Montorio: A Romance* (3 vols., 1807), introd. Julian Cowley (Alan Sutton Publishing, Stroud, 1994).

—— *Bertram; or, The Castle of St. Aldobrand: A Tragedy* (1816), introd. Jonathan Wordsworth, Woodstock Books (Oxford, 1992) [facsimile reproduction of the 1st edn. of 1816].

—— *Bertram; or, The Castle of St. Aldobrand: A Tragedy* (1816), in *Seven Gothic Dramas 1789–1825*, ed. Jeffrey N. Cox (Athens, Oh., 1992), 315–83 [follows the 1st edn. of 1816, in conjunction with the Larpent copy (LA 1922), in the Huntington Library, and the author's manuscript at Abbotsford].

—— *Melmoth the Wanderer: A Tale* (4 vols., 1820), ed. Douglas Grant, Oxford English Novels (London, 1968); repr., introd. Chris Baldick, World's Classics (1989) [follows the 1st edn. of 1820].

—— *Melmoth the Wanderer: A Tale* (4 vols., 1820), ed. Alethea Hayter, Penguin English Classics (Harmondsworth, 1977) [follows the 1st edn. of 1820].

Radcliffe, Ann, *The Castles of Athlin and Dunbayne* (1789), foreword by Frederick Shroyer (Arno Press, New York, 1972) [facsimile reproduction of the 1821 edn.].

—— *The Castles of Athlin and Dunbayne* (1789), introd. Julian Cowley (Alan Sutton Publishing, Stroud, 1994).

—— *A Sicilian Romance* (2 vols., 1790), foreword Howard Mumford Jones, introd. Devendra P. Varma (Arno Press, New York, 1972) [facsimile reproduction of the new edn. of 1821].

—— *A Sicilian Romance* (2 vols., 1790), ed. Alison Milbank, World's Classics (Oxford, 1993) [follows the new edn. of 1821].

—— *The Romance of the Forest: Interspersed with Some Pieces of Poetry* (3 vols., 1791), foreword Frederick Garber, introd. Devendra P. Varma, 3 vols. (Arno Press, New York, 1974) [facsimile reproduction of the new edn. of 1827].

—— *The Romance of the Forest: Interspersed with Some Pieces of Poetry* (3 vols., 1791), ed. Chloe Chard, World's Classics (Oxford, 1986) [follows the 1st edn. of 1791].

—— *The Mysteries of Udolpho: A Romance* (4 vols., 1794), ed. Bonamy Dobrée, notes by Frederick Garber, Oxford English Novels (London, 1966) [follows the 1st edn. of 1794].

—— *The Italian; or, The Confessional of the Black Penitents: A Romance* (3 vols., 1797), ed. Frederick Garber, Oxford English Novels (London, 1968) [follows the 1st edn. of 1797].

—— *Gaston de Blondeville; or, The Court of Henry III* (4 vols., 1826), introd. Devendra P. Varma, 2 vols. (Arno Press, New York, 1972) [facsimile reproduction of 1st edn. of 1826].

Radcliffe, Mary-Anne, *Manfroné; or, The One-Handed Monk* (4 vols., 1809), foreword by Devendra P. Varma, introd. Coral Ann Howells, 2 vols. (Arno Press, New York, 1972) [facsimile reproduction of the 3rd edn. of 1828].

Roche, Regina Maria, *The Children of the Abbey: A Tale*, 4 vols. (London, 1796).

—— *Clermont: A Tale* (4 vols., 1798), ed. Devendra P. Varma (Folio Press, London, 1968).

—— *Nocturnal Visit: A Tale* (4 vols., 1800), foreword by Robert D. Mayo, introd. F. G. Atkinson, 4 vols. (Arno Press, New York, 1977) [facsimile reproduction of the 1st edn. of 1800].

Varma, Devendra (ed.), *The Northanger Set of Jane Austen Horrid Novels*, 7 vols. (Folio Press, London, 1968) [in addition to Roche's *Clermont* (1798), listed above, includes Francis Lathom's *The Midnight Bell: A German Story* (1798); *The Castle of Wolfenbach: A German Story* (1793) and *The Mysterious Warning: A German Tale* (1796), both by Eliza Parsons; Eleanor Sleath's *The Orphan of the Rhine* (1798); *The Necromancer* (1794); and Karl Grosse's *Horrid Mysteries* (1796)].

CRITICISM

Bibliographies of criticism

Fisher, Benjamin Franklin, IV, *The Gothic's Gothic: Study Aids to the Tradition of the Tale of Terror* (New York, 1988).

Frank, Frederick S., *Gothic Fiction: A Master List of Twentieth Century Criticism and Research* (Westport, Conn., 1988).

McNutt, Dan J., *The Eighteenth-Century Gothic Novel: An Annotated Bibliography of Criticism and Selected Texts*, foreword by Devendra Varma and Maurice Lévy (New York, 1975).

Spector, Robert Donald, *The English Gothic: A Bibliographic Guide to Writers from Horace Walpole to Mary Shelley* (Westport, Conn., 1984).

General criticism

Bayer-Berenbaum, Linda, *The Gothic Imagination: Expansion in Gothic Literature and Art* (Rutherford, NJ, 1982).

Bernstein, Stephen, 'Form and Ideology in the Gothic Novel', *Essays in Literature* (Western Illinois University), 18 (1991), 151–65.

Birkhead, Edith, *The Tale of Terror: A Study of the Gothic Romance* (London, 1921; repr. New York, 1963).

Botting, Fred, *Gothic* (London, 1996).

Breton, André, 'Limites non frontières du surréalisme', *Nouvelle Revue française*, 48 (1937), 200–15; trans. as 'Limits not Frontiers of Surrealism', in Herbert Read (ed.), *Surrealism* (London, 1936), 106–11.

Brown, Marshall, 'A Philosophical View of the Gothic Novel', *Studies in Romanticism*, 26 (1987), 275–301.

Bruhm, Steven, *Gothic Bodies: The Politics of Pain in Romantic Fiction* (Philadelphia, 1994).

Carter, Margaret L., *Specter or Delusion? The Supernatural in Gothic Fiction* (Ann Arbor, 1987).

Charlesworth, Michael, 'The Ruined Abbey: Picturesque and Gothic Values', in Stephen Copley and Peter Garside (eds.), *The Politics of the Picturesque: Literature, Landscape and Aesthetics since 1770* (Cambridge, 1994), 62–80.

Clery, E. J., 'The Politics of the Gothic Heroine in the 1790s', in Philip W. Martin and Robin Jarvis (eds.), *Reviewing Romanticism* (London, 1992), 69–85.

—— *The Rise of Supernatural Fiction, 1762–1800* (Cambridge, 1995).

Cottom, Daniel, *The Civilized Imagination: A Study of Ann Radcliffe, Jane Austen, and Sir Walter Scott* (Cambridge, 1985).

Day, William Patrick, *In the Circles of Fear and Desire: A Study of Gothic Fantasy* (Chicago, 1985).

Delamotte, Eugenia C., *Perils of the Night: A Feminist Study of the Nineteenth-Century Gothic* (New York, 1990).

Doody, Margaret Anne, 'Deserts, Ruins and Troubled Waters: Female Dreams in Fiction and the Development of the Gothic Novel', *Genre*, 10 (1977), 529–72.

Duncan, Ian, *Modern Romance and Transformations of the Novel: The Gothic, Scott, Dickens* (Cambridge, 1992).

Ellis, Kate Ferguson, *The Contested Castle: Gothic Novels and the Subversion of Domestic Ideology* (Urbana, Ill., 1989).

Fiedler, Leslie A., *Love and Death in the American Novel* (New York, 1960; rev. edn., London, 1967).

Fleenor, Juliann E. (ed.), *The Female Gothic* (Montreal, 1983).

Freud, Sigmund, 'The Uncanny' (1919), in *The Standard Edition of the Complete Psychological Works of Sigmund Freud*, ed. and trans. James Strachey, vol. xvii (London, 1955), 217–56.

Graham, Kenneth W. (ed.), *Gothic Fictions: Prohibition/Transgression* (New York, 1989).

Guest, Harriet, 'The Wanton Muse: Politics and Gender in Gothic Theory after 1760', in Stephen Copley and John Whale (eds.), *Beyond Romanticism: New Approaches to Texts and Contexts 1780–1832* (London, 1992), 118–39.

Hadley, Michael, *The Undiscovered Genre: A Search for the German Gothic Novel* (Berne, 1978).

Haggerty, George E., 'Fact and Fancy in the Gothic Novel', *Nineteenth-Century Fiction*, 39 (1985), 379–91.

—— *Gothic Fiction/Gothic Form* (University Park, Pa., 1989).

Hogle, Jerrold E., 'The Restless Labyrinth: Cryptonymy in the Gothic Novel', *Arizona Quarterly*, 36 (1980), 330–58.

Holland, Norman N., and Sherman, Leona F., 'Gothic Possibilities', *New Literary History*, 8 (1977), 279–94.

Howard, Jacqueline, *Reading Gothic Fiction: A Bakhtinian Approach* (Oxford, 1994).

Howells, Coral Ann, *Love, Mystery, and Misery: Feeling in Gothic Fiction* (London, 1978).

Hume, Robert D., 'Gothic versus Romantic: A Revaluation of the Gothic Novel', *Publications of the Modern Language Association*, 84 (1969), 282–90.

Jackson, Rosemary, *Fantasy: The Literature of Subversion* (London, 1981).

Kahane, Claire, 'Gothic Mirrors and Feminine Identity', *Centennial Review*, 24 (1980), 43–64; rev. as 'The Gothic Mirror', in Shirley Nelson Garner *et al.* (eds.), *The (M)other Tongue: Essays in Feminist Psychoanalytic Interpretation* (Ithaca, NY, 1985), 334–51.

Keech, James M., 'The Survival of the Gothic Response', *Studies in the Novel*, 6 (1974), 130–44.

Kelly, Gary, *English Fiction of the Romantic Period 1789–1830* (London, 1989).

Kiely, Robert, *The Romantic Novel in England* (Cambridge, Mass., 1972).

Kilgour, Maggie, *The Rise of the Gothic Novel* (London, 1995).

Kliger, Samuel, *The Goths in England: A Study in Seventeenth and Eighteenth Century Thought* (Cambridge, Mass., 1952).

Le Tellier, Robert Ignatius, *Kindred Spirits: Interrelations and Affinities between the Romantic Novels of England and Germany (1790–1820)*, Salzburg Studies in English Literature: Romantic Reassessment, ed. James Hogg, No. 33/3 (Salzburg, 1982).

Lévy, Maurice, *Le Roman 'gothique' anglais 1764–1824* (Toulouse, 1968).

Longueil, Alfred E., 'The Word "Gothic" in Eighteenth Century Criticism', *Modern Language Notes*, 38 (1923), 453–60.

Lydenberg, Robin, 'Gothic Architecture and Fiction: A Survey of Critical Responses', *Centennial Review*, 22 (1978), 95–109.

MacAndrew, Elizabeth, *The Gothic Tradition in Fiction* (New York, 1979).

Madoff, Mark, 'The Useful Myth of Gothic Ancestry', *Studies in Eighteenth-Century Culture*, 8 (1979), 337–50.

Miles, Robert, *Gothic Writing 1750–1820: A Genealogy* (London, 1993).

—— (ed.), *Female Gothic Writing*, Special Number, *Women's Writing: The Elizabethan to Victorian Period*, 1/2 (1994).

Moers, Ellen, 'Female Gothic', in her *Literary Women* (New York, 1976), 90–110.

Morris, David B., 'Gothic Sublimity', *New Literary History*, 16 (1985), 299–319.

Morse, David, 'Gothic', in *Romanticism: A Structural Analysis* (London, 1982), 13–103.

Napier, Elizabeth R., *The Failure of Gothic: Problems of Disjunction in an Eighteenth-Century Literary Form* (Oxford, 1987).

Nelson, Lowry, Jr., 'Night Thoughts on the Gothic Novel', *Yale Review*, 52 (1962), 236–57.

Novak, Maximillian E., 'Gothic Fiction and the Grotesque', *Novel*, 13 (1979), 50–67.

Paulson, Ronald, 'Gothic Fiction and the French Revolution', *English Literary History*, 48 (1981), 532–54.

—— *Representations of Revolution (1789–1820)* (New Haven, 1983).

Platzner, Robert. L., and Hume, Robert D., ' "Gothic versus Romantic": A Rejoinder', *Publications of the Modern Language Association*, 86 (1971), 266–74.

Porte, Joel, 'In the Hands of an Angry God: Religious Terror in Gothic Fiction', in G. R. Thompson (ed.), *The Gothic Imagination: Essays in Dark Romanticism* (Pullman, Wash., 1974), 42–64.

Praz, Mario, *The Romantic Agony* (1933), 2nd edn., trans. Angus Davidson (London, 1951).

Punter, David, *The Literature of Terror: A History of Gothic Fictions from 1765 to the Present Day* (London, 1980; 2nd edn., 2 vols., 1996).

Railo, Eino, *The Haunted Castle: A Study of the Elements of English Romanticism* (London, 1927).

Restuccia, Frances L., 'Female Gothic Writing: "Under Cover to Alice" ', *Genre*, 18 (1986), 245–66.

Richter, David H., 'The Reception of the Gothic Novel in the 1790s', in Robert W. Uphaus (ed.), *The Idea of the Novel in the Eighteenth Century* (East Lansing, Mich., 1988), 117–37.

—— 'The Unguarded Prison: Reception Theory, Structural Marxism, and the History of the Gothic Novel', *Eighteenth Century: Theory and Interpretation*, 30 (1989), 3–17.

Roberts, Bette B., *The Gothic Romance: Its Appeal to Women Writers and Readers in Late Eighteenth-Century England* (New York, 1980).

—— 'The Horrid Novels, *The Mysteries of Udolpho*, and *Northanger Abbey*', in Kenneth W. Graham (ed.), *Gothic Fictions: Prohibition/Transgression* (New York, 1989), 89–111.

Roberts, Marie, *Gothic Immortals: The Fiction of the Brotherhood of the Rosy Cross* (London, 1990).

—— *A Handbook to Gothic Literature* (London, 1996).

Robertson, Fiona, *Legitimate Histories: Scott, Gothic, and the Authorities of Fiction* (Oxford, 1994).

Sade, Marquis de, 'Idée sur les romans', in *Les Crimes de l'amour* (Paris, 1800); translated extracts in Victor Sage (ed.), *The Gothick Novel: A Casebook* (London, 1990), 48–9.

Sadleir, Michael, *The Northanger Novels: A Footnote to Jane Austen*, English Association Pamphlet 68 (Oxford, 1927).

Sage, Victor, *Horror Fiction in the Protestant Tradition* (London, 1988).

—— (ed.) *The Gothick Novel: A Casebook* (London, 1990) [contains extracts from Breton, Coleridge, de Sade, Fiedler, Freud, and others].

Schroeder, Natalie, 'The *Mysteries of Udolpho* and *Clermont*: The Radcliffean Encroachment on the Art of Regina Maria Roche', *Studies in the Novel*, 12 (1980), 131–43.

Sedgwick, Eve Kosofsky, *The Coherence of Gothic Conventions* (New York, 1980; repr. New York, 1986).

—— 'The Character in the Veil: Imagery of the Surface in the Gothic Novel', *Publications of the Modern Language Association*, 96 (1981), 255–70.

Summers, Montague, *The Gothic Quest: A History of the Gothic Novel* (London, 1938; repr. New York, 1964).

Tarr, Mary Muriel, *Catholicism in Gothic Fiction: A Study of the Nature and Function of Catholic Materials in Gothic Fiction in England (1760–1820)* (Washington, 1946).

Thompson, G. R. (ed.), *The Gothic Imagination: Essays in Dark Romanticism* (Pullman, Wash., 1974).

Todorov, Tzvetan, *The Fantastic: A Structural Approach to a Literary Genre*, trans. Richard Howard (Cleveland, 1973).

Tompkins, J. M. S., *The Popular Novel in England 1770–1800* (London, 1932).

Varma, Devendra P., *The Gothic Flame. Being a History of the Gothic Novel in England: Its Origins, Efflorescence, Disintegration, and Residuary Influences* (London, 1957; repr. New York, 1966).

Wilt, Judith, *Ghosts of the Gothic: Austen, Eliot, & Lawrence* (Princeton, 1980).

Ann Radcliffe

Benedict, Barbara M., 'Pictures of Conformity: Sentiment and Structure in Ann Radcliffe's Style', *Philological Quarterly*, 68 (1989), 363–77.

Castle, Terry, 'The Spectralization of the Other in *The Mysteries of Udolpho*', in Felicity Nussbaum and Laura Brown (eds.), *The New Eighteenth Century: Theory, Politics, English Literature* (New York, 1987), 231–53.

Durant, David, 'Ann Radcliffe and the Conservative Gothic', *Studies in English Literature*, 22 (1982), 519–30.

Fawcett, Mary Laughlin, '*Udolpho*'s Primal Mystery', *Studies in English Literature*, 23 (1983), 481–94.

Flaxman, Rhoda L., 'Radcliffe's Dual Modes of Vision', in Mary Anne Schofield and Cecilia Macheski (eds.), *Fetter'd or Free? British Women Novelists, 1670–1815* (Athens, Oh., 1986), 124–33.

Grant, Aline, *Ann Radcliffe: A Biography* (Denver, 1951).

Hagstrum, Jean H., 'Pictures to the Heart: The Psychological Picturesque in Ann Radcliffe's *The Mysteries of Udolpho*', in Paul J. Korshin and Robert R. Allen (eds.), *Greene Centennial Studies: Essays Presented to Donald Greene in the Centennial Year of the University of Southern California* (Charlottesville, Va., 1984), 434–41.

Hennelly, Mark M., Jr., ' "The Slow Torture of Delay": Reading *The Italian*', *Studies in the Humanities*, 14 (1987), 1–17.

Howells, Coral Ann, 'The Pleasure of the Woman's Text: Ann Radcliffe's Subtle Transgressions', in Kenneth W. Graham (ed.), *Gothic Fictions: Prohibition/Transgression* (New York, 1989), 151–62.

Kelly, Gary, ' "A Constant Vicissitude of Interesting Passions": Ann Radcliffe's Perplexed Narratives', *Ariel*, 10 (1979), 45–64.

London, April, 'Ann Radcliffe in Context: Marking the Boundaries of *The Mysteries of Udolpho*', *Eighteenth-Century Life*, 10 (1986), 35–47.

Macdonald, D. L., 'Bathos and Repetition: The Uncanny in Radcliffe', *Journal of Narrative Technique*, 19 (1989), 197–204.

McIntyre, Clara Frances, *Ann Radcliffe in Relation to her Time* (New Haven, 1920).

McKillop, Alan D., 'Mrs. Radcliffe on the Supernatural in Poetry', *Journal of English and Germanic Philology*, 31 (1932), 352–9.

Milbank, Alison, 'Introduction', in her edn. of *A Sicilian Romance* (Oxford, 1993).

Miles, Robert, *Ann Radcliffe: The Great Enchantress* (Manchester, 1995).

Murrah, Charles C., 'Mrs. Radcliffe's Landscapes: The Eye and the Fancy', *University of Windsor Review*, 18 (1984), 7–23.

Murray, E. B., *Ann Radcliffe* (New York, 1972).

Poovey, Mary, 'Ideology and "The Mysteries of Udolpho"', *Criticism*, 21 (1979), 307–30.

Scott, Walter, 'Memoir of Ann Radcliffe' (1824); repr. in *Sir Walter Scott on Novelists and Fiction*, ed. Ioan Williams (London, 1968), 102–19.

Smith, Nelson C., 'Sense, Sensibility and Ann Radcliffe', *Studies in English Literature*, 13 (1973), 577–90.

Stoler, John Andrew, *Ann Radcliffe: The Novel of Suspense and Terror* (New York, 1980).

Sypher, Wylie, 'Social Ambiguity in a Gothic Novel', *Partisan Review*, 12 (1945), 50–60 [on *Mysteries of Udolpho*].

Talfourd, T. N., 'Memoir of the Life and Writings of Mrs. Radcliffe', in her *Gaston de Blondeville*, 4 vols. (London, 1826), i. 1–132.

Todd, Janet, 'Posture and Imposture: The Gothic Manservant in Ann Radcliffe's *The Italian*', *Women and Literature*, 2 (1982), 25–38.

Tompkins, J. M. S., *Ann Radcliffe and her Influence on Later Writers* (New York, 1980); based on an unpublished master's thesis (Univ. of London, 1921).

Ware, Malcolm, *Sublimity in the Novels of Ann Radcliffe: A Study of the Influence upon her Craft of Edmund Burke's 'Enquiry into the Origin of our Ideas of the Sublime and Beautiful'*, Essays and Studies on English Language and Literature 25 (Uppsala, 1963).

Wieten, Alida A. S., *Mrs. Radcliffe: Her Relation towards Romanticism* (Amsterdam, 1926).

Wolff, Cynthia Griffin, 'The Radcliffean Gothic Model: A Form for Feminine Sexuality', *Modern Language Studies*, 9 (1979), 98–113; repr. in Juliann E. Fleenor (ed.), *The Female Gothic* (Montreal, 1983), 207–23.

Matthew Gregory Lewis

Baron-Wilson, Margaret, *The Life and Correspondence of M. G. Lewis, Author of 'The Monk', 'Castle Spectre', &c. with Many Pieces in Prose and Verse, Never before Published* (London, 1839).

Brooks, Peter, 'Virtue and Terror: *The Monk*', *English Literary History*, 40 (1973), 249–63.

Coleridge, Samuel Taylor, review of *The Monk*, in the *Critical Review*, 2nd ser. 19 (Feb. 1797), 194–200; repr. in *Coleridge's Miscellaneous Criticism*, ed. Thomas Middleton Raysor (London, 1936), 370–8.

Grudin, Peter, '*The Monk*: Matilda and the Rhetoric of Deceit', *Journal of Narrative Technique*, 5 (1975), 136–46.

Irwin, Joseph James, *M. G. 'Monk' Lewis* (Boston, 1976).

Jones, Wendy, 'Stories of Desire in *The Monk*', *English Literary History*, 57 (1990), 129–50.

Lydenberg, Robin, 'Ghostly Rhetoric: Ambivalence in M. G. Lewis' *The Monk*', *Ariel*, 10 (1979), 65–79.

PETER GARSIDE

Macdonald, D. L., 'The Erotic Sublime: The Marvellous in *The Monk*', *English Studies in Canada*, 18 (1992), 273–85.

Parreaux, André, *The Publication of 'The Monk': A Literary Event 1796–1798* (Paris, 1960).

Peck, Louis F., *A Life of Matthew G. Lewis* (Cambridge, Mass., 1961).

Reno, Robert P., 'James Boaden's *Fountainville Forest* and Matthew G. Lewis's *The Castle Spectre*: Challenges of the Supernatural Ghost on the Eighteenth-Century Stage', *Eighteenth Century Life*, 9 (1984), 95–106.

Watkins, Daniel P., 'Social Hierarchy in Matthew Lewis's *The Monk*', *Studies in the Novel*, 18 (1986), 115–24.

Charles Robert Maturin

Dawson, Leven M., '*Melmoth the Wanderer*: Paradox and the Gothic Novel', *Studies in English Literature*, 8 (1968), 621–32.

Eggenschwiler, David, '*Melmoth the Wanderer*: Gothic on Gothic', *Genre*, 8 (1975), 165–81.

Fierobe, Claude, *Charles Robert Maturin (1780–1824): L'Homme et l'œuvre* (Lille, 1974).

Fowler, Kathleen, 'Hieroglyphics in Fire: *Melmoth the Wanderer*', *Studies in Romanticism*, 25 (1986), 521–39.

Hammond, Muriel E., 'C. R. Maturin and *Melmoth the Wanderer*', *English*, 11 (1956), 97–101.

Hennelly, Mark M., Jr., '*Melmoth the Wanderer* and Gothic Existentialism', *Studies in English Literature*, 21 (1981), 665–79.

Idman, Niilo, *Charles Robert Maturin: His Life and Works* (London, 1923).

Kramer, Dale, *Charles Robert Maturin* (New York, 1973).

Lougy, Robert E., *Charles Robert Maturin* (Lewisburg, Pa., 1975).

Ratchford, Fannie E., and McCarthy, William H. (eds.), *The Correspondence of Sir Walter Scott and Charles Robert Maturin* (Austin, Tex., 1937).

Scholten, Willem, *Charles Robert Maturin: The Terror-Novelist* (Amsterdam, 1933).

Scott, Shirley Clay, *Myths of Consciousness in the Novels of Charles Robert Maturin* (New York, 1980).

Scott, Walter, review of *The Fatal Revenge*, in the *Quarterly Review*, 3 (May 1810), 339–47; repr. in *Sir Walter Scott on Novelists and Fiction*, ed. Ioan Williams (London, 1968), 204–13.

Watkins, Daniel P., ' "Tenants of a Blasted World": Historical Imagination in Charles Maturin's *Bertram*', *Keats–Shelley Review*, 4 (1989), 61–80.

17. Essayists of the Romantic Period (De Quincey, Hazlitt, Hunt, and Lamb)

ROBERT MORRISON

ANTHOLOGIES

Woodring's anthology is the most complete, and features the work of nearly thirty Romantic prose writers, including long sections by De Quincey, Hazlitt, Hunt, and Lamb; Bromwich's anthology contains key essays in literary criticism by these four, as well as essays by Wordsworth, Peacock, and Shelley.

BIBLIOGRAPHIES

The Houtchens and Houtchens volume is still valuable for its comprehensive chapters on all four essayists, as well as on other prose writers such as Southey and Landor. Ireland's book is long since out of date bibliographically, but contains long and useful compilations of contemporary assessments of the 'character, genius, and writings' of Hazlitt, Hunt, and Lamb.

CRITICISM

'Our Prose taking it altogether, is a disgrace to the country', wrote Wordsworth in 1816. Yet even by that date powerful examples of Romantic prose had emerged and, in the years that followed, Thomas De Quincey, William Hazlitt, Leigh Hunt, and Charles Lamb transformed the range, character, and potential of the English essay. Indeed, for many critics, the finest work of these four constitutes a kind of prose counterpart to the achievement of the Romantic poets: 'The "inner world of values" evident in Romantic poems', writes Woodring (1961), 'the commitment to subjectivity, the outbreaks of imagination, the personalized solemnity, the organic or emotional unity that displaced external form, these animate the Romantic personal essay in kinship with *The Prelude* and the "Ode to a Nightingale".'

The four major essayists were all deeply involved with the anxieties and aspirations of the age, and were associates and critics of some of Romanticism's leading figures, as is evident in Hunt's essays on 'Keats' and 'Shelley' in his *Lord Byron and Some of his Contemporaries* (1828), or De Quincey's articles on 'Coleridge' and 'Wordsworth' in his *Recollections of the Lakes and the Lake Poets* (1834–9). They also commented on each other: Hazlitt's incisive essays on 'Lamb' and 'Hunt' in *The Spirit of the Age* (1825), or De Quincey's remarkably sympathetic assessment of 'Hazlitt' (1845) and his two long biographical sketches of 'Lamb' (1838, 1848) are among the most notable examples. In the first half of the twentieth century, Hazlitt, Hunt, and Lamb were most often grouped together as 'familiar essayists'. Law traces the way in which they both imitated and recast some of the central tenets of the seventeenth- and eighteenth-century essay, while Watson concentrates on their relationship to 'the essay tradition of Addison and Steele'. Recent critics explore various perspectives. Jacobus takes the theoretical structures of de Man and Ehrmann to examine what De Quincey, Hazlitt, and Lamb 'have to say about language'. Nabholtz's study details the way in which 'much of the most original prose of the early nineteenth century undertook the education of the reader *as reader* by attempting to break conventional habits of response'. Cafarelli uses works by De Quincey, Hazlitt, Hunt, and several others to demonstrate how Samuel Johnson's *Lives of the Poets* 'provided the central model for Romantic biography in shape, interpretive authority, and critical ambition'. Lindop's focus is on the massive debt De Quincey, Hazlitt, and Lamb owe to Coleridge while, in the best full-length study, McFarland shows De Quincey, Hazlitt, and Lamb as 'deeply embattled amid the convulsive disruptions and accumulating stresses that defined Romanticism'.

THOMAS DE QUINCEY

TEXTS AND LETTERS

Lindop and Wright have produced reliable and convenient paperback editions of De Quincey's better-known writings, and Jordan (1973) has edited a useful compilation of De Quincey's literary criticism. The forthcoming *Works of Thomas De Quincey* will make available for the first time an accurate edition of his entire output, reprinted in chronological order using the original texts. There is no standard edition of De Quincey's letters, though they can be sampled in editions by Bonner and Jordan (1963).

Eaton's is the standard biography, and the most thorough and factual. Sackville-West's life is a saga, vivid and memorable. Lindop's recent biography couples a great deal of new information with penetrating analyses of the paradoxes of De Quincey's personality. The standard bibliography is by Dendurent.

CRITICISM

'No Englishman cares a pin for [De Quincey]' was Nathaniel Hawthorne's assessment in 1851, and the notion persists that De Quincey is a 'marginal' figure, and that, in Cafarelli's words, 'the modern tendency to see poetry as the main expression of British Romanticism has eclipsed De Quincey's reputation'. Yet, as Morrison demonstrates, De Quincey has 'haunted, entertained and influenced some of the most significant names in nineteenth- and twentieth-century literature', including the Brontë sisters, Poe, Dostoevsky, Baudelaire, Joyce, and Borges. In the last three decades De Quincey has become a remarkably protean figure: a drug guru in popular culture in the 1960s; a writer who attracts traditional literary critics—Thron asserts that the best contemporary work on De Quincey is traditional; and an 'aesthete' and 'pure stylist' who, Leighton notes, 'lends himself . . . to deconstructive readings'. McDonagh points out that a recent 'upsurge of historicist criticism has produced yet another . . . De Quincey . . . this one more sensitive to the social and political context of his life and work'.

As the diversity of these critical interpretations suggests, De Quincey had a greater range than perhaps any other prose writer of the nineteenth century, in part because, as Lyon emphasizes, 'nearly all of De Quincey's writing was done for the periodical press'. His works include, in Barrell's neat summary, 'novels, short stories, translations of fiction mainly from the German, works of literary theory, autobiographical writings in various modes, biographical essays, essays critical, essays economic, geographical, historical, philological, philosophical, political, scientific, and so on'. Critics have discussed De Quincey's style at length. Coleridge's comment in 1809 that De Quincey's mind was 'anxious yet dilatory . . . & at once systematic and labyrinthine' anticipated a prose style that many have labelled 'flawed' and 'frustrating'. 'Pedantry, Digression, Prolixity, and Facetiousness' largely ruined De Quincey, writes Sackville-West. Yet De Quincey's style has also been greatly admired, and for a variety of reasons. Black (1985) argues that a *digressive tradition that . . . runs from Swift and Sterne to Jean Paul . . . finds its culmination . . . in the major writings of De Quincey*', while Jordan (1985) explores how De Quincey's style is informed by irony. For Saintsbury, De Quincey cannot be 'overpraised' as a writer of 'ornate' prose; and in Virginia Woolf's view, it was this style that enabled him to 'capture fuller and finer truths' than are usually the aim of the prose writer. But for Stapleton, De Quincey's 'chief originality lies in his evolution of a unique kind of narrative, in which the vision seen as the end point of experience casts an intense light upon the actual'. McFarland concludes, reasonably, that 'it is difficult to think of another figure with so varied a stylistic repertoire as De Quincey'.

Yet despite the exceptional range in subject matter and style, critics have always seen the heart of De Quincey's achievement as autobiographical, specifically the two versions of *Confessions of an English Opium-Eater* (1821 and 1856), its sequel, 'Suspiria de Profundis' (1845), and 'The English Mail-Coach' (1849). Ramsey and Lent have written the best essays on the structure of these works, while other critics have explored influences. For Whale, *Confessions* and 'Suspiria' 'derive much of their complexity from an unresolved combination of extreme experiential concerns and a politeness which is in keeping with their periodical magazine context'. Rzepka's full-length study of the 1821 *Confessions* draws on theories of gift-exchange and sacramentalism to explore the 'literary and aesthetic and socioeconomic phenomenon called "the Sublime" ... and its relationship to literary labour'. Devlin and Jonathan Wordsworth examine De Quincey's enormous debt to Wordsworth, and Leask argues that the 1821 *Confessions* is 'parasitic' on Coleridge's *Biographia Literaria*. The effects of De Quincey's opium addiction are detailed by Hayter and Cooke. Lindop (1985*a*) suggests the influence of evangelicalism in works like *Confessions*, whereas Holstein finds that 'the *Confessions* proposes an alternative entrance into mystery and spiritual grandeur to both orthodoxy and evangelism'.

One of the most intriguing disputes in recent Romantic criticism focuses on De Quincey's autobiographical writings. For commentators like De Luca, the *Confessions*, 'Suspiria', and 'The Mail-Coach' constitute virtually all that is of importance in De Quincey, and the rest of the work is dismissed. This approach has been vigorously attacked by Maniquis (1984), who wonders how it is possible to remove 'the palpitating centre' of myth-making from 'the "surrounding tissue" of "mere prose"'. For Maniquis (1976), all of De Quincey's writings are part of one interrelated project: 'we can read his journalistic pieces on the Roman Empire just as we read "The English Mail-Coach"', he writes, 'for the Opium-Eater's history and his dreams are only versions of one consistent kind of writing in which the pariah is saving himself.' Miller and Barrell concentrate on the episode in 'Suspiria' in which De Quincey describes the childhood death of his beloved sister Elizabeth. In Miller's existentialist interpretation, this death brings the destruction of a previously indissoluble unity that De Quincey bridges only when he realizes at the last that 'man knows God through the absence of God.' But in Barrell's psychoanalytic reading, the complex set of images De Quincey associates with Elizabeth's death expand outward to inform his speculations on a wide range of political and historical issues, including British imperialism, the Indian Mutiny of 1857, and much else. For more traditional critics such as Bruss and Porter, De Quincey's auto-biographical writings produce a recognizable and stable self, but for post-structuralists like Baxter and Spector 'what is named "De Quincey" is . . . without beginning, without centre, and without end.' Most strikingly, for Hopkins 'The Mail-Coach' is 'a meaningful, coherent, imaginative' work, while for Reed the 'vibrations and slippages' of the text demonstrate that 'the mail-coach could hardly be less steady'.

Several critics have found in De Quincey's autobiography and his related fictions strong links with the Gothic. 'As an essayist and autobiographer', Sedgwick asserts, '. . . De Quincey was a great Gothic novelist', and she explores his fascination with 'privation', 'immobilization', and 'the unspeak-able'. Lever examines the paradox that, 'on the one hand, the De Quincey of the *Confessions* and the "Suspiria" is a Faustian melancholiac with the world's weight of guilt on his shoulders . . . ; on the other, he is a timid, meditative, bourgeois, polite, apologetic, and hypochondriac believer in God.' Lindop (1985b) explores the 'resentment', 'guilt', and 'frustration' that inform De Quincey's finest short fiction, and Leighton's feminist perspective reveals the 'continual conflict' in De Quincey's writing 'between an aesthetics of woman as pure and perfect and therefore figuratively dead and a politics of woman as the actual victim of some external destructive force'. Plumtree's examination of De Quincey's preoccupation with violence, persecution, and hysteria con-centrates on the three famous essays in satire and the macabre, 'On Murder Considered as One of the Fine Arts' (1827, 1839, 1854). For Malkan, the final essay 'launches the reader on a free fall from polite receptivity and sympath-etic understanding to voyeurism and moral complicity'.

In a letter of 1818 De Quincey told his mother that he hoped he 'might become the intellectual benefactor of [his] species' but his intellectual claims have been doubted since at least 1825 when Carlyle denounced him as 'a man who writes of things which he does not rightly understand'. The most devast-ating attack on De Quincey as thinker is by Wellek, who largely dismissed his 'contributions to philosophy, theology, politics, and the theory of literature'; Goldman further undermined De Quincey's intellectual pretensions when he convincingly demonstrated his dependence in many essays on unacknowledged sources. Yet several scholars have made high claims for De Quincey's intellec-tual standing. Beer helps define 'the Englishness of De Quincey's ideas', and concludes that De Quincey's 'explorations, like Coleridge's, both extend the scope and question the validity of Romantic conceptions as they were being severally set forth in the various European cultures of this time'. Black (1991) argues that in so far as De Quincey 'raised a host of aesthetic problems in the course of lampooning Kant's moral philosophy, [he] unwittingly (and, we must suppose, unwillingly) pointed the way toward Nietzsche's full-blown aesthetic critique of morality in general later in the century'. Clej's fine study reveals

De Quincey as 'one of the first writers, if not the very first, to experience and work out the symptoms of modernity'. In a comprehensive survey, Jordan (1952) details De Quincey's 'method and achievement' as a literary critic, while Burwick explores his 'signal contribution' to the history of rhetoric. De Quincey's most famous critical paradigm, 'the literature of power', has been frequently discussed, but most incisively by Bate: 'it is as a development of Wordsworth's and Coleridge's faith in the high calling of the poet that De Quincey comes to define literature specifically as "a body of creative art". He was the first to define it thus, and the definition has been enormously influential: he is, if you will, the inventor of Literature with a capital "L".'

WILLIAM HAZLITT

TEXTS AND LETTERS

Cook, Lahey, and Mackerness have produced reliable editions of the best-known Hazlitt texts, and a nine-volume selected edition is forthcoming, edited by Wu and introduced by Paulin. The standard works are by Howe. The letters have been edited by Sikes, Bonner, and Lahey; Robinson has prepared an essential supplement.

BIOGRAPHIES AND BIBLIOGRAPHIES

Baker's biography is the most authoritative, and places Hazlitt firmly within the intellectual and social context of his day. Wardle gives a sympathetic account of the development of the man and the writer. Jones concentrates on the years from 1808 until Hazlitt's death, and incorporates a great deal of new information. The standard bibliography is by Houck.

CRITICISM

De Quincey was one of many contemporaries who described 'the dark sinister gloom which sate for ever upon Hazlitt's countenance and gestures', and such accounts have largely shaped what Kinnaird (1963) cites as the 'two main objections' always urged against Hazlitt: 'one, that he was prejudiced, passion-blind, wilfully or whimsically self-indulgent; the other, that he was unlearned, ill-bred and ill-read, even anti-intellectual'. But Hazlitt's unswerving radicalism and passionate intelligence earned him the admiration of many, especially Lamb and Hunt, who knew that he 'was "at feud with the world" out of his infinite sympathy with them'; recently Epstein has called Hazlitt 'one of the few authentic heroes of literature'. At the same time, the notion that Hazlitt is slipshod and impressionistic has been vigorously rebutted. 'Hazlitt', writes

Bloom, 'makes a second to Johnson in a great procession of critical essayists that goes on to Carlyle, Emerson, Ruskin, Pater, and Wilde.'

Hazlitt responded powerfully to most of the concerns of his day: Uphaus notes he produced essays on 'aesthetics, moral theory, epistemology, drama, poetry, the novel, painting, economics, and political theory', and in a great number of his essays these concerns are intimately interconnected: as Eagleton puts it, 'Hazlitt's language refuses a distinction between the literary and the political'. Much has been written about his style. De Quincey complains of Hazlitt's 'habit of trite quotation' as ' "mouth-diarrhoea" ', and describes Hazlitt's style as 'abrupt, insulated, capricious' (he had similar things to say about Lamb's). But Bate finds that 'Shakespearean quotations bring to consummation Hazlitt's own language', and Coleridge was the first in a long line to praise Hazlitt's ability to send 'well-feathered Thoughts straight forwards to the mark with a Twang of the Bow-string'. McFarland makes the valuable qualification that Hazlitt achieves this effect 'by saying just one thing clearly and directly' and 'holding back all reservations, qualifications, contradictions, and second thoughts for an entirely different occasion'. Critics have also examined structure, though they are hardly in agreement. Bromwich (1983a) notes that in 'rhetorical design' and 'intellectual temper' Montaigne seems 'the essayist most nearly related to Hazlitt', though the essays 'quest for power in a shape that would not have been understood before Rousseau and Wordsworth'. Patterson argues that Hazlitt paid 'entirely too little attention to plot and to structure' and Ready (1981) finds the essays 'de-organic', but Albrecht (1965) discerns a principle of 'organic growth', and Salvesen contends that 'the Hazlitt essay is one of the great formal achievements of English Romanticism. The form derives from Hazlitt's presence therein.'

The two most wide-ranging studies of Hazlitt's ideas are by Kinnaird (1978) and Bromwich (1983b). For Kinnaird, Hazlitt's thought 'moves with the advancing storm centre of Romantic creativity: in his mind, as in no other prose writer of the time, the great issues of Romanticism meet, intersect, and interpenetrate, or are joined in battle'. But for Bromwich, Hazlitt's thought 'gives little evidence of development', though he is close to Kinnaird when he asserts that Hazlitt conveys, 'better than any other writer of any age, the charge and retreat of its battles, the skirmishes and stray shots, and trials of valour'. Other important studies have concentrated on the centrality of Hazlitt's concept of the sympathetic imagination. Bullitt and Albrecht (1965) detail the origins and applications of this term, while O'Hara investigates 'the major supplements to sympathy in Hazlitt's criticism—associational aesthetics and the formative imagination'. Ready (1974) and Haefner focus on Hazlitt's concept of 'gusto'. Schneider traces the sources of Hazlitt's critical principles in relation to late eighteenth- and early nineteenth-century aesthetic thought and, in a seminal essay, W. J. Bate demonstrates how 'Hazlitt, in his moral, critical, and psychological premises, represents more than any other writer of his time a union of eighteenth-century English empiricism and emotional intuitionalism'. Bate's views have been developed in a number of directions. Park sees Hazlitt's 'entire critical outlook' as a war against abstraction, in which Hazlitt rejects both 'a hostile empirical epistemology' and the idealism of the transcendent-alists, but Mulvihill argues that 'Hazlitt uses the methods of empiricism to achieve a criticism that combines sensitive observation with inductive infer-ence'. Mahoney connects Hazlitt's aesthetics with the diversity of his practical criticism to show 'the master critic of English Romanticism at work, the critic who speaks for the new subjective values which become part of the early-nineteenth-century critical landscape'.

Other studies have focused on specific groups of essays, and demonstrate Hazlitt's remarkable range. The most extensive discussion of Hazlitt's Shake-spearian criticism is by Jonathan Bate. Galperin examines 'Hazlitt's dialectic of humanism and theatricality': 'Unlike Lamb, who adamantly defends and privileges a self in opposition to the theatre, Hazlitt marshals the theatre . . . in the service of more recognizably republican ends.' Sikes and Jack are among many critics to explore the powerful influence of Hazlitt's *Characters of Shake-spear's Plays* (1817) and *Lectures on the English Poets* (1818) on Keats. Hazlitt's art criticism has been described by Bryson as constituting 'the essential bridge-passage where one can hear the themes of Enlightenment aesthetics suddenly transform into new configurations, to emerge finally as the new Romantic music'. Trawick discusses Hazlitt's treatment of the eighteenth-century art critic Joshua Reynolds, and Wright emphasizes Hazlitt's importance to Ruskin. For Barrell, Hazlitt's theory of art reads as 'a statement of determined opposi-tion to the civic theories . . . that had been advanced by Reynolds, Barry, and . . . Fuseli'. Hazlitt's political essays, Foot maintains, 'gave to the English Left a perspective and philosophy as widely ranging as Burke had given to the English Right'. Hazlitt's complicated response to Burke has also been analysed by Whale and Cook, while Garnett persuasively demonstrates that in *The Life of Napoleon* (1828–30) Hazlitt 'is too favourable to Napoleon to satisfy his enemies, and not radical enough to please those of Hazlitt's modern admirers who wish to reflect their left-wing beliefs back onto their hero'. The import-ance of Hazlitt's economic writings is thoroughly considered by Albrecht (1950), and Story shrewdly assesses *The Spirit of the Age* (1825), Hazlitt's most successful collection of essays on contemporaries like Wordsworth, Coleridge, Byron, Hunt, and Lamb.

Finally, a great deal of attention has been paid to *Liber Amoris* (1823), Hazlitt's obsessional tale of his disastrous love for the 19-year-old Sarah Walker. When it appeared Crabb Robinson thought it 'nauseous' and 'disgusting', and the book can still elicit a similar reaction, Miller dismissing it recently as 'dull and dis-tasteful'. But *Liber Amoris* has also attracted sympathetic responses: De Quincey insisted 'there was no indelicacy in such an act of confidence'. More recently, Ready (1986) describes the book as 'one of the first extended treatments in a line of modern writing on men who try to make women fit their illusions'. Morgan is interested in Hazlitt as 'the sane, unsparing analyst of his own madness', and Burroughs focuses on Sarah. For Butler, *Liber Amoris* 'is in effect a counter-example' to De Quincey's *Confessions*, while in Lahey's view the book expresses a 'preoccupation with the irresolvable discord between desire and reality' and is thus 'a parable of the entire Romantic period'.

LEIGH HUNT

TEXTS AND LETTERS

There is no standard edition of the writings of Hunt, though several different modern editions enable one to piece together a fairly representative selection of his work, and a complete edition of his letters is forthcoming edited by Cheney.

BIOGRAPHIES AND BIBLIOGRAPHIES

The most comprehensive biography of Hunt is Landré's, but it has not been translated into English. Blunden's is the standard English biography; Blainey's is a shorter portrait that incorporates a good deal of new information. The important Hunt bibliographies are by Lulofs and Ostrom, and Waltman and McDaniel.

CRITICISM

When Leigh Hunt emerged from prison in 1815 after serving a two-year sentence for libelling the Prince Regent, Keats described him as 'The wrong'd Libertas', and the image of Hunt as reformer, passionately independent critic, and champion of young genius has endured; Virginia Woolf referred to him as one of those 'free, vigorous spirits [who] advance the world'. Yet two malicious attacks still haunt Hunt's literary reputation. Beginning in 1817, J. G. Lockhart tarred him in *Blackwood's* as ringleader of the so-called 'Cockney School of Poetry', and a vulgar mediocrity with ideas well above his social station; Saintsbury is one of several later commentators who have found the same 'ill-bred pertness' in Hunt's writing. Hunt suffered again when Dickens pilloried him in *Bleak House* as the insolvent and unscrupulous Harold Skimpole, an unfair portrait that has nevertheless endured because it so effectively exploits two prominent aspects of Hunt's character, 'the devotee of imagination and fancy' and 'the shameless parasite', as Altick aptly characterizes it.

At the core of Hunt's writings is what critics have almost uniformly identified as a genial and unquenchable optimism, though for some this renders
him sentimental and shallow, while for others it is evidence of his intense
humanity. Crabb Robinson's remark in 1820 that Hunt 'catches the sunny side
of everything' is echoed by Thompson who, in the most thorough recent study,
concludes that 'the mainspring of [Hunt's] character was his faith in human
nature and in the cosmos itself . . . it is difficult to resist using "kindly", "tol-
erant", and "wholesome" when describing him.' For Jack (1963), this 'chatty'
quality makes Hunt 'a dilettante, a connoisseur, with something of the
superficiality that the term implies . . . after a while we become tired of him,
as Keats did.' But according to Cameron, Hunt's kindliness produces a power
and indignation that are the 'essence' of his achievement.

Hunt's diversity as a writer is perhaps his greatest strength. 'The variety
forced by the requirement of writing to schedule', Woodring (1985) points out,
'gives us many opportunities to watch him in the freshly bathed nakedness of
anger at misconduct by those in public office and soon after in diaphanous
semi-transparency as genial observer of life in the parlours and streets of
London'. As a literary critic, most commentators rank Hunt below Lamb and
Hazlitt: 'he has humour and pathos', writes Priestley, 'but they pale before the
humour and pathos of Lamb. He has wit and an acute critical mind, but not
the wit and acuteness of Hazlitt.' Yet in a comprehensive introduction Thorpe
ranks Hunt 'next to Coleridge and Hazlitt, and above Lamb [and] De Quincey',
and Reiman finds that Hunt's 'aesthetic taste . . . proved—at least on its positive side—to be superior to that of any other critic of the nineteenth century'.
Hunt's most important piece of literary criticism is *Imagination and Fancy*
(1844), which Fogle criticizes because of Hunt's 'catchall' use of these two key
Romantic terms, but which in Smith's view demonstrates that 'Hunt had a
power of taste, in the high sense defined by Shelley and Hazlitt, that was effective in its own time and can still instruct in its own right'. Warren's appraisal
of the book finds that 'Imagination . . . for Hunt is a kind of cognitive feeling.'

Hunt's importance as a drama critic has been commented on many times
since Hazlitt credited him in 1828 with being the first to give 'the true *pine-
apple* flavour to theatrical criticism, making it a pleasant mixture of sharp
and sweet'. In the best of the more recent assessments, Wells writes that 'in
general, Hunt's interest centres firmly on the actors, and on the problems of
performers interpreting particular roles. . . . The emphasis on star actors is
itself a manifestation of Romanticism, with its fascination with individual personality.' Fenner convincingly finds Hunt the 'foremost among the musical
journalists of the early nineteenth century' (1972), and elsewhere praises the
way in which Hunt 'brings before our eyes his vision of both the faults and
triumphs of ballet in his time' (1977). As a critic of the visual arts, Hunt's
most enduring influence was on Keats: 'it is partly because of him', asserts

Jack (1967), 'that so many pages of Keats's poems . . . may fitly be described as "walls glowing with life and colour".' Hunt's abilities as 'a great introducer' (in Amy Lowell's words) are discussed by Misenheimer, who remarks that 'probably no other single phrase could better characterize his unique services as journalist, anthologist, translator, and critic'. Hunt also wrote the first major literary *Autobiography* (1850), which remains one of the most perceptive and engaging assessments of the age of Romanticism and which, as Webb notes, features Shelley as 'the hero'.

Finally, as editor of several important (though sometimes short-lived) journals, Hunt's influence was profound. 'There can be no doubt', Johnson (1927) writes, 'that as the first epoch-making step towards the modernising and demo-cratisation of journal-newspapers was taken by Defoe, the second important era of progress was inaugurated by Leigh Hunt.' The best known of these journals, the *Examiner*, which Hunt edited 1808–21, has been the subject of book-length studies by Blunden and Stout (1949) while, in a wide-ranging sur-vey of Hunt's political essays, Woodring (1962) highlights the 'passion, weekly intelligence, and education' of Hunt's *Examiner* essays. Recent critics, includ-ing Barnard and Kandl, have explored the way the politics of Hunt's journals help construct the meaning of the poetry he published. Marshall's full-length study of the *Liberal* (1822–3) details the four issues of that brilliant but ill-fated journal, which Hunt was to have edited with Byron and Shelley, and which Marshall rightly characterizes as an 'episode . . . of fundamental significance in understanding those participating in it'.

Lamb once called Hunt 'matchless as a fire-side companion' and indeed some of the key details of his life and career can be found in the biographies of other writers, including Hazlitt, Keats, Shelley, and Lamb himself. Stout (1957) examines Hunt's varying responses to Wordsworth and Coleridge, Johnson's book on Hunt and Shelley is a thorough account of their intimacy, and Gates (1986) sheds new light on Hunt's relationship with Byron. She also (1992) examines Hunt's marginal comments on Hazlitt's *Literary Remains* (1836) and concludes that the continuing dialogue between the two writers 'went on for another twenty-nine years after Hazlitt's death, which Hunt seem-ingly interpreted as merely a temporary interruption in the intellectual and emotional give-and-take of a lifetime'.

CHARLES LAMB

TEXTS AND LETTERS

Bate and Phillips have produced the best paperback editions of Lamb. The standard works and letters are edited by Lucas, though Marrs's ongoing edi-tion of the letters supersedes Lucas up to 1817.

ROBERT MORRISON

The standard biography is by Lucas; Courtney, who argues for a much more politically involved Lamb, supersedes Lucas up to 1802. Blunden's book is a valuable compilation of contemporary assessments, and Prance's a useful reference guide to the people and places associated with Lamb and his sister Mary. The best bibliography is still by Barnett and Tave.

'Charles Lamb I sincerely believe to be in some considerable degree *insane*', Carlyle wrote in 1831 as the loudest contemporary voice in a tradition of belittling Lamb that reached its climax a century later, when Thompson condemned him as 'trivial', 'sentimental', and possessing 'a regressive mind'. With enemies like this, Lamb has needed firm friends, but often attracted only besotted admirers. Notoriously, Swinburne wrote that 'no good criticism of Lamb, strictly speaking, can ever be written; because nobody can do justice to his work who does not love it too well to feel himself capable of giving judgment on it.' Yet between these two critical poles there has always been a third school that recognized that Lamb's humour arises from tragedy, and his strength from despair. 'One could have imagined [Lamb] cracking a jest in the teeth of a ghost', Hunt said, 'and then melting into thin air himself, out of sympathy with the awful.' It is this Lamb that recent criticism has fastened upon, answering Wedd's memorable call in 1977 'to put the guts back into Charles Lamb'.

The touchstone of Lamb's achievement has always been the *Essays* and *Last Essays of Elia*, most of which were first published in the *London Magazine* between 1820 and 1825. Barnett (1964) charts the evolution of the *Essays* through Lamb's letters, reading, conversation, and early writings, while Bate demonstrates that they are the product of two distinct literary traditions, one of 'learned wit and irony' initiated by the essays of Montaigne, and the other of radical self-revelation, best exemplified by Rousseau's *Confessions*. Famously, De Quincey found the prose of the *Essays* 'discontinuous', for 'the most felicitous passages always accomplish their circuit in a few sentences', but Randel argues that such 'discontinuousness' represents Lamb's 'skeptical resistance toward the more exalted claims made by his contemporaries for the power of the human mind'. Coates believes that the debt of the *Essays* to the 'civilized tradition' of seventeenth-century prose stylists like Thomas Browne makes them, in effect, a critique of the 'downright certitudes and moral clumsiness' of much of the prose of the Romantic age. Structurally, the *Essays* often dramatize a progression from the narrow perspective of the Understanding to what Nabholtz calls the 'life-giving world of the Imagination', while Haven and Frank see them as 'psychologically ordered movement[s] of consciousness' structurally reminiscent of the conversation poems of Wordsworth and Coleridge, and the odes of Keats. What Lamb once called 'that dangerous figure—irony' is everywhere in the *Essays*. Mulcahy's assertion that his 'usual practice is to interweave with his tapestry of illusion a thread of reality' is extended by Flesch, who states that 'Lamb's affectation of the figure of irony . . . provides a way for him to jump from what could be called the dream-world, that is, the world of powerful feeling, to the ironizing waking world, where he is merely a clerk.'

In what remains the single best appreciation of the *Essays*, Pater discerns that with Lamb 'the desire of self-portraiture is, below all more superficial tendencies, the real motive in writing at all—a desire closely connected with . . . modern subjectivity'. For Jessup, Elia is a 'tough-minded' philosopher who stands 'firmly in the tradition of British empiricism'; witness his dislikes of 'the dreaming Shelleys and the denying Byrons'. But for Reiman, Elia explores 'universal human problems in a truly imaginative way' by creating a 'symbol-world' of 'whist games, borrowed books, and frail china tea-cups'. More recently, Monsman's partially deconstructive reading focuses most profitably on how 'by turning the Elia persona back upon the guilty profile of his own life in a transforming and purgative act, Lamb catches within his verbal net a limping reflection of his now absent original wholeness'. Aaron's study, informed by psychoanalytic and feminist theory, reveals how the subordinate social roles played by Charles and Mary make them 'emblems of other more hidden lives, equally affected by gender and class discrimination, and by the label of madness'. Parker places the *Essays* in their original *London* contexts, and then examines how for editor John Scott, 'the slightness and the whimsical grace of Elia's contribution . . . are a reflex of their historical moment, and their complicated play of nostalgia and reminiscence a cogent resolution of social and political contradiction'.

In 1909 Bradley called Lamb 'the best critic of the nineteenth century' and, though few would agree with that estimate now, Lamb's range and insights have received high praise, particularly as they apply to drama. In the finest introduction to Lamb as critic, Park (1980) asserts that 'the term which best characterises his critical theory of literature is "dramatic", and he is, with Hazlitt, the greatest critic of the drama of his own or any other age in England.' Barnet describes Lamb's concept of dramatic illusion as 'the most sophisticated, the most discriminating, and the most accurate treatment of the problem in the history of English dramatic theory'. Commentators have responded variously to Lamb's most notorious literary opinion, that it is 'essentially impossible' to represent *King Lear* on stage: Ades (1970) stresses that Lamb 'was inclined to believe that the theatrical traditions of his time were simply inimical to the satisfactory playing of Shakespearean tragedy'; Park (1982) says that Lamb's 'case against the art of acting is aesthetic and . . . dependent on his view of the nature of the imagination'; Heller demonstrates that Lamb's argument anticipates the recent work of influential reader-response critics such as Stanley Fish. The importance of the *Specimens of English Dramatic Poets* (1808) is valuably reassessed by Shokoff, and McKenna's full-length study is most informative on the *Specimens* and *Extracts from the Garrick Plays* (1827). Lamb was also a penetrating literary critic, and especially of two of his most important friends: when Wordsworth sought Lamb's advice, Ades (1977) notes wryly that the usual pattern was for him to complain and then 'make the change as Lamb suggested'; Coleridge is similarly indebted to Lamb for criticism that was both incisive and generous, as Whalley details.

Lamb's place in the Romantic movement has often been debated. In the best-known contemporary assessment, Hazlitt finds him 'in opposition' to the Spirit of the Age: 'he has none of the turbulence or froth of new-fangled opinions.' But in the most recent full-length introduction Barnett (1976) concludes that Lamb is 'a pioneer Romantic', captivated by the world of the past, by the world of dream, and by children. Other critics find Lamb a provocative mixture: he is 'a Romantic artist' but 'no pilgrim of Eternity', states Scoggins. 'He is not the Romantic visionary of mountaintops or dizzy ravines, but of bowers and urban pastoral recesses.' Trott contends that 'Lamb's is at once the most sophisticated and regressive of Romanticisms. Its effect is simultaneously exhilarating and endearing, elusive and naive.' Whatever the verdict on this issue, Lamb's influence on the Victorians was profound. 'For anyone working in the mid-nineteenth-century field', writes Tillotson, 'Lamb is as important as Wordsworth and Coleridge, Keats and Shelley, Jane Austen and Scott. His essays were of the very mind of his successors.'

REFERENCES

ANTHOLOGIES

Bromwich, David (ed.), *Romantic Critical Essays* (Cambridge, 1987).
Woodring, Carl (ed.), *Prose of the Romantic Period* (Boston, 1961).

BIBLIOGRAPHIES

Houtchens, C. W., and Houtchens, L. H. (eds.), *The English Romantic Poets and Essayists* (New York, 1966).
Ireland, Alexander, *List of the Writings of William Hazlitt and Leigh Hunt and Charles Lamb* (New York, 1868).

Criticism

Cafarelli, Annette, *Prose in the Age of Poets* (Philadelphia, 1990).

De Quincey, Thomas, 'Recollections of Charles Lamb', in David Masson (ed.), *The Collected Writings of Thomas De Quincey*, 14 vols. (Edinburgh, 1889–90), iii. 34–92.

Hazlitt, William, *The Spirit of the Age*, ed. E. D. Mackerness (London, 1969).

Hunt, Leigh, 'Remarks Suggested by the Perusal of Mr. Hazlitt's *Plain Speaker*', in L. H. Houtchens and C. W. Houtchens (eds.), *Leigh Hunt's Literary Criticism* (New York, 1956), 243–67.

Jacobus, Mary, 'The Art of Managing Books: Romantic Prose and the Writing of the Past', in Arden Reed (ed.), *Romanticism and Language* (Ithaca, NY, 1984), 215–46.

Law, M. H., *The English Familiar Essay in the Early Nineteenth Century* (Philadelphia, 1934).

Lindop, Grevel, 'Lamb, Hazlitt and De Quincey', in Richard Gravil and Molly Lefebure (eds.), *The Coleridge Connection: Essays for Thomas McFarland* (London, 1990), 111–32.

Nabholtz, John R., *'My Reader my Fellow-Labourer': A Study of English Romantic Prose* (Columbia, Mo., 1986).

McFarland, Thomas, *Romantic Cruxes: The English Essayists and the Spirit of the Age* (Oxford, 1987).

Watson, M. R., 'The Familiar Essay and the Tradition', in *Magazine Serials and the Essay Tradition 1746–1820* (Baton Rouge, La., 1956), 69–86.

THOMAS DE QUINCEY

Texts and letters

Bonner, W. H. (ed.), *De Quincey at Work* (Buffalo, 1936).

Eaton, H. A. (ed.), *A Diary of Thomas De Quincey* (London, 1927).

Jordan, John (ed.), *De Quincey to Wordsworth* (Berkeley and Los Angeles, 1963).

—— *De Quincey as Critic* (London, 1973).

Lindop, Grevel (ed.), *Confessions of an English Opium-Eater and Other Writings* (Oxford, 1985).

Masson, David (ed.), *The Collected Writings of Thomas De Quincey*, 14 vols. (Edinburgh, 1889–90).

Tave, Stuart (ed.), *New Essays by De Quincey* (Princeton, 1966).

Wright, David (ed.), *Recollections of the Lakes and the Lake Poets* (Harmondsworth, 1970).

Biographies and bibliographies

Dendurent, H. O., *Thomas De Quincey: A Reference Guide* (Boston, 1978).

Eaton, H. A., *Thomas De Quincey* (Oxford, 1936).

Lindop, Grevel, *The Opium-Eater: A Life of Thomas De Quincey* (London, 1981).

Sackville-West, Edward, *A Flame in Sunlight: The Life and Work of Thomas De Quincey* (London, 1936; repr., ed. John Jordan, London, 1974).

Criticism

Barrell, John, *The Infection of Thomas De Quincey* (New Haven, 1991).

Bate, Jonathan, 'The Literature of Power: Coleridge and De Quincey', in Tim Fulford and Morton D. Paley (eds.), *Coleridge's Visionary Language* (Bury St Edmunds, 1993), 137–50.

Baxter, Edmund, *De Quincey's Art of Autobiography* (Edinburgh, 1990).

Beer, John, 'The Englishness of De Quincey's Ideas', in James Pipkin (ed.), *English and German Romanticism: Cross-Currents and Controversies* (Heidelberg, 1985), 323–47.

Black, Joel D., 'Confession, Digression, Gravitation: Thomas De Quincey's German Connection', in Robert Lance Snyder (ed.), *Thomas De Quincey: Bicentenary Studies* (Norman, Okla., 1985), 308–37.

—— *The Aesthetics of Murder: A Study in Romantic Literature and Contemporary Culture* (Baltimore, 1991).

Bruss, Elizabeth, 'Thomas De Quincey: Sketches and Sighs', in *Autobiographical Acts* (Baltimore, 1976), 93–126.

Burwick, Frederick, 'Introduction', in *Selected Essays on Rhetoric by Thomas De Quincey*, ed. Frederick Burwick (Carbondale, Ill., 1967), pp. xi–xlviii.

Clej, Alina, *A Genealogy of the Modern Self: Thomas De Quincey and the Intoxication of Writing* (Stanford, Calif., 1995).

Cooke, Michael G., 'De Quincey, Coleridge, and the Formal Uses of Intoxication', *Yale French Studies*, 50 (1974), 26–40.

De Luca, V. A., *Thomas De Quincey: The Prose of Vision* (Toronto, 1980).

Devlin, D. D., *De Quincey, Wordsworth and the Art of Prose* (London, 1983).

Goldman, Albert, *The Mine and the Mint* (Carbondale, Ill., 1965).

Hayter, Alethea, *Opium and the Romantic Imagination* (London, 1968).

Holstein, Michael E., ' "An Apocalypse of the World Within": Autobiographical Exegesis in De Quincey's *Confessions of an English Opium-Eater* (1822)', *Prose Studies*, 2 (1979), 88–102.

Hopkins, Robert, 'De Quincey on War and the Pastoral Design of "The English Mail-Coach" ', *Studies in Romanticism*, 6 (1967), 129–51.

Jordan, John, *Thomas De Quincey: Literary Critic* (Berkeley and Los Angeles, 1952).

—— 'Grazing the Brink: De Quincey's Ironies', in Robert Lance Snyder (ed.), *Thomas De Quincey: Bicentenary Studies* (Norman, Okla., 1985), 199–212.

Leask, Nigel, ' "Murdering One's Double": De Quincey's *Confessions of an English Opium-Eater* and S. T. Coleridge's *Biographia Literaria*', in Peter J. Kitson and Thomas N. Corns (eds.), *Coleridge and the Armoury of the Human Mind* (London, 1991), 78–98.

Leighton, Angela, 'De Quincey and Women', in Stephen Copley and John Whale (eds.), *Beyond Romanticism: New Approaches to Texts and Contexts 1780–1832* (London, 1992), 160–77.

Lent, John, 'Thomas De Quincey, Subjectivity, and Modern Literature: A Consideration of the Release of Vision in *Confessions of an English Opium-Eater* and "Suspiria de Profundis" ', *Sphinx*, 9 (1979), 36–58.

Lever, Karen M., 'De Quincey as Gothic Hero: A Perspective on *Confessions of an English Opium-Eater* and "Suspiria de Profundis" ', *Texas Studies in Literature and Language*, 21 (1979), 332–46.

Lindop, Grevel, 'Pursuing the Throne of God: De Quincey and the Evangelical Revival', *Charles Lamb Bulletin*, 52 (1985a), 97–111.

—— 'Innocence and Revenge: The Problem of De Quincey's Fiction', in Robert Lance Snyder (ed.), *Thomas De Quincey: Bicentenary Studies* (Norman, Okla., 1985b), 213–38.

Lyon, Judson, *Thomas De Quincey* (New York, 1969).

McDonagh, Josephine, *De Quincey's Disciplines* (Oxford, 1994).

Malkan, Jeffrey, 'Aggressive Text: Murder and the Fine Arts Revisited', *Mosaic*, 23 (1990), 101–14.

Maniquis, Robert, 'Lonely Empires: Personal and Public Visions of Thomas De Quincey', in Eric Rothstein and Joseph Anthony Wittreich (eds.), *Literary Monographs*, vol. viii (Madison, 1976), 47–127.

—— 'V. A. De Luca. *Thomas De Quincey: The Prose of Vision*', *Studies in Romanticism*, 23 (1984), 139–47.

Miller, J. Hillis, 'Thomas De Quincey', in *The Disappearance of God* (Cambridge, Mass., 1963), 17–80.

Morrison, Robert, ' "I here present you, courteous reader": The Literary Presence of Thomas De Quincey', *Charles Lamb Bulletin*, 90 (1995), 68–72.

Plumtree, A. S., 'The Artist as Murderer: De Quincey's Essay "On Murder Considered as One of the Fine Arts" ', in Robert Lance Snyder (ed.), *Thomas De Quincey: Bicentenary Studies* (Norman, Okla., 1985), 140–63.

Porter, Roger, 'The Demon Past: De Quincey and the Autobiographer's Dilemma', *Studies in English Literature*, 20 (1980), 591–609.

Ramsey, Roger, 'The Structure of De Quincey's *Confessions of an English Opium-Eater*', *Prose Studies*, 1 (1978), 21–9.

Reed, Arden, ' "Booked for Utter Perplexity" on De Quincey's "English Mail-Coach" ', in Robert Lance Snyder (ed.), *Thomas De Quincey: Bicentenary Studies* (Norman, Okla., 1985), 279–307.

Rzepka, Charles, *Sacramental Commodities: Gift, Text, and the Sublime in De Quincey* (Amherst, Mass., 1995).

Saintsbury, George, 'Thomas De Quincey', in *The Collected Essays and Papers*, 4 vols. (London, 1923), i. 210–38.

Sedgwick, Eve Kosofsky, 'Language as Live Burial: Thomas De Quincey', in *The Coherence of Gothic Conventions* (New York, 1980), 37–96.

Spector, Stephen J., 'Thomas De Quincey: Self-Effacing Autobiographer', *Studies in Romanticism*, 18 (1979), 501–20.

Stapleton, Lawrence, 'The Virtù of De Quincey', in *The Elected Circle: Studies in the Art of Prose* (Princeton, 1973), 119–65.

Thron, E. Michael, 'Thomas De Quincey and the Fall of Literature', in Robert Lance Snyder (ed.), *Thomas De Quincey: Bicentenary Studies* (Norman, Okla., 1985), 3–19.

Wellek, René, 'De Quincey's Status in the History of Ideas', *Philological Quarterly*, 23 (1944), 248–72.

Whale, John, ' "In a Stranger's Ear": De Quincey's Polite Magazine Context', in Robert Lance Snyder (ed.), *Thomas De Quincey: Bicentenary Studies* (Norman, Okla., 1985), 35–53.

Woolf, Virginia, 'Impassioned Prose', in *Collected Essays*, 4 vols. (London, 1966–7), i. 165–72.

Wordsworth, Jonathan, 'Two Dark Interpreters: Wordsworth and De Quincey', *Wordsworth Circle*, 17 (1986), 40–50.

ROBERT MORRISON

WILLIAM HAZLITT

Texts and letters

Cook, Jon (ed.), *William Hazlitt: Selected Writings* (Oxford, 1991).

Howe, P. P. (ed.), *The Complete Works of William Hazlitt*, 21 vols. (London, 1930–4).

Lahey, Gerald (ed.), *Liber Amoris* (New York, 1980).

Mackerness, E. D. (ed.), *The Spirit of the Age* (London, 1969).

Robinson, Charles E. (ed.), 'William Hazlitt to his Publishers, Friends, and Creditors: Twenty-Seven New Holograph Letters', *Keats–Shelley Review*, 2 (1987), 1–47.

Sikes, Herschel M., Bonner, Willard Hallam, and Lahey, Gerald (eds.), *The Letters of William Hazlitt* (New York, 1978).

Biographies and bibliographies

Baker, Herschel, *William Hazlitt* (Cambridge, Mass., 1962).

Houck, James A., *William Hazlitt: A Reference Guide* (Boston, 1977).

Jones, Stanley, *Hazlitt: A Life* (Oxford, 1989).

Wardle, Ralph M., *Hazlitt* (Lincoln, Nebr., 1971).

Criticism

Albrecht, W. P., *William Hazlitt and the Malthusian Controversy* (Albuquerque, N. Mex., 1950).

—— *Hazlitt and the Creative Imagination* (Lawrence, Kan., 1965).

Barrell, John, *The Political Theory of Painting from Reynolds to Hazlitt* (New Haven, 1986).

Bate, Jonathan, 'The Example of Hazlitt', in *Shakespearean Constitutions* (Oxford, 1989), 127–201.

Bate, W. J., 'William Hazlitt', in *Criticism: The Major Texts* (New York, 1952), 281–92.

Bloom, Harold, 'Introduction', in Harold Bloom (ed.), *William Hazlitt* (New York, 1986), 1–13.

Bromwich, David, 'The Originality of Hazlitt's Essays', *Yale Review*, 72 (1983a), 366–84.

—— *Hazlitt: The Mind of a Critic* (Oxford, 1983b).

Bryson, Norman, 'Hazlitt on Painting', *Journal of Aesthetics and Art Criticism*, 37 (1978), 37–45.

Bullitt, John M., 'Hazlitt and the Romantic Conception of the Imagination', *Philological Quarterly*, 24 (1945), 343–61.

Burroughs, Catherine, 'Acting in the Closet: A Feminist Performance of Hazlitt's *Liber Amoris* and Keats's *Otho the Great*', *European Romantic Review*, 2 (1992), 125–44.

Butler, Marilyn, 'Satire and the Images of Self in the Romantic Period: The Long Tradition of Hazlitt's *Liber Amoris*', *Yearbook of English Studies*, 14 (1984), 209–25.

Cook, Jon, 'Hazlitt: Criticism and Ideology', in David Aers, Jon Cook, and David Punter (eds.), *Romanticism and Ideology* (London, 1981), 137–54.

De Quincey, Thomas, 'William Hazlitt', in *The Collected Writings of Thomas De Quincey*, ed. David Masson, 14 vols. (Edinburgh, 1889–90), xi. 341–54.

Eagleton, Terry, 'William Hazlitt: An Empiricist Radical', *New Blackfriars*, 54 (1973), 108–17.

Epstein, Joseph, 'Hazlitt's Passions', *New Criterion*, 10/3 (1991), 33–44.

Foot, Michael, 'The Shakespeare Prose Writer', in Harold Bloom (ed.), *William Hazlitt* (New York, 1986), 89–104.

Galperin, William H., 'Lamb and Hazlitt: Romantic Antitheatricality and the Body of Genius', in *The Return of the Visible in British Romanticism* (Baltimore, 1993), 129–55.

Garnett, Mark, 'The Napoleonist', *Charles Lamb Bulletin*, 70 (1990), 185–95.

Haefner, Joel, 'Rhetoric and Art: George Campbell, William Hazlitt, and "Gusto"', *Charles Lamb Bulletin*, 63 (1988), 234–43.

Hunt, Leigh, 'Mr Hazlitt and the Utilitarians', in *Leigh Hunt's Literary Criticism*, ed. L. H. Houtchens and C. W. Houtchens (New York, 1956), 275–81.

Jack, Ian, 'The Critic: William Hazlitt', in *Keats and the Mirror of Art* (Oxford, 1967), 58–75.

Kinnaird, John, 'The Forgotten Self', *Partisan Review*, 30 (1963), 302–6.

—— *William Hazlitt: Critic of Power* (New York, 1978).

Mahoney, John L., *The Logic of Passion* (New York, 1981).

Miller, Stephen, 'The Gentleman in the Parlour', *American Scholar*, 49 (1979–80), 115–26.

Morgan, Charles, 'Introduction', in *Liber Amoris and Dramatic Criticisms*, ed. Charles Morgan (London, 1948), 7–28.

Mulvihill, James, 'Hazlitt and "First Principles"', *Studies in Romanticism*, 29 (1990), 241–55.

O'Hara, J. D., 'Hazlitt and the Functions of the Imagination', *Publications of the Modern Language Association*, 81 (1966), 552–62.

Park, Roy, *Hazlitt and the Spirit of the Age* (Oxford, 1971).

Patterson, Charles I., 'Hazlitt's Criticism in Retrospect', *Studies in English Literature*, 21 (1981), 647–63.

Ready, Robert, 'Hazlitt: In and Out of "Gusto"', *Studies in English Literature*, 14 (1974), 537–46.

—— *Hazlitt at Table* (Rutherford, NJ, 1981).

—— 'The Logic of Passion: *Liber Amoris*', in Harold Bloom (ed.), *William Hazlitt* (New York, 1986), 47–61.

Salvesen, Christopher, 'A Master of Regret', in Harold Bloom (ed.), *William Hazlitt* (New York, 1986), 29–46.

Schneider, Elisabeth, *The Aesthetics of William Hazlitt* (Philadelphia, 1933).

Sikes, Herschel M., 'The Poetic Theory and Practice of Keats: The Record of a Debt to Hazlitt', *Philological Quarterly*, 38 (1959), 401–12.

Story, Patrick, 'Emblems of Infirmity: Contemporary Portraits in Hazlitt's *The Spirit of the Age*', *Wordsworth Circle*, 10 (1979), 81–90.

Trawick, Leonard M., 'Hazlitt, Reynolds, and the Ideal', *Studies in Romanticism*, 4 (1965), 240–7.

Uphaus, Robert W., *William Hazlitt* (Boston, 1985).

Whale, John, 'Hazlitt on Burke: The Ambivalent Position of a Radical Essayist', *Studies in Romanticism*, 25 (1986), 465–81.

Wright, William C., 'Hazlitt, Ruskin, and Nineteenth-Century Art Criticism', *Journal of Aesthetics and Art Criticism*, 32 (1974), 509–23.

ROBERT MORRISON

LEIGH HUNT

Texts and letters

Brewer, L. A., *My Leigh Hunt Library: The Holograph Letters* (Iowa City, Ia., 1938).

Dibley, David Jesson (ed.), *Leigh Hunt: Selected Writings* (Manchester, 1990).

Fogle, Stephen F. (ed.), *Leigh Hunt's Autobiography: The Earliest Sketches* (Gainesville, Fla., 1959).

Gosse, Edmund (ed.), *Imagination and Fancy* (London, 1907).

Houtchens, L. H., and Houtchens, C. W. (eds.), *Leigh Hunt's Dramatic Criticism 1808–1831* (New York, 1949).

—— —— *Leigh Hunt's Literary Criticism*, with an essay in evaluation by Clarence De Witt Thorpe (New York, 1956).

—— —— *Leigh Hunt's Political and Occasional Essays*, introd. by Carl Woodring (New York, 1962).

Hunt, Thornton (ed.), *The Correspondence of Leigh Hunt*, 2 vols. (London, 1862).

Johnson, R. Brimley (ed.), *Prefaces by Leigh Hunt* (Chicago, 1927).

Morpurgo, J. E. (ed.), *The Autobiography of Leigh Hunt* (London, 1949).

Priestley, J. B. (ed.), *Essays (Selected) by Leigh Hunt* (London, 1929).

Biographies and bibliographies

Blainey, Ann, *Immortal Boy: A Portrait of Leigh Hunt* (London, 1985).

Blunden, Edmund, *Leigh Hunt* (London, 1930; New York edn., *Leigh Hunt and his Circle*).

Landré, Louis, *Leigh Hunt (1784–1859): Contribution à l'histoire du Romantisme anglais*, 2 vols. (Paris, 1936).

Lulofs, Timothy, and Ostrom, Hans (eds.), *Leigh Hunt: A Reference Guide* (Boston, 1985).

Waltman, John, and McDaniel, Gerald (eds.), *Leigh Hunt: A Comprehensive Bibliography* (New York, 1985).

Criticism

Altick, Richard D., 'Harold Skimpole Revisited', in Robert McCown (ed.), *The Life and Times of Leigh Hunt* (Iowa City, Ia., 1985), 1–15.

Barnard, John, 'Keats's Belle Dame and the Sexual Politics of Leigh Hunt's *Indicator*', *Romanticism*, 1 (1995), 34–49.

Blunden, Edmund, *Leigh Hunt's* Examiner *Examined* (London, 1928).

Cameron, Kenneth Neill, 'Leigh Hunt', in *Romantic Rebels* (Cambridge, Mass., 1973), 146–60.

Fenner, Theodore, *Leigh Hunt and Opera Criticism* (Lawrence, Kan., 1972).

—— 'Ballet in Early Nineteenth Century London as Seen by Leigh Hunt and Henry Robertson', *Dance Chronicle*, 1 (1977), 75–95.

Fogle, Stephen F., 'Leigh Hunt and the End of Romantic Criticism', in James V. Logan, John Jordan, and Northrop Frye (eds.), *Some British Romantics: A Collection of Essays* (Columbus, Oh., 1966), 119–39.

Gates, Eleanor M., 'Leigh Hunt, Lord Byron, and Mary Shelley: The Long Goodbye', *Keats–Shelley Journal*, 35 (1986), 149–67.

—— 'Leigh Hunt's Marginal Comments on Hazlitt's *Literary Remains*', *Keats–Shelley Journal*, 41 (1992), 178–225.

Jack, Ian, 'Leigh Hunt', in *English Literature 1815–1832*, vol. x of *The Oxford History of English Literature* (Oxford, 1963), 319–24.

—— 'The Dilettante: Leigh Hunt', in *Keats and the Mirror of Art* (Oxford, 1967), 1–22.

Johnson, R. Brimley, *Shelley–Leigh Hunt: How Friendship Made History* (London, 1929).

Kandl, John, 'Private Lyrics in the Public Sphere: Leigh Hunt's *Examiner* and the Construction of a Public "John Keats"', *Keats–Shelley Journal*, 44 (1995), 84–101.

Kendall, Kenneth E., *Leigh Hunt's* Reflector (The Hague, 1971).

Lamb, Charles, 'Letter of Elia to Robert Southey, Esquire', in *Charles Lamb: Selected Prose*, ed. Adam Phillips (Harmondsworth, 1985), 228–39.

Lockhart, J. G., 'On the Cockney School of Poetry. No. 1', *Blackwood's Edinburgh Magazine*, 2 (1817), 38–41.

Marshall, William H., *Byron, Shelley, Hunt, and* The Liberal (Philadelphia, 1960).

Misenheimer, James B., 'Leigh Hunt: A "Great Introducer" in English Romanticism', *Yearbook of English Studies*, 1 (1971), 135–40.

Reiman, Donald, 'Leigh Hunt in Literary History: A Response', in Robert McCown (ed.), *The Life and Times of Leigh Hunt* (Iowa City, Ia., 1985), 73–99.

Robinson, Henry Crabb, *On Books and their Writers*, ed. Edith J. Morley, 3 vols. (London, 1938).

Saintsbury, George, 'Leigh Hunt', in *The Collected Essays and Papers of George Saintsbury*, 4 vols. (London, 1923), i. 158–83.

Smith, David Q., 'Genius and Common Sense: The Romantics and Leigh Hunt', *Books at Iowa*, 40 (1984), 41–57.

Stout, G. D., *The Political History of Leigh Hunt's* Examiner (St Louis, 1949).

—— 'Leigh Hunt on Wordsworth and Coleridge', *Keats–Shelley Journal*, 6 (1957), 59–73.

Thompson, James R., *Leigh Hunt* (Boston, 1977).

Thorpe, Clarence De Witt, 'An Essay in Evaluation', in *Leigh Hunt's Literary Criticism*, ed. L. H. Houtchens and C. W. Houtchens (New York, 1956), 1–73.

Warren, Alba H., *English Poetic Theory 1825–1860* (Princeton, 1950).

Webb, Timothy, 'Correcting the Irritability of his Temper: The Evolution of Leigh Hunt's *Autobiography*', in Robert Brinkley and Keith Hanley (eds.), *Romantic Revisions* (Cambridge, 1992), 268–90.

Wells, Stanley, 'Shakespeare in Leigh Hunt's Theatre Criticism', *Essays and Studies*, 33 (1980), 119–38.

Wheatley, Kim, 'The *Blackwood's* Attacks on Leigh Hunt', *Nineteenth-Century Literature*, 47 (1992), 1–31.

Woodring, Carl, '*Inter Pares*: Leigh Hunt as Personal Essayist', in Robert McCown (ed.), *The Life and Times of Leigh Hunt* (Iowa City, Ia., 1985), 61–72.

Woolf, Virginia, *A Writer's Diary*, ed. Leonard Woolf (London, 1953), 36.

CHARLES LAMB

Texts and letters

Bate, Jonathan (ed.), *Elia and the Last Essays of Elia* (Oxford, 1987).

Lucas, E. V. (ed.), *The Works of Charles and Mary Lamb*, 5 vols. (London, 1903).

—— *The Letters of Charles and Mary Lamb*, 3 vols. (London, 1935).

Marrs, Edwin (ed.), *The Letters of Charles and Mary Anne Lamb*, 3 vols. (Ithaca, NY, 1975–).

Phillips, Adam (ed.), *Charles Lamb: Selected Prose* (Harmondsworth, 1985).

Park, Roy (ed.), *Lamb as Critic* (London, 1980).

Biographies and bibliographies

Barnett, George L., and Tave, Stuart M. (eds.), 'Charles Lamb', in C. W. Houtchens and L. H. Houtchens (eds.), *The English Romantic Poets and Essayists* (New York, 1966), 37–74.

Blunden, Edmund, *Charles Lamb: His Life Recorded by his Contemporaries* (London, 1934).

Courtney, Winifred F., *Young Charles Lamb 1775–1802* (New York, 1982).

Lucas, E. V., *The Life of Charles Lamb*, 2 vols. (London, 1905).

Prance, Claude A., *Companion to Charles Lamb* (London, 1983).

Criticism

Aaron, Jane, *A Double Singleness: Gender and the Writings of Charles and Mary Lamb* (Oxford, 1991).

Ades, John I., 'Charles Lamb, Shakespeare, and Early Nineteenth-Century Theatre', *Publications of the Modern Language Association*, 85 (1970), 514–26.

—— 'Friendly Persuasion: Lamb as Critic of Wordsworth', *Wordsworth Circle*, 8 (1977), 18–24.

Barnet, Sylvan, 'Charles Lamb's Contribution to the Theory of Dramatic Illusion', *Publications of the Modern Language Association*, 69 (1954), 1150–9.

Barnett, George, *Charles Lamb: The Evolution of Elia* (Bloomington, Ind., 1964).

—— *Charles Lamb* (Boston, 1976).

Bradley, A. C., *Oxford Lectures on Poetry* (London, 1909).

Carlyle, Thomas, *Two Note Books of Thomas Carlyle*, ed. Charles Eliot Norton (New York, 1898).

Coates, John, ' "Damn the Age! I Will Write for Antiquity": Lamb's Style as Implied Moral Comment', *Charles Lamb Bulletin*, 47–8 (1984), 147–58.

De Quincey, Thomas, 'Charles Lamb', in *The Collected Writings of Thomas De Quincey*, ed. David Masson, 14 vols. (Edinburgh, 1889–90), v. 215–58.

Flesch, William, ' "Friendly and Judicious" Reading: Affect and Irony in the Works of Charles Lamb', *Studies in Romanticism*, 23 (1984), 163–81.

Frank, Robert, *Don't Call me Gentle Charles!* (Corvallis, Ore., 1976).

Haven, Richard, 'The Romantic Art of Charles Lamb', *English Literary History*, 30 (1963), 137–46.

Heller, Janet Ruth, 'Lamb and Reader-Response Criticism', in *Coleridge, Lamb, Hazlitt, and the Reader of Drama* (Columbia, Mo., 1990), 115–27.

Hunt, Leigh, 'Keats, Lamb, and Coleridge', in *The Autobiography of Leigh Hunt*, ed. J. E. Morpurgo (London, 1949), 273–88.

Jessup, Bertram, 'The Mind of Elia', *Journal of the History of Ideas*, 15 (1954), 246–59.

McKenna, Wayne, *Charles Lamb and the Theatre* (Gerrards Cross, 1978).

Monsman, Gerald, *Confessions of a Prosaic Dreamer* (Durham, NC, 1984).

Mulcahy, Daniel, 'Charles Lamb: The Antithetical Manner and the Two Planes', *Studies in English Literature*, 3 (1963), 517–42.

Nabholtz, John, 'Drama and Rhetoric in Lamb's Essays of the Imagination', *Studies in English Literature*, 12 (1972), 683–703.

Park, Roy, 'Lamb, Shakespeare, and the Stage', *Shakespeare Quarterly*, 33 (1982), 164–77.

Parker, Mark, 'Ideology and Editing: The Political Context of the Elia Essays', *Studies in Romanticism*, 30 (1991), 473–94.

Pater, Walter, 'Charles Lamb', in *Appreciations* (London, 1889), 107–26.

Randel, F. V., *The World of Elia: Charles Lamb's Essayistic Romanticism* (Port Washington, NY, 1975).

Reiman, Donald, 'Thematic Unity in Lamb's Familiar Essays', *Journal of English and Germanic Philology*, 64 (1965), 470–8.

Scoggins, James, 'Images of Eden in the *Essays of Elia*', *Journal of English and Germanic Philology*, 71 (1972), 198–210.

Shokoff, James, 'Charles Lamb and the Elizabethan Dramatists: A Reassessment', *Wordsworth Circle*, 4 (1973), 3–11.

Swinburne, Algernon Charles, 'Charles Lamb and George Wither', in *The Complete Works of Algernon Charles Swinburne*, ed. Edmund Gosse and Thomas James Wise, 20 vols. (London, 1925–7), xiv. 281.

Thompson, Denys, 'Our Debt to Lamb', in F. R. Leavis (ed.), *Determinations* (London, 1934), 199–217.

Tillotson, Geoffrey, 'The Historical Importance of Certain *Essays of Elia*', in J. V. Logan, John Jordan, and Northrop Frye (eds.), *Some British Romantics: A Collection of Essays* (Columbus, Oh., 1966), 89–116.

Trott, Nicola, ' "The Old Margate Hoy" and Other Depths of Elian Credulity', *Charles Lamb Bulletin*, 82 (1993), 47–59.

Wedd, Mary, 'Dialects of Humour: Lamb and Wordsworth', *Charles Lamb Bulletin*, 19 (1977), 46–54.

Whalley, George, 'Coleridge's Debt to Lamb', *Essays and Studies*, 11 (1958), 68–85.

18. *Political Prose of the Romantic Period*

JOHN WHALE

The writings dealt with in this section are too multifarious to be easily defined by the word 'political'; they should not be neatly separated according to generic boundaries such as 'prose' or 'non-fictional prose'. To define the writers in this section against the 'essayists' dealt with earlier in the volume runs the risk of aestheticizing the work of liberals and polite radicals such as Hunt and Hazlitt. Taking Lamb, Hazlitt, and Hunt out of the political equation also means, of course, that the remaining figures—such as Burke, Paine, and Cobbett—lose by the arrangement. Most of the writers referred to here would not have recognized a perspective which could so easily separate the literary and the political. This is not to suggest that there were not very particular and meaningful distinctions to be made between different forms and kinds of writing in the period, but that the differences do not exhibit a clear-cut separation between what is 'political' and what is not. In the 1790s, middle-class writers self-consciously exploited a variety of kinds of writing in order to contribute to a highly politicized cultural debate. Wollstonecraft and Godwin, for example, wrote novels in conjunction with polemical journalism and political treatises; Cobbett and Paine each worked in a variety of genres stretching from history through to practical manuals. And a good case could be made out for Coleridge as the most rhetorically various political prose writer of this period, but for reasons of genre as well as canon he does not figure here. Recent critical methodologies have also taught us to be suspicious of such simple separations. Many of the most exciting recent critical and historiographical developments in this area have shown the benefits which come from treating such materials discursively. Only then can the rich heterogeneous nature as well as the historical significance of prose writing in this period be properly appreciated.

TEXTS AND TEXTUAL STUDIES

Until recently, many of the writings falling under the heading of 'political prose' have been difficult to obtain either in scholarly or popular editions. Many still are. The situation has improved considerably over the last six or seven years, however. The Wordsworth 'Revolution' Woodstock reprint series has made available many texts formerly only accessible in the best research libraries. Woodstock can be congratulated on reprinting the basic materials, but introductory matter, bibliographical guidance, and textual editing exist in these volumes only at the most minimal level. Pickering & Chatto have also published in their 'Pickering Masters' series editions of the prose works of Godwin, Wollstonecraft, Malthus, and Owen, as well as an extensive eight-volume collection entitled *Political Writings of the 1790s* edited by Claeys. This last edition brings together for the first time the many responses to Burke and Paine during the so-called 'Revolution controversy' as well as a wealth of radical and 'loyalist' writings from the second half of the decade. It also contains an extensive introduction and a helpful chronology which surveys in detail the different stages of debate in the decade. It divides the period into the following sections: 1789–91, 1791–3 'The Question of Equality', 1794–7 'The Decline of Popular Radicalism', 1797–1805 'The Origins of Counter-Enlightenment'. These Pickering editions have already become, in some instances, the standard editions to which scholars and critics refer, but they are expensive and they are variable in terms of the quality and nature of their textual editing.

As ever, popular editions have a considerable impact on the ways in which texts and their authors are received and interpreted, especially when they are accompanied by ground-breaking introductions. This is particularly true of the editions of Burke's *Reflections* edited by O'Brien and, more recently, by Pocock.

CRITICISM AND COMMENTARY

Ever since Williams suggested a set of 'contrasts' in *Culture and Society 1780–1850* (1958) which involved measuring Burke against Cobbett, literary critics working in this period have faced the challenge of looking at Romantic literature not simply in a political context, but with an awareness of the political nature of cultural production. During the intervening years there has been much valuable work which has served to place individual authors, occasionally genres and subgenres, into more precise political focus, but, it has to be admitted, relatively few far-reaching and influential attempts to offer a systematic or exemplary account of the period in the way that Williams in that and subsequent books had suggested.

In this wider context, it is not surprising that political prose still does not figure prominently in the Romantic canon. Where there is substantial work by literary specialists it is often because there is a conveniently literary point of access, the most common being that the writer concerned also happens to be a novelist. Alternatively, it might be the case that particular writers have themselves already made a link between politics and aesthetics, as in the case of Burke and Wollstonecraft. In much the same way as the recent rise of women's poetry in the period has highlighted the need for the creation of a new aesthetic through which it can be mediated (both appreciated and historically recovered), so too Romantic political prose calls for a new way of understanding the relationship between language, aesthetics, and ideology. More particularly, a new technical vocabulary may be needed to articulate the recalcitrant plainness or apparent transparency of prose styles such as those deployed by Paine and Cobbett.

BURKE

From the perspective of historians and political scientists, the main issues surrounding Burke over the last 250 years have derived from his appropriation by both liberal and conservative thinkers in the middle of the nineteenth century. The inheritance of these appropriations in this century has led to fairly extensive inquiries into the role played by natural law in Burke's thinking and the extent to which he can legitimately be seen as a forerunner of modern conservatism. Macpherson has neatly summarized this as a problem of coherence in work which exemplifies two seemingly opposite positions: 'the defender of a hierarchical establishment, and the market liberal'. Argument has also centred on the nature of Burke's complex involvement with a bourgeois revolution. While commentators have recognized the ambivalence of his position, Burke has been seen as both champion and scourge of a bourgeois order. Kramnick's powerful, but dangerous, psycho-biographical study encapsulates this ambivalence as an unconscious struggle which divides Burke's very self. This vision of a self-hating bourgeois should be read alongside O'Brien's suggestion of Burke's being a suppressed rebel against English rule. Despite the obvious dangers involved in a psychological interpretation of Burke, these two commentators have been influential in opening up their subject to important and powerful contradictions. Both the psychoanalytic reading of political representation and Burke's Irishness have been (and are likely to prove to be) fruitful areas of study.

While literary scholars and critics might see Burke's reputation over the last 200 years as a history of appropriations and interpretations, historians and political scientists have frequently written as if they were simply performing a process of scientific definition. Similarly, it has often been assumed that it is legitimate to think of Burke's writings as constituting a coherent political philosophy. Burke's thought in relation to the Enlightenment and to modern conservatism has been assessed in precisely this way. More recently, in work produced by historians and political scientists, there has been a growing awareness of the need to treat Burke's works as particular and strategic; and also to define them by their contemporary legal and political terms rather than by imposing presentist categories upon them. The work of Pocock is most influential in this respect.

The trend among commentators with a literary bias has been rather different. Over the last twenty years, Burke has frequently been analysed by literary critics who have found a particularly fruitful site for their concerns about the interrelationship between the aesthetic and ideology in the conjunction of his *Enquiry into the Origin of our Ideas of the Sublime and Beautiful* and his *Reflections on the Revolution in France*. While historians might question the validity of this tendentious selection of two texts separated by almost forty years, it is worth remembering that this kind of comparison formed the basis of many contemporary attacks and critiques of Burke in the 1790s, most notably Wollstonecraft's in her *Vindication of the Rights of Men*.

With the impact of poststructuralism in the late 1970s there came the opportunity to analyse this conjunction of the aesthetic and the political in more discursive terms. The study of 'representation' meant that Burke's texts could now be seen as indicative and constructive of the meaning of 'revolution' which could be conceived in a wider cultural context. Essays by Ferguson (1992) (and, to a lesser extent, one by Mitchell) were influential in this respect for they established the *Enquiry* as a key historical source for the gendering of identity in relation to aesthetic experience which could then also be read as the unconscious of the explicitly political *Reflections*. In this respect, Burke's *Enquiry* has provided the basis for many feminist rereadings of male Romanticism and of the Gothic. Paulson's Freudian interpretation of the narratives of revolution and his concentration on the idea of 'representation' confirmed and extended the application of roughly poststructuralist literary forms of analysis to political and aesthetic categories. In particular, because of its central concern for the competing narratives of revolution, Paulson's book signalled the possibility of reading the historical meaning of literary and artistic texts as a dynamic competition between different images and stories of sexuality, gender, and psychoanalysis. Blakemore's book represents the strengths and weaknesses of understanding revolution from a linguistic and semiotic model provided by poststructuralism. From this perspective, it is able to offer valuable insights into the unwritten nature of the English constitution, but its methodology inevitably transforms Burke into a prototypical poststructuralist. Furniss's study (1993) is, perhaps, the culmination of a literary and poststructuralist approach to Burke which has provocatively combined the *Enquiry into the Sublime and Beautiful* with the *Reflections*. His book is especially valuable for the way in which its poststructuralist, Derridian, methodology manages to encompass an awareness of political economy as well as a historical specificity which owes much to the work of Pocock.

Future work on Burke is likely to include yet more on the gender implications of his aesthetics, a more thoroughgoing analysis of his writings on India sponsored by the current interest in defining Romantic-period writing in relation to Orientalism, colonialism, and nationalism; and, not unrelated to the last, his complex writing on, and involvement in, Irish culture.

PAINE

Not surprisingly, Paine's more literal and less overtly rhetorical prose writings have proved more resistant to the kind of critical strategies which have been so extensively applied by literary specialists to Burke. Only recently have critics begun to analyse and interpret the ways in which his writings deploy reason in conjunction with a form of the sublime. His own critique of Burke's supposed excess of rhetoric in *Rights of Man* has, somewhat ironically, provided critics with an exposé of his own rhetorical manœuvres. Only rarely have critics taken Paine's writing on its own as an object of study; more frequently he has been deployed rather conveniently alongside Wollstonecraft and Burke as part of the 'revolution controversy' (Furniss 1990, Turner 1989, Whale 1991).

Appropriations of Paine, though more numerous and various than those of Burke, have received considerably less attention. The relative lack of attention paid to the intrinsic nature of his writings is a measure of the degree to which even the history of ideas can be driven by an implicit belief in originality and a conventional literary assumption about what constitutes good and bad writing. Aside from detailed biographical studies, most work on Paine has focused on his context, his intellectual and political milieu (Claeys 1989b). His affiliation to the cause of American independence has been relatively well explored. Even Philp's sympathetic recent study (1989) begins with an almost apologetic admission that 'Paine was not a particularly original political philosopher.' There has been an assumption that it is Paine's international character that makes him important and unique: 'the first international revolutionary' as Philp puts it. Equally significant is his mobilization of a mass audience through print culture. Attempts to place Paine in a conventional relationship of influence from previous political thinkers such as Hobbes and Locke, and through Enlightenment French philosophers such as Rousseau, have not been definitive.

More work certainly needs to be done on defining the nature of Paine's political rhetoric. However, the success and power of his writings clearly demand a different kind of understanding of the way in which the transmission of ideas and texts can operate upon and be modified by audiences. A new kind of socio-aesthetics is called for which could provide a more adequate account of the process of reception and the social creation and transformation of political meanings. Klancher provides one possible route of inquiry. McCalman has recently suggested others in his work on radical societies, communities, and economic, public spaces. The most significant recent work on Paine, including the popular biographies, has redefined his position in relation to a bourgeois revolution. Wilson has suggested that Paine's economic thought reveals a subscription to an empire of international free trade dominated by the USA. Once again, the force of this work is to define in greater particularity the nature of Paine's historical difference from the present and it provides a useful challenge to our assumptions as to what is left or right, reactionary or progressive. As work on so-called unrespectable radicals gathers pace and uncovers a more complex, heterogeneous, and exciting culture of British radicalism in the period our sense of Paine is bound to be redefined.

The political and historical reception of Cobbett has focused on his 'nostalgia': his dream of a well-populated and well-fed 'Old England' which underscores his critique of luxury and of burgeoning industrialization. This has often made him a difficult figure for the Left to accommodate with any degree of comfort and has made defining his political position in twentieth-century terms very difficult. As a result, he has been variously, but not necessarily contradictorily, defined as a radical Tory, a friend of the people, a gentleman farmer, and a vulgar radical. This is compounded by the other major concern of his critics and commentators: his supposed switch from a conservative to a radical mode of politics around 1802. A less presentist view of Cobbett would resist the use of left/right labels and would emphasize the underlying consistency of his views on political economy and the conditions of the agricultural labouring classes. Even in today's critical climate where there is a new impetus in the historiography of British radicalism, Cobbett's position remains difficult to define. McCalman classifies him as a 'respectable' radical outside what becomes by implication the more challenging and exciting 'unrespectable' camp. Even in Williams's stirring introductory study (1983) there is a struggle to defend him against the charges of being anti-intellectual and of possessing a petit bourgeois mentality; and, one feels, Williams switches in his book rather strategically to a more discursive set of 'themes' in order to escape some of the more disturbing particularities of Cobbett's work.

The difficulties posed by Cobbett's writing to literary analysis are those of Paine writ large: how to define a style which appears to be transparent or plain; how to account for popularity and to describe the proliferation of meaning within print culture. The sheer volume and variety of Cobbett's writing and publishing enterprises also carries with it a very significant, even daunting, challenge to the would-be commentator.

In the most substantial recent contributions to our assessment of Cobbett, he has been compared and contrasted to Paine in relation to their shared 'transatlantic connection' (Wilson); and defined meticulously and convincingly in relation to rural popular culture by Dyck. Nattrass's book is particularly welcome as the first full-length study which attempts to take us beyond the assumption of a plain style and to analyse Cobbett as a conscious artist who deploys a mixture of styles for different audiences. More contributions in this area are likely to follow as literary critics increasingly draw on a combination of historical and linguistic skills to redefine the arena of popular political culture and its semiotics.

GODWIN

Ever since Hazlitt's portrait in *The Spirit of the Age*, Godwin has been dogged with the label of unworldly idealist and subsequent commentators have often had to fight hard to win back a sense of the urgent political context which informs *Political Justice*. The history of philosophical anarchism has not, of course, had the same kind of formative influence on British politics as Burke's particularly complex brand of Whiggism. With the notable exception of books by Clark, Locke, Marshall, and Philp (1986), Godwin the political prose writer has not engendered the amount of critical interest that one might expect. The largely biographical studies of Locke and Marshall complement each other well, while Clark's book has the dual purpose of attempting to rescue Godwin's philosophical anarchism from numerous misconceptions and to make good his absence from the history of utilitarian thought.

Literary focus has tended to use the political writings, mainly *Political Justice*, to substantiate readings of *Caleb Williams* (Butler). Recent work has debated Godwin's position in relation to radical thought and, above all, has attempted to define the precise nature of his philosophical, middle-class, or polite radicalism. Philp's study has provided a clearer sense of the context which gave rise to Godwin's philosophy and has placed new emphasis on the role of private judgement and its relation to a dissenting conscience in Godwin's thought. More recently, Barrell has explored Godwin's involvement in the Treason Trials of 1794 and has offered a powerful analysis of the rhetoric involved, while Chris Jones has brought Godwin into the debate about the relationship between sensibility and radical forms of civic identity. More work on these last two topics and on Godwin's contribution to debates on education, political economy, and population is to be expected. The new Pickering edition of the 'political writings' (separate from the edition of the novels) should at least ensure greater accessibility and textual confidence so that literary scholars will be able to extend their concerns beyond *Caleb Williams* and *Political Justice*.

WOLLSTONECRAFT

More than any other writer in this section, Wollstonecraft may be said to have made it into the new Romantic canon. Work on her has been considerable over the last twenty years and it continues to grow apace. This is partly because of her position as a founding figure of modern feminism. In its definition of femininity as a form of false refinement, her *Vindication of the Rights of Woman* offers to the modern reader an illustration of the socially constructed nature of gender and secures the text's status as a landmark in the history of feminist writing. And in her deployment of the rational persona of the philosopher in both vindications, Wollstonecraft has also been seen to perform an originary act in the history of the women's movement which has powerful, but complex, implications. Most of the best work on Wollstonecraft over this period has had to negotiate her role within feminist thought and her situation as a libertarian woman writer within late eighteenth-century culture. Most attention has been centred, quite understandably, on her second vindication on the subject of the rights of woman, but, in the last ten years especially, there has been a growing interest in the full range of her fictional and non-fictional works, including *Vindication of the Rights of Men, An Historical and Moral View of the Origin and Progress of the French Revolution*, and, even more recently, *Letters Written during a Short Residence in Sweden, Norway, and Denmark*.

Cora Kaplan's two essays reprinted in her book *Sea Changes*—'Wild Nights: Pleasure/Sexuality/Feminism' and 'Pandora's Box: Subjectivity, Class, and Sexuality in Socialist Feminist Criticism'—powerfully and lucidly set the agenda for many of the recent revisions of what has been seen as Wollstonecraft's problematic subscription to an Enlightenment rationality. While recognizing her complicity with the Left's historical denial of pleasure, Kaplan calls for a reconfiguration of the relationship between reason and emotion in Wollstonecraft's writing; and, instead of simply repeating the argument in favour of a repressed rationality, she provocatively claims that even *A Vindication of the Rights of Woman* exhibits an almost Gothic libidinous energy. Over the last ten years a number of critics have taken up the challenge. From this point onwards, it has become possible to see the complex mixture of reason and feeling in Wollstonecraft's writing as a positive quality rather than a weakness. Instead of seeing Wollstonecraft as dependent upon a form of male rationality which she can sustain only fitfully, it became possible to see the distinctiveness and difference registered in her political attempt to 'melt reason to pity'. Over the same period, more precise historical definitions of Wollstonecraft have been presented. Mary Poovey's study of the ideological figure of the 'proper lady' and its impact upon the 'style' of three major writers (including Austen and Shelley) has been particularly influential in the case of Wollstonecraft and has had an impact on her non-fictional works as much as on her novels. We now have a much better-informed view not only of Wollstonecraft's involvement in the evolution of democratic ideas (Sapiro), but also of her role in a 'cultural revolution' in writing in which, according to Kelly (1992), a process of feminization takes place in the formation of national consciousness.

Placing Wollstonecraft in relation to Romanticism has always been hazardous. There is always the risk that comparison would lead to absorption,
assimilation, or domination. Valuable early attempts by Mitzi Myers (1977,
1979) situate Wollstonecraft carefully and sensitively as a proto-Romantic.
More recent work has set about redefining the categories by distinguishing
between male and female Romanticisms. Alexander's strategy is to define
women's writing, including Wollstonecraft's, against a 'Romantic feminine'
derived in part from Rousseau. Having set up an experienced difference of femininity generated by male power, she then goes on to define the unique sense
of 'bodily knowledge' available to women writers which, in Wollstonecraft's
case, is characterized not just by desire, but also by a 'fierce scrutiny' of desire.
Wollstonecraft is thus credited with the creation of a feminine Romanticism
which rewrites the male sublime as a mixture of idealism and a 'hard won
realism'. By a similar strategy of self-consciously invoking a binary divide of
male and feminine Romanticisms in which the latter, it is argued, 'resist[s] a
model of oppositional polarity for one based on sympathy and likeness', Mellor
offers a brief measured portrait of Wollstonecraft as a 'liberal feminist' devoted
to equality in her call for a 'revolution of manners'.

Recent work on conduct literature, plot paradigms, the discourses of women's
travel writing, the bicentenary of her travels to Scandinavia, and of her death
in 1797 are likely to produce even more stimulating and challenging work on
Wollstonecraft. Taylor's important essay continues the constructive negotiation
between current needs and historical awareness by helpfully addressing the
complex and complicated identity at the heart of Wollstonecraft's 'feminism'
with all its tensions, repressions, and 'transgressive aspirations'. Gubar's recent
attack on Wollstonecraft's 'feminist misogyny' provides ample evidence, if any
were needed, that Wollstonecraft's legacy to contemporary feminism is not
simply complex, but contentious.

OTHER WOMEN WRITERS

Women's writing has been one of the major areas of growth in the field of
political prose. This extends beyond Wollstonecraft to include writers to whom
little attention was paid before the 1980s. Though they all write in more than
one genre, the prose writings of Helen Maria Williams, Hannah More, Mary
Hays, and Elizabeth Hamilton have all begun to receive significant attention
and are likely to receive more in the next few years. Of these, Williams has
so far generated the most extended commentaries not only because her volu-
minous and various *Letters from France* provide a useful parallel eye-witness
account of the French Revolution to Wollstonecraft's *An Historical and Moral
View of the Origin and Progress of the French Revolution*, but also because they
demonstrate the way in which forms of romance and history intersect in the

1790s. Reading novelistic paradigms into non-fictional political prose writings has so far proved to be one of the most fruitful areas of study for critics using literary forms of analysis to investigate this material. This is apparent so far in a number of essays (Vivien Jones 1992, Keane, and Kennedy). In a similar fashion, Favret has successfully investigated the paradigmatic textual properties of the letter as fiction in order to open up the cross-generic boundaries between various prose writings and the novel. She too has provided her work with a double focus by combining a poststructuralist idea of the letter as *envoi* with a historical sense of the particularity of a shift in genres and its relationship to gender. The increased critical interest in travel literature, particularly women's travel literature, in the period has also been significant and is one of the other factors which has brought Williams to the fore.

Among the rich and diverse areas of development in this field one should also note, following Poovey, the work on conduct literature (Armstrong and Tennenhouse, Vivien Jones 1990) and the study of women writers who, like Hannah More, are complicit either with the establishment or with patriarchy (Kowaleski-Wallace, Myers 1982; Sutherland). Finding the 'feminist' potential in More, for example, can provide a healthy counter to progressivist assumptions and to the glib ascription of twentieth-century labels to late eighteenth- and early nineteenth-century politics. Women writers, including Wollstonecraft, have also figured prominently in the recent extensive critical literature on sensibility (Barker-Benfield 1992, Chris Jones). This has helpfully focused on the civic, republican identity of sensibility by examining the connections between its different subjectivities and their various capacities and commitments to forms of social contract. This story of the political mutations of sensibility has been helpfully extended by Kelly (1993), whose book also pays significant attention to Elizabeth Hamilton.

One of the most exciting developments in the last eight years has been in the history of radicalism. McCalman's pioneering historiographical study (1988) has drawn attention to the rich variety of movements, figures, and practices involved in radicalism in the period 1790–1840, including black radicals like Wedderburn. This uncovering of heterogeneity has seriously questioned previous assumptions about the clear-cut separation of forms of religious enthusiasm from rationalist radicalism which had been established, in part, by Thompson's own pioneering study in the early 1960s. It has also challenged a progressivist view of the movements for reform by exposing not just their links with irrational modes of thought and expression, but also with disturbing forms of eroticism. Important books by Chase and Worrall (the latter much more literary in orientation) have also drawn attention to the varieties— millenarian, millennialist, apocalyptic, agrarian, prophetic—and the developments of Spencean radicalism in the period. These books complement developments in Blake studies which are similarly engaged in defining his artisanal context and the affiliations of his visionary radicalism. For the literary historian and critic, this work has exciting implications, not least being the way in which it broadens the terms in which we can view the writings and publications of radical groups and individuals. Indeed, the practice of writing takes on a very different status as it is defined in relation to a variety of cultural practices and institutional pressures, including repressive legal restrictions. Written texts assume a different identity when placed in such a mixed and multifarious context. Faced with such practices, critics have sought to define writing in terms of *bricolage* rather than relying on traditional concepts of originality, individuality, and authority.

In a similar way, recent work on the French Revolution has had its impact on our understanding of British political prose in the Romantic period. Cultural historians of the Revolution such as Ozouf, Outram, Hunt (1984, 1992), and others have examined its festivals, rituals, assemblies, and crowds in anthropological and semiotic terms. This has implications not just for writers like Williams and Wollstonecraft who witnessed revolutionary culture first-hand, but also for our understanding of political culture in Britain. Such studies alert us to very different examples of literary production, the practices of reading, and the transmission of meanings from those which have traditionally preoccupied literary historians. While women's writing is currently making a welcome and significant impact on the Romantic canon and is already creating a demand for new critical strategies and aesthetic values, it will be interesting to see if the recent histories affecting political prose will usher in a new understanding of the socio-linguistic and collaborative nature of 'literary' production and transmission first called for by Williams in the 1950s.

REFERENCES

TEXTUAL STUDIES

Boulton, J. T. (ed.), *Edmund Burke: A Philosophical Enquiry into the Origin of our Ideas of the Sublime and Beautiful* (London, 1958).
Butler, Marilyn, *Burke, Paine, Godwin and the Revolution Controversy* (Cambridge, 1984).
—— and Todd, Janet (eds.), *The Works of Mary Wollstonecraft*, 7 vols. (London, 1989).
Claeys, Gregory, *Political Writings of the 1790s*, 8 vols. (London, 1995).
Cobbett, J. M., and Cobbett, J. P. (eds.), *Selections from Cobbett's Political Works*, 6 vols. (London, 1935).
Cobbett, William (ed.), *Porcupine's Works*, 12 vols. (London, 1801).
—— *Rural Rides: From Articles in the Political Register* (London, 1830).
Cole, G. D. H. (ed.), *William Cobbett: The Life and Adventures of Peter Porcupine, with Other Records of his Early Career in England and America* (London, 1937).

Conway, Moncure D., *The Writings of Thomas Paine*, 4 vols. (New York, 1902–8; repr. 1969).

Copeland, Thomas, et al. (eds.), *The Correspondence of Edmund Burke*, 10 vols. (Cambridge, 1958–78).

Foner, Philip S., *The Complete Writings of Thomas Paine* (New York, 1945).

—— *The Life and Major Writings of Thomas Paine*, 2 vols. (Secaucus, NJ, 1948).

Foot, Michael, and Kramnick, Isaac (eds.), *The Thomas Paine Reader* (Harmondsworth, 1987).

Gandy, Clara I., and Stanlis, Peter J., *Edmund Burke: A Bibliography of Secondary Studies to 1982* (New York, 1983).

Jones, Vivien (ed.), *Women in the Eighteenth Century: Constructions of Femininity* (London, 1990).

Langford, Paul, et al. (eds.), *The Writing and Speeches of Edmund Burke*, 9 vols. (Oxford, 1981–91).

McCalman, Iain (ed.), *The Horrors of Slavery and Other Writings by Robert Wedderburn* (Edinburgh, 1991).

O'Brien, Conor Cruise (ed.), *Edmund Burke: Reflections on the Revolution in France* (Harmondsworth, 1968).

Pendleton, Gayle Trusdel, 'Towards a Bibliography of the *Reflections* and *Rights of Man* Controversy', *Bulletin of Research in the Humanities*, 85 (1982), 65–103.

Philp, Mark (ed.), *Political and Philosophical Writings of William Godwin*, 7 vols. (London, 1993).

Pocock, J. G. A. (ed.), *Edmund Burke: Reflections on the Revolution in France* (Indianapolis, 1987).

Tauchert, Ashley (ed.), *Mary Wollstonecraft: A Vindication of the Rights of Woman with Political and Moral Strictures* (London, 1995).

Todd, Janet, *Mary Wollstonecraft: An Annotated Bibliography* (New York, 1976).

—— (ed.), *A Dictionary of British and American Women Writers, 1660–1800* (Totowa, NJ, 1985).

—— (ed.), *Political Writings of Mary Wollstonecraft* (Oxford, 1994).

Todd, William B., *A Bibliography of Edmund Burke* (London, 1964).

Webb, R. K., *The Working Class Reader 1790–1848* (London, 1955).

CRITICISM AND COMMENTARY

Aldridge, A. O., *Man of Reason* (London, 1960).

Alexander, Meena, *Women in Romanticism: Mary Wollstonecraft, Dorothy Wordsworth and Mary Shelley* (London, 1989).

Armstrong, Nancy, and Tennenhouse, Leonard (eds.), *The Ideology of Conduct: Essays in Literature and the History of Sexuality* (New York, 1987).

Barker-Benfield, G. J., 'Mary Wollstonecraft: Eighteenth-Century Commonwealth-woman', *Journal of the History of Ideas*, 50 (1989), 95–115.

—— *The Culture of Sensibility: Sex and Society in Eighteenth-Century Britain* (Chicago, 1992).

Barrell, John, 'Imaginary Trials, Imaginary Law: The State Trials of 1794', in *The Birth of Pandora: And the Division of Knowledge* (Basingstoke, 1992), 119–43.

Blakemore, Steven, *Burke and the Fall of Language: The French Revolution as Linguistic Event* (Hanover, NH, 1988).

Boulton, J. T., *The Language of Politics in the Age of Wilkes and Burke* (London, 1963).

Butler, Marilyn, 'Godwin, Burke, and *Caleb Williams*', *Essays in Criticism*, 22 (1982), 237–57.

Chase, Malcolm, *The People's Farm: English Agrarian Radicalism 1775–1840* (Oxford, 1988).

Claeys, Gregory, 'William Godwin's Critique of Democracy and Republicanism and its Sources', *History of European Ideas*, 7 (1986), 253–69.

—— *Citizens and Saints: Politics and Anti-politics in Early British Socialism* (Cambridge, 1989a).

—— *Thomas Paine: Social and Political Thought* (Boston, 1989b).

Clark, John P., *The Philosophical Anarchism of William Godwin* (Princeton, 1977).

Cone, Carl B., *Burke and the Nature of Politics: The Age of the American Revolution* (Lexington, Ky., 1957).

—— *Burke and the Nature of Politics: The Age of the French Revolution* (Lexington, Ky., 1964).

—— *The English Jacobins: Reformers in Late Eighteenth-Century England* (New York, 1968).

Deane, Seamus, *The French Revolution and Enlightenment in England 1789–1832* (Cambridge, Mass., 1988).

Dyck, Ian, *William Cobbett and Rural Popular Culture* (Cambridge, 1992).

Everest, Kelvin (ed.), *Revolution in Writing: British Literary Responses to the French Revolution* (Milton Keynes, 1991).

Favret, Mary A., *Romantic Correspondence: Women, Politics and the Fiction of Letters* (Cambridge, 1993a).

—— 'Spectatrice as Spectacle: Helen Maria Williams at Home in the Revolution', *Studies in Romanticism*, 32 (1993b), 273–95.

Fennessy, R. R., *Burke, Paine, and the Rights of Man* (The Hague, 1963).

Ferguson, Frances, 'Wollstonecraft our Contemporary', in Linda Kauffman (ed.), *Gender and Theory: Dialogues on Feminist Criticism* (Oxford, 1989), 51–63.

—— *Solitude and the Sublime: Romanticism and the Aesthetics of Individuation* (New York, 1992).

Foner, E., *Tom Paine and Revolutionary America* (Oxford, 1976).

Furniss, Tom, 'Rhetoric in Revolution: The Role of Language in Paine's Critique of Burke', in Keith Hanley and Raman Selden (eds.), *Revolution and English Romanticism: Politics and Rhetoric* (London, 1990), 23–48.

—— *Edmund Burke's Aesthetic Ideology: Language, Gender and Political Economy in Revolution* (Cambridge, 1993).

George, Margaret, *One Woman's Situation: A Study of Mary Wollstonecraft* (Urbana, Ill., 1970).

Gilmartin, Kevin, 'Popular Radicalism and the Public Sphere', *Studies in Romanticism*, 33 (1994), 549–57.

Godwin, William, *Memoirs of the Author of a Vindication of the Rights of Woman* (London, 1798).

Goodwin, A., *The Friends of Liberty: The English Democratic Movement in the Age of the French Revolution* (London, 1979).

Gubar, Susan, 'Feminist Misogyny: Mary Wollstonecraft and the Paradox of "It takes one to know one "', *Feminist Studies*, 20 (1994), 453–73.

Guest, Harriet, 'The Dream of a Common Language: Hannah More and Mary Wollstonecraft', *Textual Practice*, 9 (1995), 303–23.

Hazlitt, William, 'William Godwin', in *The Spirit of the Age*, in *The Complete Works of William Hazlitt*, vol. xi, ed. P. P. Howe (London, 1932), 16–28.

Hone, J. Ann, *For the Cause of Truth: Radicalism in London 1796–1821* (Oxford, 1982).

Hunt, Lynn, *Politics, Culture and Class in the French Revolution* (London, 1984).

—— *The Family Romance of the French Revolution* (London, 1992).

Jones, Chris, *Radical Sensibility: Literature and Ideas in the 1790s* (London, 1993).

Jones, Vivien, 'Women Writing Revolution: Narratives of History and Sexuality in Wollstonecraft and Williams', in Stephen Copley and John Whale (eds.), *Beyond Romanticism: New Approaches to Texts and Contexts* (London, 1992), 178–99.

—— ' "The Tyranny of the Passions": Feminism and Heterosexuality in the Fiction of Wollstonecraft and Hays', in Sally Ledger, Josephine McDonagh, and Jane Spencer (eds.), *Political Gender* (Hemel Hempstead, 1994), 173–88.

Kaplan, Cora, *Sea Changes: Essays on Culture and Feminism*, Questions for Feminism (London, 1986).

Keane, Angela, 'Helen Maria Williams's *Letters from France: A National Romance*', *Prose Studies*, 15 (1992), 271–94.

Kelly, Gary, *Revolutionary Feminism: The Mind and Career of Mary Wollstonecraft* (Basingstoke, 1992).

—— *Women, Writing, and Revolution 1790–1827* (Oxford, 1993).

Kennedy, Deborah, 'Spectacle of the Guillotine: Helen Maria Williams and the Reign of Terror', *Philological Quarterly*, 73 (1994), 95–113.

Klancher, Jon P., *The Making of English Reading Audiences, 1790–1832* (Madison, 1987).

Kowaleski-Wallace, Elizabeth, *Their Father's Daughters: Hannah More, Maria Edgeworth, and Patriarchal Complicity* (New York, 1991).

Kramnick, Isaac, *The Rage of Edmund Burke: Portrait of an Ambivalent Conservative* (New York, 1977).

Landes, Joan B., *Women and the Public Sphere in the Age of the French Revolution* (Ithaca, NY, 1988).

Lock, F. P., *Burke's Reflections on the Revolution in France* (London, 1985).

Locke, Don, *A Fantasy of Reason: The Life and Thought of William Godwin* (London, 1980).

McCalman, Iain, *Radical Underworld: Prophets, Revolutionaries and Pornographers in London, 1795–1840* (Cambridge, 1988).

Maccoby, S., *English Radicalism 1786–1832: From Paine to Cobbett* (London, 1955).

Macpherson, C. B., *Burke*, Past Masters (Oxford, 1980).

Marshall, Peter H., *William Godwin* (New Haven, 1984).

Mellor, Anne K., *Romanticism and Gender* (New York, 1993).

Melzer, Sara E., and Rabine, Leslie W. (eds.), *Rebel Daughters* (Oxford, 1992).

Mitchell, W. J. T., *Iconology: Image, Text, Ideology* (Chicago, 1986).

Moore, Jane, 'Promises, Promises: The Fictional Philosophy in Mary Wollstonecraft's *Vindication of the Rights of Woman*', in *The Feminist Reader: Essays in Gender and the Politics of Literary Criticism* (London, 1989), 155–73.

Myers, Mitzi, 'Politics from the Outside: Mary Wollstonecraft's First Vindication', *Studies in Eighteenth-Century Culture*, 6 (1977), 113–32.

—— 'Mary Wollstonecraft's *Letters Written . . . in Sweden*: Toward Romantic Autobiography', *Studies in Eighteenth-Century Culture*, 8 (1979), 165–85.

—— 'Reform or Ruin: "A Revolution in Female Manners" ', *Studies in Eighteenth-Century Culture*, 11 (1982), 199–216.

—— 'Hannah More's Tracts for the Times: Social Fiction and Female Ideology', in Mary Anne Schofield and Cecilia Macheski (eds.), *Fetter'd or Free: British Women Novelists 1670–1815* (Athens, Oh., 1986), 264–84.

—— 'Sensibility and the "Walk of Reason" ', in Syndy McMillen Conger (ed.), *Sensibility in Transformation: Creative Resistance to Sentiment from the Augustans to the Romantics: Essays in Honor of Jean H. Hagstrum* (London, 1989), 120–44.

Nattrass, Leonora, *William Cobbett: The Politics of Style* (Cambridge, 1995).

Ozouf, Mona, *La Fête révolutionnaire 1789–1799* (Paris, 1976).

Outram, Dorinda, *The Body and the French Revolution: Sex, Class, and Political Culture* (New Haven, 1989).

Paul, C. Kegan (ed.), *William Godwin: His Friends and Contemporaries*, 2 vols. (London, 1876).

Paulson, Ronald, *Representations of Revolution (1789–1820)* (New Haven, 1983).

Philp, Mark, *Godwin's Political Justice* (London, 1986).

—— *Paine*, Past Masters (Oxford, 1989).

—— (ed.), *The French Revolution and British Popular Politics* (Cambridge, 1991).

Pocock, J. G. A., *Politics, Language and Time: Essays on Political Thought and History* (London, 1972).

—— 'The Political Economy of Burke's Analysis of the French Revolution', *Historical Journal*, 25 (1982), 331–49.

Poovey, Mary, *The Proper Lady and the Woman Writer: Ideology as Style in the Works of Mary Wollstonecraft, Mary Shelley, and Jane Austen* (Chicago, 1984).

Reid, Christopher, *Edmund Burke and the Practice of Political Writing* (London, 1985).

Rendall, Jane, *The Origins of Modern Feminism: Women in Britain, France and the United States 1780–1860* (Basingstoke, 1985).

St Clair, William, *The Godwins and the Shelleys: The Biography of a Family* (London, 1989).

Sapiro, Virginia, *A Vindication of Political Virtue: The Political Theory of Mary Wollstonecraft* (Chicago, 1992).

Smith, Olivia, *The Politics of Language* (Oxford, 1984).

Spater, G., *William Cobbett: The Poor Man's Friend*, 2 vols. (Cambridge, 1982).

Stanlis, Peter J., *Edmund Burke and the Natural Law* (Ann Arbor, 1958).

Sutherland, Kathryn, 'Hannah More's Counter-revolutionary Feminism', in Kelvin Everest (ed.), *Revolution in Writing: British Literary Responses to the French Revolution* (Milton Keynes, 1991), 27–63.

Taylor, Barbara, 'Mary Wollstonecraft and the Wild Wish of Early Feminism', *History Workshop Journal*, 33 (1992), 197–219.

Thompson, E. P., *The Making of the English Working Class* (1963; Harmondsworth, 1968).

Todd, Janet, *The Sign of Angellica: Women, Writing, and Fiction, 1660–1800* (London, 1989).

—— *Gender, Art, and Death* (Oxford, 1993).

Tomalin, Claire, *The Life and Death of Mary Wollstonecraft* (London, 1974).

Turner, John, 'Burke, Paine and the Nature of Language', *Yearbook of English Studies*, (1989), 36–53.

Wardle, Ralph M. (ed.), *Collected Letters of Mary Wollstonecraft* (Ithaca, NY, 1979).

Whale, John, 'The Limits of Paine's Revolutionary Literalism', in Kelvin Everest (ed.), *Revolution in Writing: British Literary Responses to the French Revolution* (Milton Keynes, 1991), 121–37.

—— 'Preparations for Happiness: Mary Wollstonecraft and Imagination', in Philip Martin and Robin Jarvis (eds.), *Reviewing Romanticism* (Basingstoke, 1992), 170–89.

Williams, Gwyn A., *Artisans and Sans-Culottes: Popular Movements in Britain and France during the French Revolution* (London, 1969).

Williams, Raymond, *Culture and Society 1780–1950* (Harmondsworth, 1961; 1st pub. 1958).

—— *Cobbett*, Past Masters (Oxford, 1983).

Wilson, David A., *Paine and Cobbett: The Transatlantic Connection* (Kingston, 1988).

Worrall, David, *Radical Culture: Discourse, Resistance and Surveillance, 1790–1820* (Hemel Hempstead, 1992).

Notes on Contributors

JENNIFER BREEN is Senior Lecturer in the School of Literary and Media Studies, Faculty of Humanities, University of North London. She has edited *Wilfred Owen: Selected Poetry and Prose* (1988), *Women Romantic Poets, 1785–1832: An Anthology* (1992; new edn., 1994), *Victorian Women Poets, 1830–1900: An Anthology* (1994), *Women Romantics, 1785–1832: Writing in Prose* (1996), and she is the author of *In her Own Write: Twentieth-Century Women's Fiction* (1990).

PAMELA CLEMIT is a Lecturer in English at the University of Durham. Her publications include *The Godwinian Novel* (1993). She has edited five volumes in *The Collected Novels and Memoirs of William Godwin* (1992), one volume in *The Political and Philosophical Writings of William Godwin* (1993), and two volumes in *The Novels and Selected Works of Mary Shelley* (1996). She is currently writing a literary biography of Godwin for Oxford University Press.

P. M. S. DAWSON is a Lecturer at the University of Manchester and one of the editors of the Oxford English Texts edition of the poems of John Clare, of which the first two volumes devoted to *Poems of the Middle Period 1822–1837* were published in 1996; the next two are scheduled for publication in 1997. He has also co-edited Clare's *Cottage Tales* and *Northborough Sonnets*, published by the Carcanet Press. He is also known for his critical and editorial work on Shelley, most notably *The Unacknowledged Legislator: Shelley and Politics* (1980) and two volumes in the Garland Bodleian Shelley Manuscripts series.

J. P. DONOVAN teaches in the Department of English and Related Literature at the University of York. He has written on English and French Romantic literature and is one of the contributing editors to the second volume of *The Poems of Shelley* in the series Longman Annotated English Poets.

DAVID FULLER is the author of *Blake's Heroic Argument* (1988), *James Joyce's 'Ulysses'* (1992), and (with David Brown) *Signs of Grace* (1995) (on literary treatments of the sacraments). His edition of *Tamburlaine the Great* for the Oxford English Texts edition of the complete works of Marlowe is forthcoming from the Clarendon Press (1998). He is currently editing a volume of Blake for Longman Annotated Texts.

PETER GARSIDE is a Reader in English at the University of Wales, Cardiff. He is a member of the Editorial Boards of the Edinburgh Edition of the Waverley Novels and the Stirling/South Carolina Collected Works of James Hogg, and is also currently engaged on a bibliography of the English novel, 1770–1830.

JERROLD E. HOGLE is Professor of English and University Distinguished Professor at the University of Arizona, as well as the current president of the International Gothic

Association. He has published widely on Romantic and Gothic literature and literary theory, and is best known in Romantic Studies for *Shelley's Process: Radical Transference and the Development of his Major Works* (1988).

GREG KUCICH is Associate Professor of English at the University of Notre Dame, Indiana. His publications include *Keats, Shelley, and Romantic Spenserianism* (1991), as well as a series of essays on Romanticism, gender, and historiography, which are part of a book in progress. He is also co-editor of *Nineteenth-Century Contexts*.

SUSAN MATTHEWS is a Senior Lecturer at Roehampton Institute, London. She has published articles on Blake, eighteenth-century women's writing, and novels in the Romantic period. She is working on a book on Blake and epic.

ROBERT MORRISON is Associate Professor of English at Acadia University, Nova Scotia. He is co-editor of *Tales of Terror from Blackwood's Magazine* and *The Vampyre and Other Tales of the Macabre*, and editor of three volumes of the forthcoming Pickering edition of *The Works of Thomas De Quincey*.

ANDREW NICHOLSON is a Lecturer in the Department of English at the University of Bristol. He is editor of *Lord Byron: The Complete Miscellaneous Prose* (1991), and of several facsimile editions of Byron's *Don Juan* for Garland Publishing. He is currently editing a further facsimile edition for Garland, the letters of John Murray to Byron (for John Murray), and, with Donald Mitchell, *The Mahler Companion* (for Oxford University Press).

MICHAEL O'NEILL is Professor of English at the University of Durham. He is the author of *The Human Mind's Imaginings: Conflict and Achievement in Shelley's Poetry* (1989), *Percy Bysshe Shelley: A Literary Life* (1989), *Auden, MacNeice, Spender: The Thirties Poetry* (with Gareth Reeves) (1992), *Shelley*, Longman Critical Readers (1993), and *Romanticism and the Self-Conscious Poem* (1997). He is also guest editor of *Percy Bysshe Shelley: Special Issue, Durham University Journal* (July 1993), editor of *The 'Defence of Poetry' Fair Copies* (1994), co-editor (with Donald H. Reiman) of *Fair-Copy Manuscripts of Shelley's Poems in European and American Libraries* (1997), and editor of *Keats: Bicentenary Readings* (1997). His book of poems, *The Stripped Bed*, was published in 1990.

FIONA ROBERTSON is Reader in English Literature at the University of Durham. Her study of Walter Scott and Gothic fiction, *Legitimate Histories*, was published by Clarendon Press in 1994; and she has edited *The Bride of Lammermoor* for Oxford University Press (1991). She is currently editing *The Fair Maid of Perth* as well the stories of Stephen Crane and a selection of women's writing from the Romantic period, and is completing a book about representations of the United States in British writing, 1790–1840.

NICHOLAS ROE is Professor of English Literature at the University of St Andrews, Scotland. His books include *Wordsworth and Coleridge: The Radical Years* (1988) and *John Keats and the Culture of Dissent* (1997), both published by the Clarendon Press.

NOTES ON CONTRIBUTORS

MICHAEL ROSSINGTON is a Lecturer in English Literature in the Department of English Literary and Linguistic Studies at the University of Newcastle upon Tyne. He is currently working on editions of Percy Shelley's *The Cenci* and Mary Shelley's *Valperga*, and on a critical book about the work of Percy Shelley.

FIONA STAFFORD is a Fellow and Tutor in English at Somerville College, Oxford. She is editor of the New Penguin edition of Jane Austen's *Emma*, and of volume vi of *The Novels and Selected Works of Mary Shelley*. Other publications include *The Last of the Race: The Growth of a Myth from Milton to Darwin* (1994), and *The Sublime Savage: James Macpherson and the Poems of Ossian* (1988).

NICOLA TROTT is a Lecturer in English Literature at the University of Glasgow. In addition to publishing on Coleridge, she has also written on several other areas of Romanticism, including Wordsworth, Wollstonecraft, Keats, and the Gothic novel.

JOHN WHALE is a Senior Lecturer in English at the University of Leeds. His publications include *Thomas De Quincey's Reluctant Autobiography* (1984) and, as co-editor with Stephen Copley, *Beyond Romanticism: New Essays on Texts and Contexts, 1789–1832* (1992), as well as essays on aesthetics and politics, travel, and Orientalism in the Romantic period. He is currently completing a book-length study of the imagination and is editing a volume of the forthcoming Pickering edition of *The Works of Thomas De Quincey*.

Index

INDEX

INDEX

INDEX

INDEX

INDEX